Handbook of Public Protecti

Handbook of Public Protection

Edited by

Mike Nash and Andy Williams

WILLAN
PUBLISHING

Published by

Willan Publishing
2 Park Square
Milton Park
Abingdon
Oxon
OX14 4RN

Published simultaneously in the USA and Canada by

Willan Publishing
270 Madison Avenue
New York
NY 10016

First published 2010

ISBN   978-1-84392-850-8 paperback
        978-1-84392-851-5 hardback

British Library Cataloguing-in-Publication Data

A catalogue record for this book is available from the British Library

Project management by Deer Park Productions, Tavistock, Devon
Typeset by GCS, Leighton Buzzard, Beds
Printed and bound by T.J. International, Padstow, Cornwall

Mike – For my family

Andy – For Bill Thompson (KTMFCS)

Contents

Figures and tables

Figures

Tables

Abbreviations

ACOP	Association of Chief Officers of Probation
ACPO	Association of Chief Police Officers
ALEX	American Legislative Exchange Council
ARAI	Actuarial risk assessment instrument
ASBO	Anti-social behaviour order
BCS	British Crime Survey
BME	Black minority ethnic
CCA	Comparative case analysis
CIA	Community impact assessment
CJA	Criminal Justice Act
CJIA	Criminal Justice and Immigration Act
CJSW	Criminal justice social work
CST	Community Security Trust
COSA	Circles of Support and Accountability
CPS	Crown Prosecution Service
CSCP	Cognitive Self Change Programme
CSO	Community service order
CSOR	Child Sex Offender Review
DTTO	Drug treatment and testing order
ECHR	European Court of Human Rights
EM	Electronic monitoring
ESRC	Economic and Social Research Council
GLM	Good Lives Model
GPS	Global positioning system
HDC	Home detention curfew
HMCIP	Her Majesty's Chief Inspector of Probation
HMIP	Her Majesty's Inspectorate of Probation
ICM	Integrated case management
ICT	Information and communication technology
IPP	Indeterminate sentences for public protection
LGBT	Lesbian, gay, bisexual, transgender

MAPPA   Multi-agency public protection arrangements
MAPPP   Multi-agency public protection panel
MARAC   Multi-agency risk assessment conference
MHA   Mental Health Act
NACRO   National Association for the Care and Resettlement of Offenders
NDPB   Non departmental public body
NOMS   National Offender Management Service
NPIA   National Policing Improvement Agency
OASys   Offender Assessment System
ODEAT   OASys Data Evaluation and Analysis Team
OGRS   Offender Group Reconviction Scale
OLR   Order of Lifelong Restriction
PND   Penalty notice for disorder
RA   Responsible authority
RMP   Risk management plan
RoH   Risk of harm to others
RSHO   Risk of serious harm order
RSHS   Risk of serious harm screening
RSO   Registered sex offender
SFO   Serious further offence
SGC   Sentencing Guidelines Council
SMB   Strategic management board
SOO   Sex offences order
SOPO   Sexual offences prevention order
SSA   Smallest space analysis
SVP   Sexually violent predator
ViSOR   Violent and Sex Offender Register
VOO   Violent offender order
YJB   Youth Justice Board
YOT   Youth offending team

Acknowledgements

We would like to thank the contributors for their involvement in and support for this project. We would also like to thank them for their continued intellectualism and enthusiasm for the important issues of public protection that embody this work. We are grateful to Brian Willan and his team for their patience and support for this project. We also continue to enjoy working with students, academics and practitioners and thank them for continuing to invigorate our enthusiasm for this subject. Andy would like to personally thank Eve for her continuing love, help and support and the sacrifices she has made to aid the completion of this book.

Notes on contributors

Kerry Baker is based at the Centre for Criminology, University of Oxford and is also a consultant to the Youth Justice Board for England and Wales. She has been closely involved in the development and validation of the Asset assessment tool, now widely used across youth justice services in the UK. She has written extensively on the subjects of assessment, risk and public protection, especially in relation to young offenders.

Andrew Bridges started work with the probation service in 1973. During his time as an Assistant Chief Probation Officer in Berkshire, he also completed nine months in 1996 as a half-time Visiting Research Fellow at the University of Oxford Probation Studies Unit. His research was published as *Increasing the Employability of Offenders: An Inquiry into Probation Service Effectiveness* in 1998. Andrew was Chief Probation Officer in Berkshire from 1998 to 2001. He also served as Lead Officer for Offender Employment for the former Association of Chief Officers of Probation, and he chaired the interdepartmental National Offender Employment Forum. He joined HM Inspectorate of Probation in April 2001, was appointed Deputy Chief Inspector in July 2003, and then became HM Chief Inspector of Probation in April 2004.

Mark Brown teaches criminology at the University of Melbourne. He has written on a number of aspects of punishment, penal history and theory. He is currently engaged in research projects on the process of desistance from offending, on the modern history of the prison in Australia, on the jurisprudence of offender risk and is slowly writing a book on penal power and colonial rule in India.

David Carson is Reader in Law and Behavioural Sciences at the Institute of Criminal Justice Studies at the University of Portsmouth. He is an academic lawyer who has fostered collaboration between law and the behavioural sciences through original teaching, research, writing, conference organisation and editing, focusing on preventive approaches (here the prevention of poor public protection decision-making).

Tim Carson has worked for the National Probation Service since 2002, and qualified as a probation officer in 2004, initially working for London Probation. He currently works for Devon and Cornwall Probation Area, and is based in the Plymouth Local Delivery Unit, with a caseload primarily consisting of high risk offenders and life-sentenced prisoners. He is also a facilitator for the Integrated Domestic Abuse Programme.

Sarah Charman is a Principal Lecturer at the Institute of Criminal Justice Studies at the University of Portsmouth. She has published widely in the area of pressure groups in criminal justice policy-making, the role of the Association of Chief Police Officers and the politics of criminal justice policy. She is currently researching in two areas: the cultural dynamics and interoperability of the emergency services; and the impact of loss within cases of miscarriages of justice.

Bob Golding is a Senior Associate Lecturer at the University of Portsmouth, and is course leader for Masters degrees in Policing, Policy and Leadership, and Police Science and Management. As well as undertaking the role of programme manager for the ACPO/Home Office National Ballistics Intelligence Programme, and programme consultant for the ACPO Criminal Use of Firearms working group, he is also a Member of the Association of Project Management (MAPM), and an advanced practitioner in Programme Management. Previously he was an Assistant Chief Constable with Warwickshire Police, from which he retired in 2006. He also had a national profile as the lead for the Association of Chief Police Officers (ACPO) for research and development and business crime. He was with Warwickshire police since 2002, previously serving as a police officer for 25 years with the Hampshire Constabulary.

Cecil Greek is Associate Professor of Sociology at University of South Florida Polytechnic. His specialty areas include the history of sociology and criminology, mass media depictions of crime and deviance, and qualitative research methodologies. His book, *The Religious Roots of American Sociology* (Garland Press, 1992), focused on the founding generation of American sociology and their eventual turn to from qualitative to quantitative methods. His second book (co-edited with Caroline Picart), *Monsters Among and Within Us: Evil, Crime and the Gothic in Films* (Farleigh Dickinson University Press, 2007), focused on film as a medium in which discussion of the continuing existence of evil is at the forefront. As an instructor, Dr Greek works on establishing an online criminology masters degree and a unique program in computer criminology. The latter introduces students to the use of computer forensics, specialised software and online databases such as those employed by law enforcement and correctional agencies.

John Grieve CBE QPM joined the Metropolitan Police in 1966 at Clapham. He served as a detective throughout London and in every role from undercover officer to policy chair and as a Murder Squad senior investigator. He organised the 'Community, Fairness, Justice' Conference and was first

Director of Intelligence for the Metropolitan Police. He led the Anti-Terrorist Squad as National Co-ordinator during the 1996–1998 bombing campaigns. He was the first Director of the Racial and Violent Crime Task Force, in which role he gave evidence to Part Two of the Stephen Lawrence Inquiry. Now he is a Senior Research Fellow at the University of Portsmouth and Professor Emeritus at London Metropolitan University; a Commissioner of the Independent Monitoring Commission for the Peace Process in Northern Ireland; he was also appointed Independent Chair of the Home Office/Ministry of Justice Independent Advisory Group on Hate Crime in 2007. In 2008 he was awarded the ACPO Homicide Working Group Lifetime Achievement Award for contributions to murder investigation.

Nathan Hall is a Senior Lecturer in Criminology and Policing at the Institute of Criminal Justice Studies at the University of Portsmouth. He has extensively researched hate crime, particularly in relation to criminal justice responses in England and Wales and in the United States. His first book, *Hate Crime*, was published by Willan Publishing in 2005, and he is joint editor of *Policing and the Legacy of Lawrence*, also published by Willan in 2009. Nathan has also recently completed a PhD thesis involving comparative research of the policing of hate crime in London and New York. In addition to working with a number of police services across the country, Nathan has also acted in a consultative capacity to the Association of Chief Police Officers (ACPO), Her Majesty's Inspectorate of Constabulary (HMIC), the Home Office and the Ministry of Justice, and is a member of the Race for Justice Independent Advisory Group and a member of the ACPO Hate Crime Working Group.

Eric Janus is President and Dean of the William Mitchell College of Law, Saint Paul, Minnesota. His main area of interest is on the interaction of law with psychiatry and other health sciences; however, he also has an interest in the effectiveness of risk assessment, the policy implications of the current approaches to sexual violence, the boundaries of the state's ability to use civil commitment to protect the public, as well as diversity and racial justice. He is the author of *Failure to Protect: America's Sexual Predator Laws and the Rise of the Preventative State*, published by Cornell University Press in 2006. The author served as co-counsel in extended litigation challenging the constitutionality of Minnesota's Sexually Dangerous Person Law. He thanks his research assistants, Joe Phelps and Emily Polachek, for their expert assistance in preparing this manuscript.

Hazel Kemshall is Research Professor of Community and Criminal Justice at DeMontfort University. She is currently undertaking research on pathways into and out of crime for young people for the European and Social Research Council, polygraph use with sex offenders for the Ministry of Justice as well as undertaking evaluations of multi-agency public protection panels, and child sex offender disclosure pilots for the Home Office. She is the author of the Home Office risk training materials for social workers and the Scottish Executive materials for social workers. Her research interests include risk assessments and management of offenders, effective work in multi-agency public protection, and implementing effective practice with offenders.

Anne-Marie McAlinden is a Lecturer in the School of Law at Queen's University Belfast. She obtained a Master's degree in Criminology and Criminal Justice (with distinction) and a PhD from Queen's on the subject of sex offender management. She previously held posts as Lecturer in Law and Lecturer in Criminology at the University of Ulster, before completing her PhD and joining the academic staff at Queen's. She currently teaches in the areas of evidence and sentencing. Her research is in the areas of sexual offences, restorative justice and penal policy where she has published widely. Her recent book, *The Shaming of Sexual Offenders: Risk, Retribution and Reintegration* (Hart Publishing, 2007), was awarded the British Society of Criminology Book Prize 2008. Her most recent work is on the grooming of children for sexual abuse. She has a contract with Oxford University Press to publish a monograph on the subject as part of the Clarendon Series in Criminology in late 2010.

Fergus McNeill is Professor of Criminology and Social Work in the Glasgow School of Social Work (a joint venture of the Universities of Glasgow and Strathclyde) and a Network Leader in the Scottish Centre for Crime and Justice Research at the University of Glasgow. Prior to becoming an academic in 1998, Fergus worked for a number of years in residential drug rehabilitation and as a criminal justice social worker. His research interests and publications have addressed a range of criminal justice issues including sentencing, community penalties, ex-offender reintegration and youth justice. Most recently, Fergus' work has focused on the policy and practice implications of research evidence in the process of desistance from offending. His first book, co-authored with Bill Whyte, *Reducing Reoffending: Social Work and Community Justice in Scotland*, was published by Willan in April 2007. His second, co-edited with Monica Barry, *Youth Offending and Youth Justice*, was published by Jessica Kingsley in September 2009.

Mike Nash is Reader in Criminology and head of the Institute of Criminal Justice Studies at the University of Portsmouth. He is a former senior probation officer who worked in lifer and maximum security prisons. He has published extensively in the field of dangerousness and public protection and worked closely with practitioners for a number of years. His most recent books include *Public Protection and the Criminal Justice Process* (2006) and *The Anatomy of Serious Further Offending* (with Andy Williams) (2008), both Oxford University Press. He has an interest in the way in which the public protection agenda has impacted upon the diverse organisational cultures which make up MAPPA.

Mike Nellis is Professor of Criminal and Community Justice in the Glasgow School of Social Work. He started his career as a social worker with young offenders in the London Borough of Greenwich and Kent, before completing his PhD at the Institute of Criminology, University of Cambridge, and embarking on a teaching career at the University of Birmingham; it was during this time that he worked on the training of probation officers. He has written extensively on this subject as well as the supervision of offenders in the community, penal reform and popular culture, and the theory and practice of community justice. He is a leading authority on the electronic monitoring of offenders, and was involved in the Home Office evaluation of the GPS satellite tracking pilots in England and Wales. He has interests in surveillance and the use of new technology in crime control more generally.

Nicola Padfield is a Senior Lecturer at the Faculty of Law at the University of Cambridge and a Fellow of Fitzwilliam College, Cambridge. She trained as a barrister and was called to the Bar in 1978, before taking up a career in academia. Her books include *The Criminal Justice Process: Text and Materials* (4th edn, 2008); *Criminal Law* (7th edn, 2010); *Beyond the Tariff; Human rights and the release of life sentence prisoners* (2002). She has edited several collections of essays, and is editor of *Archbold Review*. She has held advisory and consultant positions to a wide variety of bodies (for example, currently as expert to the European Committee on Crime Problems of the Council of Europe on their project on Dangerous Offenders) and has provided evidence to a number of Parliamentary Committees. She sits as a Recorder (part-time judge) in the Crown Court and is a Bencher of the Middle Temple.

Francis Pakes is Reader in Comparative Criminology at the Institute of Criminal Justice Studies, University of Portsmouth. He gained his PhD from Leiden University in the Netherlands. His first book, *Comparative Criminal Justice*, was published in 2004 by Willan. The second edition appeared in 2010. Apart from comparative work Francis publishes regularly on crime, justice and social change in the Netherlands and on the intersections of criminal justice and mental health.

Herschel Prins has over 50 years experience in the Criminal Justice and Forensic Mental Health fields. He has worked as a probation officer and as a psychiatric social worker (in that latter role at the then Stamford House Remand Home and Approved School Classifying Centre for male juvenile offenders). He subsequently worked in the Probation Inspectorate and then held academic appointments at the University of Leeds (Department of Psychiatry) and Leicester University (School of Social Work and Medical School). He retired as Director of the School of Social Work in 1984. He has served on the Parole Board, the Mental Health Tribunal and the Mental Health Act Commission. For some years he chaired the Mental Health Advisory Committee of the National Association For the Care and Resettlement of Offenders (NACRO). He has chaired three forensic mental health inquiries. The first into the death of Orville Blackwood at Broadmoor, the second into the absconsion (while on day parole) from a medium secure unit, the third, a homicide inquiry for the Leicestershire Health Authority. He has served on a number of editorial boards and authored numerous books and papers. The fourth edition of his book *Offenders, Deviants or Patients: Explorations in Clinical Criminology* (Routledge) was published in June, 2010.* Currently he holds professorial appointments at the Universities of Leicester (Department of Criminology) and Lougborough (Department of Social Sciences: Midlands Centre For Criminology and Criminal Justice). In acknowledgment of his services to forensic mental health the Low Secure Unit at Glenfield Hospital Leicester bears his name.

*His memoirs *Mad, Bad, and Dangerous to Know* were published by Waterside Press earlier in 2010.

Stephen Savage is Professor of Criminology and Director of the Institute of Criminal Justice Studies, University of Portsmouth, which he founded in 1992. He has published widely on policing and the politics of criminal justice policy, including *Police Reform: Forces for Change* (Oxford University Press, 2007). He has recently researched and published on miscarriages of justice, and his current research is on the independent investigation of complaints against the police.

Bill Thompson taught at Essex, Cambridge and Reading Universities, acted as an expert witness in over 200 child sex assault cases, and helped build the miscarriages of justice movement in the UK before relocating to the USA. He is author of *Soft-Core* and *Sadomasochism* (both 1994). Bill's unique ethnographic approach has meant he has been involved in researching some of the largest miscarriages of justice over the last twenty years. His work on historical cases of child abuse in care homes was presented to the Home Affairs Select Committee in 2001. He is currently researching US miscarriages of justice for a comparative study while teaching at Hartwick.

James Vess received his PhD in clinical psychology from Ohio State University in the United States, and then spent fifteen years in a variety of treatment, assessment and supervisory roles at Atascadero State Hospital, a 1,250-bed maximum security forensic psychiatric facility in California. From that, he took a clinical academic position at Victoria University of Wellington in New Zealand maintaining a forensic practice as well as providing expert evidence to the Courts and Parole Board. He currently a Senior Lecturer at Deakin University and a member of the Clinical Forensic Research Group of the Centre for Offender Reintegration. His current research focus is primarily on risk assessment with violent and sexual offenders, as well as public policy and judicial decision-making with high risk offenders. He also has an active interest in psychometric assessment, personality disorders and psychopathy, and the relationship between these factors and treatment response, risk and recidivism. He has a further interest in the management and treatment of offenders, and outcome evaluation with forensic programmes.

Beth Weaver is a Lecturer at the Glasgow School of Social Work, Universities of Glasgow and Strathclyde, having previously worked as a social worker and MAPPA coordinator. Her main area of interest is on the desistance and implications for criminal and community justice policy and practice, specifically with regard to community penalties. However, she also has an interest in the emergence of discourses, policies and practices surrounding public protection.

Dick Whitfield is Trustee and former Chair, The Howard League for Penal Reform; former Chief Probation Officer, Kent and former Independent Member of the Parole Board. He is a prominent commentator on probation-related affairs and has an active interest in probation officer training, having been an external examiner at the University of Portsmouth. His introductory texts on the probation service and books on community service, tagging and prisons have been widely read and regarded by students for many years.

Kate White worked as a Probation Officer in Bedfordshire and then in probation officer training before joining HM Inspectorate of Probation from 2001 to 2010. As Assistant Chief Inspector of Probation she was responsible for the Offender Management Inspection programme. She has also led the Inspectorate's work in relation to issues of risk of harm across the adult offending caseload, including the management of occasional inquiries and reviews in this area.

Andy Williams is Principal Lecturer in Forensic Criminology at the Institute of Criminal Justice Studies at the University of Portsmouth. He completed his doctorate in 2003, which consisted of the only insider ethnographic account of the Paulsgrove anti-MAPPP demonstrations, which took place in August 2000. His main areas of research and interest are sexual offenders, forensic evidence, crime scene behaviour and offender profiling. He is co-author (with Mike Nash) of *The Anatomy of Serious Further Offences* (Oxford University Press, 2008) and has written in the areas of moral panics, paedophilia and public protection. For the last five years he has been involved in developing and implementing training for MAPPA personnel in Hampshire, training over 350 practitioners in understanding patterns of violent and sexual offending.

Introduction

Andy Williams and Mike Nash

In 1993 two-year-old James Bulger was abducted from the New Strand Shopping centre in Liverpool and murdered. This is a case that should be familiar to most readers, due both to the nature of the attack on James and the fact that his murderers were two young boys themselves (Jon Venables and Robert Thompson were both aged ten). Both boys were eventually convicted in one of the most highly emotive and widely publicised trials in the history of the criminal justice system. Initially the offenders' identities were kept secret, until Mr Justice Morland ruled that the two boys could be identified. From that day onwards, the names of Thompson and Venables were linked for ever to one of the most horrific murders of modern times. The judge set a tariff of eight years' detention for the two boys before they could be considered for release on licence, which was later increased to a minimum of fifteen years by the then Home Secretary Michael Howard. In 1999 there came a shift of position by the government, when the decision was made that minimum punishment periods should not be set by the Home Secretary. In 2001 Thompson and Venables were given new identities and released from custody on a life-licence. As this case from the very beginning generated immense public interest, issues of public protection have been paramount. Having spent eight years in secure accommodation, under strict secrecy, the general public knows very little of their 'rehabilitation' or 'therapy', so questions arose as to whether the boys still presented a danger to the community. Having committed such a violent offence at such a young age these concerns were obviously justified, as problems relating to the management of the two offenders in the community came to the forefront. The identified problems – such as keeping their location secret, risk assessment and managing their needs and vulnerabilities away from the relative security of their custodial accommodation – were often framed in the discourse of striking a balance between individual rights/liberty *and* community safety and public protection. It is this dichotomous discourse that runs through many of the chapters in this Handbook.

The reason we have started with the Bulger case is not for effect, nor to regurgitate what has been written many times before; but was simply because of timing. Seventeen years on, just as we were preparing to hand this Handbook to our publisher, news came through that on 2 March 2010, Jon Venables had been recalled to prison for breaching his licence conditions. The immediate visibility of this event throughout the national media, on news channels and radio 'phone-ins', indicates that it is still a case that matters. Initial reports simply stated that he had been returned to prison because of breaching his licence, but no details as to the exact nature of the breach or breaches were forthcoming. As news spread of his recall, speculation grew as to what had happened. Was he recalled for a breach in his licence conditions, or had he committed another criminal offence? These questions were put to the then Justice Secretary, Jack Straw, who said he would not disclose the details of Venables' recall:

> I'm sorry that I cannot give more information at this stage on the nature of the alleged breach. I know there is an intense public interest in why he has been recalled. I would like to give that information but I'm sorry that for good reasons I can't and that's in the public interest. (Travis 2010)

Issues of 'public disclosure' and in the 'best interest of the public' have become the sociological shorthand of public protection discourse in recent years. They are thrown at all sorts of public protection issues, from child neglect and abuse (for example the Climbié and Baby Peter cases), to police investigations into hate crime (for example the Lawrence case), through to serious further offence cases such as Anthony Rice and Dano Sonnex. Interestingly, these framed discourses are often used for diametrically opposing reasons – to both hide the truth and to find out the truth. For example, those closest to the Bulger case (including his parents) also became vocal regarding the recall of Venables, and criticised the handling of this by asking for the public disclosure of why he had been returned to prison (Blake and Roberts 2010). As usual the media had their own agenda and began to speculate into what had happened, citing the following reasons for Venables' recall: violence outside a nightclub (Blake and Roberts 2010); the abuse of ecstasy and cocaine (Booth 2010); and getting into a fight at work (Booth 2010). The bigger question this incident has raised, though, is just how successful the rehabilitation of Venables and Thompson has actually been. This is just one arm of the public protection machine. Protecting the public from danger and harm from others spans the entire process of the criminal justice system, and covers:

- **Crime prevention** – for example, through the work of proactive police investigations, the work of the National Offender Management Service, and the safeguarding children agenda.
- **Criminal investigations** – reactive police investigations into discovered or reported crimes.
- **The legal system** – where multiple agencies aid in punishing and rehabilitating a wide variety of crime and criminality.

- **Public protection systems** – where multi-agency work attempts to risk assess and manage individuals released into the local community.

The above is not an exhaustive list and these areas are not mutually exclusive. This book captures the essence of these processes of public protection through clearly identifiable themes. Our aim is not to provide simple descriptive overviews of public protection models, and readers may ask why we have avoided doing so. The main reason is because this book covers multi-jurisdictional boundaries, both in organisations and in structures involved in public protection, and also different continents and countries. Each meso and micro-level jurisdiction will have similarities and differences. Furthermore, an examination of the range of organisations involved, will reveal a complex array of public protection models, protocols and regulations. While much of public protection in the UK is based upon the principles of multi-agency working, differences among the relevant agencies do exist. It would therefore be impossible to provide a comprehensive overview of all the models in all the jurisdictions and countries that are covered in this volume. Instead, we have chosen to approach this broad subject from the viewpoint of the 'threads' or 'common themes' that we see traversing the multiple jurisdictional boundaries (Abbott 1988) that exist within the public protection domain. The two dominant themes running through many of the chapters are *risk and dangerousness* and *individual rights and community safety*. Furthermore, these two dominant themes have attempted to strengthen their own position by exploiting common fears surrounding sex offenders using the frames of 'disclosure' and 'management' of information on such offenders. Readers will find these threads running through the chapters presented here.

Risk and dangerousness

Many chapters in this volume discuss the issue of risk and dangerousness and how these concepts can inform policy and practice in how we protect the public. What we have noticed is that regardless of the country or topic at hand, issues relating to levels of risk and the dangerousness of certain types of offenders are top of the public protection agenda. Beck (1992) introduced his broad neo-Marxist perspective that examined the macro-level risks that the modern capitalist and scientific communities have 'inadvertently' created through rapid technological developments over the last 200 years. We have become a society that has opened ourselves up to all sorts of risks – from global nuclear or warfare annihilation to all sorts of diseases and natural disasters brought on by the need to use every natural resource of this planet to ensure the survival of our ever-expanding population. The discourse of risk, and the resultant risk avoidance strategies that we have developed in an attempt to avoid the dangers we have effectively brought on ourselves, have also become imbedded within our very own criminal justice systems. We talk about the level of risk of harm an individual could pose, but this question is very generic and opaque. Exactly what are we at risk from? In order to provide some clarity you need to understand risk in terms of relativity. For example, people who do not fly not only avoid the pitfalls of air travel but also avoid the risk of becoming a victim of terrorism. However, moving down a level of analysis, the likelihood of becoming a victim of terrorism via air travel is still relatively low in most countries across the globe. Another example is child abuse. Individuals who do not have children (as well as members of their family) tend not to worry on a day-to-day basis about the risk of child abuse. However, those that do have children will conceptualise the level of risk and incorporate their fears and concerns into their daily control and surveillance practices for their own children. Again, moving down a level of analysis, those who have been abused may have a heightened sense of sensitivity towards this type of risk, and will act accordingly to try to avoid those risks. In short, risk is relative and how we deal with it depends upon our own experiences, intellect and knowledge. However, it must be recognised that this is often determined by the conceptualisation of risk and dangerousness itself.

What readers will find in this volume is critical discussion of how the social construction of 'risk' and 'dangerousness' helps determine strategies for protecting the public. Once we recognise that a particular risk exists, which is usually determined by a criminal act, we then go on to assess not only the likelihood of that risk reoccurring, but the level of harm it would cause. The debate on 'what is dangerousness', and indeed who is dangerous, has been a core issue within the criminal justice system for at least 150 years. However, it was the 1970s that saw a growth in what has been called the dangerousness debate (see Nash 2006). Assigning the label 'dangerous' to a particular category of offenders enables the targeting of resources towards managing that dangerousness. What we provide in this volume is not disagreement with this position; but we hope that the critical reflection through several chapters aids in a greater understanding of what was originally expressed by Scott as dangerousness being a dangerous concept (1977).

Individual rights and community safety

The next core theme to come out of this volume is the framed discourse of offender rights versus community safety. Much of what is written in the public protection arena discusses these important issues. Just how do you strike a balance between offender rights and community safety? It is a difficult issue to comprehend for those of us that feel we should live in a democratic, free society. First there is the Human Rights Act and the European Convention on Human Rights, which has attempted to provide a more humane side to the criminal justice system. Enshrined within such legislation is the protection of individual freedoms. Individuals who have committed crimes are still afforded rights, and these are seen, depending on your own perspective, as either a good or a bad element of the criminal justice process. Second, is the issue of the right to safety. What readers will find throughout most debates on public protection is the argument that it is necessary to restrict the individual rights of an offender in order to provide adequate protection to the public. Obviously there are some individuals or groups of individuals that wish to see harm done to other members of the community. Most of us would accept that there has to be some trade-off between individual rights and public safety. That is, after all, why many countries are controlled by democratically elected governments. We put our faith in our public protection systems. However, the problem has arisen in recent years whereby an individual's freedom can be restricted simply because their behaviour fits into a particular classification system that deems them dangerous. What is of even greater concern is that the 'evidence' to support this labelling of groups is often inherently flawed, lacks systematic application across jurisdictional boundaries, has not been systematically analysed and is, in many circles, accepted uncritically. The chapters that discuss these issues bring to the forefront the need for both systematic research and critical reflection in this area. Currently in the UK we tend to err on the side of caution and take a more punitive stance towards individual freedoms, restrictive sentencing and offender management practices. All of these are 'justified' by the public protection (community safety) discourse.

Sex offenders, public disclosure and the management of information

The two dominant themes discussed above have gained their strength by utilising the fears and insecurities surrounding sex offenders, in particular child sex offenders. While it is not possible here to review the history of crusades against sex offenders (for a good general historical study see Jenkins 1998), it is important to note how influential this group has been in crystallising ideas and practices around public protection. Therefore, what readers will also find in this volume is that many of the chapters focus their discussion on public protection, individual rights, risk and dangerousness around attempts to manage sex offenders in local communities. This is indeed a huge undertaking for public protection agencies. As we develop more and more sophisticated investigative techniques, as well as increase legislation on sexual offences, we widen the net of social control (Cohen 1985). This has resulted in criminal justice agencies becoming over-burdened with offenders, which ultimately has had an influence on the effectiveness of our public protection system.

Central to the issue of sex offending is the issue of public disclosure and the management of information. In the UK, cases such as the abduction and murder of Sarah Payne, as well as the Soham murders, highlighted the need to develop policies pertaining to the sharing and managing of information on sex offenders. Again, arguments for and against the disclosing of information to the public have been framed within the discourse of individual rights versus community safety. Recently there has been a 'sea change' in thinking around this issue, with governments becoming more open to the idea of providing access to information on sex offenders to the general public. A number of chapters deal with this issue and the implications for the offender, victim and public protection policy. While this issue, as well as those discussed above, are not the only important issues, the are the ones that tie this diverse body of work together. Figure I.1 provides a simple visual representation of these issues.

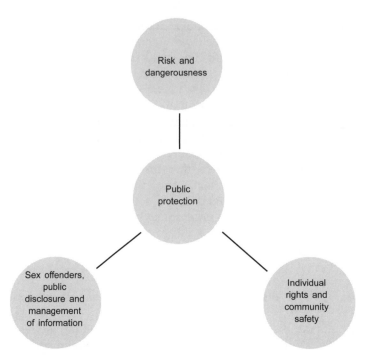

Figure I.1 Thematic threads in public protection.

Structure and organisation of the book

This book consists of five parts that examine the key threads of public protection. Each has its own individual introduction, which describes the chapters therein, so the following will provide only the briefest of descriptions of these parts. What we have tried to accomplish is the bringing together of a number of researchers, commentators and practitioners to discuss the broad range of issues, themes and threads that we have introduced above. Part One is concerned with the conceptualisation of risk and dangerousness and how these concepts are operationalised within the public protection agenda. As readers will soon discover, conceptualisations of risk are often flawed, yet they are operationalised to produce 'evidence' to predict an individual's future behaviour. The three chapters discuss these issues, among others, to try to get readers to think critically about these important issues and concepts.

Part Two links to Part One through a discussion of risk assessment. The principal way we have turned our conceptualisations of risk and dangerousness into effective ways to control and manage particular groups of offenders is through the various techniques of risk assessment. These techniques are used to identify, label and classify the 'dangerous' and the 'risky'. They also provide justifications for criminal justice agencies to restrict the human rights and liberty of those they deem to be of greater risk of reoffending. The predictive nature of risk assessment is also discussed.

Part Three is for the 'doers' out there. It provides an examination of the core developments within public protection from the perspective of practitioners that have been working at the highest level of public protection for many years. The wealth of experience and knowledge about how things are 'really done' provides the phenomenological context needed when theorising about public protection.

Part Four provides a wider perspective on public protection, covering the United States, Scotland, Australia and the Netherlands. Despite the obvious differences in the social, political and cultural contexts that have helped shape the public protection issues and arrangements in these countries, we see a clear cluster of themes that can be related to the experience of the UK.

Finally, Part Five offers a range of chapters we have generically labelled as 'contemporary issues in public protection'. As discussed above, public protection has gone from strength to strength because it has grown from a relatively small range of key issues focused around sex offenders. However, sexual offending is not the only important problem within the public protection domain. This final section introduces a broad range of issues – from electronic tagging, through to hate crime and youth offenders – and offers some interesting discussion from authors researching public protection issues in these areas.

References

Abbott, A. (1988) *The System of Professions: An Essay on the Division of Expert Labour*. Chicago: University of Chicago Press.

Beck, U. (1992) *Risk Society: Towards a New Modernity*. London: Sage.

Blake, H. and Roberts, L. (2010) 'James Bulger killer returned to jail "due to drug use and violence"', www.telegraph.co.uk/news/uknews/crime/7364719/James-Bulger-killer-returned-to-jail-due-to-drug-use-and-violence.html (accessed 4 March 2010).

Booth, J. (2010) 'Bulger killer Jon Venables "recalled to jail over fight at work"', www.timesonline.co.uk/tol/news/uk/crime/article7049248.ece (accessed 5 March 2010).

Cohen, S. (1985) *Visions of Social Control: Crime, Punishment and Classification*. Cambridge: Polity Press.

Jenkins, P. (1998) *Moral Panic: Changing Concepts of the Child Molester in Modern America*. New Haven: Yale University Press.

Nash, M. (2006) *Public Protection and the Criminal Justice Process*. Oxford: Oxford University Press.

Scott, P. (1977) 'Assessing Dangerousness in Criminals', *British Journal of Psychiatry*, 131: 127–42.

Travis, A. (2010) 'Pressure grows for answer to why Jon Venables is behind bars', www.guardian.co.uk/uk/2010/mar/03/pressure-straw-bulger-killer-prison (accessed 5 March 2010).

Part One

The Context of Public Protection

Introduction

Mike Nash and Andy Williams

This first section is intended to set the scene. The aim is to open up debates that transgress practice and theory, which in turn are covered further on in this volume. It is also intended in a way to underline why we decided to ask so many people to contribute to this handbook. It is our view that public protection, risk and dangerousness have assumed a position of very considerable influence within the wider criminal justice process. This is obvious in the more overt developments in legislation such as the introduction of indeterminate sentences for public protection (IPP), but we would argue that its influence is far more widespread. For example, the creation of multi-agency public protection arrangements (MAPPA) has not only led to closer working relationships between previously quite distinct agencies (police and probation), but has also drawn in a much wider family of agencies as those having a 'duty to cooperate'. From employment services, to victims' groups and housing authorities, the public protection network has spread its tentacles far and wide. In so doing there have inevitably been signs of cultural transference between them, none more so than between police and probation. We would argue that the public protection ethos is a powerful one, fully supported by governments and, of course, a constant source of interest for the media. It is a difficult agenda to resist and indeed has spread its influence to other areas of criminal justice practice. The probation service, for example, has significantly shifted its focus over the past two decades, and while this is not entirely due to the growth in public protection it has probably facilitated and accelerated that change. The chapters in this first section are therefore intended to explore the significance of the public protection agenda including a historical overview, a theoretical analysis and an exploration of its politics.

We start with Herschel Prins' insightful overview of dangerousness, risk and public protection. He is uniquely placed to write this chapter having been a probation officer, psychiatric social worker and academic. He has been writing in this field for over five decades and been a member of many important committees. He has been awarded numerous honorary professorships and his work is hallmarked and underpinned by his work with offender-patients, with practitioners from a variety of disciplines and as a trainer in multi-agency approaches to risk and dangerousness. His expansive chapter covers several decades of developments in assessing and managing risk and is punctuated by reference to key case studies of some of the most notorious offenders of recent times. In a world that increasingly appears risk averse, Prins takes us to a discussion on the acceptability or tolerability of risk, the difference between the two perhaps reflecting the type of society in which we live. Many of his case studies offer insights into how vital clues about the offender's behaviour were missed, overlooked or not given the significance they merited. Indeed, he makes the important point that often those 'lower down the pecking order' may have the most to contribute – if they are listened to. Prison officers in particular might come into this category as people who get to know offenders well but whose observations often fail to appear in official reports. What is striking about these cases is that, changes in legislation aside, the 'lessons to be learned' still appear in inquiries into tragedies today. Systems have undoubtedly improved but the operation and interpretation of those systems by various professionals continues to appear to cause difficulty.

Prins reminds us that human judgement is fallible and system failure is almost inevitable – as such it is important that false assurances of safety and risk minimalisation are not given. Those who choose this route (politicians might be tempted) should remember that pride comes before a fall. But perhaps Prins' main message has to be the importance of information, notably about the offender and his/her offending behaviour. Gathering this information is a painstaking process and requires an enquiring mind. His chapter might go some way to helping practitioners to think along these lines.

Mark Brown sets out to make us think about and rethink our perceptions of dangerousness. By working with the notion of the sex offender as monster he explores why certain offenders enter the realm of dangerousness and why other, equally serious offenders do not – with the more recent exception of terror suspects. Brown utilises the 'black box' model of the human mind (into which one cannot see) to try to understand why people make quite specific demands that quite specific sorts of offenders be subject to an equally specific set of measures of control and prevention. By utilising the work of Michel Foucault, Brown concludes that it is not the *difference* of sex offenders (or indeed terrorists) but their very *ordinariness* that leads to calls for these measures. He refers to Foucault for whom the monster was 'the spontaneous, brutal, but consequently natural form of the unnatural'. 'It is', Foucault said, 'the magnifying model, the form of every possible little irregularity exhibited by the games of nature ... the major model of every little deviation ... [and] the principle of intelligibility of all the forms that circulate as the small change of abnormality.' Brown argues that the regulation of these individuals is an extension of the self-regulation that ordinary men operate, and indeed are forced to operate, in their everyday interactions with vulnerable groups. It is this connectedness with 'ordinary' populations that elicits such widespread support for the precautionary measures that are in so many ways illiberal. If we can understand why we conceptualise dangerousness as we do then there may be hope that we can not only reconfigure our approach to dangerousness but also think more constructively about who these measures need to be targeted at.

The final chapter in this section is Mike Nash's review of the politics of public protection. We have indicated above that we consider this to be a highly politicised agenda and a number of chapters in this volume allude to the influence of politics at periods of key change. Perhaps one of the major points to be made is how public protection policy, even in its formative phase, did so much to shape the law and order politics of the Labour Party. It served as a catalyst for Labour's transformation from being labelled soft on crime to being 'tough' under Tony Blair. The then Home Secretary Michael Howard had worked tirelessly on developing his populist policies, not least in the hope of smoking out the soft underbelly of the Labour opposition. This he singularly failed to do, and in opposition and in power Labour has almost seamlessly assumed the Conservative law and order mantle.

The focus on policies aimed at protecting the most 'innocent' and vulnerable members of society brook little opposition in or outside of Parliament. These measures have, however, grown at an almost exponential rate to the point where huge powers can be deployed against the potentially dangerous or high risk of harm offenders. The political message given out to an anxious public is that these measures are necessary for their protection, at the same time giving a sense that the problem continues to grow and that governments are giving the agencies the powers they need to protect us. Within this debate, which is based on a more than slight distortion of reality, the rights of offenders are incrementally being reduced (see Eric Janus' chapter on how this scenario has developed in the United States). It has to be said that in some recent cases there have been successful legal challenges to certain government policies in the field. However, and again mirroring the United States, these challenges have been defeated on appeal to the higher courts. Protecting the public has assumed a dominant position in British politics which appears to continue to sweep all before it. We hope that this volume will encourage readers to pause and take stock.

Chapter 1

'Dangers by being despised grow great'*

Herschel Prins

Introduction

When the editors of this volume invited me to contribute I began to think about how long it had been since I first became interested in what is generally called *dangerousness* in both the criminal justice and forensic mental health fields. I suppose it stemmed originally from my very early days as a probation officer in the 1950s. To some extent my interest could be seen as somewhat dormant until 1977 when, in my view, two seminal papers appeared in the literature. The first was a fascinating article written from a criminological perspective by Professor Tony Bottoms (now Sir Anthony Bottoms) on the basis of an inaugural professorial lecture at Sheffield University (Bottoms 1977). The second was a most thoughtful (and thought-provoking) clinical contribution by my friend the late Dr Peter Scott. His paper was published a short while after his too early demise (Scott 1977). From then on I attempted to take a more focused interest in the phenomenon, and have written and lectured pretty extensively about it. Having said that, readers of this volume might well ask whether I have anything to say that's new. In my defence I will try to place the issue of so-called dangerousness in perspective; what follows might be deemed to be a summary of some of my previous work (for a more extended treatment of the topic see, for example, Prins 1999). The present contribution attempts to deal with the following aspects: first, a very brief historical context; second, a comment on the background of a society obsessed by 'danger' and 'risk'; third, danger and risk defined; and fourth, clinical aspects.

In the Middle Ages, and even earlier, the term 'dangerous' seems to have been applied in a general way to those persons or groups of persons who were considered to compromise the survival of the State. Rennie (1978) reminds us of the extent to which the poor and the disadvantaged were frequently referred to as the 'dangerous classes'. Indeed, such an assumption seems to be

---

*Edmund Burke, 1729–97. *Speech on the Petition of the Unitarians*. 11 May 1792.

implicit in English Poor Law legislation from the time of Elizabeth I onwards, namely that the poor were not only *idle* but *dangerous*. As Rennie states, 'For nearly four hundred years, from the thirteenth through the sixteenth centuries, the English criminal law was obsessed with vagrants and beggars, who were viewed as a great danger to society' (1978: 38). It was not until the eighteenth century onwards that the so-called *psychiatrisation* of delinquency occurred (Foucault 1978). The results of this trend were far-reaching and powerful resonances can be seen in today's society when the mentally ill are deemed by the media to be particularly prone to violence. They conveniently forget that the severely mentally ill (such as those suffering from some forms of schizophrenic illness) may be much more likely to harm themselves than others. However, in equity it must be said that there does seem to be a raised risk of violence associated with some forms of schizophrenia, but this is only most likely when the disorder is compounded by illicit drug use and social disadvantage.

So much for the brief history. I now move on to consider the current context in which we consider and deal with so-called dangerous behaviour and the risk of its occurrence. Readers will be quick to note that I have not yet attempted to define these terms. I remedy this shortly.

A risk-obsessed society

In 1992 the Royal Society made a sobering comment (1992: 3): 'Risk is ubiquitous and no human society can be considered risk free'. Human beings are made anxious about ambiguity and uncertainty and will sometimes engage in dubious and harmful practices to avoid them. Much recent and current concern about so-called dangerous people has its roots in such phenomena; unless they are properly understood, many of our efforts aimed at dealing with such people will fail. Beck puts an eloquent gloss on the matter, as follows: 'Calculating and managing risks which nobody really knows has become one of our main preoccupations. That used to be a specialist job for actuaries, insurers and scientists. Now we all have to engage in it, with whatever rusty tools we can lay our hands on – sometimes the calculator, sometimes the astrology column' (Beck 1998: 12).

Crucial to our understanding is the uncertainty of risk prediction (see later). This is particularly important at the present time when blame is so quickly apportioned in a variety of hazardous and tragic circumstances, be they homicides, train, air or sea disasters, flood damage, or infections of one kind or another.

On not being allowed to swim

Sometimes our concerns about 'risk avoidance' assume such ludicrous proportions that it requires the courts to bring an element of good sense into the situation. A few years ago the Hampstead Heath Winter Swimming Club in London took the Corporation of London to court against their decision to close their three ponds on safety grounds when they were not being supervised by lifeguards. Apparently changes to the lifeguards' duty hours meant that club members were not allowed to swim at their own risk. The doughty swimmers took their case to the High Court. The presiding judge – Mr Justice Burnton – decided in their favour, stating that in this case the law would 'protect individual freedom of action … and avoid imposing a grey and dull safety regime on every one'. His Lordship relied in part upon a previous judgment in an earlier case in which the House of Lords found against a man injured when diving into a quarry pit. 'If people want to … dive into ponds or lakes that is their affair' (*Independent* 27 April 2005, p. 7).

One could, of course, quote many other examples of this excessive preoccupation with risk avoidance. Teachers are now reluctant to comfort children physically for fear of being accused of paedophilic inclinations. They are also reluctant to engage in adventure-type school trips for fear of being taken through the civil or criminal courts if accident befalls. Far fewer children gain from the healthy exercise of walking to school for parental fear of accident or assault. Overprotection of this kind ill prepares children for the Hobbesian view of life as 'solitary, nasty, brutish and short'. In America it is said that it is becoming increasingly difficult to recruit doctors to the practice of obstetrics and gynaecology for fear of litigation when and if things go wrong. Terence Blacker went as far as to suggest in an article in the *Independent* (21 October 2005, p. 37) that such preoccupations were turning us all into 'mindless … wimps'. He describes our plight as one of terror, saying that 'fear is habit-forming, weakening. The more we allow various vested interests to frighten us with their apocalyptic warnings, the less capable we shall be of dealing with a real global crisis, if, when it comes along.' In the light of recent developments these are sobering thoughts.

Much concern about risk is, of course, media driven; if mental health, criminal justice and legal professionals are forced into making predictions, there may be an assumption on the part of the public that such professionals are capable of getting it right every time. The latter will then assume (no doubt unwittingly) a mantle of infallibility and will have to count the cost when they get it wrong, as from time to time they assuredly will. The now mandatory inquiries into homicides committed by persons known to the mental health services are a good example of this problem; it is one that needs placing in perspective. We know factually that the number of homicides committed by persons with mental disorders (particularly mental illness) is very small (and has, in fact, contrary to public opinion, actually declined over the past decade), but the media seem to have vastly influenced the politicians in their somewhat frenetic search for solutions (see, for example, Taylor and Gunn 1999; Cohen 2007; Department of Health 2008). It is also worth remembering (as a means of gaining historical perspective) that 'fashions' in criminal justice and mental health come and go. Soothill (1993) has demonstrated very usefully the manner in which this may occur. He cites as examples our almost ten-year cyclical preoccupations with, for example, homosexuality and prostitution, with rape, with physical child abuse and with so-called 'satanic' child sexual abuse.

The hazards of prediction were once described (somewhat humorously) by the former science correspondent of the *Independent* (19 September 1997, p. 10):

> Such are the risks we all run every day that, if you are an adult between 35 and 54, there is roughly a one-in-400 chance you will be dead within a year. *Homo sapiens* is a bit of a twit about assessing risks. We buy lottery tickets in the hope of scooping the jackpot, with a one-in-14 million chance of winning, when there's a one-in-400 chance that we won't even survive the year ... the evidence suggests that our behaviour is motivated by panic and innumeracy.

The varying perceptions of risk have very important implications for risk assessment and management. Measures to reduce risks may have unseen (and sometimes hazardous) consequences. For example, as the article in the *Independent* suggested, 'wearing seat belts may make drivers more reckless because they feel safer; and marking a road as an *accident black spot* may reduce accident figures so successfully that it ceases to be a black spot – it was only dangerous in the first place because people didn't know how dangerous it was'. I have sometimes wondered if the introduction of 'speed humps' and 'speed tables' will, over time, have the intended desired effect. Many drivers become frustrated by them and they may, in fact, demonstrate their frustration by acts of careless or negligent driving immediately *after* traversing them. An example drawn from much earlier times tends to lend support to these contentions. Adams (1995) cites the introduction of the Davy lamp, which was intended to save lives in the mining industry; but, as Adams suggests, it actually resulted in an increase in explosions and fatalities because the lamp permitted mining activity to be carried out at deeper levels where the explosive methane content was much higher (1995: 211).

Professional perceptions of risks

There can be little doubt that there has been a massive growth in what can best be described as the 'risk industry'. This is exemplified in well-publicised concerns about safety in the home, safety at work, the development of emergency services and currently those associated with child protection. Adams (1995) suggests that we may all tend to overdo 'risk prevention'. He cites as examples overestimates of household risks leading to unnecessary expenditure on insurance; the design of buildings that take into account hazards that can be rated as almost zero, such as earthquakes in areas where these are highly unlikely; overzealous safety measures on the railways leading to increases in passenger costs, which in turn may drive people away from the railways on to the roads, thus creating greater driving hazards; abnormal fears of mugging and similar attacks that may lead the elderly and other vulnerable people to lead unnecessarily isolated lives. Adams suggests that there are two types of human. The first is zero-risk man *homo prudens*, personifying 'prudence, rationality and responsibility' (1995: 17). He describes this creature as 'a figment of the imagination of the safety profession'. The second is a type of being within every one of us, a creature he describes as *homo aleatorius*: 'dice man, gambling man, risk-taking man'; his descriptions give further credibility to the importance of *irrationality* in human risk-taking behaviour or abstention from it.

Definitions of risk

In 1983 the Royal Society produced a report on the subject of risk which was subsequently revised (Royal Society 1992) in the light of development in knowledge and practice. In their introduction to this later report, the authors concentrated their minds on a range of terms used in the literature on risk. Some of them are quoted below:

- *Risk* is defined in terms of the probability 'that a particular adverse event occurs during a stated period of time, or results from a particular challenge' (1992: 2).

- A *hazard* is defined as 'the situation that in particular circumstances could lead to harm ...' (1992: 3).

- *Risk assessment* is used to 'describe the study of decisions subject to uncertain circumstances' (1992: 3). The Royal Society working group divided risk assessment into *risk estimation* and *risk evaluation*.

- *Risk estimation* 'includes: (a) the identification of the outcomes; (b) the estimation of the magnitude of the associated consequences of these outcomes; and (c) the estimation of the probabilities of these outcomes' (1992: 3).

- *Risk evaluation* is 'the complex process of determining the significance or value of the identified hazards and estimated risks to those concerned with or affected by the decision' (1992: 3).

- *Risk management* is 'the making of decisions concerning risks and their subsequent implementation, and flows from risk estimation and risk evaluation' (1992: 3).

The authors of that report also cautioned against equating *risk* with *danger*. To put it very simply, I see risk as the probability of an event occurring, and danger as the extent of the hazard or harm likely to accrue.[1] The term 'acceptable risk' is frequently used by decision-takers and policy-makers. The authors of the Royal Society report support the views expressed by Layfield (1987) in his report of the Sizewell B nuclear plant inquiry; they prefer the term 'tolerable'. Layfield considered that the use of the term 'acceptable' did not reflect the seriousness of the problems involved in risk-taking activities; he suggested the term 'tolerable' as being a more accurate description of what was involved. Following Layfield's report, the Health and Safety Executive defined 'tolerable risk' in the following fashion:

'Tolerability' does not mean 'acceptability'. It refers to the willingness to live with a risk to secure certain benefits and in the confidence that it is being properly controlled. To tolerate a risk means that we do not regard it as negligible or something we might ignore, but rather as something we need to keep under review and reduce still further if and as we can. (1988, in Royal Society 1992: 93)

Risk prediction

There is a vast and ever-growing literature on the prediction of risk (see, for example, Adams 1995; Royal Society 1992; Monahan *et al.* 2001, especially Chapters 1 and 7). If, by prediction, we mean the capacity to get it right every time, then the short answer has to be 'no'. If we have more modest goals, and ask if there are measures that could be taken to attempt a possible reduction in dangerous behaviour, then it is possible to give a qualified 'yes'. Pollock and Webster (1991) put the matter very succinctly: 'From a scientific perspective [the question] is impossible to answer since it is based upon an unscientific assumption about dangerousness, namely that it is a stable and consistent quality existing within the individual' (1991: 493). They suggest that a translation into more appropriate terms would produce the following question: 'What are the psychological, social and biological factors bearing on the defendant's ... behaviour and what are the implications for future [behaviour] and the potential for change?'

There has been much debate concerning *actuarial* versus *clinical* prediction. Not all of this debate has been helpful. However, one very modest and sometimes overlooked enterprise in the field of criminal justice was the pioneering work of Mannheim and Wilkins with their prediction scales in relation to the (then) sentence of Borstal Training (1955). I use the term modest because the authors stated that their scales could never replace individual assessment, largely because predictions based upon retrospective studies of case records could never take sufficiently into account subtle factors that might have been relevant at the time of sentence. We have, of course, made significant progress since those early pioneering days. However, as Fitzgibbon (2008) has shown, much depends upon the abilities of those using such scales and measurements to 'input' the relevant data. Maden's excellent book (2007) does much to clarify the usefulness of an actuarial approach. The message I take from his work is that prediction scales can alert one to the need to focus one's efforts and resources on particular *classes* of offenders/patients (see also Gray *et al.* 2008).

For some years, workers in the criminal justice and mental health fields have taken comfort from an oft-quoted statement by the American psychologist Kvaraceus that 'nothing predicts behaviour like behaviour' (1966: 8). However, as recent commentators such as Gunn (1996) have pointed out, such statements may rest upon statistical error and reinforce the fallacious view that risk is a static phenomenon and unaffected by changes in social and other circumstances. At the end of the day, as MacCulloch *et al.* stated: 'Predicting and preventing violence is a fundamental part of clinical practice

… forensic psychiatrists, psychologists and clinical criminologists are asked to assess cases to make a prediction of the likelihood of harm to others in the future' (1995: 61) (see also Kettles *et al.* 2003; Maden 2007).

Legal and administrative aspects

A number of legislatures, notably in some of the states of North America, have made attempts to define dangerousness for the purposes of incarceration of individuals adjudged to be dangerous, be this incarceration in penal or forensic mental health care institutions. Currently in the UK, the Criminal Justice Act 2003 makes it possible to impose specific sentences that take account of an offender's potential for future dangerousness. In the last few years there has been an increase in the use of the 'life' (indeterminate) sentence for cases not involving homicide. This has been justified in various court of appeal decisions on the grounds that by such means offenders considered to be dangerous (but not necessarily mentally abnormal within the meaning of the mental health legislation) can be incarcerated until such time as the authorities (for example, the Parole Board) consider, on the basis of expert advice, that they may be safely released. However, it should also be noted that decisions based solely on concerns about dangerousness appear to have recently become 'contaminated' by considerations based on political expediency. This would appear to have occurred in the case of the late Myra Hindley and some others. So far as those formally judged to be mentally disordered are concerned, current mental health legislation recognises the concept of potential dangerousness. Thus, the 1983 Mental Health Act (England and Wales) (as amended by the Mental Health Act 2007), makes provision, *inter alia*, for the compulsory detention of an individual with a view to the 'protection of other persons' and sections 37 and 41 of the Act make provision (subject to certain criteria being satisfied) for placing an order restricting discharge upon a person made the subject of a Hospital order to protect the public from 'serious harm'. In addition, the proclivities of some offender-patients are recognised in the setting up and maintenance of the three High Secure Hospitals in England and Wales (Broadmoor, Rampton and Ashworth) for those patients who 'exhibit dangerous, violent or criminal propensities' (National Health Service and Community Care Act 1990, section 4). During the past three decades the law and practice relating to both mentally abnormal and dangerous offenders have been examined by five different groups – the Butler Committee, the Scottish Council on Crime, the 'Floud' Committee, the Reed Committee and, most recently, in the joint Home Office and Department of Health report on managing people with severe personality disorder (Prins 1999).

What's in a name?

The words 'danger', 'dangerousness' and 'risk' have little real meaning on their own. It is only when placed in context that they become useful. However, any interpretation must also, to some extent, be subjective. Walker made a useful point when he suggested that 'dangerousness is not an objective quality, but an *ascribed* quality like trustworthiness. We feel justified in talking about a person as dangerous if he has indicated by word or deed that he is more likely than most people to do serious harm' (Walker 1983: 23, emphasis added). The Butler Committee, in examining the notion of dangerousness in relation to mentally abnormal offenders, considered it to be 'a propensity to cause serious physical injury or lasting psychological harm. Physical violence is, we think, what the public are most worried about, but the psychological damage which may be suffered by some victims of other crimes is not to be underrated' (Home Office and DHSS 1975: 59). Practising clinicians and others who have day-to-day contact with those deemed to be dangerous generally agree with Scott's definition that dangerousness is 'an unpredictable and untreatable tendency to inflict or risk irreversible injury or destruction, or to induce others to do so' (Scott 1977: 130). Some clinicians, for example the late Dr David Tidmarsh (1982), suggested that Scott's inclusion of unpredictability and untreatability can be questioned, since the anticipation and modification of a danger does not necessarily minimise the risk. Scott also stressed another very important element, namely that the use of dangerousness as a label might contribute to its own continuance – a point that could usefully be heeded by lawyers, sentencers and criminal justice and forensic mental health professionals. For present purposes, it is worth noting Floud's statement that 'risk is in principle, a matter of fact, but danger is a matter of judgement or opinion' (Floud 1982: 215).[2] Thus the notion of dangerousness implies a prediction, a concern with future conduct. Most authorities agree that apart from a very small group of individuals who may be intrinsically dangerous because of some inherent physical or other defect (which may make them explosive in their reactions), the general concern is with the *situation* in which the combination of the *vulnerable* individual with a *provoking incident* may spark off explosive and dangerous behaviour. As noted by the Butler Committee (Home Office and DHSS 1975), 'the individual who spontaneously "looks for a fight" or feels a need to inflict pain or who searches for an unknown sexual victim is fortunately rare, although such people undoubtedly exist. Only this last category can be justifiably called: "unconditionally" dangerous.' I would suggest that *risk* and *danger* may be distinguished in the following somewhat oversimplified fashion.

Risk may be said to be the likelihood of an event occurring, and danger may be said to be the degree of damage (harm) that may occur should the event take place.[3] The forensic psychiatrist Adrian Grounds makes the important additional point that both of these also need to be distinguished from worry. 'They are not well correlated and judgements and decisions based on worry may not be well founded. The problem is that feelings of worry are expressed by professionals in the vocabulary of risk. The feeling 'I am very worried about X' is likely to be translated into 'X is a high risk' in written and spoken communications. Worry may, however, be excessive or insufficient in relation to the risk. The test is the same as for risk: how well grounded is it in … [the offender's] history?' (Grounds 1995: 54–5).

The word 'dangerousness' will, of course, mean different things to different people. If readers of this chapter were asked to rank certain people in order of their 'dangerousness', they would probably find themselves in some difficulty. Which of the following, for example, would you consider the more 'dangerous': the bank robber; the persistent paedophile; the person who peddles dangerous drugs to children; the person who drives when knowingly unfit to do so; the swimmer who has a contagious disease but continues to use the public baths; the bigoted patriot, national leader or politician who believes they are always right, the computer hacker, the person who is HIV positive or has AIDS who persists in having unprotected sexual intercourse with a variety of partners, the consortium which disposes of toxic waste products without safeguards, forensic mental health or criminal justice professionals who always act on their own initiative without adequate consultation with colleagues and who believe that their 'personality' will 'get them by' in dangerous situations? All of these persons or bodies present hazards of one kind or another depending upon the situation in which they find themselves. Thus, it is imperative that one's subjective inclinations must be tempered by knowledge of the *facts* (see later).

Clinical issues

Sentencers (both professional and lay) and forensic mental health and criminal justice professionals have to carry out their work of limiting 'mayhem' within the constraints of the complex legislative and administrative frameworks already referred to. The current legislative framework has become so complex that even experienced sentencers find some of the legal requirements difficult to interpret. Professionals not only have to deal with these legal complications but, as stated earlier, also have to carry out their work within the current 'blame culture' and to endeavour to balance offenders' and offender-patients' needs against the need to protect the public. The current political climate continues to place a premium on the latter, and as suggested earlier this has recently been reinforced with the implementation of the Criminal Justice Act 2003.[4] In this final part of the chapter I provide several varied case examples as a prelude to some suggestions for improving practice.

One or two or these cases achieved a great deal of publicity and all involved homicidal conduct. My first examples are drawn from some that occurred before the instructions issued in 1994 by the Department of Health that an independent inquiry should be held in those cases where the assailant had been known to the mental health services.[5] In 2005, the Department updated this guidance with a view to making these requirements more precise (Department of Health 1994, 2005; see also Prins 2007 for a detailed account of the inquiry into the management of Michael Stone; also Francis 2007).

Case example 1 – Graham Young

I begin with the well-known case of Graham Young, sometimes known as the St Albans Poisoner. In 1962 Young was sent to Broadmoor under sections 60 and 65 of the Mental Health Act 1959. He had been convicted of administering poison to his father. There was also an allegation that he had poisoned his stepmother over a long period of time through the administration of antimony, finally killing her through the administration of thallium. Some eight years after his admission to Broadmoor he was conditionally discharged on the recommendation of his responsible medical officer (RMO). He was found employment in a warehouse at a photographic development company at Bovingdon in Hertfordshire, and was also found lodgings. He was supervised by a psychiatrist and a local probation officer under the requirements of his conditional discharge. In the light of subsequent events, it is of interest to note that before his discharge from Broadmoor it has been suggested that he had applied for two posts – one at a forensic science laboratory, and another at a pharmaceutical training school. Within some three months of his discharge Young had poisoned three of his workmates with thallium, which he had obtained by signing the poisons register at a firm of leading London dispensing chemists. Suspicion quickly fell upon Young (largely due to the perspicacity of the works manager and the visiting appointed factory doctor, a local GP).

Young pleaded not guilty to murder (on the facts), it is said on the basis that he wanted to obtain maximum publicity for his crimes. He was sentenced to life imprisonment on two charges of murder and two of attempted murder. On the day that the sentences were announced the Home Secretary of the day – Reginald Maudling – made a statement in the House of Commons announcing the setting up of two inquiries. The first was to be an in-depth investigation into the circumstances of Young's discharge and subsequent supervision. This was under the chairmanship of the late Sir Carl Aarvold, Recorder of London. The second was a wide-ranging review of the law and procedures relating to the management of mentally abnormal offenders, under the chairmanship of Lord Butler (Aarvold et al. 1973 and Home Office and DHSS 1975). The Aarvold inquiry made a number of important recommendations concerning the supervision of restricted offender-patients and the over-ready availability of poisons for purchase by members of the public. Following the inquiry a permanent body was established to advise the Home Secretary on restricted cases requiring special care in assessment. Initially known as the Aarvold Board, it later became known as the Advisory Board on Restricted Patients, remaining in existence until it was 'stood down' in 2003. The reason for this was that the 1983 Mental Health Act had given greater powers over the discharge of restricted offender-patients; and with these powers had come greater expertise and experience in dealing with cases such as those presented by the likes of Graham Young.

A number of important points emerged from the Aarvold Report. First, whether or not adequate attention prior to discharge was paid to Young's long-standing obsessive preoccupation with poisons.[6] Second, how much was known about his two employment applications before discharge. Third, the wisdom of allowing him to take up employment in a workplace where he could easily have had access to poisonous substances. Relevant here is the injunction in Shakespeare's King John, 'How oft the sight of means to do ill deeds makes deeds ill done' (IV, ii: 218–19). Fourth, some questions arose about the quality of the supervision given him by his community supervisors. To be fair to the probation service, it was claimed on their behalf that they were given insufficient information about his past history. It was also suggested at the time that Young was never visited at his lodgings. When the police visited following his arrest, they found a variety of chemicals and bizarre drawings of men in varying stages of dying, including some showing them with substantial hair loss – a feature of thallium poisoning.

Some three years or so after his life sentence, Young developed a mental illness serious enough to warrant his formal transfer back into the Special (Secure) Hospital system under the 1983 Mental Health Act. However, it was felt subsequently that he should be returned to prison. In a perceptive review of the case Bowden (1996) quotes the telling conclusions of a case conference held at Park Lane Special Hospital (now Ashworth Hospital): 'We can do little else but recommend that Graham be returned to whence he came and repay his debt to society and his victims in the normal way' (Bowden 1996: 23). And so it was to be. In August 1990 Young died in Parkhurst prison, aged 42, from natural causes (heart attack), although as readers may imagine there was a good deal of speculation as to the cause of death. (For a more general account of Young's life see Holden 1995, and for one written by a member of his family – his aunt Winifred – see Young 1973.)

Case example 2 – Sharon Campbell

Sharon Campbell, a psychiatric patient with a history of mental illness, stabbed to death her former social worker, Isabel Schwarz. This followed an assault some months earlier and allegations of threats by Campbell. She was found guilty of manslaughter on the grounds of diminished responsibility and made subject to a Hospital Order with Restrictions (sections 37 and 41 of the Mental Health Act 1983). One of the key factors emerging from the inquiry into her care was a history of poor compliance with medication (something of a perennial problem for which a hoped for remedy is now being sought in the community compulsory treatment provisions of the 2007 amendments to the Mental Health Act). In addition, her willingness to accept social work support and supervision was very variable. The inquiry indicated that although mental health resources were available they were not being used very effectively. The inquiry team was impressed by the effort and time put into the case by many different professionals, but in the months leading up to the fatal attack there had been a dearth of psychiatric treatment and close and regular supervision. In addition, the report had a good deal to say about the need for employing authorities to set in place procedures that would attempt to maximise the personal safety of social work and allied staff (Spokes *et al.* 1988).

Case example 3 – the shootings at Dunblane Primary School

In the early morning of 13 March 1996 Thomas Hamilton approached the car park at Dunblane Primary School where he proceeded to cut the telephone wires that served some neighbouring houses. He then entered the school armed with four handguns and 743 rounds of ammunition. He went into the assembly hall and began firing; subsequently he went into other adjacent parts of the school, firing indiscriminately. Hamilton eventually turned his weapon on himself, placing a revolver in his mouth, and died shortly afterwards – such an outcome is not uncommon in killings of this kind. As a result of this mass carnage sixteen children and one member of staff died. Hamilton inflicted gunshot wounds on ten other pupils and three other members of the teaching staff. In one of the most detailed and measured reports of its kind, Lord Cullen (Scottish Office 1996) outlined some of the background factors that might have been in Hamilton's mind on that fateful day.

> His [boys'] clubs were in decline. He was in serious financial difficulties. His mood was low and he was deeply resentful of those who had claimed he was a pervert. After a gap of about eight years his interest in firearms was resurgent. There is evidence which points to his making preparations for what he did ... in the light of expert evidence from a psychologist and a psychiatrist, I conclude that Thomas Hamilton was not mentally ill but had a paranoid personality with a desire to control others in which his firearms were the focus of his fantasies. The violence which he used *would not have been predictable*. His previous conduct showed indications of paedophilia. (Scottish Office 1996: 2, emphasis added)

At various times Hamilton's fitness to possess firearms should have been looked at more closely. For example, in 1989 his authority to possess firearms and ammunition was not questioned after he had 'behaved inappropriately in showing firearms to a family in Linlithgow'. In 1991 a detective sergeant, in a formal memorandum, challenged his fitness to be trusted with a firearm. This followed a police investigation of certain events at a summer camp run by Hamilton. Lord Cullen is highly critical of the lack of follow-up of this memorandum. He says, 'on balance, there was case for revocation which should have been acted upon. The same consideration should in any event have led to the refusal of Thomas Hamilton's subsequent application to renew his firearms certificate' (Scottish Office 1996: 2).

The inference I draw from Lord Cullen's comments is that there have been occasions when staff who are somewhat lower down in the 'pecking order' of the mental health or criminal justice hierarchy may not have been given the serious attention that their observations deserved. Other examples can be found in the inquiry reports into the cases of Jason Mitchell (Blom-Cooper *et al.* 1996) and Richard Burton (Chapman *et al.* 1996). There have also been instances of the views of close relatives not having been given the serious attention they merited (Prins 1999: Chapter 4).

Case example 4 – Daniel Mudd

Daniel Mudd had been released in 1983 on conditional discharge from Broadmoor, where he had originally been detained for non-homicide offences (arson and assault). In 1986, during his period of supervision in the community, he killed a fellow (female) resident in a mental after-care hostel. He was subsequently sentenced to life imprisonment. An internal committee of inquiry was set up by Wiltshire County Council (1988). Their findings revealed what would seem to have been a number of very serious errors of judgement and practice. I summarise them as follows:

- Too little attention had been paid to the nature of Mudd's previous offences, behaviour and convictions prior to his hospitalisation. These had included making indecent phone calls, assault with intent to commit actual bodily harm, and indecent assault on an adult female.

- Too little attention appeared to have been paid to the views of the doctors who examined him at his trial. They suggested that he was potentially very dangerous, and, because of the nature of his particular personality disorder, *might kill someone at some future date*.

- Although Mudd had been in the care of the local authority concerned with his current supervision for many years, no attempt appeared to have been made to collate the data in the numerous files about him that were available; these would have provided an extended personality profile. In addition (and very unwisely in my view) no one had thought it useful to consult the social worker who had known and supervised him as a youngster.

- Mudd had very serious drinking problems during the period of supervision. These, it was alleged, had never been properly identified or placed in the context of his past behaviour and attitudes. There were said to have been occasions when he was so affected by drink that he could not get up to go to work. This lack of identification continued, even when he was picked up on several occasions by the police for being drunk and when he had assaulted a man while under its influence. He had also been discharged prematurely from a training scheme because of alleged sexual advances to a woman trainee. His supervising social worker left and no attempt appeared to have been made to prepare Mudd for his departure. It was also alleged that he had then been left unsupervised for a month.

- The committee found that throughout the period of supervision Mudd's version of events had been accepted at face value and without challenge. The records available (which were in any case difficult to interpret) showed no indications of any critical analysis of events and attitudes. Supervision by senior management had not been effective. The supervisors seem to have adopted a preconceived notion that Mudd was someone who needed to be 'rescued' from an adverse life experience (namely having been detained in a Special Hospital) and that this preoccupation had blinded them to the realities of the case.

- Finally, it was considered that his supervisors took too much upon themselves and did not liaise sufficiently well with the relevant department of the Home Office. In addition (and perhaps even more seriously) they failed to provide that department with adequate regular updates about the progress of the case.

Case example 5 – Christopher Clunis

The inquiry into the care and management of Christopher Clunis is possibly the most well known of all mental health 'homicide inquiries'. It has served as a 'pattern' for later inquiries and practices. It was important in paving the way for the introduction of detailed guidance on the care and management of mentally disordered persons with a proclivity for violence; it also heralded the introduction of 'risk registers' for such individuals. A further development is worthy of mention here. His case led to the establishment of the Zito Trust. The work of its founder – Jane Zito and her colleagues – has been of great significance in our understanding of both victims and perpetrators.

Clunis, a diagnosed schizophrenic, stabbed to death a complete stranger – the recently married Jonathan Zito – on a London Underground railway platform. Following conviction and sentence by way of a Hospital Order with Restrictions (sections 37 and 41 of the Mental Health Act 1983) the two health authorities concerned with his care and treatment set up an independent inquiry (Ritchie *et al.* 1994). Their very comprehensive and careful account traces the care (and sadly sometimes the lack of it) of Clunis for the period 1986–1992. Although the inquiry team singled out a few instances of dedicated care and concern on the part of one or two workers, none of the various agencies concerned escaped criticism; for example, the police, Crown Prosecution Service, health and social services, the probation service and voluntary agencies. What emerged overall was not a picture of wilful or intentional neglect of duty, but a failure to spot vital behavioural cue and clues, *and a failure to communicate between agencies at every level.* Had information from a variety of sources been linked, certain deficiencies observed by the inquiry team could have been avoided. Some examples were: (1) failure to obtain a detailed and sequential history of the pattern of Clunis's lifestyle (cf. the case of Daniel Mudd above); (2) failure to consider his past record of violence and to treat it seriously enough to proceed with *prosecution* rather than *diversion* from the criminal justice system; (3) failure to act assertively enough in dealing with the steady deterioration of his mental state: the team suggested that this particular failure may have arisen because of an erroneous ideological assumption about not wishing to label Clunis as a schizophrenic in order to avoid stigmatising him; (4) failure to monitor his progress in a pro-active fashion; (5) inadequate training for mental health and criminal justice professions in this area of work.

Over the years I have used the following two examples in the course of sessions with forensic mental health and criminal justice postgraduate students and workers. They are 'fictional' but mirror real-life situations.

Two case vignettes used in training

Case example 6

'Paul' was in the community on conditional discharge from hospital (sections 37 and 41, Mental Health Act 1983). The order had been imposed for killing his wife. He had been detained in hospitals for some ten years before being conditionally discharged by a Mental Health Review Tribunal. The facts of his original offence were that having killed his wife (by manual strangulation) he had hidden her body and it was some months before it was discovered. At the time of his arrest he had been seeing another woman on a regular basis. A year after being conditionally discharged into the community he informed his supervising probation officer that he had been seeing a woman and hoped to marry her. In this case the probation officer's responsibilities seemed quite clear. In the first instance, the development would need to be reported to the Ministry of Justice (Mental Health Unit) which has central government responsibility for mentally disordered offenders. Second, the officer would need to ascertain from Paul more details of this new relationship. In the course of such discussion Paul would need to be advised that he should inform the woman of his past history (given the particular circumstances of his original offence). Should Paul refuse to do so, his probation officer (having taken advice from his line management, and maybe the Ministry) would need to tell Paul that he himself would have to inform the woman concerned.

Some might consider that this would constitute an intrusion into an offender-patient's personal liberty, but the broader issue of the protection of the public, in this case the woman Paul is seeing and maybe others, necessitates such action. The issues seem clear-cut. In other cases there are grey areas that require careful consideration of who else should be involved, as illustrated in the next example.

Case example 7

'Tom' is a 60-year-old offender released on life licence for killing a child during a sexual assault. He had been convicted on a previous occasion of indecent assault and had then been made the subject of a Hospital Order without Restrictions (section 37 of the Mental Health Act 1983). He had been living in the community on life licence for about two years, and had so far not given his supervising probation officer any cause for concern. However, the officer then received a phone call stating that Tom had been seen 'loitering' by the bus stop outside a local primary school. What should the probation officer do about this development? There are several steps that need to be taken. First, further information is required as to the source and reliability of the information received. This is of particular importance at a time when public and political concerns about paedophilic behaviour are highly charged. Did this information come via the school or, for example, from a bystander who knew Tom's history and was perhaps out to make trouble for him by deliberately misconstruing a quite innocent piece of behaviour? (After all, he *could* have been waiting for a bus quite legitimately.) Second, in order to clarify Tom's behaviour, the officer would need to arrange an urgent appointment to see Tom. Why, for example, was he at this particular bus stop? His responses would have to be judged in the light of details about his previous offences. It would be very ominous if, for example, the circumstances of the offence for which he received his life sentence were similar to his present behaviour. Third, the probation officer would have to consider whether it was advisable to contact the school and/or the local police to ascertain if any complaints or comments had been received concerning similar conduct by Tom. Whatever steps the probation officer takes, *the offender is entitled to be told of the action proposed and the reasons for it.* Such information will be likely to be received and accepted more easily if Tom had been given very clear indications at the start of his life licence (or conditional discharge, if he had been dealt with through the mental health care system) concerning his obligations under their terms. 'Tom' needs to be made aware of his supervisor's responsibilities to report any apparently untoward conduct. Sadly, there have been occasions in the past when mutual expectations and obligations have not been shared openly. In such cases an offender or offender-patient can feel legitimately surprised when speedy and sometimes apparently condign action is taken.

The foregoing selection of case examples may be considered somewhat idiosyncratic; there is some truth in this. The selection has been merely to present the variety of factors that may lead to unsatisfactory outcomes. Other examples may be found in Prins (1999) and of course in the plethora of homicide inquiry reports that have appeared since 1994. These now number several hundred. The present Director of the Zito Trust, Michael Howlett, informs me that there must now be some 400 or so (personal communication, 5 January 2009).

Trying hard but could do better

Having highlighted a number of imperfections in practice, I conclude this chapter by suggesting some possible remedies. However, a note of caution is needed before doing so. Human judgement is highly fallible. We should never give the impression to the media and the public that mistakes will *never* be made. To do so would be an indication of professional arrogance and lead to quite unrealistic expectations. This may lead to heavy 'falls from grace' when disaster occurs – as assuredly it will from time to time. All we can do is to promise to do our best. My comments are divided into four sections: aspects of communication, the concept of vulnerability, establishing an effective baseline and improving practice.

Aspects of communication

A non-forensic mental health and criminal justice professional once stated with great wisdom that 'All tragedy is the failure of communication' (Wilson 1974: 9). Such a statement embodies a number of aspects of communication – as follows:

The need for good inter-professional communication. For example, case conferences and public protection committees in their various guises sometimes fail to work as effectively as they might – for the following reasons. First, espousal of the mistaken belief that multi-agency is synonymous with multi-disciplinary, when in terms of role perceptions and 'territorial' boundaries it clearly is not. Second, the participants in such meetings are trained in different ways and their 'world views' may be markedly different (for an account of an 'imaginary' case conference see Prins 1999: 127–9). I do not propose to deal with the intricacies of current multi-agency public protection arrangements (MAPPA) as these are dealt with elsewhere in this volume. However, some of the problems involved in these have been discussed usefully by Ansbro (2006a, 2006b).

The need for adequate communication between worker and offender/offender-patient and an understanding of the impediments to this. These include ambivalence, hostility, fear and denial, not only on the part of the offender/offender-patient but also on that of the worker. Denial is by no means the sole prerogative of offenders and offender-patients. Maybe offenders, offender-patients and their professional workers should heed Banquo's advice to his fellows: 'And when we have our naked frailties hid, That suffer in exposure, let us meet, And question this most bloody piece of work, To know it further' (*Macbeth*, II, iii).

How well do professionals 'hear' the concerns of the families or others close to their charges? In the Andrew Robinson inquiry, it became clear that Andrew's parents had tried to draw attention repeatedly to their fear of his continued psychotically motivated aggression and violence towards them. Their home had become a place of terror and accounts of their fears *appear* to have gone unheard (Blom-Cooper *et al.* 1993). Such a need is graphically expressed by Falstaff in *Henry IV Part II* when he says: 'It is the disease of not listening, the malady of not marking that I am troubled withal' (I, ii).

The need for professionals to be 'in touch' with the warring and less comfortable parts of themselves. This need may show itself, for example, in misperceptions of race and gender needs; in our inquiry into the death of Orville Blackwood in Broadmoor, we considered that perceptions of young African-Caribbeans as always being 'Big, Black and Dangerous' might seriously have handicapped some of the staff's handling of this group of offender-patients (Prins *et al.* 1993).

There may also be unresolved and professionally limiting personal conflicts about some specific forms of conduct, notably those involving extreme sexual deviation. Professionals working in this field might usefully heed the statement by Pericles in Shakespeare's play of that name that 'Few love to hear the sins they love to act' (I, i).

The concept of vulnerability

The assessment and management of dangerous behaviour and the risk factors involved are concerned, essentially, with the prevention of vulnerability, namely taking care not to place the offender or offender-patient in a situation in which they may be highly likely to re-enact their previous pattern(s) of dangerous behaviour. The recognition of this reduces the vulnerability of both the public to the commission of unfinished business and the vulnerability of the offender/offender-patient (Cox 1979). (See also case example 6 above.)

Establishing an effective baseline

All the research and clinical studies in the area of risk assessment and management in criminal justice and forensic mental health attest to the importance of obtaining the basic facts of the situation. It is the evidence that decision-making bodies, such as courts, mental health review tribunals, the Parole Board and the Ministry of Justice, require in order to make the most effective decisions. This necessitates having an accurate and full record of, for example, the index offence or other incident and in addition the person's previous history, especially their previous convictions. A bare legal description tells us nothing about seriousness of intention at the time of the offence, or its prognostic significance. This has become of increasing importance today when 'plea bargaining' and advocates' attempts to persuade courts to 'downgrade' offences have become more frequent. An incident that may well have had the ingredients to justify an original charge of attempted murder may eventually end up, by agreement, as one of unlawful wounding. Neither do the bare details of an offence give any real indication of motivation. For example, burglary may take the form of a conventional break-in, or it may have more ominous prognostic implications if, say, the only items stolen were the shoes belonging to the female occupant of the premises. For example, those males who expose themselves to women in an aggressive fashion associated with erection and masturbatory activity need to be distinguished from those who are more passive and who expose from a distance without erection; the former group are those who may be more likely to go on to commit serious sexually assaultive offences. Scott, in his paper on assessing dangerousness in criminals, stressed the need to take a longitudinal and rounded view of the offender's 'career-path' and a careful scrutiny of *all* the facts (Scott 1977).

At one time high hopes had been placed upon various procedures for risk *registration*. However, some of the evidence I once gathered from the fields of childcare and probation seemed to indicate that risk registration did not *necessarily* ensure good practice (Prins 1995). We seem to live in the age of the 'tick box' and the 'protocol'. 'Audit' and clinical governance are the order of the day, but whether their somewhat obsessional hold on administrators and others really aids practice is by no means clear. One consultant psychiatrist has recently gone as far as to coin a new word for this preoccupation – 'formarrhoea' (Hardwick 2003).

Improving practice

There is no doubt that many forensic mental health and criminal justice professionals carry out very high-quality work in cases requiring risk assessment and management. They receive little credit for this. However, as we have seen, there have been instances when the quality of work has shown deficiencies. Why might this be and how could such deficiencies be remedied? Basically, it has to do with asking 'unaskable', unthinkable and uncomfortable questions. I have identified seven groups of questions in order to describe them as seven possible 'sins of omission'. Before doing so, a couple of preliminary general observations are needed. Professionals in this difficult and often highly charged area need two types of supervision and support. The first is the support and supervision that holds them accountable to their organisation for what they do. The second, and equally important, is the degree of supervision from line management that enables them to do more effective and empathic work. It is very important for workers to have the chance to share perspectives with their peers. This assists in the development of knowledge and confidence. The following seven areas of questioning may go some way to providing more effective engagement.

1 Have past precipitants and stresses in the offender/offender-patient's background been removed? If still present, are they amenable to further work and, more importantly, has the worker the courage to deal with

them? A period of long-term work with an offender or offender-patient may induce in the worker a form of 'familiarity', which may blind them to subtle changes in the individual's social and emotional worlds. If they have worked very hard to induce change through the establishment of a 'good' relationship, they may not wish to do anything that may challenge that; they may prefer not to know. Genders and Player, in their study of Grendon prison, stated that they were often reminded of the words of the old song, 'I wish I didn't know now what I didn't know then' (Genders and Player 1995: 40).

2 What is the individual's current capacity for dealing with provocation? It is useful to remind ourselves of Scott's advice that aggression may be deflected from a highly provoking source to one that may be scarcely provoking at all – the 'medea syndrome' (Scott 1977). Some of our most perplexing cases are those in which serious violence has been caused to the 'innocent stranger' in the street. Careful scanning of the immediate environment may enable us to detect (and perhaps help the individual to avoid) potentially inflammatory situations. For example, to what extent has the over-flirtatious wife or partner of a jealous husband (partner) courted a potentially dangerous situation by sarcasm, making denigrating remarks about sexual prowess, been otherwise contemptuous, or worn provocative clothing? The same is true, of course, with the male in the provocative role, as is the case from time to time in male homosexual relationships. Detailed accounts of previous provoking incidents are therefore vital in order to assess future risk and provide effective continuing management.

3 How does this offender-patient continue to view himself or herself? The need for a 'macho' self-image in a highly deviant male sex offender is often based upon unresolved past conflicts with women. This may make him likely to continue to take his revenge by way of serious sexual assaults accompanied by extreme violence and degradation of his victims.

4 To what extent have we been able to assess changes for the better in this person's capacity to feel empathy for others? Does this individual still treat others as objects rather than as persons upon whom to indulge their deviant desires and practices?

5 To what extent does the behaviour seem person-specific, or as a means of getting back at society in general, as is the case with some arsonists. The person who says, with continuing hatred in their voice, 'I know that one day I'm going to kill somebody', has to be taken very seriously. To what extent are thoughts of killing or injury still present? Is there a pleasurable feel to their talk about violent acts? Is there continuing interest in such material as violent pornography, horror videos, the occult, atrocities, torture? Sometimes the 'evidence' is less tangible and 'hunches' need to be relied upon – but always carefully followed up and checked out. Thus, Commander Dalgleish in P. D. James' *Original Sin* described his 'instinct' as something which he sometimes distrusted, but had learned not to ignore (James 1994).

6 How much continuing regard has been paid to what the offender/offender-patient actually *did* at the time of the offence? Was it so horrendous that they blotted it out of consciousness? For example, did they wander off in a semi-amnesic state or, upon realising what they had done, summon help immediately? Or did they, having mutilated the body, go off happily to a meal and a good night's sleep? How much are they still claiming it was a sudden and spontaneous crime, when the evidence shows careful planning and considerable premeditation? What was the significant role of substance abuse of one kind or another? Prisons and to a lesser extent secure hospitals are not ideal places for testing out future proclivities in such people. However, escorted periods of leave with close supervision may enable alcohol intake and its effects to be assessed. The persistent paedophile on an escorted group outing to the seaside may alert observant nursing staff to continuing abnormal sexual interest by having eyes only for the semi-naked children playing on the beach. In similar fashion, staff may report patients' interest (and arousal) when in the presence of the children of visitors to the ward, or to pictures of children on the television. How much is known about what 'aids' to sexual fantasy they are storing in their rooms or cells? (For example, newspaper clippings, graphic details from court papers.) The offender-patient who says he is writing his life history in a series of exercise books could well be asked to show them to us; somewhat surprisingly, they are sometimes willing to do so. We may find detailed descriptions of continuing violent and/or sadistic fantasies, which are being used as rehearsal for future activity. All these indicators, coupled with psycho-physiological measures, may help us to obtain a better, if not conclusive, perception of likely future behaviour (for further illustrative material see Prins 1999: 141 *et seq.*).

7 Can we discern to what extent this individual has begun to come to terms with what they did? It is important for all professionals and decision-makers to regard protestations of guilt and remorse with a degree of caution. As Russel and Russel state: 'A person who expresses guilt is to be regarded with vigilance. His next move may be to engineer a situation where he can repeat his activities (about which he expresses guilt), but this time with rationalisation and hence without guilt. He will therefore try to manipulate his victim into giving him a pretext' (1961: 141). Sometimes, an offender or offender-patient may be reluctant to acknowledge the truth of what they have done for fear of causing hurt to relatives and others close to them. The late Dr McGrath, sometime medical superintendent at Broadmoor, once cited the case of a paedophilic sadistic killer who consistently denied his guilt in order to spare his 'gentle devoted parents who could not believe his guilt'. When they died, within a fairly short while of each other, he willingly admitted his guilt, and in due course was released (McGrath 1989). Neither should we forget that in relation to confession and guilt, offender/offender-patients may, in fact, not be guilty of any crime, as numerous *causes célèbres* have so sadly demonstrated.

Concluding observations

In this chapter I have endeavoured to place notions of dangerousness and risk in context. I have tried to offer some examples of ways in which the supervision of potentially dangerous high-risk offenders might be made more effective. Although the advent of sophisticated computational techniques has undoubtedly provided a platform for actuarial advances, it is still the worker at the *individual* level who has to make prognostic judgements and undertake the hazards of ongoing supervision (see Maden 2007). It is comparatively easy and safe to predict what someone will do two weeks or even a month hence; much more hazardous to predict what they might do in a year's time.

Central to the task of the criminal justice or mental health professional in high-risk cases is a commitment to detail and to tracing connections between behaviour patterns. In a review of Gail Bell's book *The Poison Principle*, Forrester – a forensic psychiatrist – makes the following very apposite comment: 'Detail forms the substance of forensic psychiatry in the same way that the investigations of a physician might invoke various ... [tests], so the investigative forensic-psychiatrist must put together a fully corroborated personal narrative, or be charged with pitiful neglect' (Forrester 2003: 467).

It also involves a great deal of personal soul-searching in order to come to grips with behaviour that is frequently anxiety-making and sometimes horrifying. It also calls for operating with a greater degree of surveillance and close monitoring than is customary in some other areas of 'counselling'. It certainly involves a capacity not to attempt to 'go it alone' and in this area of work there is no place for 'prima donna' activities. Despite the difficulties (or maybe because of them), many workers enjoy the challenge presented by those who have shown, or are adjudged likely to show, dangerous behaviour towards others. Such were the views of a small group of consultant forensic psychiatrists when I asked them for the reasons why they chose to specialise in forensic psychiatry (see Prins 1998).

As stated earlier, sadly, but perhaps understandably, politicians and the general public have very high expectations that forensic mental health and criminal justice professionals can 'get it right' every time. Professionals can only give of their best on the understanding that they are not infallible; and if society has ordained that risks through legislation will be taken, then occasional failures are inevitable. Decision-making is often not only complex but emotive. Maybe if professionals are occasionally found 'wanting', it is because as Rumgay and Munro have suggested they feel powerless to intervene effectively (2001). In other instances it may be that people cannot take on board the notion that killers like Harold Shipman and the Austrian Josef Fritzl, for example, could behave as they did since such behaviour defies all expectations. In order to be effective we need therefore to confront our own 'demons'.

Acknowledgements

Once again I must offer my sincere thanks to Mrs Janet Kirkwood for producing the final manuscript, and with such cheerfulness.

Selected further reading

Casement, P. (1985) *On Learning From the Patient*. London: Tavistock.
Casement, P. (1990) *Further Learning From the Patient*. London: Routledge.
Casement, P. (2006) *Learning From Life: Becoming a Psycho-Analyst*. London: Routledge.

These three books written by a former probation officer turned psychoanalyst although written from a psychoanalytic perspective offer very useful insights into working with dangerous people.

Notes

1 A small journey into etymology is helpful here. It may come as a surprise to some readers (as it once did to me) to find that the word *danger* in fact derives from the Latin *dominiarium* which connotes lordship or sovereignty, thus implying, as Sarbin once suggested (1967), the importance of the relationship elements. Sarbin argued that such a meaning had important implications in relation to an individual's concept of his social identity and to the actions he (or others) might take to confirm or deny it.

2 A considerable number of pronouncements have been made in the High Court in recent times concerning the sentencing aspects of risk determination (Criminal Justice Act 2003). Readers should consult the quarterly 'In Court' sections of the *Probation Journal* written by Nigel Stone, especially for the years 2007 and 2008.

3 In the 1970s and early 1980s the words 'danger' and 'dangerousness' were much more in use than they are today. It has become much more common (and sensible) to write and speak about 'risk'. Risk *assessment* and *management* are often seen as discrete entities. In my view this is misconceived; they should be seen as part of a seamless process, since management should entail continuing *reassessment*.

4 The dilemmas involved in balancing rights and obligations are well attested to in two Home Office inquiry reports into the criminal activities of three offenders under supervision at the time of their crimes. The first, Anthony Rice, committed murder while on life licence for attempted rape. The second concerned the joint activities of Damien Hanson and Elliot White, who murdered a man and attempted to murder his wife. White was already subject to a drug treatment and testing order (DTTO), the latter having been imposed for being in unlawful possession of 2.8 grams of cocaine. Both detailed inquiries, carried out by Her Majesty's Inspectorate of Probation, indicate some of the dilemmas involved in balancing human rights against issues concerning public protection (HMCIP 2006a, 2006b). These issues have been explored more generally in a recent excellent book by my former Loughborough colleague, Kate Moss (Brookes) (2009).

5. The impetus for the 1994 instructions seems to have arisen from concerns that had been expressed about the activities of a very small number of mentally disturbed individuals, whose activities had promoted much media interest and condemnation. Examples include Ben Silcock and his foray into the lions' den at London Zoo;

Michael Fagin's entry into the Queen's bedroom; and Michael Buchanan, who killed a complete stranger (a retired police officer) in an underground car park.

6 Readers interested in knowing more about the use of a variety of poisons in homicide cases should consult the recent excellent book by the analytical chemist Dr John Emsley (2008).

References

Aarvold, C., Hill, D. and Newton, G. P. (1973) *Report on the Review of Procedures into the Discharge of Psychiatric Patients Subject to Special Restrictions*, Cmnd. 5191. London: HMSO.

Adams, J. (1995) *Risk*. London: University College London Press.

Ansbro, M. (2006a) 'What can we learn from serious incident reports?', *Probation Journal*, 53: 57–70.

Ansbro, M. (2006b) 'Serious further offence inquiry', *Probation Journal*, 53: 167–77.

Beck, U. (1998) 'Politics of risk society', in J. Franklin (ed.) *The Politics of Risk Society*. Cambridge: Polity Press (pp. 9–22).

Blom-Cooper, L., Hally, H. and Murphy, E. (1993) *The Falling Shadow: One Patient's Mental Health Care: 1978–1993*. London: Duckworth.

Blom-Cooper, L., Grounds, A., Guinan, P., Parker, A. and Taylor, M. (1996) *The Case of Jason Mitchell: Report of the Independent Panel of Inquiry*. London: Duckworth.

Bottoms, A. E. (1977) 'Reflections on the renaissance of dangerousness', *Howard Journal of Penology and Crime Prevention*, 16: 70–96.

Bowden, P. (1996) 'Graham Young (1947–1990): The St Albans Poisoner: his life and times', *Criminal Behaviour and Mental Health*, Suppl: 17–24.

Chapman, H., Ashman, M., Oyebode, F. and Rogers, R. (1996) *Report of the Independent Inquiry into the Treatment and Care of Richard John Burton*. Leicester: Leicestershire Health Authority.

Cohen, S. (2007) *Folk Devils and Moral Panics*, 3rd edn. London: Routledge.

Cox, M. (1979) 'Dynamic psychotherapy with sex offenders', in I. Rosen (ed.) *Sexual Deviation*, 2nd edn. Oxford: Oxford University Press (pp. 306–50).

Department of Health (1994) *Guidance on the Discharge of Mentally Disordered People and Their Care in the Community*, HSG/94/17: 10 May. London: Department of Health.

Department of Health (2005) *Independent Investigation of Adverse Events*. London: Department of Health. (Memorandum replacing paras 33–36 in HSG(94) (LASSL 94(4)). London: Department of Health.

Department of Health (2008) *A Review of 26 Mental Health Homicides in London Committed Between January, 2002 and December, 2006*. London: Department of Health.

Emsley, J. (2008) *Molecules of Murder: Criminal Molecules and Classic Cases*. Cambridge: Royal Society of Chemistry Publishing.

Fitzgibbon, D. W. (2008) 'Fit for purpose: OASys assessments and parole Decisions', *Probation Journal: The Journal of Community and Criminal Justice*, 55: 55–69.

Floud, J. (1982) 'Dangerousness and criminal justice', *British Journal of Criminology*, 22: 213–23.

Forrester, A. (2003) 'Review of G. Bell, *The Poison Principle: A Memoir of Family Secrets and Literary Poisonings*', *Journal of Forensic Psychiatry*, 14: 465–8.

Foucault, M. (1978) 'About the concept of the "dangerous individual" in 19th century legal psychiatry', *International Journal of Law and Psychiatry*, 1: 1–18.

Francis, R. (2007) 'The Michael Stone Inquiry: a reflection', *Journal of Mental Health Law*, 15: 41–9.

Genders, E. and Player, E. (1995) *Grendon: A Study of a Therapeutic Prison*. Oxford: Clarendon Press.

Gray, N. S., Taylor, J. and Snowden, R. J. (2008) 'Predicting violent convictions using the HCR-20', *British Journal of Psychiatry*, 192: 384–7.

Grounds, A. (1995) 'Risk assessment and management in clinical context', in J. Crichton (ed.) *Psychiatric Patient Violence: Risk and Response*. London: Duckworth.

Gunn, J. (1996) 'The management and discharge of violent patients', in N. Walker (ed.) *Dangerous People*. London: Blackstone Press.

Hardwick, P. (2003) 'Formarrhoea', *Psychiatric Bulletin*, 27: 388–9.

HMCIP (Her Majesty's Chief Inspector of Probation) (2006a) *An Independent Review of a Further Serious Offence: Anthony Rice*. London: Home Office.

HMCIP (2006b) *An Independent Review of a Further Serious Offence: Damien Hanson and Elliot White*. London: Home Office.

Holden, A. (1995) *The St Albans Poisoner: The Life and Crimes of Graham Young*, 2nd edn. London: Corgi Books.

Home Office and Department of Health and Social Security (1975) *Report of the Committee on Mentally Abnormal Offenders* (Butler Report), Cmnd 6244. London: HMSO.

James, P. D. (1994) *Original Sin*. London: Faber.

Kettles, A. M., Robson, D. and Moody, E. (2003) 'A review of clinical risk and related assessments in forensic psychiatric units', *British Journal of Forensic Practice*, 5: 3–12.

Kvaraceus, W. (1966) *Anxious Youth*. Columbus, Ohio: Charles E. Merrill Press.

Layfield, F. (1987) *Sizewell B Public Inquiry*. London: HMSO.

MacCulloch, M., Bailey, J. and Robinson, C. (1995) 'Mentally disordered attackers and killers: towards a taxonomy', *Journal of Forensic Psychiatry*, 6: 41–61.

McGrath, P. (1989) Book Review, *British Journal of Psychiatry*, 154: 42.

Maden, A. 2007 *Managing Violence: A Guide to Risk Assessment in Mental Health*. Oxford: Oxford University Press.

Mannheim, H. and Wilkins, L. (1955) *Prediction Methods in Relation to Borstal Training*. London: HMSO.

Monahan, J., Steadman, H. J., Silver, E., Applebaum, P. S., Robbins, P. C., Mulvey, E. P., Roth, L. H., Grisso, T. and Banks, S. (2001) *Rethinking Risk Assessment: The Macarthur Study of Mental Disorder and Violence*. Oxford: Oxford University Press.

Moss (Brookes), K. (2009) *Security and Liberty: Restriction By Stealth*. Basingstoke: Palgrave Macmillan.

Pollock, N. and Webster, C. (1991) 'The clinical assessment of dangerousness', in R. Bluglass and P. Bowden (eds) *Principles and Practice of Forensic Psychiatry*. London: Churchill Livingstone (pp. 489–97).

Prins, H. (1995) '"I've got a little list" (Koko: Mikado), but is it any use? Comments on the forensic aspects of supervision registers for the mentally ill', *Medicine, Science and the Law*, 35: 218–24.

Prins, H. (1998) 'Characteristics of consultant forensic psychiatrists: a modest survey', *Journal of Forensic Psychiatry*, 9: 139–49.

Prins, H. (1999) *Will They Do it Again: Risk Assessment and Management in Criminal Justice and Psychiatry*. London: Routledge.

Prins, H. (2007) 'The Michael Stone inquiry: a somewhat different homicide report', *Journal of Forensic Psychiatry and Psychology*, 18: 411–31.

Prins, H., Backer-Holst, T., Francis, E. and Keitch, I. (1993) *Report of the Committee of Inquiry into the Death in Broadmoor Hospital of Orville Blackwood and A Review of the Deaths of Two Other Afro-Caribbean Patients: Big, Black and Dangerous?* London: Special Hospitals Service Authority.

Rennie, Y. (1978) *The Search For Criminal Man*. Toronto: Lexington Books.

Ritchie, J., Dick, D. and Lingham, R. (1994) *The Report of the Inquiry into the Care and Treatment of Christopher Clunis*. London: HMSO.

Royal Society (1992) *Risk: Analysis, Perception, Management*. London: Royal Society.

Rumgay, J. and Munro, E. (2001) 'The lion's den: professional defences in the treatment of dangerous people', *Journal of Forensic Psychiatry*, 12: 357–78.

Russel, C. and Russel, W. M. S. (1961) *Human Behaviour*. Boston, MA: Little Brown.

Sarbin, T. R. (1967) 'The dangerous individual: an outline of social identity transformations', *British Journal of Criminology*, 7: 285–95.

Scott, P. D. (1977) 'Assessing dangerousness in criminals', *British Journal of Psychiatry*, 131: 127–42.

Scottish Office (1996) *The Public Inquiry into the Shootings at Dunblane Primary School on 13 March, 1996* (Cullen Report), Cmnd 3300. London and Edinburgh: HMSO.

Soothill, K. (1993) 'The Serial Killer Industry', *Journal of Forensic Psychiatry*, 4: 341–54.

Spokes, J., Pare, M. and Royal, G. (1988) *Report of the Committee of Inquiry into the Care of Miss Sharon Campbell*, Cmnd 440. London: HMSO.

Taylor, P. and Gunn, J. (1999) 'Homicides by people with mental illness: myth and reality', *British Journal of Psychiatry*, 174: 9–14.

Tidmarsh, D. (1982) 'Implications from research studies', in J. Hamilton and H. Freeman (eds) *Dangerousness: Psychiatric Assessment and Management*. London: Gaskell Books: Royal College of Psychiatrists (pp. 12–20).

Walker, N. (1983) 'Protecting people', in J. Hinton (ed.) *Dangerousness: Problems of Assessment and Management*. London: Allen and Unwin (pp. 23–38).

Wilson, J. (1974) *Language and the Pursuit of Truth*. Cambridge: Cambridge University Press.

Wiltshire County Council (1988) *Report of the Departmental Committee of Inquiry into the Discharge of Responsibilities of Wiltshire Social Services in Relation to Daniel Mudd from his release from Broadmoor in May, 1983 until his arrest in December, 1986 for the Murder of Ruth Perrett*. Trowbridge, Wilts.

Young, W. (1973) *Obsessive Poisoner: The Strange Story of Graham Young*. London: Robert Hale.

Chapter 2

Theorising dangerousness

Mark Brown

Introduction

Ten years ago John Pratt and I finished work on an edited collection titled *Dangerous Offenders: Punishment and Social Order*. The focus of that collection was historical and contemporary formulations of dangerousness and the kinds of responses engendered by the spectre of dangerousness. Though much attention was given, particularly in essays by Pat O'Malley and John Pratt himself, to continuity and change in understandings of dangerousness, what stands out most to me now is the representation of dangerousness as something apart and something distant. One important device for achieving this was the depiction of the dangerous as monsters: for O'Malley 'an image of evil that could not possibly be "us" and that is beyond the rational' (2000: 28); for Pratt it was 'embodied in the figure of today's "sexual predator", as if such monsters may surreptitiously move into our neighbourhoods, and against such eventuality the entire community must be mobilised' (2000: 46). At the same time, Pratt's analysis of dangerousness laws in western countries had suggested that while such laws might be growing in number, the most remarkable feature was that their apotheosis, the preventive detention scheme in its various forms, remained in fact little used (Pratt 1995). It was as if imagining and conjuring up the dangerous offender served an important political and symbolic purpose, but dangerousness was just that, much more a spectre than a reality of social life and practical penality. Dangerousness was thus, in a sense, a field of possibility that could, but never quite did, draw upon the resources for public protection that measures like the indefinite sentence provided.

My proposal in this chapter is that the last decade has seen if not a decisive break with this long-standing model of dangerousness, then at least a significant refiguring of the ground of dangerousness. In recent times ideas of dangerousness seem to have proliferated, taking in, for instance, anti-social 'dangerous children' whose conduct has prompted the regulation of a whole field of sub-criminal conduct. Yet at the same time, the imagination of what constitutes serious danger has both condensed and in many ways become more selective in character. Thus, while the shape and form of criminal dangers seem to have grown, there has been an odd reluctance to expand the scope of the preventive detention schemes that have traditionally marked out the domain of dangerous offender law. Globalisation, in particular, has produced many new candidates. There are people smugglers who pack innocents into shipping containers only to let them die ugly deaths of suffocation and heatstroke. Britons will recall the 58 Chinese illegal immigrants found suffocated in the back of truck at Dover in June 2000 (*Independent* 2000). Near the end of the decade, in April 2009, 62 Afghans met a similar fate as they began their long journey to the west (*Los Angeles Times* 2009). A cursory examination of the news wires shows this to be a depressingly regular occurrence throughout the first decade of the twenty-first century. People traffickers, whose victims importantly have not consented to their transport and trade as a commodity, also wreak a toll of human havoc and many of these modern-day slavers are based in our very own towns and cities. Even within the realm of 'common' criminal conduct we find the rise of 'amphetamine cooks', brewing potentially lethal drugs like 'crystal meth' or 'ice' that connect the twin evils of serious mental health breakdown and a particularly lacerating and mindless form of criminal violence. Of course, this is just a selection of dangerous offender 'candidates' for purposes of illustration. Still, none of these offender types has been drawn into the framework of preventive dangerous offender law in any coherent fashion. Yet against this backdrop of suffering there has been more than just a shoring up of existing provisions against sex offenders. Sex offenders across a range of English-speaking western jurisdictions have become subject to a whole raft of draconian and illiberal measures of prevention, anticipation and post-sentence confinement. Meanwhile, a new group – generically termed 'terror suspects' – has been added to the select coterie of dangerous individuals and in their turn become subject to an array of otherwise unthinkable measures of civil confinement and control.

All of this prompts the simple question that the present chapter seeks to answer: why? Why does the dogged old image of the sex offender – the pederast, pervert or dirty old man of earlier times – appear now so fresh and powerful as an object of danger? Why, against the backdrop of tens and hundreds of deaths of trafficked and smuggled women and children, as well as the many thousands trapped in sexual slavery in our own towns and cities, does the bearer of religious bad attitudes or revolutionary fervour appear worthy of a control order? The answer, I will suggest, does not lie in either of these figures in their own right, as if greater scrutiny or closer attention to the irregularities of their character – a finer grained analysis – would somehow 'explain' the rise of these new mechanisms for securing public protection. For one thing, neither of these figures of danger has changed much, even as the measures for securing protection against them have been built up. Moreover, it is not as if the measures in any way reflect the specific nature of the danger. If the threats posed are felt to be in some way *sui generis*, and thus requiring of special measures, the measures selected certainly are not. Rather, they have a morphological and conceptual similarity with long-standing strategies of social defence, of which civil quarantine is perhaps the most obvious example (Wood 1988).

The approach of this chapter to theorising dangerousness is somewhat different from the concerns that have animated much of the criminological literature on the subject. In his important essay 'About the Concept of the "Dangerous Individual" ', Michel Foucault charted a transformation in nineteenth-century penal power that brought 'increasingly to the fore not only the criminal as author of the act, but also the dangerous individual as potential source of acts', thus engendering a legal concern not focused on what the dangerous individual 'is by statute ... but on what he is by nature, according to his constitution, character traits, or his pathological variables' (Foucault 2000: 199). As a discipline, criminology seems to have been captured by this representation of the dangerous individual *qua* individual and its literature continually cycles around the theme. The vast bulk of criminological work on dangerous offenders is principally focused on predicting the behaviour of the dangerous through knowledge of the patterning of offenders' constitutional features and pathological traits. The results are embodied in measures and principles for risk prediction and risk management that so much characterise the modern discipline and ensure its 'relevance' to policy-makers, parole decision-makers and a concerned public (Lovins *et al.* 2009; Walters *et al.* 2009).

Where a social theoretical frame has been applied, there has been a tendency more to change the filter than the lens itself. Thus, for instance, the concern of a number of theorists to illustrate how neo-liberal government reprises J. S. Mill's notions of self-government and reasonable despotism to govern those who are either unable or unwilling to manage themselves. Nikolas Rose and Pat O'Malley both, in slightly different ways, make this point and it is no doubt an important one. Rose (2000), for example, connects ideas of the pathological dangerous individual with a wider governmental strategy that operates via what he terms 'circuits of inclusion' and 'circuits of exclusion', the latter working to hold at bay the risks such individuals pose through various mechanisms of excision from society. This governmental strategy is focused, he suggests, upon 'excluded sub-populations [who] have either refused the bonds of civility and self responsibility, or [who] are unable to assume them for constitutional reasons, or they aspire to them but have not been given the skills, capacities and means' (Rose 2000: 331). The effect is to produce 'an array of micro-circuits, micro-cultures of non-citizens, failed citizens, anti-citizens, comprised of those who are unable or unwilling to enterprise their lives or manage their own risk, incapable of exercising responsible self-government, either attached to no moral community or to a community of anti-morality' (2000: 331). Somewhere among these micro-circuits and micro-cultures reside the monstrous individuals referred to earlier by O'Malley, those who reflect 'an image of evil that could not possibly be "us" and that is beyond the rational' (2000: 28).

The remainder of this chapter will suggest a new and hopefully productive approach to the problem of understanding dangerousness. The starting point here is that the last three or four decades have seen little progress in our understanding of dangerous offenders because of our unremitting focus upon systemic responses – such as the indefinite sentence and its use, or lack thereof – and upon the characteristics of the 'pathological individuals' themselves (usually in the hope that we may predict their future conduct or manage the risks such conduct poses to the community). We have failed to escape, in other words, from the classic formulation offered by Foucault in his essay on the dangerous individual, and indeed in *Discipline and Punish*, of (a) the penal law and (b) the pathological offender who must enter it in order that a penal judgement can be made. What we cannot explain about dangerousness is surely what is most important in the broadest sense: why do certain offences and certain types of offender become available for framing in 'dangerous offender' terms, while others whose depredations make them close neighbours for all common purposes seem to escape the danger label or seem in some way unsuitable for it? Why, in modern liberal societies, do we seem so willing to trade away the liberty rights of those deemed dangerous and why in such a wholesale fashion?

From here, the chapter divides into three sections as an attempt to answer these questions is built up. First, the concept of the monster that has been continually invoked as a metaphor for difference, for abnormality and for being beyond or outside the community of normal folk is reintroduced. Here, however, that rendering will be reversed, with the suggestion made instead that careful reading of Michel Foucault's *Abnormal* lectures (Foucault 2003a) allows us to see the monster not as apart from sociality but in fact as shining a light back onto it. On this view, the monster constitutes what Foucault termed a 'magnifying model' of all the naturally occurring irregularities to be found in the human character and conduct. With this in mind we can begin to understand how mechanisms of selectivity work to render some crimes and criminals suitable candidates for framing as dangerous offenders while others remain intelligible as practical problems to be solved by the ordinary mechanisms of criminal justice. The key in this respect, however, lies in extending Foucault's genealogy of the abnormal individual to connect it with his later work on governmentality and security, set out in a series of lectures given in 1977–78 titled *Security, Territory, Population* (Foucault 2007).

The following section makes this connection, describing how the liberal governmentality of modern societies relies upon certain understandings of social phenomena, perhaps the most important of which is the idea of the naturalness of processes of population. On this view, which was largely inchoate in Foucault's thinking at the time of the *Abnormality* lectures, mechanisms of security work to contain risks inherent in the free activity of the population. Here we can begin to discern an interaction between the magnifying model offered by the monster, who most bitterly illustrates potentials naturally occurring within the population, and the development of an apparatus of security that will extend a grid of regulation over all those portions of the population in which such risks are seen to lie. The final section draws these ideas together to illustrate how they enable us to make sense of the continued prominence of sex offenders in the modern pantheon of dangerous types. In closing, an attempt is made to suggest what it is about terror suspects that has provided them with the same unfortunate cachet.

Monsters within

The monster epithet given as a way of referring to sex offenders has been almost as popular within academic discourse as it has among the popular press. We have already registered John Pratt's depiction of 'such monsters [who] may surreptitiously move into our neighbourhoods' (2000: 46). A highly cited paper by Jonathan Simon (1998) is titled 'Managing the monstrous: sex offenders and the new penology'. More recently, in the course of applying the work of Giorgio Agamben to the problem posed by sex offenders, Dale Spencer provides a useful review of the sex offender literature which, he observes, is replete with the 'signifiers … "animals" and "monsters" [that] have been attached to these offenders' (2009: 219). To it he adds Agamben's analytic of *homo sacer*, the 'accursed life … which no one can touch without dirtying oneself' (Spencer 2009: 224). As with much of this literature, this characterisation is seen as a way of further enhancing a theoretical vision of the *process* by which sex offenders are made subject to measures of illiberal government.

That is quite different from the approach taken here. In generating these process-type analyses, epithets like 'animal' or 'monster' are in a sense regarded as epiphenomenal, which is to say that they are seen as secondary phenomena, aside to the main focus of the study. Simon, for example, proposes that: 'Sex offenders are our modern day monsters, producing tidal waves of public demand' (1998: 456). Here, the idea of the monster itself is incidental, serving rather as a foil for Simon's main argument, which concerns the convergence of popular punitiveness and a new penology logic to explain developments like sexually violent predator laws that became an important feature of US society during the 1990s. The argument would have worked equally well had Simon proposed that sex offenders were our modern-day heretics: in either case the term monster or heretic functions as a bridging concept that allows the writer to move on to arguments about the main phenomenon under study. Left out of this is any reflection or theorisation of the concept of the monster (or animal, or heretic) itself and the work which that idea might be doing to frame or develop the anxiety producing Simon's 'tidal waves of public demand'. Furthermore, we have in these accounts, as indeed in much contemporary criminological theorising, a kind of black box model of the public mind. Citizens confronted with 'sex monsters' go on, by some unknown process (which early twentieth century psychologists described as like a 'black box', the interior of which cannot be observed), to produce quite specific demands that quite specific sorts of offenders be subject to an equally specific set of measures of control and prevention.

This 'bit in the middle' is one of the great untheorised elements of dangerousness. Elsewhere in criminology efforts have indeed been made to say 'why this person and not the next' and 'why this response and not some other'. Nils Christie (1986), for example, has attempted to say why certain victims of crime are more able than others to achieve a victim status and to be seen as a victim. Christie connects the achievement of victim status with wider community perceptions of social status, valued acts and personal qualities, but also with the relationship that exists between victim and offender.

Our task here is in some ways similar. It is to understand why certain types of offences and offenders can be framed in dangerous offender terms and why the special measures directed at them seem so necessary. It is in this connection that the concept of the monster will be useful, not as a bridging concept but as a theoretical notion in its own right.

Michel Foucault's genealogy of the abnormal individual

While there is an enormous body of writing on the concept of the monster in literature and history (see Sharpe 2007), perhaps the most useful theorisation in fact lies quite close to home for criminologists. Just as Michel Foucault's *Surveiller et Punir* (*Discipline and Punish*) went on sale in France in February 1975, the author gave a series of lectures elaborating some elements of that text and presaging work that would later appear in the *History of Sexuality* series and in his studies of governmentality. The lectures, titled *Abnormal*, were concerned with the emergence in the nineteenth century of the abnormal individual, a figure whose existence Foucault claimed could be traced to three individuals: 'the monster, the incorrigible and the masturbator' (2003a: 60). We can see in these lectures a continuation of Foucault's broader interest at that time with excess. Concern with the excesses of sovereign power or the problems of excessive punishment gives way here to an interest in excesses of behaviour and we are given cannibals, incestuous aristocrats and grave-robbing necrophiliacs. But when Foucault states that 'we are in the land of the ogres' (2003a: 109) he is also identifying a process of transformation wherein the abominations of monsters will be fractured and divided so that, like Tom Thumb, the great figure of the monster will be overcome by the *petit*, and one might also say petty, figure of the abnormal individual. Giving his argument rhetorical form, Foucault asks, 'How, then, could the species of great exceptional monstrosity end up being divided up into this host of little abnormalities, of both abnormal and familiar character?' (2003a: 110).

Much of *Abnormal* involves a close charting of the process whereby abnormality was incorporated by psychiatry and by which psychiatry became the study of all those little deviancies that make up the figure of the abnormal. What happens next is a kind of inversion of monstrosity itself, wherein psychiatry's claim to specialisation comes to lie not in its capacity to describe the monster (though certainly it could do so) but in its ability to recognise his descendant, the abnormal, through the reinterpretation and reinscription of otherwise normal conduct into a matrix of human irregularity. It is also out of this reformulation that the 'dangerous individual' emerges, this person 'who is not exactly ill and who is not strictly speaking criminal' (2003a: 34).

Human nature and the monster

In establishing the monster as a figure of transgression, Foucault begins to elaborate a broader vision of conduct than the disciplinary notion of prescriptive norms that lies at the heart of *Discipline and Punish*. The monster for Foucault is not simply the violator of normative frameworks. The monster represents a violation of the laws of nature itself. For Foucault, what is significant in the monster is that its 'very existence is a breach of law at both levels' (2003a: 56), the laws of society and the laws of nature. Thus, the 'monster emerges within this space as both an extreme and an extremely rare phenomenon ... [it is] the limit, both the point at which the law is overturned and the exception that is found in only extreme cases' (2003a: 56). In social terms, we might say the monster is at once an archetype and an embodiment of all that should not be allowed to be. The monster, in other words, 'combines the impossible and the forbidden' (2003a: 56).

It is worth pausing briefly here to make one observation. This shift in referent to nature and to the naturalness or unnaturalness of behaviour, though little developed in *Abnormal*, will become an important feature in Foucault's later work as his vision shifts from power to the idea of government more broadly. Though the monster violates social norms, what is significant in Foucault's treatment of this figure is its violation of the laws of nature. This reflects a marked shift from the dystopian visions of disciplinary power he had only recently finished setting out in *Discipline and Punish*. If disciplinary power aimed to dictate the way things should be and to arrange a seamless and continuous grid of control, making individuals subjects of blind obedience, a reference to the laws of nature, to the way things actually are, marked out an entirely new vision. In setting up the contrast between sovereign and disciplinary power Foucault at one point had proposed that disciplines 'refer to a theoretical horizon that is not the edifice of law, but the field of the human sciences. And the jurisprudence of these disciplines will be that of clinical knowledge' (Foucault 2003b: 38). With the shift in attention presaged here his theoretical horizon changed once again. This time it turned to human nature, to the regularities and irregularities of human behaviour as they were to be found in nature and thus to the sciences concerned not with 'the mechanics of the coercions exercised by disciplines' (2003b: 38) but with the mechanics of an unfettered human nature. And it is in this connection we can see the monster playing a special role.

Returning to *Abnormal*, the importance of the monster to Foucault lay in more than it simply being an abomination. *Contra* the vision that the monster is 'beyond the rational' and 'could not possibly be us' (O'Malley 2000: 28), an idea that has become so much the currency of criminological invocations of the monster, for Foucault the monster was 'the spontaneous, brutal, but consequently natural form of the unnatural'. 'It is', he said, 'the magnifying model, the form of every possible little irregularity exhibited by the games of nature ... the major model of every little deviation ... [and] the principle of intelligibility of all the forms that circulate as the small change of abnormality' (Foucault 2003a: 56). Thus, although the monster for Foucault was defined in the breach – of social norms, of nature's laws – it could also be understood as no more than an unencumbered human nature, as something like 'the old man of the forests with all the fundamental presocial archaisms' (2003a: 91). The significance of this for Foucault's genealogy of the abnormal individual lay in the capacity of psychiatry to divine monstrous nature behind normal behaviour, to thus link the criminal and the monster and so to underpin clinical science with a presumptive unnatural human nature to be discovered. Here, we may turn this around to suggest an altogether different insight based upon the analytic of liberal governmentality. This analytic grew out of these early explorations of natural processes, but its theoretical horizon is not the clinical sciences that would police the boundary of normality and abnormality. It is, rather, the concept of population itself and the governmental apparatus of security that works to facilitate the population's free and efficient conduct.

Dangerousness in liberal governmentality

As Foucault's focus shifted from power to government, and to the instructional texts of European governmental practice published from about the sixteenth century onwards, the concept of a disciplinary society intimated in *Discipline and Punish* rather quickly began to fade. What replaced it was a neologism, governmentality, that has caused much confusion in criminology and elsewhere, not least because until recently only one of the more than thirteen lectures Foucault devoted to elucidating the concept had been published in English (under the title 'Governmentality' in Burchell, Gordon and Miller's *The Foucault Effect* 1991).

Liberal governmentality

The term governmentality describes both 'a general economy of power' (Foucault 2007: 11) and a heuristic device by means of which Foucault hoped to 'tackle the problem of the state and population' (2007: 116). In a reordering of his previous visions of power, Foucault proposed a division between old governmentalities and modern governmentality. The former he described as a governmentality of police, in the seventeenth-century sense of the term, and the latter as liberal governmentality, in the sense that it relies upon freedom as a technique and strategy of rule. A governmentality of police was a form of rule grounded in sovereign and disciplinary strategies that took as its aim the observation, regulation and control of all that fell within the territory of the state and, as its goal, the growth and power of the state. Looking back to his earlier work, Foucault noted that 'the great proliferation of local and regional disciplines we have observed in workshops, schools and the army from the end of the sixteenth to the eighteenth century, should be seen against the background of an attempt at a general disciplinarization, a general regulation of individuals and the territory of the realm in the form of a police based essentially on an urban model' (2007: 341).

The decisive break between old and new forms of rule and the conditions of emergence for a liberal governmentality were formed by recognition that the dream of a 'homogeneous, continuous, and exhaustive' (2007: 66) form of control through domination was neither possible nor desirable. Not only was the 'exhaustive and unitary project of police' (2007: 354) not possible in a practical sense, since some things always escaped it, more importantly it was also not desirable, since it reflected a misapprehension of, and thus a fight against, reality itself. It is at this point that we return to the idea of the natural, hinted towards but never fully developed in Foucault's account of the monster who, it will be recalled, he described as the 'natural form of the unnatural ... the magnifying model ... of every possible little irregularity exhibited by the games of nature' (2003a: 56).

Liberal governmentality takes up the challenge of reality. It seeks to know reality and it aims to govern not by interfering in reality but by letting reality as far as possible take its own course. It is essentially 'a government of men that would think first of all and fundamentally of the nature of things and no longer of man's evil nature' (2007: 49). A liberal governmentality will govern in a way 'not so much to prevent things as to ensure that the necessary and natural regulations work, or even to create regulations that enable natural regulations to work' and to ensure that natural processes are not disrupted by 'clumsy, arbitrary, and blind intervention' (2007: 353). This will require an apparatus of protection and judicious shepherding of natural phenomena and thus Foucault proposes the 'fundamental objective' of this liberal governmentality 'will be mechanisms of security' (2007: 353). We have, then, on the one hand a 'game of liberalism' that will involve 'not interfering, allowing free movement, letting things follow their course' (2007: 48) and, on the other, a mechanism of security that will coordinate these disparate forms of reality, 'organizing, or anyway allowing the development of ever-wider circuits' and relying 'on details that are not valued as good or evil in themselves, that are taken to be necessary, inevitable processes, as natural processes in the broad sense ... [that are] situated at the level of population' (Foucault 2007: 45). Thus, contemporary society, which the concept of liberal governmentality aims to describe, is actualised through freedom and through the constant circulation of individuals and things. But this governmental letting go, which is such a feature of our times, also takes place against, or is framed within, a background of mechanisms of security that operate to identify and limit what Foucault terms 'the inherent dangers of this circulation' (2007: 65).

Risk, danger and security

Far from eschewing danger, liberal governmentality in fact constantly invokes it, coaxes it and relies upon its energy. But ultimately too it must also close off those dangers that threaten the social fabric and desirable processes of population. The 'motto of liberalism', claimed Foucault, is 'Live Dangerously' (2008: 66). In this sense 'fear of danger ... [is] the condition, the internal psychological and cultural correlative of liberalism' (2008: 67). But if individuals are conditioned to experience their lives in this way, that does not mean that liberalism gives itself over wholly to danger. Rather, the strategy of liberalism itself 'turns into a mechanism continually having to arbitrate between the freedom and security of individuals by reference to this notion of danger' (2008: 66). As we will see further below, the analyses that chart nature's spontaneous 'mechanisms in their innermost and complex nature' (2008: 61) will have important implications for our contemporary understandings of dangerousness.

Key among these is the way, within an apparatus of security, that risk and danger are located not upon the old disciplinary binary of normal/ abnormal but across a whole field that transects and grids the population based upon estimates of relative normality and in connection with new regulatory apparatuses that shape, coordinate and, in a sense, aim almost to purify phenomena of their natural irregularities and disturbances. Here there is regulation, but it is not regulation of the disciplinary variety, informed by a prescriptive norm, institutionalised and structured upon an axis of obedience (see Lentzos and Rose 2009). Regulation here is diffuse, grounded in studies of population dynamics and interleaved with the techniques of freedom that are the engine of liberal governmentality. But this is also the point at which the monster – the moral monster, the sex monster, the 'natural form of the unnatural' – returns to connect the putatively abnormal and normal and to mark out an important boundary between risk and danger, and between punishment and precaution.

Sex offenders and dangerousness

In tracing what they describe as a movement 'from dangerousness to precaution', Hebenton and Seddon (2009) admit to being perplexed by the centrality of sex offenders in the discourse on public security. 'Indeed', they observe, 'one may ask why it is that, across diverse cultural contexts referred to in this paper (United States, United Kingdom and Australia), the sexually violent offender has become the exemplar par excellence of this "emergent response"' of precaution (2009: 355). Why, in other words, is the sex offender the subject of now widespread regimes of prevention, anticipation, pre-emption and precaution, while the individual trafficking girls and young women into sexual slavery remains a suitable candidate for the ordinary mechanisms of justice and punishment? What separates the sex offender from the child trafficker, the amphetamine cook who invokes psychosis and random violence, or the burglar who bashes an elderly war veteran senseless? Contemporary writers on dangerousness do not seem to be able to answer this question, being able only to point, as Hebenton and Seddon describe, to a sense of generalised anxiety, to Zygmunt Bauman's (1998) 'ambient fear', or to a sense that in the 'affect rich' field of crime control emotion trumps science (or reality). This is a scene where, in François Ewald's terms, 'science ... is consulted less for the knowledge it offers than for the doubt it insinuates' (2002, in Hebenton and Seddon 2009: 346).

With their black box model of the public mind each of these approaches grossly undervalues the capacity of individuals to locate risks and to separate out those they deem suitable for 'ordinary' criminal justice processes and others of a different, more dangerous order. What is lacking here – and what the liberal governmentality thesis will be able to provide – is an explanation of the *intelligibility* of precaution to the ordinary person: in other words, what makes precaution seem a suitable response to the problem of child sex offending but not child trafficking?

Sex offenders and the intelligibility of precaution

Drawing together the theoretical insights of the previous two sections, we may make the following propositions as regards the intelligibility of precaution or pre-emption. Sex offenders become suitable targets for this *type* of illiberal government not because they are in some way 'beyond the pale' but because they are connected with 'ordinary' men across a seamless and continuous field of sexual regulation. Sex offenders become figures of danger and suitable subjects of a precautionary logic because they function as the magnifying model of all the little irregularities of male sexuality, irregularities that are targeted in an extensive, multi-modal field of regulation that grids the space of men's sexuality, not in disciplinary terms but in the reconfigured logic of security. The *extent* of precautionary encroachments upon the freedoms of action and circulation of sex offenders is rendered intelligible and indeed necessary not because of a 'diffuse anxiety' or 'ambient fear' about the state of things. Rather, such encroachments become thinkable because liberal governmentality, having charted, transacted and connected normal and abnormal population processes, invokes in the ordinary man practices of self-regulation that seek to protect him and those around him against nothing more (or less) than himself: against the eruption of natural irregularities which, of course, are given ultimate shape and form by the sex offender, the sex monster. And finally, the sex offender becomes eligible for pre-emptive strategies of security because, unlike the people trafficker or the amphetamine cook, what is being regulated is a tendency that is natural and immanent in the population as a whole. In other words, the target of pre-emptive confinement is not so much the sex offender, but human nature itself.

But how does a logic of precaution, pre-emption or anticipation – something in many ways offensive to our long-standing principles of justice, even in the face of dangerousness – come to be integrated into it? The answer, we can suggest, is that it achieves this entry into the apparatus of justice and security through its reliance upon certain supports to be found in existing processes or ways of thinking. A number of supports for the introduction of precautionary measures can be identified but just two will be mentioned here. The first, which will be developed in some detail in the next section, is the inscription of sex offending and normal male sexuality within a single field of conduct natural to population and thus the intermixture of discourses of criminal danger and male normativity. The second support, of which only brief mention will be made, is found in the problem posed by the naturalness of these processes, creating not so much a recognisable pathology but something more like what in the nineteenth century had been termed 'lesion of the will'. This term connotes a circumstance where 'the moral sentiments, not the cognitive faculties, [are] extravagantly and separately deranged' (Eigen 2006: 230), leaving a strange hybrid of the normal and abnormal in thought and conduct. The problem posed by lesion of the will is precisely the problem of the naturalness of the unnatural. It is the irruption of disorder within an otherwise properly ordered field. It is error emerging out of processes that normally produce rational thought and conduct. Research in the field of sexual offending has increasingly moved towards examining the phenomenon in this light, seeking to know how and in what way sex offenders are in fact 'just like us'. One example will illustrate the point. Ward and Gannon (2006: 83) observe that 'as human beings, sexual offenders are naturally predisposed to seek certain goals, or *primary human goods* ... (e.g., relatedness, creativity, physical health, and mastery) ... [and] it is assumed that sexual offending reflects socially unacceptable and often personally frustrating attempts to pursue [these] primary human goods' (original emphasis). Here, then, a discourse of pathology is overwritten by one of natural processes and sexual offending moves from the enclosure of pathology to the normal desires of individuals attempting, in however errant a fashion, to pursue ordinary human goods. But in doing so, this science also places a question mark over the 'passions and appetites' of all men, just as lesion of the will, or the idea of moral insanity, had in the nineteenth century raised a frightening vision of what Eigen (1999: 436) terms 'autonomous passions and [their] consequent deficiencies in self-control'.

Connecting sex monsters and ordinary men in an apparatus of security

This space of security also finds support in a discourse of risk that breaks down the old binary of normal and abnormal, replacing it instead with a gradated field of risks, dangers, anxieties that form a thread connecting ordinary men and sex monsters. Running through it are three connected discourses: of public perception and behaviour, of governmental regulation, and of scientific knowledge. What they chart is the manner in which the sex monster, as the magnifying model of all the irregularities and perturbations to be found within ordinary men's sexuality, hovers like a spectre over the field of the regulation that channels, directs and constrains the (sexual) conduct of men in general. But this is not a simple or uni-directional process, for the limitations upon freedom and natural conduct that are produced through this regulation feed back into the system to produce anxieties and concerns of their own. The system of security thus has iatrogenic effects, or what Foucault (2008: 69) termed 'liberogenic' effects, 'that is to say, devices intended to produce freedom which potentially risk producing just the opposite'. Given the limitations of space here, seven aspects will be briefly mentioned that traverse the field connecting ordinary men and sex monsters, beginning with discourses of public perception and anxiety and ending with the science of sexual aberration.

1 *One only has to surf the newswires and 'blogosphere' briefly to find evidence of the complex impacts of the regulation of ordinary men's sexuality.* The latencies of risk and danger within ordinary men against which protective mechanisms are invoked produce impacts like the following: Women want their children to have contact with men but are fearful of the consequences. In 2009 a survey by the English Children's Workforce Development Council found that '55 per cent of parents say they want a male childcare worker for their nursery-aged children, with 66 per cent of lone parent mothers saying they would like a man involved in the care and development of their young children.' Further, the survey found that '17 per cent of children from lone parent female families have fewer than two hours a week contact time with a man, while 36 per cent have under six hours' (*Children Webmag* 2009). Yet a British Mori poll revealed that: 'Ten per cent of parents would refuse to leave their children at any nursery which employed men to look after them and one in eight adults

oppose the idea of men being employed at any childcare centre' (*Herlad Sun* 2003). The resultant anxiety and confusion is summed up on one parent's blog: 'I recently returned from living in Kuala Lumpur for six months with my partner and daughter,' says the writer. 'Little did we realise we would view returning to Australia with trepidation because of the cultural anxiety surrounding children and what it does to the social relationships between them and adults.' The blog goes on to detail the way Malaysian men would walk up to and then tickle or stroke their baby: 'Imagine if an unknown male asked to hold a woman's baby, stroked its chin, made baby sounds or asked questions about the baby in Australia. He'd just as likely be lynched or at the very least the shadow of PAEDOPHILE would haunt his days with snide whisperings and anxious angry glares' (*Parenting Express* 2009).

2 *Men self-regulate their contact with children lest they should be accused of misconduct.* A multitude of surveys in this respect can be found. For example, in 2007 *The Times* newspaper reported results of a survey commissioned by a children's charity and a men's volunteer organisation. It reported: 'Men are refusing to volunteer to work with children because they are frightened of being labelled a paedophile.' Specifically, 'one in five said that they did not want to be checked by the Criminal Records Bureau, and 13 per cent said that they were scared of being branded paedophiles.' An experienced mentor of young boys described his own precautionary behaviour: 'You don't see the child alone in private. You are always in a public place, sometimes even with his parent. I suppose I subconsciously look to check that other people are around if we are in the swimming pool changing rooms' (*The Times* 2007).

3 *Teaching and childcare organisations limit contact of men with children and men report female teachers monitoring their contact.* Next, governments take up this apparatus of supervision and control as a form of 'state responsibility'. Beginning with the organisations themselves, the childcare literature is replete with reports concerning the low number of men engaged in childcare – around 1 per cent in many countries – and reports by men of surveillance of them as potential sources of environmental danger. For example, a report for the UK's Daycare Trust by Owen (2003) titled *Men's Work?* found men to be under-supported in their decisions to undertake child-care work, discriminated in respect of tasks viewed as appropriate to men, such as those involving contact or supervision, and less likely than women to envisage remaining in the profession. The social monitoring that occurs in individual workplaces was formalised as a governmental strategy in England and Wales in 2009 with a Vetting and Barring Scheme that extended the risk assessment net to cover 11 million people (later reduced to 9 million) who work or volunteer with children, young people or vulnerable adults. Included in the data used to exclude individuals from contact with these groups was what the director of the scheme termed 'soft intelligence', including hunches, suspicions, accusations and other forms of information unlikely to meet legal standards (BBC 2009). Under the banner line 'Every parent a suspect', the *Guardian* (2009) newspaper observed that 'parents are being banned from school events such as carol services and sports days unless they carry ID

such as a passport; playgrounds are being shut to parents who want to watch their kids; and volunteers have simply drifted away, disgusted by the fact that they are regarded as potential abusers.' Here, the normal strategies of liberal governmentality's population transection – locating and identifying risk groups, setting in place mechanisms of security to limit dangers – move on to such a wide footing as to create extensive anxiety effects in their own right.

4 *The dangers posed by men result not simply in men's self-regulation in relation to these risk environments, but also the training of children in strategies of safety and pre-emption in their dealings with men.* Thus, the dangers posed by men are inscribed not simply in regulatory investments directed towards potential perpetrators but so too towards their putative victims through a kind of juniors' course in responsibilisation. For example, within the early childhood education literature there has for some time existed an array of materials both for training children and for drawing parents into the field of preventive education. Plummer (1984) provides sample letters that may be sent to parents and lesson plans for the education of six to twelve year-old children in safe touch, including colouring in and match-up exercises. In Australia, Family Planning Queensland produces a teaching aid titled *Everyone's Got a Bottom – A Storybook For Children Aged 3–8 Years* (Rowley 2007), of which it says: 'This little book is badly needed for helping parents, carers, teachers and child care personnel to keep children safe.' A subsequent evaluation found that: 'More than 92% of respondents had used the book to develop strategies to help the child deal with unsafe situations involving both strangers and familiar adults, discuss sexuality, and the correct terminology for genitals' (Sanderson and Mazerolle 2008: v).

5 *Studies of internet use regularly record internet pornography sites and pornography related searches taking up a large proportion of all internet use.* Moreover, internet-based child pornography has become a rapidly expanding industry with an apparently large population of male consumers.

6 *Scientific population studies trace the distribution of errant interests in immature or child-like sexual images and ideas, evincing the simple continuum between monster and man and the distribution of risks across the population.* For example, Freel (2003) reviews the literature on population studies of men's sexual interest in children. These studies show that when men are surveyed anonymously between one in four and one in six indicate a sexual interest in children or young people under the legal age of consent. Extending this logic of population transection, Freel examines such interest among childcare workers, again finding that about one in six males (15 per cent) express a sexual interest in children, with the female rate being about one quarter of that, or 4 per cent.

7 *Finally, scientific studies within the field of evolutionary psychology chart, if not the necessity of, then at least the productiveness of certain aberrations, irregularities or perturbations in natural processes of sexuality.* For example, Quinsey (2002) notes the powerful evolutionary force of males' mate selection detectors. Key among

these evolutionary attention-grabbers include, perhaps not unexpectedly, preferences for proto-typical body shape ratios, but apparently also flags like 'neotenous (immature)' faces (2002: 5). Male mate selection preferences thus lie in a shifting balance of mature and immature markers, and sexual difference – whether that be seen as preferences for same sex, kin or youth – can be understood by scientists as minor irregularities in this complex evolutionary mechanism. Similarly, in a study of 3,978 men and 7,817 women aged 17–56, Ellis, Widmayer and Palmer (2008: 454) investigated the 'possibility that sexual assault (rape) can be comprehended as an evolved reproductive strategy'. As well as finding that males who succeed in sexual assault often secure longer lasting (rather than simply one-off) sexual intercourse partners, Ellis *et al.* were able to conclude that 'at least a minority of men may have evolved tendencies to use assaultive tactics to secure mating opportunities beyond those obtained by men who only employ "voluntary" tactics' (2008: 461).

What is illustrated in this array of anxieties, perceptions, statistics, forms of subjectification and modes of responsibilisation is the intimate connection between what the sex monster speaks to – which is human nature itself – and the process by which dangerousness laws and their attendant strategies of exclusion, sequestration, pre-emption and the like are made thinkable. Thus, the intelligibility of strategies of security directed at sex offenders relies upon various supports, one of which is this continuum of risk that connects the ordinary man and the sex monster and enmeshes each, to their required level, in a grid of regulatory control. The discourse of dangerousness that has the sex offender at its centre and which invokes these strikingly illiberal measures of control thus finds support in the intelligibility of such measures to ordinary men and women, grounded, as it is, in their experience of the regulation of ordinary men's own conduct.

Recalling the question about what makes sex offenders special, it might be hoped that this way of approaching the problem of dangerousness advances upon traditional criminological perspectives that place the sex offender next to other offender 'types' and ask, in the manner of Hebenton and Seddon (2009), why sex offenders become subjects of precaution across diverse cultural contexts while other offenders don't. Recalling Foucault's description of the monster as occupying a space that is 'both the impossible and the forbidden' (2003a: 56), it's clear that what appears dangerous about sex offenders is not their difference but rather their very recognisability. In other words, it is the very familiarity and intelligibility of the desires that animate their offending that mark sex offenders out as a danger like few others.

Finally, turning briefly to the entry of so-called 'terror suspects' into the field of dangerousness, we can suggest that something of the same process can be observed. Here, however, it may be the *imagined* naturalness, or at least a concern that there *is* a naturalness to (terrorist) violence within the religious communities from which many post 9/11 terror suspects are drawn, that raises the spectre of danger at the level of population. A sense of how this works can be found in the details of a case reported in *The Australian* newspaper in August 2009. Under the heading 'Somali extremists on a "fatwa order" from God', the article reports a pre-dawn swoop by 400 Australian Federal Police officers upon 19 homes in outer suburban Melbourne. The operation was hurriedly pulled together, the newspaper reports, because 'police were concerned that a Somali Australian who returned from [Somalia] only three weeks ago might have secretly obtained a fatwa from a sheik there and that as such 'a suicide attack on an Australian Army base might be imminent'. The four men arrested that morning and subjected to all the illiberal necessities of anti-terror legislation found themselves so placed because, like the sex offender, the target of those strategies is also partly nature itself, if we may take their religion to be an example of laws that govern the social space of nature. And like the sex offender, the normality of the terror suspect's mind, or at least the absence of clear pathology or cognitive failure, problematises the status of all within their community, suggesting inchoate tendencies that will be appropriate concerns for an apparatus of security. Here again, recent work from the field of psychology supports this prediction. In a review of current knowledge on psychological assessment of terrorists Dernevik *et al.* (2009: 510) cite as authoritative Sageman's earlier conclusion that 'three decades of research has been unable to detect any significant pattern of mental illness in terrorists'. They also accept Silke's proposal that in the absence of any 'evidence for psychological abnormalities', what is needed is 'a "normality" perspective on terrorist offenders' (Dernevik *et al.* 2009: 511).

Conclusions

The aim of this chapter has been to offer some fresh thinking on the question of why certain types of offence and offender come to be seen through the lens of dangerousness while others are relegated as ordinary subjects of criminal justice. This has become increasingly important in recent years as illiberal strategies of pre-emption and precaution, including control orders and post-sentence detention schemes, have been added to the existing armoury of dangerous offender indefinite detention laws. The proposals offered in this chapter, in this attempt to theorise dangerousness, have drawn on the work of Michel Foucault and have involved some elaboration of his theoretical work: on the concept of the monster, on liberal governmentality, and perhaps to a lesser degree on the way new measures find support in existing forms of thought or practice. It is important, however, to emphasise that such theorising is not pure abstraction and that theoretical propositions should at one level or another satisfy the demands of both inductive and deductive logic. Which is to say that theory should both emerge from existing data and be able to make predictions or claims about what new cases should look like. It is for this reason that an attempt has been made here both to illustrate the argument with the case of sex offenders, against whose circumstances most of these ideas have initially been developed and tested, and to offer terror suspects as a case for further investigation.

The main argument made in this chapter has been rather simple, even if the process of elaborating and supporting it has taken some time. The basic argument began by noting the limited scope of contemporary invocations of dangerousness. At its centre lie sex offenders, who continue to be thought of and acted against through a lens of dangerousness. Though many other forms of serious criminal harm exist, in recent years only those individuals connected with terrorism appear to have been added to the pantheon of dangerous types, together with both the language and preventive armature of dangerousness that is extended to them.

Why so? The answer proposed here is that illiberal strategies of precaution, framed within a discourse of dangerousness, are invoked in instances where the target behaviour represents something immanent in the natural processes of population itself. These forms of behaviour are thus not simply crimes in the legal sense, nor even abnormalities in the pathological sense, but rather dangers – be they biological or social in character – arising at the level of population itself. The newly raised strategies of precaution are thus part of a wider field of regulation that can be detected, clearly in the case of sex offenders, in more nascent form in regard to terror suspects, in mechanisms of security applied to manage population risks. Over this spectrum of control, embedded as it is within the mechanics of liberal governance, the risks presented by the dangerous offender mark a kind of apotheosis of the dangers inherent in population and in freedom of action and circulation. The intelligibility of strategies directed at dangerous offenders – which is to say, why they make sense and what makes them appear suitable and appropriate – relies upon and finds support in this wider field of regulation which, rather than separating the sex offender or terror suspect from sociality and community – marking them out as apart and beyond the social pale – in fact connects them through a matrix of population risks and attending strategies of risk mitigation. The intelligibility of post-sentence and indefinite detention schemes for sex offenders thus lies partly in the self-regulation exercised by ordinary men in their everyday conduct and contact with children, in its connection with the field of preventive strategies designed to protect children and in the scientific studies that identify the very naturalness of the unnatural that is represented by the sex monster and that is presupposed to be immanent in all men. It is thus the very recognisability and familiarity of the sex offender that instantiates the dangers he is felt to pose and that distinguishes him from other serious offenders, like the amphetamine cook or the people trafficker. Set against the sex offender, these individuals, cruel and unpredictable as they might be, seem remote figures whose depredations stand as proper objects of ordinary law enforcement and criminal justice.

Acknowledgements

An early version of some of the ideas contained in this chapter was presented at the Third Australian and New Zealand Critical Criminology Conference in Melbourne, Australia. Research towards this chapter was supported by a Discovery program grant from the Australian Research Council (DP0877331). Thanks to Claire Spivakovsky for drawing my attention to Rowley (2007).

Selected further reading

The question of dangerousness is something of a perennial. In its last invocation prior to current concerns over sex offenders it was violent offending that stirred public anxiety. Jean Floud and Warren Young's (1981) *Dangerousness and Criminal Justice* remains vital reading for anyone concerned with public policy responses to the spectre of danger. It provides a readable but penetrating assessment of the problems of using statistical methods to determine who should be subject to preventive measures, as well as a principled approach to the questions of prevention and public anxiety in this context. Moving into more theoretical territory, Michel Foucault's lectures provide a useful way into his work. *Abnormal*, and *Security, Territory, Population* (*STP*) have been cited extensively here, and are key texts. But the introductory lecture in *The Birth of Biopolitics* provides a useful introduction and synopsis of *STP*, even if the remainder of that text is of little relevance. Efforts by psychologists to understand sexual and other deviations through a lens of normality are now well developed. A good introduction to this work, with many citations to appropriate studies, is Tony Ward and Shadd Maruna's (2007) *Rehabilitation: Beyond the Risk Paradigm*.

References

The Australian (2009) 'Somali extremists on a "fatwa order" from God' Online at: www.theaustralian.com.au/news/nation/somali-extremists-on-a-fatwa-order-from-god/story-e6frg6nf-1225758010718 (accessed 5 August 2009).

Bauman, Z. (1998) *Globalization: The Human Consequences*. Cambridge: Polity Press.

BBC (2009) 'Vetting scheme to protect children to be outlined later', Online at: http://news.bbc.co.uk/2/hi/uk_news/education/8411399.stm (accessed 11 January 2010).

Brown, M. and Pratt, J. (2000) *Dangerous Offenders: Punishment and Social Order*. London: Routledge.

Children Webmag (2009) 'Wanted Caring Men'. Online at: www.childrenwebmag.com/articles/parenting-articles/wanted-caring-men (accessed 14 August 2009).

Christie, N. (1986) 'The ideal victim', in E. Fattah (ed.) *From Crime Policy to Victim Policy*. London: Macmillan.

Dernevik, M., Beck, A., Grann, M., Hogue, T. and McGuire, J. (2009) 'The use of psychiatric and psychological evidence in the assessment of terrorist offenders', *Journal of Forensic Psychiatry and Psychology*, 20: 508–15.

Eigen, J. (1999) 'Lesion of the will: medical resolve and criminal responsibility in Victorian insanity trials', *Law and Society Review*, 33: 425–59.

Eigen, J. (2006) 'The will of the deviant', *Harvard Law Review*, 119: 230–7.

Ellis, L., Widmayer, A. and Palmer, C. (2008) 'Perpetrators of sexual assault continuing to have sex with their victims following the initial assault: evidence for evolved reproductive strategies', *International Journal of Offender Therapy and Comparative Criminology*, 53: 454–63.

Floud, J. and Young, W. (1981) *Dangerous and Criminal Justice*. London: Heinemann Educational Books.

Foucault, M. (1991) 'Governmentality', in G. Burchell, C. Gordon and P. Miller (eds) *The Foucault Effect: Studies in Governmentality*. Chicago: University of Chicago Press (pp. 87–104).

Foucault, M. (2000) 'About the concept of the "dangerous individual"', in J. Faubion (ed.) *Michel Foucault: Power: Essential Works of Foucault 1954–1984, vol. 3*. London: Penguin, pp. 176–200.

Foucault, M. (2003a) *Abnormal: Lectures at the Collège de France 1974–1975*. London: Verso.

Foucault, M. (2003b) *Society Must be Defended: Lectures at the Collège de France 197–1976*. London: Verso.

Foucault, M. (2007) *Security, Territory, Population: Lectures at the Collège de France 1977–1978*. Basingstoke: Palgrave Macmillan.

Foucault, M. (2008) *The Birth of Biopolitics: Lectures at the Collège de France 1978–1979*. Basingstoke: Palgrave Macmillan.

Freel, M. (2003) 'Child sexual abuse and the male monopoly: an empirical exploration of gender and sexual interest in children', *British Journal of Social Work*, 33: 481–98.

Guardian (2009) 'Every parent a suspect'. Online at www.guardian.co.uk/commentisfree/henryporter/2009/dec/14/parent-suspect-vetting-barring-scheme (accessed 11 January 2010).

Hebenton, B. and Seddon, T. (2009) 'From dangerousness to precaution: managing sexual and violent offenders in an insecure and uncertain age', *British Journal of Criminology*, 49: 343–62.

Herald Sun (2003) 'Parents fear male nursery carers: paedophile panic is blamed for lack', BNet Australia. Online at: http://findarticles.com/p/articles/mi_qn4156/is_20030608/ai_n12583076/?tag=content;col1 (accessed 14 August 2009).

Independent (2000) '58 bodies found in back of truck at Dover'. Online at: www.independent.co.uk/news/uk/this-britain/58-bodies-found-in-back-of-truck-at-dover-714535.html (accessed 12 January 2010).

Lentzos, F. and Rose, N. (2009) 'Governing insecurity: contingency planning, protection, resilience', *Economy and Society*, 38: 230–54.

Los Angeles Times (2009) '62 migrants die in shipping container'. Online at: http://articles.latimes.com/2009/apr/05/world/fg-pakistan-migrants5 (accessed 12 January 2010).

Lovins, B., Lowenkamp, C. and Latessa, E. (2009) 'Applying the risk principle to sex offenders: can treatment make some sex offenders worse?', *Prison Journal*, 89: 344–57.

O'Malley, P. (2000) 'Risk societies and the government of crime', in M. Brown and J. Pratt (eds) *Dangerous Offenders: Punishment and Social Order*. London: Routledge (pp. 17–33).

Owen, C. (2003) *Men's Work? Changing the Gender Mix of the Childcare and Early Years Workforce*. London: Daycare Trust.

Parenting Express (2009) 'Care, fear and the death of childhood'. Online at www.parentingexpress.com/Stories/Stories/0050.htm (accessed 14 August 2009).

Plummer, Carol A. (1984) *Preventing Sexual Abuse: Activities and Strategies for Those Working with Children*. Holmes Beach, FL: Learning Publications.

Pratt, J. (1995) 'Dangerousness, risk and technologies of power', *Australian and New Zealand Journal of Criminology*, 28: 1–31.

Pratt, J. (2000) 'Dangerousness and modern society', in M. Brown and J. Pratt (eds) *Dangerous Offenders: Punishment and Social Order*. London: Routledge (pp. 35–48).

Quinsey, V. (2002) 'Evolutionary theory and criminal behavior', *Legal and Criminological Psychology*, 7: 1–13.

Rose, N. (2000) 'Government and control', *British Journal of Criminology*, 40: 321–39.

Rowley, T. (2007) *Everyone's Got a Bottom*. Fortitude Valley, Qld: Family Planning Queensland.

Sanderson, J. and Mazerolle, P. (2008) *An Evaluation of the Book 'Everyone's Got a Bottom'*. Brisbane: Griffith University.

Sharpe, A. (2007) 'Structured like a monster: understanding human difference through a legal category', *Law and Critique*, 18: 207–28.

Simon, J. (1998). 'Managing the monstrous: sex offenders and the new penology', *Psychology, Public Policy, and Law*, 4: 452–67.

Spencer, D. (2009) 'Sex offender as homo sacer', *Punishment and Society*, 11: 219–40.

The Times (2007) 'Men "afraid to work with children" ', *TimesOnline. Online at:* www.timesonline.co.uk/tol/life_and_style/education/article1867921.ece (accessed 14 August 2009).

Walters, G., Knight, R. and Thornton, D. (2009) 'The latent structure of sexual violence risk: a taxometric analysis of widely used sex offender actuarial risk measures', *Criminal Justice and Behavior*, 36: 290–306.

Ward, T. and Gannon, T. (2006) 'Rehabilitation, etiology, and self-regulation: the comprehensive good lives model of treatment for sexual offenders', *Aggression and Violent Behavior*, 11: 77–94.

Ward, T. and Maruna, S. (2007) *Rehabilitation: Beyond the Risk Paradigm*. London: Rougtledge.

Wood, D. (1988) 'Dangerous offenders, and the morality of protective sentencing', *Criminal Law Review*, 424–33.

Chapter 3

The politics of public protection

Mike Nash

Introduction

Protecting the public from harm has emerged as a key governmental priority for many jurisdictions around the world. In a climate where risk has increasingly become associated with loss, harm and danger (Dwyer 2007: 781), we appear to be living in a 'culture of fear' (Furedi 2002: 5). As a result, politics is very much about making reassuring noises concerning public safety, even though, as argued by Steinhert, 'the state plays it part in dramatizing risk' (2003, in Walklate and Mythen 2008: 217). Indeed these authors suggest that 'everything we do ... is becoming subject to risk assessment and classified through risk scales' (2008: 271). Yet, with the best will in the world, preventing danger is an extremely difficult if not impossible task, despite such bold moves as that of the United Nations in establishing a Commission on Human Security in 2003 with the intention of promoting 'freedom from fear' (Walklate and Mythen 2008: 209). Thus politicians seek to ensure that systems are in place that are designed to risk assess and risk manage those who pose the greatest risks to society – especially its most vulnerable members. Either that or it is a sophisticated attempt to placate public feeling at times of high emotion following the commission of particularly symbolic crimes. Embodying legislation, protocols and guidance, these systems aim to reduce potential risk of harm to the public while enabling politicians to say that they have put the necessary procedures in place – they have done *what they can*. In an area of practice where failure inevitably means tragedy, any government is acutely aware of the interest of the mass media in allocating blame. If the systems are in place, for example the 347 pages of multi agency public protection arrangements (MAPPA) guidance in England and Wales (Ministry of Justice 2009a), then it may be easier for governments to avoid that blame and pass it on. This chapter explores the political context of public protection policy and assesses the extent to which politics itself can act to exacerbate rather than mitigate an uncommon but frequently defining aspect of criminal justice.

Historical thread

It is not difficult to trace a thread of public protection policy (and politics) back over the past two decades, whereby actions against serious – and increasingly labelled as dangerous – offenders have been key to party politics. Governments wishing to be viewed as tough on offenders have found it easy to progress measures aimed at those found guilty of having committed (and even sometimes only assessed as likely or probable to commit) the most serious of offences, frequently but not exclusively predatory sex offenders. These measures, though, have had wider ramifications and influenced criminal justice policy more generally, notably in terms of an upwardly punitive turn across the board. There have been significant changes to the way in which criminal justice agencies go about their daily business, notably in much closer working between the key *protection* services such as police and probation (see, for example, Nash 1999; Kemshall and Maguire 2001).

A useful starting point in England and Wales is the period leading up to the 1991 Criminal Justice Act (CJA). The 1990 White Paper, *Crime, Justice and Protecting the Public*, introduced a noticeably more punitive trend, especially for the probation service. In essence the Conservative government attempted to meet two conflicting goals: to reduce the burden of personal taxation while simultaneously getting tougher on crime and increasing the prison population. These seemingly contradictory aims were to be achieved by a deft sleight of hand that would see probation orders become community penalties and supervision in the community transformed into punishment in the community (Worrall 1997). These developments would trigger a significant change in the role and ethos of the probation service and perhaps faced with the threat of private sector competition, the opposition to the change was less significant than might have been expected in the face of a major philosophical shift. The intended outcome of the change was an attempt to persuade the courts that so-called *alternatives to prison* were punishments in themselves, and were demanding penalties able to stand alone in the sentencing framework. Indeed, the Association of Chief Officers of Probation (ACOP) released a paper in 1988 entitled *More Demanding than Prison*, perhaps to emphasise their tough new credentials to a belligerent government. Of course, a penal policy that was essentially aimed at reducing the prison population was hardly likely to endear the Conservative government to the party faithful, so in what was essentially to become perhaps one of the last liberal criminal justice acts, a deviation from the reductivist position was taken. This involved a focus on violent offenders in particular; the current hysterical emphasis on sex offenders was yet to reveal itself. In attempting to keep more people out of prison the act re-emphasised the principle of proportionality; that sentencing should reflect offence seriousness rather than be an accumulation of previous offences and sentences. This meant that previous convictions were not to be used to inflate sentences above that warranted by the instant offence, but there was to be an exception made for violent and sexual crimes. In these cases previous convictions could be used if they represented a *pattern* of harmful behaviour. Furthermore, violent and sexual offences could be sentenced at the maximum for the crime, even if the instant offence did not warrant it, provided the court decided that the offender posed a risk of serious harm. The White Paper made the intention clear: 'Some violent offenders pose a threat to public safety: and legislation which the Government proposes will allow the Crown Court to send them to custody for longer than would otherwise be justified by the seriousness of the offences they have committed' (Home Office 1990: para. 1.8).

1991 therefore marked the beginnings of a real focus on violent and sexual offenders as being 'different' and deserving of disproportionate treatment, or in other words to be punished for *what they might do in the future*. This focus was successful in that the government of the day were able to portray themselves as tough on crime even though their flagship legislation had a basically reductivist position. Although seen as a 'bifurcated' approach (Bottoms 1977) whereby there are tougher or longer sentences for high risk of harm offenders and less severe, community-based punishments for others, it is perhaps more accurate to note an overall inflation in punitiveness as probation-run sentences also became more restrictive in their conditions and enforcement. Before moving on, however, it should be noted that the generally liberal intention of the Act was achieved quite rapidly in that the overall prison population declined from 48,000 to 42,000 within six months. That said, there had been a groundswell of objection, especially from the judiciary (Dunbar and Langdon 1998: 103–11) against the reduced importance of previous convictions in determining sentence and quite quickly other events occurred that saw the punitive turn really take hold.

There are numerous texts that deal with the period from 1991 to 1997, when the Labour Party under Tony Blair was elected to government (see, for example, Worrall 1997; James and Raine 1998; Dunbar and Langdon 1998; Matthews and Young 2003). The period was marked by unpicking a number of the 1991 CJA measures, by a virtual battle between Michael Howard as Home Secretary and Tony Blair as his Shadow, the increasingly tough stance taken by Labour on law and order issues, the government increasingly criticising the judiciary for soft sentencing, the Home Secretary intervening to extend tariffs on the killers of James Bulger (responding to the 'public voice', he said), the judiciary defending itself and the growing creep of US influence into UK legislative practice. Measures such as 'two strikes and you're out' (automatic life sentences for the second commission of certain offences) were in many ways flag-waving by the government and were a determined attempt to lure the Labour Party into an 'elephant trap' (Dunbar and Langdon 1998: 138) between the major parties. However the purpose such measures served was to ensure that the incoming Labour government was already on message for tougher law and order policies. In debating the Crime (Sentences) Bill (became an Act in 1997) Lord Ackner noted that the Home Secretary had in his view 'an unerring populist streak that sadly the Opposition seem now to wish to emulate' (*Hansard*, HL, 27 January 1997, col. 1013). Throughout this period the law and order emphasis increasingly swung towards protecting the public from harm caused by serious violent and in particular sex offenders.

At the turn of the century two very notable cases in particular flamed these particular fires: the abduction and murder of eight-year-old Sarah Payne by a released sex offender in 2000 and the murders of ten-year-olds Holly Wells and Jessica Chapman in Soham in 2002 by a man without previous convictions but who had numerous previous allegations of unlawful sexual behaviour lodged against him. Both of these cases also continued to increase the 'blame' stakes as the government moved quickly to legislate for change and strengthen existing procedures. The murder of Sarah Payne and subsequent campaign by her parents (ably supported by the *News of the World*) for community notification of sex offenders, in part led to serious disturbances on the Paulsgrove estate near Portsmouth (see Golding this volume; Williams and Thompson 2004a, 2004b). Such public protest about relocating sex offenders into the community (spawning the word 'nimby' – not in my back-yard) has contributed greatly to the near impossibility of speaking in rehabilitative terms for sex offenders and the considerable increase in cautious decision-making.

The range of chapters in this volume testifies to the scope and importance of public protection measures in many parts of the world. At the same time it is evident that these measures are often predicated upon a small number of cases, albeit each one a tragedy and, importantly, heavily reported across all news media. Indeed, a number of these cases have given rise to specific pieces of legislation and, notably in the United States but with examples elsewhere, the legislation bears the name of the victim, for example the Jacob Wetterling Act (also generally known as Megan's Law), the Adam Walsh Act and the Matthew Shepard and James Byrd Act. Garland argues that by these actions the 'projected, politicised image of the victim' (Garland 2000: 143) personalises the issue for millions worldwide, allowing and facilitating the development of 'distant suffering' (Karstedt 2002). These tragedies touch the hearts of millions of people, as perpetrators are cast as everyone's nightmare and perceptions of danger become heavily distorted around the image of predatory offenders, as well summarised by Lacombe (2008: 55): 'Indeed, in the current climate of panic, we can say without exaggeration that the figure of the sex offender has become emblematic of society's greatest fears: an amoral, impulsive predator who amuses himself by tormenting, torturing and killing the most vulnerable among us.'

If these are the thoughts lingering in the public consciousness it is not difficult to see why and how governments declare war on these offenders on behalf of the people and embark on punitive and exclusionary policies (Janus 2007, and this volume), knowing that the public are unlikely to disagree. Indeed, following Garland's work (2000, 2001) we can see that even traditional opposition as demonstrated by 'liberal elites' may have dissipated in the face of these groups feeling threatened by serious and dangerous criminals. It has long been fashionable to be tough on crime but the measures concerning potentially dangerous offenders massively increase the scale of state intervention into the lives and liberties of a particular group of offenders (but one whose ill definition leads to a constant increase in its numbers). Not only that: due to the construction of dangerousness, these interventions relate to what might happen in the future; it is what Rose describes as bringing the future into the present (2002, in Hebenton and Seddon 2009: 344–5), or as these authors describe it, 'precautionary logic'. This logic means, in practice, that public protection systems attempt to predict the unknown, to protect an often unnamed individual from harm at some point in the future. But of course, that harm may never happen.

The wider context

So who or what exactly are governments trying to protect us from? Seemingly, as noted above (Walklate and Mythen 2008: 217), it is almost everything that human beings come into contact with. However this volume concentrates on the commission of serious harm by (largely) known offenders and it is on this issue we will focus. As evidenced by a number of chapters in Part Two, the identification of those who will 'do the harm' with any degree of certainty is far from easy, yet the process of identification, assessment and risk management of such targets is precisely what the public protection process sets out to achieve and seemingly assures the public will happen. It is not so long ago that the answer to the 'who' question would have simply been 'dangerous people'. Yet even this answer is more complicated, as the notion of dangerousness is socially constructed rather than being a 'quality' of human behaviour and is therefore 'peculiarly open to abuse' (Scott 1977: 127). For example, Peelo *et al.* (2004) studied the reporting of homicide in three British daily newspapers and demonstrated how readers receive a mediated version of murder (based on a variety of research criteria and newspaper 'inclusion' factors) which informs their perception of prevalence, context, victims and motivation. That perception is likely to be distorted and increase the sense of fear of certain violent attacks when in all probability what risk there is is likely to be less spectacular and much closer to home.

Thus the unknown predator stalking the (innocent) and unknown member of the public has become the target of preventive strategies, even though, as Furedi notes, 'the intensity and the frequency of fear are not causally linked to the probability of risk' (2007, in Walklate and Mythen 2008). In maintaining the horror story terminology, Hebenton and Seddon (2009: 343) describe the position of politicians wishing to be seen to be dealing with this problem as having a 'spectre' haunting them, with 'the ghost at this particular feast (being) the seduction of securing public protection'. Public protection therefore becomes a process by which the unknown are meant to be protected from the unknowable – further distorting the true nature of risk in society. The 'public' aspect of the policy is difficult to define but would appear to be a largely nebulous group except in those few cases where a specific person is known to be at risk. The Appeal Court judgment in the Baby Peter case (see below) further underlines the difficulty in defining what or who constitutes the public as understood in public protection legislation (see the *lack* of definition in the 2003 Criminal Justice Act).

It is unlikely that the public would disagree with the notion of 'dangerous people' being at large in the community and it being the duty of government to offer protection, but the definition and understanding of 'who is dangerousness' may, of course, differ greatly over time and among different population groups. That said, serious violent and sexual offending would have undoubtedly come close to being top of the list for most people.

The commission of certain crimes, for example murder, triggering certain punishments such as the life sentence, might commonly have seen offenders automatically enter the dangerous category. Yet it is here that problems begin to arise, for there is a clear need to distinguish between offenders within *generic* offence categories to assess their *individual* risk. Prins (this volume) offers an excellent historical summary of developments in dealing with this issue. The problems unfold around the way in which these offenders are responded to; their assessment, classification, sentencing, nature of intervention, sentence length, release decisions and post-release conditions. Wrapping itself around this process is the possibility of cases *going wrong* (Nash and Williams 2008) and victims' families and the media demanding to know why offenders were initially set free to commit further serious offences (see Brooke 2009 for but one of numerous media examples). One immediate question at this point might be, what went wrong with the public protection process? While governments will be acutely aware that underpinning the process question will be a much more basic one concerning the release of potentially dangerous people into the community in the first place; in other words, whose fault was it? To avoid the second question it therefore becomes imperative that the first is responded to as fully as possible in the confidence that procedures are as good as they can be, or in the case of the British government, live up to the claim to be world leading (Home Office 2008).

The stranger-predator stereotype dominates much of the public conscious-ness of dangerousness and to a large extent it is against this stereotype that measures are developed and deployed. A clear legislative comment on this came in the appeal against sentence by a man who had received an indeterminate sentence for public protection (IPP) for his involvement in the death of 'Baby Peter'. In allowing the appeal and replacing the indeterminate sentence with one fixed at six years, Lord Justice Hughes commented that despite his complicity in the death of a seventeen-month-old boy, it was 'simply a step too far' to suggest that he might in the future commit serious offences against the public – he therefore did not meet the dangerousness criteria as required under the 2003 Criminal Justice Act – see below. Lord Justice Hughes therefore confirmed the 'frightening' public stereotype while neatly side-stepping the issue that Baby Peter was also a member of the public and he and similar victims deserve the same risk consideration as *stranger* members of the public.

For example, schemes such as the community notification of sex offenders in the United States are intended in large part to make strangers 'known' by revealing increasing amounts of information about them contingent upon the risks they are assessed as posing to the community. Again, the assessment of risk is likely to increase the closer to the stranger stereotype the offender is; thus a predatory paedophile offender may be deemed to require the greatest restrictions and consequent intrusions into his/her liberty (Human Rights Watch 2007). Yet we know that compared to so-called domestic or familial sex abusers the predatory offender is far less common; however, the former group often manages to avoid public protection and community notification processes (see, for example, Corrigan 2006). Thus a type of paradox emerges. As a result of political sensitivity it is usually the case that the public protection caseload increases rather than decreases – it is an *inclusive* process framed by *defensive* political and professional cultures. In many ways this is understandable. Therefore, as numbers grow it becomes necessary to differentiate between offenders in order to allocate resources to those deemed to pose the greatest risks. Thus, offenders are included on the basis of the worst case scenario. The thought of the most heinous crimes being committed by an offender under supervision ensures that the public protection system sweeps all before it – just in case. However, this in turn leads to a major screening process that is extremely costly in resource terms and is surrounded by a considerable bureaucracy, at least in the UK. In attempting to reduce the size of a caseload that has been in large part created out of political expediency, resources are drawn from elsewhere in organisations and as a result the same serious offences can occur in non public protection parts of the organisation (Ministry of Justice 2009b). A major report by Human Rights Watch (2007) found that in the United States there is growing concern over the ongoing growth of the registered sex offender caseload and the ability of police and probation services to manage it. At the same time those who have campaigned vociferously for public notification, such as Patty Wetterling, mother of the abducted Jacob Wetterling, are now withdrawing support for widespread notification, not least in her case due to her understanding of the low level of sex offender recidivism. When notification is triggered in thirteen states by 'public urination' then it is perhaps unsurprising that a change of policy may be under way.

Thus measures originally targeted at high risk of harm offenders tend to become all-inclusive, for example the addition of a man convicted of having 'sex with a bicycle' (Cramb 2007) to the Sex Offenders' Register in England. The 2003 Criminal Justice Act has brought 153 offences within a 'potentially dangerous' starting group, whereby a range of increased and indeterminate sentences could be imposed on those committing one of these offences and assessed as posing a serious risk of harm to the public. The CJA was another attempt, it would appear, to constrain the discretion of the judiciary by reviving the spirit of the 1997 Crime Sentences Act. The measures were in particular aimed at offenders liable by the commission of their crimes to a sentence of ten years or more or life imprisonment. The new measures proposed that if the offence was liable for a life sentence and it was 'serious enough', a life sentence must be passed. Similarly if it was not liable for life but again was serious enough, an indeterminate sentence for public protection must be passed. Even for those not liable to a ten-year sentence or more, extended periods of post-sentence supervision would be passed (five years for violence and eight years for sexual offences – not to exceed the maximum for the crime). The assessment of seriousness would include the following: all information regarding the nature and circumstances of the offence, any information regarding patterns of behaviour, and *any other information about the offender*. This last point is important as Stone reports that in IPP cases even words described as 'bravado' spoken by offenders to probation officers can be taken into account (Stone 2007: 451).

The indeterminate sentence for public protection has courted the most controversy since its inception and epitomises recent government measures to combat the so-called dangerous offender. The measure became operative in May 2005 and since that date 5,246 sentences had been passed until April 2009 (Straw 2009). Of these, 291 offenders had received a 'tariff' (the equivalent fixed-term sentence appropriate for the crime) of less than twelve months. Out of the total number of IPPs only 60 had been released by April 2009 and of these fourteen had been recalled to custody. The popularity of these sentences with the judiciary has exceeded government forecasts considerably (Stunell 2009; Prison Reform Trust 2007) and has resulted in the minimum tariff now being raised to 24 months in the Criminal Justice and Immigration Act (CJIA) 2008. The commission of one of these offences fires the starting gun for the offender to be considered dangerous under the provisions of the 2003 CJA, whereby in place of a fixed sentence proportionate to the crime committed (and other militating factors such as previous convictions and non-admission of guilt) a sentence without end is imposed. By passing such a sentence the judge in effect passes on the 'risk' of the release decision to the Parole Board. The popularity of these sentences since their inception demonstrate their appeal not only to judges but also to politicians who can project themselves as having responded to the public mood and can be seen as having acted on the problem.

These latest measures perfectly illustrate the risk control philosophy described by Hudson (2003). They tick all the boxes that have appeared since the 1990s: sentences without end, longer fixed sentences, and longer post-release supervision (control). However, even in instigating such popular measures, the government has still received periodic kicks in the teeth. For example, a number of indeterminate sentence prisoners have taken the government to court to prove that their continued detention beyond their tariff is unlawful. This related to the failure to provide them with the opportunity to demonstrate their safety by attending approved or accredited programmes in prison – up to one-third of all IPP prisoners (2,057), according to Liberal Democrat MP Andrew Stunell (2009), had not gained access to a single programme. The High Court originally found in favour of the prisoners, leading to headlines such as in the *Mail*: 'Government faces huge payouts after court rules detention of sex offender is "unlawful"' (31 July 2007). The Secretary of State appealed against this judgment and in May 2009 the House of Lords dismissed the appeals of three prisoners (James, Lee and Wells), declaring that although the Secretary of State for Justice had failed in his public duty to provide treatment courses for indeterminate prisoners, their post-tariff detention was not unlawful. Lord Brown argued that the growth of IPPs had taken NOMS by surprise and had swamped the prison system (it could be argued, of course, that this surprise was naive in the extreme). However, the Law Lords came to a view that the decision of 'unlawful detention' was unsustainable not least because if a prisoner was found to be plainly dangerous by the Parole Board on a delayed consideration, he would have had to have been released as his detention would have been unlawful during the Secretary of State's 'systemic failures'. In summing up, Lord Brown made a number of general comments on criminal justice policy. He said that he had real disquiet about the introduction of IPP and that it was regrettable that the Secretary had admitted his systemic breach of his public law duty with regard to the operation of the regime. He considered action in the field to be 'ill-considered' and quoted the old maxim, 'marry in haste, repent at leisure' (House of Lords 2009).

In a similar uncomfortable vein for the government, it has also been found (Court of Appeal, 9 July 2009) to be in contravention of Article 8 of the European Convention of Human Rights, by allowing for indefinite notification (registration) of sex offenders with sentences in excess of 30 months without a formal review. Once again this decision will be appealed in the new UK Supreme Court. However, the decision reflects a trend of continuing legal challenge to the UK public protection legislation with the Parole Board also in the firing line. In July 2009 a judicial review quashed a Parole Board decision concerning the release of a prisoner for going against all available evidence (R v Parole Board [2009]). In this case, a life sentence prisoner who had on several occasions been recommended for progressive moves to open conditions had been rejected for such a move by the Secretary of State. Following another two-day review he had been rejected by the Parole Board who, it is said, did not include prison service witness evidence in its decision letter. The case was upheld on judicial review and ordered to be heard at the earliest possible date. The performance of the Treasury Solicitor was described as 'scandalous' by the judge. This decision, of course, touches upon continuing discussions over the independence of the Parole Board (see Whitfield, this volume). Finally perhaps in this bad news section for the government is the reporting of its life and indeterminate 'tariffs'. These were once highly secretive decisions, at least in the case of lifers, but are now formally announced in court. Unfortunately it is the tariff that is emphasised rather than the indeterminate nature of the sentence. In opening up court decisions the government has opened itself to criticism, albeit highly misplaced. However, the negative reporting of tariffs in serious cases undoubtedly impacts upon decisions taken further on in the offender's custodial life. This negative publicity, highly reported in the case of Craig Sweeney (BBC 2006) has led to an amendment to the rules governing tariff setting as outlined in the Criminal Justice and Immigration Act 2008 (s.19, 223). Courts are now able to consider the relative seriousness of the case before them and instead of allowing a 50 per cent reduction in tariff to match with release rules for fixed-term sentences it can now take account of seriousness and reduce the sentence discount from 50 per cent to 0 per cent. Therefore not only is the government accused of ill thought through legislation, it also appears to quite quickly legislate for change in its measures if publicity has been negative in serious cases. Perhaps as an acknowledgement of its inability to provide adequate resources to meet the needs of indeterminate sentence prisoners to prove their 'safety' the provision to impose an automatic life or IPP sentence under the CJA 2003 has been downgraded from a *duty* to a *power* (CJIA 2008, s. 14, 197).

Recent history therefore suggests that in many ways governments such as that of the UK have attempted to tighten up the decision-making process and reduce the opportunities for personal and professional discretion. For example, judges were *required* to pass a public protection sentence if certain criteria are fulfilled by the offender (CJA 2003, s. 224–36 and Sch. 15 – but note change in CJIA 2008 as above); in effect there is a default position on dangerousness that pays less attention to the offender's individual circumstances and more to their matching group-generated criteria. The vast majority of sex offenders must be included on the register and this must be for a minimum period regardless of risk (which is in effect defined by the original sentence length). In making certain actions prescribed, the government has at the same time reduced the powers of some of the professions who have traditionally dealt with dangerous offenders – psychiatrists being a notable example. In a review of Appeal Court judgments on the risk assessment of potentially dangerous offenders, Stone (2007) identified that judges were favouring probation officers' reports and assessments over those of psychiatrists, on the basis that their assessment artefacts were the product of *significant research* (2007: 447). A number of chapters in this volume might cast doubt on the confidence of the Court of Appeal's view. Just as dangerousness has been regarded as too woolly a concept (with risk of harm preferred), then so has clinical judgement had to take something of a back seat, although dynamic change in offender behaviour is now included in OASys, the preferred NOMS offender assessment tool.

Politics, policy and practice

The politicisation of dangerousness has therefore in part led to its categorisation and compartmentalisation. Rare and often unique offending behaviour is thus classified into categories of risk of harm, defined as low, medium, high and very high by MAPPA guidelines (Ministry of Justice 2009a). As stated above, this is an aid to resource allocation but can itself lead to further public protection problems. The case of Dano Sonnex (Ministry of Justice 2009c) is a good example of the outcomes of a mis-assessment of risk. Having been (wrongly) assessed as medium risk he was allocated accordingly to a supervisor who was lacking the additional public protection experience and expertise, was also newly qualified and already covering for absent colleagues. One of the difficulties of having resources follow risk levels is that it is predicated on an assumption that only the highest risk case will commit the most serious crimes. Bridges (2006) has already identified that 80 per cent of serious further offences are committed by low and medium risk offenders but the question that needs to be asked is, should this be such a surprise? Bridges (2006) argues that rather than human dangerous behaviour being generated in clearly delineated boxes or categories, it should instead be considered as a continuum. Offenders are thus able to move up and down this continuum as circumstances change rather than remain fixed within one category of risk. This underlines the importance of dynamic variables in risk assessment but also the need to ensure that good risk assessment is spread out in an organisation rather than be confined to specific teams or pockets of excellence.

The politics of public protection therefore appears to establish a series of contradictions that could impact upon public safety. These contradictions can be the result of competing criminal justice priorities and philosophies. An example of this might be the inclusion of offenders in their own risk management plan. Kemshall (this volume) speaks of restorative initiatives such as Circles of Support which seek to unite offender and community in a common and supportive bond to aid resettlement and better manage risk. This is in marked contrast to the type of regimes described by Janus (2007 and this volume) which are non-inclusive and punitive in nature. It is, of course, for governments to determine their preferred course of action in this area but one example shows how politically sensitive these decisions can be. In a case of a serious further offence (HMIP 2006) an inquiry team concluded that the inclusion of offenders in meetings that established and monitored their risk assessment plans (MAPPA meetings) was a threat to good and effective risk management. As offenders have a right to legal representation at such meetings, the inquiry into this particular case of sexual assault and murder decided that the offender's presence at MAPPA meetings had compromised his effective monitoring as he was able to manipulate and challenge the terms of his supervision. Thus, despite practitioner support for the benefits of allowing offenders to be present, this recommendation was made: 'It is important that the core business of the MAPPA meeting, of sharing and analysing information objectively, and making decisions accordingly, is not hindered by the presence of the offender' (2006: 65). This decision was part of an attempt by the British government to address what is regarded as an imbalance between the rights of the offender and those of the public to be protected (Home Office 2006). By denying offenders the opportunity to exercise their rights those of the public were, by default, elevated.

Public protection and blame

Another discernible trend over the past two decades is perhaps the shifting of blame for serious further offences. The 1991 CJA in many ways allocated 'blame' or 'cause' to the offender – probably the right locus of attention for many people. However, it is now possible to note that, as politicians and government ministers have legislated in increasingly stringent terms against this offender group, the blame becomes shifted towards the professionals implementing legislation and policy. In other words, the politicians have 'done their bit' and it is therefore down to the professional practitioners to do theirs. They have been given the tools and it is up to them to use them. Underlying this shift in attitude is a strong belief that these tools can assist in prevention, and what is often not predictable *could* and in some cases *should* have been prevented by those professionals involved in the case. In many ways this takes us into territory where professionals are deemed to be responsible for the behaviour of those under their supervision. Implicit in this assumption is that the laws and processes are good enough to protect the public, therefore these tragedies must be attributable to a failure to use the systems effectively. Although often served up as a 'system failure' (Nash and Williams 2008), what is perhaps meant is that people have failed to use the systems properly. As a result we have witnessed high profile staff departures (for example the director of Haringey children's services and the chief officer of London probation service). In both cases the departures followed great tragedy: the murder of 'Baby Peter' and the murders of two French students. In each case the *protection* services were heavily involved and in the wake of investigations of the incidents, senior government ministers waded in to give their views and to ensure that blame was deflected from the government of the day (Cheston 2009; Tran 2009). The public anxiety and anger generated by these cases, very much part of the 'distant suffering' noted by Karstedt (2002), ensures that governments do their best to argue that they have provided sufficient resources, and the necessary legislation, to better protect the public, especially its most vulnerable members.

The politics of these high profile cases is clear in the furore following the death of Baby Peter at the hands of his mother, her boyfriend and his brother in August 2007. The then director of the responsible local authority, Haringey in London, Sharon Shoesmith, was removed from her post by the Children's Secretary Ed Balls in December 2008. There was a tremendous media reaction against her, with a 1.6 million signature petition from the *Sun* newspaper. During her High Court bid to claim her dismissal as unfair, her lawyers argued that the Ofsted report on her department, which originally had produced high ratings (three or four stars out of four) in most categories, was subsequently rewritten using the same data to include one star (inadequate) and judging the authority to be failing in four out of seven areas (Curtis *et al.* 2009). The reporting in the *Sun* of the case continued to describe Shoesmith as 'grasping' and 'grovelling' (Wells 2009). In the midst of a legal wrangle the chairman of the Commons Children's Committee, Barry Sheerman, wrote to Ofsted asking for an explanation and called for an inquiry to establish if 'high level' pressure had been put on Ofsted to alter their findings.

The politics of inclusion?

It has been noted above that the public protection agenda is more inclusive than the relatively small incidence of dangerous behaviour might warrant. Based as it is on a precautionary principle, we appear now to have a situation whereby huge numbers of offenders are initially *included* simply in order to be screened out at a later date. This process is based upon a predication that the commission of a particular offence (past or present) is an indicator that potentially serious offending could arise in the future. Previous behaviour is a not unreasonable starting point to predict the future but we know from many research studies that predicting very serious behaviour is far more difficult, not least because its baseline is relatively low (for a thorough discussion see Maden 2007). However, rather than work with ways in which responses might be further refined it appears as if the trend is to be expansive in the definition of the target group, in other words an attempt to cover all eventualities. The government is able to offer the suggestion of scientific rationality in its dealings with high risk of harm offenders and this feeds into its public reassurance programme. For example, the British government claims its offender assessment system (OASys) to be among the most sophisticated in the world and that its MAPPA process is 'world leading'. This is undoubtedly a part of the government's big message that serious offenders are being dealt with in the best way possible – although always with the *caveat* that not all risk can be eliminated. Is that, however, the message that the public hears? Their response to serious further offences suggests that it is not. By the government claims for its scientific rationale, the public could be made to feel safer, perhaps bearing in mind the extremely positive messages given out by other scientific advances such as DNA profiling. Yet there may be mistakes in developing an over-reliance on technology and tools. For example, on a recent visit to South Korea the author was shown a demonstration of the real time tracking of sex offenders in the community by GPS satellite (see Nellis, this volume). The demonstration showed a recent case of a sexual assault which the system was later able to track to the monitored offender, who was convicted. The system did not prevent the attack; it enabled the post-assault detection to be more effective. Many 'systems' deployed against high risk offenders, especially sex offenders, are reactive rather than preventive. The sex offender register, for example, is simply that: a list of details concerning convicted sex offenders. It does have a requirement on the police to visit (see above) but other than that it provides a useful database if an attack occurs. It cannot prevent an attack.

This should open up a further line of discussion related to the competing aims of public protection and how one policy could inadvertently compromise another. The irrepressible growth in the numbers on the sex offender register (for example, Devon up by 52 per cent 2008–9 and Swansea 25 per cent) inevitably causes a severe strain on resources. Wood and Kemshall (2007) in their review and evaluation of MAPPA found that home visits to low and medium risk offenders on the register were being reduced on average from two to one per year (2007: 19). It is almost a case of give with one hand and take with the other in terms of the government's public protection policy.

In a similar vein, MAPPA are a set of arrangements that offer an impression of joined-up thinking and management of offenders in the community. The government is able to point to the very low reconviction rates for the highest risk offender and naturally go on to claim that the arrangements are very successful, which indeed they are. Yet we know that the reconviction rates for serious offences among lifers for example are traditionally very low indeed, at approximately 1.24 per cent reconvicted for another homicide (Kershaw *et al.* 1997), and we also know that sex offender reconviction rates are not what many among the public might believe them to be. Thus it could be argued that the government is to a certain extent on to a winner before they start, as the default reoffending rate for those upon whom most resources have been focused is low in any case. This produces another paradox, as reflected in Bridges' figures for serious further offences (SFOs) (2006, and this volume). The big message for public consumption is that the system is working. Yet when SFOs do occur, often among lower risk offenders, the system is still held to be failing by the media and the public. Naturally at this point the government is likely to argue that people did not operate the systems effectively – the system in itself is satisfactory. The result will therefore be a strengthening of the requirements of those people in the system to do better and perhaps place more demands on them. Yet it is precisely at this juncture that politics in many ways wins out because governments rarely admit to *systemic* failings which may be caused by their own policies. It is people rather than policies, although individuals are rarely held to blame, but the trend noted above may be a sign of things to come.

What the current UK system of public protection encourages is a systematic and bureaucratic response that can compartmentalise risk and its consequent resource allocation. In the United States this type of approach has already caused significant problems in the community supervision of sex offenders according to Corrigan (2006). In the home state of Megan Kanka, she found that large numbers of sex offenders were evading or being omitted from the sex offender notification system. The particular difficulty arose from risk classification systems that heavily prioritised stranger, predatory offenders in the highest risk classification. As risk determined the levels of community notification, offenders who predominantly offended in a domestic context were frequently left out of the notification procedures. Equally a number of offenders challenged their risk assessment level and while in the appeal processes were also left out of the notification procedures. Perhaps the key message arising from Corrigan's research is that fixed and predetermined categories do not work when dealing with human behaviour, especially when that behaviour leads to people being assessed as dangerous. Flexibility is important in dealing with potentially dangerous offenders but this does not fit easily with government pressures to ensure that the public are reassured by the procedures that they have put in place. The issue here therefore becomes one of system compliance, where the effort goes into ensuring that the system is followed and maintained rather than the system itself underpinning good quality professional practice. It is a case of the tail wagging the dog.

It could be argued that system maintenance and integrity has become something of a goal of government policy at times of tragedy, with numerous recommendations made to ensure that the system requirements are adhered to, rather than the requirements themselves being considered as a causative factor of poor performance. In the Baby Peter case it was alleged in a BBC news report that social workers were spending 70–80 per cent of their time in front of computers rather than on front-line child protection work. Visitors to probation offices might be similarly struck by the number of staff sitting in front of their PCs without an offender in sight. As noted earlier, the system requirements are in themselves extremely resource intensive and the bureaucracy undoubtedly takes professional staff away from their core responsibilities, which is working with people. It appears as if demonstrating the integrity and effectiveness of public protection processes and systems relies upon ever more bureaucracy, driving a targets culture throughout the wider criminal justice system. In a piece of research on morale in the probation service, Farrow cited one probation officer as saying:

> I work with high risk offenders and I'm always chasing my tail. I don't have time for reflection ... have I done things properly? I worry that sooner or later something will go wrong, a high risk offender will do something and it will all fall back on me. I'll get little support from the service saying did you do this or that? Very little account will be taken of all the hundreds of things I have to do. (Farrow 2004: 212)

Others reported matters such as spending 80 per cent of their time on paperwork or the admin procedures, red tape and bureaucracy always being pressing (2004: 212).

Comments by Bridges and White (this volume) in part confirm this scenario. They suggest that during inspections, HMIP have found very good assessment practice among probation staff but less consistency in following through on the actions flowing from the assessment. As they rightly say, there may be a number of reasons to explain this but target culture may be one of them and if an initial assessment is completed in the required time-frame then a form of system compliance mentality may take over. The ongoing and thoughtful work of supervision is less susceptible to being measured (but see Bridges and White) and may assume less of a priority. Performance measurement therefore has to be associated with the perhaps more intangible aspects of working with high risk offenders and workload measurement needs to reflect the time necessary to reflect on what is happening in a case rather than push staff on to meet the next target.

Conclusion

Protecting the public from serious harm has been a mainstay of the political agenda for much of the past decade. It has by and large been uncontested, leaving successive Labour governments to ratchet up measures in response to each new tragic occurrence. It has been an agenda that has in many respects aped that of the United States, while managing to avoid the worst excesses of that regime. But perhaps more than the individual elements of the agenda is its impact upon policy and practice across the criminal justice sector. A fundamental aspect of this has been a transformation in the work of police officers. From being an agency primarily concerned with detection of crime they have, since the sex offender register was established, become responsible for offender supervision; at a stroke moving them much closer to the work of the probation service. With these new supervisory responsibilities they have also assumed the task of risk assessment of sex offenders in the community. It is not rocket science to work out that each year will bring an increase in sex offender registration and monitoring as new cases join those already on the register and spend years as active cases, if indeed they are ever de-registered. With other requirements to visit sex offenders in their homes, it is easy to see that there has been a considerable increase in the workload of the police without a substantial increase in resources for what was in effect a completely new area of work.

Indeed public protection is a constant resource drain at a time when public sector organisations are required to make substantial efficiency savings. The hidden problem here perhaps is that it is not only resources that are redirected to public protection teams but also experience and expertise. The other side of this coin is that resources and expertise are drained away from other parts of criminal justice organisations.

Undoubtedly an assumption behind this process is that highest risk offenders will commit the worst crimes and therefore resources and expertise are needed to better manage them in the community. This issue has been discussed in this and other chapters in this volume but it is worth emphasising that it is often medium and low risk offenders who commit serious further offences (Bridges 2006). It is sometimes the case, of course, that offenders are wrongly assessed as a lower risk than they should be (the Dano Sonnex case being an excellent example) and therefore are managed with fewer resources and less expertise. It is possible to use the wonders of hindsight to find reasons why mistakes can be made but it is rare that the system itself is blamed. However, the fact is that public protection has grown considerably and this growth impacts across the already stretched criminal justice sector. IPP sentences have led to an increase in the prison population, and perhaps more importantly put severe strain on the provision of the accredited programmes so necessary for prisoners to demonstrate the safety of their release. The work of the Parole Board has also increased very considerably, with the numbers of oral hearings increasing for life sentence prisoners predicted to increase by 69 per cent from 2008/09 to 2009/10. Oral hearings for IPP cases are predicted an even more dramatic 200 per cent increase over the same period (704 to 2,162) (Parole Board 2009). Registered sex offender numbers have increased from 28,994 (2004/05) to 32,336 (2008/09), adding to the workload of the police, as just mentioned (it should also be noted that, in respect of the point made earlier about having to filter the numbers for risk, only 4,408 of the latest figures are level two MAPPA and 424 level three). MAPPA equally is a resource drain at the top end of risk, although the low reconviction rates for high risk offenders may well make it a price worth paying. The development of the dangerous offenders database (ViSOR) will also demand a high resource input (but is, of course, designed to augment MAPPA) and the creation of a violent offender order (VOO) in 2009, similar to the original sexual offender order, will also increase demands on the police service in particular.

The growth of measures therefore brings its own problems and not the least of these is the pressure placed on criminal justice professionals to process, assess and manage the public protection caseload. This work also has to be conducted in a regime where all decisions have to be defensible, such is the high profile attached to it. Much has been written on the transition from defensible to defensive and it is apparent that caution has become a byword, notably for probation officers whose recall rates have helped to increase the prison population by 16 per cent in the period 1995–2009 (Ministry of Justice 2009b), and the Parole Board whose release rates for fixed and indeterminate sentence prisoners have fallen significantly over the past few years (see Whitfield, this volume). This cautious approach in turn produces more problems, particularly for the prison service whose inmate population continues to grow to record numbers. At times the government has been forced to vary its own policies as numbers have become unmanageable. For example, IPP sentences have seen their minimum tariff increased from twelve months to two years alongside a subtle change in the wording to remove in effect the *requirement* for judges to automatically impose indeterminate sentences in cases where criteria are met. It remains to be seen whether a growing number of challenges to public protection measures will also force further retreats by the government. Currently there are appeals in process against the length of time offenders spend registered on the sex offender register without a formal review. Added to this is an appeal by Barry George, the man acquitted, having served seven years of a life sentence, for the murder of television presenter Jill Dando, against his continued supervision under MAPPA. George is still subject to the lowest level of MAPPA supervision due to two convictions for indecent assault and attempted rape dating from 1982 and 1983 respectively. In contesting his appeal the Metropolitan Police argue that he still poses a continuing risk despite his acquittal and cites two complaints from women received since his release. However, the probation officers' trade union NAPO argued that 'if people are referred to Mappa on the basis of suspicions and intelligence or because their case is high-profile, it does open up worrying aspects around intrusion' (Laville 2009). Perhaps fractures are beginning to emerge along the public protection front? The United States, of course, has a long history of litigation in the public protection area, but America's Supreme Court has consistently upheld measures designed to protect the public. In the UK there are indications that the courts may be less sympathetic, leaving the government sitting in between the media and the law.

The government continues to use the civil law to control *potentially harmful* behaviours, with any infraction leading automatically to criminal law sanctions. It attempts to regulate future harms and risks by controlling the present and does so largely in the absence of the major rights objections raised at the time of the influential Floud Report (Floud and Young 1981). The question is, of course, where might it all end? The government's recent proposals that parents involved in regular school runs with children should go through a registration process, and also people visiting schools such as children's authors, have provoked much criticism, including a ferocious response from high profile figures such as Philip Pullman. Indeed such has been the opposition that the government is already backtracking on this measure, a common feature of some of their seemingly ill thought through ideas. It is likely that the 11 million helpers who may have been required to be criminal record checked and registered will now be considerably reduced in number, although those with regular contact (weekly, for example) may still have to do so (Helm and Syal 2009). It is now increasingly difficult for parents to take photographs of their children at events such as sports days and school plays, and anti-terrorist measures (Terrorism Act 2000, s.22) have seen a number of legitimate photographers searched and moved on when photographing landmark buildings in London and indeed elsewhere in the country (*Guardian* 2009). Unknown and unseen future risks are now determining how we live in the present, either as offenders or non-offenders. The public the government seeks to protect may now find more of their traditional freedoms under threat. So far the British public have accepted more stringent measures against offenders as they have seemingly felt themselves to be at risk from them. Yet all the evidence suggests that this risk is minimal and perhaps as the public themselves begin to be constricted by the fall-out from measures aimed to protect them, they will begin to question the need for such an extensive public protection agenda in the future.

This chapter opened by raising the issue of 'fear' and it closes in the same vein. Collective insecurities, overblown perceptions of risk and a need to be assured of safety have come to dominate public life. All misfortunes, even natural ones, lead to blame, so we conclude with the 'natural disaster' of the worst winter in the UK for 30 years. After the usual British excitement the blame culture took over with government and local authorities in the firing line for providing insufficient grit. Naturally a huge number of sports fixtures were postponed but it was left to the erudite manager of Arsenal football club, Arsène Wenger (2010), to express what no doubt many think but are cajoled in various ways to believe the opposite. He wrote on the postponement of games due to ice on the approaches to football grounds:

> But I must say it is the price we pay for living in a society with 100 per cent security. Nobody accepts any risk any more and everybody is always guided by fear. If one of 60,000 people has an accident, you feel very guilty and nobody accepts any more that the slightest insecurity could exist in our society and that's why the games are postponed when there is no real need for it.

He could have been describing public protection policy.

Selected further reading

Many of the key texts for this subject are included in the reference list. Readers might like to read in greater depth Dunbar and Langdon's (1998) *Tough Justice* if they wish to understand in more detail how a consensus seemingly emerged between Conservative and Labour politicians on criminal justice policy in the 1990s. Gordon Hughes' excellent *The Politics of Crime and Community* (2007, Palgrave) offers a perspective on how crime and its control have become a key community issue, reflecting on one of Labour's big messages that crime control and prevention was the responsibility of us all. The ongoing debates about the notification of sex offender whereabouts continue to sharpen this issue. Finally for a comparative, theoretical and broad selection of essays on the subject, readers should consult Tim Newburn and Paul Rock, *The Politics of Crime Control, Essays in Honour of David Downes*, (2009, Clarendon Series of Criminology, Oxford University Press.)

References

ACOP (1988) *More Demanding than Prison*. London: Association of Chief Officers of Probation.

BBC (2006) 'Child sex snatch jailing insult', BBC News, 12 June. Online at: http://news.bbc.co.uk/1/hi/wales/5069656.stm.

Bottoms, A. (1977) 'Reflections on the renaissance of dangerousness', *Howard Journal*, 16: 70–96.

Bridges, A. (2006) 'Working with dangerous offenders: what is achievable?', unpublished paper, School of Oriental and African Studies, University of London, 15 November 2006.

Brooke, C. (2009) 'Rapist, shielded by his "human rights" was free to live where he chose ... and kill a girl of 14', *Mail Online*, 9 May. Online at: http://www.dailymail.co.uk/news/article-565189/Rapist-shielded-human-rights-free-live-chose-kill-girl-14.html (accessed 27 October 2009).

Channel 4 (2008) 'Balls: Shoesmith had to go', 1 December. Online at: http://www.channel4.com/news/articles/society/law_order/balls+shoesmith+had+to+go/2859757 (accessed 7 January 2010).

Cheston, P. (2009) 'Balls: I was right to sack Baby P council chief', *London Evening Standard*, 9 October. Online at: www.thisislondon.co.uk/standard/article-23754536-baby-p-chief-knew-of-failings-before-sacking.do (accessed 13 December 2009).

Corrigan, R. (2006) 'Making meaning of Megan's Law', *Law and Social Inquiry*, 31(2): 267–312.

Cramb, A. (2007) 'Man who had sex with bicycle sentenced', *Daily Telegraph*, 14 November.

Curtis, P., Williams, R. and Stratton, A. (2009) 'Ofsted accused of manipulating Haringey report after Baby P', *Guardian*, 9 October 2009.

Dunbar, I. and Langdon, A. (1998) *Tough Justice: Sentencing and Penal Policies in the 1990s*. London: Blackstone Press.

Dwyer, C. D. (2007) 'Risk, politics and the "scientification" of political judgement: prisoner release and conflict transformation in Northern Ireland', *British Journal of Criminology*, 47(5): 729–97.

Farrow, K. (2004) 'Still committed after all these years? Morale in the modern-day probation Service', *Probation Journal*, 51(3): 206–20.

Floud, J. and Young, W. (1981) *Dangerousness and Criminal Justice*. London: Heinemann Education.

Furedi, F. (2002) *Culture of Fear*. London: Continuum.

Garland, D. (2000) 'The culture of high crime societies', *British Journal of Criminology*, 40: 347–75

Garland, D. (2001) *The Culture of Crime Control: Crime and Social Order in Contemporary Society*. Oxford: Oxford University Press.

Guardian (2009) 'We're photographers, not terrorists', 11 December. Online at: www.guardian.co.uk/commentisfree/libertycentral/2009/dec/11/photographers-section-44-terrorism-act (accessed 13 December 13 2009).

Hebenton, B. and Seddon, T. (2009) 'From dangerousness to precaution: managing sexual and violent offenders in an insecure and uncertain age', *British Journal of Criminology*, 49(3): 343–62.

Helm, T. and Syal, R. (2009) 'U-turn over sex-crime vetting of class helpers', *The Observer*, 14 December.

Her Majesty's Inspectorate of Probation (2006) *An Independent Review of a Serious Further Offence Case: Anthony Rice*. London: HMIP.

Home Office (1990) *Crime, Justice and Protecting the Public: The Government's Proposals for Legislation*, Cm 965. London: HMSO.

Home Office (2006) *Rebalancing the Criminal Justice System in Favour of the Law-abiding Majority: Cutting Crime, Reducing Offending and Protecting the Public*. London: Home Office.

Home Office (2008) MAPPA annual reports press release. Online at: www.syps.org.uk/press_releases/MOJPressReleaseMAPPAAnnualReports20070820October2008.pdf (accessed 7 January 2009).

House of Lords (2009) Secretary of State for Justice (Respondent) v James (FC) (Appellant) (formerly Walker and another) AND R (on the application of Lee) (FC) (Appellant) and one other action [2009] UKHL 22.

Hudson, B. (2003) *Justice in the Risk Society*. London: Sage.

Human Rights Watch (2007) *No Easy Answers: Sex Offender Laws in the US*. New York: Human Rights Watch.

James, A. and Raine, J. (1998) *The New Politics of Criminal Justice*. Harlow: Longman.

Janus, E. (2007) *Failure to Protect: America's Sexual Predator Laws and the Rise of the Preventive State*. Ithaca and London: Cornell University Press.

Karstedt, S. (2002) 'Emotions and criminal justice', *Theoretical Criminology*, 6(3): 299–317.

Kemshall, H. and Maguire, M. (2001) 'Public protection, partnership and risk penality: the multi-agency risk management of sexual and violent offenders', *Punishment and Society*, 34(2): 237–64.

Kershaw, C., Dowdeswell, P. and Goodman, J. (1997) *Life Licensees – Reconvictions and Recalls by the end of 1985: England and Wales*. London: Home Office Research and Statistics Directorate.

Lacombe, D. (2008) 'Consumed with sex: the treatment of sex offenders in risk society', *British Journal of Criminology*, 48(1): 55–74.

Laville, S. (2009) 'Cleared Dando suspect challenges surveillance order', *Guardian*, 30 November.

Maden, A. (2007) *Treating Violence: A Guide to Risk Management in Mental Health*. Oxford: Oxford University Press.

Matthews, R. and Young, J. (eds) (2003) *The New Politics of Crime and Punishment*. Cullompton: Willan Publishing.

Ministry of Justice (2009a) *Mappa Guidance 2009 Version 3*. London: Ministry of Justice.

Ministry of Justice (2009b) 'Story of the prison population 1995–2009 England and Wales', *Ministry of Justice Statistics Bulletin*, 31 July. London: Ministry of Justice.

Ministry of Justice (2009c) 'Reports into the management of Dano Sonnex within the criminal justice system'. Online at: www.justice.gov.uk/news/announcement040609a. htm (accessed 13 December 2009).

Nash, M. (1999) 'Enter the polibation officer', *International Journal of Police Science and Management*, 1(4): 360–8.

Nash, M. and Williams, A. (2008) *The Anatomy of Serious Further Offending*. Oxford: Oxford University Press.

Parole Board (2009) 'Parole Board Published Business Plan'. Online at: www. paroleboard.gov.uk/news/parole_board_publishes_business_plan_for_2009_10/ (accessed 30 December 2009).

Peelo, M., Francis, B., Soothill, K., Pearson, J. and Ackerley, E. (2004) 'Newspaper reporting and the public construction of homicide', *British Journal of Criminology*, 44(2): 256–75.

Prison Reform Trust (2007) *Indefinitely Maybe? How the Indefinite Sentence for Public Protection is Unjust and Unsustainable*. London: Prison Reform Trust. Online at: www. prisonreformtrust.org.uk/uploads/documents/Indefinitely_maybe.pdf (accessed 10 December 2009).

Scott, P. (1977) 'Assessing dangerousness in criminals', *British Journal of Psychiatry*, 131: 127–42.

Stone, N. (2007) 'In court', *Probation Journal*, 54: 446–54.

Straw, J. (2009) House of Commons written answers. Online at: http://services. parliament.uk/hansard/Commons/ByDate/20090616/writtenanswers/part022. html.

Stunell, A. (2009) 'Number of 'prisoners serving beyond their tariff continues to rise'. Online at: www.stunell.co.uk/news/000537/stunell_number_of_ipp_prisoners_ serving_beyond_their_tariff_continues_to_rise.html.

Tran, M. (2009) 'Jack Straw blames probation management over French students' murder', *Guardian*, 8 June. Online at: www.guardian.co.uk/uk/2009/jun/08/ probation-police-french-student-murder (accessed 14 December 2009).

Walklate, S. and Mythen, G. (2008) 'How scared are we?', *British Journal of Criminology*, 48(2): 209–25.

Wells, T. (2009) 'Baby P pay-off deal shame', *The Sun*, 13 October.

Wenger, A. (2010) 'Postponements guided by fear', 8 January. Online at: www.arsenal.com/news/news-archive/wenger-postponements-are-guided-by-fear (accessed 15 January 2010).

Williams, A. and Thompson, B. (2004a) 'Vigilance or vigilantes: the Paulsgrove riots and policing paedophiles in the community, part 1: The long slow fuse', *The Police Journal*, 77: 99–119.

Williams, A. and Thompson, B. (2004b) 'Vigilance or vigilantes: the Paulsgrove riots and policing paedophiles in the community, part 2: The lessons of Paulsgrove', *Police Journal*, 77: 199–205.

Wood, J. and Kemshall, H. (2007) *The Operation and Experience of Multi Agency Public Protection Arrangements (MAPPA)*, Home Office Online Research Report 12/07. Online at: www.homeoffice.gov.uk/rds/pdfs07/rdsolr1207.pdf (accessed 14 December 2009).

Worrall, A. (1997) *Punishment in the Community: The Future of Criminal Justice*. Harlow: Longman.

Assessing and Managing Risk

Introduction

Mike Nash and Andy Williams

The theme of Part Two centres on the concept of risk and how the management of risk has become *the* preoccupation within public protection. The aim is to look critically at how the notion of risk has become embedded within the criminal justice system, and how discourses of risk are often used to mask draconian policies, especially around extended and indeterminate sentencing. Following from the conceptual work in Part One, which formed the broad opinion that risk and dangerousness has come to dominate public protection, this section also considers how important issues such as human rights can be easily usurped simply by using risk assessment discursive strategies. The developments in risk assessment techniques, starting in the 1930s and continuing right the way through to the present day, can be viewed in both a positive and a negative light. One positive development with the current risk assessment techniques used – such as OASys and Risk Matrix 2000 – is that they have, to some extent, standardised the assessment process. What was once the domain of psychiatric clinicians is now open to a wider range of professions who work within public protection and are charged with 'managing' risk. Another positive is that many of the available risk assessments are 'evidence based'. While there are obvious problems with using nomothetic information to predict an individual's future behaviour, having risk assessments based upon empirical evidence is at least a step in the right direction. The negative side of the coin includes too much 'form filling' and 'box ticking' – or 'drop-down menu checking' – and not enough in-depth understanding of an offender's criminality. The potential for the deskilling of those at the business end of offender management has become a reality in some agencies. While this may be a difficult pill for some practitioners to swallow, it is nonetheless an important change that has taken place in public protection over the last twenty-years or so, and one that needs further consideration.

What readers will find here are four chapters dealing with three core issues – risk assessment, decision-making and managing offenders – all of which are placed within the framework of public protection. The message from these broad themes is clear: contemporary criminal justice policy is currently dominated by the concept of risk and this is a difficult agenda to resist. Millions of pounds have been invested (especially in the UK), on multi-agency working, which operates a vast 'bureaucracy' of forms, protocols and national standards, the like of which we have never seen before. This has resulted in more data collection and sharing than we can ever possibly exploit. Unfortunately, this ever-increasing risk-management bureaucracy has created a system whereby regulations, standard operating procedures and policies are inward-thinking and are introduced so the agency can provide a 'defensible position' to justify problems and failures with the management of offenders when they commit further offences. What is obvious when considering the chapters in this section is that very little of our current methods for managing and assessing risk is fed back into research or understanding broader patterns of criminality. Our hope is that these chapters raise some fair, yet critical points that readers can consider not only as being crucial to understanding the social and political context of risk assessment, but also illustrates the public protection framework within which the management of offenders takes place.

We begin with James Vess' comprehensive overview of risk assessment within public protection. He examines current practices in risk assessment and the associated roles that mental health professionals play within the public protection framework. His extensive experience and knowledge in this field is the result of an entire career dealing with offenders in a variety of treatment, assessment and supervisory roles within a clinical setting. Having worked in both the United States and New Zealand, his current research into risk assessment gives him a unique insight into the practical application of clinical tools. His distinctive perspective offers an important discussion on one of the core problems facing many practitioners: the juxtaposition between the creation of punitive sex offender laws and the balancing of human rights to the individual. Using some core examples from America, Vess argues that various community protection laws can be classified by the degree to which they curtail the individual rights of sex offenders. He also makes the crucial point that the fear and revulsion of sex offenders creates a system whereby practitioners are more likely to be overly cautious when risk assessing the levels of harm. These false positives produce fewer negative consequences to both the practitioner, in terms of career prospects and professional standing, and the organisation managing that particular offender. Vess notes that unfortunately, this comes at the expense of the rights of the offender. Much of his discussion focuses on the role that mental health experts play in risk assessing individuals and it is here that he makes some telling points regarding the role of the expert. The mental health expert must ensure that in a forensic setting, the client is the judicial decision-maker, and 'the expert's responsibility is to provide the best available risk assessment evidence in a way that is not misleading'. However, Vess also provides a refreshingly objective overview of risk assessment techniques used within mental health. He argues that the various problems with risk assessment methods places the mental health professional in an awkward ethical position, when using these tools in a forensic setting. He states that what should be of fundamental concern is that the use of clinical risk assessments that restrict individual freedoms and rights should be used in an ethical manner that evolves as laws develop. Vess reminds us of the inherent ethical tension between the trust and rapport that is developed in order for an offender to engage in a process of 'self-revelation', and the fact that this information could be used by social control agencies to restrict that individual's freedom or extend their sentence. He proposes that setting clear boundaries regarding the role of the assessor and the assessment process ensures a more ethical stance, even though it may result in limited disclosure.

Nicola Padfield's chapter provides an extensive overview of the UK law on public protection, and highlights the real context in which these pieces of legislation are implemented. Her epistemological background gives her a unique insight into the legal system, having trained and practised as a barrister before becoming an academic specialising in decision-making processes within the criminal justice system. It is this experience that brings to the forefront the issue of legal decision-making within the context of public protection. Padfield's intricately woven legal critique draws attention to one of the core issues within public protection: as serious further offence inquiries inform us, some of the problems with providing an accurate risk assessment have their origins in the decisions made throughout the entire legal and criminal justice process; and she traces some of these problems and issues chronologically. Starting with the application of criminal law with the first level of gate-keepers – the police – Padfield notes how the inconsistencies in decision-making pertaining to who was charged and was released led to the creation of the Crown Prosecution Service. Using examples such as mental illness and psychiatric evidence, we see how specific decision-making processes leads an individual into the public protection system. Padfield examines pre-trial decisions such as whether to give cautions or to prosecute, as well as bail and extradition decisions in order to critically examine the legal processes that are involved in protecting the public. One of the central issues for Padfield is the fact that during the trial and sentencing stages, very little is known about the reality of decision-making processes that effectively determine the level of public protection that is provided. For example, she discusses how jury decisions are shrouded in secrecy and there is a distinct lack of knowledge of the relationship between jury and judicial decision-making. The broad range of issues covered in this chapter includes how, within the public protection system, offenders have to subtly negotiate their way through the prison system via interactions with report writers and prison decision-makers (that is, the Parole Board). Once released into the community, the offender is still subject to a plethora of civil public protection laws and Padfield discusses the legal ramifications of this through the lens of MAPPA and the Sex Offenders Act 1997, which includes an interesting examination of civil protection and control orders. The concluding remarks highlight the flaws in the area of the laws concerned with public protection, and that the issues decided by courts, which include the protection of the individual's rights as well as issues of public protection, are actually constrained by many decisions taken earlier in the process.

The chapter by Andy Williams offers an in-depth description and critical overview of the Offender Assessment System (OASys). OASys is the risk assessment tool used within the prison and probation services, which assesses the likelihood of reconviction and risk of harm among adult offenders. He has been researching the development of multi-agency working for ten years and has been involved in training MAPPA personnel since 2006. During this time he has become a 'critical friend' to MAPPA, and has observed and discussed many issues with practitioners from a broad range of organisations including the police, probation, and social services, youth offending and child protection teams, as well as many health service providers. Williams reviews the aetiological development of the actuarial risk assessment instruments, and charts the rise in dominance of these techniques within the arena of public protection. Williams' main concern is how these risk tools have come to usurp the basic analytical skills of good offender assessment and rely more on ticking boxes than on an in-depth understanding of an individual's criminality. He demonstrates these concerns through his analysis of OASys. By providing readers with an in-depth discussion of all the components to the current OASys form, Williams attempts to provide a more contextual understanding to how the assessment is undertaken in practice. Following from this he provides some general critical points that feed into the overriding message within the chapter. The epistemological chasm suggests that despite the large amount of offender information that is collected within the public protection arena, there is little systematic research undertaken on these 'data enriched' records.

In the final chapter in this section, David Carson and Tim Carson build upon the ideas introduced by Padfield and Williams, by arguing that if public protection is to improve then greater focus needs to be placed on the quality of professionals' decision-making. This can be examined in terms of five 'levels', or contributions: risk prediction (assessment), risk management (interventions to control), risk decision-making (quality control), risk resource management (efficient investment), and integration of risk policies (systemic perspectives). Each level focuses on contributions by different people: for example, decision-makers, decision implementers, trainers, supervisors, and researchers and managers. They argue that failure to act at all levels will impair progress and distort decisions, not least about responsibility. In order to demonstrate their arguments, they provide an explanation of each 'level' before providing examples of their roles in relation to some recent reports and developments. The examples used in this insightful chapter demonstrate that within public protection we need to adequately predict violent behaviour (as well as identify perpetrators); to invest more effort in the potential for managing risk decisions (and they argue that this would be more efficient and effective than seeking further refinements with risk factors); to apply knowledge from the behavioural sciences, and learning from practical experience, to improve decision-making; to acknowledge the critical – albeit political – role of resource allocation in support of risk-taking; and finally to identify the extent to which organisational, procedural, cultural, policy and other factors can – albeit unintentionally – make public protection more difficult.

Chapter 4

Forensic risk assessment: public protection versus offender rights[1]

James Vess

Introduction

In May 1989, Earl Shriner dragged a seven-year-old boy off his bicycle and into the woods near the boy's home in Tacoma, Washington. The boy was raped, choked, sexually mutilated and left for dead. At the time, Shriner had a 24-year history of violence and sexual assault, for which he had been in and out of institutions since the age of fifteen. He had been released from prison two years earlier, after serving a ten-year sentence for the kidnapping and assault of two teenage girls. While in prison, he had bragged of his sadistic fantasies. Prison officials had sought to have him committed to a secure state hospital rather than released because of the risk he posed, but psychiatric evaluations concluded that he did not meet the legal criteria for confinement because he did not suffer from a recognised mental disorder that rendered him an immediate and substantial danger to others. Intense public outrage was inflamed and given expression through sensational media coverage of the crime. In 1990, the state of Washington passed the Community Protection Act, the first in a wave of statutes allowing for the indefinite civil commitment of sexual offenders considered to pose a threat to public safety. Twenty states had similar civil commitment laws by the end of 2007, with over 4,500 sex offenders under continuing confinement after serving their prison sentence (Gookin 2007). Such an offender is typically labelled a 'sexually violent predator' or SVP.

Also in 1989, eighteen-year-old Lloyd McIntosh attacked and raped a six-year-old girl, and was committed to a secure psychiatric hospital in New Zealand. Despite allegations of further sexual violence while institutionalised and concerns about his risk of reoffending, he was discharged in 1993. Within three months of his discharge, he violently raped a two-year-old girl, who was left in a life-threatening condition as a result of the attack. He was sentenced to ten years in prison for this crime. He was denied parole, and having no alternative under existing statutes, he was released in May 2003 at the conclusion of his full sentence. Although under round-the-clock supervision as specified by the Parole Board, he soon attacked an intellectually disabled woman while the staff assigned to monitor him remained outside the bedroom door, feeling constrained by the terms of the supervision from entering the room. This highly publicised sequence of events produced an intense public reaction, spurring policy-makers to respond to the fear, anger and criticism of the community. While serving the eighteen-month sentence he received for his latest assault, New Zealand's parliament passed a law allowing for the extended supervision of sex offenders who, like McIntosh, presented an alarming threat to public safety. Within Australia, extended supervision schemes for sex offenders have now also been introduced in Victoria, Queensland, New South Wales and Western Australia (David et al. 2007).

In 1994, seven-year-old Megan Kanka was lured into the house across the street from her home in Hamilton County, New Jersey, where she was sexually assaulted and killed by Jesse Timmendequas, one of three discharged sex offenders who lived there. The community was outraged that no one on the block had been notified that these sex offenders lived among them and posed a threat to their children. Their reaction resulted in Megan's Law, a registration and community notification statute that has been adopted across the United States, including a federal version that was adopted in 1995 (Winick 2003). Known as the Jacob Wetterling Crimes Against Children and Sexually Violent Offender Registration Act, this law requires states to establish sex offender registration and community notification programs or lose 10 per cent of federal law enforcement funding (LaFond 2005).

The origins of community protection laws for sex offenders

As these examples show, laws intended to provide greater public protection from sexual offenders are typically a reaction to heinous and highly publicised offences, which cause fear and outrage. The public demands that something be done. Politicians and law enforcement professionals come under intense pressure to respond with definitive actions to allay the community's anxiety. Legal controversy remains over issues of due process (the law must be fair and the government must respect all of the rights owed to a person under the law), double jeopardy (a person cannot be tried twice for an offence for which he or she has already been prosecuted or convicted), proportionality (the punishment must be proportional to the severity of the offending), and ex post facto (the retroactive application of a law that increases the punishment from that which was allowed when the crime was committed – Janus 2000; LaFond 2000). Concern has also been expressed over the precedent set by the expanded use of civil commitment as an expression of the state's police power for public protection, and the eventual effectiveness of these laws has yet to be empirically demonstrated for significantly reducing rates of sexual offending (Burdon and Gallagher 2002; LaFond 2000; Levenson 2004; Levesque 2000). It has therefore been argued that the laws themselves raise important concerns about human rights. Even if such laws are more effective for increasing public safety than less restrictive approaches, some question whether they are morally or legally justifiable (see Doren 2002; Nash 2006).

Special legislation to deal with sex offenders is not a recent development. Use of indefinite civil commitment of sex offenders in the United States began during the 1930s with the emergence of various 'sexual psychopath' statutes. The goal of these earlier laws was to protect society from future sexual offences by providing sexual offenders with treatment in order to cure the underlying mental disorder (Burdon and Gallagher 2002). As American society shifted from an emphasis on rehabilitation to an emphasis on retribution in dealing with offenders, most of these laws were eventually repealed (American Psychiatric Association 1999, in Burdon and Gallagher 2002). The recent community protection approach that emerged during the early 1990s was a response to perceived inadequacies in previous approaches to provide for public safety, and it attempts to strike a different balance between public safety and the protection of offenders' rights. In contrast to earlier approaches, the community protection model is less concerned about treatment or rehabilitation of offenders to reduce recidivism or facilitate community reintegration (Vess 2008). The primary goal of the community protection model is the incapacitation of sexual offenders for the sake of public safety. The enactment of laws under this model has sparked ongoing debate and numerous legal challenges on a variety of issues, including the need to strike a proper balance between public safety and the rights of individual offenders.

The primary distinguishing characteristic of current sex offender laws is that they provide for sanctions against offenders on the basis of their risk for future offending, rather than impose punishment for past actions. This represents a departure from most legal precedent in modern western societies, and requires an explicit consideration of the impact of such laws on the human rights of offenders. The approach taken in this chapter is to examine current practices in risk assessment and the associated roles that mental health professionals play in proceedings prescribed by these laws, in light of a specific model for human rights.

Human rights and sex offender laws

To understand the ethical issues posed by these laws, it is necessary to have a clearly articulated framework for understanding human rights. Ward and colleagues have discussed human rights in correctional clinical practice, and have specifically applied their model to the treatment of sex offenders (Ward and Birgden 2007; Ward et al. 2007). Drawing from the work of Freeden (1991), these authors develop a conceptual model in which human rights serve a protective function, so that individuals can pursue their own intentions in creating meaningful lives. Human rights thereby create a space within which individuals can lead lives that maintain a basic sense of human dignity.

In the model presented by Ward and Birgden (2007), human rights reflect the core values of freedom and well-being, based on Gewirth's (1996) assertion that these conditions are necessary for the attainment of the individual's personal goals. Freedom involves the ability to act on the basis of one's particular intentions, and well-being involves conditions that support basic levels of physical and mental functioning, as well as access to necessary social, material and psychological resources. The structure of human rights begins with these broad, intangible core values and moves towards more specific human rights objects, as formulated by Orend (2002), including personal security, personal freedom, material subsistence, elemental equality and social recognition. It is in support of these human rights objects that the more tangible rights delineated by current human rights policies are defined, such as freedom from discrimination, the right to a fair trial and due process of law (Ward and Birgden 2007; Ward *et al.* 2009). The utility of this model for forensic clinical practice is that all professional ethics can be seen as serving to protect underlying human rights, and all human rights can be seen as stemming from the core values of freedom and well-being.

Taking this human rights model into consideration, the various community protection laws can be organised by the degree to which they appear to curtail the individual rights of sex offenders. From this perspective, indefinite civil commitment of an SVP following the completion of a finite prison sentence presents the most restrictive measure, with a deprivation of liberty comparable to continued imprisonment. In these cases, the core human value of freedom is severely curtailed, and the core value of well-being may be significantly diminished. The attainment of the offender's personal goals are clearly subordinated to the state's goals for public safety. Facing a life of indefinite confinement as an identified sexual predator, with the constant attribution that one is too dangerous to be among the public, it may be difficult to maintain a basic sense of human dignity.

The next most intrusive and restrictive method is extended supervision in the community beyond the original parole period allowed by ordinary sentencing practices. In these cases, the offender is released from prison, but must abide by any restrictions imposed by the Parole Board. As currently enacted, sex offenders can be placed under extended supervision for up to ten years in New Zealand or fifteen years in Australia. In Australia, this term can be extended for additional periods of up to fifteen years, whereby living under supervision becomes a lifetime condition. While the deprivation of freedom is less than under SVP laws, the curtailment of this basic human right may still be substantial, so that in extreme cases the offender must live under conditions similar to home detention, and may be subject to electronic monitoring of his or her movements. Specific human rights such as personal freedom and elemental equality may be particularly threatened in these circumstances.

The approach to public safety with the least overt curtailment of offender rights might appear to be registration and community notification laws, whereby the offender is released after serving his prison sentence and is not subject to extended periods of active supervision in the community. However, a closer review of the enactment of community notification laws shows the substantial impact they can have on the lives of offenders. Freedom involves the ability to act on the basis of one's particular intentions, and well-being involves conditions that support access to necessary social, material and psychological resources (Ward and Birgden 2007). The effects of community notification laws, which can include social rejection, discrimination in housing and employment, and vigilante violence, are such that these core values may be severely eroded in the lives of sex offenders.

One important difference between SVP laws and extended supervision or community notification is that when an offender is committed under an SVP law, he or she is not released to the community until the risk for reoffending is assessed as sufficiently reduced. This contrast serves to amplify the issues inherent in the limited accuracy of our current risk assessment procedures. The consequences of a false positive finding, in which an offender is predicted to reoffend when in fact he or she would not, are higher under an SVP law, because the unnecessary loss of freedom is substantially greater with indefinite, involuntary commitment to a secure facility. Under either SVP or extended supervision, and some community notification schemes, the costs associated with false negatives accrue to public safety, whereby an offender is predicted not to reoffend (and available interventions or notifications are not applied), when he or she does commit a subsequent sexual offence, and new victims are created. In this context, the accuracy of risk assessment is a crucial consideration.

Risk assessment procedures

The accuracy of risk assessment

A central issue common to all recent initiatives to increase public protection from sex offenders arises from the fact that, unlike determinate sentences following conviction for a criminal offence, these laws provide for the imposition of sanctions against sex offenders based on the risk of future offences. Although actuarial measures represent a significant advance over unstructured clinical judgement (Doren 2002; Hanson and Morton-Bourgon 2007), the primary concerns about human rights in relation to judicial decisions under such laws derive from the limited accuracy of current actuarial measures to predict the likelihood of sexual reoffending. It is important to recognise that none of the statistical indices yet developed can completely answer the question of how accurate a risk assessment measure is (Gottfredson and Moriarty 2006). Some researchers (for example, Harris and Rice 2003; Quinsey *et al.* 2006) argue that relative operating characteristic (ROC) analysis offers the best index of statistical accuracy because it is independent of the base-rate variations in different samples of offenders. Yet others argue that the base rate of sexual recidivism cannot be ignored in considering the accuracy of a given measure in a particular application (Gottfredson and Moriarty 2006), especially in light of the low base rate observed for sexual reoffending. A recent meta-analysis involving over 17,000 sex offenders from 72 different studies showed a sexual recidivism rate of 12.4 per cent (Hanson and Morton-Bourgon 2007). Other studies have suggested that approximately 10 per cent to 15 per cent of sex offenders would be expected to be detected for a new sexual offence after five years in the community (Hanson and Bussière 1998; Harris and Hanson 2004), although it must be recognised that recidivism rates based on rearrests or reconvictions represent an underestimation of the true extent of sexual re-offending. Knowing the relevant base rate of sexual reoffending, and its impact on the accuracy of risk predictions based on various measures, is important for making sense of the various statements made about the risk measures used in a particular case.

Indices that are sensitive to base rates and those that are not can lead to dramatically different conclusions concerning the value of risk assessment measures. Campbell (2003) questions the value of ROC analysis, regression analysis and correlational data for judicial decision-makers, and points out the limitations of ROC values as an index of accuracy. He illustrates this point by reporting the rates of true and false positives, and true and false negatives for the Static-99, one of the most widely used and extensively validated risk measures currently available (Hanson and Thornton 2000; Doren 2004). Using the optimal cut-off score for the Static-99 reported by Sjostedt and Langstrom (2001) of >4, and assuming a 35 per cent base rate for sexual reoffending, Campbell reports that 51 per cent of the sexual recidivists would be missed (the false negative rate), and 31 per cent of those predicted to be recidivists would not reoffend (the false positive rate). As the base rate changes, as may be expected among different sub-types of offenders, the rates of false positives and false negatives for a given score on the prediction measure will also change. This is why it is incomplete, and potentially misleading, to report indices like ROC values with the implication that they provide information of sufficient accuracy without reference to the base rate. While these figures are associated with a significant improvement over predictions made without using empirically derived actuarial risk measures, they specify the degree of uncertainty still inherent in this approach.

In light of the margin for error inherent in current actuarial measures, more individualised risk assessments are desirable, preferably those that take into account dynamic and aetiological factors. Yet here too there are voices of caution in the professional literature. Campbell (2003) refers to adjusted actuarial assessments (that is, actuarial assessments adjusted by considering dynamic factors and other clinical information) as unstandardised procedures which may be administered in an inconsistent *ad hoc* way. This criticism may be minimised by considering only factors clearly associated with increased rates of sexual recidivism in the empirical research literature in the formulation of risk in an individual case. It is noted, however, that 'without a well defined decision-making procedure for adjusted actuarial assessment, these improvised judgements can also be expected to vary inconsistently from one case to another' (Campbell 2003: 275).

Peer-reviewed research identifying the accuracy levels of adjusted actuarial assessment is still in the early stages. While some like Quinsey *et al.* (2006) maintain that adjusting purely actuarial risk predictions can only diminish their accuracy, many experts in the field are advocating a more thorough understanding of individual cases through the consideration of dynamic risk factors (for example, Doren 2002; Hanson *et al.* 2007; Hanson and Morton-Bourgon 2007). The point here is that there is no clear method for adjusting actuarial results in light of factors not included in standardised measures of static risk, and little empirical data to date to provide estimates of accuracy with adjusted risk assessments.

Individual risk from group data

One of the central issues for risk assessments in public protection proceedings is the applicability of group assessment data to individual offenders. A key concern here is the use of probability statements that are based on observed reconviction rates for groups of offenders and the degree of inference about the individual that can be made based on findings about a group. This issue is reflected in the title of an article by Grant Harris (2003): 'Men in his category have a 50% likelihood, but which half is he in? Comments on Berlin, Galbreath, Geary and McGlone'.

The criticism of actuarial risk estimation to which Harris responded is the implication that it is inappropriate or misleading to treat each individual member of a risk category as if he or she were the same as every other member of the category. One argument is that predictions about individuals cannot be made using information derived from groups. But as Harris points out, virtually all decisions require clinicians to treat individuals as members of groups, and attempting to treat an offender as if he were entirely unique would require clinicians to ignore prior scientific research. The capacity to match an individual to a well-defined group with a known rate of recidivism is the foundation of the considerable progress that has been made in risk assessment through actuarial methods.

Janus and Prentky (2003) noted that there is a deep philosophical dispute about whether it makes sense to speak of probability when applied to a single individual as opposed to a group. But these authors focus on the practical matter that real-world predictions are based on formal or informal awareness of relevant group behaviour. They state that all prediction, including actuarial and clinical predictions, must be group based, otherwise it would be merely a guess. They make two points in this regard. One is that they believe that the morality of depriving people of long-term liberty based on predictions of future crimes is questionable, largely because of this issue of basing individual predictions on group membership. However, given that community protection laws exist, and that they routinely use clinical prediction, the authors concluded that actuarial risk assessment should not be rejected for being group based, because all prediction is group based. Actuarial methods currently provide the highest predictive accuracy, and therefore judicial decision-makers should rely on the most accurate available risk information.

The central *caveat* to this issue that frequently seems lost in the risk assessment information presented to the court is that rates of recidivism associated with groups of offenders, and the statistical properties of a risk measure, do not tell us an individual offender's probability of recidivism. Rather, this information tells us how a scale or measure performed in differentiating between recidivists and non-recidivists in a given study or set of studies (Mossman 2006). In the interest of protecting the human rights of the offender, the strengths as well as the limitations of current risk assessment measures must be made as clear as possible to those making decisions about the individual's freedom.

Another concern about the use of group data to quantify the risk presented by an individual is the nature of the group or groups with whom a measure has been empirically validated. The accuracy and relevance of the research findings that serve as the foundation for risk assessment reports to the courts have been criticized because much of the research literature does not distinguish among reoffence rates for different types of offenders such as rapists and child molesters (Vess and Skelton, in press; Wood and Ogloff 2006). Besides not assessing reoffence rates by offender type based on offence history, most studies do not examine the rates of specific types of reoffending, such as reoffences against child versus adult victims, or contact versus non-contact offences. Yet some public protection laws specifically require assessment of the risk for committing future specified sex offences against child victims. Without available base rates for specific types of sexual reoffending by specific types of offenders, examined as a function of different levels of actuarial risk, relevant and accurate conclusions about the probability of further qualifying offences under the Acts are difficult to reach. The issue is further complicated by evidence that offenders may not be consistent in their choice of victim. Recent research in New Zealand, for example, indicates that a significant portion of offenders who sexually reoffend do so in a way that is not 'true to type', such that 37 per cent of those with a prior offence history that included only adult victims sexually reoffended against a child (Vess and Skelton, in press). The key here is that risk assessment measures should provide reoffence information and demonstrate adequate predictive accuracy relevant to the legal question presented by a statute, such as risk of sexual reoffending against children.

Concerns over the accuracy of applying group data to individual cases are amplified when offenders fall outside the parameters of the actuarial scheme. A clear example of this concern involves risk assessment with female sex offenders. All currently available risk measures have been developed and validated with male offenders. The degree to which the same risk factors apply to female offenders is unknown. The limited recidivism data available for female offenders shows a sexual reoffending rate of approximately 1 per cent (Cortoni and Hanson 2005; Freeman and Sandler 2008). In cases of risk assessment with female sex offenders, the statistically most accurate approach will be to predict the base rate, which indicates that 99 per cent of female sex offenders will not sexually reoffend. Providing an individualised assessment which identifies factors contributing to prior offending, the likelihood of encountering these factors in the post-release environment, and evidence regarding the individual's current capacity to cope effectively with these factors, may provide useful information to judicial decision-makers in the case of a female sex offender, but it must be recognised that we cannot currently provide the empirically validated probability estimates of risk that can now be provided for males.

The role of mental health professionals

Who sets the threshold for risk?

The integrity of the risk assessment process depends on the adequacy of the expertise applied in the assessment of risk in any given case. Although different procedures are used in different jurisdictions, a common procedure is for risk assessments to be conducted by one expert who is an employee of the state agency responsible for the implementation of the law. This is not meant to imply that departmental psychologists do not strive to take an impartial approach to risk assessment based on best practice standards. Rather, the issue here involves the scope of the professional roles assumed by a psychologist employed by the government department that will be seeking a specific judicial decision. Bush, Connell and Denney (2006) presented several relevant distinctions, including the issue of objectivity and whether expert opinion reflects advocacy of a particular belief or consistently favours the retaining party, in this case the department. This distinction becomes particularly important at the point that the department's psychologist becomes an advocate for the legal outcome desired by the department, such as the goal of obtaining an order for extended supervision or civil commitment as an SVP.

A related issue concerns the threshold of risk used to determine when to make an extended supervision order or SVP application. There are different perspectives on how high the risk should be before such sanctions are warranted, but it is the departmental standard that ultimately determines the initiation of this process, and often the only opinion provided to the court is based on this standard. In some jurisdictions there is relatively little independent risk assessment expertise available to offenders (that is, few experienced experts who do not work for the Department of Corrections or other government agency), so that there are limited opportunities to effectively challenge the recommendations of the department on the basis of assessed risk. This raises a concern about adequate checks and balances in the administration of some community protection schemes. There is no clear and immediate solution to this problem. In the meantime, efforts must be taken to ensure that the level of assessed risk is presented in an objective and clearly defined way, including the limitations of current risk assessment methods, so that the court can make informed decisions based on the judge's interpretation and application of the law.

The process of assessing and reporting risk to the court in cases of civil commitment or extended supervision highlights the issue of the various roles that mental health professionals may play, and the potentially problematic boundaries of these roles. One issue in this area is being clear about who the client is. In most cases in these proceedings, the client is the court or other judicial decision-making body. The role of the risk assessor is to provide the most accurate and objective evidence regarding risk relevant to the matters to be decided by the court. This role should be non-partisan, regardless of which side has retained the expertise of the assessor.

Independence of experts and dual roles

Other concerns derive from the perceived or actual independence of the psychologist conducting a risk assessment for the department in extended supervision hearings in jurisdictions where such assessments are routinely conducted by staff of a state agency. One issue here involves the scope of the professional roles assumed by a psychologist employed or retained by the government department that will be seeking a specific judicial decision. The relevant distinctions in this issue are articulated by Bush *et al.* (2006), based on the relationship between the retaining party and the examiner. The dual role of mental health professionals in this legal context is potentially problematic as they may become increasingly viewed as agents of supervision and social control rather than as treating clinicians. In Australia, Sullivan, Mullen and Pathe (2005: 320) contend that the 'roles of health professionals in assessment and treatment under the Victorian Act are contentious and at odds with existing standards of ethical practice'.

There is a related issue when the expert explicitly occupies dual roles and the resulting potential for conflicts of interest. This most directly occurs in instances in which a psychologist is in both a treatment role and a court assessment role, but it also applies when the psychologist engages in advocacy in the role of trial consultant. As a trial consultant the psychologist essentially joins the retaining attorney's team 'to bring psychological expertise to the partisan adversarial process. Impartiality is not required of the trial consultant, but the psychologist trial consultant who holds a place on the "trial team" is cautioned against agreeing to transition into or concurrently participate in the case as an examining or testifying expert' (Bush *et al.* 2006: 40).

The clarity of these role boundaries may be difficult to maintain. As Bush *et al.* go on to say:

> Although there is no clear line distinguishing the appropriate contribution of a testifying expert from that of a nontestifying, consulting expert, practitioners may help clarify the appropriate course of action by examining their motivations. Being motivated to clarify genuine professional disagreement and its genesis, to assist an attorney in making appropriate use of one's opinion, the testifying expert is on solid ground. When the motivation is to contribute as a member of the trial team, sharing its goal to win the case, the psychologist has become an advocate whose opinions should not be offered as objective expertise. (2006: 40)

At the point of the initial risk assessment to determine whether an application for civil commitment or extended supervision should be made, the department's psychologists may be seen as unbiased experts who are seeking an objective determination of risk. After it is decided to seek an application, however, it may be that the department's psychologists are in a more difficult position to maintain a neutral and objective stance in the proceedings. This is particularly pronounced if the psychologist is an active member of the department's legal team who assists them in the goal of prevailing in the court hearing to decide the application.

This concern is amplified when there is a lack of risk assessment expertise available to offenders that is independent of the government department seeking a judicial decision against them. When such expertise is not available it may be difficult for offenders to present a competent challenge to the findings and recommendations of the state. This raises human rights issues related to equal protection under the law, and the underlying principles of freedom and well-being.

Consent

Another concern is raised by those cases in which the offender refuses to participate in the assessment process. The question has been debated as to whether it is ethical to produce an assessment report in the absence of an interview with the individual whose risk is being assessed. Embedded in this situation are two different issues. One is whether a report of sufficient accuracy and relevance can be written without a direct interaction with the offender, and the second is whether one can ethically proceed with such an assessment without the offender's consent. As for the first issue of accuracy, it is well established that actuarial risk assessment measures depend primarily upon static, historical factors that are obtained from the official record, and do not therefore require an interview. As noted, some have argued that purely actuarial assessment findings are superior to those adjusted by assessment of dynamic factors, so that direct assessment by clinical interviewing is not only unnecessary but perhaps undesirable. Furthermore, factors such as psychopathy, an important consideration in formulating risk for reoffending, can reliably be assessed based on a thorough review of adequate file documentation, although the optimal assessment process for the revised Psychopathy Checklist (PCL-R) includes interview data (Hare 2003).

Confidentiality

Underlying all of these concerns is the issue of confidentiality. It has been established that in cases of assessing risk for civil commitment or extended supervision proceedings, the offender cannot maintain confidentiality of information contained in official records associated with his offending. But the parameters of what information may remain confidential is less clear. In New Zealand, for example, the law allows for the protection of information disclosed by the offender in the context of treatment activities. It requires specific consent from the offender in order to access and include this information in any reports, including risk assessment reports to the court. The importance of this protection emphasises a critical aspect of the treatment process: the individual undertaking treatment must be able to disclose information without fear of recrimination and punishment, or the entire therapeutic process is compromised.

This issue of confidentiality also requires special consideration in the risk assessment process. It must be made clear to the offender that the evaluator is acting as an agent of the state, so that information disclosed in the risk assessment process will not be held as confidential, and will be reported to the court as part of the formulation of risk. This sets up a potential conflict that distinguishes forensic assessments in this context from most other clinical activities. On the one hand, the evaluator is encouraging the offender to open up about the factors related to his offending and potential for reoffending, and on the other this information may result in a finding of higher risk that will provide the basis for the court to substantially curtail the offender's liberty.

Confidentiality and trust

This issue therefore goes to the heart of one of the fundamental differences of the role of the forensic risk assessor as compared to other clinical roles. In order to most effectively assess an individual, including a sex offender, a certain amount of rapport is necessary. Rapport involves an element of trust. The clinician is saying, in essence, that it is best if you tell me enough about yourself that we can understand how your offending has happened, and how it might happen again. And yet this 'best' outcome is arguably best only from the state's perspective, and may not be best for the offender's interests. This is especially so in light of the limited accuracy of current risk assessment methods, and the opportunity for the offender to be among the false positives whose freedom will be diminished on the mistaken determination that they will sexually reoffend.

Conclusions and recommendations

Others have noted the fear and revulsion generated among the public by offenders who are perceived as dangerous, and the corresponding loss of offender rights (Nash 2006). In this environment, it can be challenging for those in forensic practice to consistently act in ways that safeguard these rights, especially when these rights are seen as competing with the community's right to safety from potentially dangerous offenders. At a practical level, there may be much greater pressure not to get it wrong by producing a false negative, when an offender you said was low risk goes out to commit another sexual offence. There is often much less potential for negative consequences to one's professional standing, or to one's employer, resulting from a false positive. When an offender is assessed as sufficiently high risk to warrant civil commitment or extended supervision, but would not have gone on to reoffend, often the only source of consternation is from the offender and perhaps his family.

Another argument to contend with is the assertion that because of the limited accuracy of our risk assessment methods and the potential harm to offenders' rights caused by judicial decisions based on our findings, the ethical mental health professional should not participate in such legal proceedings. Yet community protection laws exist, and the decisions will be made, decisions that have long considered expert opinions by mental health professionals. Insofar as the empirical foundations of risk assessment have undergone substantial development over the past twenty years, and have improved the nature of the information that we can provide regarding risk, our continued participation in these proceedings should be guided by ethical considerations that will also continue to evolve.

Sex offenders retain their fundamental human rights, even when the state imposes limitations on the exercising of these rights (Schopp 2003; Ward and Birgden 2007). Risk assessment experts must be properly trained and sufficiently skilled in the use of empirically validated measures and procedures. The role of the expert in such cases must always remain clear; the client is the judicial decision-maker, and the expert's responsibility is to provide the best available risk assessment evidence in a way that is not misleading. This includes risk assessment information that is directly relevant to the legal question, recognising that it is the court that will ultimately decide this legal question in light of all available information and its own interpretation of the applicable legal standards. The more specific the information is (for instance, using actuarial measures that provide reoffending rates specific to certain types of offences covered by the law and empirically validated on relevant offender populations) the more useful it is to the court. Where there are gaps in our current knowledge and error rates in our current procedures, it is an ethical responsibility to make these limitations as clear as possible in our reports.

Other ethical considerations in this area involve the clarity of role boundaries. Although the primary client is seldom the offender, we are inviting an individual to engage in a process of self-revelation that will have a direct effect on decisions made about his or her liberty. There is an inherent ethical tension between the trust and rapport that is essential to an optimal assessment process and the utilisation of information in reports to the courts or other state agencies that have the power to determine the offender's freedom. The role of the assessor and the boundaries involved in the assessment process must be made explicitly clear to the offender, even when this may result in more limited disclosure in the assessment process. It is the offender's right to make an informed decision about what he or she discloses, in full awareness of the likely consequences resulting from the use of this information in a risk assessment report.

A subsequent problem is that mental health experts, once they have completed an objective assessment of risk, may become partisan participants in the adversarial legal process. The guiding principle here is that the role of the expert is to be a source of unbiased clinical and scientific information to the court, rather than as an advisor to legal counsel whose role it is to obtain a ruling favourable to their side in the matter before the court. This may be difficult for experts retained by either the state (the prosecution) or the defence attorney. Even if attorneys accept the need for an objective and unbiased assessment of risk, both sides may expect the active advice and guidance of the expert they are working with to best present their case, attack the evidence of the opposing side, and obtain their desired judicial outcome. The degree to which the assessor engages in this role of advisor or strategist in the hearing process potentially increases the risk of becoming a partisan participant rather than an objective expert.

A broader ethical consideration is the need to provide education to a variety of parties in the nature of sex offender risk assessment and risk management. This includes attorneys, judges, Parole Board members, policy-makers and the general public. There is potentially a great deal of misunderstanding regarding the risk presented by sex offenders, as well as the strengths and weaknesses of our current methods of assessing this risk. Risk assessment experts are in an important position to disseminate information and dispel misconceptions in ways that may minimise the fear and loathing evoked among the public. Such expertise may also help not only to inform judicial decision-making in individual cases, but to set standards through case law by which risk assessments should be conducted and reported. Finally, risk assessment and risk management expertise gained through practical experience and knowledge of research findings should be introduced at every opportunity into the process of policy development. This includes policy in the form of statutory law and at the level of departmental procedures implementing these laws. Risk must be recognised as dynamic and contingent on environmental and personal factors affecting an offender's quality of life. We should move away from a risk prediction model that acts on the basis of an assessment of risk at one point in time, to a risk management model in which risk is assessed on an ongoing basis. Our approach should attempt to motivate individuals to alter their behavior in order to minimize the state's interference with their rights. This motivation may be encouraged more effectively through preserving offenders' rights at each step of the process than by sweeping initiatives that fail to distinguish the relatively few who present a high risk to public safety.

Selected further reading

For a coherent and informative overview of the issues associated with public protection from sex offenders, see LaFond (2005). The focus is largely on legislative initiatives in the US, but the empirical evidence and policy controversies are generally relevant to other jurisdictions. A useful coverage of related issues can also be found in Winick and LaFond (2003). More detailed information about current assessment and treatment procedures, including consideration of specific subgroups among the sex offender population, is provided in Beech, Craig and Browne (2009). A practical framework for risk assessment can be found in Conroy and Murrie (2007).

Notes

1 Portions of this chapter were first published as J. Vess, 'Fear and loathing in public policy: ethical issues in laws for sex offenders', *Aggression and Violent Behavior*, 14: 264–72 (2009). Copyright 2009 by Elsevier. Adapted with permission.

References

American Psychiatric Association (1999). *Dangerous Sex Offenders: A Task Force Report of the American Psychiatric Association*. Washington, DC: American Psychiatric Association.
Beech, A. R., Craig, L. A. and Browne, K. D. (eds) (2009) *Assessment and Treatment of Sex Offenders: A Handbook*. Chichester: Wiley/Blackwell.
Burdon, W. M. and Gallagher, C. A. (2002) 'Coercion and sex offenders: controlling sex-offending behavior through incapacitation and treatment', *Criminal Justice and Behavior*, 29: 87–109.
Bush, S. S., Connell, M. A. and Denney, R. L. (2006) *Ethical Practice in Forensic Psychology: A Systematic Model for Decision Making*. Washington, DC: American Psychological Association.
Campbell, T. W. (2003) 'Sex offenders and actuarial risk assessments: ethical considerations', *Behavioral Sciences and the Law*, 21: 269–79.

Conroy, M. A. and Murrie, D. C. (2007) *Forensic Assessment of Violence Risk: A Guide for Risk Assessment and Risk Management*. Chichester: John Wiley.

Cortoni, F. and Hanson, R. K. (2005) *A Review of the Recidivism Rates of Adult Female Sexual Offenders*. Correctional Service of Canada, Research Report R-169. Online at: www.csc-scc.gc.ca/text/rsrch/reports/r169/r169_e.pdf (accessed 13 July 2009).

David, A., Gelb, K., Moore, V. and Stewart, F. (2007) *High Risk Offenders: Post-sentence Supervision and Detention Final Report*. Sentence Advisory Council, State of Victoria, Australia.

Doren, D. (2002) *Evaluating Sex Offenders: A Manual for Civil Commitments and Beyond*. London: Sage Publications.

Doren, D. (2004) 'Stability of the interpretative risk percentages for the RRASOR and Static-99', *Sexual Abuse: A Journal of Research and Treatment*, 16: 25–36.

Freeden, M. (1991) *Rights*. Minneapolis, MN: University of Minnesota Press.

Freeman, N. J. and Sandler, J. C. (2008) 'Female and male sex offenders: A comparison of recidivism patterns and risk factors', *Journal of Interpersonal Violence*, 23(10): 1394–1413.

Gewirth, A. (1996) *The Community of Rights*. Chicago: University of Chicago Press.

Gookin, K. (2007) *Comparison of State Laws Authorizing Involuntary Commitment of Sexually Violent Predators: 2006 updated, revised*. Washington State Institute for Public Policy, document number 07-08-1101. Online at: www.wsipp.wa.gov (accessed 5 March 2009).

Gottfredson, S. D. and Moriarty, L. J. (2006) 'Statistical risk assessment: old problems and new applications', *Crime and Delinquency*, 52: 178–200.

Hanson, R. K. and Bussière, M. T. (1998) 'Predicting relapse: A meta-analysis of sexual offender recidivism studies', *Journal of Consulting and Clinical Psychology*, 66: 348–62.

Hanson, R. K. and Morton-Bourgon, K. E. (2007) *The Accuracy of Recidivism Risk Assessments for Sexual Offenders: A Meta-analysis*. Public Safety and Emergency Preparedness Canada. Online at: www.ps-sp.gc.ca/res/cor/rep/_fl/crp2007-01-en.pdf (accessed 23 July 2007).

Hanson, R. K. and Thornton, D. (2000) 'Improving risk assessment for sex offenders: a comparison of three actuarial scales', *Law and Human Behaviour*, 24: 119–36.

Hanson, R. K., Harris, A. J. R., Scott, T. L. and Helmus, L. (2007) *Assessing the Risk of Sexual Offenders on Community Supervision: The Dynamic Supervision Project*. Public Safety Canada. Online at: www.publicsafety.gc.ca/res/cor/rep/_fl/crp2007-05-en.pdf (accessed 25 January 2008).

Hare, R. D. (2003) *Hare Psychopathy Checklist – Revised (PCL-R), 2nd Edition*. Toronto: Multi-Health Systems, Inc.

Harris, G. (2003) 'Men in his category have a 50% likelihood, but which half is he in? Comments on Berlin, Galbreath, Geary, and McGlone', *Sexual Abuse: Journal of Research and Treatment*, 15: 389–92.

Harris, A. J. R. and Hanson, R. K. (2004) *Sex Offender Recidivism: A Simple Question*. Public Safety and Emergency Preparedness Canada. Online at: www.psepcsppcc.gc.ca/publications/corrections/200403-2_e.asp (accessed 23 August 2005).

Harris, G. T. and Rice, M. E. (2003) 'Actuarial assessment of risk among sex offenders', *Annuls of the New York Academy of Science*, 989: 198–210.

Janus, E. S. (2000) 'Sexual predator commitment laws: lessons for law and the behavioral sciences', *Behavioral Sciences and the Law*, 18: 5–21.

Janus, E. S. and Prentky, R. A. (2003) 'Forensic use actuarial risk assessment with sex offenders: Accuracy, admissibility and accountability', *American Criminal Law Review*, 40. Online at: www.forensicexaminers.com/whatsnew.html (accessed 25 April 2007).

LaFond, J. Q. (2000) 'The future of involuntary civil commitment in the U.S.A. after *Kansas v. Hendricks*', *Behavioral Sciences and the Law*, 18: 153–67.

LaFond, J.Q. (2005) *Preventing Sexual Violence: How Society Should Cope with Sex Offenders*. Washington, DC: American Psychological Association.

Levenson, J. S. (2004) 'Sexual predator civil commitment: a comparison of selected and released offenders', *International Journal of Offender Therapy and Comparative Criminology*, 48: 638–48.

Levesque, R. J. L. (2000) 'Sentencing sex crimes against children: an empirical and policy analysis', *Behavioral Sciences and the Law*, 18: 331–41.

Monahan, J. and Steadman, H. J. (1996) 'Violent storms and violent people: how meteorology can inform risk communication in mental health law', *American Psychologist*, 51: 931–38.

Mossman, D. (2006) 'Another look at interpreting risk categories', *Sexual Abuse: A Journal of Research and Treatment*, 18, 41–-63.

Nash, M. (2006) *Public Protection and the Criminal Justice Process*. New York: Oxford University Press.

Orend, B. (2002) *Human Rights: Concept and Context*. Ontario: Broadview Press.

Quinsey, V. L., Harris, G. T., Rice, M. E. and Cormier, C. A. (2006) *Violent Offenders: Appraising and Managing Risk*. Washington, DC: American Psychological Association.

Schopp, R. F. (2003) '"Even a dog ...": culpability, condemnation, and respect for persons', in B. J. Winick and J. Q. LaFond (eds) *Protecting Society From Sexually Dangerous Offenders: Law, Justice and Therapy*. Washington, DC: American Psychological Association (pp. 183–96).

Sjostedt, G. and Langstrom, N. (2001) 'Actuarial assessment of sex offender recidivism risk: a cross-validation of the RRASOR and the Static-99 in Sweden', *Law and Human Behavior*, 25: 629–45.

Sullivan, D. H., Mullen, P. E. and Pathe, M. T. (2005) 'Legislation in Victoria on sexual offenders: issues for health professionals', *Medical Journal of Australia*, 183: 318–20.

Vess, J. (2008) 'Sex offender risk assessment: consideration of human rights in community protection legislation', *Legal and Criminological Psychology*, 13: 245–56.

Vess, J. and Skelton, A. (in press) 'Sexual and violent recidivism by offender type and actuarial risk: reoffending rates for rapists, child molesters and non-contact offenders', *Psychology, Crime and Law*.

Ward, T. and Birgden, A. (2007) 'Human rights and correctional clinical practice', *Aggression and Violent Behavior*, 12: 628–43.

Ward, T., Gannon, T. A. and Birgden, A. (2007) 'Human rights and the treatment of sex offenders', *Sexual Abuse: A Journal of Research and Treatment*, 19, 195–216.

Ward, T., Gannon, T. and Vess, J. (2009) 'Human rights, ethical principles and standards in forensic psychology', *International Journal of Offender Therapy and Comparative Criminology*, 53: 126–44.

Winick, B. J. (2003) 'A therapeutic jurisprudence analysis of sex offender registration and community notification laws', in B. J. Winick and J. Q. LaFond (eds) *Protecting Society From Sexually Dangerous Offenders: Law, Justice and Therapy*. Washington, DC: American Psychological Association (pp. 213–29).

Winick, B. J. and LaFond, J. Q. (eds) (2003) *Protecting Society From Sexually Dangerous Offenders*. Washington, DC: American Psychological Association.

Wood, M. and Ogloff, J. R. P. (2006) 'Victoria's Serious Sex Offenders Monitoring Act 2005: implications for the accuracy of sex offender risk assessment', *Psychiatry, Psychology and Law*, 13: 182–98.

Chapter 5

Discretion and decision-making in public protection

Nicola Padfield

Introduction

In this chapter, I seek to place the law on public protection in the context of the reality of the implementation of that law. Law in practice is, of course, not always as it appears on the statute book or in the case law. Even where the law appears clear, it often gives wide discretionary powers to those whose duty it is to apply it. Thus, laws exist that allow both prisons and psychiatric hospitals to be used lawfully to protect the public from 'dangerous' people. The rights and freedoms of the 'dangerous' are also curtailed in numerous ways within the community. The law is used to construct complex rules that both allow huge restrictions on liberty and also create complex frameworks (safety nets) to protect the individual from the abuse of power. This chapter focuses on how these laws leave broad discretionary powers with key decision-makers, and emphasises that the key decision-makers are not always the most obvious players. There are serious holes in the 'safety nets' provided by the law. In particular, while the courts may offer a due process safety net in relation to many decisions, other equally crucial decisions may remain relatively invisible. The chapter concludes that the protection of the individual must be taken as seriously as the protection of the public: more open and accountable decision-making is essential.

The focus of this book is on public protection from 'dangerous' people. Let me start by identifying two important subjects that are not reviewed in detail in this chapter. The first is the definition of who is dangerous. Have we got satisfactory definitions? Dangerous people may or may not do dangerous things. People who do dangerous things are not always dangerous. An example: those who drive dangerously are clearly acting dangerously, but are they dangerous? And what constitutes dangerous driving? This example is provoked by consideration of recent changes to the punishment of those who operate commercial vehicles, particularly in relation to the breaches of drivers' hours rules and overloading of vehicles. It is no longer simply the police who issue fixed penalty notices, but also the Vehicle and Operator Services

Agency. Between 28 May and 7 September 2009, VOSA issued an astonishing 11,000 fixed penalty notices, with over 800 vehicles being immobilised.[1] More than half a million pounds was collected in deposit payments in the first three months of the new scheme, with over 60 per cent of penalty notices being issued to the drivers of non-UK vehicles. As far as I can see there has been no published research in this area. The public are supposedly being protected from 'dangerous' drivers by what might appear to be draconian and largely invisible decisions. This is merely an illustration of the potential breadth of a review of the laws relating to public protection. This chapter adopts a narrower focus.

The second important subject that is not developed in this chapter is a detailed theory of decision-making. Those who seek a more theoretical approach are referred elsewhere.[2] This is a chapter written by an academic lawyer, using recent case law to illustrate concerns about decision-making processes. Whereas lawyers usually focus on legal decisions, both outcome (substantive) and process (procedural) decisions, this chapter seeks to focus attention on the decision-makers rather than the decisions. In particular, we must recognise the role of the wide variety of decision-makers who stand behind, or earlier in the process than, those entrusted with a formal or legal decision. As Hawkins (2002) points out, legal rules and bureaucratic policy are merely among many 'forces' that shape outcomes. The wider forces and constraints are too easily ignored: resource constraints and interpersonal relationships being obvious examples, which are raised in this chapter.

Dangerous people who commit serious criminal offences are likely to find themselves in prison (or hospital). But some 'dangerous' people will be diverted away from the criminal justice process, and many of those who are labelled 'dangerous' may, of course, not offend or reoffend. We have to start by acknowledging that: (1) predicting who is and who is not dangerous is an unreliable business; and (2) even if predictions were reliable, they would inevitably change over time: reassessments are essential. These basic facts are explored elsewhere in this book (see the chapters by Williams, and Carson and Carson), but must be kept in mind throughout the discussion of this chapter. Another basic fact that bears repetition is that 'gate-keepers' (whether to the criminal justice system or civil detention) are there not only to protect the public but to be vigilant in ensuring that those who should not face detention, or the harsh glare of the criminal justice process, are diverted away from it.

Public protection: the use of the criminal law

Gate-keeping decisions

There is a large literature on the use and abuse of discretionary powers within the criminal justice system.[3] Traditionally the police have been seen as the gate-keepers: they have the power/duty to identify possible crimes and to investigate them. But the real gate-keepers are the public, who are responsible for the identification of most 'dangerous' people to the police. We know little about the decisions of families and friends who decide to (or not to) refer their friends or relations to the police. Victims of crime interviewed for the British Crime Survey (BCS) are asked why they did not report incidents to the police. As in previous years, in 2008–9 the most frequently mentioned reason for not reporting incidents was that victims perceived them to be too trivial, there was no loss, or they believed that the police would or could not do much about them. But these generalisations are of little use when it comes to victims of serious sexual or violent offending. The 2008/09 BCS self-completion module on intimate (domestic or sexual) violence shows that 6 per cent of women were victims of domestic abuse in the past year compared with 4 per cent of men.[4] The vast majority of these crimes are not reported to the police.

Once the police are aware of a suspect, or a suspected crime, they have broad powers to decide whether to proceed along a criminal investigation or whether to 'divert' an offender towards civil measures: see below. They may simply caution someone, formally or informally. The formal cautioning rate remains astonishingly high: in 2007 the cautioning rate for indictable offences (the number of offenders cautioned as a percentage of those found guilty or cautioned) remained the same as in 2006, at 40 per cent.[5] This is surely a remarkable figure: 40 per cent of the most serious detected crimes never reach court. As well as cautioning offenders, the police also issued 207,500 penalty notices for disorder (PNDs) and 102,500 warnings for cannabis possession in 2007.

Growing concern about inconsistent police decision-making was one of the main factors that led to the creation of the Crown Prosecution Service (CPS) in 1986.[6] In their decision whether or not to charge, how much emphasis does the CPS give to questions of public protection? Section 10 of the Prosecution of Offenders Act 1985 requires the Director of Public Prosecution to publish a Code giving guidance on general principles to be applied by prosecutors in determining whether proceedings should be instituted. The latest version of the Code for Crown Prosecutors[7] states:

> The decision to prosecute or to offer an individual an out-of-court disposal is a serious step. Fair and effective prosecution is essential to the maintenance of law and order ... It is the duty of prosecutors to make sure that the right person is prosecuted for the right offence and to bring offenders to justice wherever possible. Casework decisions taken fairly, impartially and with integrity help to deliver justice for victims, witnesses, defendants and the public (para 2.1).

The CPS must be satisfied of a 'realistic prospect of conviction' (the evidential criteria), but must also consider the 'public interest' criteria. The Code states that the more serious the offence, the more likely it is that a prosecution will be needed in the public interest. But the public interest may not require a prosecution where 'the defendant is elderly or is, or was at the time of the offence, suffering from significant mental or physical ill health, unless the offence is serious or there is real possibility that it may be repeated'. Thus

Crown Prosecutors must balance the desirability of diverting a defendant who is suffering from significant mental or physical ill health with the need to safeguard the general public. These decisions of the Crown Prosecution Service are not always transparent. A look at the case law quickly reveals interesting decisions.

Why and when is the criminal justice system chosen? For example, it would be interesting to know much more about the reality of decision-making involving mentally ill offenders and psychiatric evidence. The law on those who are 'unfit to plead' provides some graphic examples.[8] One would have thought that those who are too unfit mentally to stand trial should escape the criminal justice process entirely. Far from it: they are likely to face two juries, not just the usual one. Take, for example, the leading House of Lords' authority of *H* [2003] UKHL 1. This defendant, aged thirteen, was charged with two offences of indecent assault on a girl aged fourteen. Before his trial in the Crown Court (at Bradford) he was examined by psychiatrists instructed on his behalf and on behalf of the Crown, all of whom agreed that he was unfit to stand trial. Yet rather than simply dealing with his case through mental health services, he had to survive two jury trials (and indeed an appeal to the House of Lords). First, a jury was empanelled to decide the question whether he was fit to stand trial, and unsurprisingly, given the psychiatric evidence, they found that he was indeed under a disability and so unfit. Then at a separate hearing a different jury found that he had indeed done the acts alleged against him in the indictment. He was then absolutely discharged on both counts and his father was directed to cause him to be registered as a sex offender. We return later to the consequences of being on the sex offender register. Here I ask simply whether these proceedings really were necessary in the interest of public protection. More importantly, perhaps, were they in the interest of welfare of this thirteen-year-old defendant?[9] This is not the place to discuss in detail the law on unfitness to plead,[10] which is both difficult and artificial. The current test for determining fitness to plead dates from 1836[11] and many have argued that the test is too restrictive.[12] Here I raise the question of the choice of proceedings and the relative role of social workers, psychiatrists, police and CPS. It is somewhat chilling to read the judgment of the House of Lords, in the appeal against the second jury's verdict, which focuses (perhaps properly, but nonetheless chillingly) on the narrow question under appeal: the applicability or otherwise of Article 6 of the European Convention on Human Rights (the right to a fair trial). There is no discussion of the welfare of the child, and no questioning of why this child was subjected to this heavy-handed criminal justice process.

Let us look at another recent example: someone who all those professionally involved with had readily accepted would never be fit to stand trial (*Norman* [2009] 1 Cr App R 13). Norman was arrested and charged with child abduction on the same day as his alleged offence, in May 2006. He was clearly seen as a risk to children, but it was also well known that he suffered from Huntington's disease (diagnosed in 2003) and despite the fact that all agreed that he was not fit to be tried, he was held in Lewes Prison, where he was subject to 'unpleasant treatment' from his fellow prisoners, for just over a year.[13] As the Court of Appeal commented:

no satisfactory explanation was given to us in response to enquiries we directed be made as to why his detention for this long period of time had been in a prison. It appears that attempts were made soon after his arrest by solicitors acting for the appellant to transfer him on stringent bail conditions to a specialist home, but this failed as funds were not available from the local authority; we understand that the defence thereafter continued to press for his condition to be properly addressed. We were also told by the CPS that custody time limits were extended on several occasions because of delays in obtaining defence psychiatric reports ... what happened to this appellant is no credit to the criminal justice system. Indeed, save where the judge expedited the hearings, there is a risk of the perception that it displays certain indicia of a lack of concern for a man suffering from a devastating hereditary illness developed late in life. We hope that lessons will be learnt from what has happened in this case. (Thomas LJ, para. 8)

It is surely important to question why young H and Mr Norman were treated in the ways they were. Who made the decisions to initiate, let alone to continue with, criminal prosecutions? Have the police, CPS and psychiatrists' decisions in these cases been adequately scrutinised? The courts clearly provide an inadequate means of review, if one wants to consider the overall wisdom of the decisions taken. And, of course, the cases that reach the higher courts, and are therefore reported, will in any case be only a small sub-sample of cases.

What charge?

Once the police and CPS have taken the decision to charge, there is the question of what the charge is. This is deeply confusing for the outsider to understand. The Code for Crown Prosecutors says, at para. 6.1:

Prosecutors should select charges which:
a reflect the seriousness and extent of the offending supported by the evidence;
b give the court adequate powers to sentence and impose appropriate post-conviction orders; and
c enable the case to be presented in a clear and simple way.

This means that Crown Prosecutors may not always choose or continue with the most serious charge, where there is a choice.

One of the more difficult decisions must be deciding whether a charge is murder or manslaughter. The sentencing options, while symbolically different, are in practice very similar, and indeed it is well known that those convicted of manslaughter may serve longer in prison than those convicted of murder: rightly, perhaps, one might add, since the likelihood of reconviction is often higher. The law on diminished responsibility as a partial defence to murder has evolved because defendants in many (often high profile) murder cases have clearly been severely mentally ill. Why do so many mentally ill offenders have to endure a prosecution for murder? How and why does the CPS decide that they should stand trial? The case of *Dass* [2009] EWCA Crim 1208 concerned a man who was convicted of the murder of his grandparents and uncle in 1998.[14] He was transferred five months later to Ashworth Hospital, and in 2004 to a low level secure unit in a general hospital, where, the Court of Appeal reports, he continued to suffer from chronic paranoid schizophrenia. We will examine in due course the decision of the Court of Appeal, which rejected the argument that a hospital order should be substituted for a sentence of life imprisonment. The case turns on a sentencing issue, and the court was clearly influenced by the complexities involved in assessing the risk that the appellant might pose in the future. Was this the thinking that made the CPS decide to pursue a murder trial in the first place, when the appellant would presumably have pleaded guilty to manslaughter at the first opportunity? Where lies the public interest in prosecuting murder in this case?

Decision-making in such cases can take a long time, and this delay sometimes seems inhumane. In *Staines* [2006] 2 Cr App R (S) 61, the defendant was charged with murder. The story of her life, in the words of the Court of Appeal, was 'one of unmitigated and profound tragedy'. When she was arraigned in the Crown Court some six months later (September 2000), she pleaded guilty to manslaughter by reason of diminished responsibility. The matter was then put over for reports without the Crown indicating whether or not the plea was acceptable, and the defendant remained in custody (in Broadmoor, having been transferred from Holloway). It was only in December 2000 that the Crown indicated that the plea to manslaughter was acceptable: and then they were still relying in large measure on reports that had been written some nine months earlier. Here the delay may have been due to the lawyers. At other times it seems to be due to the psychiatrists (and perhaps unseen interpersonal rivalries?). In *House* [2007] EWCA Crim 2559 there was what the Court of Appeal calls 'a highly regrettable delay' between the time when the offender, who suffered from paranoid schizophrenia and from an anti-social personality disorder, pleaded guilty to attempted murder and attempted rape: there were ten months between plea and sentence (making a total of one year, five months and ten days served on remand: for a young man who had telephoned the emergency services himself immediately after committing his offences, giving them his correct name and address, and admitting that he had raped and stabbed a woman). In what sense are the people who make these decisions 'accountable'?

Caution or prosecution?

Much publicity has been given recently to the huge growth, noted above, in the use of cautions as alternatives to prosecutions. These may be formal or informal police cautions, or the more controversial conditional cautions, introduced in the Criminal Justice Act 2003 (and developed further in the Police and Justice Act 2006). Interestingly, the current guidance on the Crown Prosecution Service's website[15] on cautioning relies on a case from 1998:

> A caution or conditional caution will not be appropriate if there is any doubt about the reliability of any admissions made or if the defendant's level of understanding prevents him or her from understanding the

significance of the caution or conditional caution and giving informed consent. It should not be assumed that all mentally disordered offenders are ineligible for cautioning or conditional cautioning, but there is no definition of or restriction on the particular form of mental or psychological condition or disorder that may make an admission unreliable. (*R v Walker* [1998] Crim L.R. 211)

Walker was a drug addict prostitute charged with, and convicted of, robbery. She, with a man, had taken the car keys of a man in a red light district and demanded money for their return. The case turned on whether or not she had smoked crack cocaine at the police station and whether her admissions in interview were admissible. Her appeal, on the interpretation of the law on confessions to be found in s.76(2)(b) of the Police and Criminal Evidence Act 1984, was allowed. But the case gives little guidance on the question of whether or not to caution. It raises interesting questions about the sequence of decisions that were taken. If the CPS decides that a caution or conditional caution is inappropriate, the only alternative to prosecution is to take no further action. The guidance specifies that:

In considering whether the public interest requires a prosecution, prosecutors should enquire whether:
- the police or Social Services have used their powers under sections 135 or 136 Mental Health Act 1983;
- the defendant has been admitted to hospital for assessment or treatment under sections 2 or 3 Mental Health Act 1983;
- the defendant is receiving supervised community treatment under a Community Treatment Order made under section 17A Mental Health Act 1983;
- the offender has been admitted to hospital as an informal patient under section 131 Mental Health Act 1983; or
- an order for guardianship under section 7 Mental Health Act 1983 has been made.

This suggests a complex review of earlier decision-making. The existence of a mental disorder is only one of the factors to be taken into account when deciding whether the public interest requires a prosecution. The seriousness or the persistence of the offending behaviour should be considered, as should the views of the victim and 'any responsible clinician'. The fact that a person is receiving compulsory treatment under the Mental Health Act 1983, or as an informal patient under s.131 of the Mental Health Act 1983, does not prevent a prosecution. However, a prosecution must not be pursued solely to treat and manage a mental disorder. But the decision to prosecute or divert a patient receiving treatment under the Mental Health Act 1983 should be informed by:

Medical reports from the responsible clinician to explain the nature and degree of the disorder or disability, and any relationship between the disorder and the treatment and behaviour of the offender; and any other relevant information from hospital staff about the treatment and behaviour of the patient, including the treatment regime and any history of similar and recent behaviour.

Disappointingly, little independent academic research has been carried out in recent years into decision-making at police stations. The importance of gathering empirical evidence is self-evident.

Bail and extradition hurdles

We could focus on many other pre-trial decisions which concern public protection. The decision to remand someone in custody is obvious. It is much more difficult to prepare one's case for court from inside a prison or hospital. But nowadays it is not only the decision to grant bail that should be examined, but also the decision to impose bail conditions. This may be particularly important as the law gets ever more complex: the police as well as the courts are empowered to impose conditions that are necessary to make sure that defendants attend court and do not commit offences or interfere with witnesses while on bail.[16] Curfew conditions are common, with or without electronic monitoring. Sentencing judges now specify when sentencing what credit should be given for time served on remand or even, curiously, on electronic curfew, but no credit is given for time on curfews that are not electronically monitored! The increased use of bail conditions merits much more research. Are conditions being imposed where they are not necessary? And exactly what conditions are being imposed? They may include wide geographic exclusion zones (*R (Thomas) v Greenwich Magistrates' Court* [2009] EWHC 1180 (Admin) and/or the removal of passports (even on the basis of secret information: *R (Ajaib) v Birmingham Magistrates' Court* [2009] EWHC 2127 (Admin)).

Another swathe of decision-making surrounds the extradition of suspects to stand trial abroad. These decisions to extradite, too, are worthy of further exploration: do they protect the rights of those from whom the public may or may not require protection? The Extradition Act 2003 has made extradition much easier. The focus of the law and of the courts is perhaps inevitably on the role of the judge. Thus, s.91 of the Extradition Act 2003 provides that if at any time in the extradition hearing it appears to the judge that the physical or mental condition of the suspect is such that it would be unjust or oppressive to extradite him, the judge must either order the person's discharge or adjourn the hearing. There are a significant number of cases that have had to interpret this section. Gary McKinnon's case has had public attention: see *McKinnon v United States* [2008] UKHL 59; and now *R (McKinnon) v Secretary of State for Home Affairs, R (McKinnon) v DPP* [2009] EWHC 2021 (Admin). This case decided that McKinnon's extradition to the US would not infringe his rights under the European Convention on Human Rights.[17]

There are many other interesting cases. Two recent examples: *Spanovic v Croatia* [2009] EWHC 723 (Admin) concerned a Serbian who is accused of war crimes against Croatians, and is suffering from paranoid psychosis. The Court concluded that he should be extradited. In considering s.91, they said that 'It is plain to us, that the bar is set very high, and the graver the charge, the higher the bar, in that there is a heightened public interest in the alleged offender being tried: provided, of course, that the trial and the conditions in which he will be held will be fair' (para. 39). *Hewitt v Spain* [2009] EWHC 2158 (Admin) involved the extradition to Spain of a man with a mild to moderate learning disorder and significant cognitive impairment to stand trial for sexual assault. Again, in rejecting the argument that it would be unjust and oppressive to extradite him, the court held that it was appropriate that the issue of his fitness to stand trial be determined in Spain.

Those court decisions are easy to criticise. Putting faith in other legal systems may or may not be appropriate; proceedings may be unnecessarily drawn out if fundamental issues are not considered at an early stage. In particular, the argument in *Spanovic* that the graver the charge, the greater the public interest in prosecution, is curious. It is as logical to argue that the more serious the offence alleged, the more important it is to protect the mentally ill or disordered, and to review the case at an early stage. Clearly a court is required to make a decision based on the facts of the individual case. The focus here may be on the judicial decision, but behind the court is the decision of the Crown Prosecution Service, the decision of the psychiatrists and psychologists, the legal advisors and indeed the legal aid authorities who fund the defence. All these decisions merit examination.

Sentencing and public protection

Once the decision to charge is made, key decisions will be taken by magistrates, juries and judges. Little is known about the reality of their decision-making: the jury is shrouded in secrecy and is not required to give reasons for its decisions. They may acquit those for whom they have some sympathy. On the other hand, there are plenty of examples of juries' decisions to convict that turn out, perhaps many years later, to have been mistaken. For example, Sean Hodgson was convicted in 1982 of murder, and it was not until March 2009 that his conviction was quashed (see [2009] EWCA Crim 490). The complex role of psychiatric evidence on jury and judicial decision-making is well documented in the literature.[18] A recent case law example is *TS* [2008] EWCA Crim 6 where the Court of Appeal quashed the appellant's conviction for raping his ex-wife and ordered a retrial on the basis of complex and somewhat contradictory medical advice on the appellant's psychiatric diagnosis.

Here we need to explore again the relationship between judicial and jury decision-making, and the key decisions taken earlier by other bodies. We have already seen that the police and CPS decisions are crucial in decisions to prosecute. The growing use of plea bargains in this country must not be ignored. It has been commonplace for many years for an informal plea bargain to take place between prosecutors and defence lawyers: 'If you drop the charge of X against my client, he will plead guilty to Y.' With increasing pressures on legal aid budgets, it must be a concern whether defence lawyers are adequately funded to fulfil the vital function of protecting their clients' interests.

Sentencing practice remains remarkably under-researched in this country. There have been attempts to encourage greater consistency in practice: both by governments, in endless, lengthy Acts of Parliament, and the appellate courts, most obviously in guideline judgments from the Court of Appeal. The Sentencing Guidelines Council (SGC) was created in 2003 in large measure to create greater consistency in sentencing decisions, and to help structure decision-making, which it does largely by publishing guidelines to which a sentencing court must 'have regard' (s.172, CJA 2003). It also publishes a newsletter that provides information about sentencing trends as part of the Council's aim to provide reliable information in an accessible form.[19] This includes information about the sentencing of young people as well as adults, and information on local, regional and national sentencing trends in general and by specific offence. But these statistical trends give no explanation of the facts of individual cases, or the factors that will have influenced the judges or magistrates in individual cases. Nor is it obvious who studies this information: are sentencers meant to do so, and if they do, what are they meant to make of it? An ambitious academic project that sought to explore the reality of sentencing decision-making recently ended before it had really taken off. In February 2009 the SGC and the Ministry of Justice published Dhami and Souza's *Study of Sentencing and its Outcomes: A Pilot Report* (MoJ Research Series 2/09). This pilot assessed the feasibility of what would have been a much bigger sentencing study: collecting data from court records in order to help understand the reasons behind individual sentence decisions. The pilot realistically but very disappointingly revealed that much crucial information was not obtainable, making it difficult to achieve the study's objectives and so the SGC[20] and Ministry of Justice decided not to continue funding it.

So how does a judge or magistrate sentence in practice? The statutory purposes of sentencing adult offenders are found in section 142 of the Criminal Justice Act 2003, which prescribes that:

> Any court dealing with an offender in respect of his offence must have regard to the following purposes of sentencing –
> (a) the punishment of offenders,
> (b) the reduction of crime (including its reduction by deterrence),
> (c) the reform and rehabilitation of offenders,
> (d) the protection of the public, and
> (e) the making of reparation by offenders to persons affected by their offences.

The SGC's guideline, *Overarching Principles: Seriousness* (issued in December 2004) comments that 'the Act does not indicate that any one purpose should be more important than any other and in practice they may all be relevant to a greater or lesser degree in any individual case – the sentencer has the task of determining the manner in which they apply'. So not much constraint is offered by this. The Council has now provided guidelines for the most common offences: providing starting points for offences of different seriousness, and broad sentencing ranges. But decisions of the Court of Appeal still reveal some surprising sentences, which the Court of Appeal changes only where they were wrong in principle or manifestly excessive.[21] In addition, there are prosecution appeals against sentences, where the Attorney General refers what the prosecution perceive to be 'unduly lenient' sentences for the opinion of the Court of Appeal. It is not easy to know the 'right' answer in any individual case. For example, L was a drunk young man with no previous convictions who pleaded guilty to having an offensive weapon, a pen knife, at a party to which he was not invited and to waving it around causing fear to guests: is the 'right' sentence twelve months in a young offender institution? ([2009] EWCA Crim 1818) A woman of exemplary good character is arrested for dangerous driving (see *Myers* [2009] EWCA Crim 1395). She had suffered from two substantial episodes of bipolar affective disorder of the manic type. In dismissing her appeal against a suspended sentence with requirements of supervision and mental health treatment, Mr Justice Blair said, 'We would accept the submission that has been made to us that in the circumstances the appellant's culpability is greatly reduced. We cannot, however, accept that it is totally reduced. That would be in our view to have regard simply to the offender and not also to the offence' (at para. 13). Where exactly is the line to be drawn between reduced culpability and no culpability in a case like this?

The reality is that sentencers still have wide discretionary powers, and that counsel,[22] probation officers and psychiatrists have the power to influence these decisions. Let us return to *Staines* [2006] 2 Cr App R (S) 61. We have already noted that her plea to manslaughter was eventually accepted. She was sentenced to a discretionary life sentence with a minimum term of four years and hospital and limitation direction under the Mental Health Act 1983, s.45A. She sought on appeal to substitute for the life sentence a hospital order under sections 37 and 41 of the Act. The Court of Appeal upheld the life sentence. How does a judge choose between a life sentence and a hospital order? Ms Staines' lawyers argued that the life sentence should be reserved for those who may be incapable of responding to treatment: because, as it stood, the sentence meant that she would remain in hospital until she was successfully treated, when she would have to be returned to prison. The Court accepted that defendants made subject to hospital orders, whether restricted or not, are entitled to release when the medical conditions justifying their original admission cease to be met and are liable to recall only on medical grounds. On the other hand, a defendant sentenced to life imprisonment is eligible for release on the expiry of the minimum term and is entitled to be released only if he is no longer a source of danger to the public.

> But the decision whether it is safe to release him will be taken by the Parole Board, as an independent body acting judicially, which will not be confined to the medical considerations of which, alone, a Mental Health Review Tribunal may take account, and he is liable to recall indefinitely if he appears to present a danger to the public, the grounds of recall, again, being broader than in the case of a restricted patient. (para. 28, citing Lord Bingham in *Drew* [2003] UKHL 25)

In short, the court was satisfied that a life sentence affords a measure of control not available under the other available orders, and that with an order under s.45A, 'the regime to which the appellant is currently subject affords to the public a significantly enhanced and desirable degree of protection from the risk of danger from the appellant' (at para. 30). We will return to the case once more when considering release decisions, but it is important to stress here that the main consideration for sentencers sometimes appears to be the relevant release procedures. As D. A. Thomas put it in his commentary on *A* [2005] EWCA Crim 2077 at [2005] Crim LR 82:

> A sentence of life imprisonment may maximise the protection of the public, by restricting the grounds on which the offender can claim to be released and widening the grounds on which he can be recalled, but at the expense of the possibility that he may not be transferred to hospital and therefore be denied the appropriate treatment. A hospital order will guarantee the offender's admission to the specified hospital, but at the cost of some slight diminution of the protection of the public.

These medical/legal decisions involve a complex interweaving of decisions. In *Dass*, also discussed above, the appellant had argued that where there is evidence of a causal link between an offence and an offender's mental illness and the illness is of a nature or degree that makes it appropriate for him to be detained in hospital for treatment, there is a 'general rule' that a hospital order should be imposed, arguing that it is wrong in principle for the sentencer to leave it to the Executive to 'correct the injustice of committing a mentally ill person in need of treatment to prison by means of an administrative transfer'. The court disagreed: and were clearly influenced by the complexities involved in assessing the risk that the appellant might pose in the future. If he were under a hospital order, the emphasis would be on the risk of recurrence of mental illness, but under the prison regime on the risk of reoffending.

We return to the question of release below: for present purposes, the point is simply to emphasise the complex relationship between psychiatric reports, pre-sentence reports and sentencing decisions.

Since the Criminal Justice Act (CJA) 2003, another indeterminate sentence has been added to the sentencers' armoury. As well as the life sentence, 'imprisonment for public protection' (IPP) is available for a long list of violent or sexual offences. The rules for the imposition of IPP were much amended by the Criminal Justice and Immigration Act 2008 in an attempt to limit the huge increase in indeterminate sentences. The number of prisoners serving indeterminate sentences has risen in only five years from fewer than 6,000 to 11,781 (June 2009 figures, published July 2009). When considering whether he or she should impose a sentence under the dangerous offender provisions, the sentencer must first decide whether there is 'a significant risk to members of the public of serious harm caused by the offender committing further specified offences' (s.229(1)(b) of the CJA 2003). The court must obtain a pre-sentence report before deciding that the offender is a dangerous offender unless, in the circumstances of the case, the court considers that such a report is unnecessary (s.156(3) and (4)). Where the offender is aged under eighteen, the court cannot conclude that a pre-sentence report is unnecessary unless there are one or more previous pre-sentence reports, the most recent of which is in writing and is before the court (s.156(5)). As the Sentencing Guidelines Council puts it, 'the court is guided, but not bound, by the assessment of dangerousness in a pre-sentence report. Both counsel should be given the opportunity of addressing the court on the issue of dangerousness, especially if it contemplates differing from the conclusion in such a report' (SGC, *Dangerous Offenders: Guide for Sentencers and Practitioners* (2008 version) at para 6.1.4).

It is not, of course, only in the case of potentially 'dangerous' offenders that the hearing of a case listed for sentencing is adjourned for a pre-sentence report. There was a time in the 1990s when it was a probation service 'key performance indicator' whether or not the judge accepted the recommendation of the probation officer. Obviously this had the potential to skew the recommendation: if the probation officer will be rewarded for recommending what the judge accepts, there is an element of circularity. Tata *et al.* (2008) explore how and why 'judge satisfaction' must not be taken as the measure of 'quality' in pre-sentence reports. Halliday *et al.* (2009) explore the extent to which social workers in Scotland may be unduly influenced by their professional anxiety to maintain their status and gain esteem in the eyes of the sentencing judge.[23]

Another major area of discretion that merits much further analysis is the enforcement of community sentences. During the 1990s there was much effort made to encourage probation officers to initiate breach proceedings against offenders who failed to comply with the terms of their court order, in large measure in order to give community penalties greater credibility both with sentencers and with the public. The number of people jailed for breach of community orders reflects the more hidden decisions of their supervisors. Enforcement is not necessarily 'effective' (as ever, depending on what it is that is sought to be effected!). There is not nearly enough evidence. The National Audit Office, in a report entitled *The National Probation Service: The Supervision of Community Orders in England and Wales* (2008), called for much more rigorous research into the impact of community sentences,[24] and their use in relation to mentally ill offenders is particularly important. Lord Bradley's *Review of People with Mental Health Problems or Learning Disabilities in the Criminal Justice System* (2009) commissioned a cost/benefit analysis of the impact on prison places if there were to be an increase in the use of community orders for people with mental health problems and learning disabilities. Unsurprisingly, 'early indications suggest that there are significant cost savings to be made for the criminal justice system by increasing the use of community sentence alternatives for individuals with mental health problems or learning disabilities' (Bradley 2009: 95). It might well be that research would show that community sentences are as 'effective' and as economic as custodial alternatives. Yet again, we need more evidence on how community penalties are used as measures of public protection. In the next section we look briefly at decision-making in the context of MAPPA.

Getting out of prison (or hospital)

The complexity of the rules on getting out of prison are well known. Clearly, once someone is in prison, the prison authorities have enormous power in relation to how the prisoner progresses through the prison system. The key body for our purposes may be the Public Protection Casework Section (PPCS) of the National Offender Management Service (NOMS). But it is important to keep in mind the 'automatic' release of offenders at the halfway point in determinate sentences. In the last section, the question was asked whether a sentence of twelve months in a young offender institution was the 'right' sentence for a knife-brandishing first-time offender. Under current rules, the offender would serve at most only half this time in custody. A prisoner undertakes a complex journey negotiating his way towards release. Many decisions in prison clearly affect later decisions: for example, the prisoner's security categorisation[25] and allocation to a particular prison is fundamental. The complex route that a prisoner (and particular a lifer and other 'dangerous' prisoners) must tread along the snakes and ladders board of the prison regime is frequently illustrated in the case law. The relationship between different report writers and decision-makers is subtle.[26] One decision builds on the previous one. Padfield and Liebling (2000) explored how parole dossiers are built up over time, with the danger that subsequent reports, written by those who have read earlier reports, may build on earlier opinions and even mistakes (2000: 83). Good record-keeping is vital. For a recent account of the devastating impact that unsatisfactory record-keeping may have, see *Goodall v GSL UK Ltd* [2009] EWHC 2124 (Admin). The prisoner applied for a judicial review of a purported decision of an official in the privately run prison to which he was transferred to recategorise his prisoner status from Category C to Category B. Shockingly the judge concludes that 'this is not a case in which I can be at all certain exactly what happened, but in judicial review proceedings it is for the claimant to demonstrate that the facts are as he claims. This claimant has not done so and for that simple reason this claim must fail' (para. 9). It is particularly important that life sentence prisoners are enabled to progress through the prison system towards Category D (open prisons). If they are to persuade the Parole Board to release them, it is also essential that they are able to complete relevant courses. The non-availability of courses that have been deemed essential for prisoners seeking to prepare themselves for release has been loudly condemned by the courts.[27] The decisions that give priority to some prisoners over others can be equally unfair.

All determinate prisoners are eligible for half-time release, and many come out much earlier on a home detention curfew or an end of custody licence (see Padfield 2009b). These decisions to grant earlier than half-time release have hardly been studied. Contrary to what many people may believe, release from jail is never unconditional for any prisoner. Prisoners are released on licence. A standard licence might contain many of the following conditions: that the offender receives visits from his supervisor, lives somewhere specific; undertakes only approved employment; doesn't travel abroad without permission. Additional licence conditions may include:

- Attendance at appointments with a named psychiatrist/psychologist/ medical practitioner and cooperation with recommended care or treatment.
- Not to take work or organised activities with people under a certain age.

- Not to reside in the same household as children under a specified age.
- Not to approach or communicate with named people.
- To avoid a particular area.
- To address alcohol, drug, sexual, gambling, solvent abuse, anger, debt, or offending behaviour problems at a specified centre.
- A drug-testing condition.

These licence conditions are often onerous. Since s.28 of the Offender Management Act 2007 was brought into force, the license can also include a requirement that an offender participates in polygraph sessions: lie detection. The Polygraph Rules 2009 (SI 2009/619) came into force on 8 April 2009, and were challenged unsuccessfully by an offender in *R (Corbett) v Secretary of State for Justice NOMS* [2009] EWHC 2671 (Admin).[28] The case raises interesting questions about how conditions are selected for individual prisoners.

Many prisoners will be subject to supervision by a multi-agency public protection arrangements (MAPPA). Introduced in 2001, MAPPAs have become hugely important in the management and supervision of dangerous offenders in the community.[29] There are three formal categories of MAPPA offenders:

- **Category one**: Registered sex offenders (around 30,000 offenders in 2004/05; 32,336 in 2008/09).
- **Category two**: Violent or other sex offenders (around 12,600 offenders in 2004/05; 11,527 in 2008/09).
- **Category three**: Other dangerous offenders (around 3,000 offenders in 2004/05; 898 in 2008/09).

These bald figures tell us little. But MAPPA decision-making is crucial, as the annual reports and case law reveal. *R (Gunn) v Secretary of State for Justice and the Nottinghamshire MAPPA Board* [2009] EWHC 1812 (Admin) tells a story that is probably typical. Gunn, who was serving a sentence for conspiracy to supply Class B drugs, applied for judicial review of the conditions imposed on him following his release on licence. The local MAPPA assessed him as a level three risk offender. His licence conditions included a requirement to live at specified premises and another one not to enter the city of Nottingham without prior approval of the probation officer. He had lived in Nottingham for a long time and had family, children and friends in the city. He submitted that the high level of risk assessment of him that led to the licence conditions was not supported by the evidence relied upon, but the court held that it was not necessary for the various allegations made against him to be proved either by a criminal trial or by a civil balance of probabilities before they could be taken into account in a matter of risk assessment. The assessment of risk was not for the court to make, but for the MAPPA panel sharing relevant information that it considered to be credible and current and pertinent to the issues in hand. The function of the court was to review the process with an appropriate intensity of scrutiny depending on the evidence, the issues and the context; but not one of appeal or making an independent determination for itself of questions of risk. The case illustrates many of the concerns frequently raised about MAPPA, in particular whether prisoners have adequate disclosure of the information being shared at MAPPA meetings (where they are, of course, not represented). Craissati (2007) identifies certain paradoxical effects of stringent management, focusing on sex offenders. She concludes that:

> Really thoughtful risk management does not always consist of rights and wrongs, but of dilemmas ... there is a fine line between control and persecution, one that is difficult to detect at times, and that social exclusion – in the current climate – seems to be an unavoidable consequence of rigorous risk management ... The possibility that stringent risk management approaches embodied within the MAPPA re-creates – for some offenders – the disturbing experiences of their early lives seems absolutely clear. That it may paradoxically result in triggering greater levels of offending is an uncomfortable idea, as is the suggestion that in order to reduce risk, sometimes professionals and agencies may need to take risks. (Craissati 2007: 227)

Recall to prison is very common, and can happen not only because the offender reoffends but because a supervising probation officer or 'offender manager' is concerned that he might. Here again we have complex decision-making structures. The decision to recall will be taken initially by junior offender managers, in consultation with their managers. The actual decision is taken by the Public Protection Casework Section within the NOMS Public Protection Unit, which is made up of ten recall teams.[30] Collins (2007) suggests that the increasing numbers of prisoners recalled to prison is related to a decline in the use of professional discretion. Worryingly, the most likely to be recalled are the most disadvantaged (2007: 170). Until the Criminal Justice and Immigration Act (CJIA) 2008, all those recalled to prison were subject to a Parole Board review before they could be released. This had led to a surge in cases before the Parole Board. In 2007–08, the Parole Board considered 19,060 recall cases – up 30 per cent in just one year.[31] Now the CJIA 2008 allows NOMS to re-release offenders after 28 days. Will we see offenders yo-yoing in and out of prison? As Probation Circular 14/2008 (on post-release enforcement – recall and further release) says; the new provisions of the CJIA 2008 'are designed to enhance the use of recall as a flexible risk management tool'. Paragraph 12 specifies that 'the person is suitable for automatic release only if the Secretary of State is satisfied that he will not present an identifiable risk of serious harm to members of the public if he is released at the end of the 28 day period beginning with the date on which he is returned to custody.'[32]

So who gets re-released, and who stays beyond the 28 days? *R (Bektas) v Secretary of State for Justice, Probation Service* [2009] EWHC 2359 (Admin) concerned a prisoner serving eight years for conspiracy to supply class A drugs, who was remanded in custody a few months after his release on licence when he was charged with threatening to kill his wife. The case illustrates several of the problems that can arise. When do the authorities choose to revoke a licence for someone arrested for fresh alleged offences?

What happens when the police/CPS drop the new charges? Here, the license was not immediately revoked, but had been by the time the CPS dropped the charges against him. The judge holds that the decision to recall him as a standard case and not a fixed term recall was one that the Secretary of State was entitled to take. The prisoner had been recalled for allegations, now dropped: yet he was still awaiting an oral hearing before the Parole Board some nine months later. The way recall and re-release work in practice needs urgent examination.

The Parole Board's role today is limited to decisions regarding those serving indeterminate sentences, and those who have been recalled to prison and are not re-released within 28 days.[33] The role and function of the board is crucial: and indeed their caution is well known. Last year they directed the release of only 15 per cent of life sentence prisoners whose cases were considered by oral hearing, and the release rate for IPP prisoners was a great deal lower, at 8 per cent[34] (all of these prisoners, having served the minimum term specified by the trial judge, are being detained only for public protection). The case law is full of examples that underline the importance of researching and understanding the board's decision-making. Most famously, the Court of Appeal in *R (Brooke) v Parole Board* [2008] EWCA Civ 29 held that the Parole Board was not sufficiently independent of the Secretary of State, as required by both English common law and article 5(4) of the European Convention on Human Rights (ECHR).[35] But there are many other concerns. Delay remains a huge problem: see *Betteridge v Parole Board* [2009] EWHC 1638 (Admin). At first sight it might appear as if the Parole Board are the gate-keepers protecting the public from those serving life or indeterminate sentences who should not be released, but this is not the reality. In practice, there are a number of other gate-keepers, who can prevent or delay a prisoner's progress towards release: the many prison officers, psychologist and probation officers who make important decisions throughout the prisoner's sentence. The House of Lords' recognition of the Ministry of Justice's 'systemic failures' in not providing adequate courses in prison (see *Wells v Parole Board* [2009] UKHL 22) has already been noted, but the failings are not only systemic. An individual probation officer, in failing to provide a release plan, can ensure that a prisoner will not be released. And decisions that have not moved the prisoner through the system to an open prison will also ensure a negative decision by the Parole Board.[36]

A useful example of the current problems is provided by the case of *Spicer* [2009] EWHC 2142 (Admin), who was given an automatic life sentence for seven offences of robbery on 15 December 2003, with a tariff of three years, eight months, which expired on 1 July 2007. By June 2008 he was a category C prisoner. A Parole Board hearing that month considered a number of reports, including a recent OASys assessment and an HCR-20 report.[37] The former indicated a high risk of reconviction and a high risk of harm to the public. The latter indicated a moderate risk of violence. They recommended not release but a move to an open prison which was accepted by the authorities and in September 2008 he moved to an open prison. However, his allocated psychologist recommended that he should be assessed for a Cognitive Self Change Programme (CSCP), assessment for which is only carried out in closed conditions, and in December he was returned to closed conditions. But there are only 40 places on the CSCP and at the time of this hearing (August 2009) Spicer was still in closed conditions, on the waiting list for assessment. The court decided to require the Ministry of Justice

> to reconsider the claimant's categorisation, but to add to the order a proviso that the defendant shall not be obliged to embark on this exercise if within 2 weeks from the handing down of judgment [i.e. by 1 September 2009] the Parole Board has fixed a hearing for no later than 30 October 2009. This is not, in my judgment, to encourage queue-jumping before the Parole Board of the kind which has been deprecated by Collins J in *R (Betteridge) v The Parole Board* [2009] EWHC 1638 (Admin). It is simply tailoring the remedy which is required to do justice in this case, with which the Parole Board is not concerned, to the particular situation of those who are parties. (para. 39)

Queue jumping is certainly happening as the Parole Board has introduced a 'flexible' prioritisation framework. It would be interesting to hear Mr Spicer's perspective on all this. Hawkins (2003) points out that one of the unfortunate features of those parts of the criminal justice system that are concerned with the selective lifting of the criminal sanction is that they are particularly vulnerable to criticism: a successful decision outcome is invisible; only failure has the potential to come to public attention (Hawkins 2003: 211). Is it surprising that the prison authorities and the Parole Board seem so risk averse?

During the course of a sentence, a prisoner may be transferred to hospital. A recent decision which casts gloomy light on the impact of political involvement in decision-making on the hopes for rehabilitation for those detained in mental hospitals is *X v Secretary of State for Justice* [2009] EWHC 2465 (Admin). In 1996 X was convicted of two murders and sentenced to two mandatory life sentences. In 2000, when he was diagnosed as suffering from personality disorder and obsessive compulsive disorder, he was transferred to Broadmoor High Security Hospital under section 47 of the Mental Health Act 1983. The Secretary of State also directed, under section 49 of the 1983 Act, that he should be subject to the special restrictions set out in section 41. He was transferred from Broadmoor to a medium secure unit in 2007. In 2008 his responsible clinician submitted to the Secretary of State an application for him to have escorted community leave as part of his rehabilitation. The 'therapeutic goals' of the leave would be 'exploration of issues related to risk assessment; community reintegration; assessment of reaction to this'. The application was turned down, first on 15 August 2008, when a senior case worker at the Ministry of Justice's Mental Health Unit responded to the application on the behalf of the Secretary of State. She stated:

> In view of the high profile given to this case a Ministerial decision was needed, and I apologise for the inevitable delay. Unfortunately the Minister did not agree to grant [X] any leave at present, and no reasons were given for the decision. I am sorry to send what must be, for [X], a disappointing response, but it may be the case that after a period of

continued stability and engagement a more favourable outcome may result from any future requests.

The doctor unsurprisingly appealed this decision 'in the hope that some markers might emerge about how progressing his case might proceed in the future'. On 3 February 2009 the senior case worker wrote again to the doctor, stating:

> ... a further submission was put before the Minister requesting escorted leave in the local area and clarifying the exclusion areas. However, the request was again refused. The Minister commented that due to the deeply disturbing nature of the crime and, importantly, the perspective of the victim's family he would not allow escorted leave.

The Deputy High Court Judge struck down this decision as being unlawful: 'the reasons put forward for the Secretary of State's decision disclose irrationality in it' (para. 55). It would be interesting to know the eventual outcome. As we have seen, those sentenced to life in prison and then transferred to hospital still face the hurdle of the Parole Board before they can be released. The case of Staines has already been discussed to explore the different impact of different sentencing options – life sentences and hospital orders, with and without restrictions. And even at the end of a prison sentence a prisoner may not, of course, be released into the community. They may be transferred to a hospital. And they may be compulsorily treated for any mental disorder from which they are suffering (see *R (B) v Ashworth Hospital Authority* [2005] UKHL 20). I turn to civil detention in the next section of this chapter.

Public protection: the use of the civil law

The sex offender register

There has been a flood of recent laws seeking to 'protect the public' from convicted sex offenders in the community. First, the Sexual Offenders Act 1997, section 1 introduced the 'sex offender register'. Being on the register is not a sentence, but all those convicted of sexual offences are required to give the police details of their name, address and date of birth. Originally this was to be done within fourteen days of conviction, and offenders had to notify any address at which they would be staying for fourteen days or longer. The notification period was reduced to three days in the Criminal Justice and Court Services Act 2000, and a new requirement added that offenders on the register were required to notify the police if they intended to travel overseas. Regulations required that notification of travel should be made at least 48 hours prior to departure, including the identity of the carrier, all points of arrival in destination countries, accommodation arrangements, return date and point of arrival if known. These provisions were repealed and replaced by similar rules in Part II of the Sexual Offences Act 2003.

Here there is little discretion: the offender (or his parent on his behalf!) *must* register. But these draconian provisions have recently been successfully challenged. In *R (F) v Secretary of State for the Home Department, R (Thompson) v Secretary of State for the Home Department* [2010] UKSC 17[38] one of the appellants was a boy who had been aged eleven when he committed the rapes for which he was sentenced to 30 months' detention; the other, an adult, had been sentenced to five years' imprisonment in 1996 for indecent assault. They were both subject to the notification requirements of Part II of the Sexual Offences Act 2003 for an indefinite period. The issue for the Supreme Court was whether, in order to achieve the legitimate objective of assisting the police in the prevention and detection of crime, it was necessary that all sex offenders who were sentenced to imprisonment or detention for 30 months or longer should be subject to the notification requirements for the rest of their lives without the possibility of a review. The Supreme Court held that, as a matter of principle, an offender was entitled to have the question of whether the notification requirements continued to serve a legitimate purpose determined on a review. The Court of Appeal had been keen to point out that no purpose was served by keeping on the Sex Offenders Register a person of whom it could confidently be said that there was no risk that he would commit a sexual offence: the police database should not include offenders who no longer presented a risk of sexual offending. The Supreme Court agreed. The lack of a system to review those who were no longer a risk might adversely affect the efficacy of the system, as police forces became burdened with notifications from an ever-increasing number of offenders. Lord Phillips queried whether it was ever possible to be sure that an offender posed no significant risk of sexual reoffending. No evidence had been placed before the Court which answered that question one way or the other. But uncertainty as to that issue could not, even under the precautionary principle, render proportionate the imposition of notification requirements for life without review. It was obvious, the Court said, that there had to be some circumstances in which an appropriate tribunal could reliably conclude that the risk of an individual carrying out a further sexual offence could be discounted to the extent that continuance of notification requirements was unjustified. This common-sense approach is to be welcomed,[39] and it will be interesting to see how the government reacts.

'Civil' protection orders

The line between civil and criminal law is thoroughly blurred. Many discretionary powers limit freedom in the interests of public protection. We exclude many areas: perhaps most obviously the freedom to enter the country in the first place.[40] Then there are many 'low level' public protection measures: protection from harassment orders and anti-social behaviour orders (ASBOs), for example. A study of discretion in the making of protection from harassment orders (created in the Protection from Harassment Act 1997) would need to start with an examination of who applies for an injunction in the first place: normally, the individual victim and not the police. The application may result from a feeling that the police have failed to support the victim adequately, that the criminal justice system has 'failed'. A study of ASBOs is likely to be more complex: they may be initiated by the police, a local authority, or a social landlord, or imposed as a sentence in their own right. A key concern has been the length and the breadth of the restrictions often included in the ASBO. Another concern should be their efficacy.

There are a host of other orders that were originally designed for sex offenders, but can often now be applied to a wider range of offenders. Section 2 of the Crime and Disorder Act 1998 introduced sex offender orders. First proposed as 'community protection orders', these were orders for which the police could apply, and lasted for a minimum of five years. Section 66 of the Criminal Justice and Court Services Act 2000 then introduced restraining orders. These provisions were repealed by the Sexual Offences Act 2003, which introduced three new civil preventative orders: sexual offences prevention orders (SOPOs), foreign travel orders and risk of sexual harm orders.[41]

It is up to the police to apply for a SOPO in relation to anyone convicted of the offences listed in Schedules 3 and 4 of the 2003 Act, which extend to some 200 paragraphs. In 2008–09 1,512 SOPOs were ordered. Foreign travel orders have been rarely used, perhaps because their maximum duration was six months (only one was imposed in 2007–08; twelve in 2008–09).[42] The maximum duration was extended to five years by the Policing and Crime Act 2009, which also inserted a new section (117A) into the Sexual Offences Act 2003 that requires offenders (from 1 April 2010) subject to a foreign travel order that prohibits them from travelling anywhere in the world to surrender their passports at a police station specified in the order. Risk of sexual harm orders, specifically designed to protect children from sexual harm, again a civil protective order, can be used, for example, to ban someone from using the internet. The Human Rights Committee of the House of Commons commented, 'they would be very likely to have a catastrophic effect on people's lives and reputations.'[43] It is not clear if they are being used. In addition, there are notification orders, which require sexual offenders who have been convicted overseas to register with the police. As far as I know, there has been no recent research into the imposition and monitoring of these orders.[44] There is little in the public domain about how they are used, though the annual reports of multi-agency public protection panels gives examples, area by area. Only broad data is gathered nationally. There has been little litigation.

Civil detention under the Mental Health Act 1983

On 31 March 2009 there were 12,300 patients formally detained (that is, involuntarily held) in NHS facilities and 3,700 in independent hospitals[45] (NHS Information Centre 2009). The law applicable is to be found in the Mental Health Act 1983, as amended, and is well reviewed elsewhere in this book. In brief:

- Section 2: allows for the compulsory admission of people to hospital for assessment where 'he ought to be so detained in the interests of his own health or safety or with a view to the protection of other persons' (s.2(2)(b)). Obviously the decisions of the two doctors who must write recommendations, in the prescribed form, are crucial.

- Section 3: allows for the admission to hospital for up to six months for treatment. Such admissions are renewable for a further six months, then for one year at a time. Again, medical assessments are crucial: two doctors must confirm that the patient is suffering from a mental disorder of a nature or degree that makes it appropriate for him or her to receive medical treatment in hospital; that appropriate medical treatment is available for him or her; and that it is necessary for his or her own health or safety, or for the protection of others that he or she receives such treatment and it cannot be provided unless he or she is detained under this section.

- Section 4: emergency admissions under s.4 require only the authorisation of one doctor.

- Section 5: patients who are voluntarily in hospital may also be compulsorily detained. (Voluntary patients are known, somewhat oddly, as 'informal patients'.)

The role of the psychiatrist may be crucial, but a number of different players may have a role in authorising the detention and indeed the discharge of a patient. Police, key workers, care coordinators,[46] the nearest relative and 'Mental Health Act managers'[47] all play crucial roles. Thus, for example, the police may be called to someone's house and may decide that before deciding on a criminal justice response, a mental health assessment is necessary: two psychiatrists and an approved mental health professional (AMHP)[48] will then be called to the house. Clearly, at this early stage crucial decisions are taken that may direct the person into one of two very different processes: either the civil or the criminal justice system.

It may be difficult for both restricted (those sent to hospital by a criminal court under s.41 or s.45A of the MHA 1983, as amended) and non-restricted patients to challenge their detention. Release decisions, concerning both restricted and non-restricted patients, may be made by the Mental Health Tribunal[49], but a hearing before this body comes at the end of a complex series of decisions. The reports written by the medical, nursing and social care staff carry much weight, and even more important is the medical examination of the patient by a member of the tribunal. What was said earlier about the limited role of the Parole Board is relevant here: key decisions will have been taken during the period of detention that will have crucial impact on the tribunal. Holloway and Grounds (2003) concluded that 'tribunals are failing in their fundamental duty to safeguard some patients from unjustified detention in hospital' (2003: 158). These failings were put down to process issues, and to the weaknesses in the evidence upon which the tribunal based its decisions. Whether the new tribunal system affects decision-making remains to be seen. What is also influential is the 'culture' of decision-making, what Hawkins might call the 'social surround' (Hawkins 2003: 190).

Control orders

In a chapter that seeks to examine decision-making in relation to public protection issues it is impossible to ignore the control order system. Although few in number, their use has been deeply controversial, imposing vast limits on the suspect's freedom. Their origins lie in Part IV of the Anti-terrorism Crime and Security Act 2001, which provided for the indefinite detention of terrorist suspects without charge, and had that not been declared unlawful by the House of Lords in *A v SSHD* [2004] UKHL 56; [2005] 2 AC 68, it would doubtless have been a good example for this chapter. But as a result of that unanimous decision of the House of Lords, Parliament then passed the Prevention of Terrorism Act 2005. This provides for two sorts of control orders:

1 Non-derogating orders: those which the government suggests do not restrict liberty (and thereby do not contravene article 5 of the European Convention on Human Rights, the right to liberty) which may be made by the Home Secretary, subject to review by the courts.

2 Derogating control orders, which may be made only by a court.

Even though only non-derogating orders have been passed, it is unsurprising that they have resulted in a huge amount of litigation. The law on the supervision by the courts of non-derogating control orders is provided by section 3 of the 2005 Act, as amended by the Counter-Terrorism Act 2008. The language of section 3(3) makes it clear that the order will subsist unless the decision is 'obviously flawed'. The Home Secretary simply has to have 'reasonable grounds for suspecting that the individual has been involved in terrorism-related activity' and must consider that a control order is necessary to protect the public from the risk of terrorism (s.2). This is an extremely low threshold. There does not have to be any factual basis for this assessment of risk. Even if the suspicion is based on wholly inaccurate and misleading information, all that is required is that the suspicion of the Secretary of State be reasonable according to what is placed in front of him (see Justice 2009). In each case the administrative court subsequently undertakes a full judicial review under section 3(10) which will hear all the evidence in order to consider whether the decision to make the control order was 'obviously flawed'.

So far, 28 individuals have been the subject of control orders, and as of 10 December 2008 there were fifteen still in force. Of these:[50]

- One had been subject to one or more control orders for under six months.
- Seven had been subject to one or more control orders for between six and twelve months.
- Two had been subject to one or more control orders for between twelve months and two years.
- Three had been subject to one or more control orders for between two and three years.
- Two had been subject to one or more control orders for over three years.

The list of possible restrictions is very long (see sections 1(3) and (4)). Among them are curfews of up to sixteen hours enforced by an electronic tag, restrictions on the use of mobile phones and the internet, vetting of all visitors and meetings and restrictions on an individual's movements.[51] While the Prevention of Terrorism Act contains a long list of the type of activities that might be prohibited, the Home Secretary has the power to add new restrictions or obligations as he sees fit.[52] But, as Lord Carlile said in his fourth report,[53] 'it should be emphasised that nobody, least of all those who have to administer and enforce them, likes control orders. In every case alternatives are sought if available' (para. 36). They are hugely expensive, and quite often ineffective (seven people subject to control orders have absconded). A number have been struck down by the courts: notably in the House of Lords in *Secretary of State for the Home Department v JJ* [2007] UKHL 45 (where the House of Lords held by a majority of three to two that a control order imposing an eighteen-hour curfew was such a severe restriction on the liberty of the 'controlled persons' that it constituted a deprivation of liberty within the meaning of article 5 of the European Convention on Human Rights).[54]

The decision-making process remains largely secret. Within the Home Office there is a Control Orders Review Group (CORG), and the Home Secretary is also personally involved. Even before a court, the individual may not learn much about the evidence against him. 'Special advocates' are now regularly used in a wide variety of cases where a court or tribunal receives evidence and submissions not disclosed to the person most directly affected. They have special security clearance for accessing information that the government seeks to keep confidential and will not be disclosed to the suspect or their own lawyers. (Indeed, special advocates have also been used before the Parole Board, for immigration proceedings and even employment and planning proceedings involving questions of national security.)[55] In *MB v Secretary of State for the Home Department* [2007] UKHL 46 [2008] 1 AC 440, the majority of the House of Lords enunciated general principles governing the circumstances in which the special advocate procedure will comply with article 6 of the European Convention on Human Rights (the right to a fair trial), but these principles are very difficult to apply in practice. The appeal in *Secretary of State for the Home Department v AF* [2009] UKHL 28 was heard before an unusual nine-member panel of Law Lords in March 2009, the result being that the Home Secretary must now disclose the gist of the material on which a control order is based. The issue continues to dog the courts.[56]

While the number of control orders may be small, they clearly pose a stark challenge: does the 'war on terror' justify such draconian laws? What should the role of the courts be in protecting the liberties of the individual (see Kavanagh 2009)? For the purposes of this chapter I would suggest simply that the law should not allow such enormous (disproportionate?) restrictions on liberty without clear due process safeguards. The criminal law provides a better framework. But if the control order is to continue to be used, independent research into the decision-making process would be invaluable.

Conclusion

The purpose of this chapter has been to rehearse some of the most obvious areas of law concerned with 'public protection'. It has focused on recent law reports to illustrate this author's main concerns. These cases illustrate that the issues decided by courts, which include the protection of the individual's rights as well as issues of public protection, are actually constrained by many decisions taken earlier in the process. Whether we are concerned with prior decisions taken by psychiatrists before the mentally ill are detained, or the decisions taken 'administratively' by prison authorities before the case of a life sentence prisoner reaches the Parole Board, the same concerns arise: are those who make these more hidden decisions adequately accountable? Accountability and transparency are key legal principles. But many of the cases described in this chapter suggest that accountability is often an empty concept, certainly if one is relying on the law reports for data. The decisions that lawyers study in law reports are relatively visible: this chapter has also raised concerns about decisions taken rather more secretly, not only by secret services but by the police and many other agencies. It is often said that the price of freedom is vigilance. It is far too easy for us to become complacent about the adequacy of safeguards against wrongful or unnecessary limits on individual freedoms. This chapter seeks to encourage greater vigilance.

The chapter also urges lawyers to think more like sociologists (and perhaps for psychiatrists to think more like lawyers). Sociologists have long been busy identifying the impact of risk aversion and moral panics on current society,[57] and lawyers are only slowly working out the impact of risk on legal decision-making.[58] Hebenton and Seddon (2009), in their analysis of the impact of 'precautionary risk' influences on decision-making, conclude that 'the reality of a precautionary logic in contemporary neo-liberal culture cannot be gainsaid. Such a logic implores everyone to pre-empt risk by heeding warnings, being suspicious and embedding security measures in everyday life' (2009: 353). Everyone is pre-empting risk: the lawyer must wake up. We should look beyond 'the law' at the individuals behind the decisions. These individuals include, of course, the subjects of the decisions we review. Every case tells a real story. The law reports themselves document, for example, the reality that the provision of many services, such as mental health care within the criminal justice system, is often poor. But the focus must also be on the individual decision-maker. There is plenty of scope for lawyers to use their expertise to highlight the ways in which individual decision-keepers may consciously and subconsciously use and abuse their powers.

Selected further reading

There are a number of excellent general text books that have chapters relevant to this subject: for example, Ashworth (2010), Cavadino and Dignan (2007), Easton and Piper (2008), Padfield (2008), and Sanders and Young and Burton (2010). A useful series of essays on the use of discretionary powers by various players in the process is to be found in Gelsthorpe and Padfield (2003). Public protection post-release from prison is explored from a wide variety of different perspectives in Padfield (2007); and for wider European comparisons see Padfield, Van Zyl Smit and Dunkel (2010). A practical guide to the law on sentencing dangerous offenders is provided by the Sentencing Guidelines Council (2008). On risk predictors, see Annex E to Justice (2009), or Farrington, Jolliffe and Johnstone (2008).

Notes

1 See www.vosa.gov.uk/vosacorp/newsandevents/pressreleases/2009pressreleases/07-09-09fixedpenalties1stquarterresults.htm

2 For example, Hawkins (1995), (2002), (2003), and Gelsthorpe and Padfield (2003).

3 Padfield (2008).

4 Walker *et al.* (2009: 43).

5 Criminal Statistics 2007, p. 9 (2008 figures due shortly).

6 See the Prosecution of Offenders Act 1985 (and the Royal Commission on Criminal Procedure 1981).

7 The new DPP, Keir Starmer, following the practice of his predecessors, consulted on proposed changes in October 2009. The latest version was published in February 2010.

8 As well as those detailed within this chapter there are many other shocking cases in the law reports: see *Johnson* [2002] EWCA Crim 1900 where the Court of Appeal quashed the appellant's conviction for murder in 1976 because the jury should not have been allowed to proceed to a verdict while J was mentally unfit and unable to participate effectively in his trial. (The Court was also concerned that Johnson was still in prison 26 years later when the judge had recommended 20 years.) And *Grant* [2008] EWCA Crim 1870 who successfully appealed against his conviction because he had been unfit to plead.

9 Section 44 of the Children and Young Persons Act 1933 still applies: Every court in dealing with a child or young person who is brought before it, either as an offender or otherwise, shall have regard to the welfare of the child or young person and shall in a proper case take steps for removing him from undesirable surroundings, and for securing that proper provision is made for his education and training. See also s.9 of the Criminal Justice and Immigration Act 2008.

10 See the Law Commission's current review. It can be argued that these hearings provide civil liberties safeguards for mentally disordered offenders, but they seem archaic and inappropriate to me.

11 *Pritchard* (1836) 7 Car. & P. 303.

12 Mackay and Brookbanks (2005), Mackay *et al.* (2007).

13 A particularly worrying decision in this case was the seemingly inhumane application to extend custody time limits on 24 January 2007.

14 The Court of Appeal says 1992 (at paras 7 and 20) but this must be an error. Another stark example is *Moyle* [2008] EWCA Crim 3059.

15 www.cps.gov.uk.

16 See Hucklesby (2004).

17 See Padfield (2009a) As we go to press McKinnon continues to fight his extradition on the grounds of his mental health.

18 For a recent discussion, see Ward (2009)

19 See www.sentencing-guidelines.gov.uk/news/newsletter/index.html.

20 On 6 April 2010 the SGC was replaced by a new and more powerful Sentencing Council: see s.118–136 of the Coroners and Justice Act 2009.

21 There were 5,422 applications for leave to appeal against sentence to the Court of Appeal in 2008, and 1,567 successful appeals (Judicial Statistics 2008, page 22).

22 Increasingly counsel for the prosecution will address the court on relevant guidelines: sentencing hearings are no longer simply a plea in mitigation on behalf of the defendant. The relative role of the various 'players' in the sentencing process is shifting. See *Pepper* [2006] 1 Cr App R (S) 20; *Cain* [2006] EWCA Crim 3233, [2007] 2 Cr App R (S) 25; *Tongue and Doyle* [2007] EWCA Crim 561; *James* [2007] EWCA Crim 1906.

23 See also Castellano (2009) for an analysis of the way non-legal actors play a pivotal role, with a view from the United States.

24 See also Davis *et al.* (2008).

25 On which there are a large number of applications for judicial review. See for example, *Spicer* below, but also *R (Falconer) v Secretary of State for Justice* [2009] EWHC 2341 (Admin); *R (Cox) v Governor of HMP Bristol* [2009] EWHC 1862 (Admin).

26 See, for example, Liebling and Price (2003) for an account of prison officers and the use of discretion.

27 See, for example, *Wells v Parole Board* [2009] UKHL 22, where the House of Lords loudly condemned the Minister of Justice for his 'systemic failure' to provide the systems and resources that prisoners need in order to be able to demonstrate that it is no longer necessary to detain them in prison.

28 See also *R (Coney) v Parole Board* [2009] EWHC 2698 (Admin).

29 See MAPPA annual reports at www.probation.homeoffice.gov.uk/output/page30. asp.

30 Curiously, the staff list is attached as Appendix B to Probation Circular 14/ 2008.

31 See Padfield (2006).

32 Note the wording is not identical to the test set out in s.255A(5) of the CJA 2003, which does not include the word 'identifiable'.

33 See Padfield (2009b).

34 See the Parole Board's Annual Report 2008/09.

35 The Ministry of Justice's consultation paper *The Future of Parole* (Consultation Paper 14/09).

36 See Padfield and Liebling (2000).

37 Justice (2009) provides an excellent review of the various risk assessment tools currently used in sentence management: see Appendix E of that report.

38 Also known as *R (on the application of F) v Secretary of State for Justice*, a tiny example of the myriad confusions caused by the division and reorganisation of the Home Office, Lord Chancellor's Department, the short-lived Department of Constitutional Affairs and the Ministry of Justice.

39 Though the police recently won an appeal allowing them to retain a complete register of criminal convictions indefinitely: *Chief Constable of Humberside v Information Commissioner* [2009] EWCA Civ 1079.

40 See Pratt and Thompson (2008).

41 Very clearly described in Shute (2004).

42 National statistics, MAPPA Annual Reports 2008/09, www.probation.justice.gov. uk/files/pdf/MAPPA%20National%20Figures%202009.pdf.

43 Joint Committee on Human Rights, Seventh Report of 2002–03, *Scrutiny of Bills: Further Progress Report*, HC 547/HL.

44 A review of new preventive regimes in Australia should operate as a warning: 'it is not clear how prisoners are selected for applications to be made ... the process of initial selection should be clear and accountable. Perhaps if Queensland prosecutors, judges and defence lawyers were aware that more than a two year sentence for any sexual offence was likely to lead to an application for preventive detention, sentencing submissions and sentencing decisions might take this into account. It is not clear that this is the case ... It appears also that the choice of preventive detention instead of a supervision order is sometimes made because of the unavailability of resources such as appropriate housing and treatment programmes. The resource issue is clearly one that must be resolved. While placing prisoners in ghettoes on the outskirts of town with limited facilities and

little hope of reintegration is a serious problem, especially given the rehabilitative aspirations of the legislation, refusal to release because of a lack of housing is even more problematic' (Douglas 2008: 872–3).

45 In criminal justice, there is growing interest in comparing decision-making in private prisons with that in publicly run institutions. Presumably comparable literature exists in studying hospital regimes?

46 There are some wonderful blogs which underline the practical difficulties of the job: for example, fightingmonsters.wordpress.com.

47 The use and abuse of the word 'manager' is rampant. Here a manager is not a hospital manager in any usual sense of the word, but a manager of processes.

48 An AMHP used to be known as an approved social worker.

49 Major (revolutionary?) organisational changes have come into effect with the implementation of the Tribunals, Courts and Enforcement Act 2007. Most tribunals have now been combined into the First-tier Tribunal, with an Upper Tribunal created to deal with appeals from, and enforcement of, decisions of the First-tier Tribunal. Thus since November 2008 the jurisdiction of the Mental Health Review Tribunal (MHRT) moved to the newly created Health, Education and Social Care (HESC) Chamber of the First-tier Tribunal. New rules of procedure for mental health review cases have also come into effect: see the Tribunal Procedure (First-tier Tribunal) (Health, Education and Social Care Chamber) Rules 2008 (SI No 2008/2699).

50 See Ministerial Statement in HC Feb 2009.

51 On whether the suspect must submit to searches, see *Secretary of State for the Home Department v GG; Secretary of State for the Home Department v N* [2009] EWCA Civ 786.

52 For an excellent summary of the law, see Liberty (2009).

53 Carlile (2009).

54 But see *Secretary of State for the Home Department v JJ v AF* [2007] UKHL 46 (a fourteen-hour curfew was considered not to constitute a deprivation of liberty within the meaning of art. 5) and *Secretary of State for the Home Department v E* [2008] UKHL 47 (a control order which included an overnight curfew of twelve hours had not deprived E of his right to liberty in breach of art. 5). These three decisions have been much criticised for being unprincipled: see, for example, Ewing and Tham (2008).

55 For a critical review, see Chamberlain (2009), who highlights the systemic problems with the use of special advocates: the inability to call evidence, the lack of effective means to challenge the government's disclosure objections and the inability to take instructions on the closed case.

56 See *R (Secretary of State for the Home Department) v BC* [2009] EWHC 2927 (Admin).

57 Garland (2001), Beck (2004), for example.

58 For an unusual and helpful analysis of how 'risk' is the new buzzword of administrative governance, see Fisher (2003).

References

Ashford, A. (2010) *Sentencing and Criminal Justice*. 5th edn. Cambridge: Cambridge University Press.

Beck, U. (2004) *Risk Society: Towards a New Modernity*. London: Sage.

Bradley, K. (2009) Lord Bradley's Review of People with Mental Health Problems or Learning Disabilities in the Criminal Justice System (The Bradley Report). London: Department of Health.

Carlile, Lord (2009) Fourth Report of the Independent reviewer pursuant to section 14(3) of the Prevention of Terrorism Act 2005. Online at: www.statewatch.org/news/2009/feb/uk-lord-carlile-fourth-report.pdf

Castellano, U. (2009) 'Beyond the courtroom workgroup: caseworkers as the new satellite of social control', *Law and Policy*, 31: 429–62.

Cavadino, M. and Dignan, J. (2007) *The Penal System: An Introduction*, 4th edn. Sage: London.

Chamberlain, M. (2009) 'Special advocates and procedural fairness in closed proceedings', *Civ JQ* 314.

Collins, H. (2007) 'A consideration of discretion, offender attributes and the process of recall', in N. Padfield (ed.) *Who to Release? Parole, Fairness and Criminal Justice?* Cullompton: Willan Publishing.

Craissati, J. (2007) 'The paradoxical effects of stringent risk management: community failure and sex offenders', in N. Padfield (ed.) *Who to Release? Parole, Fairness and Criminal Justice?* Cullompton: Willan Publishing.

Davis, R., Rabinovic, L., Rubin, J., Kilmer, B. and Heaton, P. (2008) *A Synthesis of Literature on the Effectiveness of Community Orders*. RAND Europe.

Douglas, H. (2008) 'Post-sentence preventive detention: dangerous and risky', *Criminal Law Review*, 854.

Easton, S. and Piper, C. (2008) *Sentencing and Punishment: The Quest for Justice*, 2 edn. Oxford: Oxford University Press.

Ewing, K. and Tham, J. (2008) 'The continuing futility of the Human Rights Act', *Public Law*, 668.

Farrington, D.P., Joliffe, D. and Johnstone, L. (2008) *A Systematic review of risk assessment devices in the prediction of future violence*. Glasgow: Scottish Risk Management Authority.

Fisher, E. (2003) 'The rise of the risk commonwealth and the challenge for administrative law', *Public Law*, 455.

Garland, D. (2001) *The Culture of Control*. Oxford: Clarendon Press.

Gelsthorpe, L. and Padfield, N. (eds) (2003) *Discretion: Its uses in criminal justice and beyond*. Cullompton: Willan Publishing.

Gelsthorpe, L. and Padfield, N. (2003) 'Introduction', in L. Gelsthorpe and N. Padfield (eds) *Exercising Discretion: Decision-making in the Criminal Justice System and Beyond*. Cullompton: Willan Publishing.

Halliday, S., Burns, N., Hutton, N., McNeill, F. and Tata, C. (2009) 'Street-level bureaucracy, interprofessional relations, and coping mechanisms: a study of criminal justice social workers in the sentencing process', *Law and Policy*, 31: 405–28.

Hawkins, K. (ed.) (1995) *The Uses of Discretion*. Oxford: Oxford University Press.

Hawkins, K. (2002) *Law as Last Resort: Prosecution Decision-making in a Regulatory Agency*. Oxford: Oxford University Press.

Hawkins, K. (2003) 'Order, rationality and silence: some reflections on criminal justice decision-making', in L. Gelsthorpe and N. Padfield (eds) *Exercising Discretion: Decision-making in the Criminal Justice System and Beyond*. Cullompton: Willan Publishing.

Hebenton, B. and Seddon, T. (2009) 'From dangerousness to precaution: managing sexual and violent offenders in an insecure and uncertain age', *British Journal of Criminology*, 49: 343–62.

Holloway, K. and Grounds, A. (2003) 'Discretion and the release of mentally disordered offenders', in L. Gelsthorpe and N. Padfield (eds) *Exercising Discretion: Decision-making in the Criminal Justice System and Beyond*. Cullompton: Willan Publishing.

Hucklesby, A. (2004) 'Not necessarily a trip to the police station: The introduction of street bail', *Criminal Law Review*, 803.

Justice (2009) *A New Parole System for England and Wales*. London: Justice.

Kavanagh, A. (2009) 'Judging the judges under the Human Rights Act: deference, disillusionment and the "war on terror"', *Public Law*, 287.

Liberty (2009) Summary of the Prevention of Terrorism Act 2005. Online at: www. liberty-human-rights.org.uk/issues/2-terrorism/control-orders/index.shtml.

Liebling, A. and Price, D. (2003) 'Prison officers and the use of discretion', in L. Gelsthorpe and N. Padfield (eds) *Exercising Discretion: Decision-making in the Criminal Justice System and Beyond*. Cullompton: Willan Publishing.

Mackay, R. and Brookbanks, W. (2005) 'Protecting the unfit to plead: a comparative analysis of the "trial of the facts"', *Judicial Review*, 2: 173–95

Mackay, R., Mitchell, B. and Howe, L. (2007) 'A continued upturn in unfitness to plead – more disability in relation to the trial under the 1991 Act', *Criminal Law Review*, 530.

NHS Information Centre (2009) *In-patients Formally Detained in Hospitals under the Mental Health Act 1983 and Patients Subject to Supervised Community Treatment: 1998– 99 to 2008–09*. NHS Health and Social Care Information Centre.

Padfield, N. (2006) 'The Parole Board in Transition', *Criminal Law Review*, 3.

Padfield, N. (ed) (2007) *Who to release? Parole, fairness and criminal justice*. Cullompton: Willan Publsihing.

Padfield, N. (2008) *The Criminal Justice Process*. Oxford: Oxford University Press.

Padfield, N. (2008) *Text and Materials on the Criminal Justice Process*, 4th edn. Oxford: Oxford University Press.

Padfield, N. (2009a) 'Shining the torch at plea bargaining', *Cambridge Law Journal*, 11–14.

Padfield, N. (2009b) 'Parole and early release: The Criminal Justice and Immigration Act 2008 changes in context', *Criminal Law Review*, 166–87.

Padfield, N. and Liebling, A. with Arnold, H. (2000) *An Exploration of Decision-making at Discretionary Lifer Panels*, Home Office Research Study, 213. London: Home Office.

Padfield, N., van Zyl Smit, D. and Duenkel, D. (eds) (2010) Release from Prison: European policy and practice. Cullompton: Willan Publishing.

Pratt, A. and Thompson, S. (2008) 'Chivalry, "race", and discretion at the Canadian border', *BJ Criminology*, 48: 620.

Sanders, A., Young, R. and Burton, M. (2010) *Criminal Justice* 4th edn. Oxford: Oxford University Press.

Sentencing Guidelines Council (2008) *Dangerous Offenders: Guide for Sentencers and Practitioners*.

Shute, S. (2004) 'The Sexual Offences Act 2003: (4) New civil preventative orders', *Crim LR*, 417–40.

Tata, C., Burns, N., Halliday, S., Hutton, N. and McNeill, F. (2008) 'Assisting and advising the sentencing decision process: the pursuit of "quality" in pre-sentencing reports', *British Journal of Criminology*, 835.

Walker, A., Flatley, J., Kershaw, C. and Moon, D. (eds) *Crime in England and Wales 2008/9 Vol 1: Findings from the British Crime Survey and police recorded crime*, Home Office Statistical Bulletin 11/09. London: Home Office.

Ward, T. (2009) 'Usurping the role of the jury? Expert evidence and witness credibility in English criminal trials', *International Journal of Evidence and Proof*, 13(2): 83–101.

Chapter 6

An epistemological chasm? Acturial risk assement through OASys

Andy Williams

Introduction

As the final draft of this chapter was being prepared the Edlington case of two young boys convicted of grievous bodily harm and sexual assault against two boys aged nine and eleven came to the forefront of national media coverage. After their conviction – an indeterminate sentence with a minimum five-year tariff – sections of the media, politicians, 'experts' and social commentators all denounced the boys as evil, and criticised child protection services for failing to stop this awful attack being undertaken. What is obviously going to accentuate the influence this case has on future public protection policy is that we were in the run-up to a general election. On hearing of the conviction of the two boys, Conservative Leader David Cameron took the opportunity to make a political point by calling the case a 'symptom of broken Britain' and that we should not consider this case an isolated 'incident of evil' (Stratton 2010). To a certain extent this is not an isolated case by any stretch of the imagination. Children have been doing horrible things to each other for years and will continue to do so. However, such terrible incidents are still rare and the more robust measures of violence in society do indicate that violence in the UK has decreased in recent years. Despite most sensible criminologists knowing this, and being able to relate claims such as the ones made by Cameron to Labour's use of the American Right's populist approach to crime (Young 2003: 36–42), cases such as Edlington will enable the mass media, politicians and vested interest groups to push for an extension of the penal policies that have been a core feature of the Labour government's law and order agenda since 1997. Nowhere more have we seen this than in the responses to sexual and violent predators.

The protection of the public from 'dangerous' sexual and violent offenders has overloaded our criminal justice system to such an extent that a 'Spencerian' organic evolution (Spencer 1893a, 1893b; Swingewood 1991: 53–8) has forced a broad range of other government and non-governmental organisations to become increasingly involved in the bureaucratisation of offender management

(Weber 1978). Looking back over the last 100 years or so, we see a plethora of influences that have increased the net of social control (Cohen 1985; Garland 2001), with many suggesting that increasing the managerial and bureaucratic nature of offender management increases efficiency. Some of these influences include the rise and dominance of the medical, psychiatric and psychological professions (Abbott 1988; Cohen 1985; Conrad and Schnieder 1992; Pearson 1975); the rise in what Harcourt (2007) calls the 'actuarial age'; the cyclical sexual predator 'panics' identified by Jenkins (1998); the growth of the child abuse industry (Carol 1994; Thompson 1994; Williams 2004); and finally, the importance of the dangerousness debate (Kemshall 2003; Nash 1999, 2006; Prins 2007; Brown and Pratt 2000). A major consequence of these influences (and many more besides)[1] is that social and criminal justice public protection policies have been constructed with the main aim of enhancing the management of offenders in the community. As Part One of this volume has noted, many of these policies have been reactive and based upon poor conceptualisations of dangerousness and an even worse understanding of criminal behaviour. No better example of this reactive policy-making can be seen than in the current UK system that manages sexual and violent offenders: MAPPA (multi-agency public protection arrangements).

This chapter reviews the dominant risk assessment technique used for assessing violent and sexual offenders through the lens of MAPPA and operates from a simple assumption: in order to adequately manage 'dangerous' offenders in the community with the finite resources that are available, you need to know and understand your offender *in detail*. However, this is a loaded assumption. It comes with a lot of political, social, economic and academic baggage. As a practitioner, whether you're a probation or police officer, from housing or social services, or from forensic health services – how you manage your offender caseload will be determined by a range of what Brantingham and Brantingham (1991, in Wortley and Mazerolle 2008: 3–8) call micro, meso and macro factors. Such factors include your own education, experience and training; the organisational structure, management, resources and protocols in which you operate; as well as the broader political and social influences that impact upon what you can achieve on a day-to-day basis.

Within the MAPPA framework, two of the key duties practitioners have to undertake are a risk of re-offending assessment (the current method is OGRS 3), and a risk of harm analysis; both of these are based within the structured framework of the Offender Assessment System, or OASys for short. This chapter provides the first phenomenological critique of OASys, by critically examining this risk assessment process, and argues that while it is one of the more robust assessments we have ever had, it has the unintended consequence (Weber 1978) of deskilling workers and decontexualising offending behaviour. It does this by effectively reducing the understanding of criminality to a checklist of quantifiable causal factors, where correlations between influencing factors and behaviours are based upon studies of small offender groups. This type of assessment lacks any in-depth qualitative analysis of the important factors identified by Scott (1977) in his work with dangerous offenders. Scott rightly stated that an offence consists of three core factors – the offender, the victim, and the circumstances and context. It is the understanding of these three elements that provides a thorough understanding of the crime incident. This chapter will also discuss a core issue that is crucial if we are to develop our theoretical and applied understanding of violent and sexual criminals. As multi-agency public protection has developed over the last ten years or so, and as the myriad of protocols, procedures and risk assessment tools have grown and developed, one thing has become apparent – these developments have produced a huge amount of information about criminality (Gottfredson and Hirschi 2004) that is rarely pieced together and analysed. This information could enable us to (1) enhance the strength of our overall understanding of these offender groups' criminality; (2) be incorporated into the risk assessments that rely so heavily on such statistical information and knowledge of offender groups; and (3) enable core problems to be quickly identified and lessons learned when things do go wrong and the offender commits a further offence. The lack of this basic crime and profile analysis, from information that is generated naturally within MAPPA and the relevant authorities, is what I call an 'epistemological chasm'. There are many reasons for this chasm, some of which I discuss below. Before this, it is important to outline the current thinking and assessment techniques used within the public protection arrangements.

The actuarial paradigm

Understanding the history of social processes and developments within social policy is crucial if we are to understand the contemporary policies that exist. This is especially the case for understanding current policies related to risk assessments of sexual and violent criminals. Before readers wince at the thought of an extended historical chapter it is pertinent to remember Turvey's words:

> The study of history is for critical thinkers – those who will not blindly and politely accept what they have been handed by someone claming to be an authority... it is for those who understand the value of hunting down information and sourcing it, and who would prefer not be led by the hand into intellectual servitude. (Turvey 2008: 2)

This is one the core differences between what Bridges (see this volume) called the 'commentators' and the 'doers'. The 'doers' tend to be forced into servitude by those in power, and there is a distinct lack of historical knowledge in some of the 'doers' I have met. Fortunately, there are those 'commentators' (a poor term to express academic and scientific research) that do not have to worship at the altar of power or organisational bureaucracy. We are, of course, diminishing in number but there are still enough of us demanding objectivity and truth. Hopefully, the remainder of chapter will persuade the 'doers' that it is important to critically assess systems and policies and that 'critical friends' play that vital role; something that should be emphasised in practice, as demonstrated by Grieve (this volume).

The protection of the public from dangerous sexual and violent offenders can involve many different agencies, all with competing and/or differing organisational cultures, objectives and resources. Sections 67 to 69 of the Court Services and Criminal Justice Act 2000 attempted to align these agencies on a statutory footing, after some earlier efforts of multi-agency practice resulted in some high profile failures; for example, the inadequate risk assessment and management of Victor Burnett on the Paulsgrove estate, which resulted in the anti-MAPPP[2] demonstrations in August 2000 (see Williams and Thompson 2004a, 2004b). Ever since 2001, agencies have been forced more and more to work together, using a broad range of risk assessment techniques and protocols. The dominant actuarial assessment tool used within MAPPA is currently OASys, which has largely been developed as a result of what Harcourt (2007) calls the 'actuarial age'.

The coming of the actuary

The technique of using actuarial methods in risk assessment can be traced back to the insurance industry and it is here that assessments of an individual's probable level of risk were made on the basis of known characteristics of the statistical group that individual had been placed into. Assessments are made relating to people's characteristics and previous behaviour, in order to make predictions about their future behaviour. It is this thinking that has become endemic within the criminal justice system, the origins of which can be traced back to the early part of the twentieth century. In 1929 in the United States, the prominent sociologist Ernest Burgess stated that 'it would be possible to predict the future conduct of groups of persons on the basis of their past behaviour' (Burgess 1929: 534). Burgess, of course, was talking about developing the 'expectancy rate', which is 'a statistical statement of the probabilities of a certain type of behaviour which would apply to a group of persons rather than to a specific individual' (1929: 534). In his first major study, Burgess examined 3,000 parolees from Joliet, Menard and Pontiac in order to answer the question of 'correlation of observance or violation of parole with facts about the paroled man as recorded in prison records' (1929: 534). Once it was determined who violated parole, Burgess cross-referenced these offenders with a range of 21 risk factors based upon an offender's original or index offence, including: nature of offence, number of associates in committing offence, type of criminal (first offender, occasional, habitual, or professional offender), marital status, type of neighbourhood and so forth. Once the relevant expectancy tables were produced, Burgess proffered that one could determine whether a parolee would be a likely success for parole. Burgess' research prompted a number of criticisms. Rice (1929) highlighted a number of difficulties in the conceptualisation and operationalisation of the 21 risk factors. For example, he raised the question of why these factors were used and not others, suggesting that some risk factors were merely used because they were available, *ergo* they could be measured (1929: 556). Coincidentally, this is similar to a criticism made of the lack of static and dynamic risk factors included in contemporary risk assessment tools (see Boer and Hart 2009: 33).

Despite a number of problems, Burgess' basic idea was developed and implemented by Ferris F. Laune. In 1933, Laune assumed 'the newly created post of Sociologist and Actuary at the Illinois State Penitentiary in Joliet' (Harcourt 2007: 39). He was the first to officially implement Burgess' techniques, and in the same year he produced the first actuarial report – the *prognasio* – based 'on group-trait offending rates evaluating an individual prisoner's probability of violating parole if released' (Harcourt 2007: 39). This can be seen as the birth of the actuarial measure within the criminal justice system. Interestingly, and something missed by Downes and Rock in their review of the Chicago School (1995, 2007), is the fact that the growth and development of actuarial techniques originates in some of the major work of Chicago School researchers. Albert Reiss, Lloyd Ohlin, George Vold and George Lunday all wrote their theses on or around the predictive model of Burgess (Harcourt 2007: 40). Most criminological texts tend to ignore this very important body of work, instead concentrating on the human ecological approach of Shaw and McKay, or the ethnographic golden years (see Downes and Rock 1995, 2007; Bulmer 1986). The Chicago School and the Illinois Department of Corrections played the crucial 'entrepreneurial role' (Becker 1963) in disseminating the actuarial approach throughout the criminal justice in the United States. Lloyd Ohlin, for example, as research sociologist for the Illinois Division of Corrections, published *Selection for Parole: A Manual of Parole Prediction* in 1951. This was the first ever parole manual for prediction, and as Ohlin acknowledged, reflected 'twenty years of experimentation and research in the application of parole prediction methods' (Ohlin 1951: 8). During the 1930s through to the early 1960s, then, the 'actuarial paradigm' (Harcourt 2007) became the dominant way of assessing levels of risk of reoffending in the criminal population. Unfortunately, it is not within the remit of this chapter to provide a full overview of the various developments that took place during the twentieth century. Those readers who are interested should go to the original studies of Burgess (1929) and Ohlin (1951) (and also see Harcourt 2007 for an excellent review of the development of these techniques in the US).

Today, actuarial risk assessment techniques of all kinds proliferate the criminal justice system. They are used to determine pre-trial detention, the length of criminal sentences, whether offenders should be given extended (indeterminate) sentences (see the Criminal Justice Act 2003; Taylor *et al.* 2004: 251–8), and an offender's likelihood of reoffending score and risk of harm to others. As Harcourt (2007: 2) asserts, actuarial prediction instruments 'increasingly determine individual outcomes in our policing, law enforcement and punishment practices'. For example, in the UK actuarial risk assessments are undertaken at all three stages of the criminal justice system: at the court stage for sentencing purposes; during periods in custody and to aid parole decisions; and finally, during the probation period where the offender is being managed within the community. As such, actuarial risk assessments have become a core business activity of protecting the public, responsibility of which is clearly housed within the National Offender Management Service (NOMS – see Nash and Williams 2008); and there have been significant changes to risk assessment tools during the last fifteen years or so. Depending on the main objective of assessment (the likelihood of reoffending, risk of harm, risk management or treatment to name just a few), violent and sexual offenders can be assessed using a number of actuarial risk assessment instruments (ARAI). Harkins and Beech (2009: 102–10) summarise ten ARAIs designed to be used with sex offenders. These include Static-99, Static-2002, Risk Matrix 2000, SORAG (Sex Offence Risk Appraisal Guide), SARN (Structured Assessment of Risk and Need) and VRS: SO (Violence Risk Scale: Sex Offender version). Obviously, it is not possible here to review all of these tools in any detail. The remainder of this chapter concentrates on an examination of the OASys tool. There are a number of reasons for this: first, OASys is the dominant assessment method used within the MAPPA framework. Secondly, the NOMS website boldly claims that it 'is considered to be the most advanced system of its kind in the world'.[3] Indeed, it is a comprehensive tool that considers a multitude of criminogenic risk factors that have been identified as having an influence on offender behaviour. The current government has invested such a large amount of time and money into OASys that this risk assessment object even has an entire research team – the OASys Data Evaluation and Analysis Team (O-DEAT) – dedicated to researching its impact and viability. But how did we get to the position where OASys has dominated the risk assessment field in the UK?

Rationalising risk

Today, most social scientists have heard of the concept of 'risk', as the majority of the predictive tools used by the criminal justice system are designed to determine future behaviour and future risk. In contemporary society we are driven by the risk discourse (Hudson 2003). It forms everyday thinking, and serious decisions about future *possible* behaviour are made within this framework. Sociologically, there are two reasons why the risk discourse has become so central to criminal justice policy: because of Beck's conceptualisation of 'risk' and Weber's identification of the bureaucratisation of 'legal-rational domination'. Beck (1992) is largely responsible for many individuals embracing the concept of risk, despite the many flaws there are with this concept and the phenomenological reality within which it operates. The concept has actually taken on a life of its own, much like the self-fulfilling prophecy of deviance amplification systems (Wilkins 1964; Young 1971). In short, risk has become a reality simply because people now frame their discourses around the concept. The basic premise of Beck's work is that the consequence of global industrialisation and scientific development is a 'set of risks and hazards, the likes of which we have never previously faced' (Beck 1992: 2). To be sure, with today's technology, we certainly have access to images and information pertaining to a whole range of contemporary dangers. However, risks and hazards are all relative and we tend to drift in and out of our levels of fear. For example, I don't have any kids at the moment so I am not fearful that marauding 'paedophiles' are waiting on each corner to attack them. And even if I did have kids, through information and knowledge I recognise that kids are rarely snatched off the streets and we need to look a lot closer to home for signs of child abuse. The central problem with Beck's work is that it hides a neo-Marxist ideology that is more about the death of the grand narrative than being based upon any empirical and scientifically observable facts (*ergo* testable through verification and falsification). As Callinicos (1996) and Harvey (1990) assert, there are far more similarities than differences between modern, postmodern and late-modern changes within society. The simple fact of the matter is, these types of concepts are always class driven, with the middle classes always attempting to tell the working classes what they should be fearful of and what are the 'real' risks to their families. When you actually engage in ethnographic studies of sub-populations, social groups or social phenomena,[4] there is nearly always an alternative explanation to the 'official' one (see Williams and Thompson 2004a, 2004b for an alternative and more realistic explanation to the Paulsgrove demonstrations in August 2000). Despite these problems, the concept of risk has become intrinsic to penal policy, especially when trying to predict future behaviour. Weber's political sociology demonstrates why this has happened.

Max Weber noted that as the capitalist system of production developed, all forms of organisations engaging in economic and social endeavours would rationalise their structure and protocols. All organisations engage in a range of social actions, labelled by Weber as falling within the conceptual ideal types of rational (logical and mathematical), emotionally empathic or artistically appreciative (Weber 1978: 5). As the western world went through its process of industrialisation and urbanisation, economic and managerial imperatives derived from the protestant middle-class work ethic (Weber 1992) created a situation where central components of social action became domination and legitimacy (Parkin 1993: 71; Weber 1978: 212). One of the core themes running through Weber's political sociology is this issue of dominance and legitimacy through the exercise of power, and he noticed that rational rules and bureaucracy were the core methods of implementing power and domination over people. Legal-ration domination within modern organisations is bureaucratically driven by rules, regulations and protocols. Thus, modern officialdom functions are structured in the following way (taken from Gerth and Mills 1993: 196–8):

1 Fixed and jurisdictional areas that are governed by laws or administrative regulations.

2 The principles of office hierarchy mean a firmly ordered system of super and subordination in which there is a supervision of the lower offices by higher ones.

3 The management of the modern office is based upon written documents (the files).

4 Office management usually presupposes thorough and expert training.

5 Official activity demands the full working capacity of the official.

6 The management of the office follows general rules which are more or less stable … Knowledge of these rules represents a special technical learning which the officials possess.

While this is Weber's ideal-type conceptualisation of the bureaucratic office, and Beck's work is an overblown neo-Marxist concept, modern criminal justice systems and policy have embraced both these issues and rationalised risk by creating bureaucratic protocols for assessing violent and sexual offenders. In part, this has been fed by what criminologists wrongly call 'moral panics' (Cohen 1987, 2002) against 'dangerous' offenders (Nash 2006; Brown and Pratt 2000). Young explains that the potent mix of politicians and the media engaging in moral enterprise within the framework of law and order, coupled with what he calls 'economic and ontological insecurity in late modernity' (2003: 41), has created an almost continuous cycle of anxieties that have identified those that are more 'risky' and 'dangerous' than others. It is these fears that have driven the public protection agenda against sexual and violent criminals in the UK for the last 30 years or so. What Young has either forgotten or does not know about is that Callinicos (1996) and Harvey (1990) have long since destroyed the notion of post/late-modernity as being qualitatively no different from the modernist project of 200 years ago. As Pearson's (1983) excellent work has noted, the same fears and concerns over the 'dangerous' folk devil (Cohen 1987, 2002) that we have today were practically the same 150 years ago. For example, we were just as fearful about sexual criminals (Jenkins 1998) and dangerous youths (Pearson 1983) back then as we are today. This is nothing new. What changes over historical time periods are merely the means by which we deal with people we believe to be the most dangerous in society. Of course, because those who are seen as 'dangerous' has to do with social and political constructs, these perceptions change between what could be described as a 'see-saw continuum' of punitive penal populism and liberal rehabilitative programmes. The discourse of 'risk' (Beck 1992) in which we currently frame (Goffman 1986) public protection and criminal justice policy (Hudson 2003) has little to do with an objective assessment of fact, and who is actually dangerous and who isn't, and more to do with the failure of the grand narrative (Callinicos 1996) to deal with real economic and social problems. It is with these broader social, economic and political issues in mind that ARAIs have been able to gain dominance in the jurisdictional boundary (Abbott 1988: 2) that is risk and public protection.

Bringing the above ideas further within the context of Young's (2003) analysis of the current criminal justice system in the UK, there has certainly been an increase in the literature examining what Garland (1994) called administrative criminology (for example see Cohen 1985; Matthews and Young 2003; Stenson and Sullivan 2001; Worrall and Hoy 2005). This growing body of research charts a number of dominant trends within crime and governance policy and highlights that there is a belief that public protection has become more managerial and bureaucratic, with roles such as those within the probation service losing their autonomy to the beast that is 'national standards' and 'technocracy' (Worrall and Hoy 2005: 86). Indeed, when OASys was first introduced within the probation service, many individual officers were sceptical about the tool, and argued that they would lose discretion and control over their work (Worrall and Hoy 2005: 86). It appeared that the problems highlighted by Shaw (1987) – loss of control, acceleration of managerial and bureaucratic demands, preoccupation with minutiae of their jobs, and losing sight of wider social, economic and political influences – would become a reality. For example, in a recent training session one individual approached me with a concern that being new to risk assessment she was unsure how much the risk assessment tools overrode her own judgement, and whether she was allowed to go against the risk assessment score. This is not one isolated individual, and it is worrying that those working and making decisions at the 'business end' of the criminal justice system have to be driven by an ARAI score, even when evidence, empathy and logic skills may be telling them something different. Of course, we cannot blame MAPPA workers for this, as serious further offence independent reviews are predicated solely on the basis of whether you have followed the protocols of the risk assessment tool (Nash and Williams 2008: 30–4), and can result in practitioners being vilified and blamed for an offender's criminal actions. This drive towards a 'tick-box' culture is just another example of the bureaucratic model of criminal justice (Davies *et al.* 2005: 23–8). It is this central risk assessment (used within MAPPA) that the remainder of this chapter concentrates on. The following section provides an overview of the tool, as well as one or two critical points to consider. After that, research and epistemological issues that are consistently being neglected are discussed, alongside possible future areas of research.

OASys in action

The current risk assessment tool used by MAPPA personnel is the Offender Assessment System (known as OASys). It is the national risk and needs assessment tool that is used across all probation areas in England and Wales (Debidin and Fairweather 2009: 1) and was developed by the prison and probation services as a 'set of paper forms that break down into a number of different sections' (NPS 2003: 1). Prior to the introduction of OASys, two risk assessment tools were used: the Level of Service Inventory – Revised (known as LSI-R and developed by Andrews and Bonta 1995) and the Assessment, Case Management and Evaluation (ACE, which was developed by Roberts *et al.* 1996). In 1999 the Home Office decided to build upon these two methods, as well as 'the existing evidence base in the literature, to devise a new assessment as part of a national "What Works" strategy' (McGuire 1995, in Debidin and Fairweather 2009: 1). After a pilot scheme that tested OASys in three probation areas between 1999 and 2001 (Howard *et al.* 2006), OASys was implemented nationwide from 2001 and has moved from being paper based to its current electronic format. A prominent feature of the academic and government literature on this technique is a distinct lack of a detailed overview and critical discussion of the components of OASys and its advantages and disadvantages. Indeed, a quick trawl of the academic literature that makes reference to OASys failed to even identify its core components. Some have tried to remedy this lack of critical assessment (Kemshall 2003); however, such work simply provides only brief and descriptive overviews of this core assessment tool. For example, Kemshall's (2003) work on risk in the criminal justice system, and Craissati's (2004) work on risk assessment tools and sexual offending both provide an adequate albeit basic description of

OASys: 'The tool, labelled the Offender Assessment System (OASys) is based upon social learning theory, assesses risk factors across a number of domains and combines actuarial and dynamic risk factors' (Kemshall 2003: 70).

The core aim of this section is to provide readers who are not familiar with OASys with an overview of its components, together with a critical analysis of the tool, which hopefully moves beyond a simple descriptive summary. In doing so, several core problems with OASys have been identified and are discussed in detail below.

Counts and categories

OASys combines a number of key tools in an attempt to predict an offenders' recidivism risk. For example, it currently uses OGRS 3 (Offender Group Reconviction Scale), which is an actuarial device that examines factors such as previous convictions, age and gender (Howard *et al.* 2009: 1). The actuarial measure is a simple ordinal logistic regression model in which the following probability of proven reoffending equation is used:

$$Pro = exp(z)/(1+exp(z))$$

$$where\ z = A + B1 + B2 + B3 + B4$$

While this may seem complicated, the variables A and B1 to B4 relate to reoffending within one or two years (A); the Copas Rate, which reflects the intensity and length of an offender's criminal career (B1); sanctioning history, for example, first conviction, never cautioned/reprimanded/warned (B2); age and gender (B3); and finally, the principal current offence, for example, violence (B4). Howard *et al.* (2009: 3) found that OGRS 3 improved the prediction of proven reoffending to 80 per cent, as compared with the OGRS 2 predictive value of 78 per cent. As these results suggest, OGRS 3 appears to be a fairly robust indicator for predicting whether an offender is likely to reoffend. However, what OGRS 3 does not do is provide information pertaining to the type and level of harm and seriousness that that future crime event will take. Additional information is required and one of the advantages of OASys is that it takes both static variables, such as those used by OGRS 3, and dynamic variables, in order to try to determine an offender's risk of harm level (see below for an expansion on this). This first couple of pages of the assessment takes the form of descriptive information pertaining to the case at hand (called Case Identification). Descriptive details such as offender's forename, surname, date of birth, gender, religion, PNC number, ethnicity, purpose of assessment, sources of information and offence information are included in this section. From then on, one can identify thirteen core sections to OASys, as outlined in Table 6.1.

The core sections identified in Table 6.1 form the bulk of the risk assessment for the offender. However, a more important section of OASys follows – the Risk of Serious Harm Screening (RSHS) – and this is clearly an advantage of the tool. It is specified at the beginning of the RSHS that it must be completed in all cases. The purpose behind this screening is to identify whether the

Table 6.1 Core elements of OASys.

No.	Section description	Contents/details	Static or dynamic
1	Offending information	• This section deals with information that calculates the OGRS 3 and includes: offence description; details of sentence; number of court appearances before age of 18; age at first conviction; number of convictions, etc. • Two scores are produced: (i) general offending % within 12 months of community sentence/discharge; and (ii) general offending % within 24 months of community sentence/discharge.	Static
2	Analysis of offences	• This section deals with a more in-depth look at the offence for which the offender is being assessed on, with three themes emerging; offence details, victimology, and motivation for the offence. • *Offence*: brief offence details (qualitative description); whether the offence involved carrying or use of a weapon, any violence or threat of violence, excessive/ sadistic violence, arson, a sexual element, or physical damage to property; information pertaining to the circumstances and context of the interaction between the victim and the offender (e.g. was the victim contact targeted, was it physical violence towards a partner, or was it repeat victimisation of the same person). • *Victim*: for example, relationship between victim and perpetrator; impact on the victim; and whether the offender recognised the impact and consequences the offending had on the victim. • *Motivation*: considers the motivation and triggers towards the offending and includes: type of motivation (sexual, financial, addiction, emotional, racial, or thrill seeking); whether any dis-inhibitors influenced the offending (alcohol, pornography, emotional state or drugs, etc.); and whether there was an escalation in seriousness from any previous offending.	Static
3	Accommodation	• This section begins to discuss the offender's current situation and consists of four core questions that relate to the offender's current accommodation status and suitability. It combines quantitative data scoring with qualitative contextual information. • The four questions ask whether the offender is of no fixed abode or is in transient accommodation; what the suitability of the accommodation is (overcrowding, quality	Dynamic

Table 6.1 continues overleaf

Table 6.1 continued

No.	Section description	Contents/details	Static or dynamic
		of residence, relationships with rest of the household, etc.); the permanence of the accommodation; and the suitability of the accommodation.	
4	Education, training and employability	• This section deals with a range of issues relating to the offender's educational attainment and employment history. It combines quantitative data scoring with qualitative contextual information. • Questions within this section include employment history (number of jobs, gaps between periods of working, reasons for leaving, etc.); work-related skills (apprenticeships); attitude to employment (motivation to find work, satisfaction, attendance and performance levels etc.); school attendance; whether the offender has learning difficulties; educational or formal professional vocational qualifications; and attitude to education and training.	Mainly static with some dynamic
5	Financial management and income	• Section 5 reviews the financial position of the offender in order to try to determine if they are solvent and whether their financial position is a risk factor. • Questions include what the offender's financial situation is (lack of financial stability, debts, court costs or fines, no regular source of income etc.); financial management (budgeting skills, provision to meet bills, savings, loans, etc.); illegal earnings as a source of income; over-reliance on family and friends for financial support; and severe impediments to budgeting. • This section is mainly based upon quantitative scoring with some room for qualitative data.	Mainly static with some dynamic
6	Relationships	• The relationship section considers the offenders' relationships and includes quantitative scoring with room for qualitative details. • The scoring questions include current relationship with close family; experience of childhood (e.g. physical, sexual, or emotional abuse); current relationship status and relationship with partner; previous experience of close relationships; evidence of domestic violence or partner abuse; and parental responsibilities.	

7	Lifestyle and associates	• Section 7 deals with the offender's lifestyle and associates and incorporates both quantitative scoring and qualitative detail. • There are four core questions within this section: regular activities encouraging offenders (e.g. leisure activities creating opportunities to offend); how easily influenced they are by criminal associates; manipulative and/or predatory lifestyle (e.g. does the offender exploit others or abuse friendships, relationships or positions of trust); finally, does the offender engage in reckless or risk-taking behaviour (e.g. excessive thrill-seeking and risk-taking behaviour, intolerance for boring unchallenging situations).	Static
8	Drug misuse	• The drug misuse section provides a list of drugs in order to find out whether the offender has ever misused drugs in custody or in the community. • This list (currently section 8.1) incorporates all the main categories of drugs – from heroin to crack to solvents and steroids – and the assessor completes each category with a drop-down box with a 'yes', 'no' or 'occasionally' response choice. • The answers in section 8.1 are also split into current and previous usage. • The answers in 8.1 inform the scoring of the questions 8.4 to 8.9 which include: current drug (from section 8.1 with class A drugs scoring 2 and class B and C scoring 0); level of drug use; whether the offender ever injected drugs; motivation to tackle drug misuse; and whether drug use and obtaining drugs is a major activity for the offender.	Mainly static but some dynamic
9	Alcohol misuse	• This section deals with the offender's alcohol misuse and incorporates both quantitative scoring and qualitative information. • Questions include whether current drinking habits are problematic; binge drinking or excessive use of alcohol in the last six months; frequency and level of alcohol misuse in the past; whether violent behaviour can be related to alcohol use at any time; and whether the offender is motivated to tackle alcohol misuse.	Mainly static with minor dynamic
10	Emotional well-being	• Section 10 deals with the offender's emotional wellbeing and includes a number of quantitative scoring questions such as: whether they experience difficulties coping (e.g. emotional instability or stress, feeling low or anxious); current psychological problems or depression; social isolation (does the offender lack close friends or associates, etc.); offender's attitude to themselves; self-harm, attempted suicide, suicidal thoughts or feelings; and any current psychiatric problems.	Mainly static but some minor dynamic

Table 6.1 continues overleaf

145

No.	Section description	Contents/details	Static or dynamic
		• There is also a list of questions relating to medical and psychiatric issues, which includes evidence of childhood behavioural problems; history of severe head injuries; history of psychiatric treatment; medication for mental health problems; whether the offender has ever failed to cooperate with psychiatric treatment and so forth.	
11	Thinking and behaviour	• This section reviews the offender's thought processes linked to offending behaviour and attitudes. Like the previous sections it mainly uses quantitative scoring, with a section at the end for qualitative detail. • Questions in this section include: level of interpersonal skill; impulsivity; aggressive and/or controlling behaviour; temper control; ability to recognise problems; problem-solving skills; awareness of consequences; whether the offender sets and achieves adequate goals; understanding of other people's views; and whether the offender has concrete and/or abstract thinking.	Static
12	Attitudes	• Section 12 deals with the offender's attitudes to offending, punishment, supervision and general society, based upon six core quantitative scoring questions. • Areas covered include: pro-criminal attitudes attitudes towards staff (i.e. custodial and supervisory staff); attitudes towards supervision and licence; attitudes towards the community and society; the offender's understanding of their motivations for offending; and finally, whether the offender is motivated to address their offending.	Mainly static with some dynamic
13	Health and other considerations	• The final section examines a range of health and other considerations that may impact upon the offender's supervision and criminality. • Questions here (currently section 13.1) relate to such issues as the offender's general health; electronic monitoring (e.g. does it have an adverse effect on others at the address); whether there is fixed telephone and electricity supply at the offender's address etc.	Static and dynamic

offender is likely to: cause serious harm to others, to staff or prisoners, or to themselves; to be a risk in respect of escape/absconding, control or breach of trust; and to be at risk because of their vulnerability. RSHS consists of three components. First is the basic screening, which allows for a brief identification process, using drop-down box menus, with the following five 'screening checklists':

1 Information from other sections of OASys and risk of serious harm to others (Section R1).
2 Risks to children (R2).
3 Risks to the individual (R3).
4 Other risks (R4).
5 Other information (R5).

Second is the risk of serious harm full analysis, which follows from any risks identified in any of the sections noted above (the full analysis of sections R1 to R5). It is here that the service user should fill in as much qualitative detail as possible, from 'all available information' (quoted from the OASys form). Reviewing a number of OASys reports, I found that this is the opportunity for the assessor to investigate the offender's profile of current behaviour (section R6.1) and previous behaviour (R6.2), and to be able to move beyond a simple risk score and category. The third and final component is the risk of serious harm summary. The summary includes a brief breakdown of who is at risk; what the nature of that risk is; when the risk is likely to be greatest; what circumstance could increase the risk; and finally, the factors that could reduce the risk. Following from this is a section dealing with management issues, which includes an overview of the risk management plan (RMP). The RMP has become an important tool for quality control within NOMS, and there are strict guidelines as to the type and range of information to be included here.

As with many contemporary bureaucratic protocols, OASys is usually undertaken using a specialised computer programme. Despite being part of the official structure, there are differences across MAPPA areas in both the level and how OASys is completed, especially the RSHS (see Morton 2009a; Kemshall and Wood 2009: 539). Training in Hampshire tends to suggest that the probation officer who is completing the assessment should interview the offender, write notes and then enter the responses into OASys soon afterwards.[5] After each section is completed, practitioners click the completed box and this locks the section. What this means for actual practice is that if changes need to be made because of a change in circumstances, or new information is provided, the officer has to undertake a new OASys assessment. This can become time-consuming and because this is often combined with a high caseload and stretched resources, I know many probation officers who do not add important pieces of information in order to save time (or indeed because they do not have enough time to do so). However, 'locking' sections is required so that the programme can start its statistical wizardry. The basis on which a computer can calculate these probabilities is, of course, through the use of quantitative data. The majority of responses are coded into the following categories:

- No problems (score 0)
- Some problems (score 1)
- Significant problems (score 2)
- Missing/Explanation unknown/Unavailable (M), Disclosure (D).

A number of sections present numerical range categories and a related score for each range. For example, in the Offending Information section, which works out OGRS 3, question 1.7 asks the age at first conviction. The range categories are 18+ (score 0), 14–17 (score 1), under 14 (score 2). The point of all this categorisation and scoring is to enable a quantitative statistical analysis to be undertaken. The thinking behind this type of analysis is rooted in the actuarial paradigm (discussed briefly above); and follows from the belief that complex human behaviour can be reduced to a range of criminogenic risk variables and standardised with coded scores. This can also be linked to the debate in social sciences, such as sociology and psychology, between the positivists and humanists (Swingewood 1991; Macionis and Plummer 2002). However, this debate is redundant and to be honest is somewhat reductively ridiculous, as I personally follow Denzin's (1971) very clear rules on data and methodological triangulation. Unfortunately, an unintended consequence of OASys is that there is an over-reliance on the quantitative scoring when it comes to risk assessment and understanding the offender's criminality.

A common criticism of most ARAIs is that they are based solely upon static risk variables. As Craissati notes (2004: 40–51), static variables are those that are historical and cannot be altered and tend to fall under two categories: offending history and personal history. For example, offending history includes previous convictions, age at first conviction, use of force in index offence and so forth (see also Boer and Hart 2009: 32). Personal history variables include age, intelligence, and relationships/attachments. One of the reasons why OASys was developed was because of the dissatisfaction with previous risk assessment models that only used static risk information (see Howard *et al.* 2006; Kemshall 2003; Andrews and Bonta 1995). It was with this problem in mind that OASys has been championed, due to the fact that it provides a range of questions that deal with both static and dynamic risk variables. Dynamic variables are generally seen to be those factors that contribute to an offender's criminality, which change or are 'amenable to deliberate intervention' (Craissati 2004: 52). According to Hanson and Harris (1998, in Craisatti 2004: 52) there are generally two main categories of dynamic variables: stable and acute. Stable risk factors tend to persist for months or years and include intimacy deficits, attitudes (whether it's pro-offending or distorted views), sexual self-regulation and so forth. Acute dynamic risk factors, on the other hand, may last for only days or minutes: for example, negative interpersonal interaction and accommodation issues. Despite including dynamic risk variables, we can see from Table 6.1 that OASys is still dominated by static factors and this is not the only criticism of the assessment tool.

Criticisms of OASys

One of the first issues to assess is how dynamic variables are conceptualised and operationalised. It must be remembered that the range of questions in

OASys have been chosen because there is some empirical research that supports their inclusion. I discuss this evidence briefly below. What is important here is the issue of stable and acute dynamic variables and how we view them across the spectrum of offender management. One of the common themes to emerge from my analysis of SFO cases (see Nash and Williams 2008: 183–249) was the failure of assessors to identify changes in dynamic variables and take appropriate action. In short, once an OASys assessment was undertaken, first by the prison service and then by probation, it was very rare that it was updated as new information became available. Of course, concerns about offenders' behaviour *are* raised within probation teams, with line managers and other agencies involved in the management of the offender. However, the subtle changes that occur over various time periods and compound to eventually lead to further offending are often not analysed or incorporated into OASys. There are some obvious resource and caseload management issues that will affect a probation officer's ability to do this. This problem relates to 'operationalising' a risk variable, or, in non-academic speak, what you do with the information you have. How the variable is conceptualised is also an important factor. Maden's (2007) excellent work will be used here by way of an example. In his work on violent offenders and mental health, Maden observes that as soon as we identify a factor as being connected to an offending *incident*, it automatically becomes a static risk factor. However, Maden argues that the identified factor might not have any influence on the next criminal incident. Indeed, he states that just because someone has a mental illness such as schizophrenia does not mean that the condition was the cause of the offending behaviour, especially if the condition was under proper control (2007: 145–51). Unfortunately, because OASys has this ready-made checklist, assessors tend to think inside the box, inside the bigger box. A good analogy here is a train journey. If you look out of the window to the horizon, you see objects relatively clearly (trees, cows, houses, etc.). However, if you look directly down at the ground all you see is a blur of objects and it's difficult to pick anything out unless the train slows down. The horizon objects are the static (and some dynamic) variables that have been identified in the offenders' lives. The blurred information could be important aspects that we miss because we are training people to look too closely at the identifiable 'horizon' factors.

A second criticism relates to the empirical evidence that supports the core sections of OASys identified in Table 6.1 (see above). O-DEAT undertook a review of all pertinent research between 2002 and 2007, as evidence to support the individual components of OASys. This research 'evidence' consists of only 33 studies after the team undertook a rapid evidence assessment (REA) (Morton 2009b: 10–11), so it seems a tad bemusing that a team who is dedicated to undertaking research on OASys did not do a full systematic review of the available empirical evidence. More importantly, we should regard the evidence supporting the core sections identified in Table 6.1 as tentative and weak, not only because it is based on 33 studies, but also because in many of the studies used there is evidence that provides both positive and negative support for the risk factor in question. For example, evidence relating to the importance of education to risk of reconviction is mixed, with no clear empirical evidence supporting the view that increasing an offender's basic educational skills reduces the likelihood of reconviction (see Hollin and Palmer 1995, in Morton 2009b: 14). If we spend time reviewing the studies used to provide 'evidence' to support the inclusion of the static or dynamic risk variables, we soon find two key methodological problems. First, the sample sizes are relatively small, so generalisation from such studies should always be tentative. Moreover, inferences that are made based on these studies are not as strong as we assume, or have been led to believe. Second, much of Morton's research uses meta-analysis studies and there are some inherent methodological problems with this type of literature research. For example, problems exist when comparing lots of different studies, when the range of research uses varying research questions, and data collection and analysis techniques. To put it another way, the studies are (often) not 'like for like'. Overall, the warning here is simple: we must look closely at the research that purports to provide empirical evidence supporting OASys risk variable categories, when this research, in places, is not that scientifically robust.

A third problem relates to the scoring of questions. Even though OASys was supposed to bring a standardised form of assessment, this is only true in relation to the questions asked. It does not include how the assessor scores a category. Yes, there are standardised scoring criteria (1 = some problems; 2 = significant problems), but the final decision is still a subjective one made by the assessor, and their decision will be based upon a range of factors including level of knowledge of offending behaviour, experience and intuition. This could potentially lead to one assessor scoring 1 for a particular question, yet if you gave that same information to another assessor their perception may be that it is a more significant problem and they would give it a score of 2. There is no way we can completely eliminate 'assessor affects and bias' in scoring risk variables; however, we must at least acknowledge that this as a potential problem and more research needs to be undertaken in this area.

A fourth issue that needs be raised is the problem with threading and linking the identified risk factors throughout the sections of OASys. I have seen a number of OASys reports where an assessor has identified a factor as being a significant influence in the offending history of an individual – alcohol misuse, for example – yet in another section of the report, where it asks if alcohol is a concern, they have responded with either a 'no' or zero scoring (meaning no problems). Consistency throughout the assessment is crucial as there is often a disparity in the practitioners' ability to link (or not link), core behaviours between each section.

Finally, it could be argued that OASys does not really provide practitioners with an understanding or profile of the individual offender's criminality, but is more a bureaucratic tool that allows criminal justice agencies to do several things: first, to justify indeterminate sentences and extend punishment without further crimes being committed (McSherry and Keyzer 2009); second, to monitor and evaluate performance, as well as provide a 'defensible' position if the offender commits a serious further offence while being managed within the public protection arena (Nash and Williams 2008; Silver and Miller 2009; Worrall and Hoy 2005). To this end there is more of an emphasis placed on simply filling in the OASys at the right time (see Morton 2009a), rather than trying to understand an offender's criminality. Perhaps it is better to view OASys as providing an important *descriptive overview* of key criminogenic influences – both static and dynamic – that can then be explored in a more individualistic and qualitative manner. However, before this can be achieved, we need to actually analyse the information collected in the many thousands of OASys reports that are completed each year, in order to reduce what I call the 'epistemological chasm' that has appeared in recent years.

Epistemological gerrymandering?

In terms of how many OASys assessments were completed, the figures speak for themselves. According to Debidin and Fairweather (2009: 4), 'during 2007/08, around 700,000 were completed on almost 350,000 offenders'. Even if we take into account that there will be a small proportion where OASys is not completed, and that others may have had more than two OASys assessments, the majority of offenders will clearly have had two assessments in total. As MAPPA deals with offenders within varying risk categories (see below), we can make a basic inference that the majority of offenders will have completed one OASys assessment in prison and one when they are released into the community (undertaken by the probation team). Therefore, my earlier point about not updating OASys as dynamic risk variables alter the level of risk and likelihood of reoffending appears to be correct. This section discusses this core issue within public protection – the widening epistemological chasm.

An epistemological chasm is appearing in our understanding of criminality.[6] *What* we know about offenders and *how* we know what we know has largely become the province of criminal justice agencies involved in public protection who do not necessarily have the skills, resources or time to conduct in-depth empirical research of the crucial socio-demographic, spatial and temporal data that they produce about offending behaviour (Boba 2005; Canter and Youngs 2009). Indeed, as noted above, even the O-DEAT itself did not have the time to conduct a full systematic research review of the empirical evidence behind OASys. While the development of multi-agency joined-up thinking should be viewed in a positive light, the benefits of this system pertaining to understanding criminality are largely being wasted. In this section three core issues are examined. The first briefly discusses the structure in which knowledge of violent and sexual criminals is produced, highlighting the different levels of offender management and the different categories of offenders that fall within MAPPA. I also draw attention to the basic processes in which knowledge about offender behaviour is produced. Second, I consider the issue of differentiation in training, which creates variations in the level of risk assessment. Not only does this result in dissimilar levels of supervision and interventions for similar offender groups, it also has implications for the type and validity of knowledge about criminality that is created from these risk assessments. Finally, I discuss what I believe to be the crux of the matter: the generation of knowledge about offenders. We are wasting a wonderful opportunity to analyse OASys assessments and MAPPA cases to produce empirical knowledge about a range of issues, including profiles of offenders' actions during the commission of their crimes; the importance of forensic evidence in identifying patterns of behaviour that could feed into understanding levels of risk; and important information regarding SFOs.

Knowledge production

The Crime and Disorder Act 1998 provided the first legislative impetus for the development of multi-agency working and the management of offenders, either after their release from a custodial sentence or as part of the range of available community sentences (Davies *et al.* 2005; Nash and Williams 2008). Since then, other pieces of legislation have further enhanced and enabled the development of end-to-end offender management (Kemshall and Wood 2009; Nash and Williams 2008). In particular, sections 67 to 69 of the Criminal Justice and Court Services Act 2000 placed a statutory requirement on local authorities to create a multi-agency public protection arrangement in each region. As the Ministry of Justice's website[7] states, the protection of the public from 'dangerous' violent and sexual offenders is the remit of NOMS (National Offender Management Service), and MAPPA sits within NOMS and incorporates a range of agencies, whose level of involvement with an offender depends primarily upon what category the offender has been placed within. *Level one*, or 'ordinary management' offenders, are subject to the usual type of management by the designated agency, whether it be probation, youth offending team (YOT) or from forensic health. *Level two* is 'active multi-agency management', and incorporates the active involvement of several agencies that manage the offender through regular MAPP meetings. Finally, *level three* offenders are again involved in active multi-agency management, similar to those at level two. The difference here is that these cases are deemed to need a higher level of management and involve senior officers who have the power to authorise the use of special resources such as police surveillance. These categories are effectively the levels of management within MAPPA (Kemshall and Wood 2009).

The level of offender management will primarily depend upon the category or type of offender that is being managed, and the categories are determined by the OASys assessment discussed above. Category one offenders are registered sex offenders (RSO) and comprise the bulk of offenders managed through MAPPA (31,392 for 2007/08 figures); category two are violent or other sexual offenders (16,240 for 2007/08); and finally, category three offenders come under the salubrious title of other dangerous offenders (2,569 for 2007/08). Offenders are placed into specific categories, in the first instance, based upon their legal offence category. For example, section 327(2) of the Criminal Justice Act 2003 defines RSOs; and section 327 (3, 4 and 5) of the Criminal Justice Act 2003 defines violent or other sexual offenders. There are, of course, many problems with using legal constructions of illegal behaviour. Fielding's (2006) excellent ethnography of courtroom dynamics in cases of 'violence against the person', demonstrates how the successful prosecution of violent behaviour *ergo* its final legal classification, involves a complex interplay between various discursive and structural elements. Some of these include the level and context of documentation of the violent event, lay-participants (such as witnesses and experts) and their understanding and interpretation of these events; the language used in the courtroom; as well as legal and courtroom principles and protocols. Furthermore, we must take into account plea-bargaining. The official offence that becomes that static variable 'previous convictions' may not adequately reflect the offender's actual behaviour during the commission of the crime. Thus, the offender that comes to MAPPA as a category one, two or three offender has been through a process that has filtered important behavioural crime actions that will undoubtedly affect our understanding of that individual's criminality.

Despite these undoubtedly important issues, what the MAPPA structure generates, through assessment techniques such as OASys, is a rich range of data covering a multitude of criminogenic risk factors. Unfortunately, this immense 'data-pool' is not being efficiently exploited for the enhancement of epistemological knowledge pertaining to criminality. There are two core reasons why this is not happening – training and research.

Training and research

Anecdotal and observational evidence collected over the last seven years of this author's involvement with MAPPA, both in research and in training over 350 practitioners, suggests that there is a disparity in the levels and types of training between the criminal justice agencies involved in MAPPA and MAPPPs (multi-agency public protection panels). The epistemological issue produced from this problem is that despite having a standardised assessment tool, there is a serious differentiation in the ways in which risk assessments are undertaken *and* the types of knowledge of 'criminality' that are subsequently produced. One example of the disparity between training levels was observed during a training session, when a member of the MAPPA administrative and training team reported that some areas admitted to her that they didn't even undertake separate MAPPA or OASys training for new personnel starting within these arrangements.[8] If the number of serious further offences weren't enough to place this observation into a serious context (Nash and Williams 2008), recent research also supports the above observation. For example, Morton's (2009a: 1) findings indicate that in several core sections of OASys, similar offenders may be assessed differently and will therefore receive different levels of supervision and interventions. From a purely academic perspective, a key objective is to try to formulate a risk assessment based upon inferences made about an offender, which when undertaken time and time again produces similar results across offender and crime specific groups (Canter and Youngs 2009: 20). A more standardised and systematic approach to training will help to achieve this.

The core problem is that while bureaucratic rules and regulations, and technological advances, have increased the range and type of information that is recorded and stored about an offender, little empirical research is being undertaken on this rich pool of offender, victim and offence data. This is not a new problem. As Canter and Youngs (2009: 73) noted in their discussion of investigative databases, it is rare for law enforcement agencies to recognise the research potential of their databases. This criticism can also be applied to the multiple agencies involved in MAPPA. Because many of the computer information systems between agencies are different, there is little systematic empirical research undertaken on the data held, and there is a lack of collaboration between agencies and researchers, with the gate-keepers of this information (criminal justice agencies) failing to identify the potential benefits of opening up databases for collaborative empirical study. This is also a view shared by Carson and Carson, and Grieve (both in this volume). Grieve, for example, highlights the benefits of a full analysis of risk identification, assessment and management intelligence through models such as comparative case analysis (CCA). Now this is not to ignore the good work done by O-DEAT, who undertake research work on OASys. Unfortunately, a quick trawl through their compendium of research and analysis (Debidin 2009) highlights that the majority of this research relates to issues such as inter-rater reliability, the predictive validity of OASys and research into core factors like lifestyle/associates and offending-related problems. The range of quantitative studies is quite impressive. Unfortunately, it is not possible to reduce complex human risks and criminal actions to an equation and more research could be done. Sadly, one of the core reasons blocking such research being undertaken is what Abbott eloquently called the control over jurisdictional boundaries:

> Control of knowledge and its application means dominating outsiders who attack that control ... The professions, that is, make up an interdependent system. In this system each profession has its activities under various kinds of jurisdiction. Sometimes it has full control, sometimes control subordinate to another group. Jurisdictional boundaries are perpetually in dispute, both in local practice and national claims. It is the history of jurisdictional disputes that is the real, determining history of the professions. (Abbott 1988: 2)

Another problem stopping research is the difficulty of information disclosure and sharing between agencies. At a recent briefing on the police failures within MAPPA regarding the Dano Sonnex case (Hampshire HQ, Netley, 12 February 2010), the theme of 'non-existent information sharing' came up yet again. The DCI who was in charge of overseeing the review of procedures in the Metropolitan Police after this case was very honest in his assessment of the difficulties caused by the police in not sharing information across agencies, which resulted in the horrific murders of Laurent Bonomo and Gabriel Ferez. Unfortunately, this is a message that has been a core problem for multi-agency working for the last ten years, and I wonder if it is the right message to emphasise. It seems to me that most personnel who work within a multi-agency framework understand that information must be shared, even if they don't always do so. I believe that while we should continue to push the message that information sharing is necessary, we also need to examine more carefully what is done with that information once it is shared. You can only act on information pertaining to risk factors if you understand what you have got in front of you. Understanding the relevant intelligence or data that is either discovered or given to you involves the issue of enhanced training and research. A hypothetical example illustrates this point. If one wants to understand a set of idiographic information (Turvey 2008: 76) of child abuse and neglect, in order to generate a much more nomothetic profile of this type of social problem, one should use methodological triangulation (Denzin 1971). For example, one could use methods such as narrative action systems, smallest space analysis (SSA) (see Canter and Youngs 2009) and behavioural evidence analysis (Turvey 2008) to identify and analyse action patterns in the abuse, thereby identifying dominant criminogenic risk factors that could aid in creating a more robust risk assessment and management plan. In short, from this empirical analysis one may be able to determine a more holistic understanding of the individual case that is supported by robust empirical evidence. Prevention strategies can then be suggested to reduce or resolve the case in hand. Below are just a few examples of where research on the data-pool created within MAPPA and through OASys assessments could be conducted.

- **An aggregate analysis of OASys information** – where identified index offences are aggregated and data is analysed across the range of this type of offence/offenders. For example, all rapes could be collated to see what types of patterns emerge between the thirteen core sections of OASys. It may be that we are able to identify the common risk factors among this group of offenders, which could then be used to provide a more detailed examination of these factors.

- **Longitudinal analysis** – where an offender is reconvicted we can compare and contrast details from the original index offence to the latest offence to see if any similar risk factors emerge. The usefulness of this method enables us to see trends in risk factors over longer periods of time that could feed back into training service users on how to better spot acute dynamic risk factors.

- **Equivocal forensic analysis and offender profiling** – using the methods of investigative psychology, such as narrative action systems, multi-dimensional scaling and SSA (see Canter and Youngs 2009; Howitt 2009) and behavioural evidence analysis (Turvey 2008), the identification of salient forensic case details could be used to examine behaviour before, during and after the offence. Working out an offender's *modus operandi* through crime scene characteristics enables a stronger understanding of the possible level of harm for future offending behaviour. Forensic information also relies on more scientifically robust data collection and analysis methodologies.

- **A full analysis of all SFO cases** – instead of providing in-depth analysis of public inquiries into SFOs, where some core findings are sometimes fed back into training, an analysis of all SFOs that take place could be undertaken. This could lead to a more detailed understanding of the types of problems that exist within the offenders' lives, as well as identify any pertinent changes to important risk factors. It would also pinpoint key organisational failures (some researchers have already begun to explore this area – see Ansbro 2006a, 2006b).

Conclusions

The growth of the actuarial age has been crucial for how we manage offenders in the community and protect the public from the various risks of serious harm. The myriad of actuarial risk assessment instruments that have developed over the last 60 years have used a broad range of empirical research that identify specific static and dynamic risk factors, enabling us to predict, to a certain extent, the likelihood of an individual reoffending. Recently, ARAIs have also tried to incorporate predictions about risk of serious harm. This tries to identify the level of harm – the seriousness of the crime incident – once an offender does reoffend. Obviously this can lead to an automatic assumption that the offender *will* offend, which brings us into the realms of science fiction and of 'pre-crime'; something we should all try to avoid. However, public protection from the so-called 'dangerous' violent and sexual offenders uses the MAPPA framework and OASys risk assessment tool to make predictions using evidence-based research. The selling point of OASys has always been how it combines static and dynamic risk variables in its prediction algorithm. Unfortunately, the problems with OASys cannot be ignored and we really need to consider how making a checklist out of complex human behaviours and interactions makes OASys predictions more accurate. I am not arguing for a complete abandonment of the tool, for it is a strong development within the criminal justice system. What I am suggesting is that we use this largely quantitative ARAI in conjunction with more qualitative methodologies and research. What also needs to be examined is how OASys can lead to a deskilling of practitioners, preverting them from developing key analytical skills for understanding criminality.

Research is the key here. The rationalisation of risk through bureaucratic rational-legal domination means countless paperwork and while that paperwork is the bane of many of our lives it does have one benefit: it produces mountains and mountains of data. This data needs to be examined and researched. Organisations may fight over their jurisdictional boundaries within the multi-agency approach to public protection, but they must remember that they are public servants and are there at the behest of society. I have introduced in this chapter some core ideas of why research is so important in public protection. While some sceptical readers may see these ideas as being ideal-type, Neverland fantasies, the message still holds true: the importance of using the empirical evidence that is kept in computer databases to identify risk factors and inform prevention strategies. By ignoring the research potential, a wonderful opportunity to develop our stock of knowledge of specific offending populations and their criminal actions is largely being missed. Fortunately, over the last ten years researchers have begun making inroads and things are looking more positive. However, it is still important to ensure that decisions are based upon evidence that is supported by empirically robust methodological and theoretical techniques. This is even more crucial if we consider that the current risk assessment tool used in MAPPA, OASys, is an actuarial measure and therefore relies on our nomothetic understanding of criminal groups. Surely, we need to be constantly updating the nomothetic data-pool with more data to ensure that these techniques become more and more scientifically robust. Opening up these databases for systematic longitudinal empirical research is one way this robustness can be achieved.

Selected further reading

For a thorough review of the development of actuarial risk assessments see Harcourt's (2007) excellent *Against Prediction*, a text that is also of great use when examining the core issues pertaining to racial profiling. McSherry and Keyzer (2009) provide a succinct overview of three interesting cases of sex offenders, and consider the issues of risk assessment, punishment and the problems with striking a balance between offenders' civil liberties and the victims' human rights. For a comprehensive review on the research behind OASys see Debidin (2009). As usual Kemshall's (e.g. 2003) work provides a very good starting point for understanding risk assessment within the context of MAPPA. Finally, for an interesting analytical framework for understanding 'risky' individuals using the idiographic method, see Turvey's *Criminal Profiling* (2008).

Notes

1 Unfortunately, it is not within the remit of this current chapter to explore these influences in any great detail. For those interested in such matters, please refer to the cited works.
2 Before MAPPA became the umbrella term, multi-agency public protection panels (MAPPPs) was the dominant term. MAPPPs have since become a sub-unit of the broader MAPPA structure.
3 www.noms.justice.gov.uk/protecting-the-public/risk-assessment/ (accessed 27 January 2010).
4 The work of the Chicago School as well as other ethnographies during the period 1920 to 1970 demonstrates this. For example see the work of Polsky (1998), Pryce (1979), Liebow (1967), Foote Whyte (1993) – just a few of the many examples of the richness in detail in ethnographic work.
5 Private communication with PSO (4 December 2009).
6 The term 'criminality' is used here to denote the 'stable differences across individuals in the propensity to commit criminal (or equivalent) acts' (Gottfredson and Hirschi, 1984, in Wilson and Herrnstein 1998: 23).
7 www.noms.justice.gov.uk/protecting-the-public/supervision/mappa/ (accessed 10 January 2010).
8 Observational notes, 18 January 2010.

References

Abbott, A. (1988) *The System of Professions: An Essay on the Division of Expert Labour.* Chicago: University of Chicago Press.

Andrews, D. A. and Bonta, J. L. (1995) *LSI-R: The Level of Service Inventory – Revised.* Toronto: Multi-Health Systems.

Ansbro, M. (2006a) 'What can we learn from serious incident reports', *Probation Journal*, 53(1): 57–70.

Ansbro, M. (2006b) 'Serious further offence inquiry', *Probation Journal*, 53(2): 167–96.

Beck, U. (1992) *Risk Society: Towards a New Modernity*. London: Sage.

Becker, H. (1963) *Outsiders: Studies in the Sociology of Deviance*. New York: Macmillan.

Boba, R. (2005) *Crime Analysis and Crime Mapping*. London: Sage.

Boer, D. P. and Hart, S. D. (2009) 'Sex offender risk assessment: research, evaluation, "best-practice" recommendations and future directions', in J. L. Ireland, C. A. Ireland and P. Birch (eds) *Violent and Sexual Offenders: Assessment, Treatment and Management*. Cullompton: Willan Publishing (pp. 27–42).

Brown, M. and Pratt, J. (2000) *Dangerous Offenders: Punishment and Social Order*. London: Routledge.

Bulmer, M. (1986) *The Chicago School of Sociology: Institutionaization, Diversity and the Rise of Sociological Research*. Chicago: University of Chicago Press.

Burgess, E. W. (1929) 'Is prediction feasible in social work? An inquiry based upon a sociological study of parole records', *Social Forces*, 7(4): 533–45.

Callinicos, A. (1996) *Against Postmodernism: A Marxist Critique*. New York: St Martin's Press.

Canter, D. and Youngs, D. (2009) *Investigative Psychology: Offender Profiling and the Analysis of Criminal Action*. Chichester: John Wiley.

Carol, A. (1994) *Nudes, Prudes and Attitudes: Pornography and Censorship*. Cheltenham: New Clarion Press.

Cohen, S. (1985) *Visions of Social Control: Crime, Punishment and Classification*. Cambridge: Polity Press.

Cohen, S. (1987) *Folk Devils and Moral Panics: The Creation of the Mods and Rockers*, 2nd edn. Oxford: Blackwell.

Cohen, S. (2002) *Folk Devils and Moral Panics: The Creation of the Mods and Rockers*, 3rd edn. London: Routledge.

Conrad, P. and Schneider, J. (1992) *Deviance and Medicalization: From Badness to Sickness*. Philadelphia: Temple University Press.

Craissati, J. (2004) *Managing High Risk Sex Offenders in the Community: A Psychological Approach*. London: Routledge.

Davies, M., Croall, H. and Tyrer, J. (2005) *Criminal Justice: An Introduction to the Criminal Justice System in England and Wales*, 3rd edn. Harlow: Pearson Education.

Debidin, M. (ed.) (2009) *A Compendium of Research and Analysis on the Offender Assessment System (OASys) 2006–2009*, Ministry of Justice Research Series 16/09. London: Ministry of Justice.

Debidin, M. and Fairweather, L. (2009) 'Introduction to OASys and research on OASys 2006 to 2009', in M. Debidin (ed.) *A Compendium of Research and Analysis on the Offender Assessment System (OASys) 2006–2009*, Ministry of Justice Research Series 16/09. London: Ministry of Justice.

Denzin, N. (1971) 'The logic of naturalistic inquiry', *Social Forces*, 50(2): 166–82.

Downes, D. and Rock, P. (1995) *Understanding Deviance: A Guide to the Sociology of Crime and Rule-breaking*, 2nd edn. Oxford: Oxford University Press.

Downes, D. and Rock, P. (2007) *Understanding Deviance: A Guide to the Sociology of Crime and Rule-breaking*, 5th edn. Oxford: Oxford University Press.

Fielding, N. G. (2006) *Courting Violence: Offences Against the Person Cases in Court*. Oxford: Oxford University Press.

Foote Whyte, W. (1993) *Street Corner Society: The Social Structure of an Italian Slum*, 4th edn. Chicago: University of Chicago Press.

Garland, D. (1994) 'Of crimes and criminals: the development of criminology in Britain', in M. Maguire, R. Morgan and R. Reiner (eds) *The Oxford Handbook of Criminology*. Oxford: Oxford University Press (pp. 17–68).

Garland, D. (2001) *The Culture of Control: Crime and Social Order in Contemporary Society*. Oxford: Oxford University Press.

Gerth, H. H. and Mills, C. W. (1993) *From Max Weber: Essays in Sociology*. London: Routledge.

Goffman, E. (1986) *Frame Analysis: An Essay on the Organization of Experience*. Boston, MA: Northeastern University Press.

Gottfredson, M. and Hirschi, T. (2004) *A General Theory of Crime*. California: Stanford University Press.

Harcourt, B. E. (2007) *Against Prediction: Profiling, Policing, and Punishment in an Actuarial Age*. Chicago: University of Chicago Press.

Harkins, L. and Beech, A. (2009) 'Assessing the therapeutic needs of sexual offenders', in J. L. Ireland, C. A. Ireland and P. Birch, P. (eds) *Violent and Sexual Offenders: Assessment, Treatment and Management*. Cullompton: Willan Publishing (pp. 97–131.

Harvey, D. (1990) *The Condition of Postmodernity: An Enquiry into the Origins of Cultural Change*. Oxford: Blackwell.

Howard, P., Francis, B., Soothill, K. and Humphreys, L. (2009) *OGRS 3: The Revised Offender Group Reconviction Scale*. Online at: www.justice.gov.uk/publications/docs/oasys-research-summary-07-09-ii.pdf (accessed 4 October 2009).

Howard, P., Clark, D. and Garnham, N. (2006) *An Evaluation of the Offender Assessment System (OASys) in Three Pilots 1999–2001*. London: Home Office.

Howitt, D. (2009) *Introduction to Forensic and Criminal Psychology*, 3rd edn. Harlow: Pearson Education.

Hudson, B. (2003) *Justice in the Risk Society*. London: Sage.

Jenkins, P. (1998) *Moral Panic: Changing Concepts of the Child Molester in Modern America*. New Haven: Yale University Press.

Kemshall, H. (2003) *Understanding Risk in Criminal Justice*. Maidenhead: Open University Press.

Kemshall, H. and Wood, J. (2009) 'Community strategies for managing high-risk offenders: the contribution of multi-agency public protection arrangements', in A. R. Beech, L. A. Craig and K. D. Browne (eds) *Assessment and Treatment of Sex Offenders: A Handbook*. Chichester: John Wiley.

Liebow, E. (1967) *Tally's Corner: A Study of Negro Streetcorner Men*. Boston, MA: Little, Brown.

Macionis, J. and Plummer, K. (2002) *Sociology: A Global Introduction*. London: Prentice Hall.

Maden, A. (2007) *Treating Violence: A Guide to Risk Management in Mental Health*. Oxford: Oxford University Press.

Matthews, R. and Young, J. (2003) *The New Politics of Crime and Punishment*. Cullompton: Willan Publishing.

McSherry, B. and Keyzer, P. (2009) *Sex Offenders and Preventive Detention: Politics, Policy and Practice*. Australia: Federation Press.

Morton, S. (2009a) *Findings from the Measurement of OASys Completion Rates*. Ministry of Justice Research Summary 4/09. London: Ministry of Justice.

Morton, S. (2009b) 'The current evidence base for the offending-related risk factors included in OASys', in M. Debidin (ed.) *A Compendium of Research and Analysis on the Offender Assessment System (OASys) 2006–2009*, Ministry of Justice Research Series 16/09. London: Ministry of Justice.

Nash, M. (1999) *Police, Probation and Protecting the Public*. London: Blackstone Press.

Nash, M. (2006) *Public Protection and the Criminal Justice Process*. Oxford: Oxford University Press.

Nash, M. and Williams, A. (2008) *The Anatomy of Serious Further Offending*. Oxford: Oxford University Press.

NPS (2003) *OASys: The New Offender Assessment System*. Online at: www.probation. homeoffice.gov.uk/files/pdf/Info for sentencers 3.pdf (accessed 22 February 2010).

Ohlin, L. E. (1951) *Selection for Parole: A Manual of Parole Prediction*. New York: Russell Sage Foundation.

Parkin, F. (1993) *Max Weber*. London: Routledge.

Pearson, G. (1975) *The Deviant Imagination: Psychiatry, Social Work and Social Change*. Basingstoke: Macmillan.

Pearson, G. (1983) *Hooligan: A History of Respectable Fears*. London: Macmillan.

Polsky, N. (1998) *Hustlers, Beats, and Others*. New York: Lyons Press.

Prins, H. (2007) *Offenders, Deviants or Patients?*, 3rd edn. London: Routledge.

Pryce, K. (1979) *Endless Pressure: A Study of West Indian Life-Styles in Bristol*. London: Penguin.

Rice, S. A. (1929) 'Some inherent difficulties in the method of prediction by classification', *Social Forces*, 7(4): 554–8.

Roberts, C., Burnett, R., Kirby, A. and Hamill, H. (1996) *A System for Evaluating Probation Practice*, Probation Studies Unit Report 1. Oxford: Oxford Centre for Criminological Research.

Scott, P. (1977) 'Assessing dangerousness in criminals', *British Journal of Psychiatry*, 131: 127–42.

Shaw, K. (1987) 'Skills, control and the mass professions', *Sociological Review*, 35: 775–93.

Silver, E. and Miller, L. L. (2009) 'A cautionary note on the use of actuarial risk assessment tools for social control', *Crime and Delinquency*, 48(1): 138–61.

Spencer, H. (1893a) *Principles of Sociology: Vol I*. London: Harrison and Sons.

Spencer, H. (1893b) *Principles of Sociology: Vol II*. London: Harrison and Sons.

Stenson, K. and Sullivan, R. R. (2001) *Crime, Risk and Justice: The Politics of Crime Control in Liberal Democracies*. Cullompton: Willan Publishing.

Stratton, A. (2010) 'Edlington case is symptom of "broken society", says David Cameron'. Online at: www.guardian.co.uk/politics/2010/jan/22/david-cameron-edlington-broken-society (accessed 23 January 2010).

Swingewood, A. (1991) *A Short History of Sociological Thought*. Basingstoke: Macmillan Press.

Taylor, R., Wasik, M. and Leng, R. (2004) *Blackstone's Guide to the Criminal Justice Act 2003*. Oxford: Oxford University Press.

Thompson, W. (1994) *Soft Core: Moral Crusades Against Pornography in Britain and America*. London: Cassell.

Turvey, B. E. (2008) *Criminal Profiling: An Introduction to Behavioural Evidence Analysis*, 3rd edn. San Diego, CA: Academic Press.

Weber, M. (1978) *Economy and Society, Vol 1: An Outline of Interpretive Sociology*. Berkeley, CA: University of California Press.

Weber, M. (1992) *The Protestant Ethic and the Spirit of Capitalism*. London: Routledge.

Wilkins, L. (1964) *Social Deviance: Social Policy Action and Research*. London: Tavistock Publications.

Williams, A. (2004) '"There Ain't No Peds in Paulsgrove": Social Control, Vigilantes and the Misapplication of Moral Panic Theory', unpublished PhD Thesis, University of Reading.

Williams, A. and Thompson, B. (2004a) 'Vigilance or vigilantes: the Paulsgrove riots and policing paedophiles in the community, Part 1: The long slow fuse', *Police Journal*, 77(2): 99–119.

Williams, A. and Thompson, B. (2004b) 'Vigilance or vigilantes: the Paulsgrove riots and policing paedophiles in the community, Part 2: The lessons of Paulsgrove', *Police Journal*, 77(3): 193–205.

Wilson, J. and Herrnstein, R. (1998) *Crime and Human Nature: The Definitive Study of the Causes of Crime*. New York: Free Press.

Worrall, A. and Hoy, C. (2005) *Punishment in the Community: Managing Offenders, Making Choices*, 2nd edn. Cullompton: Willan Publishing.

Wortley, R. and Mazerolle, L. (2008) 'Environmental criminology and crime analysis: situating the theory, analytic approach and application', in R. Wortley and L. Mazerolle (eds) *Environmental Criminology and Crime Analysis*. Cullompton: Willan Publishing (pp. 1–18).

Young, J. (1971) *The Drugtakers: The Social Meaning of Drug Use*. London: MacGibbon and Kee.

Young, J. (2003) 'Winning the fight against crime? New Labour, populism and lost opportunities', in R. Matthews and J. Young (eds) *The New Politics of Crime and Punishment*, Cullompton: Willan Publishing (pp. 33–47).

Young, J. and Matthews, R. (2003) 'New Labour crime control and social exclusion', in R. Matthews and J. Young (eds) *The New Politics of Crime and Punishment*, Cullompton: Willan Publishing (pp. 1–32).

Chapter 7

Public protection: perpetrators, predictions, prevention and performance

David Carson and Tim Carson

Introduction

A number of people, in a range of professions, are employed to take risk decisions, within legal contexts, to protect the public from harm. They rely upon the extensive research into, discussion of and policy development relating to risk, danger, etc, as demonstrated by this volume (see Nash 2006). A high proportion of that research seeks to enhance our ability to identify the people who are, and the occasions when they are, more or less dangerous. It involves traditional empirical research, where the significance of different factors are investigated and compared. It allows us to make some of the inductive inferences involved in risk predictions. Researchers can focus on 'the risk', but practitioners have to make decisions. Knowing about 'the risk' 'in' a particular person, setting or event, is certainly helpful. But it only informs part of the decision. Not only must practitioners draw upon risk factor research, based upon the behaviour of other people, in other settings, but they must apply it to their unique clients within the context of a particular setting and plan to implement, control and review their decision. Practitioners need guidance on risk decision-making, implementation, control and learning from review processes.

This distinction may appear trivial, or petty. It may be argued that once the implications of the research for the particular case have been discovered and applied, then the decision follows. But that is, dangerously, wrong. Consider, for example, how 'risk' is generally understood. Many dictionaries, research studies (for example, Prins 1999) and authoritative texts (Royal Society 1992), assume that 'risk' only refers to the chance of harm or other loss. But public protection professionals, invariably, have to compare and contrast the potential harm and the possible benefits of their proposed risk decision. Should the Parole Board recommend that a life sentence prisoner be moved into a category D prison, where he will have a better chance of gaining skills necessary for making a success of eventual life outside prison, but also have a greater chance to abscond? Public protection, among much else, necessarily involves seeking to contain danger at minimal cost to taxpayers. A consequence of this too rarely challenged assumption is that there has been comparatively little research on likelihood of success factors. These are features of the person or setting that make it more or less likely that the goals sought (such as pre-release skills), will be achieved. 'Success' factors are not the same as 'protective' risk factors, which are, increasingly, being identified. 'Protective' factors identify reasons why *harm* is less likely to occur; 'success' factors identify when the potential benefits might be achieved. Beneficial goals should be sought both for their own value as well as potential justifications to balance against the chances of harm.

The extant research has also focused on risk assessment to the comparative detriment of risk management. Practitioners may be informed by a risk assessment but they must go on to make and implement a decision. For example, they may decide that it is 'safe enough' to manage a man, assessed as being a particular degree of danger, in the community. But they need to go on to consider which forms of control are necessary, or desirable, in order to implement their decision. This decision could include where he is to live, where and what he may and may not go and do, and the people with the skills and knowledge needed to support, supervise and intervene if necessary. The risk decision-makers must know about the quantity and quality of resources, including colleagues' skills, available to implement those controls. Just as we rely upon doctors and nurses to acknowledge when they have insufficient skills or knowledge, so must risk decision-makers be able to rely upon others to acknowledge their limits, and in advance (failure to do so is, in both professions, liable to constitute negligence).

The current research on risk assessment (for example, into risk factors) has had the advantage of being apolitical. It fits readily within traditional expectations of empirical research. But risk management is inextricably tied up with the quantity and quality of resources available. That makes it 'political' and less amenable to traditional forms of empirical academic research. A poor risk prediction can be saved by good risk management because people can intervene to make the beneficial outcomes more, and the harmful outcomes less, likely. But a good risk assessment may not survive poor implementation (see HMIP 2006). If public protection is to improve then greater focus needs to be placed on the quality of professionals' decision-making. This can be examined in terms of five 'levels', or contributions.

Five 'levels' for acting on risk and public protection

A five 'level' model, of risk decision-making, has been identified (Carson and Bain 2008). The levels identify different activities, or contributions, and actors. While the activities are distinct, the same actors may be involved at different levels. Each level will be briefly described before a more sustained discussion of some of the implications is provided. The core argument is that attention must be paid to all five levels if risk-taking, and public protection, is to improve.

Risk identification and assessment

This is the level traditionally identified and associated with risk-taking. It is where most of the research has been undertaken. It involves identifying and analysing the nature and degree of risk or danger. At its most basic it involves assessing whether, and if so to which extent (if not also when, where and why), someone poses or creates a risk or danger to themselves and/or others. For example, a prisoner has come to a point in his or her sentence and must be released soon. Will his release pose a danger to anyone? If so, what is its nature and extent? Risk assessment involves two elements: the outcomes – which may be beneficial as well as harmful – and their likelihood. It also involves some 'dimensions', in particular different degrees of uncertainty about each risk element. It is the uncertainty that makes it a risk decision rather than, for example, a mere choice. For example, some of the information about the outcomes and/or their likelihood will be more reliable than the rest. Decision-makers must consider the propriety of relying upon particular information (that is its uncertainty). However, that uncertainty does not affect the risk, in terms of altering the significance of the outcomes or their likelihood. That we have poor data about a particular risk, for example a particular airline's safety record, does not make a crash more, or less, likely to occur. But it does affect the propriety of making that decision, although the need for action (perhaps because an emergency or dilemma is involved), may invoke other dimensions (Carson and Bain 2008).

Risk management

The individual is too dangerous; all the risk factors scream so. But if sufficient resources are invested, human and otherwise, the risk can be manipulated, controlled and managed. With the individual restrained by a body belt, and surrounded by well-informed and motivated prison officers, the likelihood that he would escape and injure other people could be reduced, dramatically. That is the rationale for prisons. Of course it does not follow that that is what should be done; simply that it could. Risk assessment is just the first consideration. For example, a particular harmful outcome might be considered 'likely', but if effective supervision could be organised then it might be appropriate to reassess the likelihood as 'unlikely'. Assessments must be made within the context of a management or decision-implementation plan. Risk assessment and management are increasingly recognised to be iterative: part of an integrated and continuing decision-making process (NPB 2008; NPS 2008).

Risk decision-making

Extensive research has demonstrated the frequency with which, and some of the reasons why, we all are prone to making poor decisions (Breakwell 2007). What is the point of having even highly reliable data, on potential outcomes and their likelihood, if we are incompetent in using it? This relates not only to the common cognitive errors – such as our tendency not to vary sufficiently initial 'anchored' risk assessments in the light of new information – but also how the many people involved in multi-disciplinary assessment and action teams communicate about risk (Breakwell 2007). For example one person may assess a risk as 'serious'; the British probation service refer to 'low', 'medium', 'high' and 'very high'. Another person may agree. But it does *not* follow that they understood each other or meant the same thing. Indeed, did the expression refer to the seriousness of the feared outcome, to its perceived likelihood or an amalgam of both? This can easily be demonstrated by asking those involved to explain, in numerical terms, what they meant by each expression (Carson and Bain 2008). All the value of an individual's excellent risk prediction may be lost in the 'Chinese whispers' of communication to all the others involved in making and implementing the decision. It is vital that the main benefits and harms being predicted, their seriousness and their likelihood, are communicated effectively and efficiently. So attention must be paid to the quality of the decision-making generally. Professional risk-takers deserve practical support from their supervisors and managers.

Risk supervision and learning

Risk-taking is decision-making under uncertainty (Janis and Mann 1977). A quality public protection service would devote significant time and resources to reducing that uncertainty and increasing control by enhancing professional knowledge and technique. Someone needs to take charge of the opportunities for learning and generalising both from the research and the institutional experience of thousands upon millions of invariably successful risk decisions taken. The task is not just to improve risk assessment, but to gain knowledge about successful risk management and decision-making techniques (see Williams, this volume). It should include consideration of the many value judgements involved in public protection risk-taking. Assessing *likelihood* requires the assessor to identify the most scientific (the most likely to be correct) information. But assessing *outcomes* (for example, the importance of re-establishing marital relationships or preventing public fear), involve value judgements. Having readily identifiable professional standards upon these issues offers a 'win-win'. The practitioners know which standards to apply – thereby enabling them to adhere to the standard of care in the law of negligence – and those affected by risk decisions will have more explicit criteria against which they can decide whether and when they have legitimate grounds for complaint.

Risk systems: integration and management

The traditional focus, in public protection research and debate, is upon individual decisions and decision-makers. And when harm occurs – which is inevitable, for it would not otherwise be risk-taking – we tend to highlight the immediately preceding events as the causal culprits. Other systemic factors, such as organisational arrangements and cultures, will receive less critical attention, although poor communication is almost bound to be identified (see Hill 2009; Nash and Williams 2008). It is easier to identify individuals' contributions, and to assign blame to them, than to understand and ascribe responsibility to less directly visible factors. But that is a feature of our inadequate analyses of risk-taking processes. Someone must be responsible for ensuring that the parts, including the review processes, operate well together.

The rest of this chapter will identify some changes that could be made at each of these five levels. The principal argument remains, however, that to improve public protection we need to act on these, and many other issues, at all five levels.

Risk prediction: the event as well as the person

Rubin, Gallo and Coutts, in research by the Rand Corporation for the UK's National Audit Office (2008), noted that risk prediction, for public protection purposes, has focused upon identifying features 'in' individuals who pose concerns. That includes their behaviour, such as abuse of alcohol. This is unsurprising given that practitioners are working with and making decisions affecting individual clients or patients. But they also noted that social, cultural and time-related factors are significant. They recognised the roles of poverty, geography and alcohol, although they suggest that these may be symptoms as well as causes.

> There is no single intervention or practice that will solve the problem of violent crime. As the following discussion highlights, violence is influenced by individual, familial, peer, institutional, local community, societal, cultural and systemic factors. These various factors need to be taken into account when designing interventions to prevent crime or reduce recidivism. (Rubin *et al*. 2008: 17)

To this list, it is submitted, should be added the event of concern: that is, the violence. We could, and should, seek to predict the event as well as the person and the personal, economic, cultural and other social factors influencing them.

After extensive historical and ethnographic research, Randall Collins (2008) argues that most current risk factors only provide a *background* explanation for violence: 'some background conditions may be necessary or at least strongly predisposing, but they certainly are not sufficient; situational conditions are always necessary' (Collins 2008: 20). For Collins those criminological theories that emphasise the role of opportunities to commit crimes, and the absence of social control, are 'on the right track' (2008: 21); they emphasise the situational. But, he insists, violence will not occur unless the aggressor's situational tension and fear of violence are overcome. Even those who are assessed as being highly dangerous spend most of their time not being violent. Violence is difficult, not easy! Media representations are grotesquely inaccurate, implying that it is easier to undertake, lasts longer and involves more people than reality demonstrates. Even in war, most front-line infantry underuse their weapons. Referees in boxing contests are not so much needed to limit the violence as to stop the boxers remaining in clinches where they cannot damage each other for the edification of the paying public. 'All types of violence fit a small number of patterns for circumventing the barrier of tension and fear that rises up whenever people come into antagonistic confrontation' (Collins 2008: 8).

Collins analysed a wide range of forms of violence. He wished to avoid accusations of taking it out of its relative and social contexts. He highlights the patterns of violent behaviour. Before violence actually occurs there is a build-up of tension. There is a kind of 'balance' between the parties deterring actual violence. Only when something happens, often a 'slip' (which can be a physical 'loss of balance' or similar or just an 'emotional' change in the relationship between the protagonists), does it become safe for the aggressor to become violent. Violence is characterised by imbalances of power. Consider media descriptions of violent events, although they are often poorly reported. The aggressors are regularly more numerous or better armed (that is, with knives and other weapons) than the victims. Consider the prevalence of domestic violence and the power imbalances there. Violence is cowardly; the strong attack the weak when and largely because it is safe for them to do so. When the aggressors are safe there is a 'forward panic', an explosion of violence as the pent-up emotion is released:

> A forward panic starts with tension and fear in a conflict situation … There is a shift from relatively passive – waiting, holding back until one is in a position to bring the conflict to a head – to be fully active. When the opportunity fully arrives, the tension/fear comes out in an emotional rush … Running forward or backward, in either case they are in an overpowering emotional rhythm, carrying them on to actions that they would not normally approve of in calm, reflective moments. (Collins 2008: 85)

Violence, Collins emphasises, is situational and relational. It is of the moment and concerns the relationships the parties were and are in:

> The emotion of a forward panic … has two key characteristics. First it is a hot emotion … It comes on in a rush, explosively; it takes time to calm down … Second it is an emotion that is rhythmic and strongly entraining. Individuals in the throes of a forward panic keep repeating their aggressive actions … The emotion is flowing in self-reinforcing waves. (2008: 93)

Consider the frequency of reports of violence where the injuries inflicted go well beyond those that were 'functionally necessary' for subduing or simply harming the victim. However, Collins may overstate his case. Some violence is reported as being entirely 'irrational', which implies an absence of relationship between the aggressor and victim, for example with no time for a tension-building stage. But is that a function of the report of the incident, more concerned with judging than analysing? Do the reports take account of the aggressor's perspective? Perhaps the 'irrational' aggressor perceived events differently and seized an opportunity to act then when the balance of safety favoured him or her? Collins maintains that his analysis applies in many contexts, including within domestic violence. The aggressor needs to find a way around the situational confrontation with his or her partner, although that might be much easier (learned) after a series of aggressive acts. Men, often physically stronger, have that safety advantage. The woman's 'slip' may be a conciliatory concession.

> The pattern is to attack the weak, indeed precisely as she demonstrates her weakness, the attacker becomes entrained in her yielding. As she gives way, physically and emotionally, he presses forward ... The situational dynamic ... is pulling them deeper and deeper into the pattern of abuse. It is like a long drawn-out forward panic in its later phase ... it is the reciprocal entrainment of the cringing victim ... and the repetitive attacking we find in troops committing an atrocity against helpless foes. It does not appear to be stress-related, but rather an institutionalized game that he plays with her, a ritual in which he sets all the rhythms. (Collins 2008: 147)

This chapter argues that public protection professionals should include predictions of the event, not just the possible perpetrators, in their risk decision-making. It may, fairly, be asked how that could be possible given the difficulties in predicting which events and people an individual may become involved with over a period of time. But we can all predict what we will be doing, where, when, with whom and how, over future periods. How many confrontational relationships are we likely to get into? Those predictions, like risk decisions, will be imperfect to different degrees. But we can analyse and assess, to some degree, our and others' likely responses to any confrontations during those events. How does each individual identify and manage tense relationships? How 'skilled' is he or she in understanding what is happening, in avoiding increased confrontation, managing it, not making or acting upon 'slips'? And if capable how committed? It is not just Collins (2008); the Rand Report also emphasises the significance of interactional 'transactions'.

Other research also cites evidence for the significance of 'saving face', especially in instances in which the insulted party has low or unstable self-esteem: 'microanalyses of homicides have indicated that such crimes are most often the results of "transactions" in which the perpetrator resorted to lethal violence to resolve an argument involving emotional injury to the offender' (DeFronzo 1997: 397; Eisner 2003). David Luckenbill (1977) reported 'that such crimes are most often the outcome of a "character contest" in which one of the participants attacks the other's sense of value, worth, competency, or reputation' (in DeFronzo 1997: 23).

The most likely form of error, in a dangerousness prediction decision, is a false positive. That nobody is injured may explain why there are few complaints, but false (or erroneous) positive predictions remain examples of erroneous – *although not necessarily blameworthy* – decision-making (Carson and Bain 2008). The public, politicians and the media are much more concerned about false negatives, where danger was not predicted but harm occurred. Injuries to members of the public, particularly violence, are regularly rated as more important than the 'injuries' (such as unnecessary detention) experienced by the person considered dangerous. That value judgement can be justified (see the next section). But that cannot justify our lack of concern to learn from all forms of erroneous decisions. Improved decision-making will reduce false negatives as well as false positives. And over-predicting danger is not harm free. Not only does it impair some individuals' legal status, possibly making them less motivated to work with professionals, but it necessarily means that finite resources have been used inefficiently. Collins' insights could permit a reduction in false positive predictions of danger.

Risk management

Risk management here refers to the potential for targeting resources to influence the outcome of risk decisions. These resources take many forms. They include different quantities and qualities of people (their skill, experience, knowledge and training), equipment (for example, aids to identifying and restricting individuals' movements), places (prisons, bail hostels) and programmes (such as anger management courses). They can influence both what happens – that is, how valuable and/or serious are the consequences – and their likelihood. They include the enhanced legal powers of the police. Indeed it may be useful to think of the police as the lead authority on risk management in public protection, while others such as probation officers and others especially trained in the critically reflective use of risk factors can be seen as the leaders on risk assessment. In practice the roles will be blurred but the distinction is useful in terms of identifying responsibility for developing expertise and learning from experience.

Risk assessment and risk management need to be seen as complementary and iterative processes. This enables us to resolve the long-standing, often acrimonious, debates over the primacy of 'clinical' (individual specific) and 'actuarial' (background) risk factors. Actuarial factors, relying upon the highest quality relevant research based upon similar people and circumstances, should be used for risk assessment. 'Clinical' factors are more relevant for risk management. Clinicians and others who have worked closely with a patient or client will be in a good position to develop risk management plans tailored to the individual and his or her specific circumstances. They will also have extensive experience of the nature and quality of the local resources (people, programmes, facilities and procedures) available to manage the risk. Their skills and resources may make them (in)appropriate to manage different types and levels of challenge. Critically, risk decisions should be explicit about the resources to be invested in managing the decision, and the time for which they are considered valid.

Time is a critical risk management resource. Risk assessments are, explicitly or implicitly, made at and for a particular period of time. Individual assessments relate to the point of time when made and, implicitly, a future period (for example, the individual does not need further restriction today or during the next two weeks). But what is that future period, and for how long are risk assessments valid? More things, both beneficial (such as goals) and harmful, can occur in a longer period. So predictions for shorter periods are, just on this basis, more likely to be accurate. And the research, the evidence base for many risk assessments, is often based on relatively short periods. For example, the highly esteemed MacArthur studies of mental disorder and violence (Monahan *et al.* 2001), focused on violence in 'the 20 week period immediately after discharge because this represents the time period during which both patients appear to be at the highest risk for violence and clinicians of a mental health system might reasonably take steps to reduce the likelihood of violence after discharge' (Monahan *et al.* 2001: 35).

However, while the authority for a prediction may be research based upon a twenty-week risk period, decisions are both sought and regularly made for much longer periods. For example, under the Mental Health Act 1983 (as amended), predictions can be sought, and decisions made, for periods of detention as long as twelve or 24 months. And the Parole Board seeks predictions encompassing the rest of the offender's life. In a very real sense this is 'the system' (the legal and procedural framework for making official risk decisions) inviting/encouraging mistakes or, at least, requiring sub-optimal decision-making. Both risk assessments and decisions ought to be for an explicitly declared risk period; they should include 'best reviewed before' declarations. Public protection risk decision-makers ought to recognise this as a minimum requirement of professional practice.

Risk management is inherently 'political' in at least two senses. First, it depends upon the quantity and quality of the resources made available to support it. Fewer people, for example, need to be detained if there are sufficient quality resources to maintain them elsewhere. But it is not a simple relationship of more resources meaning fewer risks of harm. Nevertheless, the frequency with which the media and other commentators associate apparent risk-taking failures to individual officers' incompetence, rather than to insufficient resources for risk management, is remarkable. Public protection practitioners could help themselves by insisting that risk assessment and management are always recognised as integrative and iterative.

Risk management is also 'political' in that it necessarily involves difficult issues of value and principle. For example, should the emotional abuse of children be compared with the physical, and if so how? How should fear of crime be weighed, especially when irrational? People and events are not neutral; we are highly influenced by the manner in which they are presented to us, often by an uncritical media with its own agenda. So public protection risk-takers simply cannot be sure, before or at the time of making their decisions, how the issues will be perceived and understood some time later if and when the feared harmful outcomes occur. It is not just what will happen but how the value issues involved will be interpreted. Public protection professionals need to develop statements, or protocols, of 'evidence-based professional values'. These could make it markedly easier for decision-makers to justify, not just rationalise, their decisions.

Take, for example, the key issue of acceptable error rates. Only unthinking people could seriously assert that it is possible for risk decisions always to avoid harmful outcomes. (Either they do not understand that 'risk' necessarily involves uncertainty, or they have their own agendas.) But what should be regarded as an acceptable error rate? Errors can be false negatives (failures to predict a danger), or false positives (incorrectly believing and acting upon perceived risks of harm). But note that a simple finding that a risk proved to be a false positive, or negative, does not and cannot prove that it was a poor-quality negligent decision! To make that judgement we need to assess the whole decision-making process. Public protection professionals are entitled, in language, logic and law, to a degree of 'leeway'. They have to balance the possibility of making a wrong decision – perhaps restricting an individual more than events will suggest was necessary – against the chance that the individual would cause harm. That leeway involves value (political) judgements. A more informed debate, about acceptable error rates, could both help to reduce decision errors and redirect resources towards better risk management. Might a research-informed evaluation, of the comparative importance of false and positive errors, allow managers to target resources more appropriately?

Researchers assessed the likelihood that offenders on probation in Philadelphia (some 50,000 individuals) would be charged with actual or attempted murder in a two-year period (Berk *et al.* 2009). Probation department officials were asked to assess the comparative costs of false and positive errors.

> False negative results – failing to identify individuals who are likely to commit a homicide or attempted homicide – were seen as very costly. In contrast, false positive results – incorrectly identifying individuals as prospective murderers – were not seen as especially troubling. The primary loss would be the costs of delivering more intensive and specialized services, which might be a good idea regardless. Individuals who are identified as likely murderers are also likely to commit other serious crimes even if they are not charged with murder or its attempt. (Berk *et al.* 2009: 195)

When pressed, departmental 'administrators seemed to be in general agreement' (Berk *et al.* 2009: 195) that false negatives were ten times more serious than false positives. (The research study did not investigate whether this implicit value judgement was reflected in departmental policies or practices.) The researchers deliberately limited themselves to the data that was already available to the probation department, such as age, race, prior record and gender. They noted that from an initial sample of 30,000 cases there had been 322 charges of actual or attempted murder. So if someone had predicted that there would be no murder or attempted murder charge in all of those 30,000 cases, he or she would have been correct 99 per cent of the time! But that 1 per cent false negative rate would have been criticised!

A 'random-forests' methodology was adapted whereby a range of predictors were repeatedly applied to the data set. It included the evaluation that false negatives are ten times more costly than false positives. The resulting predictive method was then applied to the remaining sample of people on probation in Philadelphia. It distinguished those who were, and were not, predicted to be charged with murder or attempted murder.

About 43% of the probationers and parolees are correctly forecasted as being charged with a homicide or attempted homicide, given the cost ratio that was used ... It follows that, whereas about 1 in 100 of the overall population of probationers and parolees will be charged with a homicide or attempted homicide within 2 years while under supervision, a little under eight in 100 offenders within the identified high risk subgroup were charged with such crimes. The various stakeholders have found this eightfold improvement in prediction to be very promising. (Berk *et al.* 2009: 199)

The method also allowed the researchers to identify the relative importance of different predictive factors. Age was most important, then age of first contact with the adult court system. Absence of data on these issues reduced forecasting accuracy by 12 and 8 per cent respectively (2009: 201).

So the research produced a method of predicting serious harm (murder or attempted murder charges), which was eight times more accurate in relation to the 'high risk' group identified. An even higher degree of improvement ought to be possible in the United Kingdom, given that about 90 per cent of our murders (HMIC 2000), in comparison with 50 per cent of Philadelphia's, appear to be identified and processed as such. It enables the identification of a 'high risk' group of offenders on parole or probation – although in Philadelphia there are some twelve false positives to each true. While that remains a high error rate it also, as the researchers emphasise, demonstrates the importance of investing risk management resources in that high risk group. Systems have now been established in Philadelphia where some probation officers manage a caseload of fewer than twenty such offenders (Berk *et al.* 2009). And – the key points for this chapter – that 'error rate', and professional 'judgement call', has become 'evidence based'.

Managing risk decisions: procedural aids and support for decision-makers

Risk decisions should be judged by the quality of the processes involved. That includes considering the quality of the data used and the management plan devised. They should not be assessed by outcomes (positive or negative), since those can be the product of accidents, good fortune or simply the inherent risk. These risk-taking processes include the 'technology' involved, such as the decision aids and procedures utilised. Someone within public protection teams needs to take responsibility for ensuring appropriate action at this 'level'. Consider, for example, the number of variables that are involved in buying a bottle of wine (colour, grapes, nationality, alcoholic strength, age). It is not surprising that we often adopt a 'heuristic' or someone else's advice in order to avoid the cognitive overload (Kassin 2004). Public protection risk-taking should be more difficult. So are practitioners provided with decision aids, for example, tools for taking appropriate, sequential decisions on manageable amounts of information or methods for aptly combining information into smaller 'chunks'? Note that managers, not just decision-makers, can cause losses by not providing apt decision aids. Two topics that fit under this 'level' but are rarely discussed are the role of experience and the 'need' for 'risk failures'.

We know that harm may occur, even when the best possible decision has been taken, because that is a defining feature of 'risk'. So a service which never experiences adverse outcomes would appear to be ideal. It would appear to deserve commendation and praise in abundance. But no! Consider, as an example, the early release of offenders from custody. Decision-makers would aim to ensure that no such offender reoffended. Imagine they achieved that goal, without 'cheating' by making no decisions (that is, avoiding the chance of error). Have they achieved a public protection state of bliss? Adverse publicity is unlikely, but equally praise and positive publicity will also be scarce. But we cannot logically conclude that there was good decision-making. We know that there were no false negatives (erroneous assessments that it was apt to release early). But we do not know that there were no false positives (erroneous assessments that it was inappropriate to release early). The practitioners' – allegedly – highly successful decision-making record may simply be the consequence of adopting a very conservative approach, of only recommending 'certainties' for the risk. Those practitioners may actually be very poor – even unprofessional – risk-takers! The uncomfortable truths are (1) that we cannot judge risk-taking merely by the outcomes and (2) that we need some 'risk failures' in order to know that some forms of poor risk-taking (the improperly conservative) are not taking place.

It may be replied that 'risk failures' can never be condoned. But that merely exemplifies risk aversion, a misunderstanding of the nature of risk, and a willingness to expect the impossible from decision-makers. To acknowledge the need for 'risk failures' is neither to welcome nor to celebrate any occasion when harm results from such a decision. It simply draws attention to the need for managers to have systems whereby they can identify the potential for 'risk failures'. Consider the team where no early released offenders have reoffended over a significant period. Management needs to know how and why that was achieved. Good practice needs to be understood and shared. But if no failures could occur, because an inordinately conservative policy was being applied, then it needs to take action. A more likely scenario is that while failures are possible they are highly unlikely. For example, in the Philadelphia study (Berk *et al.* 2009) ten false positives to one false negative was explicitly provided for, although twelve to one was achieved. If the feedback reveals an error rate significantly out of line with that deemed professionally proper then management should intervene. Any service dedicated to learning from its risk-taking experience should be able to reduce such a ratio over time. But the managers should know that neither a nil false negative or false positive rate is consistent with good practice. The only way to achieve a nil error rate is not to take risks – which defeats the purpose and professionalism of those involved.

We may, analytically, recognise the need for 'risk failures', but it does not follow that they need to include harm or other loss. Rather, the decision-making process should include arrangements for minimising loss, even when it is an inescapable and non-negligent consequence of risk-taking. One technique involves breaking risk decisions down into component parts or steps that might be considered 'trials', where the amount of harm, if it were to occur, would be reduced. For example, instead of simply discharging a patient, arrangements might be set up to allow him or her off the ward for an hour, then two, then off the hospital grounds for another period. Each of those periods can be considered to be a separate risk. If no patient fails to return within the individually specified time then serious consideration should be given to whether too conservative a risk policy is being adopted. A virtue of this approach is that the likelihood of harm, if not the degree of harm, is less within a one-hour risk period than within two or more. The point is not to allow, let alone to encourage 'risk failures', but rather to note that all risk-taking systems must – analytically – have them and to manage and learn from that.

Acknowledging the need for 'risk failures' is more likely to help than to hinder professional risk-takers. Consider, for example, the likely effect of being able to inform any judge or official inquiry about the steps that had been taken to assure the organisation that an appropriate balance between false positive and false negative decisions had been reached. The first author was once informed of a unit that was legally empowered to detain certain individuals but also expected to prepare them for reintegration into community living. They noted that they had made 2,000 risk decisions to allow individuals off the premises for a limited period. In only seven cases had an individual not returned by the specified time. Nobody in authority over the unit had had the courtesy, courage or leadership to compliment the staff on a good risk-taking (if rather conservative) record (an academic's praise counted for little). But all the staff knew about one of those seven cases, where an individual had injured a member of the public and the media had encamped opposite the unit's entrance!

The examples just cited also demonstrate the important role of experience. Risk assessment, based upon actuarial factors, is based upon a form of experience. Researchers will have noted how often people with certain characteristics (such as age, gender or delusions) have acted dangerously. They will – or should – have done that in a rigorously methodologically controlled manner. That cannot be the same when practitioners notice similarities in cases they have dealt with. Several 'errors' are possible; in particular the features identified may have been perceived inaccurately or have little significance. Experience, it is submitted, is not relevant to risk assessment but is relevant to risk management. In particular it gives decision-makers very valuable information about the quality of the controls they use to manage the risk. It gives them information on how much they may trust different risk dimensions. For example, the experiences of patients being allowed off the ward for one hour and returning when they should will serve to reduce anxiety about repeating the exercise, or allowing a longer period. Of course, experience will always remain questionable. The individual may have manipulated decision-makers by returning within the prescribed period in order to be allowed a longer period considered necessary to effect a complete 'escape'. Decision-makers are entitled to refer to such experience when rationalising their decisions. That experience, provided they can always show that they were critical and not blindly trusting, could reasonably justify their decision.

Managing risk decision-makers

The third 'level' concerned the quality assurance of decision-making; learning the likely causes of error and minimising their frequency and effects for the future (prevention). The fourth 'level' focuses on supporting the risk decision-makers, in particular helping them to learn from their experience by ensuring apt feedback systems. Public protection decision-makers need and deserve the proactive support of their managers and employers to tackle others' poor-quality, often hasty and simplistic judgements upon their decisions. This should include a rigorous system of audit whereby a cross-section of risk decisions – whether initially associated with success or failure – is reviewed for the lessons that may be learned. Audit would be one key element towards ensuring that services adopted a 'learning paradigm'. Everyone should 'win' from progressively less ignorance about risks, even if it can never be totally eliminated. If properly designed, for example encouraging professionals to report their concerns with a measure of protection (such as airline pilots being encouraged to report 'near misses'), it would go a considerable way to tackling the blame culture.

Critically we must move from a system that emphasises learning from failure to what can be learned from success. Practitioners need to know what works rather than what does not work. The first author has heard several public protection officers, referring to an inquiry, comment resignedly: 'There but for the grace of God go I.' They believe that the outcome of professional risk-taking – and being blamed – is beyond their control; they are so disillusioned that they are beyond rational argument.

Ask any public protection worker how many of his or her risk decisions have led to harm and the likely response is a quiet counting of recalled events. Then ask the same person how many decisions have led to success, or how many professional risk decisions he or she has taken, and that person is likely to wonder why such 'stupid' questions are being asked. But without such information about the total number of decisions and the success to failure ratio, how is anyone to identify and encourage improved decision-making?

A particular problem concerns success. The goal of professional risk-taking is fewer erroneous decisions, whether false positive or negative. Improved practices, such as those identified in Philadelphia, could move us towards those goals. But how do we know when, and by how much, we are being successful? It is easy to observe, and count, when an offender on probation kills someone. It is not so easy when he or she does not kill anyone. The killing is liable – on superficial analysis – to be regarded as an example of poor risk-taking, deserving condemnation. The non-killing deserves no attention; even if it was due to probation officers' work and skills, that was their job. This may seem a trite point but unless we have some means of identifying successes we cannot identify what, when and where we ought to be learning from.

One method would be to identify any year-on-year increase, or reduction, in killings or whatever is causing concern. But consider what is likely to happen to a service where less harm (or more successes) is taking place? Resources will be withdrawn on the basis of another superficial analysis that they are superfluous. Someone within public protection needs to focus on identifying and demonstrating the rates and causes of successful risk-taking.

Managing the total system

It is necessary for someone within a public protection agency to be charged with ensuring that the total 'system' is integrated, effective, efficient and regularly renewed. As this will regularly involve liaising with other services and disciplines, and require the power to make and enforce agreements such as procedure protocols, this is likely to involve the highest echelons within the organisation. The Association of Chief Police Officers (ACPO) for England, Wales and Northern Ireland has taken such a critical step. It has agreed a statement of core principles designed to tackle risk aversion and foster an approach focused upon supporting officers and learning from experience (ACPO 2010). More is possible. The analogy, and collaboration, with health care could be increased. Medicine also involves risk-taking (in diagnosis and treatment). The evidence base for medicine may be much more extensive and highly developed but it provides a model of authoritative information open to critical review (for example, see the web-based information available from the Cochrane Collaboration, www.cochrane.org/index.htm).

The analogy could also be used to encourage radical reviews of professional risk-taking. For example, an observational study of 21 surgery teams (De Leval *et al.* 2000) revealed that mistakes and problems were relatively commonplace, on average seven per operation. The quality of the team was determined more by their skills in responding to the problems than by the number of problems (Reason 2004). Perhaps we should see problems in public protection, things 'going wrong', as normal. Does that provide a more accurate description of public protection work? Should the focus be upon managing those problems rather than slightly more accurate risk factors, on resource intensive risk management rather than 'scientific' risk prediction?

Conclusion

This chapter has identified a five 'level' model of risk-taking, provided an outline description and identified a few issues relevant to each stage, deliberately focusing upon relatively recent ideas and reports. The core argument has been that if the public are to be better protected from people who are perceived to be a danger, then action needs to be taken at each of these levels. The focus should not be limited, in particular, to those who make and implement the risk decisions on our behalf. Everyone involved has a contribution to make and a responsibility to bear. Fish, Munro and Bairstow (2009) have recently demonstrated the value and potential of a systems approach to child protection reviews. Their analyses and recommendations, consistent with the principal points made here, would emphasise these five 'levels' being seen as integrative – as contributing to a 'circle' of action – rather than a hierarchy as may have been implied. They demonstrate the importance of managers knowing what is actually happening in their service, of not allowing themselves to become divorced from the day-to-day reality of professional practice as they progress through promotion:

> The systems approach raises some fundamental questions about traditional views on accountability, power and control. In the systems approach, the front-line worker's actions are seen as, in part, due to factors in the wider system that influence the nature of the task s/he is expected to carry out and the conditions in which it can be performed. This raises the question of how to apportion accountability and responsibility. Is the front-line worker only, in part, accountable, and how do we measure the size of that 'part'? How do we apportion accountability when causation is conceptualised as diffused throughout the many layers of the system? Who has the power to produce improvement? It is possible that the heroic worker of exceptional talent can defy the adverse pressures to achieve high standards but it might be more effective on a wider scale if a senior manager re-designed the task so that is easier for the average front-line worker to do it well. (Fish *et al.* 2009: 127–8)

References

Association of Chief Police Officers (2010 forthcoming) *Guidance on Managing Operational Risk*. Cambourne: National Policing Improvement Agency.

Berk, R., Sherman, L., Barnes, G., Kurtz, E. and Ahlman, L. (2009) 'Forecasting murder within a population of probationers and parolees: a high stakes application of statistical learning', *Journal of the Royal Statistical Society*, 172(1): 192–211.

Breakwell, G. M. (2007) *The Psychology of Risk*. Cambridge: Cambridge: University Press.

Carson, D. and Bain, A. (2008) *Professional Risk and Working with People*. London: Jessica Kingsley.

Collins, R. (2008) *Violence. A Micro-sociological Theory*. Princeton, NJ: Princeton University Press.

DeFronzo, J. (1997) 'Welfare and homicide', *Journal of Research in Crime and Delinquency*, 34: 395–406.

De Leval, M. R., Carthey, J., Wright, D. J., Farewell, V. T. and Reason, J. T. (2000) 'Human factors and cardiac surgery: a multicenter study', *Journal of Thoracic and Cardiovascular Surgery*, 119: 661–72.

Eisner, M. (2003) 'Long-term historical trends in violent crime', *Crime and Justice*, 30: 83–142.

Fish, S., Munro, E. and Bairstow, S. (2009) *Learning Together to Safeguard Children: Developing a Multi-agency Systems Approach for Case Reviews*. London: Social Care Institute for Excellence.

Hill, L. (2009) *Investigation into the Issues Arising from the Serious Further Offence Review: Dano Sonnex*. Online at: www.justice.gov.uk/news/docs/noms-investigation-report-sonnex.pdf (accessed 26 August 2009).

Home Office (2008) *Saving Lives. Reducing Harm. Protecting the Public.* London: Home Office.

HM Inspectorate of Constabulary (2000) *Policing London, Winning Consent.* London: HMSO.

HM Inspectorate of Probation (2006) *An Independent Review of a Serious Further Offence Case: Damien Hanson & Elliot White.* London: Ministry of Justice. Online at: www. justice.gov.uk/inspectorates/hmi-probation/docs/hansonandwhitereview-rps.pdf (accessed 26 August 2009).

Janis, I. L. and Mann, L. (1977) *Decision Making: A Psychological Analysis of Conflict, Choice, and Commitment.* New York: Free Press.

Kassin, S. (2004) *Psychology,* 4th edn. Upper Saddle River, NJ: Prentice Hall.

Luckenbill, D. F. (1977) 'Criminal homicide as a situated transaction', *Social Problems,* 25(2): 176–86.

Monahan, J., Steadman, H. J, Silver, E., Appelbaum, P. S., Cleark Robbins, P., Mulvey, E. P., Roth, L. H., Grisso, T. and Banks, S. (2001) *Rethinking Risk Assessment.* New York: Oxford University Press.

Nash, M. (2006) *Public Protection and the Criminal Justice Process.* Oxford: Oxford University Press.

Nash, M. and Williams, A. (2008) *The Anatomy of Serious Further Offending.* Oxford: Oxford University Press.

National Probation Board (2008) *Managing High Risk of Serious Harm Offenders with Severe Personality Disorders,* National Probation Service Circular PC21/2008. Online at: www.probation.homeoffice.gov.uk/files/pdf/PC21%202008.pdf (accessed 26 August 2009).

National Probation Service (2008) *Dynamic Risk Assessment of Sex Offenders,* National Probation Service Circular PC02/2008. Online at: www.probation.homeoffice.gov. uk/files/pdf/PC02%202008.pdf (accessed 26 August 2009).

Prins, H. (1999) *Will They Do It Again?* London: Routledge.

Reason, J. (2004) 'Beyond the organizational accident: the need for "error wisdom" on the frontline', *Quality and Safety in Health Care,* 13 (Suppl. 2): 28–33.

Royal Society (1992) *Risk: Analysis, Perception and Management.* London: Royal Society.

Rubin, J., Gallo, F. and Coutts, A. (2008) *Violent Crime: Risk Models, Effective Interventions and Risk Management.* Rand Corporation, for National Audit Office.

Part Three

Doing the Job

Introduction

Mike Nash and Andy Williams

This section is, to lift Bridges and White's phrase, about 'doing the job' of public protection. However, in putting these chapters together we have no wish to perpetuate a view that theory and practice are poles apart and never the twain will meet. Our view is the opposite of this. We believe that practitioners can benefit from stepping outside of the relentless pressures of everyday life by considering other (and possibly alternate) views and ideas. Similarly by understanding better the way in which practitioners see and do their job, academics in turn can inform their research programmes. This section is a combination of those who do or have done the job in a personal capacity or have the responsibility to inspect work and inquire into those cases where something has gone wrong. In public protection work we have the situation whereby separate agencies with distinct and sometimes unique roles are obliged, in law, to work with each other. Yet often those discrete agencies know little of their partners in public protection, having been trained in different ways and usually having roles that are at best compatible and at worst regarded as opposed to those in other organisations. The essence of MAPPA is to ensure that these differences do not become barriers. Our hope, therefore, is that by reading this handbook, those who work in public protection agencies can not only learn more about their partners but also perhaps begin to understand the common and different issues faced by a diverse range of staff. At the same time those practitioners reading this volume might also benefit from the ideas of academics and indeed academic practitioners.

Dick Whitfield's chapter on the work of the Parole Board is based upon his experience both as an independent member of the board and as a former chief officer of probation. He therefore acted as both a producer and consumer of probation information. In many ways the Parole Board has assumed an absolutely central role in public protection processes. It is the end stage where offenders designated as dangerous are assessed to see if they are safe to be released back into the community. Of course, these decisions have been taken over many years but it is perhaps only in the last few years that the media and therefore the public have become aware of them. The Parole Board has therefore become the focus of blame in cases where serious further offences occur even though, of course, it is probably only as good as the information that it receives. It is a decision that, many more times than not, is 'successful' if measured by further convictions during the licence period, especially for high risk of harm offenders. As we know, though, performance in this area of practice is measured by its failures rather than its successes. Dick describes the huge increase in the workload of the board, notably as a result of the introduction of indeterminate sentences for public protection. These cases have the additional pressures of prisoner and legal representative being in attendance, and challenge to risk assessments and decisions are becoming par for the course for board members. The prominence of Parole Board decisions is a reflection of the importance of public protection processes and outcomes to the government of the day. Bad outcomes mean bad publicity and at this point governments become defensive. They aim to prove that they did what they could by creating legislation or increasing budgets and therefore, if it is not their fault, whose is it? The Parole Board has been catapulted into this arena and Dick Whitfield passes comments on the recent debates concerning its independence from political influence and indeed from its sponsoring agencies such as the prison service in recent years. This debate is not yet concluded, and nor, one suspects, is the increase in the Board's workload.

Hazel Kemshall has made a very considerable contribution to the field of public protection, contributing books, scholarly articles and influential reports and evaluation for government. She brings that together in her chapter, which both describes and critiques current official systems for assessing and managing high risk of harm offenders. She reviews ten years of MAPPA developments and is able to identify lessons learned and improvements made. She echoes the messages in chapters by McAlinden, Hall, Grieve and others in this volume, which focus very much on community and victim engagement. As Kemshall argues, it is time for MAPPA to become more outward-looking in both its management of offenders and its interactions with communities – especially if those communities feel victimised and let down. Engagement with offenders and communities is key to effective risk management – *working with* rather than *working on* should be the mantra.

Andrew Bridges and Kate White offer us a different type of practitioner take on public protection. As probation officers they have, of course, been involved in work with high risk offenders. As inspectors they also have roles in monitoring performance (quality) and also undertake inquiries into serious further offences (often with other inspectorates). They are therefore uniquely placed to observe, evaluate and influence practice. They make a number of key points not only concerning their role as inspectors but also on the nature of public protection work – and how to judge its quality. They identify that work in this challenging and often unique area does not fit easily into the types of performance measurement methods employed across the public sector in recent years. They express concern at the adoption of quantitative targets when much of their inspection work is about improving quality – one not necessarily helping the other. Their main message is for practitioners and their managers, and it is that perfection is impossible but 'doing all you reasonably can' is and should be the hallmark of a quality worker. For practitioners who have been involved in serious further offences the judgement that they have met this standard would be so much more welcome than the blame that the media so rapidly seek to allocate. Bridges and White go some way towards identifying how probation staff can best tackle this very difficult area of work and make the very important point, arising from a number of their inspection reports, that probation staff have become very good at assessment (aided by tools such as the offender assessment system OASys) but are less effective in building these assessments into good risk management plans and actions. Identifying risk and then managing it are to a certain extent separate but absolutely interconnected processes, which the authors say can be aided by good management and an increased importance given to front-line practitioners within MAPPA meetings. Their chapter is undoubtedly aimed at the 'doers' but can equally inform the commentators, offering as it does a unique insider perspective on public protection work.

Finally in this section we have Bob Golding's chapter on sex offender management in the community with a particular policing perspective. Bob has been a senior police officer and is thus very well placed to comment on 'doing the job'. In his chapter Golding writes about the anti-paedophile protests at Paulsgrove, near Portsmouth; protests that he had to police as the local commander. These disturbances, described as riots by the media, very much came to symbolise the feelings of the time, accurately reflected in the phrase 'not in my back yard' (NIMBY). Elsewhere in this volume Eric Janus describes this situation in the (more extreme) American context. Reflected in this chapter are the thorny issues surrounding community notification of sex offenders' whereabouts and the way in which communities might respond if they have access to this information. As the role of police officers has changed, with their responsibility for the sex offender register and its monitoring role, so they will increasingly be thrust in between the requirement to maintain order and enforce the law while facing an increasingly vocal lobby for a process that many of their members may well have sympathy for. Golding refers to limited notification pilots in four police areas, which are now to be rolled out nationally. He suggests that the limited take-up of requests for information may mitigate some of the concerns expressed previously by senior police officers about making more information about sex offenders' whereabouts public knowledge. Of course, the proof of this particular pudding will come with the next serious offence committed by a known sex offender.

Chapter 8

Public protection and the Parole Board in England and Wales

Dick Whitfield

Introduction

Whether you consult the Parole Board's website, read its annual report or see any of its printed material, the simple statement of purpose under its letterhead is clear and unambiguous: 'Working with others to protect the public'. The theme of public protection is emphasised in attempts towards greater openness and transparency in its decision-making; in developments such as its Review Committee, which seeks to learn from cases where a parolee has gone on to commit a further serious offence; and in all of its recruitment and training activity. Yet this was a body which earlier had an ambivalent start and a reputation for secrecy – possibly one of the least understood parts of the complex criminal justice process. The purpose of this chapter is to describe the enormous changes that have taken place to its role and independence and to see whether that claim on its letterhead is justified by the contribution to public protection that it is now able to make. This is not an official Parole Board view. After 30 years in the probation service, often on the receiving end of Parole Board decisions with which I was uncomfortable, I served as a part-time independent member of the board between 1999 and 2007 and have stayed closely in touch with the rapid pace of developments since then.

This chapter is being written at a time when the future of the Parole Board is the subject of a consultation process, which will determine more than just its sponsorship arrangements (Ministry of Justice 2009). At present it is a non departmental public body (NDPB), sponsored by the Access to Justice Group in the Ministry of Justice. The independence of sponsorship arrangements has already been called into question by the Court of Appeal, resulting in a move away from its previous position in the National Offender Management Service (NOMS), but the issue may not be fully resolved yet. It may be time for it to be integrated into the Courts Service or the Tribunals Service, but key questions – the assessment of risk, the quality of decision-making and its role in the wider process of public protection – will remain.

To examine these issues some history is necessary, together with an examination of recent key changes, some case examples and the way the process works in practice. The board's remit, dealing as it does with serious and dangerous offenders, gives it a central – and vulnerable – role in the whole business of public protection.

A historical perspective

Early release from prison, together with some form of supervision, has long been a feature of the criminal justice process in England and Wales, from early convict 'ticket of leave' systems in which reporting to the police was the only requirement, to the 'borstal licence' scheme which gave the fledgling probation service responsibility for supervising released young offenders from as early as 1908. The reality of prison – that it fractured relationships, imposed social and psychological handicaps and made employment and accommodation more difficult – was well known, as was the need for some kind of post-release help. But for many years it was left to the voluntary sector, in the shape of discharged prisoners' aid societies, to provide this. It was not until the Criminal Justice Act of 1967 that a comprehensive regime to deal with the early release of prisoners was introduced for the first time.

This new scheme allowed eligible prisoners who showed 'promise or determination to reform' to earn back up to one-third of their sentence, over and above ordinary remission (itself up to one-third of original sentence), and qualify for even earlier release. The system was presented as rehabilitative – intended to manage the difficult transition from captivity to freedom – but as has subsequently often been the case, there were political (pressure of numbers) and managerial (prison discipline) interests, also.

It is difficult, now, to recall the secrecy under which the parole system at first operated. Prisoners could not read the reports written about them. The Parole Board said only 'yes' or 'no' to applicants, with no explanation and there was no guidance to long-term prisoners about what they should do to improve their chances of early release. The whole process was regarded (and not only by prisoners) as capricious and arbitrary.

Significant change came with the 1991 and 2003 Criminal Justice Acts, which took the Parole Board from its original advisory role to the decision-making body it has now become. It was freed from direct government control by becoming an NDPB, but was still accountable to Parliament through the relevant minister (first the Home Secretary and now the Minister of Justice). Membership of the board has always been a mix of judges, psychiatrists and psychologists, criminologists and probation officers – and Independent Members, who form the largest single group. Nearly all appointments are part-time (currently for a maximum of six years). Independent members come from a wide variety of backgrounds. I was appointed on retirement from the probation service but others the same year came from police and prison backgrounds, banking, education, industry and charity work.

The board's work has changed dramatically over the years, from dealing almost wholly with cases on paper to the huge increase in oral hearings which it is now having to organise; an equally significant rise in indeterminate sentence cases; a greater role in decisions following the recall of prisoners on licence; and, above all, a need to explain its decision-making – and deal with the challenges that inevitably follow. Thus not only has the nature of the Parole Board's work changed but so has the context in which its decisions are made.

The Parole Board today

The Parole Board now has three main areas of work. It makes release decisions for all indeterminate and some fixed sentence prisoners; it decides, following recall to prison for a breach of parole licence, whether to re-release; and it makes recommendations to ministers about transfer from closed to open prison for some indeterminate sentence prisoners. All decisions are based on an assessment of risk and are made by panels of between one and three members, at either a 'paper' panel or an oral hearing. In practice, this means that the board makes the final decision in all life sentence and indeterminate sentence cases (including those serving detention at Her Majesty's pleasure) and all eligible fixed sentences up to 15 years. The board may currently only make *recommendations* in cases where the sentence length is fifteen years or more; ministers then make a final decision. This curious anomaly will soon end, once the necessary legislation has completed its parliamentary process. Other cases referred to the board include extended sentences and those extended sentence for public protection cases sentenced before the 2008 Criminal Justice and Immigration Act came into force, which included clauses on the treatment (in early release terms) of various public protection/extended sentence cases and the specific availability of hearings.

Paper consideration is often the first stage of decision-making, but prisoners can make representations for their case to be considered at an oral hearing. These are held inside the prison, with a panel of between one and three members, and they can deal with disputes of fact (such as whether a prisoner had been properly recalled) as well as hearing evidence of progress and of risk. In order to ensure an adequate assessment of risk, the board can make directions to NOMS to provide a range of information to the hearing – although it has no direct mechanism for enforcing such directions. This is not normally an issue, but reports requested from the prison service, from the home probation officer or offender manager and from psychologists or psychiatrists are, in some cases, not forthcoming. While the general expectation is that cases will be deferred until the required information is obtained, other pressures to make a timely decision also come into play and in some cases the lack of key information has been an important factor when, afterwards, inquiries are made after the commission of a serious further offence (Nash and Williams 2008).

The Secretary of State (now the Minister of Justice) issues general directions to the board on matters that must be taken into account, but it is for panels to determine, on a case-by-case basis, who meets the statutory tests for early release. For life sentence prisoners the board has to assess whether the prisoner's level of risk to the life and limb of others is more than minimal. It is for the prisoner to demonstrate that it is not. Recommendations for transfer to open conditions, as a precursor to possible release, require a balancing act between assessed risks and perceived benefits. The board must consider not just the risk of further offending but the risk of absconding, likely compliance with the open regime and whether enough progress has been made in closed conditions in tackling the attitudes and behaviour problems that contributed to the original offence. Board members are therefore in the business of constantly assessing historic and contemporary information with a view to predicting future behaviour.

Given the nature of the prisoners with whom it deals – who have all attracted long fixed sentences or indeterminate sentences – it will be apparent that the board is permanently engaged in high risk decision-making as the potentially negative outcome is of further and sometimes very serious offending. Parole started as an act of administrative benevolence, with the reduction in sentence justified in rehabilitative terms, but the pendulum has swung. Now the effect of its decisions can sometimes be to serve public protection by effectively *extending* sentences for prisoners assessed as dangerous and posing a high risk of harm.

At the same time, the parole process (or at least its outcomes) is now much more visible to the media and the public. A series of high profile cases in which parolees have committed serious further offences has also given it a much higher profile with politicians. The political view of parole has been very ambivalent in recent years. It has been a very useful device for helping to alleviate the prison overcrowding crisis. However, it has also been sufficiently independent for previous Home Secretaries to be able to distance themselves from it (and, indeed, to lead the chorus of blame) when difficult decisions about dangerous prisoners have resulted in further tragedy. Alongside this, much stricter standards of due process, the emergence of human rights legislation and increasing legal representation and challenge (now well over 300 judicial review cases) have all created a vastly different public profile for the Parole Board.

The combination of additional scrutiny and sustained criticism from press and politicians when further offences are committed has undoubtedly created a more risk-averse culture in the board and among its members. It was a process (and philosophical shift) that I experienced at first hand between 1999 and 2007 and recent figures speak for themselves. In 2007/08 36 per cent of fixed sentence prisoners were granted parole – down from 49 per cent in 2005/06. For life sentence prisoners the release rate reduced from 23 per cent to 15 per cent over the same period (Parole Board 2006, 2008). The Review Committee may have had a role to play in this (see below) but members were acutely aware of the open hostility displayed by press and politicians when things were seen to have gone wrong. Defensive decision-making was an understandable result and reflects a trend increasingly noticeable in all criminal justice decision-making (see Padfield, and Bridges and White, this volume). The board has always had to distinguish between the likelihood of any reoffending during the parole period, and the gravity of any such offence. Realistically, it is clear that many repeat and prolific offenders are likely to return to crime sooner or later, especially in terms of theft, burglary or fraud offences. So are habitual drug users, who need to finance an all-consuming habit. The decision therefore hinges upon whether releasing on parole *in the hope* that additional supervision in the community and possible additional treatment requirements will be more effective than simply keeping the person in custody for what may be only a few more months? The board's remit is concerned just with the period on licence and much panel discussion is about balancing the likelihood of further offences during this period, against the potential longer-term benefits.

A different approach has to be taken when serious sexual or violent offences have occurred. Here, the statistical risk of offending may be relatively small, given the timescale involved, but the impact of any new and similar offence, and the creation of another victim in these circumstances, demands much more caution. The issue here, of course, is one of assessing even rarer behaviour than occurs in the general prison population. The same potential benefits from early release may also accrue for sex offenders – restoration of family contacts, the chance of employment and rebuilding a crime-free life – but the price of failure may be extraordinarily high too. The Parole Board and its members have to cope with the knowledge that they are known by their failure; success is routinely expected (and largely achieved) but it creates no headlines in the press or votes of confidence from politicians.

The centrality of public protection means that the board has to see the evidence for any claim of reduced risk. The completion of accredited course programmes or one-to-one work are usually cited; so too is the development of insight into offending behaviour and the trigger factors that led to the offence. Trying to separate out these claims (often optimistically and honestly made) from the hard evidence is a painstaking task. Members will usually look first at the risk factors, which were apparent at the time of the original offence. The list might include instrumental or expressive violence; drug, solvent or alcohol abuse; gambling; and a general criminal attitude. These factors will then be considered in conjunction with longer-term personal issues such as learning disability or low IQ; poor employability; mental health issues; impulsivity; a generally poor emotional state; an unstable childhood; and, of course, the list of previous convictions, previous responses to supervision and behaviour in prison. Risk assessments build up like a jigsaw with interlocking pieces eventually producing an emerging picture of current risks. Any work undertaken in prison to reduce these risks will provide crucial information for the consideration of release.

Alcohol and drugs are all too prevalent in prisoners' backgrounds and a range of courses exist in prison to deal with them. But successful completion of such a course has to be seen in the light of the lack of opportunity to test out new behaviours – a major problem for incarcerated offenders. An assessment of release plans then becomes important. Is he or she returning to positive relationships and stable living conditions? Is it back to the same peer group with whom he has already offended? What chance is there of stable employment? Whatever the conclusion, reasons for both positive and negative decisions have to be detailed and supported by the evidence. In particular, concerns about the risk of harm have to be made clear. Board members can make use of training, a comprehensive handbook of advice, a wide range of reports, directions and precedents – but it still depends on individual understanding and analysis, moderated by one's colleagues' views, before the decision can be made.

Being a member

There is no doubt that the selection of members, training and the culture of the Parole Board all reinforce the primacy of public protection. But this has to be seen alongside the individual life stories that confront members at every panel and must influence decision-making. A description of how decisions are arrived at may help to put this in context.

For cases that are to be determined on the papers alone, the panel will have had a substantial dossier to read, on every prisoner, some three weeks in advance. The term 'substantial' refers primarily to size – it may well run to well over 100 pages – but may be less warranted in terms of the quality of reports or the completeness of information. The period before the panel meeting can be used to request any missing reports or to resolve queries, but improving the overall quality and focus of key reports remains an issue (Parole Board 2009: 19). Much of the information in the dossier is duplicated by a range of different writers; others have clearly had so little contact with the prisoner that any judgement must be treated with some caution. Reading the dossier is a sifting process; finding the nuggets of information that make the prisoner come alive and provide some real insight is the key. Court reports, previous convictions, judges' sentencing remarks and reports on courses undertaken in prison are all there. So too is the OASys report, a computer-based risk assessment form that forms the centrepiece of the dossier and provides a risk 'score' to determine the overall level of the offender's risk. The form also contains narrative sections and the option of updating the original information; if well completed it can be invaluable. But it is a long and complex form and completion is a time-consuming business. Sketchy and sometimes inaccurate data can make too much reliance on its conclusions suspect.

With growing experience, I could plough through a dossier, making notes, in about 40 minutes and would make an initial conclusion about suitability for release. If it was a case in which I was to lead the discussion and draft the reasons, it would be perhaps twice as long. Four or five key reports, including the one from the home probation officer, or offender manager, might be enough to arrive at an outline conclusion – but to be sure, and to provide the evidence that written reasons need, much more digging was required. On the day of the panel, each member would start the discussion on their 'lead' cases and would share the thinking that had led to their preliminary conclusion. The draft written report, which goes to the prisoner, would also be shared, adapted and improved. In many cases these were uncontentious, if report writers had given clear, well evidenced recommendations, release plans were good and risk was seen as manageable. Swift decisions could then be made. Conversely, other cases involved so many negative aspects, including the sheer weight of previous offending, previous failures on supervision or parole licence and the lack of a stable release plan, that a 'no' decision was also clear. But reasons still had to be carefully drafted, including suggestions of what was needed from the prisoner if a more realistic application were to be made if a further review was available, before the case could be 'signed off'.

Inevitably, most time was spent on cases where the decision could go either way, or where members took different preliminary views. Discussions could be lengthy and occasionally fierce; members do have their own prejudices and blind spots and the use of three-person panels is an important filter and safeguard. For oral hearings members would similarly get dossiers in advance but with the important difference that a colleague would already have done a preliminary 'sift' to look for anomalies, missing information or issues that needed to be resolved before the hearing date. Release plans in particular need to be firm and finalised so that decisions can be taken on the day of hearing. On the day of hearing, panel members meet first to share preliminary views and for agreement to be reached about what areas of questioning would be needed – and who should do it. But the dynamics of oral hearings are vastly different from deciding on a paper dossier. The emphasis on risk analysis remains, but decisions are bound to be more 'people influenced'. Not just the prisoner, who can be questioned at some length, but his or her witnesses and key report writers can all have their opinions tested. The quality of legal representation is also important and over the course of a two or three hour hearing my own preliminary views often had to be revisited (see also HMIP 2006 for further comments on legal representation for prisoners in parole and public protection matters).

And yet, despite the wholly positive impression that prisoners might create, the support of report writers and witnesses and effective advocacy, the statistical risk analysis in the dossier could not be ignored and often led to uncomfortable questioning. Despite OASys being the most widely used risk assessment artefact (other specialist ones would be used for sex offenders), my own preference was to focus on the OGRS (Offender Group Reconviction Scale) score, which was a component part of the overall OASys calculation. OGRS is simple to complete, with a limited number of variables and provided me with a better starting point than the 'low', 'medium' and 'high' risk categories that OASys provided.

OGRS provides a percentage reconviction score for a group of similarly convicted prisoners and, though limited, I could use this directly. For example, I might say to prisoners, 'This scale says that an offender with your background and previous convictions will have a 75 per cent chance of reconvicting within two years. How can you convince us that, if we release you early, you could be one of the 25 per cent who keep clear of crime?' The answers, whether well thought out, glib, unthinking or halting, were always instructive and seemed to focus minds much more sharply on the real issues of risk.

This approach cannot, of course, be universally used, particularly when patterns of behaviour, displayed over time, cannot be identified. In cases where extreme violence had been used in a single offence the emphasis might have to be on trigger factors and a detailed examination of what preceded the moment when the act was actually committed. Why should we believe it was a 'one-off' offence, as is so often claimed? Was drink or drugs a factor? Were there mental health issues?

When the decision comes to be made after an oral hearing, discussion between panel members often centres on the balance to be struck between static risk factors (age at first offence and previous convictions, for instance) and dynamic ones (which may be subject to change and will certainly cover relationships, and work undertaken in prison), together with the factors that are always central to reconviction studies, including accommodation and work prospects. At the end of any discussion, however, panel members will still depend not only on the weight they have placed on various factors, but also on a measure of intuition and professional judgement. All of this takes place with the sobering knowledge that 'a risk is a hazard that is incompletely understood and whose occurrence can be forecast only with uncertainty ... also, the concept of risk is inherently contextual, as hazards arise and exist in specific circumstances' (Hart *et al.* 2000: 209).

One scenario that occurs regularly and creates particular difficulties is the stalemate that arises when, for indeterminate prisoners, a move to open conditions is considered. This is a key moment – progression through open conditions (escorted and then unescorted visits, work placements and finally independent work outside the prison) is the precursor for release. Since open prisons focus on resettlement and not on dealing with any outstanding risk issues, it follows that all work on risk factors should be addressed in closed conditions, earlier in the sentence. But Parole Board panels frequently see long-serving prisoners for whom suitable courses are not available; or who have undertaken them years earlier, with limited success, and whose offence is now twenty or more years old. Panels are reluctant to 'warehouse' prisoners and often look to the positive experience an open prison can provide, as an alternative.

But a move to open prison will not in itself address underlying risk issues and moving towards a process of gradual community involvement and the development of a release plan without doing so will not meet public protection requirements. Doing well in open conditions may simply mask the risk elements which remain. There are no easy answers to this growing body of prisoners and one or two well publicised failures make it unlikely that the impasse in particular cases can be resolved.

There is no structure through which individual Parole Board members can assess the success of their deliberations. Parole licence (except for life licence) is generally fairly short term and the overall picture is positive, with – typically – over 70 per cent of parolees completing their licence satisfactorily and with many of those recalled returning to prison for breach of the licence conditions rather than the commission of a new offence. With life sentence prisoners, only 89 were recalled for any reason out of 1,646 under active supervision (Parole Board 2008/09: 12), suggesting that most decisions were appropriate. Reoffending may be years later and supplanted in the memory by the hundreds of other cases a member may have dealt with in the interim. Only when a letter from the Review Committee (see below) arrives is the impact of a 'failed' decision known.

What kept me going – and, I think, most colleagues – was a belief that Parole still represents the best way to help offenders manage the transition from captivity to freedom; that it remains the most sensible way of managing a reasonable level of risk and that it does provide some proper safeguards to the community. In the same way that the Board is wholly dependent on others for the information on which decisions are made, so it is equally dependent on the staff of probation services who supervise from the moment the prison gates shut. We all have to make the best of a system which can still deliver a measure of public protection and some real benefits to both offenders and the whole community.

When things do go wrong – the Review Committee

Nevertheless, board members have always been acutely aware of high profile cases where serious further offences, up to and including murder, have been committed by prisoners who were still on parole. They had been granted release because risk was assessed as manageable ... so what had gone wrong? In an attempt to learn from these tragedies, the board set up a Review Committee in 2003. Its remit was to look at all cases where the decision to release had been followed by an alleged violent or sexual offence. This meant, in practice, revisiting perhaps 40 to 50 cases each year. Before each quarterly meeting committee members are asked to look in depth at one or two cases and to present them to the committee so that a judgement can be made on the appropriateness of the original decision.

I was a member of this committee during its formative years and it was a formidable task. The reviewer provides the committee with detailed information on previous convictions; the original offence and the risk factors that were apparent at that time; behaviour and progress in custody; the impact any offending work in prison might have had on risk; the reports and recommendations from all who contributed to the original parole review; and a detailed look at the release plan. To these were added an analysis of the panel's written reasons – in particular, how risk issues were identified and addressed – the reasons for recall and a thorough look at any new offence (although this is not always possible as consideration might take place before a new trial). The pattern of post-sentence supervision would also be scrutinised with an analysis of the risk areas which remained.

The results of the committee's deliberations were then fed back to the members of the panel who took the original decision to release. Originally, this was in narrative form with no formal structure, but later a more structured and consistent approach was adopted, which placed the decision in one of five categories, as below:

1 **Entirely reasonable** – accepted that, on the facts available at the time, the decision was sound and properly reasoned. All relevant issues had been addressed and there was no indication that further information should have been sought. We regularly saw such cases, where the new offence was not just wholly unpredictable and unlike any previous offending,

but came 'out of the blue' when licence conditions seemed to have been conscientiously observed.

2   **Reasonable** – again accepted that the decision to release was arguably a good one, but it acknowledged that another panel on another day might equally have decided differently. We rarely knew whether these had been majority decisions, but it is a reflection of how finely balanced decisions are that this could well have been the case. Panel chairs always try to get a unanimous decision but have to proceed on a majority when this is not possible.

3   **Reasonable with concerns** – these decisions could be criticised in some respects, but would not be regarded as flawed overall. The concerns of the Review Committee might relate to missing information or gaps in the written reasons and it was useful to identify these as a way of raising standards. But the additional information might have made no difference to the resulting decision.

4   **Questionable** – this is where the committee started to express real concerns. Rarely could the decision have been characterised as wholly unreasonable, but it was assessed as one that a fully informed panel would not have made. Risk factors may have been overlooked, key information may have been unavailable (a regular frustration) or the reasons did not seem to match the information available to the Review Committee. Formal feedback is then given to the original panel, which is invited to respond and to clarify why they took the decision they did. This useful step is, however, problematic in life licence cases, where a period of years may have elapsed before any new offence. As the system has developed, panel members have been asked to comment at an earlier stage (following the single reviewer comments) so that the full committee has complete information.

5   **Completely unreasonable** – indicates that no sensible or rational panel could have come to this conclusion. During my years on the Review Committee I never came across a case that met these requirements – and one hopes that, with a three-member panel, one never will.

The committee has, I think, been successful in feeding back learning points to individual members and to panels. It is less easy for lessons to be passed on to the whole membership, but issues identified have formed the basis for wider training and development as experience has grown. In 2007/08 the committee's 'scores' were (Parole Board 2007/08):

- Entirely reasonable   8
- Reasonable   16
- Reasonable with concerns   15
- Questionable   12
- Entirely Unreasonable   0

In the context of almost 30,000 decisions a year, the numbers are, of course, extremely low. But the Review Committee has had a real impact, not least because of the high profile of some cases that come before it. Members receiving a letter from the committee about one of 'their' cases have described it as 'a sledgehammer blow', regardless of whether their decision was considered wholly reasonable or not. One member, notified that a prisoner released following a decision of a panel on which he had sat had been subsequently been convicted of rape, said: 'My first thought was to resign. If what I was doing had led to another victim, how could I justify it? How could I ever explain to her (the rape victim) what we had done? I knew he had got no previous sexual offences [he had been serving a sentence for burglary] 'but it was just awful to feel responsible and I can't describe the effect it had on me'.

Sitting on the Review Committee inevitably led to my becoming more risk averse. The mathematical risk of failure may be low, but the price can be extremely high. As this experience has spread to more members, so it has had an impact on panels and hearings and it seems to me to be one aspect of the notably more cautious approach evident in recent years. High profile failures and political pressure have also been factors – but the personalised impact of individual failures on individual panel members should not be underestimated. How much this learning can be generalised into better risk assessment is arguable. The Review Committee's independent researcher, Wendy Morgan, of the London Metropolitan University, summed it up as follows:

> the general profile (of those individuals committing new offences of serious or sexual violence) is of individuals who have progressed well during their prison sentences (e.g. participating in treatment) and who were assessed as suitable for parole by at least one, and generally two, probation officers. Contrary to expectations, those within the sample who, on the basis of criminal history, would be considered at higher risk tended to remain crime free longer than those assessed at lower risk. (Morgan 2005: 16)

Improving standards generally, rather than refining risk prediction, would seem to be the main result of Review Committee work.

Two other aspects of the Review Committee are worth mentioning. One is the introduction of eminent outside professionals to its membership. The first two, both vastly experienced, were Stephen Shaw, the Prisons and Probation Ombudsman, and Peter Neyroud, Chief Constable and Chief Executive of the National Policing Improvement Agency (NPIA). The objectivity, fierce intelligence and refreshingly different approach that both brought to the Review Committee enabled it to grow significantly. The second was born out of recognition that many of the issues uncovered concerned partner agencies just as much as the Parole Board. A Joint Review Panel was therefore formed which considers these cases and senior representatives of police, prisons, probation services and the Prison Service Directorate of Health decide how the learning – whether in terms of supervision, assessing prison behaviour, identifying warning signals and risky behaviour or mental health issues – can be passed back to the 'coal face'. The sheer size of the other agencies involved all dwarf the Parole Board, so it will not be easy. But the Review Committee and its practice offshoot, the Joint Review Panel, are widely recognised as examples of good practice in public protection terms, and need to be sustained.

Nevertheless, the newly appointed Chair of the Parole Board, Sir David Latham (a former Lord Justice of Appeal) has made the limitations clear. In a newspaper article he is quoted as saying:

> We cannot live in a risk free world and there will sadly be, and inevitably will be, some cases where release results in a serious offence being committed by a prisoner who was thought to present either no, or no significant, risk. Unless we operate a system which essentially deprives prisoners of any realistic right to release at some point, release is going to have to take place and an assessment of risk has to take place in a realistic way. (Latham 2009: 70)

The conflict with today's media assumption – so often fuelled by politicians – that we are entitled to live in a risk-free society, is obvious.

Conclusion – the future

The Parole Board's future, as noted in the introduction to this chapter, is currently under review and a consultation paper was issued in July 2009 with some four months for responses. The foreword to the document set out the reasons for the review:

> The Parole Board carries out an extremely important role in protecting the public ... [it] is no longer just a body advising the Crown on the exercise of its prerogative. It has evolved into a more court-like body that makes decisions about the safe release of offenders back into the community. This presents a number of challenges to the Board at a time when it's [sic] facing increasing pressures in terms of the mix of cases. The Board's functions, powers and status have not been systematically reviewed or revised in light of developments since its creation. This consultation paper represents an opportunity to address this ...
> (Ministry of Justice 2009)

Much of the discussion is about sponsorship arrangements – important in relation to the Parole Board's real and perceived independence. This follows the Court of Appeal's view that it was inappropriate for sponsorship to be undertaken by the National Offender Management Service, following which it was transferred to the Ministry of Justice's Access to Justice Group.

The key issue is whether the board remains a non departmental public body – free from direct governmental control, but nevertheless accountable through ministers to Parliament – or becomes a fully fledged court or tribunal under the Courts Service or the Tribunals Service.

This is not simply a bureaucratic exercise, because whatever the result there will be a new clarification of the board's role and responsibilities. It is also a chance to resolve the current impossible situation – delicately phrased in the consultation paper as 'a difficult position where it [the board] is accountable for delivering against challenging targets and yet is disconnected from and has limited influence over the resources required to achieve those targets'. Membership, and the availability of judges, will also be affected by the model eventually chosen.

Over time, with alterations to the law and a series of domestic and European Court judgments, the Parole Board has fundamentally changed. Starting as an advice-giving body, it now makes the final decision on whether or not to release prisoners convicted of the most serious offences – potentially the most risky and dangerous group of all. This has raised wider questions. Should the board's function remain, as now, limited to the release decision only? Is public protection better served by adopting a wider role – specifying what work should be undertaken in prison to reduce risk, for instance, or deciding about transfer to open conditions and other issues that would give it a sentence management function? This would certainly be resisted by NOMS, but many see it as logical for the body that has to make the end decision.

Parole Board practice is sometimes different from that of other bodies. It does not have the same rules as courts and does not test materials against the standard level of proof. It has to come to a judgement on risk based on the materials before it and can use hearsay evidence – often seen as important if its risk assessment function is to be protected. The interface with NOMS will remain a difficult area and at some stage decisions will also have to be made on the commissioning of reports, the training of reporting staff in risk assessment and the use of NOMS resources to meet the needs of prisoners when Parole Board decisions are made.

What seems clear is that significant change is needed. The latest Public Accounts Committee report into the work of the board highlighted the problems that have arisen from the switch from paper-based hearings to the much more resource intensive oral hearings. They were critical of prison and probation failures to provide timely and complete information for the assessment of serious offenders; this and other administrative delays meant that two-thirds of oral hearings had not been held in the planned month – and 20 per cent had been held more than twelve months late (Public Accounts Committee 2009).

The danger here, in public protection terms, is that panels will decide that yet further delay is the greater injustice and will make decisions on release even if information they might have wished for is not available. One or two high profile cases in the last few years have made it very clear that this is not a good option, but until the board has the powers to ensure that timely information is always provided (and many see a move to a more judicial framework as the way to achieve this) such problems will remain.

The exercise of discretion is what makes our criminal justice possible. Discretion over crime reporting and charging, discretion in sentencing and over the decision to release all help to make the system manageable. Discretion enables individual circumstances and progress to be assessed rather than compliance with rigid and inflexible rules. It also enables additional safeguards to be added in appropriate cases. In the absence of a risk-free society, unlimited prison capacity and the limitations of the tools we currently have at our disposal, parole seems to me to be the best option for the protection of the public.

References

Hart, S., Laws, D. R., and Kropp, R. (2000) 'The promise and the devil of sex offender risk assessment', in T. Ward, D. Laws and S. M. Hudson (eds) *Sexual Deviance: Issues and Controversy*. Thousand Oaks, CA: Sage.

HMIP (2006) *An Independent Review of a Serious Further Offence Case: Anthony Rice*. London: Her Majesty's Inspectorate of Probation.

Latham, D. (2009) 'Clarity essential to prisoner release process', *The Times*, 19 June 2009.

Ministry of Justice (2009) *The Future of the Parole Board*, Consultation Paper 14/09. London: Ministry of Justice.

Morgan, W. (2005) quoted in Parole Board, *Annual Report and Accounts 2004/05*. London: The Stationery Office (HC 518).

Nash, M. and Williams, A. (2008) *The Anatomy of Serious Further Offending*. Oxford: Oxford University Press.

Parole Board (2006) *Annual Report and Accounts 2005/2006*. London: The Stationery Office (HC 896).

Parole Board (2008) *Annual Report and Accounts 2007/2008*. London: The Stationery Office.

Parole Board (2009) *Annual Report and Accounts 2008/2009*. London: The Stationery Office.

Public Accounts Committee (2009) *The Work of the Parole Board Ninth Report of Session 2008/09*. London: The Stationery Office (HC 251).

Chapter 9

Community protection and multi-agency public protection arrangements

Hazel Kemshall

Introduction

Multi-agency systems for the risk assessment and management of offenders came into existence in the early 1990s, and were typified by 'case conferencing' style procedures between police and probation (the West Yorkshire police and probation area were one of the first to pursue this approach, see Maguire *et al.* 2001; see also Nash and Williams 2008: 109–12 for a history). Such arrangements were locally variable, and in some instances included other agencies such as social services and housing departments. Their development reflected growing preoccupation and widespread concern with child sexual abuse, and the spectre of the predatory paedophile gained currency during this period (Thomas 2005), fuelled by the release of notorious paedophiles Sydney Cooke and Robert Oliver and the subsequent media coverage (*Daily Mail*, 24 June 1998, p. 2; *Guardian*, 4 April 1998, p. 10). The main focus in this chapter is on MAPPA and community protection in respect of sex offenders, although violent offenders are beginning to comprise a large proportion of the MAPPA caseload and are presenting significant challenges to practice and procedures (see, for example, Nash and Williams 2008).

Multi-agency procedures became more formalised in response to the 1997 Sex Offenders Act which introduced the registration requirements for sex offenders (see Nash and Williams 2008: 110–11). The Act required greater cooperation between police and probation, and in effect sowed the seeds for the emergence of the multi-agency public protection arrangements (MAPPA). Parallel legislation such as the Crime and Disorder Act 1998 (sections 115–17 in particular) enabled information exchange for the purpose of preventing crime, and provided the backdrop against which information exchange systems between initially police and probation and then other agencies began to expand (Ericson and Haggerty 1997). These information exchange systems were initially characterised by risk aversion and precautionary approaches to risk, enmeshed in a growing penal policy of risk (Kemshall and Maguire 2001). This resulted in a growing actuarialism in risk assessment (see Kemshall 2003, chapter 4 for an overview; and Bonta and Wormith 2007). This increased focus on risk management can be summed up thus (Maguire *et al.* 2001: 3):

- In consultation with the local probation service, police forces should undertake a formal risk assessment of every offender who registers;

- Where the level of risk is considered high enough to warrant it, a plan should be drawn up to 'manage' the risk, where appropriate sharing information and tasks with other agencies; and,

- Decisions on whether to disclose information about offenders to other organisations, private individuals, or the community as a whole, should be made by the police on a case-by-case basis, taking into account their common law duty to prevent crime, as well as data protection law and relevant Articles of the European Convention on Human Rights.

MAPPA: the early years

An initial evaluation by Maguire *et al.* in 2001 found inconsistency of practice, lack of clarity about risk levels, differing systems and processes, and differing levels of participation from key agencies. Risk management plans did not necessarily follow the level of risk, although action plans were specified in most cases. Probation supervised those offenders for whom they had a statutory responsibility, using licence conditions to control offenders and breaching or recalling offenders who failed to comply. Police supervised offenders on the sex offender register, primarily through unannounced home visits, seeking intelligence:

> A key aim was to co-ordinate intelligence so as to be aware as early as possible of any warning signs of behaviour associated with the offender's individual modus operandi. For example, in one case an offender had previously used a bicycle in a particular type of area when stalking potential victims. It was discovered that he had recently bought a new bicycle and had been seen in a similar area (suggesting that he might be about to re-offend). (Maguire *et al.* 2001: 33)

Following this evaluation, multi-agency arrangements for risk assessment and management were subject to increasing central government policy guidance and formalisation, creating the multi-agency public protection arrangements (MAPPA) in 2000 (Criminal Justice and Court Services Act 2000, sections 67 and 68), and making police and probation responsible authorities. The early 2000s saw increasing formalisation, legislation and guidance (the Criminal Justice Act 2003; and MAPPA guidelines, see Home Office 2004; Ministry of Justice 2007, 2009), resulting in standard setting, improvements in structures and processes, and increased participation from key agencies (see evaluations by Kemshall *et al.* 2005; Wood and Kemshall 2007a). The Criminal Justice Act 2003 also made prisons a responsible authority, and placed a 'duty to cooperate' on a number of other agencies such as housing, education, youth offending teams and so forth. Increased central steer was also enabled through the formation of the Public Protection Unit, the formation of the National Probation Service, and more recently the National Offender Management Service.

MAPPA in the period from 1999 to 2005 has also been characterised by the use of restrictive conditions to enforce controlling risk management plans as part of an overall community protection model (Connelly and Williamson 2000; Kemshall 2008). Community protection is characterised by compulsory conditions, surveillance and monitoring, enforcement, compulsory treatment, and the prioritisation of victim and community rights over offenders (see Kemshall 2008: 13–21 for a full discussion). Interestingly, in a survey of Anglophone jurisdictions, Connelly and Williamson also identified clinical treatment and justice approaches, with treatment approaches becoming increasingly compulsory (via either sentencing or civil commitment), resulting in what Connelly and Williamson call a 'hybrid' approach to offender management. In jurisdictions characterised by such hybridisation, treatment, rehabilitation and protection are often mixed.

While the community protection model tends to dominate across the Anglophone countries, elements of deterrence and retribution also play a key role, with some commentators arguing that public protection has become a veneer for retributive and emotive sentencing (Pratt 2000a, 2000b), particularly for sex offenders (Thomas 2005). The 1990s and 2000s have seen protection used to justify disproportionate sentencing of sexual (and latterly violent offenders), particularly in response to media campaigns and political disquiet (Pratt 1997).

During the early years of MAPPA, risk management was characterised by information processing, combined with the monitoring and surveillance of offenders (Kemshall et al. 2005; Kemshall 2003), with limited attention to behaviour change or the treatment needs of offenders. For example, a typical risk management plan for a paedophile seen during the 2004–05 evaluation was as follows (Kemshall et al. 2005: 16):

- Electronic tagging
- Supervised accommodation
- Restriction of access to school locations
- Identification and intensive one-to-one work on key triggers, e.g. mood change, attitudes to and the sexualisation of children
- Use of local police intelligence about offending networks and surveillance on key movements.

However, the joint Police and Probation Inspectorate report on the community management of sex offenders conducted in 2005 found (summarised from HMIP and HMIC 2005):

- Lack of clarity and consistency about the level of MAPPA management for individual sex offender cases
- Lack of completion of OASys risk of harm sections

- Lack of clear recording in case files
- Lack of home visiting and monitoring of sex offenders
- Lack of appropriate resourcing for police visits to sex offenders
- Risk management plans not always implemented
- Poor minute-taking and actions not clear
- Lack of reviews, and no follow-up on failed actions
- Lack of appropriate and dedicated resources for MAPPA.

In addition, the joint inspection examined the quality of MAPPA supervision and oversight of cases, and against a benchmarked level assessed cases as to whether they were 'above the line'. Table 9.1 summarises the findings.

The inquiry also noted that: 'In the 100 cases we inspected interventions and their level of intensity were not proportionate to the assessed risk of harm in 35 per cent of cases which indicates either more or less input was required in those cases to manage risk of harm' (HMIP and HMIC 2005: 27). However, a Home Office report, *MAPPA – The First Five Years* (2007a), painted a rosier picture of effectiveness, based on reconviction rates for MAPPA cases. The report noted that the number of serious further offences committed by offenders managed at levels two and three in 2005/06 was only 0.44 per cent. The biggest impact was at level three, 'and such a low serious re-offending rate for this particular group of offenders is to be welcomed and supports the view that MAPPA is making a real contribution to the management of dangerousness in the community' (Home Office 2007a: 6–7). Enforcement and breach of parole licences and court orders had also risen for levels 2 and 3, in effect, taking action to prevent further offending

Table 9.1 Comparison of cases concerning risk management plans and staff involvement in child protection arrangements.

% Above the line (excellent/sufficient)	SOTI	ESI
(For high/very high risk of harm cases only)		
Has a good quality risk management plan been produced under MAPPA or other interagency arrangement?	50%	58%
Is this risk management plan being executed appropriately, with effective liaison between the agencies, particularly police and probation, including on accommodation issues?	42%	66%
Has the risk management plan been appropriately reviewed?	50%	66%
(For child protection cases only)		
Has there been probation and police involvement in child protection arrangements – e.g. core group or case conference and liaison between agencies to reduce the risk to the child(ren)?	59%	80%

SOTI = Sex Offeder Thematic Inspection
ESI   = Effective supervision inspection
Source: HMIP and HMIC 2005: 39, table 5, reproduced with kind permission of Crown Copyright.

based upon problematic behaviours or breach of conditions. Action to enforce the sex offender register requirements also increased by 30 per cent (through cautions and further convictions) and affected some 1,295 offenders, '4.3% of the total registered in the community' (2007a: 7). The period 2005/06 also saw the use of 973 sex offender prevention orders (SOPOs) under the Sexual Offences Act 2003. However, the report presented the main techniques of risk management as enforcement, breach and parole recall, and lacked any emphasis upon improving compliance, or on techniques to foster long-term self risk management.

The overuse of restrictive conditions has also been problematic. The HMIP thematic inspection on sex offenders noted that sex offenders subject to restrictive measures may struggle with social isolation and experience difficulties with community reintegration (HMIP and HMIC 2005). In the American context, Levenson and Cotter identified fourteen states that have exclusion zones prohibiting sex offenders from living within close proximity to a school, park, day care centre or school bus stop (2005: 168). They note that the zones range from 500 feet to up to 2,000 feet and in California to a quarter of a mile from a school and prohibits sex offenders residing within 35 miles of a victim or witness. Interestingly, they cite studies in which the evidence for proximity to children resulting in recidivism is mixed (see Walker *et al.* 2001; Colorado Department of Public Safety 2004; Minnesota Department of Corrections 2003). They contend that the overuse of exclusion zones may result in homelessness and transience thus making risk management harder. It also produces illogical responses to risk, potentially displacing risk onto more vulnerable people, summed up by one offender thus: 'I couldn't live in an adult mobile home park because a church was 880ft away and had a children's class that met once a week. I was forced to move to a motel where right next door to my room was a family with three children – but it qualified under the rule' (Levenson and Cotter 2005: 175).

Early guidance also tended to emphasise process and system issues within MAPPA (Home Office 2004) rather than effective interventions or the quality of supervisory practice under MAPPA. The latter was investigated under the Child Sex Offender Review (Wood and Kemshall 2007a) with key findings integrated into MAPPA guidance in 2007 and 2009 (see Ministry of Justice 2009: 178–86). This evaluation is presented in more detail below.

The first ten years of multi-agency working with high risk sexual and violent offenders has also been characterised by the precautionary principle and concerns with reputational risk management in the face of key failures (such as the murder of Naomi Bryant by Anthony Rice in 2006). The precautionary principle, or 'better safe than sorry', resulted in inflation throughout the MAPPA system, particularly at level two[1] distracting resources from case reviews, and from the management of the critical few (Kemshall *et al.* 2005). The period since 2005 has seen increased attention to quality, particularly on supervisory practice and interventions with sexual offenders.

Violent offenders are also under the remit of MAPPA, although they have often received less media and policy attention. Violent offenders have also attracted a public protection focus through the use of indeterminate public protection (IPP) sentences as created by the Criminal Justice Act 2003 under which 65 specified violent offences can be considered if the offender meets the 'serious harm' and 'significant risk' criteria (Kemshall 2008: 16). Both IPP sentences under supervision in the community and parolees on licence for violent offenders are likely to present a growing caseload for MAPPA. From 2009 violent offenders in Scotland come under the remit of MAPPA, presenting a significant resource challenge. This resource challenge is reflected in the English and Welsh MAPPA guidance 2009, in which minimum standards for visiting high risk offenders was reduced from twelve per year to four, resulting in a typical media response: 'Officers are now only expected to visit paedophiles, rapists and other sex offenders at their homes four times a year compared with once a month previously' (*Daily Telegraph* 2009). While visits are acknowledged as essential to the effective monitoring of lifestyle, and in recognising the early signs of grooming, this restructuring of the priorities of visits implicitly indicates how difficult it is to resource the community supervision of risky offenders. In this situation it is imperative that resources follow the most risk, and that contact with offenders is of high quality and effective.

Focusing on effectiveness and quality

The evaluation of MAPPA in 2007 focused on effective supervision practices and the quality of risk management (Wood and Kemshall 2007a). Importantly the evaluation interviewed and considered views of sex offenders as well as practitioners. The study found best practice MAPPA areas had a greater balance between internal and external controls. Offenders valued and benefited from attention to their personal and social problems, and to their personal goals, needs and desires – an approach promoted by the 'Good Lives Model' (see Ward and Stewart 2003a, 2003b; Ward and Maruna 2007). In addition, offenders were more likely to comply with MAPPA supervision if the role of MAPPA and their supervision requirements had been properly explained to them (Wood and Kemshall 2007a), and many saw MAPPA as having a legitimate role in helping them to avoid future offending and in reintegrating into society. Offenders were able to articulate the techniques helpful in changing behaviours and these included the following (Wood and Kemshall 2007a: 14):

- Self-risk management including the use of 'contracts' and self-reporting to police or probation if an offender believed they were about to offend.
- Clear articulation of victim issues, including the recognition of the impact of sexual offending upon children.
- The use of 'distraction techniques' to avoid inappropriate sexual thoughts when seeing children.

Staff were also interviewed, and were positive about the contribution of MAPPA to the supervision of sex offenders in the community. The following themes emerged as particularly important: effective communication and information exchange between key agencies; good links to social services and appropriate use of the relevant child protection systems, and the use of controlled disclosure to 'at risk' third parties to aid effective risk management. In addition, key facilities and resources were seen as crucial to the effective community management of offenders, including consideration of victim issues and protective measures, appropriate and supportive accommodation, rapid response to deteriorating cases, surveillance and treatment programmes. In particular, all MAPPA areas recognised the resource priorities required by critical cases managed at level three (from Wood and Kemshall 2007b: 2, 'Findings, 285'). Staff also identified a number of other factors as key to MAPPA success, most notably: timely and early preparation especially pre-release; early identification of treatment need and referral to appropriate groupwork programmes supported by one-to-one work; relapse prevention work focusing on recognising and managing triggers for offending; home visits and being 'lifestyle vigilant'; police surveillance and enforcement of appropriate external controls; and swift information exchange.

The quality of the supervisory relationship was also seen as critical to MAPPA case success, in particular 'pro-social supervision' (Trotter 1999, 2000, 2007), which was seen as important in facilitating offender disclosure about risky thoughts, attitudes and behaviours. Support combined with home visiting and focused attention on both needs and risky behaviours were seen as effective, supported by the use of 'behavioural contracts' to encourage change and compliance, such as the following (Wood and Kemshall 2007a: 18–19):

- I will attend church only at the 8.30 a.m. and 6.30 p.m. services.
- I will ensure that I sit apart from children and young people in the church.
- I will ensure that I am never alone with children and young people at church or at church groups/activities.
- I will not involve myself in any way with children and young people.
- I accept that certain people within the church will need to be aware of this contract and this will be on a 'need to know basis'. I understand that I will be aware of the people who are given this information and the reason why they need to have this information.
- I understand that if these conditions are broken the church will have no alternative but to prohibit me from attending and will have a responsibility to report this to my probation officer.

Similar contracts have been used for employment, college attendance and leisure activities, helping to achieve both rehabilitation and public protection. However, such contracts have to be used with care, based on a thorough risk assessment, and with support mechanisms and a contingency plan in the case of breakdown. Not all offenders can or will comply with such contracts, and it is important to recognise that while contracts may practically support legal requirements like parole conditions or sex offender prevention orders, they do not of themselves have legal force.

The *MAPPA Guidance 2009* reflected this growing emphasis upon quality and standards, with attention to rigour in decision-making (Ministry of

Justice 2009: 32); increased rigour in processes and systems (sections 4, 5, 7 and 10); and focus on supervisory practice in section 21 (pp. 178–86, a section based on Wood and Kemshall 2007a). Interestingly this guidance attempted to address the thorny issue of performance standards and key performance indicators (Ministry of Justice 2009: 229–33). The defensibility test set here is: 'Was everything that could reasonably have been done to prevent offenders from reoffending actually done?' (2009: 229).

Strategic management boards (SMBs) and the responsible authorities are urged to review and monitor the effectiveness of MAPPA performance. MAPPA are advised to collect both qualitative and quantitative data, particularly using quarterly data from ViSOR (Violent and Sex Offender Register; largely numerical data on categories and levels of offenders under MAPPA); qualitative audits on level two and 3 cases to determine effective management; and 'analysis of key performance indicator data to assess the extent of compliance' (2009: 229). The subsequent pages of the guidance offer specific detail on data collection and analysis about effectiveness and the quality of service delivery. Interestingly a number of the indicators are about throughputs and outputs – numbers at specific categories and levels, review dates, breaches, enforcement and so on. In terms of qualitative data, there is some attempt to audit good practice, but interestingly this is not linked to the good practice standards outlined in section 21. Thus there are no measures to capture the extent to which offenders are engaged; how behaviour contracts are used and to what effect; or to capture the range, extent and effectiveness of pro-social work with high risk offenders.

The supervision of high risk offenders, and to some extent MAPPA, was seriously challenged by the Dano Sonnex case in which Sonnex and Nigel Farmer brutally killed two French students and the media coverage of their case in June 2009. The case resulted in the departure of the Chief Probation Officer of London Probation, and a scathing attack on probation by Justice Minister Jack Straw (see Jack Straw's House of Commons statement, as printed in the *Guardian*, 4 June 2009). In brief, Sonnex was on licence at the time and subject to recall, and hence is seen as having committed this offence when 'he should have been in custody' (Straw statement). In a review of the case Liz Hill stated that:

> Assessments varied unjustifiably, and he was incorrectly assessed to present a medium risk, which in turn was the basis for the decision to allocate his supervision to a standard offender management team, rather than a more skilled public protection team in LPA. Referrals to MAPPA were not followed through. Information about an alleged offence shortly after his release was not acted on by LPA managers as it should have been. (Hill 2009: 3)

This report has resulted in all probation areas being tasked with providing a transparent and accountable system of quality assurance for the management of high risk offenders that can be actively reviewed by regional Directors of Offender Management and the centre. Thus chief officers are now required to action the following recommendation:

NOMS should design a mechanism by which the Chief Officer and the Board can assure the DOM that risks presented by higher risk offenders under supervision are being properly prioritised and managed to deliver as safe a level of public protection as is feasible. This measure should be based on numerical factors such as caseloads, staffing levels, etc. and the judgement of the Chief Officer. Accountability for delivering against this measure should be through the Board/Trust to the Director of Offender Management on a quarterly basis. The work to design this mechanism should be completed before June 30 2009 to be implemented from Quarter 2 2009. (Hill 2009: 4)

At present it is too early to judge the long-term reputational and operational impacts on probation and MAPPA in particular, but the case illustrates, as ever, that it takes only one serious failing to bring the whole system into disrepute.

More recent developments in the community management of sex offenders: the implications for MAPPA and public protection

Paralleling developments in the community protection paradigm were initiatives rooted in the voluntary sector and faith-based communities (see Kemshall 2008, chapter 5 for a full discussion). The most notable of these are Circles of Support and Accountability (COSA), initiated in Canada, and with a pilot subject to evaluation in Thames Valley, UK (see Bates et al. 2007). COSA grew out of negative reaction to the release of sex offenders into the community, and concerns that formal supervisory mechanisms could neither successfully reintegrate sex offenders nor guarantee public safety (Wilson 2003; Wilson and Picheca 2005; Wilson et al. 2005, 2007). In brief, COSA takes a broadly restorative and reintegrative approach to sexual offenders, and forms a circle of volunteers around an offender to offer a combination of both support and vigilance (see Wilson et al. 2007 for a detailed description). Interestingly in the UK setting, COSA is integrated within the MAPPA process, and each circle has 'hands on' contact with MAPPA professionals, and in addition to offer support the circle provides 'soft data' taken from offenders' self-reporting and the observations of volunteers (Bates et al. 2007: 22). This data is used by MAPPA to assess progress and compliance. In the UK context COSA has been co-opted to the community protection model, with vigilance and reporting to staff seen as crucial, and effective communication procedures with MAPPA seen as a key ingredient of COSA functioning (Bates et al. 2007: 18). While the Canadian COSA has been positively evaluated with a 70 per cent reduction in sexual recidivism against a matched sample (Wilson 2007: 37), the sample evaluated in the UK numbered only sixteen which makes general conclusions from this early pilot difficult (as of 2007, four recalls to prison out of the sixteen had occurred; Bates et al. 2007).

While the pilot is small, the importance of COSA UK is the blending of reintegrative and community protection concerns, paralleled in other initiatives such as the Good Lives Model, and increased attention to compliance and motivational issues. Disillusion with the punishment paradigm approach to sexual offenders in particular (see McCulloch and Kelly 2007 for a full review), has focused attention on the Good Lives Model which 'proposes a more holistic and constructive way of conceptualising and engaging with offenders, focusing less on individual offender deficits and more on the personal, inter-personal and social contexts required to enable offenders to live and sustain a "good life"' (McCulloch and Kelly 2007: 15). The Good Lives Model (GLM) is most often associated with the work of Tony Ward (see Ward and Maruna 2007; Ward and Stewart 2003a). In brief, GLM works with the offender to reframe his/her goals and provides the means to achieve them positively and legitimately, while assisting the offender in reconstructing a new identity that pursues personal goals legally (Whitehead *et al.* 2007). For example, a sex offender may pursue relatedness and intimacy through inappropriate relationships with children (Ward and Stewart 2003b). GLM will focus on positive and pro-social approach goals to achieve legitimately these 'primary goods' of intimacy, and emphasise avoidance goals to prevent harm. However, GLM has been subject to limited evaluation (see Kemshall 2008, chapter 5 for an overview), and comparison to more traditional risk management strategies is still required (see Bonta and Andrews 2003 for a full review). Against this backdrop, the important contribution of GLM to risk management is in its emphasis upon engagement and motivation as key processes of change. In a context of rising prison populations and the need to reduce custodial costs, there is now a greater focus on compliance and community integration, with probation services, for example, expected to reduce parole recalls and breach rates. This has already extended the remit of 'prevention of serious harm' from monitoring and surveillance to long-term behavioural change. Porporino and Fabiano (2007) have promoted their 'casework within a motivational framework' as an antidote to the public protection 'meta-narrative' (a term coined by Robinson and McNeill 2004). In brief, Porporino and Fabiano draw on extensive research on effective practice to argue that case management should be integrated and structured, utilising appropriate problem definition, pro-social style, motivational techniques which emphasise negotiated problem definition and the use of approach goals to behaviour change, and planned intervention that focuses on desistance from crime. Importantly, they note that there has to be a careful balance between the 'incentives and disincentives that operate on offenders' (2007: 202). Key techniques are reinforcement of change, removal of obstacles to change and progress, responding and dealing with relapse, building self-efficacy in offenders, helping offenders to identify and avoid triggers to offending, how to combat negative emotions with positive self-talk, and the development of strong networks of pro-social support (Porporino and Fabiano 2007).

In terms of policy, the Home Office *Child Sex Offender Review* (*CSOR*) (Home Office 2007b) has given impetus to MAPPA, but also to broader policy responses to sex offenders. The review focused on current practice with sex offenders, including work abroad and stated: 'The principal aim of all the actions in this report is to provide greater child protection. This may be achieved through reducing re-offending by known offenders, preventing initial offending, and identifying where offences are taking place by increasing people's confidence to report them' (Home Office 2007b: 5).

In essence, the report attempted to straddle two strands of thinking in the effective management of sex offenders: a strengthening of statutory responses and increased restrictive conditions; and a public awareness/education response rooted in the work of Richard Laws (2000), and expounded predominantly by the children's charities such as Barnado's, NSPCC, and Stop It Now! Their influence is represented in the following comment within the Home Office report:

> During the review, those involved in protecting children stressed the importance of public involvement in enhancing child protection. We need to give the public the means to fulfil this role, and we need to achieve a culture change whereby the relationship between the police and the public is more open, with information being shared in both directions. (Home Office 2007b: 9)

The review acknowledged that targeted public awareness and education of parents, particularly around grooming behaviours, and in order to accept and recognise that most sexual offenders are known to the victims, were important but difficult messages to achieve. To this end, action 1 of the review recommended a public awareness programme in partnership with 'non-governmental organisations', and in 2008–09 a pilot involving the Lucy Faithfull Foundation/Stop It Now! was carried out.[2] To support this, and to enhance public confidence in the police and greater dialogue between the two, action 2 of *CSOR* proposed 'increased awareness of how sex offenders are managed in the community' (2007b: 28). The report proposed easily accessible public information, especially about MAPPA. The latter was not to involve public disclosure about individual cases (although MAPPA do have the power to disclose to third parties where risk and case management justify it), but was intended to 'reassure the public that protection arrangements are in place, and to ensure a transparent system operates in which the public is fully aware of the true level of risk' (2007b: 9). The *MAPPA Guidance 2009*, however, gave little emphasis to communication with the public, providing six lines of coverage in section 25.7, stating:

> Two challenges facing MAPPA are how to effectively manage public expectations and how to handle media interest. The national MAPPA Communication Strategy requires each RA to produce and implement a media strategy and an annual communication plan. SMBs should make good use of the MAPPA leaflet, **Keeping Our Communities Safe**, to promote the work of MAPPA in its local area. (Ministry of Justice 2009: 220; and Home Office 2008 for the leaflet).

While the guidance urged SMBs to develop a 'wider strategy of communication and education of the public' (2009: 220), to date this has been largely carried out by annual reports, with limited public accessibility, and with little accountability or transparency to victims or their relatives (as reviewed by a BBC Radio Four *File on Four* programme 7 July 2009). The MAPPA leaflet comprises two pages providing a brief overview of MAPPA key functions, and it is difficult to see how this could be considered as a core feature of a public awareness and education strategy with local communities. There is no consideration of hard to reach groups, communication strategies to encompass diversity, or how to convey difficult messages about risk to the public.

It is notable that the Cosgrove Report in Scotland over ten years ago (1999) strongly placed communities 'at the centre of efforts to combat sex offending' (Cosgrove 1999: 5). The first of their measures to strengthen the response to sex offending was: 'Improved understanding within communities about sex offending and the positive involvement of communities in the development of local strategies for the management of sex offenders' (Cosgrove 1999: 5).

The report promoted community 'vigilance' as opposed to vigilante action, as the underpinning notion for 'building the community's response to the problems of sexual offending' (1999: 11). In the interim years, this underpinning commitment and the centrality of community education and engagement has been eroded by distorted media coverage of sexual offending and political expediency, in England and Wales as well as in Scotland. To a limited extent the *Child Sex Offender Review* has renewed interest in the 'community', although the centrality and prominence of community is questionable.

In response to actions 1–4 of *CSOR*, the Home Office launched a pilot allowing members of the public to seek disclosures from the police about named individuals if they had justifiable concerns (action 4 of the *CSOR*). In those cases where the offender has a conviction for child sexual offences and the risk justifies it, there is a presumption for disclosure to the applicant.[3] It is anticipated that as well as ameliorating both media and public calls for a 'Sarah's Law', such limited disclosure will enhance both public confidence and public dialogue with the police about the community management of sex offenders. This initiative, alongside a strengthening of MAPPA's use of controlled disclosure, is seen as critical to increasing child safety (Home Office 2007b). Of the twenty actions stated in the review, actions 1–4 can be broadly placed within the public health paradigm, and implicitly acknowledge that sex offenders will be part of communities over the long term, and that a proportion of sex offenders will always be among us. The *Child Sex Offender Review* is perhaps novel, in that it represents the first piece of substantial sex offender policy that attempts (perhaps rather implicitly) to integrate both the community protection and public health paradigms into a coherent strategy for managing sex offenders. However, the review is rather weak on how these approaches should be combined into a long-term effective strategy, or how these two distinct paradigms can be combined into a complementary approach. Petrunik, for example, has argued that community protection is in essence a panoptical system which uses the expertise and knowledge of professionals to exercise control, interventions and surveillance (2002). Within this system, the few watch the many. However, the system is limited, not least by finite resources, and the capacity and expertise of the experts upon whom the system rests. Petrunik contrasts this with a synoptical system of surveillance and control in which the many (in this case 'the public') watch the few (sex offenders). The move to a synoptic system is most often driven by media coverage, public outrage, and failures within the panoptical system (such as MAPPA failures or serious further incidents). The public response to such failure is to demand a 'greater say' in the risk management of sex offenders, and thus panoptic control systems elide into synoptic ones (see Kemshall 2008: 126 for a full discussion). However, it is important to recognise the differing drivers for synoptic control – these can be inclusive and reintegrative (for example, COSA), or exclusionary (to 'out' sex offenders and drive them out of communities). Differing values can influence these demands and developments, and it is important therefore that policy-makers explicitly consider them, and work coherently at complementary strategies that have a common value base – this is not readily achieved by the *Child Sex Offender Review*. In the absence of such explicit consideration, political expediency can, and often does, have greater weight. Evolutionary and pragmatic policy and practice developments are also not without their dangers. For example, COSA in its original Canadian conception was based on a commitment to community reintegration. Within the Thames Valley, COSA has been co-opted to MAPPA, and it will be important to see whether these two approaches can be blended into a 'hybrid approach' to offenders that preserves core values. To date the results are promising (Kemshall 2008), but the broader debate about how to effectively combine community protection with public awareness and more integrative approaches remains embryonic.

As Petrunik reminds us, community protection and community reintegration approaches often represent differing constituent groups and voices (2002). The protection discourse is fuelled by the media (Kitzinger 2004), and has a long history of being co-opted to political expediency, often with specific associations with high profile failures and named victims (Kemshall 2008: 127). Under the guise of prevention, the key ingredients at this approach are often retribution, punishment and exclusion. In contrast, community integration emphasises 'healing the harm' rather than 'punishing the harm'. While initially dismissed as 'being nice to sex offenders', the approach is gaining ground with its focus on effectiveness, reducing offending and risk, and holding offenders accountable for their actions. As Petrunik puts it: 'the sex offender is given the chance to redeem himself under the caring and ever so watchful eyes of a concerned community' (2002: 506).

Conclusion: where next?

The first ten years of MAPPA focused on systems and process, with an underlying concern about reputational risk rooted in a precautionary approach to risk management. This resulted in MAPPA being largely inward-looking, and in its firm rooting within a community protection legal and policy response to high risk offenders that has emphasised restrictive conditions, surveillance and control as the main techniques of intervention. More recently, work with sex offenders, particularly failures, the strain on resources, and the importation of other techniques for the effective management of sex offenders has resulted in a growing consideration of alternative strategies, most notably around disclosure, GLM and COSA. Initial evidence indicates that MAPPA now has to be more outward-looking, particularly in disclosing and also communicating with local communities about risk, but also that supervisory practice is beginning to take on board these new interventions.

On a broader front, recent developments have seen an increased 'blending' of community protection and community reintegration approaches, most notably in the co-option of COSA to MAPPA, increased attention to GLM and pro-social supervision, and the new, albeit limited, policy attention to public awareness and education. Notwithstanding the *Child Sex Offender Review*, this blending has been pragmatic, and achieved largely in the absence of a broader long-term strategy aimed at their complementary use. In order to develop a strategy aimed at the 'protective integration' of sex offenders (Kemshall 2008: 132), that is – a strategy providing both safety for victims and offenders and greater long-term effectiveness of interventions and self-regulation by sex offenders – a number of key actions are required:

- Increased policy and public debate about how to combine the community protection and community integration approaches, and in respect of sexual offenders there should be a particular emphasis upon how to improve child safety as the underpinning aim.

- Using the research literature on risk perception and risk communication to develop successful strategies and processes for discussing risk with the public. Key lessons are that communicating with targeted groups and the use of community opinion-formers is a more helpful strategy than using the news print media or blanket campaigns (see Kemshall 2008: 78–83). Citizens' juries is one helpful mechanism.

- Continued evaluation and research into new initiatives emanating from both approaches, but particularly those that are broadly integrative and where, at present, research studies are less developed. This would build an evidence base from which more informed policy decisions could be taken.

- Increased dissemination and learning from specific examples where community protection and community integration approaches have been practically blended, for example, Thames Valley and supervision of high risk offenders using GLM.

- 'Joined-up thinking' at a policy level, including the integration of learning and evaluation from various pilots that straddle both community protection and community integration (for example, polygraph with sex offenders, limited public disclosure; and the public awareness pilots are all subject to evaluations). At present such pilots are evaluated in isolation, and there is no overt mechanism for synthesising learning or outcomes from them that may enhance an overall sex offender management strategy.

- Learning from sex offenders themselves. What works best for them, particularly in the long-term management of their own risks?

Finally as the Derwent Initiative put it, the time has come to actively engage communities as 'participants in, rather than as passive recipients of, public protection' (TDI 2007: 7). Such engagement may itself do much to ameliorate the retributive response to sex offenders so prevalent, and aid their long-term 'protective reintegration' into communities where we can all feel and *be* safer.

Acknowledgement

The author gratefully acknowledges the work and colleagueship of Jason Wood on a number of the studies cited in this chapter.

Selected further reading

For a helpful overview of sex offender policy development in the United States and Canada see Petrunik (2002). The article contrasts exclusionary and re-integrative policies, and examines the key drivers behind each policy perspective. For an introduction to penal policy responses to high risk offenders across a number of Anglophone countries see Kemshall (2008). This book also examines practice and policy developments in the community management of high risk offenders, with a particular emphasis on the UK content. For a highly readable, and at times challenging perspective on 'dangerousness' offenders see Nash and Williams (2008). The book examines the practicalities and difficulties of multi-agency working, and uses the prism of serious further offending to examine the organisational and structural issues behind risk management failures.

Notes

1 **Level one: ordinary risk management** – Where the agency responsible for the offender can manage risk without the significant involvement of other agencies. This level of management is only appropriate for category one and two offenders who are assessed as presenting a low or medium risk. **Level two: local inter-agency risk management** – where there is active involvement of more than one agency in risk management plans, either because of a higher level of risk or because of the complexity of managing the offender. It is common for level three cases to be 'referred down' to level two when risk of harm deflates. The permanent membership of level two should comprise those agencies that have an involvement in risk management. Responsible authorities should decide the frequency of meetings and also the representation, taking an active role in the convening of meetings and quality assurance of risk management. **Level three: Multi-agency public protection panel (MAPPP)** – for those defined as the 'critical few', the MAPPP is responsible for risk management drawing together key active partners who will take joint responsibility for the community management of the offender. An offender who should be referred to this level of management is defined (in the *MAPPA Guidance 2004*: para. 116) as someone who:
   (i) is assessed under OASys as being a high or very high risk of causing serious harm; **AND**
   (ii) presents risks that can only be managed by a plan which requires close co-operation at a senior level due to the complexity of the case and/or because of the unusual resource commitments it requires; **OR**

(iii) although not assessed as a high or very high risk, the case is exceptional because the likelihood of media scrutiny and/or public interest in the management of the case is very high and there is a need to ensure that public confidence in the criminal justice system is sustained.

2 The pilot is currently subject to evaluation.

3 The pilot is currently subject to evaluation.

References

Bates, A., Saunders, B. and Wilson, C. (2007) 'Doing something about it: A follow-up study of sex offenders participating in Thames Valley Circles of Support and Accountability', *British Journal of Community Justice*, 5(1): 19–42.

BBC Radio Four (2009) *File on Four*, 7 July 2009. Online at: www.bbc.co.uk/iplayer/episode/b00lgj3h/File_on_4_07_07_2009/ (accessed 14 July 2009).

Bonta, J. and Andrews, D. (2003) 'A commentary on Ward and Stewart's model of human needs', *Psychology, Crime and Law*, 9: 215–18.

Bonta, J. and Wormith, S. (2007) 'Risk and need assessment', in G. McIvor and P. Raynor (eds) *Developments in Social Work with Offenders. Research Highlights 48*. London: Jessica Kingsley.

Colorado Department of Public Safety (2004) *Report on Safety Issues Raised by Living Arrangements and Location of Sex Offenders in the Community*. Denver, CO: Sex Offender Management Board.

Connelly, C. and Williamson, S. (2000) *A Review of the Research Literature on Serious Violent and Sexual Offenders*. Edinburgh: Scottish Executive Central Research Unit.

Cosgrove, Lady (1999) *Reducing the Risk: Improving the Response to Sex Offending. Report of the Expert Panel on Sex Offending*. Edinburgh: Scottish Executive.

Daily Mail (1998) 'Villagers rebel over move to house a child killer in their midst', 24 June, p. 2.

Daily Telegraph (2009) 'Home visits for sex offenders cut', 26 May. Online at: www.telegraph.co.uk/news (accessed 1 June 2009).

Ericson, R. and Haggerty, K. (1997) *Policing the Risk Society*. Oxford: Clarendon Press.

Guardian (1998) 'The challenge of child sex man', 4 April, p. 10.

Guardian (2009) 'Sonnex: Jack Straw's full statement', 4 June. Online at: www.guardian.co.uk/uk/2009/jun/04/sonnex-case-jack-straw-statement (accessed 30 July 2009).

HMIP and HMIC (2005) *Managing Sex Offenders in the Community: A Joint Inspection on Sex Offenders*. London: HMIP and HMIC.

Hill, L. (2009) *Investigation into the Issues Arising from the Serious Further Offence Review, Dano Sonnex, aged 23*. Online at: www.justice.gov.uk/news/docs/noms-investigation-report-sonnex.pdf.

Home Office (2004) *MAPPA Guidance (Version 2)*. London: Home Office.

Home Office (2007a) *MAPPA – The First Five Years: A National Overview of the Multi-Agency Public Protection Arrangements*. London: Home Office.

Home Office (2007b) *Child Sex Offender Review*. London: Home Office.

Home Office (2008) *Keeping our Communities Safe: Managing Risk Through MAPPA*. London: Home Office.

Kemshall, H. (2003) *Understanding Risk in Criminal Justice*. Maidenhead: Open University Press/McGraw-Hill.

Kemshall, H. and Maguire, M. (2001) 'Public protection, partnership and risk penality: the multi-agency risk management of sexual and violent offenders', *Punishment and Society*, 3(2): 237–64.

Kemshall, H. (2008) *Understanding the Community Management of High Risk Offenders*. Maidenhead: Open University Press/McGraw-Hill.

Kemshall, H., Wood, J., Mackenzie, G., Bailey, R. and Yates, J. (2005) *Strengthening Multi-Agency Public Protection Arrangements (MAPPA)*. London: Home Office.

Kitzinger, J. (2004) *Framing Abuse: Media Influence and Public Understanding of Sexual Violence Against Children*. London: Pluto Press.

Laws, R. (2000) 'Sexual offending as a public health problem: a North American perspective', *Journal of Sexual Aggression*, 5(1) 30–44.

Levenson, J. and Cotter, L. (2005) 'The impact of the sex offender residence restrictions: 1,000 feet from danger or one step from the absurd?', *International Journal of Offender Therapy and Comparative Criminology*, 49(2): 168–78.

Maguire, M., Kemshall, H., Noaks, L. and Wincup, E. (2001) *Risk Management of Sexual and Violent Offenders: The Work of Public Protection Panels*, Police Research Series Paper 139. London: Home Office.

McCulloch, T. and Kelly, L. (2007) 'Working with sex offenders in context: which way forward?', *Probation Journal*, 6(2): 197–218.

Ministry of Justice (2007) *MAPPA Guidance 2007, Version 2.0*. MAPPA team, National Offender Management Service Public Protection Unit. London: Ministry of Justice.

Ministry of Justice (2009) *MAPPA Guidance 2009*. London: Home Office.

Minnesota Department of Corrections (2003) *Level Three Sex Offenders Residential Placement Issues*. St Paul, MN: Minnesota Department of Corrections.

Nash, M. (2006) *Public Protection and the Criminal Justice Process*. Oxford: Oxford University Press.

Nash, M. and Williams, A. (2008) *The Anatomy of Serious Offending*. Oxford: Oxford University Press.

Porporino, F. and Fabiano, E. (2007) 'Case managing offenders within a motivational framework', in G. McIvor and P. Raynor (eds) *Developments in Social Work with Offenders. Research Highlights 48*. London: Jessica Kingsley.

Petrunik, M. (2002) 'Managing unacceptable risk: sex offenders, community response and social policy in the United States and Canada', *International Journal of Offender Therapy and Comparative Criminology*, 46(4): 483–511.

Pratt, J. (1997) *Governing the Dangerous*. Sydney: Federation Press.

Pratt, J. (2000a) 'The return of the wheelbarrow men or the arrival of postmodern penality?', *British Journal of Criminology*, 40: 127–45.

Pratt, J. (2000b) 'Emotive and ostentatious punishment: its decline and resurgence in modern society', *Punishment and Society*, 2(4): 127–45.

Robinson, G. and McNeill, F. (2004) 'Purposes matter: the ends of probation', in G. Mair (ed.) *What Matters in Probation*. Cullompton: Willan Publishing.

TDI (The Derwent Initiative) (2007) *Tackling Sex Offending Together*. Newcastle upon Tyne: TDI.

Thomas, T. (2005) *Sex Crime: Sex Offending and Society*. Cullompton: Willan Publishing.

Trotter, C. (1999) *Working with Involuntary Clients: A Guide to Practice*. London: Sage Publications.

Trotter, C. (2000) 'Social work education, pro-social modelling and effective probation practice', *Probation Journal*, 47: 256–61.

Trotter, C. (2007) 'Pro-social modelling', in G. McIvor and P. Raynor (eds) *Developments in Social Work with Offenders. Research Highlights 48*. London: Jessica Kingsley.

Walker, J., Golden, J. and VanHouten, A. (2001) 'The geographic link between sex offenders and potential victims: a routine activities approach', *Justice Research and Policy*, 3(2): 15–33.

Ward, T. and Maruna, S. (2007) *Rehabilitation*. London: Routledge.

Ward, T. and Stewart, C. (2003a) 'Criminogenic needs and human needs: a theoretical model', *Psychology, Crime and Law*, 31(3) 282–305.

Ward, T. and Stewart, C. (2003b) 'The treatment of sex offenders: risk management and good lives', *Professional Psychology: Research and Practice*, 34(4): 353–60.

Whitehead, P. R., Ward, T. and Collie, R. M. (2007) 'Time for a change: applying the good lives model of rehabilitation to a high risk offender', *International Journal of Offender Therapy and Comparative Criminology*, 51(5): 578–98.

Wilson, R. J. and Picheca, J. E. (2005) 'Circles of Support and Accountability: engaging the community in sexual offender risk management', in B. K. Schwartz (ed.) *The Sexual Offender*, vol. 5. New York: Civic Research Institute.

Wilson, R. J. (2003) 'Risk, reintegration and registration: a Canadian perspective on community sex offender risk management', *ATSA Forum*, 15.

Wilson, R. J. (2007) 'Out in the open', *Community Care*, 19–25 April 36–7.

Wilson, R. J., Picheca, J. E. and Prinzo, M. (2005). *Circles of Support and Accountability: An Evaluation of the Pilot Project in South-Central Ontario*. Correctional Service of Canada.

Wilson, R. J., Picheca, J. E. and Pinzo, M. (2007) 'Evaluating the effectiveness of professionally facilitated volunteerism in the community management of high-risk sexual offenders: part two, a comparison of recidivism rates', *Howard Journal*, 46(4): 327–37.

Wood, J. and Kemshall, H. (2007a) (with Maguire, M., Hudson, K. and Mackenzie, G.) *The Operation and Experience of Multi-Agency Public Protection Arrangements (MAPPA)*, Home Office Research and Statistics Department online report 12/07. Online at: www.homeoffice.gov.uk/rds/pubintro1.html.

Wood, J. and Kemshall, H. (2007b) *The Operation and Experience of Multi-Agency Public Protection Arrangements (MAPPA)*, Home Office, Research and Statistics Department online summary 285.

Chapter 10

Public protection work: achieving the possible

Andrew Bridges and Kate White

Introduction

This chapter has been written for the doers rather than for the commentators. Given that we represent an organisation prominent for its commentating on probation and youth offending practice generally, and commentating on matters of public protection specifically, this might seem a strange claim. Nevertheless our focus is on the people who have to carry out in practice what public money pays them to do, and we consider it vital that they know what they are being asked to do on behalf of the public, and that all should understand what is achievable. Accordingly our theme is not to criticise practitioners and managers for failing to do the impossible; instead it is about encouraging a belief in achieving the possible, and illustrating what that looks like in practice.

It may be worth noting at the outset that there are some striking parallels between 'public protection' work (as we define it here) and 'Safeguarding', the work done to protect children and other vulnerable individuals from coming to harm either from themselves or from others. We will not be discussing safeguarding specifically in any further depth in this chapter, but it might be helpful to observe here that while safeguarding work focuses on potential victims and the risks of harm to them, usually from others, public protection work focuses on potential (re)offenders and their *Risk of Harm to others (RoH)*.[1]

A further point to get out of the way at the start is to confirm that HM Inspectorate of Probation does not see public protection (or safeguarding for that matter) as the 'be-all and end-all' of probation or youth offending work. We also support all the wider *constructive interventions*, as we call them, undertaken with individuals under supervision; it is simply that in recent years for a number of reasons we have found it necessary to give particular attention to the public protection aspects of such work – which is what we are once again doing here in this chapter. We consider that as an inspectorate we bring a specific 'added value' to this subject because we can provide it with both an independent perspective and a means of performance measurement. However, it is for others to look at what we say and what we do, and come to their own opinion about whether or not our claims for this inspectorate are justified.

We now begin to explore what 'doing public protection work well' might look like in practice, starting with some general principles. The first of these is to confirm that work with sentenced offenders is not a 'one-size-fits-all' service. On the contrary, all the work aimed at tackling offending behaviour involves a wide range of services and interventions, some *constructive* and some *restrictive*, each of which has to be tailored to the individual being supervised. Although there has to be in addition a fair, consistent and equitable carrying-out of the sentence imposed by the court – promoting compliance and enforcing when necessary – even the detail of doing that involves a certain degree of skilful individual judgement by the practitioner in charge of the case. Once we include the constructive and restrictive interventions as well, it is evident that work with individuals who have offended requires *doing the right thing with the right individual in the right way at the right time*. That *right thing* that needs to be done at any particular time is an especially complicated picture with children and young persons under the age of eighteen, because with this age group there is a duty to improve the well-being of the supervised child or young person, as well as a duty to make that individual less likely to reoffend (see Baker, this volume).

Nevertheless, with both adult offending work and youth offending work the aim is to achieve good quality individualised practice – how do we start to do that? The first thing we have to do is to help practitioners be clear precisely what we are asking them to achieve, including defining clearly 'what success looks like'. We have to do this in a way that is as simple and straightforward as possible, always acknowledging that 'simple' is most certainly not the same thing as 'easy', because what we are asking them to do is of course very difficult.

But we will be in trouble if our approach to defining success consists solely of long lists of procedures and instructions. It is easy for managers to fall into this trap, particularly in response to when something has gone wrong, especially something catastrophic like a current supervisee committing a serious further offence. It is both tempting and relatively easy for management to respond to an identified shortcoming in the way a particular case had been managed by issuing a new instruction designed to prevent a repetition of that shortcoming in any future case. Unfortunately, over time this will lead to ever longer and ever more complicated procedures and instructions (rules) in order to try and cope with the variety of possible eventualities that can arise with any individual case, which in turn has damaging consequences.

The more the individual practitioner has to look up a procedure or an instruction in a manual in order to be sure of doing what management requires the more difficult it is for that practitioner to make decisions and act on them in a responsible manner in accordance with the individual need of the case. Not only does it become more difficult to identify what to do in any individual circumstance, but one can also almost lose sight of the object of the exercise itself. Procedures and rules can have a value in providing a

[handwritten marginalia: use own judgement – to easy blinded by wes + regulations.]

useful framework, but unless one is careful, following the procedures correctly can itself become the object of the exercise, whereas the object should be to *do the right thing with the right individual in the right way at the right time.* Managers might well have intended to design all the procedures with the aim of achieving that purpose, but it is not possible to achieve that in practice. Pursuing this approach has a disabling effect on the practitioner, who will either take the risk of not following every procedure as prescribed or will become detached from taking responsibility for the case by asserting that 'I followed all the procedures correctly in this case' (rather like some MPs who kept saying in 2009 that their outrageous expense claims were within the rules).

Therefore, while 'practitioner compliance with procedures and instructions' might at first seem an attractive 'proxy measure' for doing public protection work well, the benefits of this approach to performance measurement are illusory. What are the alternatives? Management by objectives is normally a sound principle – couldn't we define successful public protection by the means of setting quantitatively measurable targets or objectives? Such target-based outcomes are in many circumstances a good and useful mechanism, but they don't work well with public protection (or for safeguarding either, for that matter). The committing of a serious further offence is a very rare event statistically, about one in 200 or so cases per year (depending how you count them) – but it is a very high profile event when it does happen, as most managers and practitioners are nowadays only too well aware. Such events are very low probability – but very high impact. So, for public protection work, what happens if we try to set a measurable quantitative objective as our definition of what success looks like?

For adult offenders, consideration was being given at one time to setting such a quantitative target, but rightly this option was discarded. Inevitably it would have involved setting a target of increasing by a minuscule amount a figure that was already extremely high: a target of increasing the success rate (of cases where a serious further offence was not committed) from 99.4 per cent to 99.5 per cent. This had looked at first like an attractive option, particularly because an apparently similar aim had been recently achieved with prison escapes – an already low statistical rate of escapes (but high profile when they happened) had been successfully reduced as a consequence of giving prominence to it as a quantitative performance measure. But the similarity was illusory: prison escapes are about the management of people in institutions and are much more within the control (albeit not the total control) of the managers of each prison. The degree of direct control available to the probation service and its allied agencies when managing offenders in the community is far less than that available to those managing offenders within an institution.

Worse still, once you localise such a marginal quantitative target of public protection it becomes quickly apparent that it can readily be achieved in each locality by perverse means – by organising for such cases to move out of the local area, and/or by taking steps to ensure that as few of the difficult cases move into the local area as possible! On careful consideration it was realised that although it is important to keep monitoring at a national level the rate of serious further offending, it would be counter-productive to set such a rate as a localised performance target.

So we have discarded the procedure manual and the quantitative performance measure – what other options are available? And are there any ways in which the practitioner in person can keep track of how they are doing? We consider that it is extremely beneficial if a practitioner has the means of being able to tell at the time whether or not they are doing their job well, rather than being dependent on being told months (or years) after the event how effective their work has been. Rates of reoffending, or even positive changes achieved during an accredited programme, inevitably depend on such a *post hoc* approach, which we agree is necessary in such instances – however, where it *is* possible to have some immediacy it is very beneficial to make use of it.

Going back to first principles, we as an inspectorate have emphasised in our published reports since 2005 that it is not possible to eliminate risk when managing an offender in the community, but it is right to expect staff to do their job properly. This is in keeping with our aim not to criticise people for failing to achieve the impossible – individuals who are not locked up and who are at liberty in the community have the means and the opportunity to commit a serious offence if they are so minded. Probation and youth offending practitioners can make such an eventuality less likely, but they cannot eliminate that risk altogether. We have explicitly recognised that, but we have said instead that they must do their job properly – what do we mean by that?

In our view we need to ensure that there are concepts that practitioners can carry around in their own heads so that they can *tell for themselves* whether they are doing what they are being asked to do, and so that they can tell for themselves whether they are doing it well enough or not. We can do this by introducing high order outcomes that practitioners are being asked to achieve during the course of supervising each case.

There are broadly three separate but overlapping purposes to be achieved when supervising sentenced offenders of any age:

- Ensure that they comply with the requirements of their sentence.
- Make them less likely to reoffend.
- Keep to a minimum their *Risk of Harm to others*.

Each of those purposes can be described using a range of terms, the different terms favoured in different organisations. For example, the terminology of the NOMS agency (National Offender Management Service) usefully uses the plain English terms of *punish, help, change* and *control*; *punish* equates to the first purpose above, *help* and *change* to the second purpose, and *control* to the third. This inspectorate refers to *constructive interventions*,[2] which are aimed primarily at achieving the second purpose above, and to *restrictive interventions*[3] which are aimed primarily at achieving the third purpose. But the specific language is less important than the idea that practitioners should relate to these three broad purposes and also be conscious of how they can and will be measured. There are National Standards that prescribe the quantity, frequency and timing of contact that the individual under supervision must maintain in order to comply with the requirements of their sentence – and the National Standards also prescribe what the officer must do, and in what timescale, should there be a failure to comply. It is therefore possible for the officer to keep track of whether or not they are fulfilling that first purpose as required.

Reduced Likelihood of Reoffending (LoR as we sometimes abbreviate it) can be measured in at least two different ways. One is by measuring at the start of supervision, using a dynamic scale with numeric scores such as the one used within OASys, and then measuring at the end, and where there has been a change in the 'dynamic factors' in the individual's life that had been making that individual very likely to offend the progress can be logged as a reduction in that numeric score. Another option is to record achievements made by the individual during supervision that make that individual less likely to reoffend – for example, gain better accommodation or employment, reduce addictive behaviours or improve thinking skills. These are the constructive achievements that, when they happen, a practitioner will usually experience as personally the most rewarding.

But public protection is principally about the third purpose, and this has a qualitatively distinct and different performance measure. Here the outcome is *to be able to demonstrate that all reasonable action has been taken to keep to a minimum each individual's Risk of Harm to others.* Or, in plainer language, if anything bad were to happen, would the relevant public services be able to show that *they did all they could*?

It is worth mentioning here, in fairness to practitioners, that this is a striking example of something that is both simple and difficult: simple to say, and difficult to do. We can add here that this is also true for the task of measuring this work: it is simple for us to say that it is about judging whether staff did all they could, but in practice it is difficult to arrive at fair, consistent and accurate judgements for each item of work, and to aggregate those judgements accordingly – though that is what our inspectorate can do. While on this subject of measuring public protection work by means of inspection, we will take this opportunity to add here that we have identified two distinct components to the work that we inspect – we call them the Joint Purpose and the Individual Contributions.

Many people quite rightly say that for public protection work to be effective (and safeguarding for that matter) *everyone* has to play their part – they all have to talk to each other, and work together, and it's all a shared piece of work. And they're absolutely right, that it is only when people work together as an extended team that the team effort, or joint purpose, can be achieved; that is, all reasonable action is taken by all the agencies working jointly with each other to keep to a minimum each individual's Risk of Harm to others. But that joint purpose is also made up of individual contributions to the team effort, each of which has to be in place in its own right if the joint purpose is to be achieved. For example, if the initial assessment by a probation or youth offending practitioner is inadequate the case might not even enter into the *joined-up system.* Inspectorates therefore need to spend some time looking at how well each component service makes its own individual contribution, as a step in the process towards assessing whether or not the joint purpose of protecting the public is being achieved.

Therefore we assess during our routine inspections the individual contributions to public protection made by probation and youth offending in each locality, and award scores accordingly. We do this in addition to contributing to joint inspections that assess how well the joint purpose is being achieved by all the agencies working together. As with any other team effort, there is a need to assess both how well each individual makes its specific contribution to the team effort and how well the team as a whole works together: we aim to ensure that we cover both.

This is all still rather abstract, and given that we said we would focus on the doers rather than the commentators it is clearly now time to try to close in on what this means in practice. A key element of this is to be clear what it is possible for the doers to achieve. We aim to use language that helps to set expectations at the right level. We say that when managing former offenders in the community it's not possible to eliminate risk in the community, but the public is entitled to expect that people will do their job properly. We go on to say that doing the job properly consists of taking all reasonable action (did they do all they could?), which we can judge by inspecting individual cases, and we aim to be both transparent and fair in the way that we arrive at such judgements. This approach indicates that we recognise that sometimes a catastrophic event will still occur despite the best endeavours of those in charge of the case, and that such a catastrophe should not necessarily be assumed to be a sign of a failure – that is a question that requires a skilful and fair judgement to be made by whoever is reviewing the case.

This is a critical point, since many practitioners now understandably fear that if there is a death of a child, or a serious further offence, somebody like an inspector will come along, pick over the file, find a fault, and will always, with 20/20 hindsight, simply blame the practitioner. But that's not what this inspectorate does – and we can evidence that that's not what we do, as in the example in the next paragraph. On the one hand, we readily acknowledge why the fear exists. Many people have heard of our reports where we have been critical of practitioners and managers – after all, we're not usually called in unless people think there was a problem in the first place.

But on the other hand we can also point to our report in 2007 on the probation hostels in Bristol,[4] when we also reviewed a couple of cases where murder had been committed by people on licence. Although the practice wasn't perfect, we basically said that in these cases *all reasonable action had been taken*, and it was pleasing (in a strange way) to find that this was actually reported in the *Sun* newspaper. They said that we 'ruled that there was nothing to suggest that two murders committed by freed offenders could have been foreseen by probation officers'.

This was not our precise wording, of course, but it was right in essence about what we were saying. Our report on this occasion, plus the fact that it was reported in the newspapers, provides evidence that we do and will say if we think that practitioners have taken all reasonable action despite the ensuing serious further offence. However, this now raises the question of how one makes that judgement that *all reasonable action* had been taken – what determines whether a particular piece of work passes that test? A checklist approach does not work. At first sight it might seem an attractive solution to try to identify all the components of a good assessment or other action, and then turn them into a checklist. Under this approach the item of work might be assessed according to how many of those components have been identified by the assessor as being present. But a quality job requires more than simply the presence of a number of desired components – something has to be functioning well. Inevitably it has to be a *qualitative judgement*, made by a human being, which is needed to determine whether or not an item of work is performing its intended function. This is the core element of our inspection methodology – a team of inspectors and assessors making a whole series of numerous qualitative judgements of that nature.

Although there are some differences between our adult offending and our youth offending inspections, we expect the heart of our methodology to be broadly the same. Our whole case inspection process works by examining work with a representative sample of individual cases, and, with each case inspected, asking in relation to each item of work that was relevant to that case, the key question: was it done sufficiently well (or above the line, as we sometimes say). Where the item of work applies to the particular case there is a 'tick' for doing it *sufficiently well or better*, or a 'cross' for doing it *insufficiently well or worse*, and there's *no score either way* if that item of work wasn't *relevant to that case*. Each of those judgements is a *qualitative judgement*, not dependent on a rule book or a checklist or an algorithm to provide the answer, because ultimately such tests of sufficiency or of reasonableness have to be qualitative judgements.

We have to be as sure as we can that different inspection teams would mark the same work in the same way, so we ensure that we train and quality assure, and thereby benchmark, a shared understanding among them. This enables them to draw a line consistently between sufficient and insufficient – between *good enough* and *not good enough*. Though it's not possible to achieve perfect congruence between different inspection team members, our efforts mean that we do have a sufficient level of consistency across our qualitative judgements. We also maintain constant attention to quality assurance throughout all aspects of our own inspection processes.

This, therefore, is why we say that the way to measure the public protection purpose of supervision is by individual case assessment, a whole series of skilful qualitative judgements. In principle this can be done either by external independent inspection, as this inspectorate does now, or it can be done (additionally, but not instead) by carefully managed internal assessments – self-assessment – though we wish to make a major *caveat* about that. The clear benefit that self-assessment can bring is that regular internal reviews of cases can promote steady long-term improvement in practice through regular feedback and learning. Self-assessment is therefore potentially an excellent vehicle for self-development in public protection work. However, it does require discipline and organisation by the local managers and practitioners, and in particular it requires care to benchmark the judgements of quality. Setting too low a benchmark will have a detrimental effect on practice by normalising poor practice – and will lead to disappointment when the independent inspection comes round! Setting too high a benchmark will risk debilitating the practitioners by making them feel that it is impossible to achieve effective practice.

In particular, our strong *caveat* to the managers in both the probation and the youth offending services is not to use self-assessment of public protection as a local performance measure or target. There is too strong a temptation to focus on total scores, and to try to influence those scores, when the purpose of self-assessment should be to stimulate learning and improvement in case practice. Performance measurement using this approach will need to be made externally. Self-assessment should be used for self-development only, and not for performance management. So our message to practitioners and managers – the doers – is that success is when you can demonstrate with each case that you have been taking all reasonable action. We know that it is impossible for you to eliminate risk completely, but it is possible for you to take all reasonable action. To express that more fully, you should identify and carry out all the actions (especially *restrictive interventions*) that could reasonably be taken in each particular case, so that the opportunities for that individual to inflict harm are kept to a minimum – reviewing that work regularly.

This is sometimes called 'defensible decision-making'. Some people hear that as a very negative term, fearing that it is simply about watching your back – but in our view it is a positive test, as Professor Hazel Kemshall illustrates in her material on public protection work.[5] The idea of defensible decision-making confirms that it is perfectly possible for a practitioner to make a carefully considered thought-out decision, find in subsequent events that it didn't work out and a catastrophe happened – and yet we might come along and arrive at the judgement that it was a reasonable action or decision to make at the time, as we did in the Bristol hostels case cited earlier. Later on in this chapter we say more about the evidenced practice that is more likely to lead us to come to such a judgement. Furthermore it is a *qualitative judgement* as to whether or not they are doing it *well enough*: a whole series of them about a whole series of items of work, as relevant to each individual case. But what are these items of work? Well, with each case, the headline items we cover are:

- Assessing and planning the case sufficiently well
- Intervening sufficiently well
- Responding to changing event and/or new information sufficiently well
- And thereby: achieving sufficient outcomes.

With public protection and safeguarding the outcome is *being able to demonstrate that you took all reasonable action*, and so on, with the particular case.

What we are describing here, and further below, is a different kind of *performance culture*, but it is one that complements rather than conflicts with the quantitative performance measures employed by NOMS and by the YJB (Youth Justice Board). Too often a performance culture in the probation or youth offending world has been wrongly interpreted as having a very narrow meaning, consisting solely as a context within which targets are met and standards adhered to. But when we, as an inspectorate, talk or write about a *performance culture* we mean to describe something rather broader.

We completely understand the need of NOMS to manage probation performance to common standards and to promote constant improvement. National Standards and the targets linked to them have been important in showing that the probation service has moved forward in recent years and has the ability to measure its work to some extent – but only to some extent, because quantitative measures do not have the capacity to speak of quality. Having a narrow performance culture in place which recognises the need to work within standards and strive to achieve targets undoubtedly has a value, but it needs more breadth. Some probation areas (now Trusts) had gone a long way down the 'narrow' road, sometimes learning how to meet targets even at the cost of reduced quality. Typically such areas have not fared well when subjected to our inspection regimes, when we apply our largely qualitative judgements. Our point is that the kind of performance culture that is solely about meeting quantitative targets is a fragile one that will not make for improved quality in the longer term. We seek to promote a broader concept of performance culture by employing our system of qualitative judgements.

This raises that bigger issue about the role of independent inspectorates which we can only touch on here: in essence we believe that our work can add value in a way that *complements* rather than *conflicts* – because the very highest performing areas recognised both by NOMS centrally and by us as an inspectorate manage to achieve well against both types of measure. With probation and youth offending work, if both practitioners and managers are committed to the highest professional quality then the likelihood is that they will, almost incidentally, be doing well against the more quantitative measures too.

What does that look like in practice? Well, starting at the beginning of that process: with each case, as a key part of the initial *assessment*, we want the practitioner to have identified any potential public protection or safeguarding issue in that case. Then to have assessed its nature: who is at risk of harm? (Self? Identified other? Others in general? Specific groups?) How likely is it that something will happen? What degree of harm is likely to take place if it does happen? What might trigger it? And is this someone who shows other signs in his other behaviour when he's about to do something harmful? All of this is a whole practice training session on its own. Then, equally important to assessment, comes *planning*. In both probation and youth offending work we inspectors find that practitioners are better at assessing *what the problem is*, and not so good at saying *what they plan to do about it* – a practice point from our inspections where we frequently find that improvement is needed. Saying what you plan to do about it (planning) and then doing it (implementing) is what we refer to as *management*, as distinct from assessment, of RoH.

We stress this distinction because we have long had concerns as an inspectorate that much attention was being given by some managers to the assessment of offenders and rather less to their management. This is probably true of both likelihood of reoffending (criminogenic need) and *RoH*, but the consequences for public protection are generally more serious in relation to *RoH*. We welcomed both OASys and Asset, the assessment systems for probation and youth offending work respectively, which we saw as a major step forward in the assessment of individuals under supervision. However, both systems appear to have been stronger in promoting assessment and classification, and weaker in promoting effective planning. There was a period in the probation world when the main emphasis by many managers was on assessment, linked to apparent assumptions that if we sort out assessment, good management will automatically follow. To counter this, we have continually stressed that what is required is specific attention paid to both effective assessment and management of RoH, and we welcome the fact that this is now more widely recognised within both probation and youth offending work.

For in a system where so much emphasis is often given to getting an accurate assessment, there are inherent dangers. For example, there is some comfort in having worked through a detailed and comprehensive RoH assessment process and come up with a classification of low, medium, high, or very high RoH. This classification decision can bring a feeling of satisfaction and, falsely, of a task completed – something that is potentially appealing to busy staff and can boost morale. However, although we have sometimes found it seen in this way, such a classification should never be seen as an end in itself, and should instead be seen as the first step in a longer process. What we therefore seek in addition is the answer to the 'so what?' question – we are looking for *consequent action*. In other words, where are the clearly articulated and enacted interventions that flow from the assessment? Too often we have found this piece of planning work to be either entirely absent or flawed. Sometimes there is simply no match between the assessed level and nature of RoH, and the interventions lined up to address and mitigate it. Time and again in our core inspection programmes since 2003 – about a third of the time on average – we have found that the quality of supervision/sentence planning needed to improve markedly. There undoubtedly needs to be a much better connection between *assessment* and *management* of individuals under supervision – with practitioners being better supported in doing both.

Ministers, officials, journalists and others often ask us the reasons for the shortcomings in quality of practice. It is therefore worth mentioning here that there is almost always a strong desire by staff to do a good job, but often some uncertainty about how to do it. When we inspect we usually meet staff who want to do the very best job they can. This has been true in both the community and custodial settings. There are few people who do not care about the quality of their work or who are resistant to improving it. So why does their standard of work sometimes fall short? Our frequent conclusion in response to that question is twofold: they have not been shown what doing it well looks like, and/or they are unclear about their own professional boundaries in carrying it out.

Most people, when given a clear picture of what good practice would be in a given situation, will willingly aspire to it. Often, however, there is little peer-learning, scant dissemination of good practice through teams or the wider area, and insufficient input from managers to raise the levels of practice among their staff. There may be understandable reasons for all of these factors existing (see below), but the result can be stagnation in terms of practice improvement and a negative culture in relation to staff application to the job. An enduring issue that we find on inspection when we interview staff in relation to the cases they manage is that they are uncertain about the parameters of their role and responsibilities. That is, they have a general understanding of what being a probation officer is about, but are unsure how proactive they can be – particularly in relation to the *control* part of their job, and they are not always confident about how to work alongside fellow professionals from other disciplines.

Often this uncertainty shows itself in relation to individuals who represent a *Risk of Harm to others* – most particularly sex offenders, domestic violence perpetrators, child safeguarding cases, and other cases with identified victims who may be at risk. We have found many instances where the proper need to respect the confidentiality with which victims are rightly treated by the probation area or youth offending team manifests itself as a total lack of communication between offender/case managers and victim liaison staff. This silence represents a misunderstanding of the primary need in such scenarios – to preserve victim safety at all costs. Similarly we still sometimes hear probation staff saying, 'I didn't know I could contact the Domestic Violence Unit', or 'I've never thought of exploring the possibility of doing a joint home visit with the police'. Also, probation staff are now required to demonstrate much more proactively a concern for children's welfare in *all* cases – not just those in which the index offence relates to child abuse. Frequently we find that they are unaware of the implications of this, and when asked describe themselves as ill-equipped and anxious.

In contrast, it is undoubtedly the case that the very best probation and youth offending practitioners we come across on inspection have in their armoury of skills and knowledge an ease in working creatively with partner agencies, and a confidence about their own role and its boundaries. When these elements are embedded, practitioners feel comfortable talking about their own responsibility for managing a case well. It is perhaps worth reiterating here that the majority of public protection work that we inspect, usually over two-thirds of it, meets the level of quality that we are looking for.

Accordingly, one of our core aims as an inspectorate is to promote continuous improvement as an integral element of that wider performance culture discussed above. We don't directly manage the work we inspect (of course), but our inspection practice can help to enable continuous improvement. What can help practitioners and their managers to improve the quality of public protection practice? Earlier we touched on the problem of prescribed procedures from a strategic perspective – why at first they can seem a good idea, but in practice usually prove not to be. From a practitioner perspective, 'rules' can sometimes help to set a framework, but they certainly don't ensure good practice. We don't want practice that follows the rules, but misses the point – we need to grow a much more positive and responsible performance culture than that.

The well-managed cases we have seen during our inspections and *RoH* inquiry work rarely have 'the rules' as their bedrock. Instead they have a practitioner who is exercising sound judgement and being alert and responsive, often in conjunction with other practitioners as well as their own managers. These are some of the behaviours of someone we could call the *perfect practitioner*. In our hypothetical world, what does the perfect practitioner look like? What are their characteristics? Two important sets of factors apply here: first, the personal and professional attributes, and second, a productive and supporting work environment. Let us deal with these in turn. On the personal and professional front, the perfect practitioner has a commitment and desire to work to the highest level of quality and strive for continuous improvement. They are open to increasing their knowledge and enhancing their skills throughout their career. They are well organised and order their workload and their diary so that they work efficiently, taking a short time to carry out straightforward tasks and devoting enough time to more demanding work. They recognise the importance of good planning – both in relation to their own administration and in relation to their management of the individuals under their supervision. They are mindful and reflective – traits that are too often seen as a luxury or as optional extras. They proactively seek to work closely and creatively with partner organisations, as relevant. They are alert to changing levels of *RoH*, and responsive in managing it. They are able to accommodate a heavy workload without lowering their standards.

Their day-to-day practice is better than those practitioners who do an adequate job, adhering to standards and meeting targets, but who rarely impact on an offender's future behaviour successfully because they do not see the whole picture. The perfect practitioner has a perspective beyond the office setting, and understands that their task is not simply to keep in touch with the person they see reporting to them in the probation office each week or each month – often a compliant, sanitised version of the reality. This practitioner realises that their task is to manage the offender who exists *outside* of probation premises – this might be a very different person indeed.

There is a need to be able to hypothesise as follows: what kind of person is this when I'm not with them? Is what I see typical of their behaviour? How would I test that out and seek evidence that would give me a fuller picture? Is it possible that I see them on their very best behaviour? What does their very worst behaviour look like and who is subject to this? How might my practice alter if I were to try and impact them outside of the office rather than just inside?

This holistic approach certainly involves digesting the sometimes gruesome details of witness statements, CPS documents, and the Judge's sentencing comments in order to grow the picture of the offender. It means working alongside victim liaison staff to protect victims and potential victims. It means challenging the views of colleagues and partnership professionals if their views differ from your own, so that between you the true picture can emerge. It will usually mean visiting the offender at home. New opportunities are afforded both by the NOMS offender management model and by YJB requirements that prescribe a much greater degree of joined-up working between staff based in prison and those based in the community than has been common practice in recent years. Staff *inside* and *outside* can jointly compile a more detailed picture of an offender than they have ever achieved before, maximising the likelihood of safe and productive containment post-release.

No practitioner, however capable, is immune from collusion with offenders on their caseload, but with professional discipline (and proactive challenge from confident line managers) much can be done to avoid the frequency of this. Sometimes probation and youth offending staff suffer quite simply from being too nice. Even in these times when professional probation training has long since been removed from the sphere of social work, many staff are attracted to the probation service because of their desire to help, to make things better for both offenders and the public. This is neither surprising nor, of itself, problematic. The legacy of a welfare-based system is a long and enduring one – still some practitioners equate their role with seeing the best in people. But the perfect practitioners are those who can enact the *control* part of their task without feeling they have sold out in the care part. All over England and Wales that tricky balance is being successfully achieved by determined probation and youth offending practitioners who understand their public protection role properly. But, as we have already indicated, good management and a supportive working environment also have a key role in the work of the *perfect practitioner*. We will therefore now look at certain aspects of direct practice management, and then the vexed question of resources and workloads.

To start with, the perfect practitioner will only function at their very best if they are actively supported by their immediate manager. This requires having in place a first-line manager who understands and enacts the three-pronged approach to line management and supervision: staff development, staff support and staff accountability. Such a manager has in person sufficient knowledge and skills of offender management to be able to promote high quality work in their front-line staff, including by being alert to and challenging practitioner collusion, as already mentioned above. This is not the place to produce an exhaustive list of positive traits, but our point here is that robust, well-trained and supported first-line management plays a key role in supporting effective front-line practice.

There is probably insufficient acknowledgement that those managing offenders often have a difficult and sometimes unpleasant task, and so it is good when we find that an organisation has taken care to promote good first-line management. We have found some of the best quality practice where the local organisation has done this, and taken the professional support of their staff seriously as an ongoing need to be met. For example, when we inspected offender management work by Leicestershire and Rutland Probation in 2007 we were pleased to find additional professional supervision and/or support sessions were made available to those staff managing high *RoH* cases and sex offenders. But there are further specific ways in which wider management can make effective front-line practice either more likely or less likely. Taking first the example of MAPPA (multi-agency public protection arrangements), where these have worked effectively they have contributed towards improvement in the management of some of the most challenging offenders. It has, however, been a steep learning curve for many probation and youth offending bodies, and also for prisons, to establish how best they should contribute to them. Some of the issues outlined above about practitioners lacking confidence in partnership working have not helped. On occasion the perceived bureaucracy of MAPPA has deterred potential referrals. The gateways into MAPPA have not always been clearly understood by staff and the profile of cases within MAPPA has been skewed.

However, probably more than all of these has been a failure by many of the managements involved to recognise the centrality that practitioners need to have within these arrangements. Perhaps because there is a need for middle and senior managers to be involved in MAPPA anyway, the presence and contribution of the *practitioners* at panels has too often been seen as unnecessary and has even been discouraged – often citing resource constraints. In our inspections we have frequently found that MAPPA minutes were not finding their way on to the main case file – that is, the practitioner in charge of the case was not even being told what actions and decisions had been agreed upon in their absence. This dislocation has been extremely unhelpful in the past and has sometimes left practitioners and managers alike in an indefensible position when something has gone badly wrong. Fortunately, more recent inspections have shown improvements in MAPPA and a greater clarity about what they are for and how they operate, though further improvement is needed – a task for managers.

An equally important task for managers is how to respond effectively when a catastrophic event takes place, classically a serious further offence (SFO) committed by an individual under current supervision. When a high profile SFO takes place local management face a number of difficult handling issues. A lot of energy is understandably expended in dealing with concerns from politicians, the media and the public. However, just as important are the handling issues in relation to the staff group itself. We have seen one or two probation areas (now Trusts) which, even several years after the event, are still living with the consequences of an SFO that had originally been dealt with within a *blame* culture rather than a *learning* culture. This has made local staff very cautious and risk averse, anxious about getting it wrong, often leading them to err on the side of caution when making their assessments of offenders under supervision. This can result in an overestimate of the classification of *RoH* in a particular case, followed by a failure to identify necessary interventions that matched that classification (unsurprisingly!). Ironically, this can leave practitioners *more* rather than *less* exposed to later criticism, because of the resulting recorded mismatch between assessment and interventions. Therefore, despite the obvious difficulties, it is a key task for managers to promote a *learning* rather than a *blame* culture in their organisation, while not compromising on accountability and continuous improvement.

It is worth acknowledging here an unattractive current fact of life. When an SFO or similar catastrophe occurs, more than one organisation is often actually at fault alongside the probation service and this is usually acknowledged in the official review – but almost always probation suffers disproportionately in the wider public debate and at the hands of the media in particular. What is rarely articulated successfully is the fact that probation is disadvantaged by having a less tangible and easily understood role than, say, the police or prisons. Blame is perhaps easier to attach to such a body, and its role is certainly trickier to defend. In recent years, it has therefore been especially difficult for probation to deal with the aftermath of a high profile SFO within the learning culture we are proposing here – a fact that has made life at times extremely tough for probation staff and managers.

To some extent youth offending has experienced similar difficulties, but it is striking to us that the media has not yet developed the wolfpack mentality in relation to youth offending that they have directed towards probation in recent years (and they did for social services and/or children's services from the mid-1970s onwards). We can reiterate here that the role of HMI Probation with such catastrophes has been to emphasise since 2005 that risk cannot be eliminated but that people should do their job properly. We aim not only to help managers and practitioners to learn lessons when practice has been deficient, but also to define and promote effective practice in terms of what it is possible to achieve. Although we continue to be willing to undertake individual case reviews where appropriate, we find we can better fulfil those aims when we undertake inspections of representative samples of cases.

In relation to the role of management, that leaves the outstanding issue of resourcing and workloads to consider at this point. Debates on this subject have sometimes been polarised between a claim that resource limitations and unrealistically high workloads make it impossible to undertake effective *RoH* practice, and a counter-claim that resource issues are completely irrelevant here.[6] Such polarised debates obscure some mundane truths. On the one hand, it is a convenient but erroneous myth to claim that adequate resource would guarantee adequate standards of case management. This is quite simply because resource is far from being the only, or even primary, factor promoting good practice. Average numbers of cases per practitioner are in probation over double that in youth offending teams and services, and there are some variations between individual probation and youth offending teams, but we have found it hard to identify any direct correlation between levels of resourcing and quality of practice. Even where we inspect the work of hard-pressed teams of practitioners we find that some make good active purposeful use of the (sometimes very limited) available time that they can spend with each individual under supervision, while others retreat into a kind of 'passive diarising' of the contacts they are having with each case.

However, having made that point, we would also acknowledge that it would be difficult even for our perfect practitioner to flourish in a working environment that was seriously under-funded over a very prolonged period of time. The mundane truth is that, except at the extremes, while favourable levels of resource and workloads can make effective practice more likely to take place – and thus unfavourable levels can make it less likely – there is no direct causal relationship between resourcing and effective practice. Most of the time, the focus of our inspection findings is not principally about the need to spend more time on each case. More pertinently it is on how the existing time being spent with individuals under supervision could be used more effectively.

We will illustrate this point with an example, a probation officer – we shall call him John – who was newly qualified and managing his first sex offenders. During inspection he was able to convey his evident interest in the work and his commitment to doing a good job. He described managing a rapist – we shall call him Bob – who on one occasion turned up for his appointment looking much smarter than usual, well groomed and wearing new clothes.

John remembered noticing this transformation, and we could see that he had even noted it in his contact log records. However, he did not fully consider the potential significance of this change to the Risk of Harm posed by Bob – there was no *consequent action*. A more experienced officer would have heard alarm bells ringing. Something had prompted this change in Bob – what was it? Bob had changed – so what? Could it be that he was planning to try to forge relationships with women again? Did he already have a specific woman in his sights? John had a vague idea that this new fact mattered but had no idea in what way. He almost asked himself the 'so what?' question, but then came nowhere close to *answering* it. Had he been managed more tightly and supervised more capably he might have teased this out with his manager – as it was, this only emerged through a conversation some months later with an inspector. And the remedy involved making better use of the time already being spent on the case.

HMI Probation and the other public service inspectorates all believe that a key purpose of inspection generally is to promote service improvement. That is why we have aimed to address the doers here, rather than the commentators – 'doers' being managers as well as practitioners. Therefore, in relation to the specific topic of public protection, we very much hope that our words, and the practical experience of our current inspection practice, will confirm for practitioners and managers that they are not being 'set up to fail' by a system of regulation working on '20/20 hindsight'. On the contrary, we hope that they will be encouraged to believe that our 'all reasonable action' definition of success is achievable, and one that will be recognised when they achieve it. Accordingly, they will find that they can in fact 'achieve the possible'.

Selected further reading

The standard texts by Hazel Kemshall, and by Nash and Williams, are referenced elsewhere and are recommended. For examples of other work by HM Inspectorate of Probation on this subject, go to the relevant page on the Inspectorate's website: www.justice.gov.uk/inspectorates/hmi-probation/risk-of-harm-to-others.htm. It provides access to some reviews of individual cases in 2005/06, and to some broader inspections, mainly based on assessing samples of cases. These include *Not Locked up, But Subject to Rules* (March 2007), the report of an inquiry requested by the Home Secretary following a *Panorama* programme in 2006 about the supervision of offenders in approved premises (hostels) in Bristol, and a Risk of Harm Inspection Report, *A Stalled Journey: An inquiry into the management of offenders' Risk of Harm to others by London Probation* (November 2009). A paper setting out HMI Probation's general perspective on public protection and safeguarding can be found on the same web page.

Notes

1   We put this in title case, and often in italics too, to emphasise that we have given this term a specific meaning. Our abbreviation *RoH* should be recognised as always meaning specifically *Risk of Harm to others*.

2   A *constructive* intervention addresses an individual's Likelihood of Reoffending (LoR), and is when the individual under supervision learns something that means that they are more likely to *behave more positively* in future.

3   A *restrictive* intervention addresses *Risk of Harm to others*, and is when the authorities take action to *restrict the opportunity* that the individual has to *be of harm to others*.

4   HMIP (2007) *Not Locked Up, But Subject to Rules*. London: HMI Probation.

5   Hazel Kemshall has written, co-written and co-edited numerous works on the subject since 1996, such as Kemshall, H. (2003) *Understanding Risk in Criminal Justice*. Buckingham: Open University Press.

6   An example was the exchanges reported in the media between the former Chief Officer for London Probation and the Justice Secretary in June 2009 following the conviction for murder of Dano Sonnex.

Chapter 11

Sex offender management in the community: who are the victims?

Bob Golding

We don't have ethnic cleansing here. It is social cleansing. These campaigners have a list of twenty names of people they say have committed crimes against children. But no-one knows where the list comes from, who has written it or what evidence it is based on. Now four innocent families are in hiding because of it. (Father Waddington, local priest, as reported in Perry (2000), during the paedophile demonstrations at Paulsgrove, Portsmouth)

Introduction

The above statement was made at a moment in time in the 'history' of the development of risk-based community management strategies for sex offenders. It is perhaps inevitable that this is an emotive subject, especially for those communities within which such offenders are 'managed' by the authorities. But notwithstanding the strategic approach to community based risk management which has generated the concerns reflected in the Paulsgrove example (and elsewhere), it has been said that current strategies represent a 'narrow range of responses which are defensive and focused on risk rather than on treatment and rehabilitation' – effectively 'the demonization of sex offenders' (Matravers 2003b: 3).

It is against this background that this chapter will examine, in the context of development of community based risk strategies in relation to sex offender management, the related impact on policing and communities. Three themes will be considered.

First, the developments in policy and the law relating to the management of sex offenders in the community and the emerging trends that can be identified are considered as a context-setting exercise. This involves some consideration of the risk management approach and the implications arising from it in the context of public safety. Second, a 'real world' example is used to explore the impact of public opinion on policy, showing the relative power of 'events' – particularly in the context of a prevailing policy context of risk management. Finally, the chapter considers the implications currently of that analysis in terms of the current regime of 'piloting' the disclosure in the context of its 'fit' in policy terms to addressing 'victims' in the wider sense of community sex offender management.

Policy and law development – a context

Kemshall and McIvor (2004b) identify three trends in relation to sex offender policy, which can be reflected in the timeline of legislative developments – selective incapacitation, preventative sentencing and community risk management (2004b: 9). The first phase of selective incapacitation, they argue, is a response to increasing prison populations in the 1980s and 1990s, with imprisonment used for 'the most dangerous, the most serious and habitual recidivists' (Murray 1997, in Kemshall and McIvor 2004b: 9). Developing alongside and then beyond this approach was the concept of preventative sentencing, epitomised by the 'three strikes and you're out' approach to a number of offences, and, in the context of sex offences, 'special measures' whereby public protection was 'prioritised over proportionality' (Kemshall and McIvor 2004b: 10: see also Bottoms 1995: 40: and Kemshall 2003). One of the important manifestations of this phase is what Henham has called 'predictive confinement' (2003: 59), particularly relevant in relation to sex offenders, who, he argues, were a target for sentencing in this way – although there have been strong critics who have challenged the questionable approach to 'risk prediction' to justify excessive sentencing, let alone the questions that arise over the effectiveness of this 'preventative sentencing' approach to harm reduction (see Von Hirsch and Ashworth 1996; Pratt 1997, in Kemshall and McIvor (2004b: 10).

This 'preventative sentencing approach' was underpinned legislatively by section 2.2b of the Criminal Justice Act 1991, where it might be argued that sex offenders were a 'target' through risk prediction – although its efficacy has been questioned by some commentators (Pratt 1997; Von Hirsch and Ashworth 1996; Wood 1988).

The third phase, and the one that provides the primary context to this chapter, saw the development of a risk management approach in the 1990s, with approaches to dangerous or 'risky' offenders focusing on tactics like surveillance, containment, restriction and risk management generally (Kemshall 2003; Kemshall and McIvor 2004b). The concept of management in the community through partnership and collaboration between police and probation services included, for sex offenders, statutory provision for joint risk assessment and offender management (see, for examples, sections 67–68 of the Criminal Justice and Court Services Act 2000 and the development often from the precursor public protection units (PPUs) of multi-agency public protection arrangements or MAPPA (see Maguire et al. 2001). The effective management of high risk offenders in this way has been described as presenting a 'severe challenge' (Kemshall and McIvor 2004b: 13) – a point that will be elaborated on later in this chapter.

This approach to risk management and public protection had been developing, incrementally, prior to this key piece of legislation. As Maguire and Kemshall point out:

> In the early 1990s 'probation managers ... began to liaise more closely with the police about dangerous offenders under their supervision, establishing joint protocols on information sharing that disregarded cultural traditions against the passing of confidential information between 'welfare' and 'enforcement' agencies. (2004: 211)

This period of time also saw the development in some areas of public protection panels bringing together professionals on a multi-agency basis to plan the management of risk posed by sex offenders and other 'dangerous' individuals moving into an area. While the primary responsibility arguably rested with the probation service, the police, for example, could provide intelligence and covert activity like surveillance in appropriate cases; housing could provide 'suitable' accommodation for these offenders; and other professionals similarly could inform and contribute to the developing risk management 'plan'.

A key element of the developing approach was the sex offender register (Home Office 2002; Plotnikoff and Woolfson 2000) – arguably an example of policy transfer from the United States, supported by some police staff associations and subject to a building political momentum as evidenced by two unsuccessful private member's bills seeking to introduce a UK sex offender registration system before its final adoption into the Sex Offenders Act 1997, after much debate (see Thomas 2005: 154). Later strengthening of the Act, by providing police powers to fingerprint and photograph (on first reporting) of offenders, and by enhancing sanctions for non-compliance, followed. These changes were introduced as a consequence of pressure following the murder of Sarah Payne in 2000 and the direct influence of Sarah's parents, and general public concern, at least in the reported view of the then Home Secretary Jack Straw (Thomas 2005: 162; Home Office 2000). Technological developments like ViSOR (the Violent and Sex Offender Register – an IT solution provided to police forces) were developed to support this initiative. The strengthening of the approach, in terms of policy and process (such as multi-agency joint risk assessment and management; multi-agency public protection panels (MAPPPs) for high risk offenders) was subsequently supported and underpinned by other measures, for example, sex offender orders under section 2 of the Crime and Disorder Act 1998; extended periods of supervision on public protection grounds for certain high risk sex offenders under the same Act; requirements for sex offenders to notify foreign travel under the Criminal Justice and Court Services Act 2000 with increased penalties for failure to register; and measures aimed to protect children from 'grooming' (Home Office 2002: Kemshall and McIvor 2004b: 11).

The legislative developments for this phase of risk management should not be seen in isolation, as they would not and did not develop in a vacuum. Mention has already been made of the influence of the Sarah Payne case on policy development in this area, in terms of strengthening the 'risk management' approach. The old criminological concept of moral panics (after Cohen 1972) has been used to describe the period in the 1990s, in the context of paedophiles and paedophile rings; satanic abuse; and 'stranger danger' – associated with significant and widely reported cases (Kemshall and McIvor 2004b: 14; Kitzinger 1999; Thompson 1998). Particular cases arguably raised the temperature even higher, with concerns around failures to manage sex offenders in the community (for instance, the Steven Leisk case, or the Sydney Cooke case), along with general issues emanating from the Home Office at that time around the effectiveness and caseloads of the probation service. Mention has already been made here about the concept of policy transfer from the United States, and publicity around Megan's Law (allowing disclosure to communities of the details of sex offenders), developed following the *News of the World* campaign in and around 2000 to introduce a similar 'Sarah's Law' in the wake of the Sarah Payne case in the UK. While not taking a view here as to the efficacy of the moral panic argument in this particular context, it is apparent that these pressures operated at a moment in time that was concurrent to the practical and developing joint agency approaches to risk; and the subsequent underpinning legislation and guidance to agencies which determined practice and procedure throughout England and Wales. The argument here therefore is simply one that recognises the potential significant impact on public policy and practice of public and media 'concern', however that may be generated.

Having set the risk management approach 'scene', it is important to recognise also some of its most significant limitations of the risk management approach as they have emerged. First, there are the practical limitations, so ably set out by Kemshall and McIvor (2004b: 16), who broadly summarise them as follows.

Initially they identify the inherent difficulty in the identification of those who pose a risk to meet the threshold for 'special measures', while at the same time seeking to avoid what they describe as 'net-widening'. Identifying and predicting potential to commit future serious harm is problematic.

Then there is the point that practices and tools used for assessment have not proved reliable or user friendly, and can fail to distinguish between 'types' of sex offenders – and not helped by delay by some agencies in adopting such tools (McIvor *et al.* 2002).

Next is the concept of a blame culture within and between agencies resulting in 'defensive practice and over inflation of risks ... to avoid litigation and blame' (Kemshall 2003; Carson 1996). And finally, in this analysis, is the point that different agencies may adopt different risk assessment tools, which may be used in different contexts, and by staff at different levels with different levels of training, knowledge and experience (McIvor *et al.* 2002). Taken together, Kemshall and McIvor argue that this serves to 'hamper' and 'impinge upon' the 'quality and utility of risk assessments' (2004b: 17). Added to that, particularly if one accepts the concept of net-widening, are the organisational limitations of resources, which may consciously or subliminally inform thinking. The resource implications of net-widening, for example, with respect to high risk offenders, are significant. Surveillance, monitoring and supervision of sex offenders in the community are resource intensive processes, at a time where organisational imperatives, and the centralising demands and direction of new public management in public services are in the ascendancy; and where resources to meet new and changing demands are under acute pressure. It can only ever be a rhetorical question as to whether resource implications impact on risk assessment decision-making.

Second, there are the potential limitations imposed by the philosophical approach of the current dominant community protection model. Matravers (2003b: 3) describes this in terms of the 'demonisation of sex offenders', which has generated 'sex offender management ... focused on registration and risk assessment, with treatment and rehabilitative measures taking a back seat'. The result, she argues, suggests that practitioners 'are likely to focus their attention on defensive (as opposed to "defensible") decisions about risk rather than optimising the circumstances for the reintegration of offenders' (see also Lieb 2003). She argues for a shift in thinking based on a more holistic approach, which sees sex offenders as 'ordinary people and responsible agents', thus allowing for 'the deployment of resources into primary prevention, treatment and rehabilitative measures'. This thesis, in her analysis, is underpinned by arguments suggesting a lack of empirical evidence to support what she describes as 'punitive responses' (Matravers 2003b: 4); together with a series of popular myths, for example a 'current preoccupation with predatory violent sex offenders which cannot be explained by reference to their increasing numbers' (2003b: 5); or a myth relating to 'their general proclivity for re-offending', not justified by recidivism studies of offenders against children, for example, showing that under 20 per cent will commit further or similar offences (2003b: 5–6; see also Hanson and Bussière 1998). The development of risk assessment and management in this thesis is described as a rapid rise in 'actuarial justice' and the 'marginalisation of treatment' (Matravers 2003b: 9).

Third, and again using Matravers' analysis, is the point that the problem of sex offenders is not getting worse (2003b: 7). So, she asks, in the context also of 'better management' of sex offenders, 'how do we account for continuing political and public preoccupation with these offenders?' She argues that 'what is new is the instantiation of the sexual predator as a constant and central threat to children and communities ... the result of a circular process in which popular fears give rise to populist policies that respond to and thereby reinforce popular fears' (2003b: 7).

Therefore, in a modern historical context, the 'panic' about sex offenders, in this thesis, is an 'interpretation of a problem' at a particular place in time which serves as a 'focus for the broader social concerns and anxieties of its time' (2003b: 7). In policy terms, the consequences in this thesis are therefore, for sex offenders, politicised and knee-jerk policy, 'reflecting a primary concern with public opinion and displaying a fine disregard for adverse side effects such as over inclusiveness and the erosion of offenders' rights' (2003: 11).

The next section considers using a real example the efficacy of this thesis, at least in terms of the extent (within the limited parameters of the example) that 'events' drive policy.

A real example – the power of public opinion on policy?

The example used here to consider the impact of the development of the risk management approach in practice has been selected for a number of reasons. First, it occurred at a point in time when the risk management/multi-agency approach was in its 'early days' (from 2001 onwards), and prior to the legislation requiring the formalisation of what had hitherto been in some areas (including the area in the example here) locally developed 'public protection' arrangements. Nonetheless, policy arrangements were sufficiently mature to 'test' the policy when under stress. Second, it was arguably a high profile critical incident influencing, or at least informing, subsequent policy development. Third, it demonstrates the potential, dependent on a particular congruence of circumstances, for the risk management sex offender policy approach to 'victimise' communities and individuals beyond the circle of those who might be under more immediate consideration. This is an important point in this analysis – the context described earlier is arguably narrowly focused in terms of victimology (for example, who is the victim addressed by policy in an actuarial process underlying a risk management philosophy). Matravers (2003b: 3) argues that the 'subject' is victimised by the current policy approach, as well as the subjects' victims or potential victims. But are the perceptions of victim too narrow when the implications of policy produce unanticipated consequences demonstrating – arguably – a policy weakness or failure? Fourth, and finally, the author is able to bring to bear a particular perspective, as the then Police BCU commander involved – a benefit in terms of insider awareness, but an acknowledged risk in terms of the potential subjectivity of any analysis; that will be a matter for the reader to determine.

The summer of 2000 arguably represented a critical point in the chronology of sex offender risk management. In examining the events of that year, or more accurately that summer, there is an interesting and perhaps atypical congruence of circumstances, culminating in what has been described elsewhere as a media frenzy (Thomas 2001, 2004: 234).

The Home Office in June that year announced a review of the sex offender register, which was seen as having been effective (Home Office 2000); shortly thereafter the Home Office evaluation of the register was produced (Plotnikoff and Woolfson 2000). While broadly positive, that report nonetheless found that the sex offender registration process, in terms of enhancing community safety, had no effective quantitative means by which it could be subject to appropriate performance management and measurement (Plotnikoff and Woolfson 2000, in Thomas 2004: 235).

Within that short period came the abduction in July (and subsequent murder) of Sarah Payne, and the media coverage that followed the investigation. Rebekah Wade, then editor of the *News of the World*, on the back of the Sarah Payne case, championed a campaign to make the sex offender register publicly accessible, and mounted a sustained media campaign throughout that summer which became sufficiently newsworthy in its own right to attract support elsewhere in the media (for example in the *Sunday People*). The campaign itself involved the publication of photographs and some details of sex offenders in support of its campaign (Thomas 2004: 235, 2005: 24); and championed the adoption of the Megan's Law approach (public disclosure of sex offender details and whereabouts) in the USA (see Thompson and Greek, this volume).

Two years previously a convicted child sex offender, Victor Burnett, had been located and housed in Paulsgrove, a housing estate on the outskirts of the city of Portsmouth, and had been subject to risk assessment and monitoring under local public protection arrangements, with no indications of any problems or issues arising. He had been subject to two public protection conferences involving police, probation and social services as a matter of normal procedure, and no evidence was forthcoming of regression to previous offending behaviour. It was the official view that 'the system designed to protect the public against paedophiles works' (the then Director of Social Services at Portsmouth, quoted in Hill 2001).

However, as part of the *New of the World*'s naming and shaming campaign in the summer of 2000 following the murder of Sarah Payne, Burnett was identified in the *News of the World*, with further coverage in the local press and media following. The *News of the World* was subject to pressure to stop naming and shaming, given concerns about possible adverse consequences (including the risk of vigilantism), and on 4 August the paper agreed to 'suspend' its campaign following meetings with the Association of Chief Police Officers (ACPO), the NSPCC, the National Association for the Care and Resettlement of Offenders (NACRO), and the Association of Chief Officers of Probation (ACOP) (Thomas 2004: 233).

Arguably part of the impetus for this was informed by the events of the previous day – 3 August – in Paulsgrove, Portsmouth. An impromptu demonstration involving some 150 local residents, local youths and others had resulted in Burnett's flat being broken into and trashed; in the throwing of missiles at police and the injury of an officer; damage to a local authority housing office; and the turning over and 'torching' of a car that demonstrators believed was owned by Burnett's sister. Burnett had, following the *News of the World* exposé, been relocated in anticipation of the potential risk to his well-being as a consequence of the media campaign by the *News of the World*. One of the concerns of the authorities was the risk of Burnett, and others who were being managed in the community, of going 'underground' and as a consequence not being capable of being monitored or risk managed.

There followed over days and weeks that summer continued protests in Paulsgrove, with the development of a self-appointed 'organising group' calling itself Residents Against Paedophiles (or RAP) using mobile phone networks and other means to 'advertise' their activity, and the targeting of twenty or more other local residents by the demonstrators, who developed a 'list' based on information and gossip elicited locally. The demonstrations almost night after night targeted people and homes on the list, resulting in damage and 'blockading' of homes. Subsequently, when police were able to obtain details of some of those on the 'list', it transpired that some had no criminal record or charges pending whatsoever, some had convictions, but none had convictions for sexual offences against young children. So protestors' targets were, it might be assumed, 'victims of rumour, gossip, and in some cases, sheer spite' – although one of the ringleaders asserted that 'only the undeserving got the doorstep treatment' (Hill 2001).

Much of this continuing activity, and its policing, was subject to continued media and national and international TV coverage. Sustained policing, multi-agency work behind the scenes, public and private meetings designed to reassure and encourage peaceful rather than violent protest, prosecutions for offences and use of tenancy conditions to restrain anti-social behaviour were all considered to control and manage the continuing disturbances. In addition, some families targeted who were 'innocent' had to be relocated for their protection. What was revealing in the author's experience was the exposure of the self-appointed ringleaders of RAP to a meeting with community organisations, groups and representatives, where it was abundantly clear that there was no broad community support for RAP and its activities from this quarter. But it seems (a personal observation) that the incident ran its course when the media spotlight moved on, and the headlines in an otherwise period of 'slow news' focused on the loss of a Russian nuclear submarine in the Baltic.

This example perhaps demonstrates the wider victimology of the risk management policy and its potential consequences. Subsequent policy developments (described earlier) including the formalised MAPPA arrangements, are arguably an elaboration and development of the underlying philosophical approach to sex offender management in the community and the management of risk and dangerousness. But in this case, those besieged or terrorised in their own homes were not the only victims; as was quoted at the time, 'there are those children who witnessed the demos or took part; some of them were only 4 or 5 years old. Then there were others in the area, intimidated by what was happening and too scared to speak out' (Hill 2001). As observed by Hill: 'The legacy of bloodlust may be hardest to erase. Most of those who had their collars felt were just boy rowdies, out for fun. But it's the images of women and their children marching through the night that stick most in the mind; infants toting cardboard coffins, mothers chanting hate.'

It should also be noted that the Paulsgrove incidents, while perhaps the highest profile, were not isolated in the context of the media campaign, and incidents were occurring in other parts of the country – even the mis-identification of a paediatrician in South Wales whose home was vandalised and who was 'driven out of home by vigilantes' (Thomas 2005: 26). Incidents that summer also occurred in Croydon, Lewisham, Billingham in Cleveland, Plymouth, Bristol, Manchester, and Cumnock in East Ayrshire (Perry 2000).

But the Paulsgrove incident and the role of the media, though high profile, is not unique in recent history. In Thomas' analysis, one of the trends of the late 1990s 'was the media's discovery of the paedophile', and the 'explosion of interest in the topic [of paedophiles] amongst the newspapers since 1996' (Thomas 2005: 21; see also Soothill *et al.* 1998). Thomas goes on to equate this with pushing 'the country into something of a moral panic about sex offending, especially when that offending was against children' (2005: 22). Press naming and shaming examples were not new – Thomas provides several examples from the 1990s (2005: 23), and he goes on to observe that 'these press activities were mirrored by local communal activities involving demonstrations, protests and vigilante action against sex offenders', some of which are described as 'large and beyond control' – for example, the destruction of a house by 100 demonstrators in June 1997 on the Logie estate in Aberdeen where it was thought by the demonstrators that a sex offender was living (Thomas 2005: 23–4).

Thomas draws parallels with crowd reactions decades earlier, for example with respect to the Moors murderers Myra Hindley and Ian Brady at their trial in 1965; or the violent demonstrations outside a Bristol police station in 1998 in relation to the presence of the paedophile Sydney Cooke; or the murder in Edinburgh of a known sex offender Lawrence Leyden in 1995; and subsequently the murder of Arnold Hartley in Redcar in 2003 (Thomas 2005: 25). But in the context of community risk management, the impact of all of this, at least from one perspective, is provided to us by Thomas, who quotes a spokesperson for ACOP as saying that 'there is firm evidence that real damage is being done to innocent children and adults by taking the law into their own hands. Existing vital and effective supervision and surveillance operations are being destroyed' (Thomas 2005: 28). Additionally, Thomas cites the Chief Officer of Probation stating that hostels were refusing to take offenders because of the consequences from the local community doing something 'very stupid and silly to the hostel and staff there' (Thomas 2005: 23).

It may be possible to overstate this case, however. While the extension of the scope of 'victims' can demonstrably occur in the context of a risk management policy approach, and an undermining of that policy in certain circumstances when a moral panic develops, Matravers suggests that 'it is possible to identify ebbs and flows in concerns about sex crime in general and the threat posed by external predatory offenders in particular' (2003b: 8). The intensity and longevity in the current era can, in her analysis, be linked to late modernity and an emphasis 'not on the reform of offenders ... but on the risk management of those who may go on to commit offences in the future' – what she describes as the rise of 'actuarial justice' and the 'marginalisation of treatment'. In this thesis, sex offenders are seen as 'abnormal', as presenting an 'intolerable risk to children and communities', and increasingly subject to what she describes as the 'paraphernalia of late modern penality', as exemplified by incapacitive sentencing, risk management techniques and surveillance' (2003b: 9). On the basis of the ebb and flow argument, and the cyclical model of responses (after Jenkins 1998, in Matravers 2003b: 10), a liberal climate is, it can be argued, 'overdue'. However, the 'institutionalisation' of child protection and the self-interest of welfare and other agencies 'with a stake in the maintenance of concern about sex crime' has, it is argued by Jenkins and others, broken the cycle (Jenkins 1998: 232, cited in Matravers 2003b: 10). Arguably, recent developments on controlled disclosure of sex offender information support the Jenkins and Matravers thesis – that risk management has been institutionalised within a model of 'late modernity risk thesis'.

In policy terms, the events of 2000 did not, at that time, extend the risk management approach to adopt a policy of disclosure along the lines of the so-called Megan's Law as introduced in the United States. The objections were significant, from ACPO, ACOP, child protection agencies and others – largely that 'disclosure would drive sex offenders underground, decreasing compliance with registration and disrupting community treatment programmes' (Matravers 2003b: 17). Matravers reports that government response was to beef up risk management of sex offenders in the community (see, for example, the development of MAPPA), while remaining 'steadfast in its opposition to widespread community notification' (2003b: 17; see also Bryan and Doyle 2003: 197).

But there are signs of change in the recent history of sex offender risk management. The next section of this chapter looks briefly at more recent developments in the context of disclosure, arguably the latest iteration following on from the events of 2000, which might be seen as a response in navigating a policy route between the adverse consequences identified through this analysis and case study of current risk management policies, and the risks of exacerbating those consequences further by the adoption of a Megan's Law approach of full 'disclosure' of sex offenders in the community.

A policy response: towards 'Sarah's Law'?

Some of the significant developments this decade, including the development of multi-agency public protection arrangements and associated legislation have been well documented elsewhere (see, for example, Bryan and Doyle 2003: 189). In the context of this chapter, perhaps one of the most critical developments was in 2007, with the publication by the Home Office of a comprehensive review of the arrangements for protecting children from sex offenders. The review produced twenty recommendations around the following four broad areas (Home Office 2007):

- Providing the public with the information and understanding needed to protect children – this included the issue of the public disclosure of information about child sex offenders. Notably within this review, and infoming its recommendations, was an investigation into how Megan's Law within the United States was working and its impact on child protection. In simple terms, Megan's Law allows communities direct, uncontrolled access to information on offenders, mainly through websites.

- Minimising the risk to children posed by certain individuals through the provision of treatment.

- Maximising the effectiveness of the management of known sex offenders by the authorities.

- Harnessing new technologies to provide additional management capabilities.

However, this additional direction from central government arguably presented further policy initiatives that were not matched by the resources to deliver them. A joint report in 2005 by the chief inspectors of constabulary and probation, Sir Ronnie Flanagan and Andrew Bridges, on the management of sex offenders was critical of the risk management approach, insofar that, in reality, 'competing demands' on police time meant that generally surveillance is 'difficult to obtain' when it comes to tracking sex offenders, particularly in the context of the demands on surveillance resources in undertaking counter terrorism activity. Such resource concerns generally are echoed elsewhere, for example from the NSPCC, whose head of policy is reported as saying that the sex offender management system 'lacks sufficient funding and manpower and often struggles to cope with the workload' (Gething-Lewis 2009).

With that *caveat*, however, following on from the Home Office recommendations (Home Office 2007) in September 2008, pilot schemes were launched in four police force areas (Warwickshire, Cambridgeshire, Hampshire and Cleveland – and later extended further in March 2009) to allow parents and guardians the option to ask police whether individuals who have access to their child have committed child sexual offences. Police then may release information under conditions if their assessment is that children may be at risk, subject to a confidentiality requirement.

This was one of the recommendations of the 2007 Home Office review, and arguably a response to the lobbying for a 'Sarah's Law' in the UK (after the Sarah Payne case), inspired by the Megan's Law approach in the United States. (Megan's Law is however, qualitatively different, involving the general publication of names, addresses and pictures of paedophiles in states adopting this approach.) The risks of the scheme, according to some experts and children's charities, are reportedly that they:

- May prompt vigilante actions (although none have been reported in the trials and a confidentiality requirement is made where disclosures are undertaken, the experience outlined in this chapter, based on the actions in 2000 in Portsmouth and elsewhere, suggests that this will remain a potential risk to be managed).

- Could create a false sense of security as not all paedophiles are on the sex offender register.

- Could drive paedophiles underground, making them more difficult to track.

These risks are balanced against the benefit, as reported by one chief constable, that public awareness of child protection issues has been raised, and that 'for those parents and carers who have made inquiries, we trust that it has helped give them confidence that their children are safe' (Warwickshire Police Press Release 16 March 2009). The take-up of the scheme appears modest to date, with indications that as of March 2009 just ten disclosures were made after requests for information, with 153 inquiries about the scheme and 79 applications for information. To that extent it is perhaps relatively premature to pass judgement on the success of the initiative at the time of writing.

However, for the purpose of the issues considered in this chapter, it is a significant and interesting initiative in addressing the wider potential victimology of a risk management approach to sex offenders in the community – that being the community itself, and those who may be at risk of vigilantism through information and misinformation. It is a matter for conjecture as to whether such a policy initiative would or will be sufficient to prevent the consequences of a critical incident, or 'moral panic', at a particular place and time as experienced in the Paulsgrove (Portsmouth) example discussed earlier.

Conclusion

This chapter has in its analysis sought to briefly set out the policy context for community sex offender management, and tentatively pointed out through a worked example a consequence which, it is argued, needs to be recognised and addressed in policy terms. It is perhaps inevitable that the emotiveness of the subject, and media interest, will from time to time have the potential to lead to a 'moral panic', either local or national in character, as demonstrated by the Paulsgrove example. This is, arguably, a phenomenon that is predictable and therefore one demanding of a policy response. This chapter has briefly touched on the disclosure pilots, which represent a significant contribution to such a policy approach, and has identified in the literature some critiques of current and previous policy, in particular Matravers' concerns about policy that demonises sex offenders, and policy reflective of concerns over public opinion with consequences that have an adverse affect on offenders' rights (2003b: 11).

However, it is argued here that any policy approach to community sex offender management requires a holistic consideration of policy consequences, and a recognition of the reality of public concerns, justified or not, around this emotive issue; the Paulsgrove example perhaps indicates the consequences of a failure in policy terms to do just that. The current (at the time of writing) disclosure pilots would seem to be an attempt, again in policy and practical terms, to find a way through some of the competing issues involved. Time will tell whether this proves to be sufficient. What is clear, however, in the light of the example discussed here, is that community sex offender management policy approaches do require a broad recognition of who the actual or potential victims might be, all of whom require and deserve recognition in any policy approach – the offender, the offender's victim, the community within which the offender is located, and those who might be victimised inappropriately by the community and, perhaps, the media. As Thomas tells us, 'the assessment and management of risk posed by sexual offenders have become an all-consuming task' (2005: 173). And as Hudson advises, 'risk control strategies throw into sharp relief the perennial questions of whose rights matter' (2003: 76).

Selected further reading

For an interesting consideration of managing and reducing sex offender risk in the community, which goes beyond a narrow risk-focused agenda that traditionally has been the focus of academic consideration, *Sex Offenders in the Community* (Matravers

2003a) is an important read. Kemshall and McIvor (2004a) edit a useful collection of contributions on multi-agency collaboration and approaches to dealing with the predatory paedophile, helpfully drawing on key research as well as offering practical guidance on this topic. Finally, for a consideration of the context, extent and nature of sex offending, including a consideration of both criminal justice and civil processes in providing protection from sexual offending, Thomas (2005) is an excellent introduction.

References

Bottoms, A. (1995) 'The politics and philosophy of sentencing', in C. Clarkson and R. Morgan (eds) *The Politics of Sentencing*. Oxford: Clarendon Press.

Bryan, T. and Doyle, P. (2003) 'Developing multi-agency-public-protection-arrangements', in A. Matravers (ed.) *Sex Offenders in the Community*. Cullompton: Willan Publishing.

Carson, D. (1996) 'Risking legal reperscussions', in H. Kemshall and J. Pritchard (eds) *Good Practice in Risk Assessment and Risk Management, Vol. 1*. London: Jessica Kingsley.

Cohen, S. (1972) *Folk Devils and Moral Panics*. Oxford: Martin Robertson.

Gething-Lewis, J. (2009) in 24.dash.com, communities, Central Government, 16 March.

Hanson, R. and Bussière, M. (1998) 'Predicting relapse: a meta analysis of sexual offender recidivism studies', *Journal of Consulting and Clinical Psychology*, 66(2): 348–62.

Henham, R. (2003) 'The policy and practice of protective sentencing', *Criminal Justice*, 3(1): 57–82.

Hill, D. (2001) 'After the purge', *Guardian*, 6 February.

Home Office (2000) *Setting the Boundaries: Reforming the Law on Sex Offences*, Vols 1 and 2. London: HMSO.

Home Office (2002) *Protecting the Public: Strengthening Protection Against Sex Offenders and Reforming the Law on Sexual Offences*, Cmnd 5668. London: HMSO.

Home Office (2007) *Review of the Protection of Children from Sex Offenders*. London: Home Office.

Hudson, B. A. (2003) *Justice in the Risk Society: Reaffirming Justice in Late Modernity*. London: Sage.

Jenkins, P. (1998) *Moral Panic: Changing Concepts of the Child Molester in Modern America*. New Haven: Yale University Press.

Kemshall, H. (2003) *Understanding Risk in Criminal Justice*. Buckingham: Open University Press.

Kemshall, H. and McIvor, G. (eds) (2004a) *Managing Sex Offender Risk*. London: Jessica Kingsley.

Kemshall, H. and McIvor, G. (2004b) 'Sex offenders: policy and legislative developments', in H. Kemshall and G. McIvor (eds) *Managing Sex Offender Risk*. London: Jessica Kingsley.

Kitzinger, J. (1999) 'Researching risk and the media', *Health, Risk and Society*, 1: 55–70.

Lieb, R. (2003) 'Joined up worrying: the multi-agency public protection arrangements', in A. Matravers (ed.) *Sex Offenders in the Community*. Cullompton: Willan Publishing.

Maguire, M. and Kemshall, H. (2004) 'Multi agency public protection arrangements: key issues', in H. Kemshall and G. McIvor (eds) *Managing Sex Offender Risk*. London: Jessica Kingsley.

Maguire, M., Kemshall, H., Noaks, L. and Wincup, E. (2001) *Risk Management and*

Violent Offenders: the Work of Public Protection Panels. Police Research Series Paper 139. London: Home Office.

Matravers, A. (ed.) (2003a) *Sex Offenders in the Community.* Cullompton: Willan Publishing.

Matravers, A. (2003b) 'Setting some boundaries: rethinking responses to sex offenders', in A. Matravers (ed.) *Sex Offenders in the Community.* Cullompton: Willan Publishing.

McIvor, G., Kemshall, H. and Levy, G. (2002) *Serious Violent and Sexual Offenders: The Use of Risk Assessment Tools in Scotland.* Edinburgh: Scottish Executive Social Research, Crime and Criminal Justice.

Murray, C. (1997) *Does Prison Work? Choice in Welfare, No. 38.* London: Institute for Economic Affairs.

Nash, M. (2006) *Public Protection and the Criminal Justice Process.* Oxford: Oxford University Press.

Perry, K. (2000) 'Families flee estate hate campaign', *Guardian,* 10 August 2000.

Plotnikoff, J. and Woolfson, R. (2000) *Where Are They Now? An Evaluation of Sex Offender Registration in England and Wales,* Police Research Series Paper 126. London: Home Office.

Pratt, J. (1997) *Governing the Dangerous.* Sydney: Federation Press.

Soothill, K., Francis, B. and Ackerley, E. (1998) 'Paedophilia and paedophiles', *New Law Journal,* 12: 882–3.

Thomas, T. (2001) 'Sex offenders, the Home Office and the Sunday papers', *Journal of Social Welfare and Family Law,* 23(1): 103–4.

Thomas, T. (2004) 'Sex offender registers and monitoring', in H. Kemshall and G. McIvor (eds) *Managing Sex Offender Risk.* London: Jessica Kingsley.

Thomas, T. (2005) *Sex Crime: Sex Offending in the Community,* 2nd edn. Cullompton: Willan Publishing.

Thompson, K. (1998) *Moral Panics.* London: Routledge.

Von Hirsch, A. and Ashworth, A. (1996) 'Protective sentencing under section 2(2)b: The criteria for dangerousness', *Criminal Law Review,* 43: 175–83.

Wood, D. (1988) 'Dangerous offenders and the morality of protective sentencing', *Criminal Law Review,* 35: 424–33.

Part Four

A Comparative Perspective

Introduction

Mike Nash and Andy Williams

While much of this book deals with public protection issues from the perspective of various English systems, public protection is also a global phenomenon. The globalisation of social problems, as authors such as Bauman (1997) and Young (1999) have suggested, has created a modernist project of mobilisation against our fears and insecurities regarding crime. Part of this alleged 'global insecurity' can be seen in the changes to the criminal justice system within the area of public protection. While we do not advocate the overblown neo-Marxist framework that has been applied to the notions of modernity and postmodernity, we do acknowledge its influence at the grassroots level of the criminal justice system. As the ideology of risk has become an imbedded paradigm that transgresses national criminal justice jurisdictional boundaries, it is important to provide a comparative perspective to public protection. Part Four is an attempt to provide that comparative perspective. We see these chapters as providing an important wider understanding of how models of public protection across different countries follow similar patterns and deal with similar concerns and issues. This commonality, as Francis Pakes states, can be seen in the framed discourses of public protection that examine issues such as crime prevention, public protection, surveillance and the identification of public incivilities, prolific offenders and individuals and groups deemed to be risky or dangerous. Readers may view these chapters as repeating some of what has come before, but it is important to see the subtle intricacies of how different countries have dealt with the same problems. We are not trying to suggest that there is a consensus over these issues. Our wish is merely for readers to approach the issues in these chapters with a critical eye.

The first chapter in this section sees Francis Pakes providing an overview of public protection in the Netherlands, where public protection and community safety are subsumed into the term *veiligheid*, meaning both safety and security. Pakes is ideally placed to discuss public protection for his research examines the criminal justice system in the Netherlands, concentrating on crime, social change and mental health. The first issue he examines is the essential local nature of community safety policy. It is within these localities where visible local safety programmes – such as the Rotterdam approach – place public protection at the heart of the community. The second issue Pakes discusses is that of youth crime. He notes that the overriding concern with public protection in the Netherlands is also connected to fears and concerns over groups such as youths and ethnic minorities, particularly those teenagers with a Moroccan and Turkish background. This, he argues, has become a highly racialised discourse, where Moroccan background and Muslim identity are connected with masculine narcissism and violence. Pakes then goes on to highlight the shift in dynamics of the integration and exclusion of mentally disordered offenders. A final issue is how safety and public protection policies in the Netherlands are seen as a 'grand design' flagship project. In order to demonstrate this Pakes examines the ambitious Amsterdam 1012 project, an attempt to clean up the city's red light district. His concluding remarks note that the spread of public protection as the driver for change is uneven. It contains paradoxical elements that are in essence a balancing act between interventionism and the strong tradition of *laissez-faire*. He suggests that the current public and parliamentary discourses on public protection has toughened in recent years with crime, youth, ethnicity and immigration becoming 'political footballs' where these groups are used as folk devils to justify punitive public protection policies.

Beth Weaver and Fergus McNeill's chapter describes the recent changes in the purpose and focus of probation practice and how wider community based criminal justice social work services in Scotland have placed a specific emphasis on the public protection agenda. The central difference in how offenders are supervised between the Scottish and English and Welsh systems is that in Scotland the responsibility lies with criminal justice social workers employed by local authorities. Weaver and McNeill have a unique insight into these developments through their practitioner and academic research. Weaver's role as a social worker and MAPPA coordinator placed her at the heart of the development of public protection in Scotland, while McNeill's work in drug rehabilitation and as a criminal justice social worker provides a wealth of practitioner experience. They demonstrate how the development and adoption of public protection is actually a meta-narrative emanating from official discourses. Their review of policy and practice developments emphasises the introduction of MAPPA in Scotland, showing how many of the developments within public protection have been introduced without adequate critical reflection. Indeed, we argue that an uncritical approach to the introduction of public protection policies and systems is a common issue throughout the various chapters of this volume. Their chapter concludes by discussing a range of arguments for an approach to public protection that is placed within the wider framework of rehabilitation. Here the authors locate rehabilitation as being operationalised through the emphasis on the notion of rights and justice. Their chief argument is that an alternative way forward to public protection could be framed within a broader 'integrative enterprise' such as the development of opportunities, the promotion of social inclusion and social capital. In order to achieve this, offenders must have access to the necessary resources, something the rehabilitative and reintegrative side of public protection attempts to achieve in many guises. Weaver and McNeill expertly examine these issues and show how contemporary official discourses and policies are consistent with the pursuit of both public protection and 'rehabilitation'. Their contention is that public protection should be more balanced and framed within a humane and integrative approach to offender supervision, management and rehabilitation.

Bill Thompson and Cecil Greek's chapter provides a comprehensive discussion of the development of sex offender notification laws in the United States. Their analysis centres on the policy imperatives and their effectiveness and consequences for public protection, and their review is an attempt to draw some universal lessons from US practice. They review the origins, consequences and subsequent criticism of a variety of public notification systems, and argue that these developments have been far from uniform. One can draw parallels here with what is currently being introduced in the UK. As the public notification pilots have started to be extended across the test counties, we are moving closer to a constrained version of Megan's Law. Thompson and Greek's excellent analysis provides us with some food for thought on the difficulties in implementing sex offender public notification policies. They start by examining the growth in the demand for the right to know where sex offenders are living in local communities. This is not an issue restricted to the US, of course. Issues of the public wanting information on where offenders live, and more importantly how they are being managed and supervised in the community, are common to many countries around the world. What Thompson and Greek examine is how some very visible cases of child abduction and murder by 'known' sexual predators created entrepreneurial activity, the result of which has been the creation of a broad range of public protection legislation used for the surveillance and control of such offenders. Thompson is best placed to write on issues of moral enterprise having spent the last 25 years undertaking ethnographic research into some of the biggest moral crusades and miscarriages of justice issues in the UK. Greek's work on offender databases and the construction and control of information means that their chapter offers a unique fusion of knowledge and experience within the realm of public protection. After charting the introduction of notification and sex offender legislation, the authors examine the implementation of Megan's Law in practice. Because the US system of public protection is complex – largely due to the federal, state and county policing structure – Thompson and Greek spend some time highlighting the disparities in public notification practice. Indeed, they find that the only uniformity in practice is that every internet database warns users against the misuse of that information. What is of further interest in this chapter is their discussion of the constitutional issues regarding registration requirements, as well as an interesting take on civil commitments as being an extension of community control. They suggest that civil commitments conveniently bypass many of the legal arguments concerning the constitutionality of criminal registration and notification provisions. What Thompson and Greek also discuss is a common problem we find here in the UK – system overload. As laws are expanded and the net of social control widened, the public protection system has become overloaded with offenders, as well as the resultant surveillance and supervision requirements. They demonstrate this by considering the way teen offenders are being automatically perceived as 'budding paedophiles'. They highlight how many US states treat teen sex offenders as they treat adult ones, which ultimately leads to excessive labelling and contributes to registration overload. We have noticed this 'sea change' happening in the UK, which makes Thompson and Greek's point about risk assessments being arbitrary in nature with a tendency to overcategorise offenders as 'high risk' even more telling.

Using his wealth of experience and knowledge, Eric Janus offers us a distinctive overview of what he calls new types of prevention. He has spent most of his career researching the interaction of law with psychiatry and other health sciences. He very much believes that a public health approach to prevention would produce a more comprehensive and systematic empirically based understanding of the root causes of violence. He argues that since 1990, laws based on prevention have taken a serious paradigmatic change, with a new form of social control coming to dominate public protection policy. Janus calls this new form the 'preventive state' and suggests that we have taken a wrong turn when it comes to public protection. He notes how we have adopted 'counter-empirical, interstitial laws' that identify and remove risky persons before they can cause harm. While this may be good for the bureaucratic model of criminal justice, there are a number of factors that make this approach harmful. Janus examines these factors by suggesting that the legal innovations that have brought about the preventive state provide the conditions that devour precious limits on government power. He calls this new form of prevention 'radical prevention' and it's this concept that is the thread running through his chapter. Janus suggests that radical prevention are counter-law schemes that establish alternative justice systems of prevention, and it is these schemes that cause harm. For example, they distort resource allocation, focusing on individual risk rather than patterns of risk, identifying correlates for violence rather than root causes. They also often push interventions further and further 'downstream' by disregarding empirical knowledge. Janus then goes on to make the telling observation that radical prevention is corrosive of the basic principles of liberal democracies. This can be seen through the lens of the change from guilt to risk as the prime predicate of interventions that attempt to strike a balance between liberty and security. This liberty/security balance is further upset, Janus argues, by the shift from crime detection to radical prevention. In the radical prevention schemes, surveillance replaces investigation, and anyone who fits the 'profile' for risk becomes a suspect. It is this 'outsider' jurisprudence that Janus sees as being the most dangerous aspect of radical prevention schemes. While today we target people who are sexually dangerous, the problem is that we do not know which class of people we will target tomorrow; and therein lies the danger of relying on a preventive state mentality that replicates the outsider template.

References

Bauman, Z. (1997) *Postmodernity and its Discontents*. Cambridge: Polity Press.

Young, J. (1999) *The Exclusive Society: Social Exclusion, Crime and Difference in Late Modernity*. London: Sage.

Chapter 12

Public protection and community safety in the Netherlands

Francis Pakes

Introduction

Public protection and community safety tend to be multi-headed beasts. That is as true for the Netherlands as it is elsewhere. Looking at public protection and community safety in the Netherlands a multitude of initiatives can be discerned across many spheres whose similarity can only be properly understood by the application of public protection and community safety-esque concepts. Rather like many other western democracies, much public discourse and policy-making is characterised by a newfound preoccupation with crime prevention, public protection, surveillance and the energetic targeting of public incivilities, prolific offenders and individuals and groups deemed to be risky or dangerous. And as is the case elsewhere, many of these initiatives have a local flavour.

Looking at such concepts it must be conceded that discussing public protection and community safety in a different context involves to an extent efforts to 'translate the untranslatable' (Pakes 2004). In the Netherlands both public protection and community safety are subsumed into the term *veiligheid*. This translates as both 'safety' and 'security'. *Veiligheid* is the 'persuasive expression' that both drives and legitimises policies that can be both unorthodox and intrusive. *Veiligheid* has become a key policy objective within criminal justice, but also beyond, in spheres such as public health, housing, transport and, nowhere so poignantly as immigration and integration. The latter two are particularly relevant and highlight the fact that much of society's unease that has furthered public protection measures has been affected by perceptions and discourses of race, ethnicity and the conviction that individuals of certain backgrounds are more risky or dangerous than others. I will return to that at various points in this chapter.

This chapter examines four seemingly disparate strands of community safety and public protection initiatives. The first is the essential local nature of community safety policy-making *via* highly visible local safety programmes. The Rotterdam approach – comprehensive, far-reaching and committed – will be highlighted as a pioneering example. The second involves shifts in the dynamics of integration and exclusion of mentally disordered offenders, an area where public protection has become an overriding concern. Third is a discussion of juvenile offending, which has become dominated by a highly racialised discourse, and finally I look at community safety and public protection not as an amalgamation of projects and policies but expressed *via* a 'grand design' flagship project. I examine Amsterdam's ambitious 1012 project to clean up the city's red light district as an example and the politics and pragmatics that gives it its distinctive shape.

Community safety and public protection

Despite over twenty years of criminological protestations the cosy picture of the Netherlands as a place where difference is celebrated and punishment regarded as unnecessary and distasteful is persistent (see Pakes 2006; Cavadino and Dignan 2006; Downes and Van Swaaningen 2007 for recent examples, and Franke (1990) to show the by now substantial history of Dutch scholars discussing Dutch tolerance in less rosy terms). Van Swaaningen (2005) is particularly outspoken about that anachronistic picture, which he compares with the stereotypes of tulips and clogs. He has a point: the Dutch prison population has shot up in the last twenty years and penal capacity for youngsters, the mentally disordered and illegal immigrants have all massively expanded. That no doubt is a reflection of the fact that the population is concerned about, perhaps even consumed by, worries about immigration, street crime and other insecurities that are often associated with globalisation. A strong response by those in power is asked for, and increasingly they have obliged.

However, simply to accept that the Netherlands has swung the other way and that all endeavour is about *otherisation* and punishment is not fair either. Instead, the Dutch approach to issues of public protection is inconsistent, paradoxal at times, and prominently pragmatic. While it can be agreed, with Downes and Van Swaaningen (2007), that Garland's vision of cultures of control (2001) is more applicable to the Netherlands than before, it must not be forgotten that recent legislative changes have included the legalisation of brothels, that the governance of cannabis products remains refreshingly defiant and that usage of life imprisonment, certainly as compared to the UK, remains a rarity. Difference continues to exist and that makes a comparative perspective useful.

As elsewhere, though, the Netherlands has been increasingly consumed by concerns of safety. The context in which the term safety (or security) is used has rather changed. Safety and security in post-war Netherlands had a lot to do with international concerns. The Cold War and the nuclear arms race were the backdrop to which issues of safety and security were normally addressed: that is, in relation to threats from abroad. Only since the 1980s has the discourse on safety and security become inward-looking to become national, and latterly local, concerns.

In the 1990s so-called *integraal veiligheidsbeleid* emerged, translatable as 'comprehensive safety policy' (Cachet and Ringeling 2004). The novelty of comprehensive safety policy initially was found in the fact that security policy was desired to be comprehensive and needed to be given shape in partnership. In addition the use of administrative (civil) law and techniques was billed as the novel way of enhancing security policy. Another departure from the traditional approach to security was the judgement that security or safety is a concern that goes beyond observable events and any official reaction to that. It is to do with feelings and perceptions of insecurity and, in keeping with the international *zeitgeist*, the identification and management of risk.

The government produced its first comprehensive safety report in 1993 and the first policy paper called *Veiligheidsbeleid (Security Policy)* was published in 1995. From then on policy pillars have been identified, including youth, drugs, prolific offenders and surveillance (Cachet and Ringeling 2004). Thus, the rise of community safety and public protection was kick-started at a national level but responsibility for the implementation of any number of initiatives soon became a local matter. That may suggest a policy implementation trajectory that is tidy and clean: a national framework to be implemented locally with sensitivity to local needs. However, the process is on the one hand more dialectic than that and on the other is affected by external factors. Three strands need to be considered here that help explain why the policy journey from the national to the local is not straightforward.

The first is the tug of war between local and national players in owning security and safety policy. Initially, much local community safety activity was project based. They were often given shape by zealous individuals, were small-scale and typified by a lack of strategic direction. Already in 1998 the government warned against that approach, as it was perceived as having a lack of coherence. Policy had become bitty, poorly visible and too often the hobby horse of particular individuals. In particular Tops (2007), in the case of Rotterdam, has been scathing about the project-based approach to community safety that was perceived to have failed to bring about a much needed overhaul in community safety cultures in the various organisations that are involved. In a subsequent phase, national frameworks were established to bring about an impetus and cohesiveness to local efforts. However, national frameworks are often diluted and quite frequently transformed beyond recognition at the local level. This highlights a classic tension. Although community safety is only sensibly implemented at the local level, the national level finds it terribly difficult to leave the local to it (see also Edwards and Hughes 2005).

The second is the role of criminal law, policing and punishment in safety policy. Much has been made of the multi-agency aspect of community safety that includes housing, transport, voluntary agencies, local authorities, health care and so on. It alludes to the limited prowess of criminal justice in solving social problems and highlights the problem-solving and pragmatic nature of community safety. In particular, licensing laws can be utilised effectively, and I discuss examples of that later. It suggests on the one hand that community safety cannot or should not be owned by police or the criminal justice system. It is no doubt the case that ownership has shifted to a degree towards local authorities. On the other hand, and paradoxically so, the belief in the leverage of criminalisation and policing as the default mode of intervention remains unabashed. Buruma (2004) calls this the 'minitiaturisation' of criminal law. In Rotterdam, begging has been outlawed and a great many petty delinquents have been brought to court for such matters including violations of the obligation to carry some form of ID. Thus, where on the one hand it is undisputed that criminal justice can only do so much, on the other hand it is invoked more readily for ever smaller infringements. At the same time, the embracing of community safety and public protection by agencies with an ethos of care has led in places to the usage of the term 'safety care' (Boutellier 2001) to highlight their desire to 'look after' rather than 'control' vulnerable groups of the population. That this creates operational and strategic areas of dispute is obvious.

The third is the role of external factors. One set of external factors refers to events. In the Netherlands the big events were, as I have observed elsewhere (Pakes 2004), the events of 11 September 2001 and the murders of politician Pim Fortuyn in 2002 and film-maker and TV personality Theo van Gogh in 2004. Van Swaaningen (2005) has argued that the Netherlands identifies more strongly with the US than many other mainland European countries and that 9/11 was felt as an attack on the Dutch way of life as well. The assassination of maverick politician Pim Fortuyn just prior to the 2002 general elections led to a sustained phase of public disarray. Although the guilty party was in fact a native Dutch environmental activist, the Fortuyn murder stirred racial tension that caused a great deal of commotion in the normally quite sedate public life of the Netherlands. The murder of Theo van Gogh was committed by a Muslim extremist. Van Gogh had just been involved with the making of a documentary film on the treatment of women in Muslim communities, and he did insult Muslim communities regularly in newspaper columns and media appearances. These events have helped shape social and political discourse in the Netherlands beyond recognition (Pakes 2006).

Another external factor refers to the hegemony of the term *veiligheid*. Edwards and Hughes's insight that the fact that community safety in various European countries is not just referred to in different terms but is actually a different entity in each locality is important (Edwards and Hughes 2005). In the Netherlands the term *veiligheid* has had competition from the concept of *leefbaarheid* (liveability). *Leefbaarheid* emerged as a strictly local phenomenon and has been described as the interplay between various characteristics of a person's immediate environment, including its physical, structural, social and economic characteristics. 'Liveable' became a buzzword in local politics from the 1970s up to the present day. Local parties took part in local elections particularly in cities; *Leefbaar Utrecht* or *Leefbaar Rotterdam* were two of the most visible and successful local parties, focusing on local issues with remarkable success. In 1999 this led to the establishment of *Leefbaar Nederland*, a political party with a national platform. Pim Fortuyn initially emerged as the figurehead of the party but was suddenly sacked following inflammatory statements in a media interview. Fortuyn then went it alone and founded the List Pim Fortuyn party, with even greater success.

Although the political fortunes of the liveable movement in its various guises is decidedly mixed – the party *Leefbaar Nederland* is close to meltdown – the term liveability has retained a lot of meaning and part of that fits the community safety/public protection banner. Edwards and Hughes explain its appeal cogently:

> Central to this punitive turn has been the rise of the LPF (List Pim Fortuyn) named after its charismatic political figurehead who had built his political power-base among the increasingly disaffected white Dutch working classes of Rotterdam through a focus on *leefbaarheid* or 'live-ability'. The LPF advanced a narrative of Dutch decline arguing that the Netherlands has become unliveable not least because of the liberal elite's tolerance for communities, such as Muslims from the North and Horn of Africa, who do not share a commitment to Dutch norms and traditions. In the Dutch context this conception of safety as a problem of unregulated migration has created a broader political climate rejecting the liberal, pragmatic, rationalism for which Dutch crime control had become renowned. Whereas previously 'safety' had signified a more social democratic politics of urban renewal, as in the *Integraal veiligheidsbeleid* or 'integral safety policy', the LPF were successful in capturing this term and re-articulating it to signify a range of external threats from post-9/11 terrorism to street violence and new objects of control, specifically street populations from ethnic minority communities. (Edwards and Hughes 2005: 357)

Nowhere has the term *leefbaar* had more mileage than in Rotterdam where in early 2002 *Leefbaar Rotterdam* actually won the local elections. It furthered a transformation of the Rotterdam Safety approach that is carefully chronicled by Tops (2007). Although by no means the birthplace of the *leefbaar* movement, Rotterdam is where the transformation of public protection and community safety has been most eye-catching and comprehensive. Van Swaaningen explains that the focus is mainly on street crime and also incivilities (roughly, anti-social behaviour). The discourse is one of claiming back and cleaning up the streets, with prolific offenders, street prostitutes, illegal immigrants and beggars very specifically targeted, as well as drug addicts refusing to be connected to services. He refers to it as a focus on 'banning the urban poor' (Van Swaaningen 2005: 295). Uitermark and Duyvendak (forthcoming) refer to the Rotterdam approach as 'revanchist urbanism'. It is presented as an effort to take back public places that have been surrendered to danger and disorder.

Notable about Rotterdam is not the fact that it has an integrated comprehensive safety plan (they are now part and parcel of local authority policy up and down the country) but that it uncompromisingly put 'safety first' as its overarching priority over all local authority policy-making. This was on the one hand made possible by the new political configuration of the council but also by burgomaster (Mayor) Opstelten, who embraced the transformation and served as a driving force. The fact that burgomaster Opstelten was a trailblazer exemplifies a number of wider trends. One is the often observed development in various countries that safety policy has been pushed downward from the national to the local level. Edwards and Hughes (2005) mention that France, Italy and Belgium and the Netherlands fit this trend. The figure of the burgomaster, until recently a largely apolitical pre-retirement post, has become highly influential in local community safety and public protection matters. I have discussed elsewhere how burgomasters have become formidable agenda setters in the governance of cannabis in the Netherlands (Pakes 2009). In addition, the Rotterdam project did attract a great deal of national interest and praise and as such went far beyond the strictly local. In fact, the Rotterdam approach has been facilitated by enabling national legislation, and national politicians frequently look to Rotterdam for inspiration. Although Rotterdam may not be exactly archetypal, the city has certainly played a pioneering role. Thus, the local–national relationship here is one of dialectic and symbiosis at the same time.

A mantra for safety policy is for it to be 'comprehensive'. That includes a multi-agency approach and the inclusion of issues well beyond crime, to include environmental risks, housing, transport, incivilities, community building and race relations. There is little doubt that in Rotterdam, comprehensive actually means comprehensive. It involves a statistical measure called the Safety Index, which measures safety *via* an extensive set of both objective and subjective variables. They measure safety at the level of areas. The 72 areas that comprise Rotterdam all have a *wijkveiligheidsprogramma* (local safety programme). Key areas are allocated a 'city marine', an individual with a wide remit in order to 'make policies happen' on the ground, whereas so-called 'intervention teams' operate across the city. The vagaries of the concepts of liveability, safety, public protection and community safety defy boundaries and that includes limitations on the extent to which officialdom can interfere in the lives of citizens. This is of particular relevance to intervention teams. Their trade is house visits to investigate compliance with health and safety regulation, benefits, irregular habitation, subletting, council tax debt, cannabis growing, the presence of illegal immigrants, and so on. The remit of these intervention teams is, worryingly, 'everything really' (Rotterdam Ombudsman 2007: Pakes 2010, in press). The teams can be of considerable size and frequently gain entry due to overwhelmed citizens agreeing to it or because of vague and under-protocolised official rights of entry. These teams undertake a whopping 25,000 visits per year. It is not clear exactly how addresses are selected nor is it always specified exactly what the main reason is for the visit. The Rotterdam Ombudsman argues that the instrument of the intervention team has multi-faceted aims including help, repression and control, and that serves to confuse the citizen and leads to anxiety. In addition, there is insufficient internal and external oversight as to the actual conduct of these teams. Visits are often on an *ad hoc* basis, the Ombudsman argues, but it is clear that visits only occur in the most deprived areas and sometimes unfair pressure is exerted in order to gain entry. To be fair, the local authority has since tightened its operational protocol for these teams. Teams should be not larger than three individuals (there is anecdotal evidence that visits were on occasion undertaken by at least ten people). Representatives of non-state bodies (such as utility companies) should no longer be an integral part of intervention teams. Training for 'front-line' staff is also part of the package of reform. Finally, there is central point for the registration of complaints and improved procedures for the registration of visits, findings and outcomes (Rotterdam City Council 2008).

The Rotterdam intervention teams embody the unease often associated with the overzealous pursuit of safety policy as opposed to crime and crime prevention policies. Boutellier (2001) argues that it puts crime and anti-social behaviour ideologically on a par with floods, pests and fires: it advocates administrative modes of control and removes the separate sphere that crime has traditionally been wrapped in – with separate agencies to deal with it governed by separate laws with different levels of proof and laws of evidence. Crime is now intermingled with other concerns and has, as the saying goes, become everyone's business, public, private, national and local. Boutellier describes this as the merging of criminal policy with social policy, which is probably what the Rotterdam intervention teams do at a practical level. This is much to the distrust of many a criminologist, such as Stenson (2000). At the same time, however, it cannot be concluded that safety policy is necessarily reduced to cold-blooded technocracy. Apart from investigation and control, the Rotterdam intervention teams provide a great deal of help. It is often difficult if not impossible to say where looking for trouble and infringements ends and looking after citizens starts but it is that very merging of roles and meanings that is a concern from a civil liberties perspective.

Despite these criticisms, the Rotterdam transformation (referred to by Tops (2007) as 'regime change') is nothing short of remarkable. It particularly defies the often stated truism that safety policy is almost impossible to be comprehensive due to competing priorities and perceptions between the various agencies assumed to give it shape. Usually comprehensive safety policies end up diluted and are implemented unevenly. Not so in Rotterdam and that is an achievement to be recognised.

Public protection and the problem of youth

In the Netherlands moral panics about youth cannot be separated from worries about ethnic minorities. It is in particular teenagers with Moroccan and Turkish backgrounds that bear the brunt of the public discourse on youth out of control. Although it is clear that youngsters of Moroccan descent and also those from the Dutch Antilles are disproportionately present in police statistics (Moroccans and Antilleans by three to five times, Surinamese about two times), there is rather a moral panic that conflates a Moroccan background and Muslim identity with masculine narcissism and violence.

Ethnicity and identity are laden subjects in the Netherlands. The main distinction in public and official discourse is between *allochtones* (roughly speaking, 'those not from here') and *autochtones* ('natives'). Precise definitions are difficult but involve a consideration of birthplace, nationality of parents and whether an ethnic group is of elevated risk of social exclusion. By these virtues, a teenager born in Amsterdam but with one of the parents born in Morocco is likely to be seen as (and perhaps not unlikely to view themselves) as an *allochtone*, which in practical terms means a foreigner or a stranger. The Dutch concern with the 'other' is mainly directed at *allochtones*, many of whom have Dutch nationality (but possibly hold another nationality as well), are Dutch speakers and whose ties to life in Morocco,

Turkey or Surinam might well be much looser than their bonds to Dutch society.

An incident in 2004 exemplifies the potency of a racialised public discourse on youth. Deputy head teacher Hans van Wieren was shot and killed in the secondary school where he worked, by a 16-year-old pupil, Murat D., a troubled youngster of Turkish ethnic background. The motivation for the act seemingly had to do with issues of respect and discipline. The event caused uproar in the Netherlands, with best-selling and most populist newspaper *De Telegraaf* immediately highlighting the ethnic issues involved. The commotion was fuelled when two days later about 30 youngsters from the school engaged in an impromptu demonstration in support of Murat. Banners with the message 'Murat we love you' were on display and teenagers, most of whom were of ethnic minority origin, were heard arguing that Murat was no criminal and that the victim in a way deserved his fate because he had 'picked on' the pupil. There was a minute's silence held the next day in all the secondary schools in the country. Murat had by then turned himself in; although a minor, he was tried under adult provision, a classic instance of what Muncie and Goldson (2007) call the adulteration of youth justice.

The tragic incident remained in public consciousness for quite some time. The victim possessed all the characteristics of the 'good guy'; a hard-working teacher in a challenging environment, an active community member and a family man, father of two teenage daughters. In contrast, the offender and his domestic situation, coupled with the showings of support, allowed for the vilification not only of the individual concerned but also of his *milieu*. It highlights fundamental tensions in youth justice: it varies from catering for troubled youngsters teetering on the brink of criminality to having to deal with seemingly heartless, remorseless and incorrigible young people.

Youth justice in the Netherlands traditionally has been highly caring. There is a long and successful tradition of alternative disposals, and one scheme in particular, HALT, has had considerable international recognition. HALT is a diversionary scheme that allows the offender to engage in targeted local community work to avoid a criminal record. Over 20,000 HALT disposals are carried out each year. HALT is a success story that spawned a little brother: STOP. STOP is designed for the under-twelves who have committed minor offences. It also involves reparation-type activities, of which one of the most common is the writing of a letter of apology. It is important to note that the age of criminal responsibility in the Netherlands is twelve years. STOP therefore technically sits outside the criminal law but is administered very similarly to HALT and can therefore be construed as a case of interventionist net-widening.

Despite the emphasis on diversion and on community penalties, there is an enduring practice of the incarceration of young people. Youngsters can be held in juvenile detention centres or in centres of further treatment or rehabilitation. However, the waters are severely muddied. Young people can be detained as part of a punishment or under a civil referral. They are routinely placed in the same institutions, so that those deemed to be in need of protection or rehabilitation mix with those sent there for punishment. The vulnerable are therefore mixing with the criminal, which led in 2004 to adverse comments from the UN Committee on the Rights of the Child (Weijers and Liefaard 2007).

Co-placement probably occurs out of necessity rather than principle. Cutbacks in the 1980s led to a substantial shortage of homes for vulnerable children so that many ended up in juvenile detention centres. About 500 children might be in a juvenile detention centre while waiting for a place in a more appropriate treatment centre. The current Minister for Youth and Families, André Rouvoet, has vowed to remedy the situation and has released funds to bring this about but practice is patchy. The shortage in appropriate placements is striking, given the increase in places that has occurred in the last twenty years. In 1985 there were 660 places; in 1995 that had increased to 1,045, and in 2005 the capacity is no less than 2,579, almost a fourfold increase. Looking at the development of child detention capacity in the Netherlands it is clear that the Dutch response to youth is increasingly interventionist, if not punitive. The majority are detained under civil law and it is this group that tends to stay longer than those sentenced. Of those held under criminal law provisions, most are held on remand.

A further disturbing finding is that the majority of youngsters held are not born in the Netherlands; 60 per cent in 2004, according to Eggen and Van der Heijde (2004). This has been the case for well over a decade. The damning statement made by Cavadino and Dignan (2006) about the 'wildly disproportionate number of foreigners and members of ethnic minorities in Dutch prisons' seems to extend to the juvenile estate as well. Official figures concerning arrests and juveniles interviewed by police similarly highlight this disproportionality in terms of background of the youngsters that come to the attention of the police. Arrest data show that from twelve-year-olds upwards, ethnic minority youths are over-represented in the arrest and interview statistics by two and a half to four times. It is interesting that ethnic minority twelve-year-olds are over four times more likely to be interviewed or arrested by police than 'native' twelve-year-olds (Eggen and van der Heijde 2004).

Cavadino and Dignan (2006) also mention the rise of 'neo-correctionalist' measures. However, as they (and also Van Swaaningen) have argued, it would be incorrectly alarmist to simply argue that the Netherlands has gone full throttle towards a punitive style of youth justice. The situation is more mixed than that, with alternative and rehabilitative measures being furthered in equal measure to the rise of detention. However, it is clear that youth crime has become an industry of substantial size, within the police, local government and the prison service. Uit Beijerse and Van Swaaningen (2006) rightly warn that a structure of planning and control and a discourse of morality and discipline might serve to further erode any emphasis on care, rehabilitation and children's rights.

Mentally disordered offenders

Individuals with severe mental health problems who have committed an offence can be sentenced to TBS (placed under a hospital order), which involves the involuntary admission into secure psychiatric care (Koenraadt and Mooij 2007). It often is imposed in conjunction with a prison sentence that normally is served first. Technically TBS is a measure not a sentence, with the primary aim of public protection. It is imposed following a detailed psychiatric assessment to establish to what extent mental health difficulties preclude the assignment of culpability to the offender. It is a sliding scale: an offender can be deemed to be fully capable, not at all, or somewhere in between. It is in the latter scenario that an offender might serve a prison sentence, as it were to punish the culpable part of him, after which a spell of psychiatric hospitalisation may take place. As is the case in the UK, the management of these individuals hovers between care and rehabilitation on the one hand and control on the other (Laing 1999). Recently, however, the discourse is particularly one of control. A panic was sparked following TBS patients committing occasionally quite graphic offences while out on leave. One committed murder, another kidnapped a thirteen-year-old girl. This led to a review of leave arrangements that subsequently have been substantially tightened.

At the end of 2006 there were 1,699 detainees in forensic psychiatric hospitals held under TBS arrangements. Of these, 151 were in so-called 'long stay units', and their number is on the increase. In the 1990s there was a threefold increase in capacity which currently is filled near maximum. It leads to conflicting pressures on the service. On the one hand there has been an emphasis on effective treatment working towards release with a continuation of care in the community subsequent to release. On the other hand the system is clogging up. Annually 150 to 200 individuals are sentenced to TBS and only 50 to 70 are released. That creates a waiting list, currently in the order of 200. An increasing number of individuals have the TBS measure imposed but wait in prison until a bed becomes available.

In addition, there has been a telling development with the aforementioned long stay units. These hold individuals for whom rehabilitation with an aim to return to society is no longer the objective. The aim of these units has been reduced to containment. Although a bi-annual review procedure is in place, placement in a long stay unit will effectively often equate to a life sentence. This is important from another perspective that relates to the imposition of the TBS. Where a defendant refuses to cooperate with the psychiatric reporting that is required for the court to consider, the court will often impose a prison sentence. The developments in the management of TBS increasingly cause defendants to refuse psychiatric assessment as it is seen to be an alternative route towards what may be a life sentence. Despite that, the number of individuals placed in long stay units has substantially grown. Needless to say, long stay with its low intensity treatment is cheaper. Although there always have been individuals held under TBS indefinitely, the emergence of long stay has emphasised the increased size of this group, and the perceived limitations of the rehabilitative ideal for these individuals.

The rise of TBS as a measure to contain where decision-making is dominated by considerations of risk is exemplary of public protection thinking but with highly adverse consequences. Mentally disordered offenders are less likely to be allowed out on leave, which might hamper their rehabilitation process towards release; they are more likely to be judged not suitable for rehabilitation and end up on long stay units. They are also more likely to stay in prison, either because their TBS measure cannot be implemented due to capacity problems or because, having developed psychiatric problems while in prison, no transfer to hospital can be made for the same reason.

Public protection in Amsterdam: the battle against seediness

It was observed earlier that public protection efforts come under various banners. Where *leefbaar* has been a slogan-esque concept with, at least in the short term, political mileage, the *leefbaar* movement was relatively unsuccessful in the capital city of Amsterdam. As with London in the UK, Amsterdam tends to be a case of its own. The 'Amsterdam is unique' case, however, should also not be overstated. Van Swaaningen mentions that in terms of overall approach, Amsterdam and Rotterdam may not be all that different. However, there is a project in the nation's capital that does stand out and that highlights local difference in community safety and public protection initiatives. The project has been sold to the city as a cleaning up project of Amsterdam's notorious red light district. It is called Project 1012, in reference to the area's postal code. The persuasive expression is 'seediness' (*ranzigheid*). The expression legitimises the operation and gives it focus but it hides as much as it reveals. The association of seediness with prostitution is easily made and it invokes an image of illicit sex, exploitation, anti-social behaviour during stag parties, and the pungent smell of urine. With a sense of nostalgia that is in vogue, the project aims to restore the area rather than reinvent it. It should result in a reduction in the number of prostitution windows, coffee shops and other businesses thought to be either lowering the tone or intermingled with organised crime, such as phone shops.

Labour coming man and city councillor Lodewijk Asscher has been a driving force behind the project that initially was well received. However, in Amsterdam any operation with moral undertones needs to tread carefully. The area under scrutiny is no doubt thoroughly corrupted by organised crime but it is a popular tourist destination at the same time. Both the prostitution phenomenon and the coffee shops are on thousands of tourists' travel itinerary and the city is obviously keen not to throw out the lucrative baby with the seedy bathwater. This situation differs from that in Rotterdam where the focus on safety and security is not conceived of as a balancing act, highlighting another key difference between the two cities. In many of Rotterdam's deprived areas the problem is a lack of jobs and entrepreneurs. In Amsterdam it is the wrong entrepreneur that is being tackled. This refers back to the two cities' differing demographics and position. Rotterdam has a large blue-collar workforce under threat by globalisation. Cosmopolitan Amsterdam on the other hand is home to people for whom globalisation is more a matter of opportunity, be it legal or otherwise. This has impacted on how community safety and public protection are given shape.

The fact that the Amsterdam 1012 project is more of a balancing act has on occasion led to uneasy compromises. Crucial in the tackling of organised crime and sex entrepreneurs with associations with organised crime is the so-called BIBOB legislation (Pakes 2010, in press). It allows local authorities and other bodies involved with licensing the opportunity to background check applicants before awarding permits or contracts. It is not the same as a criminal records check, however. BIBOB is not uncontroversial from a legal and ethical perspective, as it allows limited means of appeals and accepts grey judicial information to be used to inform the BIBOB's office judgement. In addition, BIBOB is not under any obligation to make its evidence available to the applicant. These issues aside for the moment, there is little doubt that very few sex entrepreneurs and coffee shop owners would pass the BIBOB test. That makes BIBOB a potent weapon in the war against seediness and one that casts its shadows at that. Where licence renewal is at issue it gives licensers a strong bargaining position. Some of Amsterdam's most iconic sex establishments have indeed been closed following a negative BIBOB judgement. However, when the northern city of Groningen sought to do the same thing and close five sex establishments, it ran into difficulties. The *Raad van State* (Council of State, an administrative law appeals body) argued that BIBOB judgements had been unsafe and that closures solely on the basis of BIBOB results were unjustified (Robles 2008). It looks as if BIBOB will need to review its ways and that might reduce its potency in weeding out unsavoury entrepreneurs.

Certain measures in Amsterdam demonstrate the intense pragmatism required to assume a level of control over the goings on in the red light district. A city housing corporation has bought several properties that were in use for prostitution. It has been justified as a 'buy out' prior to a strategy of 'smoking out'. It shows that where other options fail, local government may simply throw cash at criminals. The money that has changed hands may well be in the order of £20 million. If doing business with criminals is the way to get them out, the city does not hesitate. In an ironic way, it highlights a historical tension in the city that has been there since its seventeenth-century heyday: a tradition of successful entrepreneurism coupled with, but at the same time detached from, a strong sense of moral imperative (Schama 1987).

Community safety and public protection in the Netherlands

A number of features of community safety and public protection in the Netherlands are quickly discernible. An obvious and disturbing one is its entanglement with race. This is not restricted to youth justice and the wider discourse on ethnic minority teenagers wreaking havoc in public spaces. Instead, race, immigration and integration, in particular in relation to Muslim communities, is discussed in the news media on a daily basis. The idea that Muslim youngsters in particular have emerged as an evil from which the population needs to be protected, on public transport and at swimming pools and other public spaces, is persistent. However, the Dutch approach remains essentially twin-track, with lots of project work to involve these individuals, but at the same time various restrictive, coercive and punishment-based efforts exist to curtail them.

It is also clear that traditional criminal law is only one of the weapons brought to bear. Civil measures of a restricting nature have become commonplace, while the BIBOB framework is administrative in nature and in principle highly effective in weeding out organised crime's entanglement with legal or quasi-legal business. Despite this, the criminal law is invoked in cases big and small and expectations regarding the criminal justice system to sort society's problems remains high.

Public protection has become a local matter and is coloured by local circumstances and agendas. Rotterdam's far-reaching and in places highly intrusive integral safety programme has been the flagship although many of its features are now replicated elsewhere – nowhere, however, with Rotterdam's commitment and poise. Its most impressive feature is how all-encompassing it has become with an impressive level of commitment from virtually all agencies in the city, so that it is fair to speak of a transformation.

Conclusion

In conclusion, the spread of public protection as the driver for change is uneven. It contains paradoxical elements that are particularly discernible in youth justice, but are equally present even in Rotterdam where the discourse is often tough, although much of the interference in people's lives no doubt improves the very lives that were intruded upon. The reforms put in place further to the Rotterdam Ombudsman's damning report will only serve to secure that further.

Public protection in the Netherlands remains a balancing act. There is interventionism but at the same time there has been a strong tradition of *laissez-faire*. Amsterdam fights seediness, but let's face it, the city likes it too. Despite the harsher tone that characterises the debate on youth, the nation's youth remain confident and casual, and that is very obvious in the way they address their teachers and their parents. It is therefore difficult to discern an authoritarian turn of any magnitude. Between psychiatric institutions where mentally disordered offenders are held there are wide disparities in ethos and treatment practice. In some isolation and coercion is commonplace whereas in others it is not. The state of TBS is not easily pinpointed in the face of substantial autonomy in the various institutions but it is clear that capacity pressures and staff shortages will be drivers for an emphasis of control over rehabilitation.

Overall, the Netherlands has calmed down since the tumultuous days of 2001 and 2002. The public discourse has toughened and parliamentary discourse with it. Populist parties outside the traditional bastions of power have become major agenda-setters and both the style and the content of their politics has affected the traditionally consensus-focused and serene political way of doing business. Crime, youth, ethnicity and immigration have become political footballs and are likely to remain so in the foreseeable future. The global economic troubles from 2008 onwards have also impacted on the Netherlands and it is quite well known that any economic crisis is likely to hit ethnic minority groups hardest in terms of employability and spending power. That may well bring about a further hardening of both attitudes and measures against these groups who are already, as Cavadino and Dignan say, subject to 'the casting of the migrant as an international scapegoat or "folk devil" against whom harsh treatment is legitimated' (2006: 125).

However, the latest trend in imprisonment is that of a sharp decline in prisoner numbers. It is not entirely clear why this is the case, but a combination of a drop in offending, an increase in foreign prisoners serving their sentence in their home countries and an increase of community penalties might account for this development. However, where Downes and Van Swaaningen (2007) argue that the Dutch development should be viewed with pessimism, it is refreshing to note the stance taken by Ministry of Justice Secretary of State Nebahat Albayrak. Her initial plan was to fill the empty prison spaces with inmates from neighbouring Belgium, which suffers from capacity problems. The negotiations, however, did not get completed. Subsequently, and doggedly, the government's intention is to close several prisons with the argument that the demand for those prison cells is simply not there and will not be there in the foreseeable future. The government utilises an evidence-based approach to estimate the prison capacity required in the future and is boldly sticking to its plan despite protestations from right-wing opposition parties. If anything, it shows that the 'road to dystopia' is not without detours. Crime and justice in the Netherlands has not yet lost its ability to positively surprise us.

Selected further reading

A classic text on criminal justice in the Netherlands is Downes (1988), although a more recent discussion that focuses specifically on community safety is provided by Van Swaaningen (2005). Pakes has provided several treaties on the general criminal justice climate in the Netherland (see Pakes 2004, 2006). In addition, an interesting and very readable book on how the Netherlands is affected by globalisation is Lechner (2008), which demonstrates the importance of global processes in local developments and paints a picture of the 'social state' of the Netherlands with great acuity. Finally, for those with an interest in how national cultures come about from a historical perspective, Simon Schama's (1987) detailed and wonderfully written book on Dutch culture in the Golden Age of the seventeenth century is strongly recommended.

References

Boutellier, H. (2001) 'The convergence of social policy and criminal justice', *European Journal on Criminal Policy and Research*, 9: 361–80.

Buruma, Y. (2004) 'Onoprechte Handhaving', in B. van Stokkom and L. Gunther Moor (eds) *Onoprechte Handhaving? Prestatiecontracten, Beleidsvrijheid en Politie-Ethiek.* Dordrecht: Stichting Maatschappij, Veiligheid en Politie (pp. 19–34).

Cachet, A. and Ringeling, A. B. (2004) 'Integraal veiligheidsbeleid: Goede bedoelingen en wat er van terechtkwam', in E. R. Muller (ed.) *Veiligheid: Studies over inhoud, organisatie en maatregelen.* Alphen aan den Rijn: Kluwer (pp. 635–62).

Cavadino, M. and Dignan, J. (2006) *Penal Systems: A Comparative Approach*. London: Sage.

Downes, D. (1988) *Contrasts in Tolerance*. Oxford: Clarendon Press.

Downes, D. (2008) *Contrasts in Tolerance: Post-War Penal Policy in the Netherlands and England and Wale*s. Oxford: Clarendon Press.

Downes, D. and Van Swaaningen, R. (2007) 'The road to dystopia? Changes in the penal climate of the Netherlands', in M. Tonry and C. Bijleveld (eds) *Crime and justice in the Netherlands*. Chicago: University of Chicago Press (pp. 31–71).

Edwards, A. and Hughes, G. (2005) 'Comparing the governance of safety in Europe: a geo-historical approach', *Theoretical Criminology*, 9: 345–63.

Eggen, A. T. J. and Van der Heijde, W. (2004) *Criminaliteit en rechtshandhaving, 2004*. Voorburg: CBS.

Franke, H. (1990). 'Dutch tolerance: facts and fables', *British Journal of Criminology*, 30: 81–93.

Garland, D. (2001) *The Culture of Control*. Chicago: University of Chicago Press.

Koenraadt, F. and Mooij, A. (2007) 'Mentally ill offenders', in M. Boone and M. Moerings (eds) *Dutch Prisons*. The Hague: BJU Publishers (pp. 167–86).

Laing, J. M. (1999) *Care or Custody? Mentally Disordered Offenders in the Criminal Justice System*. Oxford: Oxford University Press.

Lechner, F. J. (2008) *The Netherlands: Globalization and National Identity*. New York: Routledge.

Muncie, J. and Goldson, B. (2007). 'States of transition: convergence and diversity in international youth justice', in J. Muncie and B. Goldson (eds) *Comparative Youth Justice*. London: Sage (pp. 196–218).

Pakes, F. (2004) 'The politics of discontent: the emergence of a new criminal justice discourse in the Netherlands', *Howard Journal of Criminal Justice*, 43(3): 284–98.

Pakes, F. (2006) 'The ebb and flow of criminal justice in the Netherlands', *International Journal of the Sociology of Law*, 34: 141–56.

Pakes, F. (2009) 'Globalisation and the governance of Dutch coffee shops', *European Journal of Crime, Criminal Law and Criminal Justice*, 17: 243–57.

Pakes, F. (2010, in press) 'The comparative method in globalised criminology', *Australian and New Zealand Journal of Criminology*.

Robles, M. (2008) 'Minister eist beter werk van Bureau Bibob', *Binnenlands Bestuur*. Online at: www.binnenlandsbestuur.nl/nieuws/2008/05/.

Rotterdam City Council (2008) *Stand van Zaken Toezeggingen Interventieteams*, letter dated 17 July 2008. Rotterdam: Rotterdam City Council.

Rotterdam Ombudsman (2007) *Baas in eigen huis: 'Tja, wij komen eigenlijk voor alles'*. Rotterdam: Rotterdam Ombudsman.

Schama, S. (1987) *The Embarrassment of Riches: An Interpretation of Dutch Culture in the Golden Age*. New York: Random House.

Stenson, K. (2000) 'Crime control, social policy and liberalism', in G. Lewis, S. Gewirths and J. Clarke (eds) *Rethinking Social Policy*. London: Sage (pp. 229–44).

Tops, P. (2007) *Regimeverandering in Rotterdam. Hoe een stadbestuur zichzelf opnieuw uitvond*. Amsterdam: Atlas.

Uit Beijerse, J. and Van Swaaningen, R. (2006) 'The Netherlands: penal welfarism and risk management', in J. Muncie and B. Goldson (eds) *Comparative Youth Justice: Critical Issues*. London: Sage (pp. 65–78).

Uitermark, J. and Duyvendak, J.-W. (forthcoming) 'Civilizing the city: populism and revanchist urbanism in Rotterdam', *Urban Studies*, 45.

Van Swaaningen, R. (2005) 'Public safety and the management of fear', *Theoretical Criminology*, 9: 289–305.

Weijers, I. and Liefaard, T. (2007) 'Youngsters', in M. Boone and M. Moerings (eds) *Dutch Prisons*. Den Haag: Boom (pp. 127–66).

Chapter 13

Public protection in Scotland: a way forward?

Beth Weaver and Fergus McNeill

Introduction

Perhaps the starting point of this chapter is to clarify that unlike arrangements in England and Wales, the supervision of offenders in the community in Scotland is the responsibility of criminal justice social workers employed by local authorities. That said, the origins of and developments in the purpose and focus of practice share similarities with England and Wales (see, for example, Robinson and McNeill 2004; McIvor and McNeill 2007). This chapter, however, intends to concentrate on more recent changes in the purpose and focus of probation practice and indeed of wider community-based criminal justice social work services in Scotland, with a specific emphasis on the rise and implications of the public protection agenda.

The official purposes of probation or criminal justice social work (CJSW) in Scotland have evolved over the past century and have been described, in chronological order as reflecting central preoccupations with supervision (as an alternative to punishment), treatment, welfare, responsibility, public protection and offender management (for more detail see McNeill and Whyte 2007). However, it should be understood that these shifts in emphasis and approach have been gradual and through each of these transitions much of the 'old' survived alongside the 'new'. This chapter will attend to the development and adoption of 'public protection' as a 'meta-narrative' emanating from official discourses which ultimately presents a fundamental purpose or objective of probation and criminal justice social work more generally (Robinson and McNeill 2004). We then proceed to address those policy and practice developments, which reflect and express this shift, with specific reference to the relatively recent introduction of the multi-agency public protection arrangements (MAPPA) in Scotland. We go on to examine some of the difficulties and challenges that an uncritical commitment to public protection as an end in itself might present. The chapter concludes by advancing some arguments for an approach to public protection that foregrounds a wider concept of rehabilitation than is currently operationalised by CJSW services by reinstating an emphasis on the notion of rights and justice. We conclude by considering how a reframing of public protection as part of a broader integrative enterprise might offer some ideas for an alternative way forward.

The evolution of public protection in Scotland: a CJSW perspective

In the mid to late 1990s, Scottish CJSW was affected both by a growing policy emphasis on public protection and by the introduction of significantly higher risk populations of offenders to caseloads. Legislative changes in the early 1990s required prisoners serving sentences in excess of four years to undertake compulsory community supervision on release (Prisoners and Criminal Proceedings (Scotland) Act 1993). Thereafter, in Scotland, advances in both the rhetoric and the practice of public protection were rapid (Robinson and McNeill 2004). Although it did not appear as an objective in the original national objectives and standards for CJSW (SWSG 1991a), by the time of the publication of *The Tough Option* (Scottish Office 1998) the minister then responsible was declaring both that 'Our paramount aim is public safety' (s.1.2) and that the pursuit of reductions in the use of custody 'must be consistent with the wider objective of promoting public and community safety' (s.1.2.3). Revisions to the Scottish standards on throughcare services (SWSG 1996) and court reports (SWSG 2000), as well as other central reports and guidance (SWSI 1997, 1998) both presaged and reflect this shift in emphasis, which has gained in momentum over the last decade.

Indeed, ever since these developments, public protection has received significant attention in official discourses or statements of objectives and priorities for probation and criminal justice social work services in Scotland. For example, the first of the three priorities mentioned in the Scottish statement of *National Priorities* for criminal justice social work is to make a 'contribution to increased community safety and public protection' (Justice Department 2001: 3). Significantly, however, and commensurate with the long-standing association between the rise of public protection as an official purpose and a continuing commitment to 'anti-custodialism' (Nellis 1995) in Scotland, this commitment to public protection has been accompanied by an enduring commitment to a reduction in the use of custody and, pertinently, to the social inclusion of offenders through their rehabilitation; an approach consistent with the social welfare philosophy underlying the Social Work (Scotland) Act 1968, which placed offenders alongside others in need of such services. In this context, therefore, rehabilitation is cast as the means of progressing towards two compatible and interdependent ends: not only the reduction of reoffending but also the social inclusion of offenders (Robinson and McNeill 2004). These commitments are articulated in the second and third of the *National Priorities*, respectively, which are to 'Reduce the use of unnecessary custody by providing effective community disposals' (Justice Department 2001: 3) and to 'Promote the social inclusion of offenders through rehabilitation, so reducing the level of offending' (2001: 3). The same three-pronged approach is manifest in the *National Objectives for Social Work Services in the Criminal Justice System: Standards – General Issues* (Scottish

273

Executive 2004a: 6.3) (it is further emphasised in Scottish Executive 2004b, 2006a, 2006b; Scottish Government 2007, 2008; Scottish Prisons Commission 2008.

Simultaneously, however, an emergent distinction in emphasis is evident in official discourses, policies and legislative reform, between risk management approaches for what one might term 'the general offending population' and for serious violent, or mentally disordered or sexual offenders. In 2000, the MacLean Committee on Serious Violent and Sexual Offenders was established to consider sentencing disposals for, and measures for the future management and treatment of, serious violent and sexual offenders who may present a continuing danger to the public (Scottish Executive 2000). On the committee's recommendation, a new sentence for the life-long control of this group of offenders, the Order of Lifelong Restriction (OLR)[1] was introduced into Scotland in June 2006. As we shall proceed to illustrate, here, significantly, we see not only the origins of the emergence of a system of differential justice in relation to specific categories of offender. We also see conceptions of offender by offence type, as well as a shift in sentencing and offender management on the basis of the perceived 'riskiness' of the individual offender in terms of what they *might* do as opposed to simply what they have done. In response to this, we have also witnessed a growing orientation towards operationalising public protection through mechanisms of control (see, for example, Hudson 2003; Kemshall 2003, 2008). For example, one can be placed on an OLR at any age, following the commission of an offence 'the nature of which, or circumstances of the commission of which, are such *that it appears* to the court that the person has *a propensity* to commit' either a sexual or violent offence or one that endangers life (s.210B, Criminal Justice (Scotland) Act 2003) (emphasis added). Among other recommendations, the MacLean Committee recommended the establishment of a 'Risk Management Authority' (the RMA) to 'establish, promulgate and continuously update best practice in risk assessment and risk management' (Scottish Exeuctive 2000: 2) and to assume operational responsibility for approving and monitoring the risk management plans for those offenders who receive an OLR.

The MacLean Report was swiftly followed by the Cosgrove Report, *Reducing the Risk: Improving the Response to Sex Offending* (Scottish Executive 2001). Lady Cosgrove's 'Expert Panel' was established to take forward the recommendations of earlier proposals, *A Commitment to Protect: Supervising Sex Offenders* (SWSI 1997), which essentially reviewed existing arrangements for the supervision of sex offenders in the community. Among the 73 recommendations of the Cosgrove Report was the identification of a need for greater inter-agency working, and a more consistent, coordinated and formalised approach to the assessment, treatment and management of sex offenders. This was encapsulated in recommendation 49, which proposed that a 'statutory duty should be placed on Chief Constables and Chief Social Work Officers to establish joint arrangements for the assessment, monitoring and management of risk', which duty was enacted in sections 10 and 11 of the Management of Offenders (Scotland) Act 2005 and thereafter resulted in the introduction of the multi-agency public protection arrangements in Scotland, to which we will return in due course.

The Criminal Justice (Scotland) Act 2003 and the Management of Offenders (Scotland) Act 2005 took forward many of the recommendations of the MacLean and the Cosgrove Reports. The Criminal Justice (Scotland) Act 2003[2] tightened legislation on sexual offending and broadened its scope; it legislated for the inclusion of electronic monitoring as a condition of licence, it increased the terms of imprisonment for certain sexual offences and widened the criteria for imposition of an extended sentence to include not only those convicted on indictment[3] of a violent or sexual offence, but also abduction.[4] In addition to extant legislation providing for extended sentences for registered sexual and violent offenders, the Management of Offenders (Scotland) Act 2005 further provided the statutory basis for the establishment of MAPPA in Scotland and legislated for the creation of a short-term sex offender licence, which can include a condition of electronic monitoring. The short-term sex offender licence applies solely to registered sex offenders who are sentenced to between six months and four years custodial sentence, effectively abolishing unsupervised release for registered sex offenders. Meanwhile, the same Act introduced the home detention curfew (HDC) for those short-term prisoners who would not be classed as serious violent or sexual offenders – the 'general offending population'. The HDC allows for prisoners to be released subject to electronic monitoring during the last part of their sentence, *prior* to the period of automatic early and unsupervised release.[5] The stated objective underpinning this initiative is to facilitate a more gradual reintegration into the community, and to reduce unnecessary continued detention in custody. In Scotland, the 'general offending' population, not placed on a HDC, who are sentenced to less than four years, are granted automatic unsupervised release at the mid-point of their custodial sentence. What this effectively demonstrates, therefore, is the differential treatment of sex offenders, certainly in the context of early, unsupervised release, not on the basis of evidence of higher rates of recidivism, but in part on the basis of public and media perceptions and the politicisation of their ensuing concerns surrounding sex offenders. No attempt is made to differentiate between types of sex offenders, or the associated differences in the levels of harm posed. Certainly, the Sentencing Commission articulated a view to this effect to the Scottish Executive, who nonetheless proceeded with the implementation of this initiative (see, for example, MacFadyen 2005; Jamieson 2005).

While this is something of a continuation of Malcolm Rifkind's (1989) 'twin-track' policy that custody should be 'used sparingly' and reserved for those offenders who pose a serious risk to the public,[6] it also points to a growing distinction between those who can be socially included and reintegrated and those who cannot, differentiated more by their potential to cause harm than the likelihood of their recidivism. Such distinctions point towards the adoption of a dual approach to risk management that extends beyond the question of the use, or otherwise, of custody, to one which Kemshall and Wood (2007: 391) respectively term an 'integrative approach' (emphasising inclusionary techniques) and a 'coercive approach' (emphasising or prioritising restrictive techniques that exert external controls and impose sanctions in the event of non-compliance) (see also Feeley and Simon 1992; Rose 2000).

By 2006, building on the Cosgrove Report (2001) and the Management of Offenders (Scotland) Act 2005, the then Scottish Executive emphasised throughout their *Reducing Reoffending: National Strategy for the Management of Offenders* report (Scottish Executive 2006a) that: 'Protecting the public from the most serious harm must be the first priority for all those dealing with offenders. It is therefore critical that agencies prioritise the management of the most serious sexual and violent offenders' (2006a: 10). There are two points of note to recognise from this statement. The first is the increasing emphasis on a more formalised, consistent and multi-agency framework for the assessment and management of offenders and public protection, evident in the reference to 'all those dealing with offenders', alongside whom criminal justice social work services are ascribed a 'common purpose' of public protection to be realised through the shared 'task' of 'reducing reoffending' (2006a: 1; see also pp. 3 and 5) (more on this later). This shared, multi-agency approach to risk assessment and management is yet further reflected in the implementation, by the Scottish Prison Service (SPS), of the integrated case management (ICM) model of sentence management in 2006 (Scottish Executive 2006c). This essentially extended the concept of end-to-end sentence management to all prisoners, as opposed to solely long-term prisoners as previously, and widened the scope of the process by adopting a multi-agency case conference approach. The intensity of the ensuing interventions differs according to assessed risk and not, as was previously the case, the length of sentence, with prioritisation afforded to 'short term' sexual offenders. This is consistent with the second point of note, in the latter part of the aforementioned quote, which places an explicit emphasis on the targeting or prioritisation of resources towards those who pose the greatest risk of serious harm; those offenders who 'raise the most serious concerns about public protection' (Scottish Executive 2006a: 6).

In the same year, and following the publication of the Sentencing Commission's report, *Early Release from Prison and Supervision of Prisoners on their Release* (Sentencing Commission for Scotland 2006), whose task was to review the current arrangements in the Prisoners and Criminal Proceedings (Scotland) Act 1993 covering the release of offenders, the then Scottish Executive, building on the Management of Offenders (Scotland) Act 2005 and the SPS's ICM system, proposed changes to the existing system of 'automatic', unsupervised, early release to apply to *all* short-term prisoners serving in excess of fourteen days' custodial sentence and proposed a new structure,[7] which would seek to determine release arrangements on the basis of risk, as opposed to sentence length,[8] or offence type. In so doing, this proposal placed a renewed emphasis on the importance of supported resettlement for *all* offenders in allowing for a structured plan, specific to the individual's needs and risk, to be followed from the point of sentencing and post-release.

In November 2007, the Scottish Government published its report *Reforming and Revitalising: Report of the Review of Community Penalties* (Scottish Government 2007). This report made explicit the twin-track approach of reserving custody for the highest risk offenders, while articulating its commitment to managing lower risk offenders in the community: 'This Government is determined to develop a coherent penal policy that uses prison for serious and dangerous offenders but deals with lower-risk offenders in the community' (2007: 1).

Indeed, this report was significant in its restatement of the 'traditional' objectives of Scottish criminal justice social work, in terms of its articulated commitment to using custody sparingly, social inclusion through rehabilitation, and public protection. For the first time, however, the futility of short-term prison sentences, when viewed through either a rehabilitative or public protection lens, was articulated, accompanied by an emphasis on governmental *duties* 'to ensure that punishments do all they can to make offenders face up to their crimes whilst supporting [offenders] to return to a positive life in the community' (2007: 1). This acknowledgement of a state duty to support (ex)-offender reintegration implies a duty on public agencies to make sure that the punishment stops when it is supposed to stop, and to do everything at the disposal of the state and civil society to bring about reintegration. In so doing, this commitment arguably signals recognition of offenders' rights to reintegration. Significantly, what we additionally see surfacing in this report, and reflected in subsequent proposals for legislative and policy change is, arguably, the emergence of a new, and possibly competing, 'meta-narrative' of reparation.

> Where an offender can remain in the community they should be made to pay back. Crime causes damage – wherever possible punishment should include an element of reparation to make good on that damage and force offenders to face up to their actions. (2007: 3)

> The Government believes that penalties which involve the offender having to give something back to their community should be increasingly used as an alternative to prison, in cases where prison is not a necessary response to protect public safety. (2007: 11)

In this report, the Scottish Government announced their intention to legislate for a new version of the community service order (CSO), which will subsume supervised attendance orders (SAO). The intention was that the revamped CSO, which would no longer be a direct alternative to custody but instead would allow the courts to consider using a reparative penalty in response to a wide range of offending and comprise between 20 and 300 hours of unpaid work, which would be available to all courts including the District Courts, thus resurrecting the heretofore somewhat neglected restorative aspect of community service and extending its scope.

Building on these insights and proposals, the report of the Scottish Prisons Commission (2008), appointed to examine the proper use of imprisonment in Scotland, further re-establishes penal reductionism as a priority for criminal justice services in a manner consistent with the pursuit of *both* public protection and 'rehabilitation' as a reintegrative and reparative enterprise. The Commission was chaired by Henry McLeish, the one-time Minister for Home and Health in the Scottish Office (pre-devolution) and later a First Minister of Scotland. The report (often referred to as the McLeish Report) was published in July 2008; the Criminal Justice and Licensing Bill currently before the Scottish Parliament contains a range of measures that respond to the recommendations of this report, including revisions to the Custodial

Sentences and Weapons (Scotland) Act 2007.[9] The report contains a very sharp analysis of why the Scottish prison population has risen rapidly in recent years. The key conclusion and central recommendations of the report are these:

> The evidence that we have reviewed leads us to the conclusion that to use imprisonment wisely is to target it where it can be most effective – in punishing serious crime and protecting the public.
> 1. To better target imprisonment and make it more effective, the Commission *recommends* that imprisonment should be reserved for people whose offences are so serious that no other form of punishment will do and for those who pose a significant threat of serious harm to the public.
> 2. To move beyond our reliance on imprisonment as a means of punishing offenders, the Commission *recommends* that *paying back in the community should become the default position in dealing with less serious offenders.* (Scottish Prisons Commission 2008: 3, emphasis added)

Thus, while the idea that we should pursue a parsimonious approach to imprisonment in particular and punishment in general is not a new one, the Commission clearly thought it a good one. Their remedy for Scotland's over-consumption of imprisonment centres on a range of measures considered necessary to enact their second recommendation and make 'paying back in the community' the 'default position' for less serious offenders. Many of these measures speak directly to the nature, forms and functions of probation or criminal justice social work, whether in relation to its court services, the community sanctions it delivers, or its role in ex-prisoner resettlement.

Extending the allegorical language of *Reforming and Revitalising: Report of the Review of Community Penalties* (Scottish Government 2007) the Commission's report seeks to recast both court services and community penalties around the concept of 'payback', which it defines as follows:

> In essence, payback means finding *constructive* ways to compensate or repair harms caused by crime. It involves making good to the victim and/or the community. This might be through financial payment, unpaid work, engaging in rehabilitative work or some combination of these and other approaches. Ultimately, *one of the best ways for offenders to pay back is by turning their lives around.* (Scottish Prisons Commission 2008: 3.28, emphasis added)

Several ways of paying back are identified here and elsewhere in the report – through restorative justice practices, through financial penalties, through unpaid work, through restriction of liberty (meaning in this context electronically monitored curfews) and, perhaps most interestingly in this context, through 'paying back by working at change'. Working at change in turn is linked to engagement in a wide range of activities that might seem likely to address some of the issues underlying offending behaviour (drug and alcohol issues, money or housing problems, peer group and attitudinal issues, family difficulties, mental health problems and so on). The report also recognises the need for offenders to opt-in to rehabilitative modes of reparation; their consent is required for both practical and ethical reasons.

The Commission's report places further emphasis on the importance of a shared, multi-agency response to the issue of ex-prisoner resettlement.

> It is in society's interests that all public services – education, employment, health, housing and so on – play an active part in helping ex-offenders to lead a law-abiding life in the community. Communities also need to play their part in giving people who have served their sentence a fair chance for a fresh start (2008: 43).

Critically, the Commission's report is infused with a level of realism that recognises that for ex-prisoners, as well as offenders subject to community penalties, the process of desistance and resettlement is one that is likely to be punctuated by periods of lapse and relapse (see Weaver and McNeill 2007, for example). The Prisons Commission argued strongly that the Scottish Government should legislate for 'progress courts' to hold swift and frequent reviews of progress and compliance with community sentences.

> There is a great deal of convincing evidence that the process of giving up offending is extremely difficult and complex – especially for persistent offenders ... It is in all of our interests that the new progress courts would deal with lapses and setbacks by the offender as swiftly and effectively as possible. Where these setbacks raise concerns about public safety, the progress court will need to take swift and proportionate action. But they would also have an equally crucial role in encouraging, recognising and supporting progress ... the emphasis would be on persevering, where possible, in making community sentences work. (Scottish Prisons Commission 2008: 37)

At the time of writing, proposals to introduce the community payback sentence, which, it should be noted, will replace the existing sentences of community service, probation and the supervised attendance order (and thus incorporate the aforementioned proposed 'new' community service order), and the end-to-end sentence management for those serving custodial sentences as delineated in the Criminal Justice and Licensing (Scotland) Bill, are currently before parliament.

Multi-agency public protection arrangements (MAPPA) in Scotland

Within this rapidly changing policy context, it might be said that a level of caution should accompany the optimism that these new proposals suggest. MAPPA in Scotland have a much shorter history than those in England and Wales and it remains to be seen how MAPPA might influence criminal justice social work policy and practice more broadly. The arrangements were introduced through sections 10 and 11 of the Management of Offenders

(Scotland) Act 2005 and were operationalised on 2 April 2007. Unlike England and Wales, MAPPA excludes much of the young offender population, who are managed through the Children's Hearing system,[10] as it is only *convicted* offenders who are managed under MAPPA. Essentially, as in England and Wales,[11] the legislation requires the 'responsible authorities' – the police, the Scottish Prison Service and local authorities (and in the case of restricted patients or mentally disordered offenders, Health Boards) – to put in place joint arrangements for the assessment and management of risks posed by certain categories of offenders.[12] The legislation also allows the Scottish Parliament to specify 'duty to cooperate' agencies who, as the name suggests, must cooperate with the responsible authorities in establishing and implementing the arrangements; these include but are not limited to Health Boards (in respect of registered sex offenders, housing providers, relevant voluntary organisations and SERCO (the company responsible for electronic monitoring of offenders in Scotland and the management of the oldest of the two private prisons in Scotland).

Again, as in England and Wales, there are three categories of offenders and three levels of risk management. The three categories of offenders are registered sex offenders, violent offenders, and other convicted offenders who are deemed to pose a risk of serious harm. Restricted patients or mentally disordered offenders, who are also sexual or violent offenders and fall within categories 1 to 3, are also included under MAPPA. In Scotland the implementation of MAPPA has been phased. The current arrangements were extended on 30 April 2008 to include restricted patients,[13] in addition to registered sex offenders[14] who were included under MAPPA from its inception in Scotland on 2 April 2007. The Scottish Government is yet to agree the operational detail of including violent and other dangerous offenders within the MAPPA structure. To provide some idea, however, of the different scale of MAPPA in England and Wales and MAPPA in Scotland, on 31 March 2009 MAPPA in England and Wales managed a total of 44,761 offenders, of which 32,336 were registered sex offenders.[15] In Scotland, the MAPPA oversee the management of a total of 3,145 registered sex offenders and restricted patients, with 2,967 of this number categorised as registered sex offenders.[16] The three levels of management are: level one, 'ordinary risk management' (where the risks posed by the offender are such that they can be competently managed by a single agency without significantly involving other agencies), level two, 'interagency risk management' (where the level of risk posed or the complexity of managing the risk posed reuires the active involvement of more than one agency); and level three, multi-agency public protection panel (MAPPP) cases (where the 'critical few' very high risk or 'notorious' offenders require the full panoply of MAPPA coordination). We noted above that in law these arrangements apply only to adult offenders, but of course there is no technical reason why MAPPA meetings should not be informally extended to consider children and young people in respect of whom significant concern exists.[17]

The implementation of MAPPA in Scotland has raised a number of issues – just as they have in England and Wales. Constructively, there is widespread support for the development of a consistent approach across Scotland; an aspiration that is particularly challenging given the absence of a centrally coordinated national probation service and some evidence of disparate practices in different areas, particularly in relation to assignation of risk thresholds and associated levels of management. This may be attributable, at least in part, to a degree of defensive decision-making due to the difficulties that the responsible authorities and duty to cooperate agencies encounter in attempting to assess risk of serious harm, and indeed imminence, in the absence of a validated tool for such purposes. This can lead in some cases to an over-inflation of levels of risk, and in turn levels of management. Again, to provide a level of context, reference to annual reporting statistics for MAPPA in England and Wales, for the period 2008–09, indicate that, taken as a whole (n = 32,336), 13.6 per cent (n = 4,408) of registered sex offenders were managed at level two and 1.3 per cent (n = 424) were managed at level three.[17] In Scotland, 31.7 per cent (n = 941) of 2,967 registered sex offenders were managed at level two and 2.2 per cent (n = 64) of registered sex offenders were managed at level three. Beyond these differences north and south of the border, an examination of the individual statistics reported within Scotland evidences a wide variation between some areas in relation to the levels at which offenders are managed ranging from 15 per cent of registered sex offenders managed at level two in one community justice authority (CJA) to 38 per cent of registered sex offenders managed at level two in another CJA.[18]

Notwithstanding this, practitioners and policy-makers do share a common concern to see the development of effective and efficient risk management arrangements that are parsimonious; that is, which manage offenders at the lowest and least intrusive level that is consistent with public safety, which concern is itself a stated objective underpinning the operation of MAPPA.[19] That said, there are a number of legal and moral concerns about the sustainability of this parsimony in the context of the obvious political sensitivities about the management of the risk of seriously harmful offending at the local and national levels, and the obvious public and media scrutiny in this area. Indeed within the MAPPA guidance itself – specifically around the management of 'notorious' offenders – there is more than a hint of preoccupation with 'reputational risk' to national and local government, rather than risk to the public *per se*.[20] Of course, this preoccupation itself generates the risk that far from favouring parsimonious interventions in the lives of offenders which respect their rights, MAPPA may contribute significantly to the net-widening and mesh-thinning through which the late-modern state increases its carceral reach (Cohen 1985), partly as a means of offsetting its increasing economic impotence in the face of globalisation, and the challenges to its legitimacy thus created (Bauman 2000; Garland 2001; McCulloch and McNeill 2007). That MAPPA function as an administrative (and at best *quasi*-legal) process with no obvious right of appeal or judicial review or even offender representation is concerning, especially given that under the twin pressures of a risk-averse society and its blame culture there are anecdotal reports of practitioners in England and Wales reverting to 'constructive breach' or 'pre-emptive enforcement'; that is, in cases where released offenders pose very serious concerns, the temptation is to load licences with untenable conditions in order to precipitate breach and recall to custody (McNeill 2009a).

Practising public protection?

Reference to recent research on practitioners' perspectives illuminates some of the subtleties of how these ideological transitions, accompanying the ascendance of public protection in official discourses and policy, are navigated by social workers. Reflecting on in-depth interviews conducted in one Scottish local authority between 2001 and 2002, Robinson and McNeill (2004) found evidence that public protection was regarded as a legitimate policy purpose by all of those interviewed. More specifically, almost all of those interviewed described their own understanding of criminal justice social work's purpose in a manner commensurate with the 'principle': 'to reduce re-offending by assisting people so as to protect the community and enhance its welfare' (2004: 289).

However, what Robinson and McNeill reveal is that despite this widely held recognition of the legitimacy of public protection as a policy purpose for criminal justice social work, there were variations in the way in which this purpose was both interpreted and operationalised by social workers. Concerning the interpretation of public protection, Robinson and McNeill (2004) identified two distinct positions emerging. Some workers regarded assisting individuals as an *intrinsic* good, an end in itself, albeit one the pursuit of which should also serve to protect the interests of the wider public. Others construed the provision of assistance as an *instrumental* good, a means to the end of reducing reoffending and thus protecting the public.

The variations in the way in which public protection was operationalised was identified by Robinson and McNeill as manifesting along three distinct but interrelated lines, that sought to reconcile public protection with the traditional CJSW concept of rehabilitation as a reintegrative and socially inclusive endeavour. First, workers argued that helping communities required helping offenders and used this to lend renewed legitimacy to 'welfare' activities. Second, workers characterised the social work relationship as the key vehicle for change, emphasising the relational aspects of their work. Third, workers stressed the broader social contexts of offending behaviour and located individual change processes within this context. Indeed, as Robinson and McNeill observe, what this demonstrates is how, in practice, ideological transitions can be 'negotiated, mediated and managed' by 'finding differing ways to re-inscribe existing purposes and practices with evolving imperatives' (2004: 292). Workers related the necessity for such manoeuvres to the perceived legitimacy of criminal justice social work in the eyes of its external audiences in the justice system and in society in general.

An analogous process of social workers manipulating and reframing discourses surrounding risk and public protection as a means of lending new legitimacy to existing practices was evident in the findings of a recent ethnographic study of social enquiry and sentencing in the Scottish courts (McNeill *et al.* 2009). This study used participant observation and other methods to explore the nature of the practice of social enquiry, in which CJSW prepare pre-sentence reports to assist sentencers in Scottish courts, and it explored the extent to which this aspect of CJSW practice was being reconstructed in accordance with contemporary accounts of penal transformation. In particular, given the centrality of discourses of risk and public protection in accounts of penal transformation, and, as we have illustrated, in official, policy discourse, the focus of the enquiry was on how discourses and practices of risk assessment were constructed in the production of social enquiry reports (SERs).

McNeill *et al.* (2009) found that despite shifts in policy discourse, the evidence of changes in penal discourse and practice was indeed more partial. Their analysis of SERs revealed that despite the ever-increasing emphasis on risk assessment in policy documents and to some extent in workers' practice discourse, even where risk assessments were integrated into the SER the assessment of risk itself remained a fairly peripheral concern in most cases. Rather, the principal focus of social enquiry seemed to be on assessing offenders' responsibility, their moral character, their motivation to change, their attitudes to future responsibilisation, their capacities and their likely compliance with community-based penalties, which the authors correlate with Hannah-Moffat's (2005) assertion that contemporary practices of risk assessment are primarily concerned with the construction of the 'transformative risk subject' as opposed to creating fixed actuarial risk subjects to be simply managed and processed, as contemporary accounts of penal transformation would suppose. Thus, while there is some evidence of traditional welfarist oriented practices persisting in criminal justice social work practice, this approach to rehabilitation is less, as was traditionally the case, an end in itself, and more as a means to the superordinate end of public protection (Robinson and McNeill 2004; McCulloch and McNeill 2007).

The promise of public protection

As we have attempted to illustrate, recent developments in official discourse testify to an emergence of 'public protection' as a principal objective of probation, and criminal justice social work services generally in Scotland. Beyond this 'official' discourse, public protection also appears to be emerging, increasingly, as a 'meta-narrative' for CJSW in practice. Indeed, as Robinson and McNeill (2004) state, and as McNeill *et al.* (2009: 294) illustrate, a level of 'ideological co-optation' has occurred in CJSW practice, in that workers are tending to identify with this recently instated official objective, rather than denying or resisting it, although as we have shown, this can at least in part be ascribed to its utility as a mechanism for re-legitimating existing practices in new ways, not least in some cases in response to a self-conscious awareness of the 'gaze' of the external audience (Robinson and McNeill 2004: 293), but more generally, in the context of an increasing loss of faith, credibility and legitimacy in traditional penal welfarist aims among the stakeholders, or 'consumers' of criminal justice social work services (McCulloch and McNeill 2007: 223). In the process, we are witnessing a marked departure away from the pursuit of rehabilitation as an intrinsic good, an end in itself, towards rehabilitation as an instrument of risk management, as a means to the end of public protection. A further explanation for the espousal of public protection as a 'core purpose' or meta-narrative in Scotland might reside in criminal justice social work's adoption of a more victim-centred approach, coherent with

Nellis' prescient observation that 'the placing of offenders' needs and interests *above*, as opposed to *alongside*, the rights of victims and the requirements of public safety lacks moral justification and, in the 1990s, political credibility' (1995: 26, cited in Robinson and McNeill 2004: 294).

As a narrative for probation practice, then, public protection possesses a certain flexibility. On the one hand, in Scotland we find it correlating neatly with the somewhat milder objectives of social inclusion and anti-custodialism in the context of criminal justice social work. On the other hand, as we have already inferred, particularly in reference to official discourses and policy objectives surrounding the management of high risk, serious offenders, it simultaneously correlates just as neatly with rationales and justifications for ever increasing levels of monitoring, supervision and surveillance. Relatedly, and in the context of youth justice in England and Wales, Phoenix (2009) puts forward a convincing argument that in the absence of an available and appropriate welfare response, which she sees as reflecting 'the state's abrogation of its responsibilities towards young marginalised individuals' (2009: 125), managerialism and risk oriented thinking actually create the conditions in which responses which are more punitive in their effects become justified on apparently welfare grounds. She argues that the identification of need, and the association, or rather presentation, of that need with being 'at risk', generates ever more intrusive forms of monitoring and intervention, in the name of welfarism, which are not, therefore, bounded by the principle of proportionality in punishment and justice, and which in turn signal a shift away from the punishment of the offence, to the control and punishment of the risk-bearer (Hudson 2003).

The problems with public protection

Thus, the flexibility of the concept of public protection creates problems as well as apparent 'solutions' for criminal justice social work practices. One potential problem with public protection's flexibility is that it stretches as an overriding purpose across a range of criminal justice agencies (Robinson and McNeill 2004) with traditionally discrete functions, alongside whom, as we have seen, criminal justice social work is increasingly ascribed not least in official discourses the common purpose of delivering public protection, within a multi-agency framework. While this probably makes some sense in terms of promoting efficiency, coherency and continuity in relation to the administration of criminal justice, and in dismantling those professional boundaries that have historically impeded this process, it is problematic in that it is effectively dispossessing criminal justice social work of any claim to a distinctive ideological identity and in so doing threatening to eclipse the unique contribution that criminal justice social work has historically claimed (Nellis 1999a, in Robinson and McNeill 2004). Indeed, in the absence of a distinctive ideological identity or a unique repertoire of skills and approaches, the very concept of rehabilitation is under threat. Any moral and ethical arguments for rehabilitation as an intrinsic good in itself, as a means of helping disadvantaged people through rehabilitation, are becoming increasingly marginalised. Instead, the justification for the existence of rehabilitative approaches seems to progressively rest on a purely technical debate about the relative efficacy of different measures and sanctions in delivering protection, among which rehabilitative measures have become just one of a variety of possible means to an end, with no particular moral or ethical dimension of their own.

Additional difficulty with the concept of public protection is the assumption of a shared understanding about who or what criminal justice social work services aim to protect. Clearly victims and communities are specified in official discourses as the beneficiaries of such strategies. But there is an important difference between protecting potential *future* victims in communities through rehabilitation and risk management and providing services (including protection and support) for those who have *already been* victimised (which, relatedly, includes offenders). Similarly, and particularly in terms of the management of high risk, serious offenders, there is a debate to be had about whether policy-makers and practitioners are becoming too preoccupied with the offender that someone may become rather than with repairing the harms that they have already done, with the person that they are now and with their positive potential (McNeill 2009b). One might also question the extent to which criminal justice social work services really work with communities in the present, as opposed to working with offenders on behalf of the future well-being of imagined communities. This tension between working with real victims, offenders and communities *now* – as opposed to working for merely imagined victims, working on offenders as bearers of imagined risks and working towards merely imagined communities – distorts discourses and practices because focusing too much on the imaginary and the anticipated permits neglect of the present and the real (see Carlen 2008).

Ultimately, however, as Robinson and McNeill (2004: 293) observe, 'there is a paradox at the heart of protection' in that in promising to protect, we are not only confirming and reinforcing the (understandable) fears and anxieties of the public but we are making a promise that, despite our collective will and efforts, we cannot hope to keep in every case. Paradoxically, in the wake of the occasional, inevitable, highly publicised and disturbing crimes (for example, in the cases of Dano Sonnex, Damien Hanson and Elliot White and Anthony Rice) – and in the ensuing heightened climate of fear, insecurity, and loss of public confidence in the criminal justice system to protect – the state reacts by deploying an expressive, punitive and self-serving display of power, manifest in its reassertion of the need to punish and protect. In so doing, it further raises expectations and amplifies these same fears and anxieties and utilises them as a mechanism through which it might display its 'sovereign might' in order to regain credibility and garner popular and political support (see for example Bottoms 1995; Garland 1996, 1997, 2000; Hall 1988). This is evident in the imposition of ever more reactionary, indiscriminate, constraining and coercive methods of crime control, which, effectively legitimises the dichotomisation of the interests of offenders and the interests of victims and communities in a zero-sum attitude (Hudson 2003; McCulloch and McNeill, 2007; McNeill 2009b), wherein the assurance of rights of victims and potential victims must result or manifest in the reduction or denial of rights for offenders or potential offenders (Hudson 2003; McNeill 2009b).

This leads to a further problem with public protection: CJSW's traditional approaches to risk management and the reduction of crime reside in long-term reintegrative change processes, which in contrast provide relatively little security and reassurance to the public in the short term, particularly when placed alongside the anticipated dangers and risks they fear, and which they find substantiated by the media and official rhetoric. This would suggest a need to communicate and engage with communities to develop more realistic expectations about what type and how much protection criminal justice services can actually provide. As Bottoms and Wilson (2004) highlight, recent research would suggest that when citizens are actively engaged in criminal justice decision-making, they are less punitive and more likely to support community alternatives. Beyond punitiveness, McCulloch and McNeill (2007: 230) point to a number of research studies examining public attitudes that would suggest a level of public receptivity to penality as not only punitive but as restitutive, reformative, restorative and reparative which, *prima facie*, would appear at least in principle to accord with the tenor of recent official discourses and policy orientations (see, for example, Bottoms and Wilson 2004; Greene and Doble 2000; Maruna and King 2004). Taken together, this would suggest that the 'meta-narrative' of public protection might be moderated by the compatible, if not competing, ascending narratives of reparation, rehabilitation and reintegration, particularly within a Scottish context.

A safer Scotland?

Although probation services need to attend to the problem of what works in reducing reoffending, it is not in itself sufficient. Probation services are not merely crime reduction agencies; certainly in Scotland, where probation is subsumed within criminal justice social work services, they are also justice agencies. Although our haste to control crime, manage risk and protect the public can sometimes lead to the neglect of questions of justice, due process and legitimacy, ultimately the pursuit of justice – social as well as criminal – is the most effective route to building safer communities. In this respect it is important to recognise the important role that criminal justice social work services play in enabling constructive reparation by offenders and in advocating for offenders so that they can access the social goods and resources they so often have been denied. Of course, it is inequality and the social injustice that it represents that so often underlies not just crime and offending but a number of wider social problems (Wilkinson 2005; Wilkinson and Pickett, 2009).

By way of contrast, the concept of 'community safety' stresses that we are all part of communities and that it is in our collective interests to respond thoughtfully and rationally to our crime problems. Moreover, the recognition that tackling crime requires that we foster the collective efficacy of communities acknowledges that we are all part of the solution. It is approaches such as these that point to an alternative way forward, towards a collective, non-pathologising, individualised response to crime and desistance which addresses the wider social contexts of the offender and other key stakeholders which include victims and communities (see, for example, McNeill 2009b; Weaver 2009). Such an approach would require a move away from correctional, instrumental models of rehabilitation towards a relational model of rights-based rehabilitation, foregrounding social reintegration through the development of human and social capital. For McWilliams and Pease (1990), rights-based rehabilitation serves a moral purpose on behalf of society by limiting punishment and preventing exclusion by working to re-establish the rights and the social standing of the offender. By contrast, Lewis (2005) has drawn on the work of the 'new rehabilitationists' (Cullen and Gilbert 1982; Rotman 1990) to revive the case for a rights-based approach to rehabilitation: meaning one that is concerned with the reintegration of offenders into society as 'useful human beings'. According to Lewis, the principles of the new rehabilitationists include commitment to, first, the state's duty to undertake rehabilitative work; second, somehow setting limits on the intrusions of rehabilitation in terms of proportionality; third, maximising voluntarism in the process; and finally using prison only as a measure of last resort because of its negative and damaging effects (see also Weaver and McNeill 2007). Not dissimilarly to Robinson and McNeill (2004), she reaches the conclusion that 'current rehabilitative efforts are window-dressing on an overly punitive "managerialist" system' (Lewis 2005: 119) although, like Robinson and McNeill (2004), and as McNeill *et al.* (2009) would suggest, she retains some hope that practitioner-led initiatives at the local level might allow some prospects that these principles could be applied. Certainly in Scotland in the current policy climate, which continues to emphasise the importance of the offender's consent to the imposition of community penalties, which is committed to using prison sparingly, and which acknowledges a duty to support (ex)-offender reintegration, such prospects do not seem as distant as perhaps they once did.

Protective integration

So what might an inclusive, collective, non-pathologising, individualised response to crime and desistance, which not only addresses the social contexts of offenders, but also victims and communities, entail? Hazel Kemshall (2008) develops some of these themes and analyses two strategies for the management of high risk offenders. The protection strategy aims to protect through the control of risk; the reintegration strategy aims to reduce risk and thus protect through integration. This mirrors the distinction between more secure short-term incapacitation-based approaches and less secure, but ultimately more effective, long-term change-based approaches and, in that, the distinction in official discourses in contemporary penal policies for high risk serious violent and sexual offenders and the 'general offending population'. Kemshall's contention is, however, that although different discourses of risk, conceptions of the offender and conceptions of justice underpin the protection and reintegration strategies, they can and should be blended. The approach to 'blended' protective integration that she advances combines strategies, which aim at (2008: 133):

- situational crime reduction within the environment which aim to reduce opportunities to commit crime;
- public education to enhance awareness about risks and how to manage them;
- support and integration of offenders to help them and thus reduce risks (as in the Circles of Support and Accountability that are now used with sex offenders in Canada and in some areas of England and Wales);
- pro-social supervision with an emphasis on the Good Lives Model;
- appropriate and balanced restrictions on offenders, consistent with their rights and with European standards;
- combining vigilance within communities with vigilance by statutory agencies;
- and effective partnership working.

In line with the argument above about pursuing community safety as opposed to public protection, Kemshall stresses the need for communities to be *active participants in* rather than *passive recipients of* protection.

Conclusion

As Kemshall's approach to reintegration suggests, the imposition of external controls on offenders' behaviour and the risk focused, within individual transformative orientation of treatment programmes, geared to the development of internal controls characteristic of contemporary practice approaches to public protection, are not in themselves sufficient for change. It is necessary to unite such approaches with broader integrative strategies, including the development of opportunities, the promotion of social inclusion and in that the development of social capital. Thus, offenders attempting to reintegrate into their communities require to (re)gain access to the necessary resources. Yet these people, particularly sex offenders, face additional barriers in this regard, for a variety of reasons including personal shame, stigma, damaged personal and familial networks, community hostility and distrust and not least the exclusionary public protection strategies and criminal justice policies that actively inhibit such processes (Burchfield and Mingus 2008) which, in turn, send the message that sex offenders and high risk violent offenders are never going to be rehabilitated (Kemshall 2008).

In this chapter we have illustrated how in Scotland contemporary official discourses and policies are, for the general offending population at least, consistent with the pursuit of *both* public protection and 'rehabilitation' as a reintegrative and reparative enterprise. However, as we have attempted to demonstrate, the continued dominance of a 'risk' or 'protection' discourse surrounding the management of high risk violent and sex offenders is likely to frustrate its own purposes if it identifies offenders with the worst aspects of themselves, if it leads practitioners to the neglect of offenders' needs, strengths, goals and aspirations and if it reinforces a social climate that creates practical and attitudinal barriers to ex-offenders' prospects of social integration and of living differently.

We have attempted to provoke some reflection not just about the kinds of CJSW services we want to develop and deliver but about the kinds of communities and societies to which we want to belong. Our contention is that public protection is better served in the pursuit of a more balanced humane and integrative approach to risk, where ex-offenders are supported to develop more meaningful and fulfilling lives, than one where the risks that they present are simply managed and surveilled, if not reinforced and further embedded by their continued stigmatisation and exclusion as risk-bearers.

Selected further reading

For a comprehensive and critical account of the historical development and contemporary management of offenders in Scotland, see McNeill and Whyte (2007). The theoretical discussions pursued in this book extend beyond paradigm shifts in practice to explore the changing theoretical contexts within which criminal justice social work practice in Scotland has emerged. Kemshall (2008) engages with both policy and practice to provide a detailed, evidenced-based and in-depth review of current approaches to the management of high risk offenders in the community in particular. In this book she also examines contemporary issues in risk assessment, multi-agency working, and recent policy and legislative initiatives in this area. For wider normative debates, see Barbara Hudson (2003), who reviews the impact of the 'risk society' and contemporary preoccupations with public protection on political, philosophical and ethical dimensions of perspectives on justice and the nature of punishment.

Notes

1 The OLR was ultimately established by s.210F of the Criminal Procedure (Scotland) Act 1995 as inserted by s.1 of the Criminal Justice (Scotland) Act 2003.

2 It may be of interest to add that at this time, the Sexual Offences Act 2003 (commenced in Scotland 2004) also introduced two new civil preventative orders: the sexual offences prevention order (SOPO) and the risk of sexual harm order (RSHO). A court may make a SOPO at the time of dealing with certain sexual offenders (as amended by s.17 of the Protection of Children and Prevention of Sexual Offences (Scotland) Act 2005) or when the police make a special application on account of the offender's behaviour in the community. A SOPO will require the subject to register as a sexual offender and can include only prohibitive conditions as opposed to positive action conditions, for example to prevent the offender loitering near schools or playgrounds (although proposals to include conditions allowing for positive action are proposed in the Criminal Justice and Licensing Bill). If the offender fails to comply with (i.e. breaches) the requirements of the order, he can be taken back to court and may be liable to up to five years' imprisonment. An RSHO places restrictions on someone who is behaving in such a way that suggests that they pose a risk of sexual harm to a particular child or to children generally. The person's behaviour need not constitute a criminal offence, and s/he need not have any previous convictions.

3 Criminal cases are prosecuted under either summary or solemn procedure in the Scottish courts, depending on the seriousness of the crime, and any

previous convictions of the accused. Minor offences are usually prosecuted under summary procedure before a Justice of the Peace (District)/Sheriff Court. More serious cases will usually be prosecuted 'on indictment', that is, under solemn procedure.

4 A court may impose an extended sentence on a person convicted on indictment of a sexual or violent offence if it considers that the period (if any) which the offender would have otherwise been subject to a licence would not be adequate for the purpose of protecting the public from serious harm from the offender. Extended sentences are available to the court for a sexual offence (as defined in section 210A(10) Criminal Procedure (Scotland) Act 1995) (which may be extended by the proposed Criminal Justice and Licensing Bill to include a conviction of an offence which discloses, in the court's opinion, a significant sexual aspect to the offender's behaviour) for which a determinate sentence of imprisonment of *any length* has been imposed or for a violent offence (as defined in section 210A(10)) for which a sentence of at least four years' imprisonment has been imposed. The duration of an extended sentence is determined by the court's opinion of the need to protect the public from serious harm from the offender, and can be up to five years for a violent offence and up to ten years for a sexual offence, for a period not in excess of the statutory maximum for the offence.

5 In Scotland, once a short-term prisoner (sentenced to less than four years custody) has served one-half of their sentence, the Scottish ministers are under a duty to release them without supervision unless such a prisoner has been made the subject of a supervised release order imposed at the date of the original sentence. We use the term unsupervised here, as opposed to unconditional (as it is termed elsewhere) deliberately. On release a short-term prisoner is not under any form of compulsory supervision but may be returned to custody by the courts under section 16 of the 1993 Act if he or she commits another imprisonable offence before the expiry of the original sentence, thus the use of the term unconditional is misleading in this regard.

6 Indeed, Malcolm Rifkind's statement is reiterated in the *National Objectives for Social Work Services in the Criminal Justice System* (Scottish Executive 2004a).

7 The intention is that the custody part will be a *minimum* of 50 per cent of the overall sentence. However, the court will have the power to increase the statutory minimum 50 per cent if required in any particular case and this will be articulated at the point of sentencing. That said, once in prison, all offenders would be reviewed as part of the sentence management process. If that assessment shows that an offender may be a high risk of reoffending and/or poses an unacceptable risk to the public, Scottish ministers will refer the case to the Parole Board with a recommendation to consider continued detention up to the three-quarter point of the sentence. At the end of the custody part, the offender will be on licence for the entire community part of the sentence. The licence conditions will enable provision for a variable and flexible package of measures including supervision if required and will detail what obligations the offender has to meet.

8 This is legislated for in the Custodial Sentences and Weapons (Scotland) Act 2007, although it is yet to be implemented.

9 Particularly in relation to the length of custodial sentence, which would trigger 'supervised' or 'conditional' release.

10 Children's Hearings are lay tribunals headed by tribunal members of the Children's Panel, often from the local community, and as such an appearance before the Children's Panel does not result in conviction.

11 In England and Wales, the Responsible Authorities are the Police, Probation and the Prison Service (MAPPA Guidance Version 3 (2009).

12 It is important to note that in Scotland the 'responsible authority' in MAPPA is not the social work department, but rather the local authority as a whole.

13 The term 'restricted patients' refers to those persons defined within sections 10, 11(a)–(d) of the Management of Offenders etc (Scotland) Act 2005. See www.opsi. gov.uk/legislation/scotland/acts2005/asp_20050014_en_1#pb3-l1g10.

14 The term 'registered sex offenders' refers to those individuals who are subject to the notification requirements of Part 2 of the Sexual Offences Act 2003 (as defined within Section 10 of the Management of Offenders etc (Scotland) Act 2005). See www.opsi.gov.uk/Acts/acts2003/ukpga_20030042_en_1.

15 See www.justice.gov.uk/news/docs/**mappa**-figures-2009.pdf.

16 See www.scotland.gov.uk/Publications/Search/Q/Subject/479.

17 The good practice document, *Getting it Right for Children and Young People who Present a Risk of Serious Harm*, was published in May 2008. This document sets out how agencies should be working together, sharing information and assessing and reviewing circumstances in line with the planning approach being promoted through *Getting it Right for Every Child*.

18 It should be noted that the percentage figures are indicative, although comparable. The recording of offenders managed at level two are taken over a whole year, whereas in England and Wales, the total number of offenders, at all levels, are reported as a snapshot, on 31 March 2009 *only*. They do not publish figures for the number of offenders managed at level one over the whole year. Thus the Scottish figures have been calibrated in the same manner for comparative purposes.

19 As calibrated by dividing the number of offenders managed at level two in the annual reporting year, by the number of offenders managed at all three levels throughout the reporting year.

20 For further information, see MAPPA Guidance V.4 (2008) at www.scotland.gov. uk/Publications/2008/04/18144823.

21 See, for example, MAPPA Guidance V.4 (2008: 27) which states that offenders may be managed at the highest level (level three) in those circumstances where 'the case is exceptional because the likelihood of media scrutiny and/or public interest in the management of the case is very high and there is a need to ensure that public confidence in the criminal justice system is sustained'.

References

Bauman, Z. (2000) 'Social issues of law and order', *British Journal of Criminology*, 40(2): 205–21.

Bottoms, A. E. (1995) 'The philosophy and politics of sentencing and punishment', in C. Clarkson and R. Morgan (eds) *The Politics of Sentencing*. Oxford: Clarendon Press.

Bottoms, A. and Wilson, A. (2004) 'Attitudes to punishment in two high-crime communities', in A. Bottoms, S. Rex and G. Robinson (eds) *Alternatives to Prison: Options for an Insecure Society*. Cullompton: Willan Publishing (pp. 366–405).

Burchfield, K. B. and Mingus, W (2008) 'Not in my neighbourhood: assessing registered sex offenders' experiences with local social capital and social control', *Criminal Justice and Behavior*, 35(3): 356–74.

Carlen, P. (ed.) (2008) *Imaginary Penalty*. Cullompton: Willan Publishing.

Cohen, S. (1985) *Visions of social control: Crime, punishment and classification*. Cambridge: Polity Press/Blackwell.

Cullen, F. T. and Gilbert, K. E. (1982) *Reaffirming Rehabilitation*. Cincinnati, OH: Anderson.

Feeley, M. and Simon, J. (1992) 'The new penology: notes on the emerging strategy of corrections and its implications', *Criminology*, 30: 449–74.

Garland, D. (1996) 'The limits of the sovereign state: strategies of crime control in contemporary society', *British Journal of Criminology*, 36(4): 445–71.

Garland, D. (1997) '"Governmentality" and the problem of crime: Foucault, criminology and sociology', *Theoretical Criminology*, 1(2): 173–214.

Garland, D. (2000) 'The culture of high crime societies', *British Journal of Criminology*, 40(3): 347–75.

Garland, D. (2001) *The Culture of Control: Crime and Social Order in Contemporary Society*. Oxford: Oxford University Press.

Greene, J. and Doble, J. (2000) *Attitudes Towards Crime and Punishment in Vermont: Public Opinion about an Experiment with Restorative Justice*. Englewood Cliffs, NJ: John Doble Research Associates.

Hall, S. (1988) *The Hard Road to Renewal*. London: Verso.

Hannah-Moffat K. (2005) 'Criminogenic needs and the transformative risk subject: Hybridizations of risk/need in penality', *Punishment and Society*, 7(1): 29–51.

Hudson, B. (2003) *Justice in the Risk Society*. London: Sage.

Kemshall, H. (2003) *Understanding Risk in Criminal Justice*. Buckingham: Open University Press.

Kemshall, H. (2008) *Understanding the Community Management of High Risk Offenders*. Maidenhead: Open University Press.

Kemshall, H. and Wood, J. (2007) 'High risk offenders and public protection', in L. Gelsthorpe and R. Morgan (eds) *Handbook of Probation*. Cullompton: Willan Publishing (pp. 381–97).

Jamieson, C. (2005) *Sex Offenders: Release from Prison and Post-Release Supervision*. Online at: www.scottishsentencingcommission.gov.uk/docs/Options%20Paper%20Response.pdf.

Justice Department (2001) *Criminal Justice Social Work Services: National Priorities for 2001–2002 and Onwards*. Edinburgh: Scottish Executive.

Lewis, S. (2005) 'Rehabilitation: headline or footnote in the new penal policy', *Probation Journal*, 52(2): 119–35.

MacFadyen, D. (2005) *Sex Offenders: Release from Prison and Post-Release Supervision*. Online at: www.scottishsentencingcommission.gov.uk/docs/Chairman's%20letter%20to%20Minister%2014-07-05.pdf.

McCulloch, P. and McNeill, F. (2007) 'Consumer society, commodification and offender management', *Criminology and Criminal Justice*, 7(3): 223–42.

McIvor, G. and McNeill, F. (2007) 'Probation in Scotland: past present and future', in L. Gelsthorpe and R. Morgan (eds) *Handbook of Probation*. Cullompton: Willan Publishing (pp. 131–54).

McNeill, F. (2009a) 'Young people, serious offending and managing risk: a Scottish perspective', in K. Baker and A. Sutherland (eds) *Multi-Agency Public Protection Arrangements and Young People*. London: Policy Press.

McNeill, F. (2009b) 'What works and what's just?', *European Journal of Probation*, 1(1): 21–40.

McNeill, F. and Whyte, B. (2007) *Reducing Reoffending: Social Work and Community Justice in Scotland*. Cullompton: Willan Publishing.

McNeill, F., Burns, N., Halliday, S., Hutton, N. and Tata, C. (2009) 'Risk, responsibility and reconfiguration', *Punishment and Society*, 11(4): 419–42.

McWilliams, W. and Pease, K. (1990) 'Probation practice and an end to punishment', *Howard Journal of Criminal Justice*, 29(1): 14–24.

Maruna, S. and King, A (2004) 'Public opinion and community penalties', in A. Bottoms, S. Rex and G. Robinson (eds) *Alternatives to Prison: Options for an Insecure Society*. Cullompton: Willan Publishing (pp. 83–112).

Nellis, M. (1995) 'Probation values for the 1990s', *Howard Journal of Criminal Justice*, 34(1): 19–44.

Phoenix, J. (2009) 'Beyond risk assessment: the return of repressive welfarism?', in M. Barry and F. McNeill (eds) *Youth Offending and Youth Justice*, Research Highlights 52. London: Jessica Kingsley (pp. 113–31).

Rifkind, M. (1989) 'Penal policy: the way ahead', *Howard Journal*, 28(2): 81–90.

Robinson, G. and McNeill, F. (2004) 'Purposes matters: examining the ends of probation', in G. Mair (ed.) *What Matters in Probation Work*. Cullompton: Willan Publishing (pp. 277–304).

Rose, N. (2000) 'Government and control', *British Journal of Criminology*, 40: 321–99.

Rotman, E. (1990) *Beyond Punishment: A New View of the Rehabilitation of Criminal Offenders* (MacLean Report). Westport, CT: Greenwood Press.

Scottish Executive (2000) *Report of the Committee on Serious Violent and Sexual Offenders*. Edinburgh: Scottish Executive.

Scottish Executive (2001) *Reducing the Risk: Improving the Response to Sex Offending: The Report of the Expert Panel on Sex Offending* (Cosgrove Report). Edinburgh: Scottish Executive.

Scottish Executive (2004a) *National Objectives for Social Work Services in the Criminal Justice System: Standards – General Issues*. Online at: www.scotland.gov.uk/Publications/2004/12/20471/49283.

Scottish Executive (2004b) *Re:duce Re:habilitate Re:form: Analysis of Consultation Responses*. Edinburgh: Scottish Executive.

Scottish Executive (2006a) *Reducing Reoffending: National Strategy for Offender Management*. Edinburgh: Scottish Executive.

Scottish Executive (2006b) *Release and Post Custodial Management of Offenders*. Edinburgh: Scottish Executive.

Scottish Executive (2006c) *JD Circular 8/2006 Integrated Case Management (ICM) Notification of commencement*. Online at: www.scotland.gov.uk/Publications/2006/12/newpage.

Scottish Government (2007) *Reforming and Revitalising: Report of the Review of Community Penalties*. Edinburgh: Scottish Government.

Scottish Government (2008) *Protecting Scotland's Communities: Fair, Fast and Flexible Justice*. Edinburgh: Scottish Government.

Scottish Office (1998) *Community Sentencing: The Tough Option – Review of Criminal Justice Social Work Services*. Edinburgh: Scottish Office.

Scottish Prisons Commission (2008) *Scotland's Choice: Report of the Scottish Prisons Commission*. Edinburgh: Scottish Prisons Commission.

Sentencing Commission for Scotland (2006) *Early Release from Prison and Supervision of Prisoners on their Release*. Online at: www.scottishsentencingcommission.gov.uk/docs/Early%20Release%20%20Report%20-%20finalised%20draft%20-%2020-12-05.pdf.

Social Work Services Group (1991a) *National Objectives and Standards for Social Work Services in the Criminal Justice System*. Edinburgh: Scottish Office Social Work Services Group.

Social Work Services Group (1996) *Part 2. Service Standards: Throughcare*. Edinburgh: Social Work Services Group.

Social Work Services Group (2000) *National Standards for Social Enquiry and Related Reports and Court Based Social Work Services*. Edinburgh: Social Work Services Group.

Social Work Services Inspectorate (1997) *A Commitment to Protect – Supervising Sex Offenders: Proposals for More Effective Practice*. Edinburgh: The Stationery Office.

Social Work Services Inspectorate (1998) *Management and Assessment of Risk in Social Work Services*. Edinburgh: Scottish Office.

Weaver, B. (2009) 'Communicative punishment as a penal approach to supporting desistance', *Theoretical Criminology*, 13(1): 9–29.

Weaver, B. and McNeill, F. (2007) 'Giving up crime: directions for policy', *The Scottish Consortium for Crime and Criminal Justice*. Online at: scccj.org.uk/documents/SCCCJ%20giving%20up%20crime%20content.pdf.

Wilkinson, R. G. (2005) *The Impact of Inequality: How to Make Sick Societies Healthier*. London: Routledge.

Wilkinson, R. G. and Pickett, K. E. (2009) *The Spirit Level: Why More Equal Societies Almost Always Do Better*. London: Penguin/Allen Lane.

Chapter 14

Sex offender notification: policy imperatives, effectives and consequences in the USA

Bill Thompson and Cecil Greek

Introduction

British academics are not alone in denouncing the demand for public notification of sex offenders as a moral panic (Zgoba 2004; McAlinden 2007; Radford 2008; Schultz 2008). However, while the US public remain fearful, and the registers' regulations generate more crimes in their transgression, panic designation has drawn attention away from the issues behind the headlines; not least the fact that there are not one but two laws associated with the Megan Kanka tragedy (New Jersey (1994) and Federal (1996)), and that these laws form only part of the registration, monitoring and public notification systems in the USA. Apart from the demand for the 'right to know', which was born of a lack of confidence in the authorities rather than blind panic, the systems that emerged reflected the ongoing demands to 'get tough' on sex offenders from both sides of the political divide in the 1980s (Jenkins 1992), the perennial conflicts between federal and state power, the crime control and due process approaches to criminal justice (Bohm and Haley 2007), and the political exploitation of the victims' relatives' desire to establish a positive legacy (McAlinden 2007).

As a result, the various states' public notification systems are far from uniform, and do not reflect any systematic public safety philosophy, be it an 'empirical-based what works' or 'risk elimination' model. Although recent higher court decisions *do* reflect the trend in dismissing long-held individual rights in favour of the 'collective good', there is a clear difference between 'scarlet letter' punishments imposed by state courts like Texas, which publicly stigmatise 'dead beat' dads, drug-dealing mothers, and drunk drivers, and the intent behind notification of sex offenders; while the former deliberately sought to shame the offender into mending their ways, notification *was* always intended to help protect the public, and any subsequent 'shaming' was a latent effect given that the legislatures were convinced that sex offenders would never desist.

In order to draw some universal 'lessons' from US practice we review the origins, consequences and subsequent criticism of these public notification systems, offering what follows as a contribution to the literature on public policy formation.

Citizens demand the right to know

Sex offender registers in the US predated the victims' rights movement, as California started systematically listing sex offenders in 1947. Arizona followed six years later, and Florida, Nevada, Ohio and Alabama by 1967. These systems were, however, solely for the benefit of the law enforcement agencies, and it took the publicity surrounding several abduction-murder cases in the late 1980s and early 1990s to change that practice.

Megan's Law was passed following public realisation that the authorities knew that Megan Kanka was living next door to no fewer than three two-time sex offenders, and 100,000 NJ residents immediately signed a 'right to know' petition as a vote of no confidence in the authorities. Yet, the legislation creating the registers upon which notification relies, the Crimes Against Children and Sexually Violent Offender Registration Act (1994), was *already* making progress in Congress when Megan went missing. Named after an eleven-year-old abductee, Jacob Wetterling, this law made 10 per cent of federal assistance to state law enforcement agencies dependent upon maintaining a sexual offender register. The bill had gained further impetus from the 1993 kidnap-murder of Polly Klaas, and owed much to the lobbying efforts of the National Center for Missing and Exploited Children, the federally funded awareness raising group, co-founded in 1984 by John Walsh whose son had been abducted from a shopping mall.

Given that the public worry that every molester is not merely a hopeless recidivist but also a potential killer (Finn 1997; Kelley 2008), and that every other law followed the relatively rare abduction-murder cases which receive extensive media attention, it is not surprising that some critics see the registration and notification laws as exemplars of panic. Other federal initiatives controlling sex offenders include:

- **Joan's Law (1988)** – denying parole for sex-homicide offenders not on death row, ensuring that the most dangerous offenders are never released.

- **Pam's Law (1996)** – imposing life sentences for some offences and recidivists, thereby keeping more offenders in jail, and tracking others who are released.

- **Aimee's Law (1999)** – imposing financial penalties on states that free violent offenders who commit related offences in other states, thereby encouraging a safety first policy by parole boards and the subsequent civil commitment of those reaching the end of their criminal conviction.

- **Jessica's Laws (2005–06)** – a federal initiative adopted by 43 states, including GPS tracking of 'high risk' offenders, quarterly re-registration for others, increasing first time registration to twenty years, and the extension of 'predator free zones'.

- **Adam's Law (2007)** – established a national registry, expanded the definitions of sexual offences, increased the type of offender requiring registration, and extended tracking across state lines.

However, while abduction-murder stories focused public attention on 'the worst of the worst' and legislators continued to overload both the registers and their regulations rather than risk public censure the next time a released offender struck in deadly fashion (Janus 2006), public demands for controls had far more to do with wishing to be forearmed and eliminate unnecessary risks than panic. On the other hand, this *ad hoc* approach to public safety also led to a growing chorus of criticism from civil rights advocates, academics and researchers questioning the laws' increasingly obvious self-defeating ramifications.

Megan's Law in practice

Though the federal initiatives fostered the growth of sex offender notification databases, their form still differs from state to state. Contrary to the first impression given by the now easily accessible websites, registration and notification is far from simple. Under the Wetterling Act, courts, police departments and prisons were duty bound to inform offenders to register and notify the appropriate authorities of the offenders' impending destination. While every state's attorney general was then made responsible for the register's accuracy, by excluding juvenile, federal, military and out-of-state offenders, then allowing each state to determine their own registration requirements, and only requiring the authorities to allow access deemed 'necessary to protect the public', that measure ensured that it was not until the Lyncher Act – with its mandated ten-year minimum registration and 'life' for those who had used violence – that any uniformity was established. As the following examples – based on reviewing the websites, telephone follow-ups, and recourse to Finn's earlier review (1997) – demonstrate, variations are still the rule.

Unlike the 'full' registers, web data often excludes 'low risk' offenders, though Hawaii and Illinois, which don't designate by risk, post everyone including juveniles. The amount of data offered can be extremely limited, like in Connecticut, or extensive like in Utah with its interactive map, a means to track offenders, and the DIY notification flyer template provided by the OffenderWatch® company which runs the site. Otherwise, the public are able to gain access to the offender's name, aliases, address, mug shot with physical description, driver's licence number, motor vehicle plate, place of employment, date of birth, nature of the crime, conviction and sentence. Some sites offer email updates for those who sign up, and/or highlight and solicit information about absconders, and/or post a 'most wanted' list, and/or provide links to educational material and even activist websites. While these components may suffice for some, the demand for complete access continues, as the 2000 campaign in New Jersey to open up the complete register online demonstrates (Fodor 2001).

Consequently, the only uniformity among the web databases is that every user is warned against the misuse of the information, with Arizona's being typical and representative:

THE INFORMATION PROVIDED ON THIS SITE IS INTENDED FOR COMMUNITY SAFETY PURPOSES ONLY AND SHOULD NOT BE USED TO THREATEN, INTIMIDATE, OR HARASS. MISUSE OF THIS INFORMATION MAY RESULT IN CRIMINAL PROSECUTION. (http://az.gov/webapp/offender/main.do)

A minority of sites also publish their state's complete law, which usually includes a clause like Idaho's:

PENALTIES FOR VIGILANTISM OR OTHER MISUSE OF INFORMATION OBTAINED UNDER THIS CHAPTER. Any person who uses information obtained pursuant to this chapter to commit a crime or to cause physical harm to any person or damage to property shall be guilty of a misdemeanor and, *in addition to any other punishment*, be subject to imprisonment in the county jail for a period not to exceed one (1) year, or by a fine not to exceed one thousand dollars ($1,000) or both. (www3.state.id.us/cgi-bin/newidst?sctid=180830026.K, – our emphasis)

There is no doubt that public interest is high, and that the websites are extremely popular; California's had 131 million hits in 2007 alone. They are easy to use and cost nothing whereas accessing the full register sometimes requires a personal visit to the designated agency – state police, highway patrol, or county sheriff – and a fee for each search; or running up a telephone bill when accessing call-in services that states like New York offer, only to discover that they only confirm whether a person is registered or not (http://criminaljustice.stateny.us/nsor/search_index.htm).

The registers are usually maintained by the state's Public Safety Department, another name for the police; though exceptions include the Bureau of Investigation of Colorado, the Assessment Committee in Arkansas, the Department of Corrections in Utah, and the state of Tennessee which leaves it up to the local law enforcement agencies to decide what a 'significant danger' is (Finn 1997).

The method of determining risk levels, a vital part of most systems, also differs from state to state. In New Jersey, the task was given to local prosecutors who used the attorney general's Task Force guidelines in consultation with the Corrections Department and the local treatment community to set risk levels. Oregon's probation officers used their state's sex offender assessment scale to draw up a notification plan, and have their own review mechanism for ambiguous and 'level three' cases, turning each decision into a learning experience for assessors. In Washington State, the process begins earlier with the Sentence Review Committee, though local law enforcement agencies can make their own assessment by using the Sheriff and Police Chief Association guidelines. Approximately half of the states use sliding risk scales based on the 'seriousness' of the offence, criminal history, psychological characteristics, and the level of 'support' available from family and friends upon release. Washington State's scale, for example, consists of low – non-violent family setting assault; intermediate – multiple non-family offences or a violent assault; high – history of predatory crimes or multiple violent offences, and/ or expressed desire to reoffend. A minority of states, like Arkansas, have added a 'level four' designation specifically for those who used violence. Some states like Oregon add other indicators including *non*-sexual offences, use of weapons, and the gender of the victim(s). While these centrally agreed criteria may have advantages, such as reducing inconsistencies between jurisdictions; contrary to Finn's suggestion (1997) they do *not* necessarily eliminate 'subjectivity' given the importance of the offender's individual circumstances, a problem recognised by Washington State which redrew their guidelines for that very reason.

States also distinguish between the different 'publics' who should be alerted when using designated risk to determine restrictions on data release:

- **Level one/low risk** – law enforcement or other government agencies.

- **Level two/intermediate** – schools and community centers *may* be notified automatically; as are housing departments, public libraries, churches and youth groups in some states.

- **Level three/high** – all local residents *may* be notified by various means, including official announcements in the local media.

Once again, there are numerous exceptions. Probation officers in Connecticut, whose notification protocol was created with input from a victim advocacy group and the Center for the Treatment of Problem Sexual Behavior, still retained the discretion to notify *anyone* with *any* information. Tennessee's Bureau of Investigation and Police Departments have the same power (Finn 1997). Apart from press releases and/or advertisements in local papers, proactive public notification can include posting public flyers around town or having police officers dispensing the flyers door to door as they do in the Catskill town of Walton, NY. Numerous county sheriffs and/or probation services call public meetings. Louisiana even places the burden on the offender, who has to send postcards to all residents within a three-block radius of their residence, or go door to door informing neighbours of their status (Maddan 2008).

The lifestyle restrictions created by registration regulations, designed to reduce direct contact with children, are exceedingly varied too. Missouri insists that offenders must stay inside their houses and post signs – 'no candy or treats at this residence' – on Halloween between 5 p.m. and 10.30 p.m., while New York believes it more important to prohibit offenders' employment opportunities in mobile ice cream trucks. In Corpus Christi, Texas, offenders have had to place a sign outside their house:

DANGER
Sex Offender Lives Here
Report suspicious activity to:
(361) 854-4122 NCCSCD
(361) 826-2900 NCSO
(361) 886-2600 CCPD (8573)

Consequently, it was no surprise that registration and notification were immediately challenged on the constitutional validity of the statutes' retroactive application and imposition of double jeopardy.

Constitutional issues related to registration requirements

Legal decisions at state level can appear contradictory, though less so once the nature of the legal arguments, petitioners' particular circumstances, and relevant case law is taken into account. The precedent set in Louisiana's *State v Babin* ensured that the Appellate Court ruled portions of their statute unconstitutional because of retroactivity. A US District Court declared parts of New Jersey's Megan's Law unconstitutional too for the same reason, although the US Third Circuit Court vacated that decision in *Artway v Attorney General* (1996). As their constitution specifically prohibited retrospective laws, Missouri's *Doe v Phillips* (2008) upheld an injunction removing pre-adjudicated offenders from the register, and two subsequent attempts to alter the constitution ran out of time. Several challenges based on the Eighth Amendment's prohibition against cruel and unusual punishment failed; but given that Alaska's constitution includes a specific right to privacy, a restraining order against notification was almost inevitable, though the 1975 US Supreme Court ruling in *Cox Broadcasting v Cohn* outlawing restrictions on publishing official court records ensured that appeals at federal level on privacy grounds would fail.

Legal assaults on the risk-level assessment process also had mixed results. In New Jersey, *Doe v Poritz* (1995) overturned a lower court decision prohibiting the local prosecutors from determining risk levels on the grounds that being a 'biased party' they violated offenders' due process rights; but as long as the offender was granted a hearing, the prosecutors could carry on. Hawaii's *State v Bani* (2001) came to the same conclusion. *Public Safety v Doe* (2003) then ensured Connecticut avoided that problem by ruling that a *procedural* as opposed to *substantive* due process violation was acceptable. To avoid the courts, other states initiated risk assessment reviews by other officials, or allowed offenders to petition for relief, or granted hearings, although that added to the existing gridlock in the US courts ensuring considerable delays in determining cases.

Ultimately, although various sections of state laws were struck down, community notification as a principle and practice gained the constitutional go ahead when the issues of retroactivity and risk assessment were apparently laid to rest by the US Supreme Court's *Smith v Doe*, which decided that as long as the law intended to protect the public and not punish the offender, almost any regulation was acceptable. The same argument was used to justify public access too, given that 'The purpose and the principle effect of notification are to inform the public for its own safety, not to humiliate the offender. Widespread public access is necessary for the efficacy of the scheme, and the attendant humiliation is but a collateral consequence of a valid registration' (*Smith v Doe* 2003).

However, that decision did *not* end Eighth Amendment arguments as even the concurring Supreme Court Justice, Souter, as well as the three dissenting justices, knew that the rationale offered was spurious. Far from offenders being 'free to move where they wish and to live and work as other citizens, with no supervision', the extremely restrictive nature of registration regulations and requirements, especially when it comes to work or accommodation, can make it near impossible, as we shall see. As for notification: 'Selection makes a statement, one that affects common reputation and sometimes carries harsher consequences, such as exclusion from jobs or housing, harassment, and physical harm' (Justice Souter, *Smith v Doe*, 2003). As a consequence, Adam's Law has led to a new round of legal challenges on the same grounds as before.

Civil commitment as an extension of 'community control'

Although complete coverage of post-incarceration civil commitment in mental facilities is beyond the scope of our review, the growing recourse to this means of controlling offenders deemed too dangerous to be returned to the community under any type of supervision is an extension of the registration and notification movement. Being a civil matter it conveniently bypasses many of the legal arguments concerning the constitutionality of criminal registration and notification provisions; though it provoked legal debates of its own.

Following two horrific crimes perpetrated by released offenders, Washington State led the way in confining 'high risk' offenders in mental facilities after their time served. Similar local events led Arizona, California, Florida, Illinois, Iowa, Kansas, Massachusetts, Minnesota, Missouri, New Jersey, North Dakota, South Carolina, Texas, Virginia and Wisconsin to follow suit; with Pennsylvania even incarcerating teen offenders in this way (Doren 2002). While it avoided the usual constitutional restrictions on criminal punishments, sections of the mental health profession have vehemently objected to its use. The American Psychiatric Association even denounced it as an 'abuse of psychiatry' (1996, cited in Janus 2006: 23); and Janus' (2006) account of the fifteen-year battle over committing Dennis Linehan illustrates why they did.

Incarcerated in 1965 for killing a fourteen-year-old, Linehan became eligible for parole in 1992, and the subsequent defence of his civil liberties against commitment included three appearances before the Minnesota Supreme Court, one before the US Eighth Circuit Appeals Court, and two petitions to the US Supreme Court. Prosecutors argued that Linehan's record of violence *before* the murder made him unfit for treatment in the community; and despite his successful completion of both sex offender and chemical dependency programmes, they argued that he had duped the psychologist recommending his release. Ironically, everyone had forgotten that the state's power to commit people under the sexual psychopath law of 1939 was subject to US Supreme Court precedent, the Pearson Test, which sought to inhibit the misuse of commitment by insisting that those targeted had to be suffering from both a recognised mental illness *and* a clear defect in their character compared to others: 'an utter lack of power to control their sexual impulses'. Consequently, when Linehan's commitment was upheld in the lower court because the state 'expert' insisted that it was Linehan's 'controlling nature' that made him so dangerous, an immediate reversal was assured. A public uproar generated by the local *Star Tribune* followed, and led to legislators lining up to 'tighten the law' ensuring Linehan was then committed under a new sexually dangerous persons law which merely required offenders to have a 'sexual, personality, or other mental disorder'. The Appeals Court, facing public scrutiny, dismissed Linehan's viable appeal on the bizarre grounds that an act of masturbation following a visit by his wife who had been accompanied by her nine-year-old daughter was proof that Linehan could not 'adequately' control his sexual impulses towards *children*!

Consequently, anyone facing commitment is caught in a Catch 22. Anything and everything that they have said or done can be used *against* them whatever its diagnostic value, good behaviour can be offered as evidence of deviousness as much as feigning, any confession matches 'denial' as an indicator of 'dangerousness', and the catch-all diagnoses found in the DSM (Kirk and Kutchins 1992) can easily fulfil the mental illness requirement.

Effectiveness of sex offender community registration

If the registration and notification of, and the restrictions placed upon, sex offenders are judged from the public's desires and legislators' intent there can be no doubt that the systems are a qualified success. Known offenders are either spending more time in jail or being more rigorously regulated upon release and thereby have less access to children. The critics, however, are not convinced that the ultimate results are effective. They question the laws' viability on several interrelated grounds; not least the fact that no one has demonstrated that public notification reduces the *overall* risk to children from sexual victimisation, given that notification focuses on known offenders (Coffey 2006).

The present system has clearly been driven by the fear of the worst case scenario rather than a rational approach to a far more complex problem; a point demonstrated by Radford's account of the role of TV coverage in generating fear-inducing myths – such as 'the problem is getting worse' because 'sex offenders are incurable' – which then shaped policy. Two myths in particular illustrate how this occurred. After 2000, the continual attempt to control the internet by the authorities found a new rationale: one in five teens aged between ten and seventeen had been approached by an online 'predator'. That 'fact' led to a scramble to add new restrictions on offenders' web use despite the claim being belied by its very source. The Youth Internet Safety

Survey actually revealed that only 3 per cent of those approaches (that is, one in 1,000) were made by an unknown adult and only then after the targeted teen had entered a clearly demarcated adult oriented chat room! Likewise, the claim that there were 50,000 active predators online, cited by Attorney General Gonzales when justifying Adam's Law, was merely a guesstimate emerging from MSNBC's sensational *Dateline* TV show (Radford 2008).

Sample's systematic study of the relationship between media stories, public perceptions and policy-making in Illinois provides even stronger evidence that misperceptions were directly driving policy. The legislators admitted seeking new laws and regulations precisely because they thought that the media coverage reflected both the most pressing threat and public concern though the coverage grossly misrepresented the real nature of local offending by stressing the online myths and examples of the 'worst of the worst' (Sample 2001, summarised in Maddan 2008). As a result, it is not surprising that critics identify the ever increasing number of offences requiring registration and the ever increasing actions being regulated as *the* core problem (Gonzalez 2008). This system overload can be illustrated by just some of the many additions to Missouri's system during 2008. Registration was extended to juveniles who committed aggravated sexual assault, and to those committing physical abuse that touched genitalia. Anyone 'promoting child pornography' involving obscene material *'portraying what appears to be a minor'* is ineligible for probation; and all registrants, rather than those moving outside the county, now had three days to report their changes in circumstances rather than ten. To be fair to Missouri, they also removed a registered offence: parents 'kidnapping' their own child; but while some states like Arizona attempt to restrict the number of offenders on registers by waiting for a second or third incident in categories like exhibitionism, most follow the trend towards increasing the requirements to be followed by the growing types of offenders mandated to register. This has dramatically added to the attendant costs and burdens on those charged with monitoring registrants, which explains why so many states 'lost track' of so many offenders. Connecticut was always rare in 'road testing' their system first, adding a parallel treatment programme, and establishing a 1:25 caseload limit for probation officers. Far more typical was the rocketing caseloads in Louisiana. Even though New Jersey was one of only two states that supplied extra funding, prosecutors discovered that the registration process took so long that a backlog quickly developed despite their extra efforts (Finn 1997). This led to two types of criticism.

The first 'critical' response was to highlight the lack of any agreed criteria for success, whether it be the recidivism rate or the number of all reported molestations. Though registration enables repeat offenders to be apprehended more quickly (Finn 1997), the law has done little to reduce the number of sex crimes against children (Maddan 2008). Despite the paucity of studies on registrants (Maddan 2008), and the marginal difference in the only comparative recidivism study – 19 per cent among the registered and 22 per cent exhibited by those whose last known offence occurred before registration was compulsory (Finn 1997) – recidivism rates have become *the* major argument in the reformers' contention that registration and notification are self-defeating. The belief that sex offenders exhibit an unusually high rate of recidivism was used to justify not only state and federal policies but the numerous court decisions that upheld them, despite varying research findings with their figures invariably inflated by groups like exhibitionists (McAlinden 2007). Yet, the real rate appears to be much lower. Between 1990 and 1997, sex offences in Illinois not only remained stable at 1.2 per cent of all criminal charges, most involved adult victims rather than the stereotypes of ravaged children and 'sexploited' teens appearing in media accounts reviewed by Sample and Bray (2003). Over five years the rearrest rate for sexual offenders did not rise above 7 per cent, and those offences against children were outnumbered by those including adult victims and the possession of child pornography (Sample and Bray 2003). A larger Bureau of Justice study, covering fifteen states, involving 9,700 sex offenders and 262,420 non-sexual offenders, uncovered similar results; and though the sex offenders were four times as likely to be arrested for the same offence, that still only amounted to 3.3 per cent of the total because most recidivism involved non-sexual offences such as DUI or shoplifting (Langan *et al.* 2003). If one then compares those figures with the 68 percent average recidivism rate reached by *all* released offenders, the core premise upon which the registration and notification of sex offenders is justified is not only questionable, it may be completely erroneous.

However, before accepting these new rates at face value we really need to know who is and who isn't engaging in repeat offences; are they the 'opportunists' within the family and its 'zone of association' – teachers, coaches, friends – or the stereotypical 'predatory' paedophile? If it is the former, as the most violent, dangerous and persistent are being incarcerated for longer, subjected to civil commitment, and/or being more rigorously monitored, the apparent decline in recidivism rates could just as easily be presented as evidence for the viability of current registration and notification systems. Low recidivism rates could likewise negate the critics' preferred alternative to the incarceration and monitoring of low risk offenders: community-based treatment, which is being offered as an effective low cost alternative to incarceration in cash-strapped times. For although meta-analysis has been used to argue that graduates of treatment programmes exhibit much lower rearrest rates (Lotke and Hoelter 2008), the innate weakness of meta-studies and the lack of research exploring the link between the various treatment programmes, the different monitoring systems, and recidivism make any conclusions about successful treatment tentative too.

What is not in doubt is the lack of treatment programmes; for although the US has a large range on offer, they are only available to a small minority of offenders (McAlinden 2007); and that drawback, caused by the cost of the highest per capita prison population in the world, is exacerbated by the way treatment is sometimes used. When Oregon discovered that many offenders fearing the potential ramifications of notification suddenly began to fight for places on treatment programmes in an effort to secure a low risk designation, the obvious implications were lost on some probation officers who not only used fear of notification to secure compliance with registration requirements but even boasted of using the threat of public notification to manage offenders in community settings (cited in Finn 1997).

The second 'enforcement' criticism led to demands for more laws. In 2007 the National Center for Missing and Exploited Children increased public fear when they claimed that one in six sex offenders were non-compliant and 'missing' because of inconsistent inadequate state laws, and listed the complaints – 25 states where non-compliance was treated as a misdemeanour; four states which left it to the offender to notify their new authority when moving to another state; another eight where the law on notification of new authorities when the offender moved was too ambiguous; and the fact that only seven states made a failure to register an automatic parole violation.

These problems had, of course, already been dealt with by the Adam Walsh Child Protection and Safety Act (Adam's Law) of the year before, with its national sex offender registry database and website, federal felony charge for non-compliance, mandated regulations for the states; and which gave the job of tracking down missing offenders to the US marshals. However, while it is easy to ridicule self-defeating fears, not only are current critiques far from watertight, it is all too easy to peddle myths about public ignorance and legislator foolishness too, especially when any sensible reform will require both groups' support. Rather than simply dismiss their perspective, it would make far more sense to try and understand it. Far from being naive, senators like Charles E. Schumer, who supported federal funding of the Parents For Megan's Law's continent-wide zip code-based email alert, warning residents when an offender is moving to their locality, really believed that: 'With dangerous predators continuing to prey on vulnerable children, the new funding will provide us with the tools we need to remain vigilant and proactive in protecting them' (PFML 2008a).

To dismiss this as a delusion requires one to ignore the potential of proactive parental vigilance and the need to offer a more viable alternative to this form of public empowerment. Likewise Congressman Steve Israel, a Member of the House Appropriations Committee, explained that: 'Parents can never be too vigilant when it comes to protecting their children from sex offenders, but we must continue to expand and sharpen the resources available to them' (PFML 2008a).

Those who oppose 'the right to know' need to explain why they do so, and what 'tools' they would prefer the public to have instead; or better still, address the problem of funding shortfalls that helps ensure the high rate of non-compliance, which is as much as 28 per cent in Tennessee. Pejorative criticism which treats all forms of DIY public protection as 'vigilantism' forgets that public support for self-defeating measures follows not only from their zero tolerance for *any* threat to their children (Fodor 2001), but also because 'myths' about and stringent demands to control sex offending were promoted as much by progressive social movements as by conservatives during the 1980s and 1990s, if not more so (Jenkins 1992). Far from being irrational, many DIY activists do not conform to the critics' description of them as 'vigilantes' either. While websites like Parents for Megan's Law's repeat the 'one in five online predator' myth they clearly draw their visitors' attention to the source of most threats: '93% of juvenile sexual assault victims know their attacker, 34.2% of attackers were family members and 58.7% were acquaintances and only 7% of the perpetrators were strangers to the victim' (PFML 2008b).

Consequently, if one wishes to co-opt the public to reform, one needs to understand that what worries PFML, like the defamed Paulsgrove protesters in Portsmouth, UK (Williams and Thompson 2004a, 2004b), is that while they *can* be vigilant about family members, acquaintances and coaches, they would prefer not to have to worry about the 650,000 registered offenders who have already proven their untrustworthiness; and that those opposing public access stop hiding behind the alleged threat of vigilantism which can clearly be exaggerated too.

Vigilantism and community rejection

While fears about 'vigilantism' dominated the UK government's response to open access campaigns until January 2010, when they embraced extending four pilot programmes, the issue rarely surfaces in the US, which could and should act as a test case, given that the home addresses of registered offenders are available to anyone. At first sight the level of harassment appears far more extensive than is publicly admitted. Depending upon the survey cited, 30 to 50 per cent of registered offenders *claim* to have experienced the loss of jobs or accommodation, and suffered property damage or threats; and 5 to 16 per cent *claim* to have been physically assaulted (Maloy 2008). However, before accepting these claims, one needs to consider how monitoring can also increase in 'public vigilance' rather than 'notification vigilantism'.

Some states went to considerable lengths to avoid any adverse consequences, and the dire warnings against misuse of information on websites, or details printed on notification flyers posted in public buildings (like those in Bloomville, NY's village hall), reflect the authorities' determination to deter any extra-legal 'justice' by making that a separate crime over and above the form of harassment undertaken and not merely an aggravating circumstance. These warnings are often matched with educational initiatives. Oregon probation officers, for example, do not inform the local media about impending arrivals until they have distributed notification flyers door to door in order to discuss the implications with residents first. Some agencies hold community meetings to explain both the law and the characteristics of offenders, with probation officers in Seattle taking the opportunity to stress the greater threat from relatives at least three times in their presentations.

As a result, agencies have found that notification has had several beneficial effects: more positive community responses to policing, enhancing residents' understanding of community corrections, and producing far fewer cases of harassment than had been expected. In the first three years of Washington State's notification programme there were only fourteen reports of harassment. An Oregon Sex Offender Supervision Network survey, covering 35 counties with 2,160 supervised offenders, uncovered a 10 per cent harassment rate, consisting of name-calling, graffiti or minor vandalism. The worst two cases consisted of one offender having a gun pointed at him, and another being threatened with having his house torched (Finn 1997). While one could quibble with the definitions of 'minor' and 'extreme' harassment if one wished, it is clear that Finn's review inadvertently uncovered an explanation for the apparent disparity between self-reported cases and the official records; public notification has led to a dramatic increase in reports from the public, including employers, of suspicious behaviour by offenders. As it is unlikely that every public report was mistaken or malicious, some of the cases of 'harassment' reported by offenders may be an attempt to explain away the consequences of their own dubious behaviour. If one then considers the way that the registration and notification process has been accredited in states like New Jersey, with enhancing inter-agency cooperation and greater regulation enforcement, we may have an explanation for the discrepancy. The community control of sex offenders has in many localities drastically improved real community policing involving residents, law enforcement and probation officers.

Practical criticism of notification is on far stronger grounds when identifying *direct* counter-productive consequences of various registration requirements than false fears about vigilantism or non-existent panics. The former have a far greater potential to undermine public safety given that they can increase the 'stressors' commonly associated with recidivism, which include isolation, disempowerment, shame, depression, anxiety and lack of social support.

The most pressing issue was and remains the 'no-go areas' imposed upon registrants, because the historic placement of schools, parks, malls and other forbidden places ensures that exclusion zones overlap to the point where ex-offenders have serious problems securing accommodation, employment, or even going to the local store. The issue went public during 2007 following reports that 22 registered offenders were living rough under the Julia Tuttle Causeway that links the city to Miami Beach because local 'no-go areas' had made it impossible for them to find housing (*New York Times* 2007). *USA Today* then uncovered the alarming fact that two-thirds of the 136 high risk sex offenders in Boston lacked a permanent address, 100 in New York City were living in two homeless shelters, and 500 had registered as 'transient' in California since the state increased its exclusion zones to 2,000 feet in 2006 (*USA Today* 2007). Michigan attempted to avoid that problem by exempting those who were already working within these zones before January 2006 or when a school or other forbidden facility had been relocated to their housing area afterwards. That state, unfortunately, is an exception; although the sheer numbers involved has subsequently forced two-thirds of states to allow homeless offenders to register as such, listing a shelter or a public location as their home address as long as they stay in touch with police. Maryland was forced to adopt this approach when an appellant court ruled that having made no provision for such an eventuality, the homeless offender was exempt from housing restrictions.

However, not every problem can be accredited to self-defeating registration regulations and the following case reveals how the authorities can generate public disquiet too. In December 2007, Washington County Sheriff Rob Gordon used the standard notification flyers to lead public opposition to the policies being pursued by the Connell House facility for offenders in Cornelius, Oregon. He had initially supported the new residential treatment plan supervised by the Oregon Psychiatric Security Review Board, whose designated insane inmates included three sex offenders, one of whom had raped a three-year-old, having absconded from the state hospital five years before. Gordon's objection followed his discovery that the facility had ordered unarmed staff not to tackle offenders who attempted to flee when on outside 'walks'. While one could castigate the sheriff for spreading fear, and the hundreds who attended the subsequent community meeting for not being impressed by the argument that these offenders' recidivism rate was lower than average, to do so would be disingenuous. It would ignore the fact that the 'secure residential treatment center' was not the halfway house for 'the cured' that the community had been led to believe it was during the planning phase. The fact that one inmate had already demonstrated a proclivity for an 'escape rape' on a toddler also explains the insight one resident, 'Lindi McGee, 41, mother of four children', gave to the local paper: 'It's scary, especially if they are mentally ill. I have mixed feelings: I understand that these people have to go somewhere; but I don't know that this is the option with so many families living nearby' (*The Oregonian* 1 March 2008).

The community agreed with the sheriff that the no-restraint policy was a step too far, putting residents at risk, and the licence was revoked (*The Oregonian*, 29 December 2007; 1, 3, 5, 9 and 12 January 2008). Given that the community had initially accepted the facility, it is pointless to denounce the residents of Cornelius as NIMBYs when what they were doing was not even insisting that the authorities prioritise residents and children's 'rights' over those of the offender, but that the facility adopt sensible and rational policies and procedures to accommodate public fear. Misreading that reasonable request is reminiscent of the way in which the residents in Paulsgrove were widely denounced when they finally lost their patience during the summer of 2000 even though the media reports castigating them refused to inform their readers that they were protesting against the authorities' refusal to activate what was then called a sex offender order on an active sex offender despite numerous complaints and an increasing number of victims (Williams and Thompson 2004a, 2004b).

While academics constantly raise the spectre of restorative justice turning vigilance into vigilantism (Morris and Gelsthorpe 2000, cited in McAlinden 2007: 205), far too many are erroneously passing off heightened vigilance as vigilantism, denouncing rather than educating the public; and that leads us to the question of the alternatives to the present policies regarding sex offenders and the attempts to encourage communities to take some responsibility for offenders as a means to reduce crime.

Alternatives

Psychologists and civil libertarians would prefer to see treatment become an integral part of the monitoring programmes rather than a substitute because they want to make community corrections *per se* a more viable alternative to the 'get tough' regimes like 'three strikes'. Some states, like Washington, have worked hard to establish, maintain and extend community-based programmes for first-time non-penetrative molesters, but it is in the distinct minority. Following the 2005 Lunsford Act (Jessica's Law), many states from Arizona to Washington introduced a split life sentence for serious offenders

– permanent electronic tagging after 25 years' incarceration; although, to date, tagging remains an expensive headache. While it could obviously offer *the* means to monitor offenders while circumventing 'no-go' zones', tagging is very costly, and its effectiveness is hotly contested, as are the medical side-effects of chemical castration, which is restricted to half a dozen states – California, Florida, Georgia, Texas, Louisiana and Montana – and has fallen out of favour despite a large number of studies showing that it too promotes low recidivism rates (McAlinden 2007).

Community treatment would not only cost far less than incarceration, it addresses the often ignored question of the best means to reintegrate sex offenders into the community as part of a comprehensive strategy to reduce sexual offences championed by groups like the Stop It Now organisation, which promotes treatment and community integration as well as monitoring to protect children.

No reform will succeed until those promoting them take on the major source of get tough policies – the American Legislative Exchange Council (ALEC), which is funded by the very companies that profit from the rise in private prisons and subsequent demand for correctional equipment. This little-known group has had an inordinate direct effect on state penal policies, as the regulations controlling relationships between state legislators and lobbyists are even less stringent than those in Congress. As a result, ALEC has not been held accountable for creating the bizarre situation in which correction systems have been overloaded with non-violent offenders of all kinds, while simultaneously releasing hundreds of untreated sexual offenders during the 1990s, which further fuelled public support for the very 'get tough' policies ALEC had drafted for legislators. And then there is the awkward issue of the dominant psychological perspectives behind the present difficulties in sex offender policies.

As most of these issues have been dealt with at great length elsewhere, and McAlinden offers a review of the academic debates (2007, chapters 7–9), we will concentrate on an issue that needs far more public consideration than the specialist literature has generated to date: the way teen offenders are being automatically perceived as budding paedophiles, and thereby have become a symbol of what is wrong with current risk designation practices such as their arbitrary nature and tendency to over-categorise offenders as 'high risk'.

Juveniles and sex offender risk assessments

Those who treat the juveniles, who commit no fewer than 25 per cent of sexual offences against eleven to seventeen-year-olds in the USA, oppose the assumption that they are paedophiles in the making, unless they were considerably older than their victim, *and* exhibited the constant sexual fantasy, arousal and behaviour patterns associated with deviant proclivities (Rich 2003; Epperson *et al.* 2006). Few teen offenders do; and they do not exhibit sexual disorders in the same way as adult offenders do either (Hunter and Becker 1994; Coffey 2006; Prescott 2006). Their offences do not even necessarily indicate a sexual disorder, let alone predict their future behaviour (Bancroft 2006; Barbaree and Langton 2006). Indeed, far from reflecting an 'abusive' intent (Prescott 2006) their crimes often reflect very common instrumental attitudes to sex, which like teens' approach to alcohol and recreational drug use is almost a norm if reports from university campuses are anything to go by (Schwartz and DeKeseredy 1997). Consequently, theoretical models based on adult offenders have little to do with the risk factors that turn common teen instrumentalism into coercion or aggressive acts (White *et al.* 2006); and the work of Worling and Langstrom demonstrates that we do not even know which risk factors are paramount (2003, 2006).

However, the differences between teen and adult offenders, the lack of agreement over the viability of different treatment methods, and the inability of actuary instruments to determine the likelihood of recidivism, let alone justify civil commitments, has not inhibited treating teens like adults and contributing to registration overload (Prescott 2006, Doren 2006; Sipe *et al.* 1998). The Texas Youth Commission, for example, by using a score of '4' rather than the scale authors' own recommendation of '6' when assessing risk level using Static-99, ensures that the youth's age at first offence and their non-marital status puts them halfway towards a 'high risk' designation simply because they are teens (Prescott 2006). Likewise, diagnoses of teen 'disorders' have been inflated both by including their use of alcohol or marijuana, despite the lack of evidence that either constitutes a contributory factor in the offence, and by the widespread application of 'conduct' or 'oppositional defiant' disorders, even though they are as controversial as the diagnosis of an 'anti-social personality disorder'. Concepts like 'a lack of empathy' and 'denial' are not only poor predictors of recidivism, they are – like sexual preoccupations, 'distorted attitudes', 'shallow emotions' and 'a lack of self-management' – almost normative in teens today (Righthand and Welch 2001; Seagrave and Grisso 2002; Hanson and Morton-Bourgon 2004; Prescott 2006). As these over-diagnoses reflect ascertainment bias, given that sex offenders often exhibit fewer conduct problems than their delinquent peers, and the younger a juvenile is, the less likely adult risk factors will apply; the continuing debate over the merits of clinical assessment versus actuarial scales has an extra significance for teens. To paraphrase Rich, existing theory is too poor and the research too flawed to accept 'the dogma of one-stop cognitive-behavioural treatment' and its corollary, the obsession with finding *the* typical profile, because 'teens are kids' and 'not hardened serial rapists, deviant sexual maniacs, or psychopaths' (Rich 2003; Seto and Lalumiere 2006; Doren 2006; Quinsey *et al.* 1998, in Prescott 2006; Epperson *et al.* 2006; Hart *et al.* 2002; Litwack 2001). While some fixated teens do exist, most offending appears to follow from their disadvantaged development and subsequent lifestyle and not from deliberate injurious intent; and as two-thirds of US teens engage in sex before leaving high school, those who 'assault' may have simply misread social cues, or could be expressing their powerlessness, or simply see themselves as getting what they want (Kirby 2001; Rich 2003). Yet, young teens continue to be designated as dangerous paedophiles.

This criticism reflects a growing belief among treatment veterans that sexual aggression in teens does *not* necessarily follow from sexual deviance and that treatment needs to be related to the offender's personality and learning style rather than the current tendency to impose an ideological-led 'one-size-fits-all' approach, long considered to be counter-productive for low risk offenders (Andrews and Bonta 2003).

In the case of teens, these problems found an exemplar in seventeen-year-old Genarlow Wilson of Georgia, who was jailed for ten years without parole for having *consensual* oral sex with a fifteen-year-old female at a party. Even if Wilson had been fifteen too, he would still have had a year in jail and then been registered; a situation so ridiculous that even Matt Towley, the Representative who sponsored the legislation, went on record that he had been trying to protect children not 'to put kids in jail for oral sex' (cited in Zott 2008: 109). We also know a SUNY student had to fight for two years against designation as an offender in an even more absurd case. The seizure of his home computer during an unrelated investigation led to charges of possessing child pornography because it contained a dozen images of sixteen-year-old females. Fortunately, the court-appointed psychiatrist pointed out that the images were 'age appropriate' given that the accused was also sixteen at the time; otherwise jail time, registration, and the Campus Sex Crimes Prevention Act 2000, which effectively 'outs' offenders, would have ended his studies. Some states like Michigan take different measures for thirteen to seventeen-year-olds who are within three years of their victims' age, judging each case on its merits. As teens have very low recidivism rates (Worling and Langstrom 2006; Smallbone 2006), the Association for the Treatment of Sexual Abuse opposes community notification in all but extreme cases, and is set against civil commitment (Trivits and Repucci 2002). What is ironic, however, is that some prosecutors, also worried about the consequences of labelling teens for life, have apparently indicted the youths on other charges, excluding them from treatment (Letourneau 2006).

Unfortunately, the questioning of the pedantic approaches being enforced upon teens and the need for more appropriate multi-factor assessment and treatment, has yet to meet mainstream media, let alone the politicians and the public (Prescott 2006; Rich 2003; Beutler 2000; Association for the Treatment of Sex Abusers 1997). This is not merely a case of public ignorance. Numerous 'experts' have failed to see the obvious weakness of treating teens like hopeless recidivists simply because some adult offenders' proclivities can be traced back to their youth, and universities promote this erroneous orthodoxy in psychology courses too.

Conclusion – panics and policy

Dismissing notification laws as a panic response does not address the cause of public concern or the possibility of utilising its qualified success to address the issue of sex offenders in the community, and certainly does not resolve ongoing problems. Continuing media concentration on the 'worst of the worst', the lack of relevant comparative research, an overloaded and increasingly costly system generating counter-productive effects, the lack of comprehensive strategies for community reintegration, and serious questions about the core rationale for the current notification systems offer a solid basis for useful criticism, and issues for reform.

While we agree that retributive perspectives have effectively failed, addressing these problems requires education rather than simply castigating the public for being fearful and ignorant of the alternatives, especially as they have to be convinced that combining treatment programmes and community integration strategies would prove far more useful than perpetuating the problems caused by 'no-go zones' and other registration requirements including the alienating features that encourage fear of the unknown, punitiveness and harassment. Far from blaming the public, we need to see them as potential allies, though the first hurdle to be overcome is the academic and 'expert' obsession with 'one-size-fits-all' solutions that fuel the media obsession with the 'worst of the worst', that continues to justify more self-defeating controls. As the costs of current policies escalate there is clearly a need to prioritise public education and consider adopting more community-based monitoring schemes, like Stop It Now, that offer a holistic approach enhancing monitoring, reinforcing treatment, and aiding the offender's integration into society.

Selected further reading

The most informative volume covering the political difficulties generated by the conception, legal framework, and the practicalities of sex offender notification and monitoring in the US remains Zott's collection (2008). Being part of the Current Controversies series designed for US students it presents diametrically opposed opinions and analysis from policy-makers, government attorneys and defence lawyers, treatment specialists, journalists and child protection activists, enabling the reader to understand the perspectives behind the current problems. Maddan's detailed study of Arkansas offenders (2008) is a major contribution to the opponents' conviction that the high rate of sex offender recidivism is mythical. These can be complemented by McAlinden's (2007) wide-ranging review of academic perspectives and community group approaches to risk, restitution and the reintegration of offenders, although some of the interpretations are contentious; and Janus' (2006) provocative thesis on the inherent problems presented by the rise of 'the preventative state'. We are also pleased to reveal that Rich's guide to the misconceptions involved in the policing of juvenile offenders (2003), much of which can also serve as a critique of the problems and conflicts in contemporary 'risk' psychology upon which the success of the wider policy rests, is being revised to incorporate developments since it was first issued.

References

Andrews, D. A. and Bonta, J. (2003) *The Psychology of Criminal Conduct*, 3rd edn. Cincinnati: Anderson.

American Psychiatric Association (1996) *Dangerous Sex Offenders: A Task Force Report on Sexually-Dangerous Offenders*. Washington, DC: APA.

Associated Press (2007) *Sex Offenders Living Under Miami Bridge*. www.nytimes.com/2007/04/08/us/08bridge.html?_r=1&scp=2&sq=Julia%20Tuttle%20Causeway%202007&st=cse.

Association for the Treatment of Sex Abusers (1997) *Ethical Standards and Principles for the Treatment and Intervention with Abusers*, Position Paper. Beaverton.

Bancroft, J. (2006) 'Normal sexual development', in H. E. Barbaree and W. L. Marshall (eds) *The Juvenile Sex Offender*, 2nd edn. New York: Guildford Press (pp. 19–57).

Barbaree, H. E. and Langton, C. M. (2006) 'The effects of child sexual abuse and family environment', in H. E. Barbaree and W. L. Marshall (eds) *The Juvenile Sex Offender*, 2nd edn. New York: Guildford Press (pp. 58–76).

Beutler, L. E. (2000) 'David and Goliath: when empirical and clinical standards of practice meet', *American Psychologist*, 55: 997–1007.

Bohm R. M. and Haley, K. N. (2007) *Introduction to Criminal Justice*, 4th edn. New York: McGrawHill.

Coffey, P. (2006) 'Forensic issues in evaluating juvenile sex offenders', in D. S. Prescott (ed.) *Risk Assessment of Youth who have Sexually Abused: Theory, Controversy, and Emerging Strategies*. Oklahoma City: Wood and Barnes (pp. 75–86).

Doren, D. (2002) *Evaluating Sex Offenders: A Manual for Civil Commitment and Beyond*. Thousand Oaks, CA: Sage.

Doren, D. (2006): 'Assessing juveniles' risk within the civil commitment context', in D. S. Prescott (ed.) *Risk Assessment of Youth who have Sexually Abused: Theory, Controversy, and Emerging Strategies*. Oklahoma City: Wood and Barnes (pp. 100–17).

Epperson, D. L., Ralson, C. A., Fowers, D., DeWitt, J. and Gore, K. S. (2006) 'Actuarial risk assessment with juveniles who offend sexually: development of the juvenile sexual offence recidivism risk assessment tool – II (JSORRAT-II)', in D. S. Prescott (ed.) *Risk Assessment of Youth who have Sexually Abused: Theory, Controversy, and Emerging Strategies*. Oklahoma City: Wood and Barnes (pp. 118–169).

Finn, P. (1997) *Sex Offender Community Notification*, NIJ Research in Action. US Department of Justice.

Fodor, M. D. (2001) *Megan's Law: Protection or Privacy*, Berkely Heights, NJ: Endslow.

Gonzalez, A. R. (2008) 'Tough laws and vigilant prosecution are the best defense against sexual predators', in L. M. Zott (ed.) *Sex Offenders and Public Policy*. New York: Thomson Gale.

Hanson, R. K. and Morton-Bourgon, K. E. (2004) *Predictors of Sexual Recidivism: An Updated Meta-analysis*. Online at: www.psepc.gc/ca/publications/corrections.

Hart, S. D., Watt, K. A. and Vincent, G. M. (2002) 'Commentary on Seagrave and Grisso: Impressions of the state of the art', *Law and Human Behaviour*, 26.

Hunter, J. A. and Becker, J. V. (1994) 'The role of deviant sexual arousal in juvenile sexual offending: etiology, evaluation, and treatment', *Criminal Justice and Behavior*, 21: 132–49.

Janus, E. J. (2006) *Failure to Protect: America's Sexual Predator Laws and the Rise of the Preventative State*. Ithica: Cornel University Press.

Jenkins, P. (1992) *Intimate Enemies: Moral Panics in Contemporary Great Britain*. Hawthorne, NY: Aldine de Gruyter.

Kelley, D. D. (2008) 'Child molestation has reached epidemic proportions', in K. M. Zott (ed.) *Sex Offenders and Public Policy*. New York: Thomson Gale.

Kirby, D. (2001) 'Understanding what works and what doesn't in reducing adolescent sexual risk-taking', *Family Planning Perspectives*, 33: 276–81.

Kirk, S. A. and Kutchins, H. (1992) *The Selling of DSM: The Rhetoric of Science in Psychiatry*. Hawthorne, NY: Aldine de Gruyter.

Langan, P. A., Schmitt, E. L. and Durose, M. R. (2003) *Recidivism of Sex Offenders Released from Prison in 1994*. Washington DC: Bureau of Justice Statistics.

Letourneau, E. J. (2006) 'Legal consequences of juvenile sexual offending in the United States', in H. E. Barbaree and W. L. Marshall (eds) *The Juvenile Sex Offender*, 2nd edn. New York: Guildford Press (pp. 275–90).

Litwack, T. R. (2001) 'Actuarial verses clinical assessments of dangerousness', *Psychology, Public Policy, and Law*, 7: 409–43.

Lotke, E. and Hoelter, H. J. (2008) 'Clarifying the facts can strengthen public policy', in L. M. Zott (ed.) *Sex Offenders and Public Policy*. New York: Thomson Gale.

Maddan, S. (2008) *The Labeling of Sex Offenders*. Lanham: University Press of America.

Maloy, M. L. (2008) 'Registries and community notification target the wrong people', in L. M. Zott (ed.) *Sex Offenders and Public Policy*. New York: Thomson Gale.

McAlinden, A. N. (2007) *The Shaming of Sexual Offenders: Risk, Retribution, and Reintegration*. Oxford: Hart Publishing.

Morris, A. and Gelsthorpe, L. (2000) 'Re-visioning men's violence against female partners', *Howard Journal*, 39: 412.

PFML (2008a) Online at: www.parentsformeganslaw.org, 1 October 2008.

PFML (2008b) Online at: www.parentsformeganslaw.org/public/statistics_childSexualAbuse.html, 1 October 2008.

Prescott, D. S. (ed) (2006) *Risk Assessment of Youth who have Sexually Abused: Theory, Controversy, and Emerging Strategies*. Oklahoma City: Wood and Barnes.

Quinsey, V. L., Harris, G. T., Rice, M. E. and Cormier, C. A. (1998) *Violent Offenders: Managing and Appraising Risk*. Washington DC: American Psychological Association.

Radford B. (2008) 'Americans exaggerate threats posed by sexual predators', in L. M. Zoot (ed.) *Sex Offenders and Public Policy*. New York: Thomson Gale.

Rich, P. (2002) *Survey Results: Student Self Reports of Sexually Aggressive Behaviors, 2002*. Available from Stetson School, Inc. 455 South Street, Barre, MA 01005.

Rich, P. (2003) *Understanding, Assessing and Rehabilitating Juvenile Sexual Offenders*. New Jersey: John Wiley.

Righthand, S. and Welch, C. (2001) *Juveniles who have Sexually Offended: A Review of the Professional Literature*. Washington, DC: Office of Juvenile Justice and Delinquency Prevention, US Department of Justice.

Sample, L. L. (2001) 'The social construction of the sex offender', doctorial dissertation, unpublished.

Sample, L. L. and Bray T. M. (2003) 'Are sex offenders dangerous?', *Criminology and Public Policy*, 3(1): 59–82.

Schultz P. D. (2008) 'Treating sex offenders makes sense', in L. M. Zott (ed.) *Sex Offenders and Public Policy*. New York: Thomson Gale.

Schwartz, M. D. and DeKeseredy, W. S. (1997) *Sexual Assault on Campus: The Role of Male Peer Support*. Thousand Oaks, CA: Sage.

Seagrave, D. and Grisso, T. (2002) 'Adolescent development and the measurement of juvenile psychopathology', *Law and Human Behavior*, 26: 219–39.

Serin, R. C. and Brown, S. L. (2000) 'The clinical use of the Hare psychopathy checklist – revised in contemporary risk assessment', in C. G. Gacono (ed.) *The Clinical and Forensic Aassessment of Psychopathy*. Mahwah, NJ: Lawrence Erlbaum Associates (pp. 251–68).

Seto, M. C. and Lalumiere, M. L. (2006) 'Conduct problems and juvenile sexual offending', in H. E. Barbaree and W. L. Marshall (eds) *The Juvenile Sex Offender*, 2nd edn. New York: Guildford Press (pp. 166–88).

Sipe, R., Jenson, E. L. and Everett, R. S. (1998) 'Adolescent sexual offenders grown up: Recidivism in young adulthood', *Criminal Justice and Behavior*, 25: 109–24.

Smallbone, S. W. (2006) 'Social and psychological factors in the development of delinquency and sexual deviance', in H. E. Barbaree and W. L. Marshall (eds) *The Juvenile Sex Offender*, 2nd edn. New York: Guildford Press (pp. 105–27).

Trivits L. C. and Repucci, N. D. (2002) 'Application of Megan's Law to Juveniles', *American Psychologist*, 57: 690–704.

USA Today (2008) www.usatoday.com/news/nation/2007-11-18-homeless-offenders_N.htm.

Weinrott, M. R. (1996) *Juvenile Sexual Aggression: A Critical Review*, Center Paper 005. Boulder, CO: University of Colorado, Center for the Study and Prevention of Violence.

White, J. W., Kadlec, K. M. and Sechrist, S. (2006) 'Adolescent sexual aggression within heterosexual relationships', in H. E. Barbaree and W. L. Marshall (eds) *The Juvenile Sex Offender*, 2nd edn. New York: Guilford Press (pp. 128–47).

Williams, A. and Thompson, B. (2004a) 'Vigilance or vigilantes: the Paulsgrove riots and policing paedophiles in the Community, part 1: the long slow fuse', *Police Journal*, 77: 99–119.

Williams, A. and Thompson, B. (2004b) 'Vigilance or vigilantes: the Paulsgrove riots and policing paedophiles in the community, part 2: the lessons of Paulsgrove', *Police Journal*, 77: 199–205.

Worling, J. R. and Langstram, N. (2003) 'Assessment of criminal recidivism risk with adolescents who have offended sexually', *Trauma, Violence and Abuse*, 4(4): 341–62.

Worling, J. R. and Langstrom, N. (2006) 'Risk of sexual recidivism in adolescent who offend sexually: correlates and assessment', in H. E. Barbaree and W. L. Marshall (eds) *The Juvenile Sex Offender*, 2nd edn. New York: Guilford Press (pp. 219–47).

Zgoba, K. M. (2004) 'Spin doctors and moral crusaders: the moral panic behind child safety legislation', *Criminal Justice Studies*, 17(4): 385–40.

Zott, L. M. (ed.) (2008) *Sex Offenders and Public Policy*. New York: Thomson Gale.

Legal cases

Artway v Attorney General (1996) 872 F. Supp. 66 – D.N.J. 1995; 81F 3rd 1235

Artway v Attorney General of New Jersey (1996) 64 USLW 2707: 81 F.3d 1235

Connecticut Dept. of Public Safety v Doe (2003) 538 U.S. 1

Cox Broadcasting v Cohn (1975) 420 U.S. 469, 470

Doe v Phillips (2008) 194 S.W.3d 837

Doe v Poritz (1995) 662 A.2d 367 N.J.

Smith v Doe (2003) 01-729 538 U.S. 84, 259 F.3d 979

State v Babin (1994) 637 So 2d 814 – La. App. 1st Cir. Louisiana

State v Bani (2001) 36 P.3d 1255. Hawaii

Websites

http://az.gov/webapp/offender/main.do

www3.state.id.us/cgi-bin/newidst?sctid=180830026.K

http://www.meganslaw.ca.gov/disclaimer.aspx?lang=ENGLISH

http://criminaljustice.state.ny.us/nsor/search_index.htm

www.parentsformeganslaw.org

Chapter 15

The preventive state: when is prevention of harm harmful?

Eric Janus

The statute is designed to confine an extremely limited number of dangerous and mentally abnormal persons because they are too dangerous to be at large, where the criminal justice system has failed in its duty to protect society ... (Brooks 1992: 735)

(A) majority [of Guantánamo detainees] will be held in some kind of prolonged detention ... administration officials have said that some detainees cannot be prosecuted but are too dangerous to release. (Finn 2009)

Introduction

Subsequent to 1990, laws based on prevention have taken a serious turn, a change in paradigm that, I assert, brings many dangers. Spreading rapidly, this new form of social control can come to dominate our polity, creating a ominous presence – the preventive state (Steiker 1998: 744). This chapter examines the new type of prevention, and assesses its risks.

Protection from harm is generally a good. It is the ubiquitous – and proper – purpose of state regulation. It is a large part of the reason for government. But prevention in the last two decades has taken the wrong fork in the road. A public health approach to prevention would have produced comprehensive and systematic, empirically-based campaigns to understand and change the root causes of violence. Instead, we have adopted counter-empirical, interstitial laws designed to identify and remove risky persons before they can cause harm.

I want to identify the factors in this new type of prevention that make it harmful. I am interested in identifying the kinds of prevention that are inherently dangerous – not dangerous contingently. For example, the criminal law is a primary vehicle in the prevention of harm. The criminal law can be used well or poorly – it can be too harsh or too lenient – but these are contingent problems, not based on some inherent flaw in the system that we call the criminal law. But other approaches to prevention, I claim, do have an inherent danger. Many of the laws developed in the United States to address 'sexual predators' fall into this category (see Thompson and Greek, this volume). It is not that these laws lack a legitimate purpose – their purpose (the prevention of sexual violence) is not only legitimate, but is also critical. It is not that they cannot be well or poorly executed. Rather, I will argue, there is an inherent danger in their structure that cannot be cured through wise administration or design. In short, I will claim that the legal innovations of the late twentieth century are harbingers of a 'preventive state'. These laws provide the conditions, a template, in which a cancerous meme can expand and devour precious limits on government power that are central to our liberal democratic way of life. I identify this new form of prevention as 'radical prevention'.

Perhaps the key feature of 'radical prevention' is its claim to exemption from the suite of constitutional constraints that the United States has developed over the years to limit governmental power, particularly in the criminal justice system. In place of the usual rules, radical prevention sets up an alternate system of social control, subject to a different set of rules that are more tolerant of governmental deprivation of liberty. It is based on an argument of necessity: certain people are 'too dangerous' to be at large, and thus the usual rules need to be abandoned because they will obstruct the task of protecting us from this high level of danger. In this sense, these new schemes are called by some 'counter-legal' because they are specifically designed to circumvent the usual legal rules governing the deprivation of liberty (Ericson 2007: 24).

It will not have gone unnoticed that the rules to be abandoned are 'constitutional' rules, and one might think that this sort of rule – being constitutional – is not so easily abandoned. But it is not that simple. The constitutional texts that constrain state power are (at least in the United States) aimed at placing limits on the powers of the government in the criminal justice context. Radical prevention systems claim to be something else. Though they take away liberty in a comprehensive way, and the resulting confinement looks for all the world identical to criminal punishment, these alternate systems claim that they are not 'criminal' and therefore are not bound by the constitutional constraints on the power to punish. Indeed, nothing in the Constitution of the United States explicitly says that the highly constrained criminal justice system is the only system that can take away people's liberty.

This textual lacuna is underscored by the existence of two exceptions to the criminal justice constraints – public health and mental health powers – that are traditional and well accepted, yet not explicitly permitted in the Constitution. Added to this are some fundamental ambiguities, explored below, in what we mean when we talk about the deprivation of liberty. As a result, the legitimacy of exempting certain types of harm from the strict criminal justice rules is somewhat complex and problematic. The lack of bright line boundaries on the power of the state to deprive people of liberty contributes to the urgency of understanding the aspects of radical prevention that make it inherently dangerous.

I argue that there are three aspects of radical prevention that, in combination, make it inherently harmful. First, radical prevention rests on 'risk' as the predicate for government intervention. Second, because radical prevention schemes seek exemption from the normal rules, they must conform to the principle of exceptionality (Agamben 2005: 1–6; Ericson 2007: 26). Third, when combined with the first two conditions, a 'politics of prevention' inevitably pushes radical prevention towards excess and distortion. Taken together, these three factors unmoor governmental intervention from some of the key benchmarks – moral as well as legal – that serve as a natural brake on excessive government power.

When courts and commentators talk about 'deprivation of liberty', they can mean it in two subtly different ways. Understanding, and clarifying, this ambiguity will assist in our discussion. A starting point for this discussion is the 1905 US Supreme Court case of *Jacobson v Massachusetts*. Henning Jacobson refused vaccination for smallpox, 'claiming that he and his son had had bad reactions to earlier vaccinations' (Mariner *et al.* 2005: 582). Pursuant to the applicable statute, he was convicted of failing to be vaccinated, and fined $5. He appealed to the Massachusetts Supreme Judicial Court, which upheld the fine against a challenge that it violated Jacobson's constitutional rights. On review, the US Supreme Court rejected Jacobson's challenge (*Jacobson v Massachusetts*, 1905).

There are several points about *Jacobson* that are noteworthy. Least of these is that the court upheld the statute against constitutional challenge, for there was not much doubt that the 'police power' of the states was broad enough to cover important public health measures (Mariner *et al.* 2005: 582). More noteworthy was that the court acknowledged that the right to refuse the vaccination was part of the 'liberty' interest that was protected in the Constitution, an interest that comprised 'a sphere within which the individual may assert the supremacy of his own will and rightfully dispute the authority of any human government, especially of any free government existing under a written constitution' (*Jacobson v Massachusetts*, 1905: 29). The court characterised the vaccination requirement as a 'restraint' of that liberty, but justified because 'the rights of the individual in respect of his liberty may at times, under the pressure of great dangers, be subjected to such restraint, to be enforced by reasonable regulations, as the safety of the general public may demand' (*Jacobson v Massachusetts*, 1905: 29). Unsurprisingly, the court went on to hold that the prevention of smallpox through vaccination was one such circumstance (*Jacobson v Massachusetts*, 1905: 39).

Two decades later, *Jacobson* was cited as constitutional support for the forced sterilisation of allegedly mentally deficient women in the infamous case of *Buck v Bell* (1927). Citing *Jacobson* as its main authority, the US Supreme Court said: 'We have seen more than once that the public welfare may call upon the best citizens for their lives ... The principle that sustains compulsory vaccination is broad enough to cover cutting the Fallopian tubes ... Three generations of imbeciles are enough' (*Buck v Bell*, 1927: 207).

I shall have more to say about the progression from *Jacobson* to *Buck*. Here, it is enough to point out that to use *Jacobson* as precedent for forced sterilisation required multiple transformations, not the least of which was a shift from one type of 'restraint' on liberty to another. In *Jacobson*, there was no provision in the statute to actually force vaccination on anyone, a point that was central to the Massachusetts Supreme Judicial Court, whose decision turned precisely on this point: 'If a person should deem it important that vaccination should not be performed in his case, and the authorities should think otherwise, it is not in their power to vaccinate him by force, and the worst that could happen to him under the statute would be the payment of $5' (Mariner *et al.* 2005: 582).

Buck, in contrast, involved forced surgery – cutting the fallopian tubes. The Massachusetts statute deprived Mr Jacobson of his liberty in the way that most laws do: they prohibit certain conduct, and establish a penalty for those who are convicted of violating the prohibition. *Buck*, on the other hand, enforced the law in a way that few laws do: directly on the body of the individual. All state regulation, all criminal prohibitions, deprive people of their liberty. Mostly, the deprivation is indirect: citizens face a criminal prohibition, and make a choice whether to obey or to violate and take the chance of a criminal penalty. Contrast this with the deprivation of liberty suffered by Carrie Buck on the operating table: the distinction is not simply the vastly different level of intrusion, but also because of the means of enforcement – direct enforcement on the body of the individual. The progression is a fateful one. Instead of standing merely for the rather uncontroversial proposition that the state could design criminal prohibitions for the good of the public, *Jacobson*, as transformed in *Buck*, became authority for the direct, physical, pre-crime incapacitation of individuals for the good of the public.

This expanded meaning of *Jacobson* was solidified in the 1975 concurrence of Chief Justice Burger in *O'Connor v Donaldson*, a mental illness civil commitment case in which he said, citing *Jacobson*: 'There can be little doubt that in the exercise of its police power a State may confine individuals solely to protect society from the dangers of significant antisocial acts or communicable disease' (*O'Connor v Donaldson*, 1975: 582–3). The transformation of *Jacobson* continued and was strengthened in *Kansas v Hendricks* (1997), a case in which the court approved sexual predator commitment laws. This time, the court was explicit in transforming *Jacobson* into a case involving 'physical restraint' in the 'civil context' (*Kansas v Hendricks*, 1997: 346). 'There are', the court stated, 'manifold restraints to which every person is necessarily subject for the common good' (*Kansas v. Hendricks*, 1997: 357). But, as in *Buck* and *O'Connor*, the court did not in any way explain the radical progression from *Jacobson*'s straightforward holding, approving a prohibition in the criminal law, to the much more radical legitimating of civil pre-crime deprivation of liberty. I shall suggest below that the transformation contains the seeds comprising the danger of radical prevention.

A taxonomy of liberty deprivation

I propose three major modes of liberty deprivation. The first, and most ubiquitous, is the criminal law, referred to by the Supreme Court as the 'charge and conviction' paradigm (*Foucha v Louisiana*, 1992: 82). This, according to the Supreme Court, is the 'ordinary' and 'the normal means of dealing with persistent criminal conduct' (*Foucha v Louisiana*, 1992: 82). The criminal process involves restrictions on liberty in both senses discussed above. Pre-crime, liberty is deprived, but only in the sense of legislative prohibition that creates the deterrence of threatened future punishment. The physical imposition of the deprivations, 'forcing' the deprivation of liberty, takes place only after charge and conviction of a crime.

Attached to this ordinary criminal process is a suite of constraints on government power: the principle of legality (or *nulla poena sine lege*) (Jeffries 1985: 190); the prohibitions against double jeopardy (*United States v Halper*, 1989: 440) and *ex post facto* laws (*Collins v Youngblood*, 1990: 41–2); *Artway v Attorney General*, 1995; *Young v Weston*, 1995); the rights to juries as fact finders (*Duncan v Louisiana*, 1968: 149), to witness confrontation (LaFave *et al.* 1999, §24.4(b)), and to the highest standard of proof (*In re Winship*, 1970); the requirement that the crime be manifest in some act (*actus reus*) with criminal intent (*mens rea*) (Torcia 1993: §25, 27); the prohibition against criminalizing a status (Robinson 1993) and on basing criminal conviction on predicted, rather than committed, crimes (LaFave and Scott 1986: §3.2); immunity from self-incrimination (LaFave *et al.* 1999: §6.5(a)); prohibitions on arrest and search in the absence of some cause to believe that a specific crime has been committed (Bergman and Duncan 2007: §23.6); and the requirement that prosecutions be based on written charges specifying the law and the facts constituting the crime (*American Jurisprudence* 2008).

The second category, which I refer to as radical prevention, departs from the criminal paradigm in that it imposes pre-crime confinement. Prevention is accomplished not through deterrence but through physical confinement in anticipation of harm. Because it is an 'elementary' principle that the 'justification for the criminal process and the unique deprivation of liberty which it can impose requires that it be invoked only for commission of a specific offense prohibited by legislative enactment' (*O'Connor v Donaldson*, 1975: 586), this sort of 'pre-crime' deprivation of liberty may not be (and, by definition, is not) part of the criminal process – it must be 'civil'. Put another way, pre-crime confinement does not require a conviction, and therefore may not involve punishment (*Foucha v Louisiana*, 1992: 84–6).

By eschewing the intent to punish (and thereby the 'criminal' label), the state frees itself from most of the constraints listed above. Because of this, one might think that schemes authorising pre-crime confinement might be hard to justify, especially because the conditions of confinement in pre-crime detention facilities often look astonishingly like post-crime (criminal) confinement. But courts have been tolerant of governmental protestations of a non-punitive purpose, accepting at face value official avowals that the razor-wire barriers around pre-crime facilities are intended to incapacitate (and perhaps secondarily to facilitate 'treatment') rather than to punish (*Kansas v Hendricks*, 1997; *In re Commitment of Travis*, 2009).

There is a third, hybrid form, which I will designate 'control orders'. These orders are directed at particular individuals, deemed or proved to be 'dangerous'. The orders set restrictions on the individual's liberties, and are enforceable by criminal punishment. In general, the restrictions prohibit activities that are not themselves inherently dangerous or risky, but are thought to be precursors of criminal acts. Thus, these schemes lack several of the normal indicia of the criminal system. Their prohibitions are not pre-described by law, and do not apply to the broad population uniformly. In addition, because the activities they prohibit are not inherently risky or dangerous, they can be said to lack the requirement of *mens rea* (Ericson 2007: 211).

Radical prevention in the United States

In the United States, radical prevention schemes have been targeted at two vaguely defined (but clearly labelled) out-groups: paedophiles (or more broadly, sexual predators) and terrorists. In both arenas, the legality of the liberty deprivation schemes has been hotly litigated, and is highly problematic. But the core idea justifying the schemes is the same: that the normal 'charge and conviction' paradigm of the criminal law is inadequate for addressing the risks posed by members of these groups, and this necessitates an alternate system for liberty deprivation outside the charge and conviction paradigm. In both cases, the formula for liberty deprivation is a two-factor formula: risk plus status. In the terrorism arena, the status is nominally 'terrorist' or 'enemy combatant', though arguably it is foreign and Muslim (McCulloch and Pickering 2009: 635; Ericson 2007: 36–71; Cole 2009; Ansari 2005; Hagopian 2004; Harris 2002). In the other case, the status is generally characterised as 'mentally disordered', 'mentally abnormal' or 'sexual predator'.

Sexual predator laws

Beginning in 1989, jurisdictions in the United States enacted a series of laws that have come to be known as sexual predator laws. These laws are part of a larger set of developments in which laws addressing sexual abuse have been revised, reformed and strengthened. These developments reflect a number of underlying themes, but the most explicit and visible is a heightened societal concern about the safety of women and children, in particular from sexual assault (Janus 2006: 75–92).

Many of the reforms have been in the criminal justice system. The innovations generally referred to as sexual predator laws are outside of that system, and it is in that way that they are counter-law. In the US, these counter-laws have taken three major forms. Sex offender commitment laws, often referred to as sexually violent predator (SVP) laws, use the form of traditional mental health civil commitment to control (most often by physical confinement) sex offenders who are found to have a mental disorder that impairs their ability to control their behaviour, and who for that reason pose a risk of future sexual harm. Twenty states have enacted SVP laws. Registration and notification laws impose on sex offenders an ongoing obligation (often decades long) to register with law enforcement, and an obligation on public authorities to notify the public (or some portion of the public) about the presence of offenders (Logan 2009). Because of federal mandates, all 50 states have registration and notification laws. Residential restrictions limit the areas in which sex offenders can live (Yung 2008). In recent years, at least 23 states and hundreds of local governments have passed laws that prohibit registered sex offenders from living within specified areas of a community (Laney 2008: 18–26). Often, restricted zones are based on areas where children are likely to congregate, such as parks, playgrounds, recreation centres, swimming pools, schools, bus stops, libraries, convenience stores, nursing homes, and places of worship (for an expansion on these laws and prohibitions see Thompson and Greek, this volume).

Terrorism laws

In the United States, prevention as a response to terrorism has taken two major forms in the late twentieth and early twenty-first centuries. The first, identified by Professor Robert Chesney (2005: 26–7), is the government's adoption, following 9/11, of a 'prevention paradigm' in its criminal justice efforts to combat terrorism. Symbolised by the USA Patriot Act, this approach comprises the aggressive use of the criminal law to effectuate prevention. This has been accomplished by attenuating the requirement that acts – to be defined as criminal – need to have some significant proximity to real harm (Ericson 2007: 36–71). But despite this paradigm shift, these approaches have been firmly grounded in the criminal justice system (Zabel and Benjamin 2008).

The archetype of the second category of anti-terrorism approaches is Guantánamo. The government has claimed the right to detain indefinitely individuals based on a status, 'enemy combatant'. Substantial pressure to close Guantánamo and regularise the status of the detainees has led to a vigorous debate about detention without criminal trial, in which a number of commentators have pointed to the SVP laws as constitutional precedent for such an alternative system of justice (Cole 2009).

Public health and mental health laws

Two forms of radical prevention are not new, and are widely thought to be unproblematic from a constitutional perspective. Traditional civil commitment laws exert non-criminal control over individuals with severe mental illness. Public health laws authorise comprehensive and direct deprivations of liberty, in the form of quarantine, isolation and perhaps mandatory vaccination, to prevent widespread contagion (Mariner *et al.* 2005: 581–2; Richards 1989: 332–7). But there is general acknowledgement that even these laws have serious substantive limits on, for example, their power to force individuals to be medicated or vaccinated against their wills (Mariner *et al.* 2005: 586–7; *Jarvis v Levine*, 1988).

Historical prevention laws

The United States has a long history of alternative systems of justice that seek to segregate or otherwise incapacitate 'dangerous' persons, often identified by their membership in outsider groups. In liberal democracies, the full panoply of rights is reserved not for all, but for 'we the people'. '"Heathens" and "infidels" were legally presumed to lack the rational capacity necessary to assume an equal status or to exercise equal rights' (Williams 1990). Jim Crow laws are perhaps the most notorious example, along with the Japanese exclusion orders. Other such laws include eugenics laws, vagrancy and poor laws, and laws criminalising addiction. Almost without exception, over the years these approaches have been soundly rejected, either by the courts (*Papachristou v Jacksonville*, 1972; *Robinson v California*, 1962), or by public opinion (Civil Liberties Act of 1988).

Control orders

In the United States, control orders have been most commonly used to address domestic violence (Ver Steegh 2000), though recently the state of Texas has enacted an 'outpatient' sexually violent predator law that bears close resemblance to control order schemes (Civil Commitment of Sexually Violent Predators 1999). Historically, some US jurisdictions authorised the use of 'peace orders'. In Australia, preventative detention orders allow law enforcement officers to hold suspects for up to fourteen days to prevent acts of terrorism or the destruction of evidence related to such actions. While these individuals are detained, 'prohibited contact' orders prevent the detainee from contacting any person named in the order (White 2008). In the United Kingdom, the Prevention of Terrorism Act 2005 allows for similar measures to be taken with terrorist suspects. The House of Lords held that the Act does not violate the provisions of the European Convention on Human Rights (*Secretary of State for the Home Department v JJ*, 2007).

What is the problem with radical prevention?

The undesirable qualities of prevention emerge most strongly when the underlying legal structure comprises three characteristics. The first factor is present when 'risk' replaces 'guilt' as the predicate for state intervention. The second is present when the legal regime relies on some assertion of exceptionalism for its legitimacy. And the third factor is what I will term the 'politics of prevention'. These factors are present most strongly in what I have labelled radical prevention, schemes that directly and severely intrude on individual liberty pre-crime. When these three factors combine, prevention becomes virulent and dangerous because it lacks the essential limits against arbitrary government deprivation of liberty.

Risk

In radical prevention schemes, risk, as an attribute of persons, replaces guilt as the predicate element whose proof triggers intervention. In ordinary prevention regulation, risk plays a ubiquitous role – but it is risk as an attribute of behaviour (or things), rather than as a characteristic of a person, that is the active ingredient.

Guilt must be replaced by risk in the radical prevention schemes, because these schemes eschew the criminal paradigm, whose key characteristics are deterrence and retribution, the latter a concept bottomed on guilt. Further, the radical prevention schemes are designed to prevent future harm, and the only way that future harm justifies present detention is by conceptualising risk as a characteristic of the person rather than of behaviour (this is embodied in risk assessment techniques – see Williams, this volume). It is only by conceptualising risk as a quality of the individual – more or less enduring, in the same manner that 'intelligence' is more or less enduring – that predictions can sensibly be made.

Because these laws are based on risk as an enduring trait of persons, they escape from one of the key self-limiting features of criminal intervention – the principle of proportionality (Richards 1989; Frase 2005). In the criminal justice system, the proportionality of the duration of liberty deprivation can be roughly proportional to the person's culpability for a particular historical act. But detention based on risk, if justified at one moment in time, will be justified in the next as well, if the risk remains constant. The cumulative burden of detention over time is irrelevant. Since risk is conceptualised as a stable trait, it is not surprising that many risk-based detentions are tantamount to life detention. Thus, unlike many instances of mental health or public health interventions, where treatments can mitigate risk, many radical prevention schemes lack a key form of built-in self-limitation (Richards 1989).

Risk presents itself as a morally neutral concept, a natural artefact susceptible to scientific investigation and measurement. But this apparent scientific neutrality masks strong normative judgements about which risks demand responses, and which do not, based on complex factors (Gardner 2009: 102–24; Sunstein 2005). The danger is that the patina of science in risk assessment hides the normative nature of the judgements, supporting facile arguments that the judgements are scientific rather than political. In contrast, the normative judgements in the criminal law are plainly on display (Janus 1997). Risk-based pre-crime detention schemes require ever broadening systems of surveillance. In traditional post-crime schemes, state intervention is triggered by the commission of a crime. Police activity is directed at identifying the perpetrator and collecting evidence to obtain a conviction. Principles of probable cause limit the intrusive gathering of evidence to a narrow group of persons who have some observable connection to the crime. But in pre-crime, risk-based systems, the focus shifts. The group at 'risk' of committing a future crime is, by definition, substantially larger than the group of individuals who actually commit a crime. And the identification of 'at risk' groups requires gathering information on even larger groups. In the SVP laws, surveillance is most intense among those who have been convicted of a sex crime. But this is a contingent limitation, and there is nothing about the notion of surveillance and risk detection that would prevent the deployment of a broader net utilising screening tools to identify individuals, perhaps children or adolescents, with the psychological profile of a future sex offender. In the national security arena, such broad-based screening has already taken root. For example, the Automated Targeting System is an 'approach for data management, analysis, rules-based risk management' in which 'every traveller' entering the United States is 'subject to a real-time rule based evaluation' to develop individual 'risk assessment scores' (US Department of Homeland Security 2006).

Risk as a characteristic of persons is paradoxically both individual and group based. Both aspects have harmful consequences. Radical prevention laws seek to intervene with respect to individuals, and therefore demand individualised risk assessments. These types of assessments provide tools that rank risks, and thus facilitate a search for the riskiest, the worst of the worst, the potential sources of catastrophic harm. This search for the 'riskiest' directs attention away from root causes toward downstream harms, distracts attention from the more common and ubiquitous forms of harm, and valorises tertiary rather than primary interventions. This distraction is exacerbated by the scientific tools for risk assessment, which focus on identifying factors that are correlated with – rather than cause – risk. Focus on individual risk thus leads to downstream interventions and away from interventions that seek to change root causes of harm. At the same time as risk is conceived as an individual characteristic, it is measured and quantified using group-based methodologies. In this way, risk-based interventions encourage and legitimate 'profiling', or assigning risk to individuals based on characteristics that place them in a 'group' that is associated with a measured historical frequency of violence (Savage 2009).

Both aspects of risk – individual and group based – contribute to the process of reification of risk as an enduring, internal attribute of persons – a quality of who the person 'is'. If group risk is to be attributed to an individual member of the group, the membership must be understood as based on some real differentiating characteristic of the individual. Group-based reasoning contributes to the notion that individuals who pose 'risk' are different in kind from the norm. This conclusion, in turn, supports, and is supported by, the principle of exceptionalism, to which we turn.

Exceptionalism

Radical prevention schemes set up alternative systems of justice that demand limitation. The criminal justice system – the charge and conviction paradigm – derives its legitimacy in large measure from the tightness of the constraints it imposes on governmental power. The availability of an alternative system of social control allows escape from those constraints. Unless those escapes are bounded, the existence of the alternative system poses a threat to the rights of all. If legislatures or courts ground such systems on broadly expandable factors – such as risk – they have, in effect, approved of a method for a radical expansion of governmental power to deprive citizens of their liberty. This is a politically untenable position.

Thus, in order to preserve the legitimacy – or at least the appearance of legitimacy – of the state's social control enterprise (and in particular, the criminal justice system), alternative systems of control must be authoritatively and persuasively described as exceptional. The US Supreme Court expressed this notion clearly in *Foucha* (1992). It described the 'charge and conviction' system as the 'normal means' of dealing with criminal conduct. A state wishing to depart from this norm must justify the departure by 'explain[ing] why its interest would not be vindicated by the ordinary criminal processes involving charge and conviction' (*Foucha*, 1992: 82). The court directly warned against 'substituting confinements for dangerousness for our present system which, with only narrow exceptions and aside from permissible confinements for mental illness, incarcerates only those who are proved beyond reasonable doubt to have violated a criminal law' (*Foucha*, 1992: 83). And the Minnesota Supreme Court stated the principle of exceptionality even more clearly, declaring that 'the judiciary has a constitutional duty to intervene before civil commitment becomes the norm and criminal prosecution the exception' (*In re Linehan*, 1996: 181).

There are several ways in which an alternate legal system might be legitimised as exceptional. The government might claim that some 'emergency' requires a departure from the usual limits on its power. An emergency, as an exceptional state, is by definition temporally or geographically limited (Gross 2000: 1834). Second, a statutory scheme might claim exception because it belongs to a traditionally recognised alternative system of prevention, such as mental health commitment or public health commitment. Third, the principle of exceptionality might be satisfied because the individuals or group to whom the alternative system applies are exceptional – 'outsider' groups distinguishable or distinguished from the 'norm', and thereby un-entitled to full participation in the rights inherent in citizenship in a liberal democracy.

Though all three of these sorts of claims are made for the radical prevention schemes currently in vogue, there is good evidence that the real, operative claim for exception is the third. The first category of exceptionality, based on the claim that extraordinary danger requires exceptions to the normal constitutional order, is exemplified in laws as mundane as curfews or evacuation orders, or as consequential as the Japanese exclusion orders. But there is good reason to think, as I suggest below, that this sort of justification lacks enduring appeal in that ordinary citizens begin to feel vulnerable as they see themselves as potential targets for such state power expansions.

The second form of justification – reliance on traditional forms of preventive detention – is of limited utility in justifying exceptional laws because these traditional forms are very narrow. The last – establishing an outsider jurisprudence – unfortunately has resonance in American jurisprudence, and appears to be a persuasive rhetorical ploy in ameliorating public and political worry about exceptional exercises of government power.

Outsider jurisprudence has strong roots in American jurisprudence, and, some argue, in the very foundations of liberal democracies (Janus 2006: 101–9; Young 1992). But the civil rights revolution has taken its toll on the ideology of difference. So, it is rare in proper conversation to hear a frank acknowledgement that some outside group occupies a degraded position in the civic polity. But radical prevention schemes are providing a template for reinvigorating this discredited and dangerous jurisprudence. In a rare explicit invocation of this principle, political scientist Jeffrie G. Murphy argued for an alternate system of justice for 'psychopaths' in his 1983 essay 'Moral death: A Kantian essay on psychopathy'. 'Psychopaths', he wrote, 'are morally dead, and hence not entitled to be treated as "persons"'. They don't merit 'that special kind of respect which is entailed by a moral commitment to justice rather than mere utility' (Murphy 1972).

The same reasoning underlies many of the court decisions approving radical prevention schemes for sex offenders. For example, in upholding Minnesota's sex psychopath law in 1939, the Minnesota Supreme Court characterised the targets of the law as 'types of "unnaturals"' (*State ex rel. Pearson v Prob. Ct. of Ramsey County*, 1939: 299). Decades later, in *Crane*, the US Supreme Court held that the mental condition required for commitment 'must be sufficient to distinguish the dangerous sexual offender whose serious mental illness, abnormality, or disorder subjects him to civil commitment from the dangerous but typical recidivist convicted in an ordinary criminal case' (*Kansas v Crane*, 2002: 413).

Two mini case studies will support the assertion that it is the outsider logic that has the enduring power to legitimise radical prevention. First, consider a contemporary example, comparing public reaction to two forms of radical prevention: SVP commitment laws of the early 1990s, and the proposed Model State Emergency Health Powers Act (MSEHPA), proposed after the 9/11 attacks. Both forms adopted radical prevention approaches to serious societal threats – sexual violence in the former case, and the potential for uncontrolled contagion from natural or terrorist causes in the second. Arguably, the threat from the second exceeded that from the first, at least in terms of the extent of potential harm. Also, the MSEHPA was more squarely in line with historical conceptions of state power than the SVP laws. No one seriously contests the state's power to control contagion through the tools of quarantine and isolation, while the SVP laws audaciously stretched a historical legal form – mental health commitment – to cover an area more traditionally in the remit of the criminal law. Yet the MSEHPA provoked substantial public outcry, while politicians and the news media rushed to support SVP laws. Much of the critique of the MSEHPA came from right-wing libertarian fringe groups, to be sure (A 'news' article on the WorldNetDaily website was headlined: 'Police State, USA: Bill Would give Governors Absolute Power; Health-emergency proposal has "little concern" for personal liberties'). But even mainstream groups, such as the legislature of the state of Minnesota, insisted on provisions in the state version of the MSEHPA that were far more protective of civil liberties than laws governing HIV and TB and sexual offenders (Individual Refusal of Treatment 2005; Preventive Measures under Health Order 1997; Health Threat Procedures 1995; Judicial Commitment Pre-hearing Examination 2005). The only explanation for the more vehement concern about the MSEHPA was that it was directed at the populace as a whole, rather than an identifiable and despised outsider group.

As a second example, consider again the early twentieth century progression from *Jacobson v Massachusetts* to *Buck v Bell*. As mentioned above, in *Jacobson*, the US Supreme Court upheld the constitutionality of a law requiring everyone to receive smallpox vaccinations, enforced by the threat of misdemeanour prosecution, punishable by a fine of $5. The public safety rationale for the regulation was plain, the intrusion on liberty minimal, and the enforcement mechanism unremarkable (*Jacobson*, 1905). *Jacobson* was the central authority some twenty years later in *Buck v Bell*. In *Buck*, the court upheld the forced sterilisation of 'mentally defective' people (1927: 207). From *Jacobson* to *Buck*, the regulation moved from scientifically sound to scientifically dubious; from mildly intrusive to radically intrusive; and from enforcement via normal regulatory means to direct enforcement outside of the charge and conviction system. One could argue that the court in *Buck* had simply loosened its standards for approving restrictions on liberty (Mariner *et al.* 2005: 584). But it can hardly be seen as immaterial that the deprivation in *Jacobson* was universally applicable, whereas in *Buck* the deprivation was limited to a degraded group clearly designated (and perceived as) outsiders, 'mental defectives' who constitute a 'kind' of people who are 'degenerate', criminal and imbecilic, and 'sap the strength of the State' (*Buck*, 1927; Markel 2003). It seems clear that the severity of the intrusion in *Buck*, enforced in an alternate legal system, could be justified only on the grounds of exceptionality.

The principle of exceptionality thus requires that radical prevention be aimed at outsider groups. These groups are marked as different in kind, rather than degree. Differences in degree suggest a continuum with arbitrary cut points, subject to political manipulation and expansion. Differences in kind, on the other hand, suggest that legal distinctions are based on 'real' or 'natural' differences among people, rather than arbitrary or political differences – thus seemingly protecting the in-group from eroding civil liberties based on policy creep. Differences in kind have natural stopping points – the boundaries of taxonomic categories. Differences in degree provide no stopping point and thus provide no assurance of real limitations on the radical prevention schemes.

'Risk' can be understood as a continuous variable, and as such is problematic as the sole predicate for radical prevention. There are two solutions to this problem. The first is to identify some other factor – such as mental disorder – that is a marker of difference. The second is the reification of risk: turning risk itself into the kind of taxonomic difference that satisfies the principle of exceptionality. The demand for exceptionality pushes us to think of risk not as a circumstantial statement about a person in a particular context, a particular stage in his or her life in a particular set of relationships and personal circumstances (Hiday 1997), but rather as a constitutional aspect of who the person is. Thus, the natural progression in justifying radical prevention schemes is for 'riskiness' to become a marker of taxonomic difference and outsider status.

This reification of risk is encouraged by the new technology of risk measurement. Actuarial risk assessment tools, standardised and research based, have the flavour of other forms of scientific testing – psychological as well as physiological – that we think of as measuring something real, stable and internal to the person. If 'riskiness' denotes something internal, stable and real in a person – a taxonomic difference – then pressure grows to identify it early, perhaps even before it is manifested in harmful action. Surveillance and screening are essential tools in the public health arsenal. The reification of risk will exert pressure to expand screening, extending it to broader segments of the population, including young children, so as to identify not only problems of development, but also the early markers of sexual predation, terrorism and other forms of deviance.

The politics of prevention

Combined with exceptionality and risk, the 'politics of prevention' provides the motive force and kinetic energy that can drive prevention to harmful extremes. The politics of prevention has several driving forces, several frames that give it its energy. Most fundamental is the lack of clear boundaries around prevention. Unlike desert-based systems, where there is a conceptually clear demarcation between guilt and innocence, risk-based detention lacks any logical, or *a priori* point at which continuously variable risk justifies intervention.

This feature of risk prevention generates and supports the notion, sometimes referred to as the precautionary principle, that any risk is too much and requires governmental intervention (Sunstein 2005: 13–108). When prevention of risk seems *possible*, it becomes obligatory (Hebenton and Seddon 2009). The logic is quite simple. If you, as a politician or a bureaucrat, *could* have done something to prevent tragedy, you *should* have done it. Of course, this way of thinking involves a logical fallacy: what looks like an inevitable and self-evident chain of events after the tragedy, was, looking from before, a low probability exercise in prediction. But the fallacy goes unnoticed. To fail to use the available tools – to respond to the available information about risk – is to commit malfeasance.

The politics of prevention depends, also, on the science of fear. Statistically equivalent risks are not politically equal risks. Texting while driving is as risky as driving while drunk – yet the tools of the criminal law are only slowly being brought to bear on the former, while the latter attracts widespread opprobrium and harsh penalties. Such examples are legion, and the causes of this differential concern are increasingly understood (Gardner 2009). When risk attains heightened salience the politics of prevention becomes a powerful force, disabling the normal deliberative and reflective mechanisms of representative democracy (Sunstein 2005). This explains the highly unusual unanimity, or near unanimity among legislators exhibited in both the sexual predator and the anti-terrorism arena. It also is manifested in the explicit and unabashed admission that empirical evidence is irrelevant when it contradicts strongly held beliefs (Gardner 2009: 110–13) – as in the unprecedented and unanimous Congressional condemnation of a peer-reviewed scientific article that dared investigate the nature of the harm caused by child sexual abuse (Abrams 1999).

In the sexual violence arena, the politics of prevention was fuelled initially by rather straightforward factors such as the dread that people feel from random violent crime. The newly developing legal schemes, with their need for exceptionality, gave new life to an old monster – the mentally deranged stranger rapist/child-molester. Whether this was an opportunistic resuscitation or a calculating one is not clear. What is clear is that the portrayal of the 'sexual predator' in this way was congruent with the culture wars of the 1990s. The sexual predator became a powerful symbol that sexual violence was aberrant rather than normal, that it was not the 'patriarchy' that allowed sexual violence to flourish (a notion favoured by feminists but reviled by social conservatives), but rather deviant, aberrational outsiders, and that people should ignore the growing body of evidence that women are statistically most at risk at home and in intimate relationships than in parking lots and dark streets (Janus 2006: 82–7).

This, then, is a further synergy that leads to excess. The risk, the politics of prevention and the principle of exceptionality reinforce each other. The principle of exceptionality requires a strengthened outsider threat to explain the need, and thereby contain the danger to the legal order posed by radical prevention. As the image of the outsider is strengthened, the sense of outrage and injustice is heightened, fuelling the politics of prevention. The lack of bright-line limits in a risk-based system allows the politics to push for more and more extreme measures. The project to insure safety, to take every last precaution, is never fully complete, because it is based on an impossible task – the prediction of rare events. Each time there is a failure, the politics of prevention seeks to locate blame (Ericson 2007: 14), and the cycle of prevention politics is re-energised.

Conclusion

Radical prevention – counter-law schemes that establish alternative justice systems of prevention – do harm in multiple ways. They distort resource allocation, focusing on individual risk rather than patterns of risk; identifying correlates for violence rather than root causes; pushing interventions further and further downstream; assessing interventions in disregard of empirical knowledge. Radical prevention has an inevitable expansiveness, as it strives fruitlessly to plug every last loophole, always seeking to prevent the next iteration of the latest catastrophe to slip through the cracks.

The logic of radical prevention is corrosive of basic principles through which liberal democracies have sought to strike a balance between liberty and security. In the switch from guilt to risk as the prime predicate of intervention, the moral force of the law is diluted, for risk – at least on the surface – is a naturalistic concept, and moral concepts are necessarily banned from consideration in setting the boundaries of legal intervention in the alternate non-criminal setting. The fact that risk, exceptionality and the politics of prevention are all highly normative is buried out of sight.

The liberty/security balance is further upset by the shift from crime detection to radical prevention. In the former, intrusive attention from the government is triggered by the commission of a crime and increasing intrusion requires increasing levels of probability linking an individual to a specific crime. In the radical prevention schemes, surveillance replaces investigation, and anyone who fits the 'profile' for risk becomes a suspect. Of necessity, the scope of surveillance broadens, as the politics of prevention pushes public officials to close every last loophole.

Perhaps the most dangerous aspect of radical prevention schemes, however, is their necessary reliance on an outsider jurisprudence. Is it a coincidence that these new laws have gained favour just as the last of the traditional outsider categories – sexual orientation – was taken off the table, struck down by the US Supreme Court in Lawrence (*Lawrence v Texas*, 2003)? The new radical prevention schemes keep the outsider template alive and well. But we should have learned that outsider jurisprudence is a powerful meme that should be exiled. As Associate Justice Alan Page of the Minnesota Supreme Court said: 'Today the target is people who are sexually dangerous. Which class of people, who are different from us and who we do not like, will it be tomorrow?' In the end, it is the replicability of the outsider template, the new legitimacy it receives, that is the enduring danger of radical prevention schemes.

Selected further reading

For more on sexual predator laws, see my book, *Failure to Protect* (Janus 2006), and LaFond (2005). Wayne Logan's *Knowledge as Power* (2009) is the authoritative text on registration and notification laws. For more on the eugenics movement and *Buck v Bell* (1927), see Lombardo (2008). For a survey of sexual violence policy from a therapeutic jurisprudence perspective, see Winick and LaFond (2003). On adolescent sexual offending, a good source is Zimring (2004). A good introduction to the statistics of sexual offending can be found in a report from Lawrence Greenfield of the US Department of Justice (1997). An excellent and dispassionate look at paedophilia is Seto (2008). For a fascinating look at the use of sexual psychopath laws against homosexual men in the 1950s, see Miller (2002). For a more technical look at assessment of sex offenders, see Campbell (2004).

References

Abrams, J. (1999) 'House condemns child sex abuse study', *Associated Press*, 12 July. Online at: www.prevent-abuse-now.com/rebuttal.htm#Lost (accessed 30 December 2009).

Agamben, G. (2005) *State of Exception* (trans. K. Attell). Chicago: University of Chicago Press.

American Jurisprudence (2008) 'Indictments and informants', 2nd edn, vol. 41. Saint Paul, MN: West Publishing.

Ansari, F. (2005) 'British anti-terrorism: a modern day witch-hunt', *Islamic Human Rights Commission*. Online at: www.ihrc.org (accessed 29 March 2007).

Bergman, B. E. and Duncan, T. M. (eds) (2007) *Wharton's Criminal Procedure*, 14th edn. Deerfield, IL: Clark Boardman Callaghan.

Brooks, A. D. (1992) 'The constitutionality and morality of civilly committing violent sexual predators', *University of Puget Sound Law Review*, 15: 709–54.

Campbell, T. (2004) *Assessing Sex Offenders: Problems and Pitfalls*. Springfield, IL: Charles C. Thomas.

Chesney, R. M. (2005) 'The sleeper scenario: terrorism-support laws and the demands of prevention', *Harvard Journal on Legislation*, 42: 1–89.

Civil Commitment of Sexually Violent Predators 1999. Stat. Ch. 841, Texas: Legislative Council.

Cole, D. (2009) 'Out of the shadows: Preventative detention, suspected terrorists, and war', *California Law Review*, 97: 693–749.

Ericson, R. V. (2007) *Crime in an Insecure World*. Malden, MA: Polity Press.

Finn, P. (2009) 'Key Democrats would let Guantanamo detainees be tried in US', *Washington Post*, 8 October, p. A7.

Frase, R. S. (2005) 'Excessive prison sentences, punishment goals, and the eighth amendment: "proportionality" relative to what?', *Minnesota Law Review*, 89: 571–651.

Gardner, D. (2009) *The Science of Fear*. New York: Plume.

Greenfield, L. (1997) *Sex Offenses and Offenders: An Analysis of Data on Rape and Sexual Assault*. US Department of Justice, Office of Justice Programs, Bureau of Justice Statistics.

Gross, O. (2000) 'The normless and exceptionless exception: Carl Schmitt's theory of emergency powers and the "norm-exception" dichotomy', *Cardozo Law Review*, 21: 1825–68.

Hagopian, E. (2004) *Civil Rights in Peril: The Targeting of Arabs and Muslims*. London: Pluto Press.

Harris, D. (2002) *Profiles of Injustice: Why Racial Profiling Cannot Work*. New York: New Press.

Health Threat Procedures 1995. Stat. § 144.4172, Minnesota: Office of the Revisor of Statutes.

Hebenton, B. and Seddon, T. (2009) 'From dangerousness to precaution: managing sexual and violent offenders in an insecure and uncertain age', *British Journal of Criminology*, 49: 343–62.

Hiday, V. A. (1997) 'Understanding the connection between mental illness and violence', *International Journal of Law and Psychiatry*, 20: 399–417.

Individual Refusal of Treatment 2005. Stat. § 12.39, subd. 1, Minnesota: Office of the Revisor of Statutes.

Janus, E. S. (1997) 'The use of science and medicine in sex offender commitments', *New England Journal of Civil and Criminal Confinement*, 23: 347–86.

Janus, E. S. (2006) *Failure to Protect: America's Sexual Predator Laws and the Rise of the Preventive State*. Ithaca, NY: Cornell University Press.

Jeffries, J. C. Jr. (1985) 'Legality, vagueness, and the construction of penal statutes', *Virginia Law Review*, 71: 189–245.

Judicial Commitment Pre-hearing Examination 2005. Stat. § 253B.07, subd. 4, Minnesota: Office of the Revisor of Statutes.

LaFave, W. R. and Scott, A. W. (1986) *Criminal Law*, 2nd edn. Saint Paul, MN: West Publishing.

LaFave, W. R., Israel, J. H. and King, N. J. (1999) *Criminal Procedure*, 2nd edn. Saint Paul, MN: West Publishing.

LaFond, J. Q. (2005) *Preventing Sexual Violence: How Society Should Cope with Sex Offenders*. Washington, DC: American Psychological Association.

Laney, G. P. (2008) *CRS Report for Congress: Residence Restrictions for Released Sex Offenders*, RL34353. Washington, DC: Congressional Research Service. Online at: www.criminallawlibraryblog.com/CRS_RPT_DomesticViolence_02-05-2008.pdf (accessed 9 November 2009).

Logan, W. A. (2009) *Knowledge as Power: Criminal Registration and Community Notification Laws in America*. Stanford, CA: Stanford Law Books.

Lombardo, P. (2008) *Three Generations, No Imbeciles: Eugenics, the Supreme Court, and Buck v. Bell*. Baltimore: Johns Hopkins University Press.

Mariner, W. K., Annas, G. J. and Glantz, L. H. (2005) '*Jacobson v. Massachusetts*: It's not your great-great-grandfather's public health law', *American Journal of Public Health*, 95(4): 581–90.

Markel, H. (2003) 'The ghost of medical atrocities: What's next, after the unveiling?', *New York Times*, 23 December p. F6.

McCulloch, J. and Pickering, S. (2009) 'Pre-crime and counter-terrorism', *British Journal of Criminology*, 49: 628–45.

Miller, N. (2002) *Sex-Crime Panic: A Journey to the Paranoid Heart of the 1950s*. Los Angeles: Alyson Publications.

Murphy, J. G. (1972) 'Moral death: a Kantian essay on psychopathy', in J. Deigh (ed.) 1992. *Ethics and Personality: Essays in Moral Psychology*. Chicago, IL: University of Chicago Press (pp. 207–22).

Preventive Measures Under Health Order 1997. Stat. § 144.4806, Minnesota: Office of the Revisor of Statutes.

Prevention of Terrorism Act 2005 (c.2), London: HMSO.

Richards, E. P. (1989) 'The jurisprudence of prevention: the right of societal self-defense against dangerous individuals', *Hastings Constitutional Law Quarterly*, 16: 329–90.

Robinson, P. H. (1993) 'Foreword: the criminal-civil distinction and dangerous blameless offenders', *Journal of Criminal Law and Criminology*, 83(4): 693–717.

Savage, C. (2009) 'Loosening of FBI rules stirs privacy concerns', *New York Times*, 29 October, p. A1.

Seto, M. C. (2008) *Pedophilia and Sexual Offending Against Children: Theory, Assessment, and Intervention*. Washington: DC: American Psychological Association.

Sunstein, C. R. (2005) *Laws of Fear: Beyond the Precautionary Principle*. Cambridge: Cambridge University Press.

Torcia, C. E. (ed.) (1993) *Wharton's Criminal Law*, 15th edn. Deerfield, IL: Clark Boardman Callaghan.

US Department of Homeland Security (2006) *Privacy Impact Assessment for the Automated Targeting System*. Washington, DC: US Department of Homeland Security.

Ver Steegh, N. (2000) 'Silent victims: children and domestic violence', *William Mitchell Law Review*, 26: 775–809.

White, L. (2008) *Terrorism Laws on Preventative Detention and Prohibited Contact Orders: Australia*. Online at: www.loc.gov/law/help/australia-preventative-detention.php (accessed 30 December 2009).

Williams, R. A. Jr. (1990) 'The American Indian in western legal thought', in L. Bender and D. Braveman (eds) (1994) *Power, Privilege and Law: A Civil Rights Reader*. Saint Paul, MN: West Publishing (pp. 169–72).

Winick, B. J. and LaFond, J. Q. (eds) (2003) *Protecting Society From Sexually Dangerous Offenders*. Washington, DC: American Psychological Association.

Young, I. M. (1992) 'Five faces of oppression', in L. Bender and D. Braveman (eds) (1994) *Power, Privilege and Law: A Civil Rights Reader*. Saint Paul, MN: West Publishing (pp. 66–80).

Yung, C. R. (2008) 'One of these laws is not like the others: why the Federal Sex Offender Registration and Notification Act raises new constitutional questions', *Harvard Journal on Legislation*, 46: 369–422.

Zabel, R. B. and Benjamin, J. J. (2008) 'In pursuit of justice: prosecuting terrorism cases in the federal courts', in *Human Rights First*. New York.

Zimring, F. E. (2004) *An American Travesty: Legal Responses to Adolescent Sexual Offending*. Chicago: University of Chicago Press.

Legal cases

Artway v Attorney General (1995) 876 F.Supp. 666 (D. N.J.)
Buck v Bell (1927) 274 US 200
Collins v Youngblood (1990) 497 U.S. 37
Duncan v Louisiana (1968) 391 U.S. 145
Foucha v Louisiana (1992) 504 U.S. 71
In re Commitment of Travis (2009) 767 N.W.2d 52 (Minn. Ct. App.)
In re Linehan (1996) 557 N.W.2d 171 (Minn.)
In re Winship (1970) 397 U.S. 358
Jacobson v Massachusetts (1905) 197 U.S. 11
Jarvis v Levine (1988) 418 NW2d 139 (Minn. S. Ct)
Kansas v Crane (2002) 534 US 407
Kansas v Hendricks (1997) 521 U.S. 346
Lawrence v Texas (2003) 539 US 558
O'Connor v Donaldson (1975) 422 U.S. 563
Papachristou v Jacksonville (1972) 405 US 156
Robinson v California (1962) 370 US 660
Secretary of State for the Home Department v JJ (2007) UKHL 45, 2007 WL 3130861
State ex rel. Pearson v Prob. Ct. of Ramsey County (1939) 287 N.W. 297 (Minn. S. Ct.)
United States v Halper (1989) 490 U.S. 435
Young v Weston (1995) No. C94-480C LEXIS 12928 (W.D. Wash.)

Part Five

Contemporary Issues in Public Protection

Introduction

Mike Nash and Andy Williams

It could be argued that public protection policy is an issue in itself, so why have a separate section? Well, we believe that there are issues that have either arisen from the growth in public protection measures or indeed are issues that are regarded as more tangential which we think should be more central. A few of those issues are dealt with here.

Mike Nellis takes us on a different journey, away from emotions to hardware and technology (although, as he notes, fading opposition to surveillance and tracking technologies may reflect a shift in feelings about their use and impact upon 'innocent' members of the public). As Nellis explains, aspects of the fading opposition may relate to a promise of a 'crime-free utopia' although the jury is very much out on this as at its best this technology may facilitate detection rather than prevention. Nellis takes us through technological developments in the UK and around the world, all the time linking this to a range of criminological theories while coining some of his own terminology such as 'technomanagerialism' when referring to the New Labour governments in the UK. He describes 'prisons without walls' and 'walking prisons' as well as zapping devices which could punish infractions instantly – the move from passive to active control. Futuristic as many of these ideas may appear, they do have a sound basis in reality, especially when that reality is driven by the financial imperatives of private companies. Clearly these electronic 'prisons' are much less expensive than the real thing and, as Nellis describes, allow policy-makers to stretch their imagination about offender control with, of course, perhaps the ultimate goal of real-time monitoring. He refers to the sex offender tracking scheme in South Korea which appears to fit this ideal (and of which the Koreans are very proud) but, in essence, it still locates an offender close to an incident rather than preventing the incident. As in other areas of policy development, the power of the public protection agenda is such that issues of rights in a surveillance society rapidly take a back seat. From its current relatively modest beginnings perhaps Nellis' message has to be to keep your eyes, as well as cameras, on this particular ball – it isn't going to disappear.

Hate as a factor in serious offending is explored by Nathan Hall. In many ways his chapter complements that of Prins, which argues for really knowing and understanding the offender. As Hall explains, it could be argued that hate crime is different from other crimes in that it is targeted at the victim's identity and may (although subject to debate) impact differentially on the way they feel about the crimes they have suffered and how they recover. What it does offer practitioners, however, if recognised, is a powerful motivator for violent and abusive behaviour – behaviour that may well be resistant to change. If assessing future risk of harm is a key aspect of public protection work then recognising hate-related attitudes, and indeed looking for them, must be an essential element of risk assessment related interviews with offenders. Hate crime offers a text for 'public' protection systems. As we know, stranger danger and unknown predators dominate our perception of the 'public at risk' – even though the reality is very different. Hate crime perpetrators at one and the same time narrow and broaden the target population. For example those who are racially biased may narrow down to a *particular* ethnic grouping but then it can be seen that *any* member of that group is vulnerable to attack. Therefore being aware of what offenders say, which organisations they affiliate to and how they dress are all crucial indicators of intent. They may not result in hate victimisation attacks but should at least be flagged up as potentially so. As Hall says, MAPPA agencies may see more of such individuals under their supervision.

Anne-Marie McAlinden discusses a topical and sensitive 'issue' – that of sex offender notification. We have dealt with this as an issue even though it is of central concern for public protection, but its high media profile makes it very topical and concerning. McAlinden describes and analyses 'what is' in terms of sex offender management and suggests that this is not conducive to effective public protection. Instead she argues that a more reintegrative or restorative approach could work. Citing evidence from around the world McAlinden suggests that even serious doubters can be persuaded that the punitive approach is not always the best approach; indeed, a number of chapters in this volume attest to changes in already hardened attitudes in the face of greater information (education) about sex offender risk. In essence she suggests that 'shame' can be understood in a number of different ways in this context and that current policy and legislation is very much about stigmatisation and exclusion rather than victim and community engagement and repair. As with much of public protection policy, the underlying assumption is that there is 'one way' of doing things, and problems and failures only result in that way being strengthened. McAlinden suggests that there are viable alternatives that should be considered – those who disagree should read Eric Janus' chapter on recent US developments.

John Grieve brings his vast experience of policing at a senior level, alongside his work on the Independent Monitoring Commission for Northern Ireland, to consider 'protecting the people' in its broadest sense. He takes the reader through a number of developments in which the police have evolved in the face of 'external' factors such as the Human Rights Act, numerous inquiries into tragedy, and legislation, requiring them to work in a multi-disciplinary way. He makes a number of points that appear in various guises throughout this volume, notably the need for as much good quality information (or intelligence) as possible, the importance of understanding the context to which that information relates, working with victims and communities to understand their perceptions and being a critical reviewer of everything. Readers might observe that policing has made huge strides in recent years as Grieve outlines a road leading to ever greater professionalism, yet he reminds us that tragedies continue to happen and for similar reasons to those of two or three decades ago. He produces a number of risk assessment methods that have resonance outside of policing and could be used by any agency with an interest in reducing harm and victimisation in our communities. The range of differing 'protection' experiences upon which this chapter is based cannot but inform a diverse range of practitioners, and indeed non-practitioners, who think about vulnerable communities and how they might be better protected.

Kerry Baker takes us into an area mentioned by Bridges and White, namely public protection work with young people. This is an area that has had little academic attention until recently, in particular the volume edited by Baker and Sutherland (2009). Although this chapter has not been written by a 'doer' or practitioner, it both explains a process that is not yet well known and asks the important questions that practitioners and policy-makers need to think about. We feel therefore that it is rightly placed in this section. If public protection work with adults is difficult, then it should be much more so with young people. Moreover, if adult offenders dominate the field, then does this become the default position for working with high risk of harm young people? As Baker says, are they the 'same but different'? The focus of public protection work is, of course, the management of future risks or the reduction of future harm. The assessment for this is often (but not exclusively) predicated upon an established pattern of behaviour. In young people this pattern may be more about their vulnerability than their 'risk'. Baker explores some of the differences between adult and young offender public protection work, noting along the way some potential positives. In particular she has observed less reliance on standardised risk assessment tools and a greater focus on the individual in their context – a lesson perhaps for adult services. Working with young offenders has always been a difficult balance between regarding them as children with needs and regarding those needs (problems) as risks. If this dilemma is uploaded into the public protection agenda then it becomes exaggerated. As Baker argues, is it the case that difficult behaviour by young people is regarded as more troublesome than dangerous? If so it would be wise to remember the case of Graham Young (see Prins, this volume). At the same time it is surely wrong to effectively damn them far into their future when they are at a stage in their lives when change and maturity can be rapid. Not least is the thorny issue of human rights and their specific applicability to young people. If there is to be an increasing incursion of adult public protection values into the young offender system it is evident from existing practice that young people's rights could begin to take a back seat. It is appropriate for Baker to raise this important issue.

Finally in this section, Steve Savage and Sarah Charman in many ways take us straight to the heart of the matter in discussing the role of victims in the development of what they describe as 'public protectionism'. However, more than just the significance of the victims' movement and/or lobby at key stages (for example, victim impact statements in court, victims interviewed by probation officers prior to a prisoner's release and their representation on Parole Board Meetings) they refer specifically to their role in campaigns, and in particular to the role of mothers. Their chapter specifically focuses on the case of Sarah Payne and considers both the role of influence held by mothers as victims and the potential for their status to be exploited. Savage and Charman take us into research on the grieving process and how women in particular in part deal with their loss by attempting to answer the often unanswerable question – why? Their energies are often channelled into campaigns, such as that for Sarah's Law and as seen in a number of similar situations in the United States. The authors remind us of the power of campaigns that target feelings that are close to home, that engender a belief that it could be me or us – campaigns that become inclusive for those who are not even likely to suffer. Savage and Charman therefore describe and analyse the changing nature of policy influence with a particular emphasis upon mothers as victims and their place in garnering support for changes in public protection policy. Rather than being exploited for political purposes the authors argue that the forces of motherhood, loss and grieving are, in this unique context, irresistible.

Reference

Baker, K. and Sutherland, A. (2009) *Multi-Agency Public Protection Arrangements and Youth Justice*. Bristol: Policy Press.

Chapter 16

Electronic monitoring, satellite tracking and public protection[1]

Mike Nellis

Introduction

Since its inception in the 1980s, the electronic monitoring (EM) of offenders has been rationalised and presented by government to the British public as something that is both more punitive and controlling than traditional community penalties, and increases public protection in the sense of reducing crime and preventing victimisation, or revictimisation. Other European countries, particularly Sweden, have been more concerned to portray EM as a controlling adjunct to rehabilitation, highlighting its reintegrative rather than its punitive aspect, but the assumption that public protection will be enhanced by EM remains much the same. In the case of EM curfews (the commonest form of EM), where offenders are required to stay in their own homes (or other designated place such as a hostel) for a period of weeks or months, public protection is supposedly achieved by the simple fact of punitive sequestration – keeping offenders off the streets, especially at night. An element of deterrence in the longer term may also be assumed, on the grounds that offenders, having once experienced it, may wish to avoid such an ostensibly onerous sentence in the future. While no directly rehabilitative effect can be attributed to EM itself – it does not seek to change attitudes or behaviour or to reform character – Hucklesby (2008, 2009) has shown that periods of enforced domestic confinement can have a 'bad-habit breaking' effect on some offenders, and in that sense can contribute to desistance. Nonetheless, worldwide – EM is now used in approximately 30 countries – there is precious little evidence that it is as good at crime reduction/public protection as governments initially hoped it would be (Renzema and Mayo-Wilson 2005). This is partly because, as Renzema and Mayo-Wilson rightly claim, there have been too few methodologically sound studies of EM, but also because the use of it, and political expectations of it, have all too often been ill thought out.

And yet it has gained a significant place in many criminal justice systems, still attracts new users (Norway in 2008, Poland in 2009) and shows no sign of being dislodged. Why is this? In respect of England and Wales (the largest EM curfew scheme in Europe), Mair (2005) has cogently argued that the government's commitment to using EM curfews was never quite warranted in terms of evidence of their effectiveness at reducing crime or even reducing prison use – although it has certainly acted as a safety valve to manage rising numbers of prisoners. Only in a minimal sense, then, has the expansion of EM been 'evidence-led policy', at least in England. Other factors have been in play here (and may well apply abroad). Symbolically, it has been used as a stick with which to beat the English probation service, whose humanistic and relational ways of working with offenders in the community were increasingly found wanting from a public protection perspective, however constructive they were with offenders themselves. Commitment to EM has largely transcended the vicissitudes of British party politics, suggesting that something deeper and more enduring than competitive law and order strategies is in play. The Conservatives, who introduced it while in government in the 1990s, have become disdainful of it in opposition, while the once cautious and pragmatic New Labour government, who rolled it out as a fully national scheme in 1999, became major ideological enthusiasts for it, steadily infusing the option of EM curfews into all forms of community supervision: bail, community sentences, early release from prison for both short sentence prisoners and parolees, as well as multi-agency public protection arrangements (MAPPA) – even, with control orders, the management of terrorist suspects (Nellis 2007a; Walker 2009).[2]

Explaining the broad appeal of EM for public protection, despite its limited impact on recidivism, becomes easier when one examines the discourse surrounding the establishment, and projected benefits, of the admittedly short-lived satellite tracking pilots in England and Wales, using technology that would trace and record an offender's movements and monitor the perimeter of designated exclusion zones, rather than simply restricting them to one place.

The satellite tracking pilots in England and Wales

The New Labour government enacted anticipatory legislation for satellite tracking in England and Wales in 2000, following the murder of an eight-year-old girl by a known paedophile (Nellis 2005). At the time the USA had been using satellite tracking for only a few years, and there was negligible evidence as to its value (Nellis 2004). Pilot schemes were nonetheless run in three sites in England between 2004 and 2006, as part of a larger strategy to stabilise the then rising prison population at 80,000 (Nellis 2009a). The official discourse surrounding the pilots – which were expected at the outset to segue smoothly into mainstream provision – illustrated with striking clarity how integral remote location monitoring in some approximation to real-time had become to New Labour's conception of public protection. Satellite tracking represented a more meticulous and fine-grained control over offenders in the community – control over routine movement – than had hitherto been possible, and reflected New Labour's defining commitment to the micromanagement of governmental processes (including offender management), and the intensified use of information and communication technology (ICT) – of which EM is an example – to achieve this. It was also consistent with New Labour's determination to modernise and transform government: EM technologies generally, and satellite tracking in particular, were seen as quintessentially modern, distinctively twenty-first century approaches which had the power to galvanise change in (or undermine once and for all) archaic, tradition oriented public services like probation. They seemingly offered new solutions to old problems, and brought in new organisations and new experts, usually in the private sector (which was considered more adept at technological innovation than the public sector) to challenge the hegemony of established interest groups (Haggerty 2004; Nellis 2006a).

Through the ideological lenses of *technomanagerialism* (as one might call New Labour's fusion of managerialism and ICT) and modernisation, traditional conceptions of control over offenders in the community, especially but not only after release from prison, began to seem anachronistic. Remote monitoring technologies which promised constant and immediate knowledge of an offender's whereabouts were, to technocratic sensibilities at least, an obvious improvement upon merely intermittent, face-to-face contact with offenders by probation, police or youth justice officers (see Home Office 2004). Even if this monitoring capacity was not actually used to the full, it could, New Labour reasoned, add something substantive to the idea of public protection, which might assuage the anxieties of an insecure and volatile electorate, and sustain the government's political edge in crime control debates. In this sense, to adapt what Thomas Mathiesen (1990) once said of imprisonment, EM's capacity for incessant oversight became an *action signifying* intervention, appealed to by politicians as proof that something is being done, by them, to address the crime problem and improve public protection. Despite media scepticism about EM, which (in Britain at least) has questioned whether the *action* can actually deliver public protection, this is not an entirely hollow gesture on the part of politicians. It is grounded in the affordances offered by electronic information and communication networks, which have reconfigured the space in which policy-makers can seek solutions to crime and disorder.

The English satellite tracking pilots were targeted on prolific and persistent offenders (especially drug-using burglars), juvenile offenders, sex offenders and some domestic violence offenders. The government minister who introduced it likened it, hyperbolically, to a 'prison without bars' – implying punishment – but in every official statement relating to the pilot 'public protection' was a prominent rationale, because of the unprecedented levels of information that would be given about offender locatability – even though tracking would not be total and not, in the main, in real-time. During the pilots 517 offenders were tracked, very few of whom had been convicted of sexual or domestic violence. The official evaluation concluded, against the grain of many of the police and probation fieldworkers involved, that there were still too many problems with GPS technology, and that it was not as yet a cost-effective measure (Shute 2007; Nellis 2009a). In the past, such critical evidence might not have impacted very significantly on an EM initiative in which there had clearly been considerable political investment, but in this instance the pilots were discontinued, not mainstreamed. This may have had as much to do with the fact that by the time the pilots ended the Ministry of Justice was no longer seeking to stabilise the prison population, but to expand it beyond 80,000, and money had ceased to be available for expensive new alternatives, or even adjuncts. Nonetheless, satellite tracking's credibility as a solution to certain aspects of offender management was not entirely dented, not least because the Dutch and the French have continued to use it (albeit on a small scale), and technological developments in the field are being kept under review. [3]

At the time of writing (September 2009), tracking is in fact once again under consideration, this time in the South London and Maudsley National Health Service (NHS) Trust, as a means of increasing security for offenders with mental disorders in and around the medium secure units at Bethlem Royal and Lambeth Hospitals. This follows the escape of a patient (serving life for rape and robbery) the previous year, and his subsequent murder of a 73-year-old man. He had feigned illness and eluded his guards while attending an outside hospital, and spent nine weeks on the run. Thus far, only staff have tested the tracking equipment, pending the deployment of an ankle bracelet that could only be removed using 'industrial bolt cutters' rather than the easily cut plastic bracelets currently in use (*Daily Telegraph*, 2 July 2009; also personal communication, Patrick Gillespie, Lambeth Hospital, 17 September 2009).

GPS technology and the network society

Sociologically, the global positioning system (GPS) must be understood as an aspect of Castells' (2004: 3) 'network society' – a society to whose organisation 'micro-electronic based information and communication technologies' are structurally constitutive. GPS is a satellite-based navigation system created by the US military in 1974, using 24 solar-powered satellites orbiting 12,000 miles above the earth, four of which are notionally 'visible' at any one time from any terrestrial location. The system was made available for civilian use in the 1980s, since when an abundance of commercial applications have developed. It works as follows:

> Essentially, the GPS receiver compares the time a signal was transmitted at the speed of light with the time it was received by the receiver. By triangulating with at least three GPS signals from satellites, longitude and latitude (2-D) can be determined; with four or more satellites sending data to a GPS receiver, longitude, latitude and altitude (3-D) can be determined. This information can then be displayed graphically on a map. (Buck 2009a: 2)

In terms of its ability to pinpoint objects and individuals on the earth's surface, in real time, to within a matter of metres, GPS technology has undeniably been transformative, but various factors can still affect the quality and accuracy of the GPS signal. Atmospheric conditions can affect its speed.

Objects on the ground – tall buildings – can deflect it slightly. Timing errors result from discrepancies between the clock in the receivers and the super-accurate atomic clocks in the satellites themselves. Satellites that waver in their orbits and the periodically variable geometry between the four visible ones, which in any patch of sky may be spaced out, lined up, or any combination in between, can cause inaccurate readings. Even if four satellites are available, the relatively weak signal strength available to civilian users means that 'GPS units often do not work indoors, underwater or underground' (Buck 2009a: 3). Various ways have been developed to address these limitations: both assisted GPS (A-GPS) and advanced forward link trilateration (AFLT) link to the cellular radio network to fill in the gaps when GPS is not available (Buck 2009b).

According to Paul Benshoof (2007: 147), director of a GPS applications research centre, innovative 'commercial applications of GPS far exceed those of the military ... the private sector continues to use GPS in ways that the original developers could never have imagined'. Customising it for crime control is one such new use, although government remains as much a player in this as the private sector. The sheer ubiquity of GPS technologies and 'location-based services' in everyday life often goes unnoticed (Graham 1997); only recently have 'satnav' devices in cars and GPS-enabled mobile phones given them a certain public visibility. Over and above its role in positioning and navigation, the accuracy of the GPS timing signal (and its low cost compared to alternative systems) is being used to increase the synchronisation of global telecommunication networks and to time-stamp electronic financial transactions. The military, for obvious reasons, dominate the development of GPS protection technologies – with the right kit, the satellite signals can be systemically jammed – but the need for them extends to civilian as well as military systems: there would understandably be alarm if thousands of tracked offenders suddenly went 'off the grid' for a sustained period.

Tracking and community supervision

In terms of its emergence as a means of supervising offenders, there is a paradox in respect of electronic tracking. Chronologically, it was *second* rather than first generation technology; it developed *after* the house arrest versions of EM, although it had been imagined first, and arguably it was the prospect of monitoring offenders' general whereabouts in an approximation to real time that inspired the whole EM movement, luring governments and commercial organisations alike to exploit affordances in the new national – and later global – communications architecture. When the concept of electronic surveillance of offender locations was first imagined, in the 1960s and early 1970s, the tracking of an offender's movement seemed far more significant, desirable and commanding than confinement to a single location, which *merely* modernised the ancient penalty of house arrest (Ball *et al.* 1988). Tracking seemingly offered the prospect of an omniscience that had not previously been possible in crime control. The imagined technology was not – at least at the start – tracking with satellites, despite the imminent creation of the GPS system.

Rather, a variety of terrestrial tracking technologies were envisaged. Harvard psychologist Ralph Schwitzgebel (1963: 12, 1964), for example, experimented with a portable communication device (tones only) on a number of volunteer delinquents, which, because it also contained equipment adapted from a guided missile system, enabled 'the experimenter unobtrusively to record the location of the [delinquent]' and ascertain where he 'spends his time' (1963: 13). Schwitzgebel envisaged using this technology in a rehabilitative way, to give offenders on the move *positive reinforcement*, but a few years later another proto-tracker (who never conducted any trials), mathematician and computer scientist Joseph Meyer (1971), put deterrence (and public protection) at the heart of his proposed system. He envisioned a 'transponder surveillance system' in which a nationwide network of computer-linked transceivers, high on the walls of buildings (outside and in) in every neighbourhood would pick up in real time a unique radio-frequency identifier signal from unremovable *transponders* attached to the wrists of some 25 million convicted criminals (usually released from prison) in the USA.[4] Curfew and territorial restrictions could be programmed into the system, tailored to individual offenders, and some transceivers would cause any nearby transponder to sound an alarm, warning the wearer to keep away and (probably) drawing attention to them.

Even the kind of EM that was shown in the Spiderman comic which (loosely) influenced Judge Jack Love and Michael Goss to create the first actual EM house arrest scheme in Albuquerque, New Mexico was of the tracking variety (complete with explosive device if Spiderman tried to remove it). Similarly in England and Wales, Tom Stacey, the founder of the Offender's Tag Association in 1981, saw tracking – not with satellites – rather than curfews as the ideal form of EM, and remained a tireless champion of it (Nellis 1991; Stacey 1995). The idea that pinpointing the whereabouts of an offender would enable public protection entered American thinking well before it became possible to achieve it. The process of translation from imagination to practice is not entirely clear from the available literature, but a futurological article by a Colorado probation officer, Max Winkler (1993), who proposed the idea of electronic 'walking prisons' (a concept already explored in a science fiction story by Cynthia Bunn (1974)) played a part. Winkler's own thinking erred towards science fiction,[5] but several US electronics companies were already pursuing the basic idea of offender tracking, shorn of additional 'zapping' devices, for example Westinghouse (funded by the National Institute for Justice in 1994) and Motorola, plus Canadian company Strategic Technologies Inc (Blakeway 1995). Winkler was, however, specifically taken up by Dr Joseph Hoshent of Lucent Technologies. Together they proposed several viable tracking technologies – not all using GPS – in a sister journal to the one in which Meyer had published a quarter century earlier (Hoshen *et al.* 1995), and later the same year Hoshen was awarded the first patent for such technology. Parallel to this the New Mexico Corrections Department had asked Sandia National Laboratories to explore real-time tracking technologies. Sandia and Spectrum Industries (in California) came close to marketing a device, but like Hoshen's patent, nothing came of it, though both initiatives paved the way for ProTech, a Florida company who tilted offender tracking technologies decisively towards GPS-based systems (Drake, no date).

The timing of these technological developments was propitious because of growing concerns at state level about the high financial cost of imprisonment. Numbers of incarcerated offenders had increased massively since the 1980s, made possible by an extensive prison-building programme – though overcrowding still occurred. The effect of this on many state budgets was proving catastrophic, and provided an incentive to consider the further development of supervision in the community, which itself had been increasing. Intermediate sanctions (midway between probation and imprisonment) were one of the first responses; measures that permitted at least some lessening of custodial sentence length were the second (Pew Centre on the States 2009; Moore and Thurston 2009). Public safety concerns about released prisoners – especially those convicted of violence to children – led to demands for more controlling measures, and the incessant oversight provided by GPS satellite tracking seemed to offer precisely this. By following movement on a 24/7/365 basis it could generate more data for supervisors; by permitting *exclusion zones* it could better protect former or prospective victims; and by creating small *inclusion zones* it could replicate house arrest. By constantly reminding offenders – who were assumed to be rational calculators – that their locations were traceable it was expected to increase deterrence.

In the USA the *Journal of Electronic Monitoring* undertook surveys of EM provision in 2002–03 and 2008–09. In the earlier period only two companies, ProTech and iSecuretrac, offered GPS products; in the later period, 'ten companies offer GPS and all then have [them] under contract and in use' (Conway 2009: 5) with more planning to do so. BI Incorporated (a pioneer in the original RF (radio frequency) EM market, founded in 1978), developed GPS products, as did Elmotech, an Israeli company established with an eye on the US market, but which (unlike BI) rapidly acquired a global presence. These companies have since been joined in the GPS market by G4S Justice Services, iSecuretrac, Serco Geograpfix; Satellite Tracking of People (STOP); Corrections Services; Digital Technologies 2000; ActSoft Inc; Guidance Monitoring Ltd; Alert System Corporation; and Omnilink Inc. These companies – some large, some small, some with an array of products and interests (not all related to law enforcement) and some geared very specifically to EM – form part of what has been called 'the commercial-corrections complex' (Lilly 1992; Lilly and Deflem 1996; Lilly and Knepper 1993). It is precisely because they understand EM technology and its potential better than the government agencies who seek and purchase their services that the companies must be regarded as active contributors to the emergence of *technocorrections* and not simply as neutral vendors, responding to a law enforcement market that emerges independently of them. They are, to a degree, creating the market, highlighting the limitations of existing crime control systems by advertising something 'better', stimulating professional (and managerial) imaginations and expanding the horizons of what is possible (Nellis 2009b). Compared to the total number of offenders under supervision in the community in the USA, one should not exaggerate the current size of the tracking market. Estimates suggest that 44,000 such units were in daily use in 2009 (compared to 30,000 in 2008), with more than half of these in Texas, Florida and California (Drake 2009) but these are arguably early days for this technology, and in terms of public protection it is less the technology itself than what its use signals – the incorporation of real-time locatability into the very meaning of *control* – that is important.

The practical operation of satellite tracking

While there are technical elements common to all products, there is no single GPS tracking technology – different companies market different systems – and potential users must become aware of the different kinds of regime that the combined hardware and software can create for particular offenders: 'With the wide range of technologies now available', says the *Journal of Electronic Monitoring* (2009: 8), 'it is possible to meet a monitoring requirement in different ways: sometimes there is more than one way to design a solution to a problem.' More fundamentally, introducing GPS into probation and parole agencies requires a transformation of their knowledge base, not only in a technical sense. The complexity of the technology puts the vendors in a strong position:

> One of the most challenging aspects for community corrections agencies is determining when and what type of GPS tracking to use for which offenders ... sometimes it is just a matter of agency preference or comfort level. The variety of GPS systems and transmission modes allow for a high level of customisation, making GPS tracking suitable for many types of offender ... A basic understanding of GPS and its correctional applications is an important first step for agencies considering the technology as an offender management tool. (Buck 2009a: 5)

The levels of 'protectiveness' offered by EM inhere partly in the design of the technology itself, partly in the social and organisational structures in which it is used, and partly in the legitimacy accorded the measure by offenders themselves. Most of the current GPS products are 'two piece units' incorporating a waist-worn tracking unit linked (by RF signals) to a conventional ankle bracelet, but four 'one piece units' (combining all the kit in an ankle bracelet) are already on the market, with more promised. Some companies market both, envisaging different purposes for them. Joseph Meyer's (1971) suggestion that tracking systems would only be credible forms of control if the bracelets worn by offenders were unremovable has not been followed. The bracelets used in the American (and European markets) are made of hard plastics or rubber that can – if the offender is so motivated – be cut through and discarded. To deter offenders from doing this, however, and to gather evidence that it has occurred, or been attempted, sophisticated (and often patent protected) anti-tamper devices have been incorporated into the bracelets. These register in the monitoring centres whenever an attempt is made to remove or damage a strap, or to open the transmitter itself. Anti-tamper devices are commonly based on electrical circuits or optical fibres, but some include 'body proximity detectors' (based on temperature) or 'motion detectors' (the protracted stillness of the transmitter may indicate that it has been removed, or that the wearer is dead). Straps cannot be stretched and removed without damaging the devices – the plastic is either unstretchable even when heated or, when heat is applied, would burn the offender before the stretching threshold was reached.

Supervisors must learn to understand what tamper alerts mean when they appear on screen. All current tamper detection methods generate both false positives and false negatives – they can be affected by abrupt movements, wear and tear and improper fitting, as well as deliberate stretching, cutting and manipulation – making it hard for supervisors to know how to react. Ostensibly, all tamper alerts warrant a response, to check that the equipment is still in reliable working order, but in practice this is easier said than done. Short of full removal of the bracelet, the tamper technology it contains can reset itself, though it will still report it (and the reset) for a further 24 hours, ensuring that a tamper which occurs out of range of the docking device (and which may otherwise go unreported) will be picked up once it comes in range again, when the offender returns home to recharge the battery. Some devices can only be reset manually after a tamper, requiring contact between monitoring staff and offender.

Current EM technologies in the US and Europe are strongly *participant dependent* – a term used by some EM vendors to denote the extent to which offenders must actively comply with the technology if it is to fulfil its locatability function. The experience of being tracked is as much one of 'regulated self-regulation' (Crawford 2003) as one of passive, externally imposed control. Compliance always remains a choice. Offenders have to take responsibility for recharging the battery, remember (with two-piece, wearable units) to carry the kit with them when they go outdoors and – knowing that they could if they wished – resist temptation to cut and discard the bracelet. Almost from the start, tracking technology has permitted one-way communication with the offender – using audible or visual signals, or vibration, which can automatically indicate 'battery low' or that the supervising officer should be called, or warn the offender that they are nearing an exclusion zone. Most audible alerts take the form of a soft tone that only the offender can hear, but recalling Meyer's (1971) suggestion, SecureAlert sells equipment which incorporates a 'very loud siren ... designed to draw attention to the client [and which] can be used as punishment or negative reinforcement' (*Journal of Offender Monitoring* 2009: 68). It is unclear whether this has ever been used in practice.

Some equipment permits two-way communication, allowing the offender to acknowledge receipt of alerts sent by the authorities, either by pager or text, although this makes the kit more costly, and harder to miniaturise. At the very least, 'alerts and alert acknowledgement reinforce the client's awareness that he or she is under surveillance', but increasingly 'more and more agencies are requiring two-way voice communications' – in essence the inclusion of a mobile phone in the kit – enabling the supervising officers to engage in periodic dialogue with the mobile offender. Five equipment manufacturers now offer this facility, with a sixth aiming to. The rationale is 'to follow-up on violations and to reinforce supervision strategies. It allows officers to interact with their clients about their clients' behaviour on a real-time basis' (*Journal of Offender Monitoring* 2009: 68). There may, however, be a downside to two-way communication; a supervisor who is in contact with an offender as he breaches the perimeter of his exclusion zone, desperately trying to dissuade him from his assumed course of action, may incur greater liability for any subsequent crime in the exclusion zone than they would have done if they had merely seen on a map where the offender was going, and primed the police to apprehend him. This fusion of counselling and surveillance harks directly back to Schwitzgebel's (1964) aspirations for EM, and while attractive in some ways, is not without drawbacks.

Real time tracking (the symbolic ideal), which requires constant signalling of the monitoring centre and generates vast amounts of superfluous data – is very expensive, and has not been deemed necessary for all offenders. Three standard operating modes have evolved for GPS technology depending on whether it is operating in real time or not.

1 **Passive mode**. The GPS unit records location (data points) throughout the day and uploads *via* landline of cellular means when the offender returns home, probably under curfew, at the end of the day. Supervising officials typically do not read the data until the day afterwards.

2 **Active mode**. This provides a continuous flow of data points in real time using cellular technology. This is both technologically more expensive, and requires constant watching by officials. Costs may be offset by requiring the offender to pay towards the daily cost of the equipment.

3 **Hybrid mode**. GPS remains in passive mode, or uploads data points at preset intervals unless the offender violates the rules he is subject to – for example, goes to the perimeter of an exclusion zone – in which case the active mode kicks in, alerts are sent to monitoring officials, and to the offender, and movement is now monitored in real time.

The continuing need for people within these technical systems is illustrated by 'drive by' monitoring, in which mobile correctional personnel unobtrusively use hand-held devices to detect (or not!) signals from one or more bracelets and identify the wearers thereof at a distance of 250–400 feet. Although introduced to back up house arrest – doing spot checks on the locations in the community where offenders were expected to be, or not supposed to be – they have also been used in conjunction with passive tracking systems, or when GPS signals have been lost. 'Drive by units ... are used for sweeps of high-risk locations such as bars and drug dealing hot spots ... [or] to check attendance at court ordered meetings and other required activities' (*Journal of Electronic Monitoring* 2009: 13).

GPS tracking and sex offenders

It has been suggested that sex offenders are the single largest category of offender on whom GPS technologies have been used in the US (Monmonier 2004; Drake 2009), and it is true that in other countries which have considered or used tracking, sex offenders are invariably a key target group. This reflects the particular fear and dread that 'predatory' offenders and their 'heinous' crimes against women and children evoke in the public mind. There is a core of rightful concern here, but it is relatively easy for media, politicians and victim advocacy groups to exaggerate the dangers and mobilise concern about sex offenders, especially at the point of release from prison. In the US, as elsewhere, much recent policy towards such offenders has been driven by the scandal of specific criminal incidents – often the killing of children by known sexual predators – that stimulate citizen initiatives and demands for political action. The community notification movement in the 1990s, which notionally enabled ordinary citizens to protect their children by publicising the addresses of local sex offenders, was an early response. Indefinite detention in psychiatric hospitals was another, pursued by some states. Amitai Etzioni's (1999: 74) suggestion that convicted sex offenders be sequestered in special towns in remote places where they could live freely, with confinement achieved 'by the use of electronic bracelets rather than barbed wire and armed guards' was never taken up, but satellite tracking came to be seen, by a cluster of politicians, correctional agencies and commercial organisations, as a near perfect solution, and spread relatively fast.

The use of tracking with sex offenders, however, has arguably been indiscriminate, and perhaps even misconceived. Contrary to received wisdom, though it has developed in the same time-frame that saw slightly increased use of EM to reduce incarceration, in this instance, with sex offenders, it was simply used to intensify the supervision process. 'The same number of sex offenders will be placed on civil confinement', write Payne, DeMichele and Button (2008: 3), 'the number of sex offenders sent to prison will not decrease and the lengths of prison sentences will not be shorter because of GPS monitoring. In effect, GPS monitoring costs are additive ones, not replacement costs.' Paradoxically, however, the 2006 federal legislation that requires US states to use EM with sex offenders (in some instances for life) has been insufficiently funded to implement the legislation (which may cause, at local level, transfer of funds away from other sorts of parole supervision to EM). Button, DeMichele and Payne's (2009) content analysis of legislation relating to EM in all 50 American states (only three did not have it) showed that nineteen of the 27 states with sex offender legislation specifically mandated the use of EM for such offenders. The legislation varies in detail and prescriptiveness as to the type of EM to be used and the length of time spent on it. Florida, Missouri and Ohio all specify the use of GPS for life on sexually violent predators; others specify a period of not less than ten years. The assumption seems to be that sex offending is largely a question of 'opportunity and availability' and that without blanket surveillance over long periods it will inevitably recur. The ethos of tracking is thus punitive rather than rehabilitative, even more so in respect of offenders' against children. Exclusion zones have become routine and by 2006 19 states had passed laws limiting victim–offender contact.

The EM sex offender legislation poses numerous difficulties for correctional agencies. Button *et al.* (2009) see no meaningful theoretical match between the indiscriminate adoption of EM, particularly GPS tracking, and the concrete motivations of particular offenders. They echo Mair's (2005) observation about the use of EM in England and Wales, that as it becomes both cheaper and technically more proficient, policy-makers turn to it regardless.[6] They note also that parole officers may be forced to subordinate more social (and useful?) forms of supervision to the servicing of data-flows generated by EM, and fear that EM may become the mainstay of sex offender supervision rather than an additional tool to complement rehabilitative and reintegrative measures. They are particularly concerned that GPS tracking is being used specifically on more violent and dangerous offenders, without an evidence base to justify this. They seemingly accept Padgett, Bales and Blomberg's (2006) claim that EM of various kinds has a crime suppression effect over the duration of a (relatively short) monitoring period, if not afterwards, but are rightly sceptical of the researcher's inference that the same suppressive effect could be maintained if the duration were simply extended for years (see also Nellis 2007b). Current evidence suggests that EM becomes cumulatively less bearable to those subject to it, such that lifetime tracking may create false expectations of protectiveness, quite apart from the human rights implications.

Electronic monitoring and victim protection

Hoshen, Sennott and Winkler (1995) anticipated that tracking technologies might be used for victim protection. In fact, both house arrest and tracking systems have been developed to do this, particularly but not only in cases of stalking, domestic violence and sexual assault, where restraining orders or no-contact orders may be in force. Equipment can either be installed in the victim's home or carried by the victim as they move around in the community. Those installed in the home are in effect variants of the transceivers installed in the offender's own home – they register the presence of the ankle bracelet when it comes into range, giving the victim's audible warning that the offender is nearby. Some notify the authorities (usually the police) too, others are usually accompanied by a panic button with which the victim can call for help. The *Journal of Offender Monitoring* (2009: 19) notes: 'While victim monitoring products are believed to deter clients from unauthorised contact, and maybe programmed to notify authorities to dispatch law enforcement, their primary function is to record contact incidents for use as evidence of violations.'

Edna Erez has undertaken the only research into the use of EM as a means of protecting victims. She calls it 'bilateral' EM because a second party – in this instance a victim of domestic violence – is enrolled into the programme. Such victims, once they separate from the abuser, can benefit from protection orders, the aim of which is to keep the defendant/offender away from the victim at the pre-trial, sentence or post-release stage, but they have proved difficult to enforce. Simply because women are vulnerable at the separation stage – and former partners may assault or stalk them – EM has been seen as a way of increasing the deterrent effect of protection orders. Erez, Ibarra and Lurie (2004) studied two US schemes, one in a large metropolitan urban area (which used it preventively, pre-trial), the other in a city in a largely rural county (which used it reactively, post-conviction), both using RF technology.

Offenders were subject to house arrest, and told to keep a certain specified distance from the victim's residence: between 1,000 feet and one mile. A receiver identical to the one that monitors the offender's curfew is installed in the victim's home, and is sensitive to the proximity of the tagged offender if he comes within a 500-feet radius. 'In addition, the victim may be given a pager to receive messages from the monitoring centre, a duress pendant, and/or a cellular phone pre-programmed to notify authorities' (Erez *et al*. 2004), and some programmes give field monitoring devices to victims that notify them of the offender's approach when they are away from home. This added an element of extra security to the protection orders, but limitations remained:

> The defendant is not tracked while away from home, as is the case with GPS based systems. It is important to note that the equipment does not provide physical protection of the victim. It will simply provide a warning (and notification to the police) when the defendant is nearby, as long as the ankle transmitter is worn. Thus the equipment will not prevent someone who is determined to hurt a 'protected' party, and is not concerned with the consequences to himself. We observed that [monitoring] personnel emphasise this technological limitation to victims during the installation. (Erez *et al*. 2004)

In the urban area, approximately 5,000 cases used bilateral EM over three years, in the rural area approximately 40 cases over nine years, for periods averaging 48 days and 72 days respectively (a variation probably accounted for by the tighter restrictions in the former programme, with more offenders being 'violated out'). In the main there were relatively few 'radius penetrations' in either scheme and victims professed themselves satisfied with the increased security EM offered them and their children. Some became dependent on the technology, fearing its removal at the end of the order, but the researchers were sufficiently impressed with RF-EM as a form of victim protection to recommend its more widespread adoption. Erez is now researching the use of bilateral GPS technology in the victim protection field, which in effect turns each victim into 'a mobile exclusion zone to the offender' (a technology that has subsequently been adapted as a means of gang disruption, to keep individual gang members apart from each other, not just from particular locations (Drake 2009: 4).

Sweden (Wennerberg and Holmberg 2007) undertook a small and admittedly unrepresentative survey of 73 victims of violent crime, sexual crime and robbery whose offenders had been placed on EM curfew as a sentence or early release from prison. Of the 42 who responded, opinions ranged widely, with those who had been victims of more serious crimes being the most negative, particularly of early release. Those who were positive appreciated the preventive and reintegrative aspects of EM compared to imprisonment, and, when the victims were female partners of abusive men, were inclined to think that by dint of their being less punitive than prison, EM curfews would make the men feel less vengeful towards them.

The attitudes of victims towards EM remain under-researched, but if EM is to have credibility as a means of protecting them it does seem important that they understand the strengths and limitations of its various modalities. There is no reason to think that fully informed crime victims would be systematically hostile to EM and it should be noted that, in England, it was a support group for victims of childhood abuse, Phoenix Survivors, which first suggested the idea of implant tracking for sex offenders to the Home Office (Bright 2002), and that the Buddi device being proposed for the NHS tracking trials was developed by entrepreneur Sara Murray (personal communication, 8 September 2009), whose commercial interest in tracking technologies arose in part after her young daughter once went missing in a supermarket.

Conclusion

In Nellis (2006b), drawing particularly on Scheerer (2000), I argued that the development of criminal justice policy worldwide was still governed by the political and professional interplay of three distinct discourses – the punitive-repressive, the managerial-surveillant and the humanistic-rehabilitative – and that in any given country (or region) the actual contours of a criminal justice system, and the parameters of penal practice, would be set by the influence that the institutional champions of each 'credo' had, by the alliances they made and/or by the checks and balances they imposed on each other. At any given time, a criminal justice system may embody influences from all three discourses, but not fully or in equal measure: one discourse may be in the ascendant, others in decline. They may be contradictions, tensions and antagonisms in a given criminal justice system, depending on the strength of commitment to different 'credos' among the different professional and occupational groups that make it up. Each of these criminal justice discourses is typically more strongly aligned with, and permeable by, particular external influences, traditions and imaginaries than others – the punitive-repressive to Hobbesian conceptions of statecraft more generally; the humanistic-rehabilitative to discourses focused on democracy, rights and social inclusion; and the managerial-surveillant to commercial, actuarial and technological innovations. Over time, the respective positions and influence of the discourses may change, reflecting both wider sociocultural and political realignments, and also internal reconfigurations and innovations within the discourses themselves.

It is largely from within 'managerialist-surveillant' discourse that public protection, conceived as something that can be consciously and continually engineered, has emerged as a social and political ideal in its own right, rather than as a haphazard and merely hoped-for consequence of imposing punishment or rehabilitation on convicted individuals. It blends thinking from managerialism, various policing strategies, situational crime prevention, victim support and deterrence theory, and in extremis conjures up a 'safety utopia' (Boutellier 2004), a place where crime will either never occur or will always be pre-empted by the omniscience of the authorities or where the bad elements, *CSI*-style, will always be caught and controlled. Precise and continuous knowledge of an offender's location – which was simply not possible in the past – is becoming integral to this new imaginary of incessant and ubiquitous public protection, whether through CCTV, online community notification of sex offenders' whereabouts, the remote location monitoring of tagged criminals or the matrix of electronic trails and traces in which, to greater or lesser degrees, all citizens are enmeshed. Current technologies offer only imperfect realisations of the ideal, but the ready availability of mundane geolocation technologies and 'location-based services' in everyday life makes it seem feasible. In this sense the customising of pinpointing technologies for crime control purposes reflects the far broader 'commodification of locatability' (Monmonier 2004: 139) that has been occurring in the late modern era for a vast range of commercial and governmental reasons. There is no end in sight: the ever increasing sophistication of the GPS, coupled with the development of rival geolocation satellite networks by the Russians (GLONASS), the west Europeans (Galileo) and the Chinese, together (and in conjunction) with the advent of more localised terrestrial tracking systems using cellular networks, will give crime controllers of the future ample means of regulating the spatial and temporal behaviour of offenders and, rhetorically at least, of protecting the public.

Within an ascendant 'managerial-surveillant' discourse,[7] crime scene correlation, *via* pre-programmed data-exchange between police and probation computer systems, may be one of these technologies. Pinpointing an offender's whereabouts in relation to known crime incidents (which may incriminate or exonerate him) was thought likely in the USA to intensify the deterrent effect of tracking even in the late 1990s, but is only now catching on, as the software improves, as large concentrations of tracked offenders in particular states and cities make it worthwhile, and as liberal resistance dissipates:

> ... automated systems will cross-reference crime scene data ... with the location history of all offenders being monitored. The tolerances of the systems are adjustable. One agency may want to know if any offender has been within 1000 feet of any reported crime scenes within 1 hour of the offence occurring. Other agencies may want to narrow the search by asking for a list of offenders who were within 250 feet of any crime scene within 15 minutes of the crime occurring. Most systems on the market offer simple correlation software as part of their basic service. The address of a single known crime scene can be checked against recorded locations of all offenders being monitored. Although this is a valuable tool, it is not nearly as powerful as the automated systems that check all recorded crime scenes against all offender locations at one time. (Drake 2009: 5–6)

Outside the USA, there is negligible interest in crime scene correlation, but it cannot be assumed that such indifference will remain constant, not only because penal sensibilities themselves change but also because 'location-based services' and expectations of immediate knowledge (as a means of risk management) will become so commonplace and normal in popular consciousness that their absence from criminal justice will come to seem untenable. Dystopias are easily conjured in respect of such scenarios, and it is not as if there is nothing to fear from a technology that could potentially displace humanistic forms of offender supervision, significantly infringe human rights, and reduce political incentives to pursue greater social justice (and the reduced crime dividend that greater equality and social cohesiveness would probably deliver). Furthermore, the internal dynamics and political reach of the commercial corrections complex, both globally and locally, remain hard to fathom and without better studies of how technocorrectional innovation has occurred in the past, and is occurring now, the case for applying the precautionary principle is easy to make.

And yet, despite the ease with which dystopian scenarios can be constructed, it can also be argued that liberal penal traditions and regard for human rights in Western Europe has already constrained and shaped the development of EM, muting its impact and blunting its worst excesses – but perhaps also limiting its potential? This muting may only be apparent if one looks comparatively at the deployment of EM in more authoritarian penal cultures (on which data is admittedly limited). Even in the US, however, there are EM house arrest projects that do amount to 24-hour lockdowns, making the experience very similar to imprisonment, far more so than the part day/usually night-time curfews that prevail in Western Europe (Roberts 2004). Without knowing that Max Winkler (1993) had envisaged tracking technology with a capacity to 'zap' non-compliant offenders, South Africa recently considered establishing a system of satellite tracking that would have enabled the monitoring agency (when judicially authorised) to remotely administer a temporarily immobilising electric shock to a tagged offender known to be entering an exclusion zone (by discharging the powerful long-life battery all at once). As much for technical as well as ethical reasons, they now seem unlikely to incorporate this device (House 2009). Less dramatically, the Korean government have subjected more than 500 adult sex offenders to real-time satellite tracking from a monitoring centre in Seoul in which probation officers watch movement on large screen maps on the office wall. Offenders found to have tampered with the devices can be sentenced to up to seven years' imprisonment, or a fine of up to 20,000 *won* (Ministry of Justice Republic of Korea 2009: 6).[8] Set against these examples it is easier to see that the uses to which EM has actually been put in Western Europe have not, so far, been excessive. That is not so much because precaution has prevailed (though there have been elements of that), as because (in England and Wales) punitive-repressive discourses have held them in check, while elsewhere in Europe they have often been more embedded in humanistic-rehabilitative discourses. An untrammelled commitment to managerial-surveillant interventions, if it occurs, will generate a highly technological approach to public protection, and while satellite tracking itself may or not flourish within this framework, technologies that facilitate locatability will probably become indispensable to the control of offenders, and to the very meaning of such protection.

Notes

1 I remain grateful to Bob Lilly and Marc Renzema for continuing insights into the use of EM in the USA.

2 Control orders in England have only included EM curfews, but in Canada the suggestion was mooted that people charged or suspected of terrorist activity would be subject to GPS monitoring: a Mr Harkat was subject of such speculation (CBC-TV national news, 10 July 2006, quoted in John Howard Society of Alberta 2006: 22).

3 In Scotland (where GPS tracking was considered but never used) it was mooted in 2009 as a means of keeping better control over the inmates of open prisons following the escape of armed robber Brian Martin (Spencer 2009). It was in fact a somewhat tentative recommendation, but was picked up by the press as if it were the mainstay of the review – 'Satellite tracking for killers in open prisons', reported *The Scotsman* (1 July 2009) – neatly illustrating the way that, in Britain at least, an EM-sceptical media have typically sensationalised and mocked proposals to use it.

4 For Meyer the non-removability of the bracelet was essential to the effectiveness of the system. He did not specify what material it should be made of, but insisted that it should only be removable using an 'abrasive grinding disk or an acetylene burner' (Meyer 1971: 13).

5 Although it echoed a rather notorious article by US criminologists Ingraham and Smith (1972), some of Winkler's thinking was in fact science fiction; he speculated on the potential of computerised implant chips that could monitor the bodies of offenders for physiological signs that they might be about to commit an offence, sexual or otherwise, and then tranquillise them.

6 Intriguingly, Button *et al.* (2009) suggest that more integrated, inter-agency working with sex offenders would probably be more effective than reliance on technology. Inter-agency working is less common in the USA than in Britain, and it may be that its absence is one reason why Americans turn so readily to technology in this context, while the British err in the opposite direction.

7 Cotter and De Lint (2009) drew on the three-discourse model for their questionnaire-based survey of 26 EM tracking schemes in the USA. They interpreted their data as saying that practitioners envisaged GPS in equal measure as expressions of both managerial-surveillant and rehabilitative credos. While accepting that the rhetoric of rehabilitation dies hard, and remains important to the self-presentation of some correctional officials, I would argue that EM technology cannot be understood as rehabilitative in itself. It is an inherently managerial-surveillant approach, which can, however, be used in the context of a programme whose overall goals and methods may well be rehabilitative, and as such can add value these programmes. Equally, as Button *et al.* (2009) show, EM can be pressed into the service of punitive supervision programmes, but that does not make it intrinsically punitive.

8 I am grateful to Professor Younoh Cho of Dongguk University, Korea for insights into the use EM in her country (meeting on 28 July 2009).

References

Ball R. A., Huff G. R. and Lilly, J. R. (1988) *House Arrest and Correctional Policy*. New York: Sage.

Benshoof, P. (2007) 'Over-reliance on any technology could leave us vulnerable', *Border and Transportation Security*, 147–8.

Blakeway D. H. (1995) 'Electronic supervision systems: innovations in technology', in K. Schulz (ed.) *Electronic Monitoring and Corrections: The Policy, the Operation, the Research*. Vancouver: Simon Fraser University.

Boutellier, H. (2004) *The Safety Utopia: Contemporary Discontent and Desire as to Crime and Punishment*. Utrecht: Kluwer Academic.

Bright, M. (2002) 'Surgical Tags Plan for Sex Offenders', *The Observer*, 17 November.

Buck, J. (2009a) *The Basics: GPS Tracking in Community Corrections*. BI Incorporated White Paper. Online at: www.bi.com.

Buck, J. (2009b) *Autonomous GPS: Assisted GPS or AFLT: What and Why?* BI Incorporated White Paper. Online at: www.bi.com.

Bunn, C. (1974) 'And keep us from our castles in analog science fiction', reprinted in J. D. Olander and M. H. Greenberg (eds) (1977) *Criminal Justice through Science Fiction*. New York: New Viewpoints (pp. 168–94).

Button, D. M., DeMichele, M. and Payne, B. K. (2009) 'Using electronic monitoring to supervise sex offenders: legislative patterns and implications for community corrections officers', *Criminal Justice Policy Review*, 20: 414–36.

Castells, M. (2004) 'Informationalism, networks and the network society', in M. Castells (ed.) *The Network Society: A Cross-cultural Perspective*. Cheltenham: Edward Elgar Publishing.

Conway, P. (2009) 'Editor's welcome', *Journal of Offender Monitoring*, 20, special issue on the 2008–2009 Electronic Monitoring Survey.

Cotter, R. and De Lint, W. (2009) 'GPS electronic monitoring and contemporary penology: a case study of US GPS electronic monitoring programmes', *Howard Journal of Criminal Justice*, 48(1): 76–87.

Crawford, A. (2003) 'Contractual governance of deviant behaviour', *Journal of Law and Society*, 30(4): 479–505.

Drake, G. B. (no date) *Elements of a Successful GPS Offender Tracking Programme*.

Drake, G. B. (2009) 'Offender tracking in the United States', paper presented at the Conférence Permanente Européene de la Probation event: 7–9 May.

Erez, E., Ibarra, P. R. and Lurie, N. A. (2004) 'Electronic monitoring of domestic violence cases: a study of two bilateral programmes', *Federal Probation*, 68(1).

Etzioni, A. (1999) *The Limits of Privacy*. New York: Basic Books.

Graham, S. (1997) 'Imagining the real-time city: telecommunications, urban paradigms and the future of cities', in S. Westwood and J. Williams (eds) *Imagining Cities: Scripts, Signs, Memory*. London: Routledge.

Haggerty, K. (2004) 'Displaced expertise: three constraints on the policy relevance of criminological thought', *Theoretical Criminology*, 8(2): 211–31.

Home Office (2004) *Confident Communities in a Secure Britain: The Home Office Strategic Plan 2004–2008*, CM 6287. London: Home Office.

Hoshen, J. Sennott J. and Winkler, M. (1995) 'Keeping tabs on criminals', *Spectrum IEEE*, 32(2): 26–32.

House, D. (2009) '*Shadow tagging systems*', paper presented at the Conférence Permanente Européene de la Probation event, 7–9 May.

Hucklesby, A. (2008) 'Vehicles of desistance? the impact of electronically monitored curfew orders', *Criminology and Criminal Justice*, 8: 51–71.

Hucklesby, A. (2009) 'Understanding offender's compliance: a case study of electronically monitored curfew orders', *Journal of Law and Society*, 36(2): 248–71.

Ingraham, B. L. and Smith, G.S. (1972) 'The use of electronics in the observation and control of human behaviour and its possible use in rehabilitation and parole', *Issues in Criminology*, 7(2).

John Howard Society of Alberta (2006) *Electronic (Radio Frequency) and GPS Monitored Community Based Supervision Programmes*.

Journal of Offender Monitoring (2009) Vol. 20 No. 1 and 2.5. Special issue on the 2008–2009 Electronic Monitoring Survey.

Lilly, J. R. (1992) 'Selling justice: electronic monitoring and the security industry', *Justice Quarterly*, 9: 493–503.

Lilly, J. R. and Deflem, M. (1996) 'Profit and penality: an analysis of the corrections-commercial complex', *Crime and Delinquency*, 42: 3–20.

Lilly, J. R. and Knepper, P. (1993) 'An international perspective on the privatisation of corrections', *Howard Journal*, 31: 174–91.

Mair, G. (2005) 'Electronic monitoring in England and Wales: evidence-based or not?', *Criminal Justice*, 5: 257–77.

Mathiesen, T. (1990) *Prison on Trial*. London: Sage.

Meyer, J. A. (1971) 'Crime deterrent transponder system: Transactions on aerospace and electronic systems', *AES*, 7–1, 1–22.

Ministry of Justice Republic of Korea (2009) *High Risk Offenders GPS Tracking Program in Korea*. Seoul: Ministry of Justice.

Monmonier, M. (2004) *Spying with Maps: Surveillance Technologies and the Future of Privacy*. Chicago: Chicago University Press.

Moore, M. and Thurston, J. (2009) *County Correctional Issues: Adapting in an era of Jail Overcrowding, Tight Budgets, Rising Costs, and Changing Inmate Demographics*, BI Incorporated white paper. Online at: www.bi.com.

Nellis, M. (1991) 'The electronic monitoring of offenders in England and Wales: recent developments and future prospects', *British Journal of Criminology*, 31(2): 165–85.

Nellis, M. (2004) 'The satellite tracking of offenders: A brief literature review', unpublished report.

Nellis, M. (2005) '"Out of this world": the advent of the satellite tracking of offenders in England and Wales', *Howard Journal*, 44(2): 125–50.

Nellis, M. (2006a) 'NOMS, contestability and the process of technocorrectional innovation', in M. Hough, R. Allen and U. Padel (eds) *Reshaping Probation and Prisons: The New Offender Management Framework*. Bristol: Policy Press.

Nellis, M. (2006b) 'Electronic monitoring, satellite tracking and the new punitiveness in England and Wales', in J. Pratt, D. Brown, M. Brown, S. Hallsworth and W. Morrison (eds) *The New Punitiveness: Trends, Theories and Perspectives*. Cullompton: Willan Publishing.

Nellis, M. (2007a) 'Electronic monitoring and control orders for terrorist suspects in England and Wales', in T. Abbas (ed.) *Islamic Political Radicalism*. Edinburgh: Edinburgh University Press.

Nellis, M. (2007b) 'Surveillance, rehabilitation and electronic monitoring: getting the issues clear', *Criminology and Public Policy*, 5(1): 103–8.

Nellis, M. (2009a) '24/7/365. Mobility, locatability and the satellite tracking of offenders', in K. Franco Aas, H.O. Gundus and H. M. Lommell (eds) *Technologies of Insecurity: The Surveillance of Everyday Life*. London: Routledge.

Nellis, M. (2009b) 'Electronically monitored punishment and penal innovation in a telematic society', in P. Knepper, J. Doak and J. Shapland (eds) *Urban Crime Prevention, Surveillance and Restorative Justice*. New York: CRC Press, Taylor and Francis.

Padgett, K., Bales, W. and Blomberg, T. (2006) 'Under surveillance: an empirical test of the effectiveness and implications of electronic monitoring', *Criminology and Public Policy*, 5(1): 61–92.

Payne, B. K., DeMichele, M. and Button, D. M. (2008) 'Understanding the monitoring of sex offenders: background and implications', *Corrections Compendium*, 33(1): 1–5.

Pew Centre on the States (2009) *One in 31: The Long Reach of American Corrections*. Washington, DC: Pew Centre on the States.

Roberts, J. V. (2004) *The Virtual Prison*. Cambridge: Cambridge University Press.

Renzema, M. and Mayo-Wilson, E. (2005) 'Can electronic monitoring reduce crime for moderate to high risk offenders?', *Journal of Experimental Criminology*, 1: 215–37.

Scheerer, S. (2000) 'Three trends into the new millennium: the managerial, the populist and the road towards global justice', in P. Green and A. Rutherford (eds) *Criminal Policy in Transition*. Oxford: Hart Publishing.

Schwitzgebel, R. R. (1963) 'Delinquents with tape recorders', *New Society*, 31 January.

Schwitzgebel, R. (1964) *Streetcorner Research: An Experimental Approach to the Juvenile Delinquent*. Cambridge, MA: Harvard University Press.

Shute, S. (2007) *Satellite Tracking of Offenders: A Study of the Pilots in England and Wales*, Research Summary 4. London: Ministry of Justice.

Spencer, A. (2009) *Balancing Risk and Need: Review of the Decision to send Brian Martin to open conditions in the light of his subsequent absconding from the Open Estate on 18th May 2009 and issues highlighted as a consequence*. Edinburgh: Scottish Government.

Stacey, T. (1995) 'Innovations in technology', in K. Schulz (ed.) *Electronic Monitoring and Corrections: The Policy, the Operation, the Research*. Vancouver: Simon Fraser University.

Walker, C. (2009) *Blackstone's Guide to Anti-terrorism Legislation*, 2nd edn. Oxford: Oxford University Press.

Wennerberg, I. and Holmberg, S. (2007) *Extended Use of Electronic Tagging in Sweden: The Offenders and Victims Views*. Report 2007:3. Stockholm: National Council for Crime Prevention (Brå).

Winkler, M. (1993) 'Walking prisons: the developing technology of electronic controls', *The Futurist*, July–August.

Chapter 17

Hate crime offending and victimisation: some considerations for public protection

Nathan Hall

Introduction

Hate crime is defined by the UK government as 'any crime or incident where the perpetrator's hostility or prejudice against an identifiable group of people is a factor in determining who is victimised' along the recognised diversity strands of disability, race, religion or belief, sexual orientation, and transgender (Home Office 2009a). In criminological and criminal justice terms 'hate crime' is a relatively new concept. It is, however, an issue that has rapidly ascended the criminal justice agenda and continues to do so. From the murder of Stephen Lawrence in 1993, which ultimately served to place hate crimes firmly on the criminological map, through to the deaths of Anthony Walker, Jody Dobrowski, Brent Martin, Sophie Lancaster, Johnny Delaney, Christine Lakinski, Fiona Pilkington and Francecca Hardwick, and numerous others, all targeted because of some aspect of their identity, to the various victim surveys that consistently demonstrate the disproportionate victimisation of minority groups, to the government's recent Hate Crime Action Plan (Home Office 2009b), concerns about identity motivated violence have moved hate crime from the periphery towards the centre of criminal justice attention.

In addition to responding to a form of criminal activity, the need to respond to hate crime is exacerbated by two key issues that relate to the very nature of identity motivated offending. In essence, hate crime is held to be unique, and therefore of particular interest to the agencies of the criminal justice system, first because of the specific interest that needs to be paid to the specific motivations behind such offending, and second because of the disproportionate impact that hate crime can have on victims. The 'unique victimisation' perspective is underpinned by a growing body of evidence that suggests that hate crimes have disproportionate physical and psychological impacts upon both the victim and the wider community as compared to equivalent crimes that are not motivated by 'hate' (Chahal and Julienne 2000; Craig-Henderson and Sloan 2003); that hate crimes are socially divisive and can heighten tensions between communities (Levin 1999; Home Office 2009a); that they are more likely than other crimes to involve repeated victimisation (Bowling 1999; ACPO 2005); and that they can increase the risk of civil disorder through retaliatory attacks along inter-group lines (Levin 1999).

The focus on 'motivation' is similarly of interest for two reasons. First, in light of the above, the motivations behind hate crimes seemingly cause disproportionately negative outcomes as compared to other motivations for crime. Second, this places the criminal justice system in the position of not only needing to respond to the offence that has occurred, but also to consider *why* it occurred. In other words, for example, securing a conviction for a hate crime under existing legislation requires evidence of a crime *and* evidence of 'hate' as the motivation behind the crime. Without the latter a hate crime would simply be an 'ordinary' crime. Given the importance of these issues, this chapter examines the literature relating to both the nature of hate victimisation and the motivations behind hate offending. In placing this within the context of public protection, Maden's (2007) 'risk assessment and management checklist' (Table 17.1) provides a useful framework for discussion. Although there is not the space here to address all of the questions Maden poses, this chapter focuses predominantly on the issues raised in Step 1, and to a lesser extent those raised in Step 2.

The origins of prejudice and discrimination

The Home Office definition of hate crime, cited above, points to the concept of prejudice as the motivation for hate crimes, and when we speak about 'hate' crimes, it is really crimes motivated by prejudice that we are referring to. It is therefore with the concept of prejudice that this chapter begins. There are numerous competing perspectives that seek to identify and explain the origins of prejudice and discrimination. Arguably the most significant contribution has been that of Gordon Allport in his seminal work, *The Nature of Prejudice*. Although competing ideas have since been advocated, Brown (1995) acknowledges that Allport's work has come to be regarded as the departure point for all modern research into aspects of prejudice. Furthermore, Brown states that so significant was Allport's contribution that his theorising has provided the basis for programmes designed to improve race relations in American schools for the past 60 years or so.

According to Allport (1954) prejudice is a normal and rational human behaviour by virtue of our need to organise all the cognitive data our brain receives through the formation of generalisations, concepts and categories whose content represents an oversimplification of our world and experiences therein. This process is essential to our daily living and the forming of generalisations, categories and concepts based on experience and probability helps us to guide our daily activities and to make sense of the world around us. However, our oversimplification of the world leads us to one of Allport's more significant points: that the formation of our generalisations is just as likely to lead to irrational generalisations, concepts and categories as it is to rational ones.

Table 17.1 Risk assessment and management checklist.

Step 1: Describe likely scenario	Step 2: Develop management strategy	Step 3: Determine priority
Nature What kinds of offences might this person commit? Who are the likely victims? What is the likely motivation?	*Risk factors* What events or circumstances might increase or decrease the person's risk? Are those circumstances present? Are they capable of being created or manipulated?	*Priority* What level of effort or intervention will it take to prevent this person from committing further serious offences?
Severity What would be the harm (physical or psychological) to victims? Is it likely the offending might escalate to life-threatening levels?	*Monitoring required* How can we monitor warning signs? What events or circumstances should trigger a reassessment? What level of monitoring and by which agency(ies)?	*Immediate action* What steps should be taken immediately to prevent reoffending?
Imminence How soon might the offending occur? In what context is it more likely to occur? Are there warning signs to suggest the offending risk is increasing or imminent?	*Interventions* What type of intervention could help to reduce the offending risk? Help/treatment/counselling? Basic needs (e.g. accommodation)	*Case review* Who has overall responsibility for case coordination? When should the case be scheduled for routine review? What should trigger early review?
Frequency/duration How often might the offending occur – once, several times, frequently? Is the violence risk chronic or acute (i.e. time-limited)?	*Supervision* What supervision or surveillance could be used to manage this person's violence risks? Control/restraint? Exclusions?	
Likelihood In general, how frequent or common is this type of offending? How frequently has this person committed this type of offending? How likely is it that this person will commit this type of offending?	*Victim safety planning* What steps can be taken to protect likely victims? Exclusion zones?	

Source: Adapted from Maden (2007: 110).

Similarly, Allport suggests that in order to further simplify our lives human beings naturally homogenise, often for no other reason than convenience, which in turn creates separateness among groups. According to Allport, humans tend to relate to other humans with similar presuppositions for the purpose of comfort, ease and congeniality. However, it is this separateness, coupled with our need to form generalisations and categories, that lays the foundations for psychological elaboration and the development of prejudice. Allport argues that people that stay separate have fewer channels of communication, are likely to exaggerate and misunderstand the differences between groups, and develop genuine and imaginary conflicts of interests. It is this, according to Allport, that contributes largely to the formation of 'in-groups' and 'out-groups' and therefore to the *potential* formation and development of in-group loyalty and out-group rejection and the subsequent *potential* expression of prejudice and discriminatory behaviour towards those out-groups.

Although this is a simplified account of the foundations of prejudice as defined by Allport (readers are advised to see the original for his comprehensive account), it is from this basis, he argues, that people develop their prejudicial nature, both positive and negative. Allport also stated that any negative attitude tends somehow to express itself in action, although the degree of action will vary greatly based upon the individual and the strength of the prejudice. To illustrate this Allport (1954: 14) provides a five-point scale to distinguish different degrees of negative action (see Figure 17.1).

Antilocution is simply the discussion of prejudices, usually with like-minded friends. *Avoidance* represents a more intense prejudice and leads the bearer to avoid members of the disliked group, although he or she does not inflict direct harm upon them. *Discrimination* is where the prejudiced individual makes detrimental distinctions of an active sort. Under conditions of heightened emotion prejudice may lead to acts of violence or semi-violence, categorised as *physical attack*. Finally, *extermination* marks the ultimate degree of violent expression of prejudice.

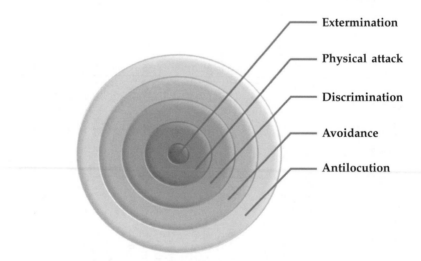

Figure 17.1 Allport's five stages of prejudice.

Allport is at pains to point out that most people never go beyond antilocution, and those that do will not necessarily move progressively up the scale, but it does serve to call attention to the range of potential activities that may occur as a direct result of prejudiced attitudes and beliefs.

Hate crimes as they are currently socially and legally constructed are rarely motivated by pure hate, but rather by prejudice, and this presents a number of problems. First, we do not know for certain what prejudice is, nor where it comes from, nor how it develops. But we do know that prejudice is entirely natural to the human condition, and is perhaps even definitive of it. As Sullivan (1999) suggests, we are social beings. We associate and therefore we disassociate and one can't happen without the other. Humans necessarily differentiate.

Second, there are many kinds of prejudice that vary greatly and have different psychological dynamics underpinning them and this has important implications for responding to hate crimes. Third, because prejudices are independent psychological responses they can be expressed in a bewildering number of ways, ranging from a mild dislike or general aversion to others to extreme acts of violence. But as Green, McFalls and Smith (2003: 27) have suggested: 'It might take the better part of a lifetime to read the prodigious research literature on prejudice ... yet scarcely any of this research examines directly and systematically the question of why prejudice erupts into violence.'

The same might also be said for more specific criminological understanding of hate offenders. Although the Stephen Lawrence Inquiry (Macpherson 1999) cemented hate crime in the criminal justice agenda (see Hall *et al.* 2009 for a discussion of this) Bowling (1999) suggests that academic and professional interest in issues of race and racism in relation to crime (and therefore, by analogy, the emergence of interest in hate crime) can be traced back to the early 1980s in the UK through two key events. The first was the urban riots of 1981, most notably in Brixton, that saw the emergence of race, prejudice and discrimination as significant social issues. The second was the emergence of victimology in the late 1970s and early 1980s, and the subsequent development of large social surveys that for the first time began to provide a wealth of data relating to the plight of the victim, and in particular the disproportionate victimisation of minority groups.

Together, these two developments served to ensure that the victim was placed at the centre of the criminal justice, criminological and political focus: a situation that remains to date. While the victim of any crime should be of central concern to all parties in the criminal justice system, this dominant focus on the victim has meant that the perpetrator as an actor in the equation has been largely ignored. This is particularly true for perpetrators of hate crime and poses something of a problem for criminology and criminal justice. The following two passages from Bowling (1999) outline the challenges that criminal justice professionals have historically faced as a result of the predominantly victim-oriented focus.

There has been almost no research on perpetrators. Whilst the most basic of descriptions have been formulated, they remain something of an effigy in the criminological literature ... The perpetrator is unknown and, consequently, the possibility for any understanding or interpretation of his or her behaviour becomes impossible. (1999: 163)

What is needed for the purposes of explaining [hate crime] is for attention to be turned away from an analysis of the characteristics of victims to focus on the characteristics of offenders: their relationship with those they victimise; the social milieux in which anger, aggression, hostility, and violence are fostered; and the social processes by which violence becomes directed against minority groups ... Criminologists operate with scant evidence about what is going on in the lives of these people. Instead, we have only a devilish effigy for symbolic sacrifice. (1999: 305)

Writing of this situation from the United States, Barbara Perry (2003) has argued similarly. In addition to the impact of the victim-oriented focus of which Bowling speaks, Perry has suggested that theorising about perpetrators has been scant partially because hate crime is relatively 'new' to the criminological horizon, and also because of the lack of agreement about how exactly 'hate crime' should be defined. In addition, Perry has pointed to the fact that historically, when criminology has taken an interest in minority groups *per se* the focus has tended to be on their criminality, rather than on crimes committed against them.

In spite of this, however, there are signs that this trend has reversed somewhat. There is a growing body of emergent literature on the subject of perpetrators, and while being still relatively small this has started to fill some of the gaps to which Bowling and Perry have both referred. It is clear from the various definitions of hate crime (see Hall 2005 for a discussion of these) that the words 'prejudice', 'discrimination' and 'bigotry' frequently appear. Perry (2003) has suggested therefore that these concepts mark the starting point for this emerging theorising about the perpetrators of hate crime. However, as noted above, the existent literature tells us remarkably little about how prejudice transforms into actions that would constitute hate crimes.

Hate crime offending

While Allport (1954) hypothesised that all prejudice will likely manifest itself in physical action of one form or another at some point in time, he also noted that not all prejudices will necessarily and automatically be transformed into an action or actions that would likely constitute a crime. It is also unclear from the wider psychological literature as to why and how prejudice transforms into negative action. Criminological literature has similarly failed to find a satisfactory causal explanation. In presenting a critique of traditional criminological theories, Perry (2003: 97) points out: 'Criminology has yet to come to terms with the phenomenon we have come to know as hate crime. Existing theory tends to neglect either or both the structural underpinnings of hate crime, and the situated process that it entails.'

There is not the space here to discuss the shortcomings of criminological theory in explaining hate crimes (see Perry 2003 for a discussion of these); however, the failings of traditional theorising have served to open up the field to empirical research into hate offenders and their motivations. In her review of the socio-psychological literature Kellina Craig (2002) identifies specific areas that relate to the characteristics of hate crime perpetrators, and in doing so notes the difficulties and limitations of theorising hate crime. Craig suggests:

> Although several explanations may be applicable to hate crime occurrence, no existing one can fully account for all types of hate crime. This is because the factors that contribute to hate crime (i.e. perpetrators' motives, victims' characteristics, and cultural ideologies about the victim's social groups) differ markedly for each incident ... Thus, in order to explain hate crimes, a consideration of all potentially relevant explanations is necessary. (2003: 120)

Craig presents evidence from a range of disciplines that supports the view that hate crime represents a unique form of aggression and has both symbolic and instrumental functions for the perpetrator. In other words, the victim is a symbol, or is representative, of the social group the offender despises, and whose victimisation can be instrumental in impacting upon and altering the actions and behaviours of others in the group to which the victim belongs. In other words, by victimising one member of an identifiable group the offender is able to create numerous secondary victims who share the same characteristics of the original victim (see also the discussion of the '*in terrorum*' effect, below). Craig also identifies that many hate offenders will carry a deep-seated resentment of minority groups and their members, and committing hate crimes helps perpetrators to maintain a positive social identity by lauding their in-group through the denigration of an out-group. Thus, she suggests, victims will often be the targets of extreme negative stereotypes.

Craig also presents evidence to demonstrate that this resentment may be fuelled by actual or imagined economic competition and frustration, the presence of certain religious values, the greater presence of psychopathological traits among hate offenders as compared to other criminals, and the presence of authoritarian personality traits among a large number of haters.

Simply, then, hate crime perpetrators can effectively be motivated by one or more of a wide range of social, psychological, political, cultural and other factors. On the basis of Craig's research, the search for a single, universal causal factor for hate crime is likely to be fruitless. Rather, it is the interplay of a number of different factors that produces perpetrators.

This situation is recognised by Rae Sibbitt (1997) in her study of the perpetrators of racial violence and racial harassment in London. By reviewing existing literature combined with her own empirical research involving interviews with offenders, community members, and statutory and non-statutory agencies in two London boroughs, Sibbitt suggests that there are essentially two strands of theories to explain why certain people commit racially motivated offences. The first, she argues, links racist behaviour to crime in general in that the psychological and contextual factors that facilitate wider criminal and anti-social behaviour will also facilitate racist behaviour.

The second approach suggests that racial harassment is a logical and predictable expression of underlying racism in society at large. In this sense, then, prejudice is felt by a community towards a minority group, perhaps fuelled by perceptions of strain, but there is a context in which a minority of that majority will 'cross the line' and express their prejudice in some physical form, in this case through harassment and violence. This approach assumes that the perpetrator is simply expressing the views that are felt but not necessarily expressed criminally by the wider majority community.

In addition to asking why these individuals 'cross the line', this also raises the question of how the wider community develop their prejudices. We have already noted the 'normality' of prejudice, but Sibbitt presents historical evidence to suggest that in particular, the rapid demographic changes in England and Wales during the 1960s, coupled with the inability of some communities to cope with this change, has played a part in the development of community prejudice. The situation is somewhat amplified, Sibbitt suggests, by factors such as unemployment, economic hardship and/ or deprivation, competition for scarce resources (for example, housing), and a lack of community facilities (particularly in relation to youth and leisure facilities). Thus, strain is not always the sole cause of hate crime, but may instead provide a platform from which it can emerge. In this sense people will require a scapegoat upon which to blame the situation in which they find themselves. Here the problems experienced by certain communities are inevitably perceived as being not of their own making or a product of circumstance, but as the fault of certain groups who are seen as responsible for causing or intensifying these social problems.

Sibbitt (1997) therefore argues that it is the interplay of these contextual factors and the psychology of certain individuals that produces perpetrators. Offenders are likely to be involved in other forms of criminal or anti-social behaviour, of which hate offending is a part, and will operate with the passive support (or at least without the condemnation) of some sections of the wider community who share similar views but who are not necessarily inclined towards criminal behaviour themselves. Sibbitt's research also includes a typology that suggests that the perpetrators of racist offences span all age ranges, from young children to old age pensioners, and involve both sexes who often act in groups.

Sibbitt's typology is useful because it sheds light on a number of the dynamic risk factors that inform racist offending. Despite Perry's identification of flaws in strain theory as a complete explanation for hate crimes, Sibbitt's research nevertheless highlights the role of localised perceptions of strain in the commission of hate crimes. Furthermore, Sibbitt's work lends empirical support to Perry's (2003) theorising concerning expressions of power and the significance of perceptions of appropriate positions within social hierarchies.

A further offender typology has been developed in the United States by McDevitt, Levin and Bennett (2002). These researchers analysed 169 Boston police case files in an attempt to produce a typology of hate offenders based upon the motives cited in interviews by police officials, victims and some of the perpetrators themselves. The research of 2002 built upon their 1993 typologies, and concluded that while the underlying motivation for all hate offences is bigotry, there are often additional motivating factors present in this type of offending behaviour.

Using indicators nationally accepted in the United States to identify the hate element of an offence (for example, the use of language by the offender, the perpetrator's offending history, the presence of 'triggering' events, the use of hate graffiti, and the location of the offence), McDevitt et al. concluded that hate offenders can be placed into one of four categories based on motivation.

Of the 169 cases analysed, they concluded that 66 per cent (or 111 of the total) of the offences, mostly committed by youths, were motivated by the thrill or for the excitement of the act. In other words, the vast majority of hate offences were motivated by the offender's desire for a 'thrill' often because they were bored or were seeking some form of 'excitement'. This finding supports Sibbitt's contention, above, that many younger racist offenders commit offences out of a sense of boredom and a need for excitement in their lives. McDevitt et al. report that in 91 per cent of these 'thrill' cases the perpetrators left their neighbourhood to search for a victim, and deliberately selected their target because they were 'different' from themselves. The researchers also suggest that many of the offences analysed in this category were underpinned by an immature desire to display power and to enhance the offender's own feeling of self-importance at the expense of others.

In 25 per cent (or 43) of the cases analysed, McDevitt et al. categorised the motivation as being 'defensive' in its nature. In these cases, the offender committed hate offences against what he or she perceived to be outsiders or intruders in an attempt to defend or protect his or her 'territory'. Echoing the view that hate crimes are 'message crimes' (discussed below), the researchers found that many 'defensive' offenders believed that minority groups had undeservedly moved into their neighbourhood and that their hate crimes served to send a message to the victim and other members of the victim's group that they are unwelcome and should relocate. McDevitt et al. suggest that defensive attacks are often associated with demographic shifts at a local level, particularly where neighbourhoods or communities begin to experience a transition from being dominated by one ethnic group towards a more diverse population.

The third category of hate motivation the researchers identified is 'retaliation', accounting for 8 per cent (fourteen cases) of the sample. This is based on the finding that a hate offence is often followed by a number of subsequent hate attacks. They state that retaliatory offences are not a reaction to the presence of a particular individual or group, but rather are a reaction to a particular hate offence that has already occurred, be it real or perceived. Retaliatory offenders are therefore retaliating against, or avenging, an earlier attack.

Perhaps the best example of retaliatory offending can be seen in the escalation of offences committed against Muslims (or those mistaken to be Muslims) in the US and also in Britain in the period following the terrorist attacks in the US on 11 September 2001 (see NYPD 2002). This lends support to McDevitt *et al*.'s suggestion that retaliatory offences based on revenge have the greatest potential for fuelling further offences, resulting in a cycle of offending that is often difficult to end.

The final category they identified is that of the 'mission' offender, representing less than 1 per cent (one case) of the sample. Here the offender is totally committed to his or her hate and bigotry, and views the objects of their hate as an evil that must be removed from the world.

While these typologies have been somewhat simplified here (see McDevitt *et al*. 2002 for a comprehensive overview) and despite the study's methodological limitations, most notably the size of the sample and the use of police case files, the study has nevertheless provided some interesting supplementary information about the commission of hate offences, as illustrated in Table 17.2.

It is clear from Table 17.2 that the majority of hate offenders are young adults, as is the case for offenders generally. Here, however, the typology varies from that proposed by Sibbitt (1997), who found that race hate perpetrators spanned a range of age groups. This discrepancy in the findings may, however, be more to do with differences in research methodologies and terminology.

Also of interest, and in line with Sibbitt's findings, is the suggestion that hate crime is often a group activity. Furthermore, hate offences often involve whatever 'weapons' happen to be at hand, and occur often with little or no victim–offender history. This lends support to the contention that hate crimes are impersonal and that victims are interchangeable, although we should note here the contrast with Sibbitt's findings concerning the victimisation of neighbours that suggests that in many cases the victim and offender are in fact known to each other.

Table 17.2 Characteristics of hate crimes by offender motivation.

Attack characteristics	Thrill	Defensive	Retaliatory	Mission
Number of offenders	Group	Group	Single offender	Group
Age of offender(s)	Teens–young adults	Teens–young adults	Teens–young adults	Young adults–adults
Location	Victim's turf	Offender's turf	Victim's turf	Victim's or offender's turf
Weapon	Hands, feet, rocks	Hands, feet, rocks	Hands, feet, rocks, sticks, guns	Bats, guns
Victim offender history	None	Previous acts intimidation	Often no history	None
Commitment to bias	Little	Moderate	Moderate	Full
Deterrence	Likely	Unlikely	Unlikely	Most unlikely

Source: McDevitt, Levin and Bennett 2002: 311.

The final points of note in Table 17.2 relate to the last two categories. The offender's commitment to their hatred is a significant factor, particularly in relation to whether or not they can be deterred from their actions. Thrill offenders are not particularly committed to their prejudice, where in contrast mission offenders are fully committed to their erroneous beliefs. Defensive and retaliatory offenders fall somewhere inbetween the two ends of this spectrum. These latter findings serve to highlight the complexity of prejudice as a psychological phenomenon. The hate of the mission offender, for example, is considerably different in its nature from the hate of the thrill offender.

Just as there are different degrees of hate, so there are different degrees of culpability. The finding that hate crimes are often committed by offenders operating in groups rather than alone has also led McDevitt *et al.* (2002) to advance a 'continuum of culpability' to assist criminal justice decision-makers in determining the role of group members in the commission of an offence, and to develop sentencing options based upon that degree of culpability. Identifying differing degrees of involvement in an attack, and thereby different degrees of culpability for those operating in groups not only serves to potentially aid prosecution decisions but also furthers our understanding of offender behaviour.

Just as there are four offender typologies, so McDevitt *et al.* have identified four levels of culpability in group offending. The most culpable group member is the 'leader', who may suggest to the group that they commit a hate offence for any of the reasons outlined above (for example, for the thrill, or to retaliate). The second category, 'fellow travellers', do not initiate the offence but once suggested are happy to comply with the suggestion of the leader, making them only slightly less culpable than the 'leader'. The third identifiable category is the 'unwilling participant', who while disapproving of the situation that is occurring, still does not actively attempt to intervene in the crime, or report it to the police. For these individuals, the need for acceptance and peer group approval is the key factor in the failure to intervene. The final category is that of the 'heroes' who actively attempt to stop the offence from taking place. McDevitt *et al.* suggest that this behaviour should be rewarded because their actions require immunity to social influence and a strong conscience in order to put the needs of a person they have never met before above the desires of their friends or peer group.

In addition to providing academics with useful information about offenders, this typology is now widely used in law enforcement in the United States and has had numerous implications in terms of policy development in this area. As McDevitt *et al.* point out:

> One reason why the original typology has been so widely adopted by law enforcement is that, early on, it offered a way to categorize hate crime offenders and suggested some clues as to methods of identifying hate offences ... Understanding different types of hate motivation and specific indicators associated with these have been shown to be useful in identifying and prosecuting hate crimes and providing appropriate services to hate crime victims ... Tools that assist government agencies in understanding and effectively dealing with hate crime incidents

may be our best effort toward curtailing this brand of violence (2002: 315).

While the body of academic research into perpetrators continues to grow, it is clear that a comprehensive understanding of why some people commit hate crimes is yet to be achieved. Yet developing an accurate understanding of hate offenders is crucial if the criminal justice system is to respond effectively and appropriately. We are fairly safe in our assumption that hatred as a human emotion has its roots in prejudice, but we know that simply being prejudiced is not enough. Not all people act upon their prejudices in a negative way, and certainly not in a way that would constitute a crime.

Rather, there has to be something more that transforms erroneous beliefs and negative emotion into criminal behaviour, and that 'something' could be one or more of a great many social, psychological, criminogenic and contextual factors. The interplay that occurs between these factors that ultimately produces perpetrators is complex and unclear, and would appear to be context-specific. For example, Iganski highlights the rather uncomfortable reality that the majority of hate offenders are not hate-fuelled bigots who actively seek out their victims in a calculated and premeditated manner, but rather are 'people like us' (2008: 42) who offend in the context of their everyday lives. As such, he suggests, hate crimes predominantly result from 'the normal frictions of day-to-day life' (2008: 45) and his research reveals a myriad distinctive features of city life in particular that provide potential opportunities for 'everyday' hate victimisation.

What is certain, though, is that the word 'hate' that is used as a catch-all term in the current context in fact masks a wide range of human emotions and behaviours that manifest themselves in many different ways with varying degrees of consequence. Hate is not a single emotion or behaviour, but instead stands for a variety of complex psychological phenomena that can be expressed in many different ways by different people. Why some people express 'hate' in the form of criminal behaviour is something that is not yet fully understood.

Hate crime victimisation

In mirroring the state of knowledge on perpetrators, Iganski (2001) has pointed out that while there has been much speculation about what the distinct harms of hate crime might be, there has in fact been relatively little empirical research undertaken into the impact of hate crime victimisation. In addition, Perry (2003) has suggested that the existing literature on hate crime victims has tended to be rather broad and non-specific in its focus. Nevertheless, this body of literature, as with that relating to offenders, has recently grown in terms of its depth and scope, and is providing some valuable insights into this area of hate crime. As such, this part of the chapter examines some of the recent research studies into the qualitative aspects of hate crime victimisation. Bowling explains that racist hate crime should be viewed as an ongoing *process*, rather than as a series of isolated, distinct and separate incidents. He suggests that:

Conceiving of violent racism as processes implies an analysis which is dynamic; includes the social relationships between all the actors in the process; can capture the continuity between physical violence, threat and intimidation; can capture the dynamic of repeated or systematic victimization; incorporates historical context; and takes account of the social relationships which inform definitions of appropriate and inappropriate behaviour. (1999: 158)

Put simply, crime victimisation does not begin and end with the commission of an offence. Hate victimisation may involve one crime or, more likely, a great many crimes to the extent that it is not always clear where one ends and the next begins. It may also involve actions that border on being criminal offences but might not be easily defined or recognised as such – a situation that can have serious implications for policing and prosecution (see Hall 2005 for a discussion of this). There is evidence to suggest that these events can nevertheless have a disproportionate effect on the victim and their community, and that the fear and intimidation that result will transcend far beyond just the moment when the incident or incidents occur.

As Martin (1996) suggests, the belief that bias motivation produces negative effects, even in crimes not held to be very serious in terms of criminal law, is one of the key rationales for giving hate crimes special attention. This is recognised by police services in both the UK and the US. In their guidance to police officers, the Association of Chief Police Officers (2000: 11) state that 'hate crime can have a devastating effect on the quality of life of its victims, those who fear becoming victims and the community. That is why we must give it priority.'

Clearly, then, the widely held view that hate crimes have a disproportionately greater impact on victims than 'normal' crimes, regardless of their apparent seriousness in legal terms, is one of the central justifications for both the recent recognition of hate as a distinct form of criminal behaviour and the imposition of harsher penalties for hate offenders.

One of the most comprehensive studies of hate victimisation to date, conducted by Herek, Cogan and Gillis (2002), examined victim experiences in cases of homophobic hate crime in the United States. The research built upon an earlier pilot study conducted in 1997, which found that hate crime victims experience greater long-term post-traumatic stress disorder symptoms, including higher levels of depression, anxiety and anger when compared to victims of similar non-hate motivated offences. Significantly, the 1997 research also found that some hate crime victims took up to five years to overcome the effects of the crime, compared to up to two years for victims of comparable non-hate motivated offences.

The larger 2002 study supported and extended the earlier findings. Herek *et al.* (2002) found that hate crimes based on sexual orientation most frequently occurred in public locations and were perpetrated by one or more males unknown to the victim. However, the researchers point out that victimisation is not confined to these dynamics and that members of sexual minorities are effectively at risk of victimisation wherever they are identified as being gay, lesbian or bisexual. Herek *et al.* also state that while hate and non-hate personal crimes did not significantly differ in their general severity, they were struck by the physical and psychological brutality of the hate crimes they encountered. The effect of this greater brutality, they suggest, is twofold. First, as was the case in the initial report, victims generally suffered greater psychological distress, which persisted over a longer period of time, than non-hate victims. These findings are consistent with other studies on hate victimisation by Erlich (1992) and Garofalo and Martin (1993).

Second, the research also found that hate crime victimisation extends beyond the immediate victim and has consequences for the wider LGBT (lesbian, gay, bisexual and transgender) community. Because offenders are motivated against an impersonal characteristic over which the victim has little or no control, Herek *et al.* argue that hate crimes act as a form of terrorism in that they send a 'message' to other members of the community who share the same traits or belong to the same social group as the victim that they are not safe either. In this sense, then, it would appear that the Home Office (2009a) are justified in their view that:

> Hate crime is different to other forms of crime. Hate crime targets people because of their identity. It is a form of discrimination that infringes human rights and keeps people from enjoying the full benefits of our society. Research has shown that hate crimes cause greater psychological harm than similar crimes without a motivation of prejudice. Hate crime creates fear in victims, groups and communities and encourages communities to turn on each other. The effects of hate crime vary, but often include: anger and fear of repeat attacks; depression and a worsening of existing health conditions, including mental health issues; a financial burden, for example, having to replace and repair vandalised property, or having to take time off work; victims changing their personal appearance, accommodation and, or daily patterns to avoid being victimised.

Other studies have also indicated a 'unique' impact associated with hate crime victimisation. McDevitt, Balboni, Garcia and Gu (2001) surveyed a sample of victims of hate and non-hate motivated aggravated assaults in the US city of Boston, in an attempt to establish the extent to which hate crime has a differential impact. In terms of behavioural reactions the study found no significant difference between hate and non-hate victims in their post-victimisation behaviour. The majority of victims of both groups stated that they paid more attention to where they walked and that they tried to be less visible following the incident, and some stated that they had subsequently become more active in the community.

However, McDevitt *et al.* (2001) did uncover significant differences between hate and non-hate victims in terms of their psychological reactions. Overall, the study found that hate victims experienced adverse and intense psychological sequelae more often than non-hate victims, were found to have greater difficulty coping with their victimisation, and experienced problems with their recovery process because of increased fear and more frequent intrusive thoughts. In addition the research suggested that hate crime victims experience increased fear and reduced feelings of safety than non-hate victims following an attack, largely, McDevitt *et al.* suggest, because of concern over the likelihood of future attacks often based upon the experience of repeat victimisation in the past. With regard to other consequences of victimisation, the research found that hate victims were more likely to lose their job, suffer health problems, experience more post-incident traumatic events, and have greater difficulty in overcoming the incident than victims of comparable crimes without the hate element.

More recent research by Craig-Henderson and Sloan (2003) argued that victims of racist hate crime experience a range of unique reactions and are different from both crime victims generally, and also victims of other forms of hate crime, in at least two ways. The first is that because race hate victims are targeted specifically because of their race (or ethnicity), the characteristics of which are always visible and easily recognised, victims are unable to take comfort in the belief that the offence was simply random and could have happened to anyone. Rather, they are forced to view their experience as an attack on their identity. The researchers suggest that this differs from other victims of crime, and indeed many other victims of hate crime, because their race (or more broadly, the reason for their victimisation) cannot be hidden from the view of others, cannot be changed, and therefore the attack cannot be easily attributed to other factors.

Craig-Henderson and Sloan argue that the second factor that distinguishes race hate victims from other hate crime victims is that they are almost always members of negatively stereotyped or stigmatised social groups. Furthermore the recognition of these factors is predominantly present in the motivation of offenders and is usually pervasive and resistant to change. It could reasonably be argued, however, that all victims of hate crime are the subjects of negative stereotypes so the extent to which this is conclusively and solely attributable to race hate victims is open to debate. Nevertheless the researchers highlight the additional issue that anti-black hate crime in particular also has the potential to invoke emotions that relate to a lengthy history of racism and discrimination, both in terms of criminal behaviour towards blacks and discrimination in other areas of their lives such as employment and housing, and so on.

While most of the studies referred to above are American in origin, many of the findings are supported by a British study examining the impact of racist victimisation on the lives of those that experienced it. Chahal and Julienne (2000) found that victims were significantly hindered or affected in several key areas of their lives. Most notably problems were associated with the victims' relationships with their partners or spouses and their children, the frequency and duration of visits from friends and family members, disruption to their routine activities and their use of space (both public and private), their general health and well-being and their overall feelings of security and safety.

Beyond this, hate crime is also held to be a 'message' crime. Essentially the victim is interchangeable and it is some feature over which the victim has no control that is the target for the offender, rather than the individual traits of victims themselves. Therefore the perpetrator, through his or her crime against an individual or small group, is 'telling' a particular wider community that its members are different, unwelcome and that any member of that community could be the next victim. As such, hate victimisation creates an *in terrorum* effect that extends beyond the individual victim and is projected to all community members, creating a sense of group vulnerability and community tension and fear (Chahal and Julienne 2000; Craig-Henderson and Sloan 2003).

The situation described above, while problematic enough in its own right, can lead to other problems in wider society, as identified by Levin (1999: 18). His research in the US revealed that:

> Hate crimes involve a heightening of tension along already fragile intergroup lines, and a heightened risk of civil disorder. Even in the absence of explosive civil strife, the lessening of trust and a change of behaviour among affected groups in a community creates a distinct harm to the public interest.

Levin also points to evidence suggesting that the wider impact of hate crimes increases the risk of further civil disorder through retaliatory attacks along intergroup lines, and also through an increased risk of copycat offending. In short, hate crimes are held to be socially divisive.

Conclusions and future direction

Thus far this chapter has examined some of the findings of an emerging literature base concerning the apparent unique nature and impact of hate crime. The shortcomings of quantitative accounts of victimisation are increasingly being replaced in importance by qualitative research studies. In essence these are effectively 'fleshing out' the bare bones of numerical data, thereby allowing a greater insight into hate victimisation. While these studies are relatively small in number, and have various methodological and practical shortcomings, they are beginning to provide valuable information. The evidence is not conclusive, and continues to attract critics and sceptics, but the emerging research literature increasingly and consistently suggests that hate crime is indeed a unique form of offending that results in unique forms of victimisation. More recent research examining wider aspects of diversity continue this trend. The scope of the literature in the field of hate crime has broadened considerably in recent times to reflect more recent practitioner and academic concerns with the broader concept of diversity. Specific examples of more recent publications reflecting this shift in focus include those relating to hate crimes in rural settings (Chakraborti and Garland 2004; Garland and Chakraborti 2006, 2007), disability hate crimes (CPS 2007; Scope 2008), homophobic hate crime (Williams and Robinson 2004; Dick 2008); transgender hate crime (Dittman 2003), and hate crimes against gypsies and travellers (James 2007). The continuance and furtherance of research in this area is therefore crucial, not just for our understanding of hate crime but also, as Iganski (2001) has suggested, because understanding the harm caused by hate crime should help us to better help its victims – a key issue for contemporary criminal justice in this area.

Although hate crimes have arguably not featured heavily in multi-agency public protection arrangements in the past, this growing body of evidence concerning the nature of hate crime, coupled with increasing interest from government and the criminal justice sector, suggests that it may well feature more heavily in the future. Indeed, this prospect is clear from the language employed in the government's hate crime *Action Plan* (Home Office 2009b). Despite acknowledging that the evidence base on the nature and extent of hate crime is currently 'patchy' and that 'this patchy picture makes it difficult to devise, monitor and evaluate action to tackle hate crime' (2009b: 11), the 2008 document entitled *Saving Lives. Reducing Harm. Protecting the Public: An Action Plan for Tackling Violence 2008–11* (Home Office 2008) committed the government to producing a dedicated cross-government strategy to assist local partners in developing their responses to hate crime. The *Cross-Government Action Plan* to tackle hate crime therefore sets out the strategic actions government will take, in England and Wales, in the short to medium term to tackle hate crime and support hate crime victims (2009b: 4).

The Home Office state that the *Action Plan* will:

> contribute to the overarching objective of improving public confidence in the criminal justice system and to the achievement of PSA 23 (to make communities safer) and PSA 24 (to deliver a more effective, transparent and responsive criminal justice system for victims and the public). Our Action Plan reflects the two main approaches of the updated Crime Strategy 2008–11, (a) 'addressing crime at all points in the cycle, from prevention and early intervention through to stopping offenders from reoffending', and (b) 'tackling the root causes of crime'. (Home Office 2009b: 4)

More specifically, the *Action Plan* includes the objectives of increasing the evidence base to fill existing gaps in knowledge and 'apply[ing] the lessons learnt from efforts to tackle domestic and sexual violence to tackling hate crime – in particular, learning lessons regarding increasing reporting, *risk assessment and management*, police training, *multi-agency working and appropriate interventions*' (2009b: 16, emphasis added). The *Action Plan* also commits the government to equipping criminal justice agencies and other public bodies with new guidance, tools and standards, including guidance on applying existing powers in relation to restorative justice and anti-social behaviour to address the behaviour of the perpetrators of hate incidents and hate crimes (2009b: 10). Finally, the *Saving Lives* document (Home Office 2008) has also committed the government to assisting local partners and supporting victims by exploring the extent to which multi-agency risk assessment conferences, specialist courts and the Independent Domestic Violence Advisor approach could be applied to tackling hate crime (2009b: 24).

In short, hate crime raises some interesting issues for public protection, and in addition provides some arguably unique yet incomplete answers to the questions posed by Maden (2007; Table 17.1 above). As the body of literature continues to grow in this field and the government's action plans begin to unfold, those involved in MAPPA may find the perpetrators of hate crime appearing more frequently.

Selected further reading

British-oriented literature exploring hate crime as a distinct form of offending behaviour is relatively sparse, perhaps reflecting the recent nature of academic interest in this field. However, this limited body of literature has in recent years begun to expand. For an overview of the subject area and a discussion of specific forms of hate crime, Garland and Chakraborti's *Hate Crime* (2009) offers a useful and accessible single-volume account of the issues. Similarly, Chakraborti's edited collection (2010) provides an account of the subject area from a range of leading authors in the field. Barbara Perry's (2009) five-volume edited collection offers a comprehensive analysis of the subject area from a more international perspective.

References

ACPO (2000) *ACPO Guide to Identifying and Combating Hate Crime*. London: Association of Chief Police Officers.

ACPO (2005) *Hate Crime: Delivering a Quality Service; Good Practice and Tactical Guidance*. London: Association of Chief Police Officers.

Allport, G. W. (1954) *The Nature of Prejudice*. Massachusetts: Addison-Wesley Publishing Co.

Bowling, B. (1999) *Violent Racism: Victimisation, Policing and Social Context*. New York: Oxford University Press.

Brown, R. (1995) *Prejudice: Its Social Psychology*. Oxford: Blackwell.

Chahal, K. and Julienne, L. (2000) *'We Can't All Be White!' Racist Victimisation in the UK*. York: York Publishing.

Chakraborti, N. (2010) *Hate Crime: Concepts, Policy, Future Directions*. Cullompton: Willan Publishing.

Chakraborti, N. and Garland, J. (eds) (2004) *Rural Racism*. Cullompton: Willan Publishing.

CPS (2007) *Disability Hate Crime: Policy for Prosecuting Cases of Disability Hate Crime*. London: Crown Prosecution Service.

Craig, K. M. (2002) 'Examining hate-motivated aggression: a review of the social psychological literature on hate crimes as a distinct form of aggression', *Aggression And Violent Behaviour*, 7: 85–101.

Craig-Henderson, K. and Sloan, L. R. (2003) 'After the hate: helping psychologists help victims of racist hate crime', *Clinical Psychology: Science and Practice*, 10(4): 481–90.

Dick, S. (2008) *Homophobic Hate Crime: The Gay British Crime Survey*. London: Stonewall.

Dittman, R. (2003) 'Policing hate crime – from victim to challenger: a transgendered perspective', *Probation Journal*, 50(3): 282–8.

Erlich, H. J. (1992) 'The ecology of antigay violence', in K. T. Berrill and G. M. Herek (eds) *Hate Crimes: Confronting Violence Against Lesbians and Gay Men*. London: Sage.

Garland, J. and Chakraborti, N. (2006) 'Recognising and responding to victims of rural racism', *International Review of Victimology*, 13(1): 49–69.

Garland, J. and Chakraborti, N. (2007) 'Protean times? Exploring the relationships between policing, community and "Race" in Rural England', *Criminology and Criminal Justice*, 7(4): 347–65.

Garland, J. and Chakraborti, N. (2009) *Hate Crime: Impact, Causes and Consequences*, London: Sage.

Garofalo, J. and Martin, S. E. (1993) *Bias-Motivated Crimes: Their Characteristics and the Law Enforcement Response*. Carbondale: Southern Illinois University.

Green, D. P., McFalls, L. H. and Smith, J. K. (2003) 'Hate crime: an emergent research agenda', in B. Perry (ed.) *Hate and Bias Crime: A Reader*. New York: Routledge.

Hall, N. (2005) *Hate Crime*. Cullompton: Willan Publishing.

Hall, N., Grieve, J. and Savage, S. P. (eds) (2009) *Policing and the Legacy of Lawrence*. Cullompton: Willan Publishing.

Herek, G. M., Cogan, J. C. and Gillis, J. R. (2002) 'Victim experiences in hate crimes based on sexual orientation', *Journal of Social Issues*, 58(2): 319–39.

Home Office (2008) *Saving Lives. Reducing Harm. Protecting the Public: An Action Plan for Tackling Violence 2008–11*. London: Home Office.

Home Office (2009a) *Definitions of Hate Crimes and Hate Incidents*. London: Home Office. Online at: www.crimereduction.homeoffice.gov.uk/hatecrime/hatecrime002.htm.

Home Office (2009b) *Hate Crime: The Cross-Government Action Plan*. London: Home Office.

Iganski, P. (2001) 'Hate crimes hurt more', *American Behavioural Scientist*, 45(4): 626–38.

Iganski, P. (2008) *Hate Crime and the City*. Bristol: Policy Press.

James, Z. (2007) 'Policing marginal spaces: controlling gypsies and travellers', *Criminology and Criminal Justice*, 7(4): 367–89.

Levin, B. (1999) 'Hate crimes: Worse by definition', *Journal of Contemporary Criminal Justice*, 15(1): 6–21.

Macpherson, W. (1999) *The Stephen Lawrence Inquiry*, Cm 4262. London: The Stationery Office.

Maden, A. (2007) *Treating Violence: A Guide to Risk Management in Mental Health*. Oxford: Oxford University Press.

Martin, S. (1996) 'Investigating hate crimes: case characteristics and law enforcement responses', *Justice Quarterly*, 13(3): 455–80.

McDevitt, J., Balboni, J., Garcia, L. and Gu, J. (2001) 'Consequences for victims: a comparison of bias and non-bias motivated assaults', *American Behavioural Scientist*, 45(4): 697–713.

McDevitt, J., Levin, J. and Bennett, S. (2002) 'Hate crime offenders: an expanded typology', *Journal of Social Issues*, 58(2): 303–17.

NYPD (2002) *Hate Crime Task Force 2001 Year End Report*. New York: New York City Police Department.

Perry, B. (2001) *In the Name of Hate: Understanding Hate Crimes*. New York: Routledge.

Perry, B. (ed.) (2003) *Hate and Bias Crime: A Reader*. New York: Routledge.

Perry, B. (2009) *Hate Crimes*, Westport, CT: Praeger.

Scope (2008) *Getting Away with Murder: Disabled People's Experiences of Hate Crime in the UK*. London: Scope.

Sibbitt, R. (1997) *The Perpetrators of Racial Harassment and Racial Violence*. Home Office Research Study 176. London: Home Office.

Sullivan, A. (1999) 'What's so bad about hate? The illogic and illiberalism behind hate crime laws', *New York Times Magazine*, 26 September.

Williams, M. and Robinson, A. (2004) 'Problems and prospects with policing the lesbian, gay and bisexual community in Wales', *Policing and Society*, 14(3): 213–32.

Chapter 18

Punitive policies on sexual offending: from public shaming to public protection

Anne-Marie McAlinden

Introduction

'Public protection' and 'risk management' have become the bywords of recent legal and policy initiatives in relation to sex offenders. In the United Kingdom, from the late 1990s onwards, a panoply of legislation was introduced in order to enhance supervisory methods and increase controls on released sex offenders in the community. These have included, most notably, sex offender notification and related orders and a range of measures based around pre-employment vetting. The media and the public have become a pivotal part of this policy cycle, with increased demands for measures that 'name and shame' known sex offenders. Many of these initiatives have stemmed from the United States, which has also witnessed punitive state-led and popular responses to the risks posed by violent and sexual offenders *via*, for example, preventative sentencing and registration and community notification under 'Megan's Law'. Although the UK has thus far resisted the wholesale adoption of public disclosure of information about sex offenders under a similarly constituted 'Sarah's Law', such measures have the potential to seriously undermine reintegrative efforts with sex offenders.

This analysis will argue that recent responses by the media, the public and the legislature to sex offender management and reintegration are based largely on 'public shaming' and have failed to secure effective risk management and public protection. The chapter explores alternative rehabilitative strategies based on restorative or reintegrative justice as a more proactive, holistic and ultimately more effective response to the issue of public protection from the risk posed by sex offenders.[1]

The chapter is divided into two main parts. The first part critically examines the retributive regulatory framework on sex offending. This includes a brief outline of the theoretical framework on risk penality that has informed recent penal policy on sex offending; an analysis of state and public responses to sex offending in terms of recent developments in the law, policy and practice on the management of sex offenders and public reaction to these; and the limitations of regulatory punitive responses which are framed in terms of public protection and public shaming. The second part outlines alternative responses to managing the risk posed by sex offenders in the community from a reintegrative standpoint, given the failure of traditional regulatory approaches. This includes an analysis of the core elements of the theory of restorative or reintegrative justice as applied to sex offending; examples of restorative practices with sex offenders and their proven effectiveness; and finally, the core critiques of restorative justice when applied to serious forms of offending. The chapter concludes with some practical suggestions as to how such an alternative response could be taken forward within the context of the current prevailing retributive framework.

Retribution: the political and public response

'The new penology': public protection, risk and preventative governance

In the United Kingdom from the late 1990s onwards, sexual offending was placed firmly on the political agenda. In tandem with broader theoretical concerns about heightening state security and crime control *via* ever more expansive modes of regulation (Beck 1992; Braithwaite 2000; Shearing 2000), the risk assessment and management of sex offenders became the structuring principle of legislative frameworks and organisational policies and practices (Parton *et al.* 1997; Kemshall and Maguire 2001). A central task of 'the new penology' (Feeley and Simon 1992) was a concern with 'actuarial justice' (Feeley and Simon 1994) – with proactively managing knowledge about offenders in order to develop appropriate preventative measures designed to classify and control risk (Hebenton and Thomas 1996).

More recently, we have witnessed the extension of the theoretical and policy frameworks on risk *via* the preventative governance of sexual offending (Ashenden 2002). A proliferation of risk-averse policies have attempted to apply the logic of precaution (Ericson 2007) and respond pre-emptively (Zedner 2009) to all potential risks posed by sex offenders (Seddon 2008; Hebenton and Seddon 2009), particularly those who offend against children (McAlinden 2010).

At the same time, public fears and anxieties concerning released sex offenders, in large part invigorated by the media (Greer 2003), fuel the demand for risk-based penal policies. The media have succeeded in particular in conflating anxiety and risk in the public imagination in that all sex offenders are deemed to pose the same degree of very high risk. The resulting notion of the sex offender as the omnipresent sexual predator helps perpetuate the cycle of regulatory populist penal policies on sex offending (McAlinden 2007: 27).

State responses: the recent legislative and policy framework on sex offending

In the United States, legislation has been enacted in response to the problems posed by recidivist violent and sexual offenders in the community. Measures have included the civil commitment of sexual predators on release from prison, and criminal provision *via* chemical castration and sex offender registration and community notification, which eventually became embodied in Megan's Law (Bedarf 1995; Kimball 1996). Through the process of 'policy transfer' (Jones and Newburn 2006), these developments have broadly been reflected in the United Kingdom. Although there are parallels in relation to the legislative arrangements put in place for preventative detention of dangerous offenders, the enactment of a range of orders to manage sex offenders on release from custody most clearly reflects the shared concern with risk management and public protection.

A comprehensive review of legislative provision for sexual offending in the mid to late 1990s (Home Office 1996a, 1996b) eventually became embodied in a plethora of new legislative measures,[2] the most notable of which was sex offender notification. These measures were founded on the basic premise that the most effective way to protect the public was through increased surveillance and monitoring of released sex offenders in the community (Kemshall 2001). Sex offender notification, or registration as it is more colloquially known, was first enacted by Part 1 of the Sex Offenders Act 1997. This measure required certain categories of sex offender to notify their name and address, and any changes to these details to the police. The conditions attached to notification and the degree of public disclosure permitted to the local community vary depending on the assessed level of risk. In England and Wales there are now multi-agency public protection panels (MAPPP), comprising representatives from the police, probation, social services and other agencies, to perform this task (Maguire *et al.* 2001; Bryan and Doyle 2003; Lieb 2003).

This framework was subjected to a good deal of academic criticism and debate (see Soothill *et al.* 1997; Soothill and Francis 1998; Cobley 2003), not least in terms of loopholes in the legislation that undermined effective public protection. As a result, it was first tightened by the Criminal Justice and Court Services Act 2000 and later replaced completely with a much broader regulatory framework contained in Part 2 of the Sexual Offences Act 2003. Offenders, for example, were now required to notify their details within three days and in person, and not fourteen days and by post as was previously the case.

The 2003 Act also introduced a range of other regulatory measures aimed at increasing public protection from this particular category of offender. The risk of sexual harm order (RSHO) and the sexual offences (SOPO) preventive order were introduced as civil orders further designed to protect children from sexual harm (Shute 2004). The former can be used to prohibit specified behaviours, including the grooming of children, and can be used whether or not the individual has a prior record of offending. The latter can be used as a variant on an exclusion order to prohibit the offender from frequenting places where there might be children, and thus posing an immediate danger to their safety, such as parks and school playgrounds.

More recently, the Safeguarding Vulnerable Groups Act 2006 gave legislative effect to many of the recommendations of the Bichard Inquiry (2004) into the Soham murders of 2002 and introduced an extended new regulatory framework (Gillespie 2007) on vetting. The Act combines previously separate disqualification lists and establishes a centralised system of continuous criminal records monitoring of every person who works with children or vulnerable adults whether on a paid or voluntary basis. The extensive remit of the new legislative framework means that virtually everyone who comes into contact with children, in respect of their education or social or leisure activities, will be intensely regulated (McAlinden 2010). As is discussed further below, these draconian and retributive penal penalties harness the need to publicly identify and control sex offenders in the community in order to protect the public. As a result, however, the civil liberties of the offender, together with their chances of rehabilitation, may be seriously undermined (McAlinden 2007).

In the United States, developments have gone further still. A range of measures have been developed by the judiciary in response to the limitations of the traditional options of prison and parole. A minority of American judges have begun to use 'shame penalties', in the form of 'signs' and 'apologies', as part of modern probation conditions for sex offenders (Massaro 1991: 1886–90; Kahan 1996; Karp 1998: 281–3). In one case,[3] for example, the court placed a convicted child molester on probation for five years subject to a requirement that he place a sign on both sides of his car and on the door of his home in large lettering which read: 'Dangerous Sex Offender – No Children Allowed' (Brilliant 1989: 1365–6; Kelley 1989: 760; Massaro 1991: 1887–8). Similarly, courts have also required sex offenders to place ads in the local newspaper publicising their offences or urging others to seek treatment (Massaro 1991: 1880).

Such 'scarlet letter' measures (Earl-Hubbard 1996; Van Dujn 1999) are symbolic of the moral and public condemnation of the offence (Tavuchis 1991) and clearly appeal to judges and the public because they satisfy punitive retributive impulses (Karp 1998: 277–8). The central component of these penalties is undoubtedly, however, public exposure – to bring the crime to the community's attention so that it may respond with shaming (Karp 1998: 281). Their primary purpose is protect potential victims by warning them of the danger these offenders pose rather than to specifically humiliate the offender or subject them to public ridicule. As is discussed further below, however, the risk of stigmatisation and social exclusion attaches to those who are subject to such penalties (Kelley 1989: 775).[4]

Popular responses: the 'naming and shaming' of sex offenders

The popular response to the presence of sex offenders in the community by the media and the public can also be characterised by exclusionary, retributive practices. In this respect, recent press and public campaigns for the 'naming and shaming' of sex offenders, particularly paedophiles, provide an archetypal example of popular responses to the perceived risk posed by released sex offenders.

The 'name and shame' campaign launched by one of Britain's leading tabloid newspapers, the *News of the World*, began following the abduction and murder of eight-year-old Sarah Payne. Sarah was abducted and murdered near her grandparents' home in Sussex in July 2000 by a known paedophile, Roy Whiting. This campaign centred on the 'outing' of suspected and known sex offenders, particularly those against children, by printing their photographs, names and addresses, along with details of their offending history.[5] The newspaper promised to continue publishing such details until they had 'named and shamed' all of the child sex offenders in Britain. Accompanying this was a demand for 'Sarah's Law', to be the equivalent of Megan's Law in the United States, which provides for a much greater degree of community notification. This issue is discussed further below.

The media crusade provoked widespread hysteria and vigilante activity particularly in Portsmouth where a number of residents protested nightly at the presence of paedophiles in their community and the failure of the authorities to notify them of their whereabouts. During a week of disturbances on the Paulsgrove estate, protesters demonstrated outside the homes of suspected paedophiles, daubed slogans on their walls, issued threats and overturned and burned cars. As a result of this activity, several families fled, one convicted paedophile disappeared and two suspected paedophiles committed suicide (Ashenden 2002: 208). The aftermath of the Sarah Payne case is demonstrative of the fact that public shaming approaches may lead to harassment or even physical attack by vengeful members of the community on suspected paedophiles (Williams and Thompson 2004a, 2004b). As is discussed below, stigmatisation of the offender, however, in the form of both state-led and popular responses to sexual offending, may have a number of other harmful consequences for the offender.

Public protection and public shaming

The range of legislative measures for identifying and controlling known sex offenders in the community may be subjected to two broad lines of critique. The first relates to arguments about the efficacy of the legislation which may undermine effective public protection. The second relates to the effects of public shaming of sex offenders which may hinder their social reintegration.

Public protection

As noted above, sex offender registration or notification is one of the core regulatory measures for managing sex offenders in the community enacted in the last decade. The proposed development of these and other measures were framed around the twin aims of deterrence and protection (Home Office 1996a: para. 43). Notification in particular, however, has been subject to sustained academic criticism and debate that indicates that these objectives may have been undermined. In the main, the legislation appears to have been enacted to satisfy the public's demand for tough legislative action against this particular category of deviant and to convey the necessary social reassurances that 'something is being done'. In particular, there are key unanswered questions about the operation of the notification scheme in practice that may undermine its chances of realising effective public protection. These relate chiefly to offender compliance, the use made of information by agencies and adequate policing resources.

The question of how the register would actually operate in practice, however, appears to have been little considered, even during the process of the recent reforms. The particular issue of public notification of the presence of sex offenders in the local community remains controversial in the UK and is certainly nowhere near as widespread as in the United States under Megan's Law. Until relatively recently, calls for the public to have a general right of access to the information notified to the police, a so-called 'Sarah's Law', have been firmly rejected and the government have been unwilling to legislate on the use made of this information (Silverman and Wilson 2002: 125–45; Power 2003; Thomas 2003). The introduction of pilot schemes in February 2009, however, to allow single parents in particular to check whether those with unsupervised access to their children have a history of sexual offending, potentially brings the UK one step closer to such a position.

Moreover, failure to address a number of key practical issues, such as likely effectiveness and adequate policing resources, may mean that the legislation is of limited practical effect in managing the risk posed by released sex offenders. As Cobley has suggested (2003: 60–1), the success of the 'register' depends on two factors: the first is offenders' compliance with the notification requirements, and the second is the use made of this information by relevant agencies. In relation to the first of these elements, a few years after the implementation of the 1997 Act, the national compliance rate with the registration requirement was over 97 per cent (Home Office 2001: 5). However, on balance, such a figure is likely to decrease incrementally as registration procedures are tightened and the number of offenders subject to the requirement increases annually.

In relation to the second of these factors, several critics have pointed out that too many sexual offenders would potentially be subject to such measures for them to be realistic policing options. Marshall, for example, estimated that 125,000 men aged 20 or over in the 1993 population of England and Wales had a conviction for an offence that would have been registerable had the Sex Offenders Act 1997 been in force at that time (Marshall 1997). In any event, those figures did not take account of cautions so that the actual figure was thought to be even higher (Soothill et al. 1997; Soothill and Francis 1998: 289).

In addition, several studies have examined the effectiveness of some of the other measures recently enacted as part of the revised regulatory framework on sex offending. The legislative predecessors to the sexual offences preventive order (SOPO) under the Sexual Offences Act 2003 were the sex offenders order (SOO) and the restraining order (RO), both of which were combined and replaced with the more expansive SOPO. Research indicates that the power to apply for an SOO was not widely used, with fewer than 100 orders being made within the first three years of implementation. Action for breach, however, was taken in respect of approximately 50 per cent of the orders made (Knock et al. 2002). This may indicate that such measures are of limited deterrent effect for sexual offenders.

The overriding limitation of all such measures is that they are by their nature aimed at those sex offenders who have already come to notice. As such, they can have no impact on managing the risk presented by 'unknown' sex offenders who remain beyond the scope of the regulatory framework. This is highly significant since research suggests that fewer than 5 per cent of sex offenders are ever apprehended (Salter 2003).

Public shaming

Public shaming approaches to sex offender management and reintegration have a number of negative effects on sex offenders. Rather than achieving the goal of successful community reintegration, state measures such as registration and notification, in common with popular 'name and shame' campaigns, may only serve to label and stigmatise the offender and isolate them from the rest of the community (Winick 1998: 539, 556). This singling out of the offender may have a significant negative effect on a number of levels.

First, it may impede offender reintegration into the community, his or her ability to get a job or accommodation and therefore ultimate offender rehabilitation (Bedarf 1995: 885, 910–11; Cobley 1997: 103; Soothill and Francis 1998: 291). Second, isolating the offender from the rest of the community may increase the chance of reoffending behaviour as a coping mechanism (Edwards and Hensley 2001: 101). Third, via 'deviancy amplification spiral'[6] (Wilkins 1964) the offender who is isolated from 'normal' law-abiding society may be forced to associate with other sex offenders where they learn more sophisticated techniques. Fourth, if a sex offender becomes ostracised in the area where he lives he will simply go underground where he could be of even greater danger and commit crime elsewhere (Soothill and Francis 1998: 288–9). Risk, in other words, is not effectively managed but simply displaced elsewhere.

Disintegrative shaming practices (Braithwaite 1989), therefore, in the form of retributive state and public responses to sex offending, will not deter offenders or protect victims in the longer term. In a number of jurisdictions, however, the negative feelings and emotions about sexual offenders have been used more effectively. These communities have adopted innovative reintegrative shaming practices with sexual offenders with the broad aims of reducing the incidence of child sexual abuse, preventing future offending and reintegrating the offender back into the community.

Restorative justice as an alternative response to sex offending

The case for alternative responses to sex offending commonly rests upon the failures of traditional regulatory approaches, which have been broadly outlined above. In this respect it has been argued, for example, that child sexual abuse is a small component of the broader category of 'gendered and sexualised violence' (Hudson 2002), which causes significant trauma for victims (Herman 1997) yet continues to evade traditional justice approaches. The failure of the formal regulatory framework with respect to sexual offences means that there is considerable scope for examining alternative forms of justice. These may offer a realistic prospect of not only managing the risk posed by sex offenders in the community and reintegrating them more effectively, but also improving levels of public protection and the outcome for victims and communities affected by sexual offences (Finstad 1990; Braithwaite and Daly 1994). Restorative or reintegrative justice, in this sense, is presented as a viable and more holistic solution to the many and varied problems presented by sex offences.

Restorative or reintegrative justice

Restorative approaches routinely involve the three central actors: the victim, the offender and the community (Zehr 1990). While there have been a number of definitions of the term, as a concept, however, it is not easy to define. One recent and much used definition is that put forward by Marshall as 'a process whereby all the parties with a stake in a particular offence come together to resolve collectively how to deal with the aftermath of the offence and its implications for the future' (Marshall 1999: 5). Essentially, it focuses on 'changing the normative orientation of law from retribution to restoration' (Hudson 1998: 238). It views crime not as a violation of a general legal category but as harm to individual people and relationships and, as the term suggests, seeks to redress or restore such harm (Consedine 1995; Van Ness and Strong 1997).

The term 'restorative justice' is in many senses an umbrella one that seeks to cover a growing range of procedures and practices. The term has been used to cover a variety of measures that seek to respond to crime in what is seen to be a more constructive way than through the use of conventional criminal justice approaches. The main variants include victim–offender mediation (Marshall 1991; Davis 1992; Umbreit 1994), family group conferencing (McElrea 1994; Retzinger and Scheff 1996; Morris and Maxwell 2000), and Circles of Support and Accountability (Cesaroni 2001; Petrunik 2002; Wilson et al. 2002, 2007a). The latter is of particular relevance to reintegrative efforts with sex offenders and is discussed further below.

Restorative justice approaches in various jurisdictions differ but are based on a number of agreed aims and principles. The central components of the theory include the following: changing the focus of justice intervention from retribution to reparation; altering the justice process to bring informal justice processes closer to local communities and increase citizen and victim involvement in the process of restoration (and reintegration); considering the impact on victims and significant others; empowering victims and offenders; engaging with offenders to help them appreciate the consequences of their actions and the impact on their victims; encouraging appropriate forms of reparation by offenders towards their victim or the wider community; seeking reconciliation between the victim and offender where possible, and reintegrating the offender within the community (Zehr 1990; Van Ness 1993; Bazemore and Umbreit 1995). These common elements are the subject of this analysis, which will focus on the benefits of restorative or reintegrative justice as a whole in managing the risk posed by sex offenders in the community, thereby increasing levels of public protection.

Shaming

The development of the theory and practice of restorative justice owes much to Braithwaite's notion of 'reintegrative shaming' (Braithwaite 1989; Ahmed et al. 2001).[7] The essence of his theory is that the ways in which not only the state but also society, the community and the family sanction deviance affect the extent to which individuals engage in criminal behaviour. According to Braithwaite the type of shaming that is important is not 'the shame of the remote judge or police officer but the shame of the people they most care about' (1993: 37). Shaming, therefore, can be achieved in a variety of ways and contexts (Hay 2001: 133–5). Braithwaite makes the distinction between two types of society and two types of shaming practice. He argues that communitarian societies are better able than others to informally sanction deviance and reintegrate lawbreakers by shaming the offence, rather than permanently stigmatising the offender through harsh formal penal codes (Braithwaite 1989: 84–5). In this vein, he contrasts the reintegrative shaming of the good parent, who makes clear their disapproval of bad behaviour without rejecting the child, with the stigmatising shame of modern criminal justice.

There are two components of reintegrative shaming: the overt disapproval of the delinquent act (shaming) by socially significant others; and the ongoing inclusion of the offender within an interdependent relationship (reintegration) (Zhang 1995: 251). Thus, shaming is reintegrative when it reinforces an offender's membership in civil society. This prevents the shamed individual from adopting a 'deviant master status' (Becker 1963) and is accomplished by four core elements: (1) the shaming maintains bonds of love or respect between the person being shamed and the person doing the shaming; (2) it is directed at the malevolence of the offence rather than the malevolence of the person; (3) it is delivered in a context of social approval; and (4) it is terminated with gestures of acceptance and forgiveness (Braithwaite 1989: 100–1).

Reintegrative shaming can be contrasted with stigmatisation which is disintegrative in nature. In this, little or no effort is made to forgive offenders and thus reinforce their membership in law-abiding society. Stigmatisation is essentially shaming in the absence of a reintegrative element and is the opposite of each of the four elements mentioned above (Garfinkel 1956). The primary relevance of stigmatisation is that it shuns offenders and treats them as outcasts and may provoke a rebellious and criminal reaction from them (Karp 1998: 283; Maxwell and Morris 1999). As Vagg (1998: 254) has argued, labelling, therefore, is the key element that separates reintegrative from disintegrative shaming.

As demonstrated above, disintegrative shaming has for the most part informed contemporary state and public responses to the risk posed by released sex offenders in the community. Such responses have publicly shamed sex offenders by labelling and marking them out socially as different. Other jurisdictions, however, have developed alternative responses with sex offenders that embrace the restorative and reintegrative paradigm. Moreover, by shaming the offence rather than the offender and to positive effect they have also been successful in securing public protection and public confidence in the process of sex offender management and reintegration.

Restorative and reintegrative shaming practices with sex offenders

In general terms, restorative schemes with sexual offences are not widely used in comparison with its more accepted uses in the context of first-time and minor offending. However, there are a few isolated examples of schemes that use reintegrative or restorative principles with sex offenders. In South

Australia, for example, young people charged with sexual offences who have admitted their behaviour are diverted from court *via* a family conference process (Daly 2006). Similarly, the 'family decision-making model' in Australia and North Carolina has used a conference-style process with children and families affected by sexual abuse and domestic violence, although usually the perpetrator is not involved in the process (Pennell and Burford 2001; Pennell 2006). In Arizona, the RESTORE programme uses restorative justice to address date and acquaintance rape by first-time adult offenders and those charged with minor sexual offences (Koss *et al.* 2003). One of the best known and well established schemes, however, is Circles of Support and Accountability (COSA), which operate with selected high risk sexual offenders who are re-entering the community on release from prison (Cesaroni 2001; Wilson *et al.* 2002; Petrunik 2002: 503–5).

At a broad level, Circles involve the development of restorative support and treatment networks for sex offenders where the community works in partnership with the offender and professional and voluntary agencies. Circles initially grew out of the restorative work of the Canadian Mennonite Church and developed as a community faith response to an immediate social problem. More recently, Circles have been extended to other jurisdictions such as Northern Ireland and England and Wales on a pilot basis. In this context, they have been used to support the multi-agency approach to sex offender risk assessment and management outlined above. It has been noted, however, that there is a clear distinction between the dominant models adopted in Canada and England and Wales, for example. While the Canadian model is organic, the English model is more systemic (Quaker Peace and Social Witness 2005: 6), where, as noted further below, it is used primarily as a risk management tool to report areas of concern back to MAPPP.

Circles are based on the twin elements of safety and support – they operate as a means of addressing public concerns about effective protection from sex offenders and also the offender's needs concerning rehabilitation and social reintegration. The circle is focused on the development of a network of informal support and treatment individually tailored around the offender, who is the core member, involving the wider community in tandem with state and voluntary agencies. The offender and other members of the circle enter into a signed covenant, which specifies each member's area of assistance. The trained circle volunteers are involved in assisting the offender with reintegration in a number of ways, from assisting in the search for suitable housing and employment to helping them change their attitudes and behaviour and avoid situations that might lead to reoffending. The offender in turn agrees to relate to the circle of support, pursue treatment and to act responsibly in the community. The offender has contact with someone from the circle each day in the high risk phase just after release. Normally, a minimum commitment of one year is expected from all circle members. The life of a circle, however, will extend as long as the risk to the community and the offender are above average.

Circles of Support meets the aims of reintegrative shaming in particular that were outlined earlier in this chapter (McAlinden 2005: 380–81). First, they are accompanied by one of the principal features of reintegrative shame cultures – they aim to control wrongdoers within a communitarian society and informally sanction deviance by reintegration into cohesive networks, rather than by formal restraint (Braithwaite 1989: 84–5). Second, Circles also meets both facets of reintegrative shaming: the overt disapproval of the delinquent act (shaming) by socially significant members; and the ongoing inclusion of the offender within an interdependent relationship (reintegration) (Zhang 1995: 251). Third, reintegrative shaming is accomplished when the four conditions mentioned above are fulfilled (Braithwaite 1989: 100–1):

1 *The shaming maintains bonds of love or respect between the person being shamed and the person doing the shaming* – this is demonstrated by the dual commitment on the part of the offender and circle members which is enshrined in the signed covenant.

2 *It is directed at the evil of the act rather than the evil of the person* – the circle confronts offenders about their deviant behaviour and holds them accountable to their commitment not to reoffend.

3 *It is delivered in a context of general social approval* – circles provide intensive support, guidance and supervision for the offender, mediating between the police, media and the general community to minimise risk and assist in reintegration.

4 Finally, *it is terminated with gestures or ceremonies of acceptance and forgiveness* – the net result is that sex offenders receive social support in reintegration, and not just hostility, from at least some members of the community.

The effectiveness of restorative justice with sexual offenders

On a more practical level, Circles of Support aim to allay the fears of the local community concerning effective public protection, and at the same time reduce the likelihood of further offending by holding the offender accountable to their commitment not to reoffend. To this end, early evaluations have produced positive results.

One early evaluation of Circles in Ontario found that offenders receiving assistance *via* a circle reoffended at a lower rate in comparison with a control sample (Wilson *et al.* 2002). In comparing the expected recidivism rate with the observed rate sexual recidivism was reduced by more than 50 per cent (2002: 378). Moreover, each incident of reoffending was less invasive and severe than the original offence for which the offender had been imprisoned (2002: 378). Further research has established that circles have contributed to sex offender desistance by increasing offender responsibility and accountability as well as enhancing community safety (Wilson *et al.* 2007b). In this vein, in the most recent evaluations a sample of 60 high risk sex offenders who participated in the circles programme had significantly lower rates of reoffending than those that did not: a 70 per cent reduction in sexual recidivism, 57 per cent reduction in all types of violent recidivism, including sexual recidivism, and 35 per cent reduction in all types of recidivism (Wilson *et al.* 2007c).

Early evaluations of the pilot projects in England and Wales have also shown that circles have been effective in reducing expected rates of recidivism and assisting in offender rehabilitation. Furthermore, despite tentative beginnings, communities were willing to play a constructive and supportive role in this process (Quaker Peace and Social Witness 2005). A follow-up to the Thames Valley project investigated the outcome of Circles with 16 core members. None of the core members had been reconvicted of a new sexual offence and of the ten core members displaying recidivist behaviour, in six cases this was detected by the circles and the information passed to the relevant professional agencies (Bates *et al.* 2004). These findings are indicative of the accountability aspect of circles and demonstrate effectively the critical role that they may play in managing the risk posed by dangerous sex offenders in the community.

Moreover, they also highlight that the circle model potentially offers professional agencies a clear means of actively and positively engaging with the local community concerning the often contentious issue of sex offender reintegration (Quaker Peace and Social Witness 2005: 18; Wilson *et al.* 2007a). Circles have proven effectiveness in enhancing perceptions about community safety and in providing reassurance to the local community. Circles have opened up the work of statutory agencies by providing an opportunity for the general public to contribute to the resettlement of individual offenders. Furthermore, a small group of community members may also offer a practical means of addressing the concerns of the wider community in relation to public protection and the placement of sex offenders in their area.

Addressing the concerns of critics

There are a number of traditional objections when restorative justice is applied to serious forms of offending such as sexual crime. For these critics, sex offending is considered too sensitive or serious an area within which to use a restorative response. To summarise the main arguments, opponents contend that restorative justice trivialises what are very serious criminal offences, particularly where victims include children or the vulnerable; it fails to promote genuine offender accountability; it reinforces the power imbalance that lies at the heart of abusive relationships and so leads to revictimisation; and it encourages vigilantism (Cossins 2008).

Proponents have addressed these concerns by countering in turn the critiques concerning 'hard' cases and how they can be overcome: even though the criminal law remains as a symbol of state and public denouncement, restorative processes that involve the offender's family and the wider community can more effectively meet the need for censure in sex offence cases; that while traditional retributive justice fails to hold offenders accountable and address ingrained forms of offending, restorative justice seeks real engagement with offenders to help them acknowledge the consequences of their behaviour; it empowers victims in a supportive environment in which the victim can convey to the offender how they have been affected by the abuse; that by offering constructive rather than purely punitive solutions, it may be employed at an earlier stage in the offending cycle; and finally, that distortions of power, including abuse of community control, are minimised when programmes adhere closely to restorative principles (Hudson 1998, 2002; Daly 2002, 2008; Morris and Gelsthorpe 2000; Morris 2002; McAlinden 2005, 2007).

In addition, critics of reintegrative theory in particular also argue that there are a number of more practical difficulties, including the lack of empirical research to date; the lack of social and norm cohesion in contemporary western society; the difficulties in promoting social inclusion; and the contestable nature of 'community' and 'partnership'. These difficulties, they argue, mean that such schemes will not implemented without difficulty in western society. Advocates, however, counter that restorative justice has outcome measures that are much broader than a pure consideration of recidivism rates (Maxwell and Morris 1999, 2002); popular responses to sex offending demonstrate that there is public consensus concerning the wrongness of sexual relationships between adults and children (Hacking 1999); the provision of accurate information about the nature of sexual crime and responses to it would hopefully shift public opinion and help to promote social inclusion (Grubin 1998); and finally, that the involvement of professional agencies in community-based schemes helps to ensure both state and community accountability (Crawford 1999).

Conclusion: restorative justice – the way ahead

Restorative justice is envisaged as a more proactive and ultimately more effective response to addressing the multiple interests implicit in the sex offender problem. It provides a proven means of addressing not only the offender's needs, in terms of reducing recidivism levels and securing successful community reintegration, but also the needs and concerns of victims and the wider community, in terms of providing effective reassurance about risk management and public safety.

Restorative approaches to sexual offending, however, must operate in carefully managed contexts. In particular, cases must be screened carefully and voluntary and consensual participation must be the cornerstone of practice. Such programmes may not be appropriate for all sex offenders, particularly high risk offenders, but they may provide an effective alternative for low to middle risk offenders, particularly when operated on a voluntary basis. It is envisaged that Circles of Support could be further extended as a part of the mainstream criminal justice response. Schemes could, for example, be further integrated into existing multi-agency arrangements on sex offender risk assessment and management as they have been in England and Wales.

It is submitted that for known high risk offenders, restorative schemes should be put in place on release from custody. For known low to middle risk offenders, Circles could operate as a fully fledged alternative to prosecution, with the criminal justice system as a back-up if things should go astray. Moreover, restorative justice offers a crucial means of probing the much talked about yet to date essentially illusory 'dark' category of unknown risk – those sex offenders who have as yet gone undetected. In short, by removing the overtly retributive, punitive element from state and public responses, the fuller adoption of restorative policies with sex offenders may encourage more victims and offenders to come forward and report offences, thereby breaking cycles of abuse.

Selected further reading

For a comprehensive overview of the risk-based legislative and organisational frameworks for governing sex offenders in the community, in the context of England and Wales in particular, see Cobley (2003) and Kemshall and Maguire (2001) respectively. Massaro (1991) and Karp (1998) provide very readable accounts of the contemporary and historical use of 'shame penalties' by the legislature and the judiciary for various classes of offenders in the context of the United States. In terms of the response by the media and the public, see Ashenden's (2002) account of the aftermath of the Sarah Payne case in England in Wales and the ensuing media driven campaign to publicly 'name and shame' known sex offenders. Those interested in the dynamics of 'shaming' should read Braithwaite's (1989) seminal text. For detailed information on the operation of circle programmes and their effectiveness see Cesaroni (2001), Petrunik (2002) and the body of work by Wilson and colleagues (2002, 2007a).

Notes

1 Note that the broad arguments in this chapter are based on work previously published by the author (see McAlinden 2005, 2006, 2007).
2 This included, for example, extended supervision of sex offenders on release from custody (Crime (Sentences) Act 1997 and Crime and Disorder Act 1998); DNA testing on blood samples taken from convicted sex offenders in prison (Criminal Evidence (Amendment) Act 1997); supervised access by defendants to victim statements and photographs (Sexual Offences (Protected Material) Act 1997); measures to prevent sex offenders from seeking employment involving access to children (Criminal Justice and Court Services Act 2000); and a system of registration (Sex Offenders Act 1997).
3 *State v Bateman* 95 Or. Ct. App. 456, 771 P.2d 314 (1989).
4 In this vein, several American writers have questioned whether this is appropriate territory for judges. Indeed, these measures, like registration and notification measures generally, have faced constitutional challenges (Brilliant 1989; Kelley 1989).
5 See, e.g. some of the headlines which appeared in *News of the World* 23 July 2000: 'Named and Shamed'; 'If You Are A Parent Read This'; 'Does A Monster Live Near You?'
6 The amplification spiral begins with social intolerance of certain forms of behaviour. This leads to more acts being defined as deviant, since people are now more aware of this behaviour. Consequently, there is more action against criminals, who are more severely punished or segregated, and more alienation of deviant groups who now only interact with each other. This in turn generates more crime by deviant groups. The net result is further intolerance of deviants by conforming society and the process begins again.
7 There is also a debate concerning the precise nature of the relationship between reintegrative shaming and restorative justice – in particular whether the terms 'reintegration' and 'restoration' are inter-changeable or even complementary (Walgrave and Aersten 1996). There are those who do not see shaming as a vital part of restorative justice and suggest that emotions such as empathy and remorse

are more important in effecting a reparative response (Maxwell and Morris 2002, 2004; Van Stokkom 2002).

References

Ahmed, E., Harris, N., Braithwaite, J. and Braithwaite, V. (eds) (2001) *Shame Management Through Reintegration*. Cambridge: Cambridge University Press.

Ashenden, S. (2002) 'Policing perversion: the contemporary governance of paedophilia', *Cultural Values*, 6(1–2): 197–22.

Bates, A., Falshaw, L., Corbett, C., Patel, V. and Friendship, C. (2004) 'A follow-up study of sex offenders treated by Thames Valley sex offender group work programme 1995–99', *Journal of Sexual Aggression*, 10: 29–38.

Bazemore, G. and Umbreit, M. (1995) 'Rethinking the sanctioning function in juvenile court: retributive or restorative responses to youth crime', *Crime and Delinquency*, 41(3): 296–316.

Beck, U. (1992) *Risk Society: Towards a New Modernity*. London: Sage.

Becker, H. (1963) *Outsiders: Studies in the Sociology of Deviance*. New York: Free Press.

Bedarf, A. (1995) 'Examining sex offender community notification laws', *California Law Review*, 83(3): 885–939.

Bichard, Sir M. (2004) *The Bichard Inquiry Report*. London: Home Office.

Braithwaite, J. (1989) *Crime, Shame and Reintegration*. Sydney: Cambridge University Press.

Braithwaite, J. (1993) 'Shame and modernity', *British Journal of Criminology*, 33(1): 1–18.

Braithwaite, J. (2000) 'The new regulatory state and the transformation of criminology', *British Journal of Criminology*, 40(2): 222–38.

Braithwaite, J. and Daly, K. (1994) 'Masculinities, violence and communitarian control', in T. Newburn and E. Stanko (eds) *Just Boys Doing Business? Men, Masculinity and Crime*. London: Routledge (pp. 189–213).

Brilliant, J. A. (1989) 'The modern day scarlet letter: a critical analysis of modern probation conditions', *Duke Law Journal*, 5: 1357–85.

Bryan, T. and Doyle, P. (2003) 'Developing multi-agency public protection arrangements', in A. Matravers (ed.) *Sex Offenders in the Community: Managing and Reducing the Risks*. Cullompton: Willan Publishing.

Cesaroni, C. (2001) 'Releasing sex offenders into the community through "circles of support" – a means of reintegrating the "worst of the worst"', *Journal of Offender Rehabilitation*, 34(2): 85–98.

Cobley, C. (1997) 'Sentencing and supervision of sex offenders', *Journal of Social Welfare and Family Law*, 19(1): 98–104.

Cobley, C. (2003) 'The legislative framework', in A. Matravers (ed.) *Sex Offenders in the Community: Managing and Reducing the Risks*. Cullompton: Willan Publishing.

Consedine, J. (1995) *Restorative Justice: Healing the Effects of the Crime*. Lyttleton: Ploughshares Publications.

Cossins, A. (2008) 'Restorative justice and child sex offences: the theory and the practice', *British Journal of Criminology*, 48(3): 359–78.

Crawford, A. (1999) *The Local Governance of Crime: Appeals to Community and Partnerships*. Oxford: Oxford University Press.

Daly, K. (2002) 'Sexual assault and restorative justice', in H. Strang and J. Braithwaite (eds) *Restorative Justice and Family Violence*. Melbourne: Cambridge University Press.

Daly, K. (2006) 'Restorative justice and sexual assault: an archival study of court and conference cases', *British Journal of Criminology*, 46(2): 334–56.

Daly, K. (2008) 'Setting the record straight and a call for radical change: a reply to Annie Cossins', *British Journal of Criminology*, 48(4): 557–66.

Davis, G. (1992) *Making Amends: Mediation and Reparation in Criminal Justice*. London and New York: Routledge.

Earl-Hubbard, M. (1996) 'The child sex offender registration laws: the punishment, liberty, deprivation and unintended results associated with the scarlet letter laws of the 1990s', *North Western Law Review*, 90(2): 788–62.

Edwards, W. and Hensley, C. (2001) 'Contextualising sex offender management legislation and policy: evaluating the problem of latent consequences in community notification laws', *International Journal of Offender Therapy and Comparative Criminology*, 45(1): 83–101.

Ericson, R. V. (2007) *Crime in an Insecure World*. Cambridge: Polity Press.

Feeley, M. and Simon, J. (1992) 'The new penology: notes on the emerging strategy of corrections and its implications', *Criminology*, 30(4): 449–74.

Feeley, M. and Simon, J. (1994) 'Actuarial justice: the emerging new criminal law', in D. Nelken (ed.) *The Futures of Criminology*. London: Sage.

Finstad, L. (1990) 'Sexual offenders out of prison: principles for a realistic utopia', *International Journal of the Sociology*, 18(2): 157–77.

Garfinkel, H. (1956) 'Conditions of successful degradation ceremonies', *American Journal of Criminology*, 61: 420–4.

Gillespie, A. (2007) 'Barring teachers: The new vetting arrangements', *Education and the Law*, 19(1): 1–18.

Greer, C. (2003) *Sex Crime and the Media: Sex Offending and the Press in a Divided Society*. Cullompton: Willan Publishing.

Grubin, D. H. (1998) *Sex Offending Against Children: Understanding the Risk*, Police Research Series Paper 99. London: Home Office.

Hacking, I. (1999) *The Social Construction of What?* Cambridge, MA: Harvard University Press.

Hay, C. (2001) 'An exploratory test of Braithwaite's reintegrative shaming theory', *Crime and Delinquency*, 38(2): 132–53.

Hebenton, B. and Seddon, T. (2009) 'From dangerousness to precaution: managing sexual and violent offenders in an insecure and uncertain age', *British Journal of Criminology*, 49(3): 343–62.

Hebenton, B. and Thomas, T. (1996) 'Sexual offenders in the community: reflections on problems of law, community and risk management in the USA and England and Wales', *International Journal of the Sociology of Law*, 24(4): 427–43.

Herman, J. (1997) *Trauma and Recovery*. New York: Basic Books.

Home Office (1996a) *Protecting the Public: The Government's Strategy on Crime in England and Wales*, Cm 3190. London: HMSO.

Home Office (1996b) *Sentencing and Supervision of Sex Offenders: A Consultation Document*, Cm 3304. London: HMSO.

Home Office (2001) *Consultation Paper on the Review of Part I of the Sex Offenders Act 1997*. London: Home Office Communication Directorate.

Hudson, B. (1998) 'Restorative justice: the challenge of sexual and racial violence', *Journal of Law and Society*, 25(2): 237–56.

Hudson, B. (2002) 'Restorative justice and gendered violence: diversion or effective justice?', *British Journal of Criminology*, 42(3): 616–34.

Jones, T. and Newburn, T. (eds) (2006) *Plural Policing: A Comparative Perspective*. London: Routledge.

Kahan, D. M. (1996) 'What do alternative sanctions mean?', *University of Chicago Law Review*, 63: 591–653.

Karp, D. R. (1998) 'The judicial and the judicious use of shame penalties', *Crime and Delinquency*, 44(2): 277–94.

Kelley, R. K. (1989) 'Sentenced to wear the scarlet letter: judicial innovations in sentencing', *Dickinson Law Review*, 93: 759–88.

Kemshall, H. (2001) *Risk Assessment and Management of Known Sexual and Violent Offenders: A Review of Current Issues*, Police Research Series Paper 140. London: Home Office.

Kemshall, H. and Maguire, M. (2001) 'Public protection, partnership and risk penality: the multi-agency risk management of sexual and violent offenders', *Punishment and Society*, 3(2): 237–64.

Kimball, C. M. (1996) 'A modern day Arthur Dimmesdale: public notification when sex offenders are released into the community', *Georgia State University Law Review*, 12: 1187–221.

Knock, K., Schlesinger, P., Boyle, R. and Magor, M. (2002) *The Police Perspective on Sex Offender Orders: A Preliminary Review of Policy and Practice*, Police Research Series Paper 155. London: Home Office.

Koss, M. P., Bachar, K. J. and Hopkins, C. Q. (2003) 'Restorative justice for sexual violence: repairing victims, building community, and holding offenders accountable', *Annals New York Academy of Sciences*, 989: 384–77.

Lieb, R. (2003) 'Joined-up worrying: The Multi-Agency Public Protection Panels', in A. Matravers (ed.) *Sex Offenders in the Community: Managing and Reducing the Risks*. Cullompton: Willan Publishing.

Maguire, M., Kemshall, H., Noakes, L., Wincup, E. and Sharpe, K. (2001) *Risk Management of Sexual and Violent Offenders: The Work of Public Protection Panels*, Police Research Series Paper 13. London: Home Office.

Marshall, P. (1997) *The Prevalence of Convictions for Sexual Offending*, Home Office Research Bulletin 55. London: Home Office.

Marshall, T. (1991) *Victim–Offender Mediation*, Home Office Research Bulletin 30. London: HMSO.

Marshall, T. (1999) *Restorative Justice: An Overview*, a Report by the Home Office Research Development and Statistics Directorate. London: HMSO.

Massaro, T. M. (1991) 'Shame culture and American criminal law', *Michigan Law Review*, 89: 1880–944.

Maxwell, G. and Morris, A. (1999) *Understanding Re-offending*. Wellington: Institute of Criminology, Victoria University of Wellington.

Maxwell, G. and Morris, A. (2002) 'The role of shame, guilt and remorse in restorative justice processes for young people', in E. Weitekamp and H. J. Kerner (eds) *Restorative Justice: Theoretical Foundations*. Cullompton: Willan Publishing (pp. 267–84).

Maxwell, G. and Morris, A. (2004) 'What is the place of shame in restorative justice?', in H. Zehr and B. Toews (eds) *Critical Issues in Restorative Justice*. Monsey, NY: Criminal Justice Press/Cullompton: Willan Publishing.

McAlinden, A. (2005) 'The use of shame in the reintegration of sex offenders', *British Journal of Criminology*, 45(3): 373–94.

McAlinden, A. (2006) 'Managing risk: from regulation to the reintegration of sexual offenders', *Criminology and Criminal Justice*, 6(2): 197–218.

McAlinden, A. (2007) *The Shaming of Sexual Offenders: Risk, Retribution and Reintegration*. Oxford: Hart Publishing.

McAlinden, A. (2010) 'The vetting of sexual offenders: state over-extension, the punishment deficit and the failure to manage risk', *Social and Legal Studies*, 19(1): 25–48.

McElrea, F. W. M. (1994) 'Justice in the community: the New Zealand experience', in J. Burnside and N. Baker (eds) *Relational Justice: Repairing the Breach*. Winchester: Waterside Press.

Morris, A. (2002) 'Critiquing the critics: a brief response to critics of restorative justice',

British Journal of Criminology, 42(3): 596–615.

Morris, A. and Gelsthorpe, L. (2000) 'Re-visioning men's violence against female partners', *Howard Journal*, 39(4): 412–28.

Morris, A. and Maxwell, G. (2000) 'The practice of family group conferences in New Zealand: assessing the place, potential and pitfalls of restorative justice', in A. Crawford and J. Goodey (eds) *Integrating a Victim Perspective in Criminal Justice*. Aldershot: Ashgate (pp. 207–25).

Parton, N., Thorpe, D. and Wattam, C. (1997) *Child Protection: Risk and the Moral Order*. Basingstoke: Macmillan.

Pennell, J. (2006) 'Stopping domestic violence or protecting children? Contributions from restorative justice', in D. Sullivan and L. Tifft (eds) *Handbook on Restorative Justice: A Global Perspective*. New York: Routledge (pp. 286–98).

Pennell, J. and Burford, G. (2001) 'Family group decision making: resolving child sexual abuse', in G. Burford (ed.) *Broken Icons*. St John's, NF: Jesperson Press.

Petrunik, M. G. (2002) 'Managing unacceptable risk: sex offenders, community response, and social policy in the United States and Canada', *International Journal of Offender Therapy and Comparative Criminology*, 46(4): 483–511.

Power, H. (2003) 'Disclosing information on sex offenders: the human rights implications', in A. Matravers (ed.) *Sex Offenders in the Community: Managing and Reducing the Risks*. Cullompton: Willan Publishing.

Quaker Peace and Social Witness (2005) *Circles of Support and Accountability in the Thames Valley: The First three Years – April 2002 to March 2005*. London: Quaker Communications.

Retzinger, S. M. and Scheff, T. J. (1996) 'Strategy for community conferences: emotions and social bonds', in B. Galaway and J. Hudson (eds) *Restorative Justice: International Perspectives*. Monsey, NY: Criminal Justice Press (pp. 315–36).

Salter, A. (2003) *Predators, Pedophiles, Rapists, and Other Sex Offenders: Who They Are, How They Operate, and How We Can Protect Ourselves and Our Children*. New York: Basic Books.

Seddon, T. (2008) 'Dangerous liaisons: personality disorder and the politics of risk', *Punishment and Society*, 10(3): 301–17.

Shearing, C. (2000) 'Punishment and the changing face of governance', *Punishment and Society*, 3(2): 203–20.

Shute, S. (2004) 'The Sexual Offences Act 2003: (4) new civil preventative orders – Sexual Offences Prevention Orders; Foreign Travel Orders; Risk of Sexual Harm Orders', *Criminal Law Review*: 417–40.

Silverman, J. and Wilson, D. (2002) *Innocence Betrayed: Paedophilia, the Media and Society*. Cambridge: Polity Press.

Soothill, K. and Francis, B. (1998) 'Poisoned chalice or just deserts? The Sex Offenders Act 1997', *Journal of Forensic Psychiatry*, 9(2): 281–93.

Soothill, K., Francis, B. and Sanderson, B. (1997) 'A cautionary tale: the Sex Offenders Act 1997, the Police and Cautions', *Criminal Law Review*: 482–90.

Tavuchis, N. (1991) *Mea Culpa: A Sociology of Apology and Reconciliation*. Stanford, CA: Stanford University Press.

Thomas, T. (2003) 'Sex offender community notification: Experiences from America', *Howard Journal of Criminal Justice*, 42(3): 217–28.

Umbreit, M. (1994) *Victim Meets the Offender: The Impact of Restorative Justice and Mediation*. Monsey, NY: Criminal Justice Press.

Vagg, J. (1998) 'Delinquency and shame: data from Hong Kong', *British Journal of Criminology*, 38(2): 247–64.

Van Dujn, A. L. (1999) 'The scarlet letter branding', *Drake Law Review*, 47(3): 635–59.

Van Ness, D. (1993) 'New wine and old wineskins: four challenges of restorative justice', *Criminal Law Forum*, 4(2): 251–76.

Van Ness, D. and Strong, K. H. (1997) *Restoring Justice*. Cincinnati, OH: Anderson Publishing.

Van Stokkom, B. (2002) 'Moral emotions in restorative justice conferences: managing shame, designing empathy', *Theoretical Criminology*, 6(3): 339–60.

Walgrave, L. and Aersten, A. (1996) 'Reintegrative shaming and restorative justice: interchangeable, complementary or different?', *European Journal of Criminal Policy and Research*, 4(4): 67–85.

Wilkins, L. (1964) *Social Deviance: Social Policy, Action and Research*. London: Tavistock.

Williams, A. and Thompson, B. (2004a) 'Vigilance or vigilantes: the Paulsgrove riots and policing paedophiles in the community, part 1: the long slow fuse', *Police Journal*, 77(2): 99–119.

Williams, A. and Thompson, B. (2004b) 'Vigilance or vigilantes: the Paulsgrove riots and policing paedophiles in the community, part 2: the lessons of Paulsgrove', *Police Journal*, 77(3): 193–206.

Wilson, R. J., Huculak, B. and McWhinnie, A. (2002) 'Restorative justice innovations in Canada', *Behavioural Sciences and the Law*, 20(4): 363–80.

Wilson, R. J., McWhinnie, A., Picheca, J. E., Prinzo, M. and Cortoni, F. (2007a) 'Circles of Support and Accountability: engaging community volunteers in the management of high-risk sexual offenders', *Howard Journal*, 46(1): 1–15.

Wilson, R. J., Picheca, J. E. and Prinzo, M. (2007b) 'Evaluating the effectiveness of professionally-facilitated volunteerism in the community-based management of high-risk sexual offenders, part 1: effects on participants and stakeholders', *Howard Journal*, 46(3): 289–302.

Wilson, R. J., Pichea, J. E. and Prinzo, M. (2007c) 'Evaluating the effectiveness of professionally-facilitated volunteerism in the community-based management of high-risk sex offenders, part 2: a comparison of recidivism rates', *Howard Journal*, 46(4): 327–57.

Winick, B. (1998) 'Sex offender law in the 1990s: a therapeutic analysis', *Psychology, Public Policy and Law*, 4(1/2): 505–70.

Zedner, L. (2009) 'Fixing the future? The pre-emptive turn in criminal justice', in B. McSherry, A. Norrie and S. Bronitt (eds) *Regulating Deviance: The Redirection of Criminalisation and the Future of Criminal Law*. Oxford: Hart Publishing (pp. 35–58).

Zehr, H. (1990) *Changing Lenses: A New Focus for Crime and Justice*. Scottdale, PA: Herald Press.

Zhang, S. X. (1995) 'Measuring shame in an ethnic context', *British Journal of Criminology*, 35(2): 248–62.

Chapter 19

Policing, public protection and minority groups

John Grieve

Introduction

I am concerned with the wider interpretations of policing and the effects this has had on thinking about public protection, in particular threats to minority groups. This chapter explores some of the thinking that has contributed to the development of risk analysis and safety measures in policing. It is concerned with both groups and individuals, although it is specifically about minority groups as, it is argued, this has relevance for all. The mantra used was 'everyone benefits'. It uses three main exemplars: the black minority ethnic (BME) community, the Jewish community, and some aspects of the Northern Irish (NI) experiences. This is a huge and dynamic topic, to which this chapter makes a limited contribution. However, it is largely based upon my experiences as a police officer concerned with these matters for 37 years; as a researcher into the practical lessons from miscarriages of justice and other *causes célèbres*; as a commissioner for certain aspects of post conflict in Northern Ireland from 2003 to the present; and finally from my more recent career as independent chair of multi-agency and multi-minority advisory groups concerned with drugs and hate crimes.

In this chapter I argue that the development of public protection and the analysis, intervention and management of an individual's risks and threats to them predate both the Crime and Disorder Act 1998 and Health and Safety Executive Legislation 2000 when risk analysis passed into common parlance in policing. The development of policing policy is therefore argued to be incremental and evolutionary, rather than revolutionary, as those who might claim it is mere political correctness allege. Risk models and analysis are also at the heart of this chapter. I will further argue that the increasing police leadership interest in project management as it influenced both intelligence-led and intelligent policing was a major factor in this evolution.

Although much of the policing renaissance described here concerns hate crime, I am arguing it has wider implications. I have also included some practical instruments that I have used and taught for some years for public protection assessments. Lastly, I explore the high volume, high risk discrete events experienced as series dilemmas of some policing. I do not deal with anti-social behaviour orders (ASBOs) except when considering aggregate problems. Before discussing these issues in relation to public protection, some brief comment on the three areas identified above is required.

Policing

This chapter concentrates on and emphasises roles and activity in the wider concept of policing, including but beyond the public police, all those agencies and individuals who are concerned with the wider maintaining of the public peace – 'the Queen's Peace her crown and dignity' as the clerks at the Central Criminal Court used to announce: what is also sometimes called the common good. It is also called the wider police family.

Critical incidents

The 1980s and 1990s saw an accelerating trajectory of learning from widely reported miscarriages of justice, all interpreted as critical incidents. This was powered by the increasing involvement of psychologists, criminologists and other social scientists (not least from their police postgraduate students, see Grieve 2007). Of particular importance was Rhona Flin's work, which influenced both police public order thinking after the Hillsborough disaster of 1989 (Flin 1996; Flin *et al.* 2008; Crego and Alison 2008) and also counter-terrorist thinking during the possible endgame in Northern Ireland (see below, under Independent Monitoring Commission). She identified critical incidents as significant for organisations. Flin and her colleagues have pointed out that risk identification skills as a management tool, though non-technical, are vital to public protection from the impact of critical incidents. She identifies seven skills (Flin *et al.* 2008):

- Situational awareness
- Decision-making
- Communication
- Teamwork
- Leadership
- Managing stress
- Coping with fatigue

We explored all seven elements in a hundred exercises about critical incident management with different agencies, largely examining the protection of black minority ethnic (BME) individuals and communities. We also used scenarios involving the Irish traveller community, children at risk, Muslims, asylum-seekers and others. Over 2,000 police delegates attended over three-day workshops (see Grieve *et al.* 2007; Crego and Alison 2008).

Flin's work had given us some useful instruments for exploring her seven skills. Of particular use was her 'dream team', a collective of a variety of disciplines to examine a high risk situation – for example, a terrorist bomb threat in a shopping centre. During the 1996–1998 Provisional Irish Republic Army (PIRA) bombing campaign, these dream teams evolved into 'gold groups' examining the tactical and strategic consequences of the decisions made. In turn these gold groups became 'diamond groups' in training in a post-Stephen Lawrence Inquiry policing environment (see below and Grieve *et al.* 2007; Savage *et al.* 2007; Crego and Alison 2008).

Community liaison, engagement, cohesion, the Crime and Disorder Act and protective services, fear of crimes

At this juncture it is important to note that for some decades there have been some officers who specialised in community safety and liaison. My experience of them predates the Scarman Inquiry into the Brixton disorders (1981). It is nothing new to consider the needs of public protection, either for minorities or for policing to seek to reduce the hazards that threaten them. I concede that there has been an increasing shift in concern about fear of crime from at least the advent of the British Crime Survey, which is related to the long gestation and improvement in the service delivery to victims (not least from the exposure of failure in the early 1980s towards rape victims; see Savage 2007; Blair 1985). There is a reality to being a victim and also being black, young, disabled, gay, female, Jewish, or any of the other minority labels that transcend political correctness.

Although governments for years had stressed public protection in vague terms, it was not until the Crime and Disorder Act (1998) that whole units were set up to deal with the multi-agency issues that evolved. This was a major Labour government drive at reforming the police and their relationships through policing to all the other bodies (not least local government) that were tasked under the new Act (see Savage 2007). The fifth Home Secretary in a decade demonstrated his continuing commitment to this aspiration in 2009, which had still not been achieved, when he was quoted speaking about a minority family (with learning disabilities) driven to despair and suicide by fearful bullying:

> This is about core policing values which is also core Labour business of looking after communities. It is about responding to people's needs at a time when they need the police to be there. The Pilkington's [*sic*] is an exceptional case, but one that should never have happened. (Summers 2009)

The article went on to call for closer cooperation between local authorities, agencies, and police in problem areas and to share information. The Crime and Disorder Act 1998 as amended by other, later legislation had created Crime and Disorder Reduction Partnerships, which included membership from the local council (of whatever size), the local chief officers of police, probation, police authority, fire and health primary care trusts. This should have ensured, a decade earlier, the kind of cooperation and information sharing that the Home Secretary now required (see, for example, Harfield and Harfield 2008: 73–4). As Her Majesty's Chief Inspector of Constabulary Denis O'Connor has pointed out, over the last two decades the Queen's Police Medal obverse reads 'To guard my people'. From this came his thinking about policing protective services for all, but especially to minorities (personal communications 1989–2009).

Community impact assessment

The murder of Stephen Lawrence and the subsequent public inquiry (Macpherson 1999) gave rise to the development of a particular tool, which is an instructive case study in the matters we are considering. Professor Betsy Stanko and her postgraduate students, particularly Laura Richards, made a substantial contribution *via* the Violent Crime Research Project for the Economic and Social Research Council about the impacts of different kinds of violence on different communities. This was incorporated into the strategic response to the public inquiry and developments in policing protective services. In turn this led to community impact assessments (CIA), which are a Human Rights Act requirement. As a risk, gap or threat analysis CIAs:

- Are ethical, transparent, inclusive, evidence and intelligence based, wide ranging and therefore tailored to community and minority needs.

- Are primarily local community based, using existing contacts and prior arrangements for the exchange of information using a variety of methods, therefore very specifically designed to abstract information of relevance to public protection.

- Use measures and categories – high, medium, low – likelihood or impact of identified possible consequences.

Impact analysis for minority groups used by Greater Manchester Police explains the thinking behind this well:

> [The] starting point will be any disparities or potential disparities identified … a judgement whether these amount to adverse impact … systematically evaluating … against all the information and evidence assembled … using as a benchmark, and making a reasonable judgement whether the policy is likely to have significant negative consequences for a particular diverse group or groups. (Greater Manchester Police 2002/05)

Learning from public order, intelligence, terrorism, murder manual and the National Intelligence Model (NIM)

Where else did this thinking come from? Public order, intelligence, terrorism, the murder manual, and the National Intelligence Model (NIM) were, of course, all very influential. I have already identified a pre-Scarman involvement but Scarman (1981) on the public disorders in Brixton (mostly but not exclusively involving minority youths) and the Taylor Report (1989) on the Hillsborough football disaster had a huge effect. An earlier model from project management had used the social technical environmental economic political legal ethical safety (STEEPLES) model, which placed an emphasis on the following factors: health, impact/likelihood, consequence/reputation, temporal/urgency/importance, vulnerability, high medium low, and financial. What I am suggesting here is that we recover the word 'intelligence' for communities. This poses a dilemma for some people, policing by communication as it seems to some, particularly those who are pursuing a war on terror as opposed to the democratic use of the criminal justice system. So my argument is along the following lines:

- The creation of a general thesis to 'make intelligence non-threatening to communities'.

- See that community impact assessments are an intelligence and public protection instrument.

- Try to get across the idea that it is not a politically correct imposition to use risk analysis and human rights in policing.

- The idea that informed consent by educated customers is not a threat to the operational independence, wider policing agencies, or to covert intelligence operations.

- Intelligence should be viewed as an education and is a step on that journey.

One of the endemic risks of using an intelligence-based risk model is the potential for the system to fail. There are a number of pathologies that can be found within operational, strategic and tactical policing failures and remedies. George and Bruce (2008) describe a range of other intelligence problems for protective services:

- Estimative misjudgement, uncritical acceptance of established positions or assumptions.

- Analysts doing what the boss wants, absence of breadth of research, and not building knowledge (a point made by Williams, this volume, in his review of risk assessment of sexual and violent offenders).

- Failing to confront organisational norms, political context or culture, no competitive analysis, no challenge groups.

- Failing to understand the task of predictive warning.

- Emphasis on short-term products, not long-term major trends.

- Overreaction to previous errors.

Much of the evolution about the protection of the public explored in many public inquiries was concerned with public disorder/return to normality thinking (see Savage 2007: 44, Grieve *et al.* 2007). However, the clarity from law enforcement and hard-edged crime investigations came from project management of policing improvements as applied to intelligence thinking. Ratcliffe (2004 and 2009) examines the international dimension, which also includes a review of the UK National Intelligence Model. As there have been a large number of major changes in public protection policing over a number of years, it is not possible to discuss them all here. However, the works of Harfield and Harfield (2005, 2008) and Harfield, MacVean, Grieve and Phillips (2008) critically examine the type of evolution I am describing. This latter work explores in depth the concept of consilient thinking in intelligent policing, where multiple disciplines and logic systems come together to find solutions to policing problems, not least of public protection (see Grieve 2008; Harfield and Harfield 2008; Stanko 2008, Juett *et al.* 2008).

All these books provide useful further reading vistas away from the core perspective discussed here. Harfield and Harfield (2008), for example, provide highly instructive policing and public protection activity that cuts across a range of minority groups and their protection (2008: 142). Their chapter on risk is especially significant, and includes important issues regarding risk that can be tied to the next crucial area of assessment.

Assessment

Grant's (1981) assessment vehicle, as amended by Butler (2004) and Fricker (2002), is helpful both for intelligence analysis and its evaluation, and also for any education and arguments. It is based on a unit Ian Grant wrote for the Open University. I have added the importance of including dissent from Lord Butler's review of intelligence on the Iraq War and Miranda Fricker's thinking about how some testimony, voices, and evidence counts far more in some debates or decision-making than in others in what she calls 'epistemic imbalance'. Grant (1981) uses the following process:

- Present clear synopsis of thesis to ensure a complete understanding.
- Does the assessment distinguish between fact, value, empirical, interpretation and evaluation?
- Are propositions tested or is there immunity from tests?
- What is the status of evidence, testimony; are collection methods explained and records available?

- Is the logic of argument articulated clearly?
- Are there alternative hypotheses; are other evidence explanations offered?
- Is there a conspiracy of silence, or any form of dissent? Is this explored and explained (this is Lord Butler's contribution) and are there gaps in the assessment articulated?
- Have the generalisations been checked?
- Is there any bias or epistemic imbalance?
- Finally, do you identify with the argument? How persuasive is the case? And why?

Some models of risk analysis used by the police service and in multi-agency working

Savage (2007: 136) has shown the relationship between Sir Kenneth Newman's reforms imported from his community policing experiences, his service with the Royal Ulster Constabulary, the Palestine police, at the Police Staff College, and his adoption of project management techniques towards risk analysis tools. One of these imports was an American system, known as 'policing by objectives' (Lubans and Edgar 1979), which applied project management techniques to policing programmes including increased consultation with community stakeholders.

The late 1990s saw a further shift with the introduction of the European Convention on Human Rights, which was enshrined in law in 1998. The United Nations Code of Conduct for Law Enforcement and the Council of Europe Declaration on Policing also provided a framework for our thinking on multi-agency working. During this intensive period of development, where ECHR became imbedded in legislation and public protection policy, a number of relevant public protection 'articles' from the convention can be indentified:

- Article 2: Right to life
- Article 5: Rights of liberty and security
- Article 8: Right to private and family life

Regarding Article 2 (the right to life), it was paramount that an effective investigation was undertaken. Case law advises on the competencies and criteria that were important. For example, those agencies and individuals protecting other people would need to be thorough and rigorous, competent and comprehensive in their work; incumbents needed to have appropriate skills and knowledge; an appropriate level of supervision of the investigation was required; they would be required to prepare thorough and complete documentation at every stage as was possible; an element of review needed to be included in the process, in other words a revisiting and checking of material and reports. Article 8 required similar competencies and criteria to be applied by those charged with delivering policing protective services (Neyroud and Beckley 2001).

PLANBI

When considering the weaving of human rights legislation into the fabric of criminal investigations, PLANBI is a useful acronym, especially when using human rights based risk assessment. Any activity that might be argued to breach people's human rights needed to fulfil the following specific criteria (Neyroud and Beckley 2001):

- *Proportional*
- *Legal*
- *Accountable*
- And any *Action* taken should be necessary;
- It needed to show that it was using the *Best Information* available, and did not accept information on face value, and that they had explored, examined, and investigated, as well as considering the consequences for an individual, and ensuring that due weight was given to what would be the family, group or community impact of that activity.

3PLEM

Comparative case analysis (CCA) has been at the heart of my work for over 30 years, and from CCA we developed a model about the way some risks to individuals or groups, particularly the vulnerable, could be assessed and how they might interact. An acronym, 3PLEM – standing for physical, political, psychological, legal, economic (including financial) and moral risks – was developed in 1985. It was originally derived in-house from work we were undertaking in the field of CHISs (covert human intelligence sources), then called participating informants. 3PLEM is a descriptive phrase that clearly identifies the legal risks involved, and in time it came to be a tool we used widely. Examining and comparing a series of dysfunctional consequences of police activity in a range of cases led us to the conclusion that when assessing 3PLEM, an assessment would be derived on whether the risks could be acceptable. The usual categories of risk were used – high, medium or low – and once assigned we were able to provide a fairly robust measure of whether we might prevent more failures. At the time it was the only risk analysis model that was known to us.

The genesis of this work came from policing reforms driven by continuing policing scandals involving detectives and informers and also the management thinking of Sir Kenneth Newman (see, for example, Savage 2007: 115; Punch 2009: 54–136). Newman's thinking was especially influential and led to a wider programme of police intelligence reform. These reforms were in part based on a project management system called 'policing by objectives', which emphasised project management often and more specifically involved an introduction to risk management. A slight variation on the model can be found in Roberts (2002: 29–31) who examined the informant dilemma a decade and a half later. Billingsley (2006) sought to advance police thinking with his PLAICE model (an acronym standing for physical, legal, assets, information technology, compromise and environment). He also proposes the TTTT as a model of risk management – terminate, treat, transfer or tolerate. Although this is helpful, it is not as broad an assessment as RARARA (see Harfield and Harfield 2008: 148–53, and below).

Steps are being taken to replace 3PLEM but the report by Mrs O'Loan (the Police Ombudsman for Northern Ireland) in 2007 on Operation Ballast, another case concerning the relationships of police officers with sources of covert intelligence (Punch 2009: 155–7), makes me think that 3PLEM has provided a waterproof jacket for the witness box for over 20 years, and worked for me recently in the High Court in London. However, it should be noted that the various forms of risk assessment models – 3PLEM, PLAICE, RARARA and TTTTs – are not mutually exclusive.

Independent Monitoring Commission Northern Ireland (2003–09)

I have already referred to Rhona Flin's influence on some aspects of the Irish potential endgame in terms of counter-terrorism investigations in England and Wales. The IMC was set up by the Irish and UK governments to offer information to all concerned with public protection from the paramilitaries. Flin's list of skills is a way of considering what the four commissioners and two joint secretaries brought to the analysis and assessment that went into our reports. What follows is an account of how we went about our tasks, not what we found. The IMC Fifth Report, published in April 2005, detailed how our methodology had evolved, which have been extensively reproduced below:

1.09 We have been asked a number of times how we make our assessments and on what information we base them. Some have asked us to put more material in the public domain. Some have challenged us on grounds that we may be or appear to be biased, and we continue carefully to consider that issue. We hope it would be helpful if we say something about the way we work.

1.10 We believe it is a great strength that the four Commissioners come from different backgrounds and have different perspectives. We seek to maximise the benefit this gives us by challenging each other's thinking as well as challenging those we meet. We try to develop assessments based on more than one source. We see if there are links between what we learn from different people and we expect to be able to triangulate different perspectives before we reach conclusions. We probe the nature and logic of the information we receive. We examine whether there are any inconsistencies. We challenge any gaps there appear to be. We question whether there might be any bias either in our own approach or in that of others and take steps to ensure it does not influence our conclusions inappropriately. We ask ourselves and our interlocutors whether other conclusions might as reasonably be drawn from the same set of circumstances. We test the confidence placed in the material and in opinions associated with it. We do all this before we come to any view, and before we write our reports. The conclusions we draw are our own.

1.11 Our sources are wide ranging. They include the law enforcement and other agencies of the UK and Ireland, as well as of any other country from which we have things to learn. But they are much wider than that. In addition to government officials and police officers we have met people from the following categories in Great Britain, Ireland North and South and in the United States:

> Political parties; government officials; police; community groups; churches; charities; pressure groups and other organisations; former combatants, including ex-prisoners; representatives of businesses; lawyers; journalists; academics; victims; private citizens, individually and as families.

We urge everybody with something material to our work to get in touch with us. We also try to take account of the work of other boards, commissions and similar bodies in Northern Ireland and elsewhere.

1.12 We are very careful what we say in our reports. From the beginning we have adhered to one firm principle. We treat everything we hear, including the identities of those who communicate with us, in complete confidence. Only in this way can they be expected to impart information to us, and without that information we cannot do the job the two Governments have charged us with. We will therefore not reveal our sources, though those people are free to say what they like about their communications with the IMC. The International Agreement lays down other constraints on us, for example so that we do not prejudice legal proceedings or jeopardise anybody's safety. But the most significant restraint is self-imposed: we will not say anything, or draw any conclusion, unless we have confidence in it, and we will qualify conclusions if we think that is necessary. We did this, for example, in our initial attribution of certain robberies in late October 2004.

1.13 We are not infallible, but we do believe we are thorough in our methods and measured in our assessments. If we find one of our conclusions does not stand up in the light of later information we will acknowledge this in a subsequent report.

It can be seen that this account of the role of monitoring in protective services from the depradations of paramilitaries in part is very close to, and owes its origins to, the model created by Grant (1981) as amended by the thinking of Fricker (2002) and Butler (2004). When the IMC was challenged in the High Court in London, Grant's assessment thinking and our 3PLEM provided the framework for my response. Moreover, the extract records our process of trying to achieve Rhona Flin's seven-part model (situational awareness, decision-making, teamwork and methods of communication). Having a psychiatrist as a fellow commissioner helps us to consider, if not manage, 'stress and fatigue'. It is for others to decide if our role amounts to 'leadership'.

DASH 2008

DASH 2008 is a model that takes its methodologies from our learning from domestic violence (DV). It is debated whether DV should be included either as a crime against a minority group or as a hate crime. What is not in doubt is the transferable learning from DV investigations, *causes célèbres* and changing policing practices (covered extensively in Richards *et al.* 2008).

There had been earlier models but these coalesced into DASH 2008. It must be emphasised here that this is a preventive model and is not easily used as a predictive assessment of further offences. There are extremely detailed risk factors covering every possible source of information including the importance of the perceptions of the victim; and it is the inclusion of the victim into the risk model that is a highly significant development and contribution to public protection. Very briefly, the model comes in three stages: risk identification, assessment, and management. Each records multiple components, for example, high risk factors such as harassment, including third parties (friends, family, colleagues, neighbours, persuading others to assist), loitering near home or workplace, and previous violence. Of course, such factors may be directly translatable to evidence or as intelligence, especially if recorded on whatever database the relevant police force is using. The model also involves a tactical menu of options to manage the risks (Richards *et al.* 2008). In considering the management of risks and describing decision-making, Laura Richards designed a model called RARARA (record, analyse, remove, accept, reduce, avoid – and averse). The 'record and analyse' were added later (Richards *et al.* 2008: 84).

MARAC/MAPPA

This is covered in detail by Kemshall (this volume) so I will not deal with it at length here. For completeness of my account in reviewing key risk models and developments the following descriptions will suffice. MARACs are multi-agency risk assessment conferences, created to consider the ways in which agencies can fulfil their obligations and commitments to each other, while caring for people at risk in DV, child protection and other cases of serious harm. They can assist decision-making and inform tasking and coordinating activities and the deployment of resources. Multi-agency public protection panels (MAPPP), while taking a strategic overview of public protection, also overlook MARACs. They may act to prevent repeat victimisation or chronic offending. They can also improve record-keeping and promote reporting to assist comparative case analysis, as well as seeking to promote better information sharing between agencies.

Health and Safety Executive (HSE)

Again, for completeness of my analysis of current influences I include HSE. The HSE is often blamed for creating an overly safety or risk-averse environment in the public protection agencies. However, although they reinforced some existing thinking and extended the remit of some models, much of the foundations had already been laid and did not originate with the HSE. Their major contribution is in the codifying and exploration of the equation: Risk = Likelihood x Consequences. This is sometimes expressed as Risk = Threat x Vulnerability.

OASys

Williams (this volume) covers OASys in detail. It is merely for completeness that I offer the following brief description to emphasise its significance and importance here. It is a system developed by the prison and probation services but adopted by DV and other areas of policing. It has definitions of what amounts to high, medium and standard risks to or from an individual:

- **High** – where there are identifiable indicators of risk of serious harm, which could occur at any time, and its impact would be serious.

- **Medium** – where there are identifiable indicators of serious harm, and where the offender has the potential to reoffend, but is unlikely to do so unless there is a change in the circumstances.

- **Low** – where the current evidence does not include any likelihood of causing serious harm.

Learning from public inquiries, child abuse, racist hate crimes, domestic violence, homophobia, mental disorder

Grieve (2007) includes a table that shows the volume of public inquiries over the past 50 years that have been concerned with public protection. Bichard's (2004) public inquiry into what was known about the murder of two young girls in Soham and how that information was exchanged (or not, as was actually the case) included his most damning criticism of the whole area of public protection; that our knowledge of dangerousness is largely predicated on the effectiveness of joined-up information sharing between agencies. The Fiona Pilkington case referred to above appears to confirm that poor communication and information disclosure between agencies is still problematic, with 'agencies meeting regularly but failing to share information or establish basic facts' (Walker 2009: 3).

Historically, the Victoria Climbié inquiry (Laming 2003) examined the incompetence, not least through blurred roles, that led to the failure to appropriately analyse or assess the risks and highlighted the numerous missed opportunities in identifying and solving them. Lord Laming and his police adviser, John Fox, had heard much evidence of multi-agency failure to intervene in the ghastly chronology of violence suffered by a BME young girl at the hands of her so-called guardians. Lord Laming concluded that merely accepting information about someone alleged to be at risk was not enough. What was needed to properly assess the situation was an open mind, an investigative approach and a healthy scepticism. Though this was relevant to all agencies, it was particularly important for the police. Unfortunately, although child protection has advanced since the Climbié tragedy, the case of Baby Peter, which occurred in the same child protection area as Climbié's death, served to warn us all that we should not rest on our laurels.

Community Security Trust (CST)

CST is a paradigm of a public protection system designed and controlled by a minority community in partnership with others. In contrast to MAPPA and MARAC, CST is a Jewish community programme promoted, financed and staffed by the community itself. They nevertheless pride themselves on their ability to work with statutory agencies. A previous Commissioner of the Metropolitan Police once said to me that if CST had not existed, the police would have had to invent it. There are a number of features of this remarkable organisation that could be valuable if other such community-based public protection organisations were developed by other minorities. First is the importance CST attaches to reliable data: this is primarily but not exclusively information about anti-semitic activity, carefully categorised and consistently recorded. It also collects open source material about potential threats to the safety of the community. Second, it supplies protective services to the Jewish community: protection at schools and synagogues and at activities and functions where Jews might be at risk. These protective services vary, and include highly skilled security physical search teams who can check premises for threats of any kind, up to and including terrorism. They also provide search and security teams for entrances to functions or events. Third, they work hard at education programmes not just for their own community but also for the wider public, politicians, and other agencies including the police about the nature of anti-semitism and its practitioners. Fourth and last for my account, they engage with other communities and share their experiences and skills. These have included Muslims, Sikhs, Hindus, Christians and other minority groups not just in the UK but internationally. A recent publication showed how everyone in every minority group at risk could learn from the Holocaust (Smith 2008). They showed how this learning could be applied to police personnel across the protective services and especially to minority communities.

The Stephen Lawrence Public Inquiry

In some ways this was a paradigm shift in thinking. In other ways it was a summation of all that had gone before. Stephen, a BME young man, was murdered by racists, and his BME friend viciously assaulted. Among the findings of a long-running public inquiry were those related to the experiences of the family, friends and community of the murdered boy of not being protected by policing. These included not least the finding of institutional racism in policing and in wider society (TSO 1999; Hall *et al.* 2009). Interestingly, Walker asked if the Pilkington case (see above) was a 'Lawrence moment' (Walker 2009: 3), by which he meant a shift in police awareness of the reality of being, for example, BME, disabled, gay, or Jewish on the streets. Of the many products for policing to come from Mr and Mrs Lawrence's hard work, I have selected two to include here – Independent Advice and community impact analysis. I have already explored CIA above (but also see Bhatti 2008, cited in Harfield *et al.* 2008). Independent Advice grew out of the need to explore how communities were experiencing policing during a crisis of public protection failure; how different perspectives could influence initially tactically but then strategically police decision-making. The way this is included in police training for public protection is covered in Grieve *et al.* (2007), Crego and Allison (2008) and Hall *et al.* (2009). These independent advisors were chosen because they were 'critical friends' of policing, and were sometimes their staunchest and most outspoken critics. Their value was their identification of matters of public protection that had been lacking from previous policing assessments. The influence of families, communities and small campaign groups – from whom many of these advisors were drawn – has been a feature of many famous cases about public protection and is discussed in Savage *et al.* (2007), Savage (2007) and Charman and Savage (2009).

Some analysis

The following list brings together the elements of what has been examined above in considering how policing can provide the best protective services and the context in which they may now operate:

- **Risk factors identification** – this is the stage at which pieces of information are linked. Information has to be gathered in a coherent, consistent and shareable way that allows the analysis and prioritising of different factors, different categories and allows some comparative case study.

- **Risk assessment** – this is the stage at which some priorities are explored: whether risks are immediate, whether high, medium or low, and whether they are serious.

- **Community impact assessments and individual risks assessments** – this is where risks can be aggregated and the context can be explored in detail by an analyst. The immediate environment of a borough, for example, or a comparative case a 1,000 miles away can both influence an assessment.

- **Risk management** – this is where priorities and resources are allocated. The assessment must lead to some intervention. Some safety plan is prepared, some activity by the agencies, or even some records of why no action is necessary.

- **Aggregating risks** – long and short term, distal and proximate. Aggregated risks are those experienced directly as a series by a victim or, over time and distance, by victims or communities, or a neighbourhood; hence proximate and nearby or distal, at some remove. They may be negotiated through media such as television and newspapers, which may provide some 'megaphone' effect to emphasise relationships between risks. For example, the media may link cases or agency responses that have only a conceptual or category relationship.

Part of the problems of protecting the vulnerable appears to be how a series of events are conceptualised and perceived by the victims, which may be different from how they are conceptualised and perceived by the authorities. As Ben Bowling (1998) pointed out, what is *an event* for the police or other agencies is experienced as a series of *ongoing activity* by minority communities. The fear is ever present and continuous; the sense of panic is often being ratcheted up over a period of time and over a series of events. This is one aspect of the high volume crimes that are each of themselves high risk, both to the victim and to the agencies concerned with preventing them.

Conclusion

A positive obligation is placed on policing to obey both Human Rights Act requirements to protect people and morally by UK policing philosophy 'to guard my people'. The experience with hate crime is transferable to wider public protection by policing, as Hall (2006) has shown: whether this is the racist experiences of the Lawrence family, the bullying of those with learning disabilities as of the Pilkington family, or the community response to anti-semitism by CST.

I have drawn some general conclusions from my experiences. First, the public police are not the only party to such responses for public protection. Second, even though the ranges of multi-agencies of MAPPA or MARAC are necessary, they are not sufficient to deal with the problems. Third, formal bonding of concerned citizens, as with the learning disabilities charities such as Victims' Voice or highly structured organisations such as CST, is not enough either. Fourth, leadership is essential, both as ongoing activity by politicians and formal leaders such as senior police officers, probation or prison staff, but also by charismatic leaders of minorities, be they gay, challenged, Jewish, black, religious, neighbourhoods, campaigns, estates or any other minorities. Critics as leaders, including the academically critical, are vital. Fifth, while legislation, both enabling and law enforcement, is necessary, it is also not of itself sufficient to deal with the public protection of minority communities. Finally, despite all that is said about immigration and the sneer of political correctness gone mad, the benefits that minority views bring to the richness of life of neighbourhood, community or state – not least that of challenge or dissent – are vital to twenty-first century society. This should be included within the consilient way of thinking.

I have also argued in this chapter that the issue of public protection and the individual's risk and threat analysis predates human rights and Health and Safety legislation (2000) and the Crime and Disorder Act (1998). The kinds of milestones in policing described in Grieve (2007) stretch back 50 years. Each identified a further shift in the widening concept of policing and the variety of roles that different agencies would play in protecting minority communities.

Outside of current counter-terrorism assessments, which I have not dealt with here (see for general information the UK Government CONTEST and Prepare, Prevent, Pursue and Protect 2009), I consider the kind of thinking that has gone into DASH and CIA the most comprehensive so far prepared. The work on risk factor analysis that has gone into DASH, when combined in a matrix with CIA models, seems a useful tool. The OASys concept of serious harm is also useful, but has not sufficient factors for considering aggregate damage and risk, as the Pilkington case showed for minority communities. Finally, statutory agencies such as the police, probation and local authorities, working in conjunction with community organisations like CST and other independent advisors, seems to offer a good way forward.

Selected further reading

Hazel Kemshall and Andy Williams, both in this volume.

References

Bhatti, A. (2008) 'The mobiles are out and the hoods are up' in C. Harfield, A. MacVean, J.Grieve, and Phillips, D. (2008) The Handbook of Intelligent Policing, Consilience, Crime Control, and Community Safety. Oxford: Oxford University Press.

Bichard, Sir M. (2004) The Bichard Report Inquiry. Online at: http://homeoffice.gov.uk/publications/operational-policing/bichard-inquiryreport.

Billingsley, R. (2006) 'Risk management: is there a model for covert policing?', Covert Policing Review: 98–100.

Blair, I. (1985) Investigating Rape: A New Approach. London: Croom Helm.

Bowling, B. (1998) Violent Racism: Victimisation, Policing and Social Context. Oxford: Clarendon Press.

Butler, Lord (2004) Review of Intelligence of Weapons of Mass Destruction. Report of a Committee of Privy Counsellors. London: The Stationery Office.

Charman, S. and Savage, S. P. (2009) 'Mothers for justice? Gender and campaigns against miscarriages of justice', British Journal of Criminology, 49(6): 900–15.

Crego, J. and Alison, L. (eds) (2008) Policing Critical Incidents: Leadership and Critical Incident Management. Cullompton: Willan Publishing.

ESRC Violence Research Project (2002) Taking Stock. What do we know about Interpersonal Violence. Swindon: UK Economic and Social Research Council.

Flin, R. (1996) Sitting in the Hot Seat. Chichester: Wiley.

Flin, R., O'Connor, P. and Crichton, M. (2008) Safety at the Sharp End. Surrey: Ashgate.

Fricker, M. (2002) 'Power, knowledge and injustice', in J. Baggini and J. Stangroom (eds) *New British Philosophy: The Interviews.* London: Routledge.

George, R. and Bruce, J. (2008) (eds) *Analyzing Intelligence: Origins, Obstacles and Innovations.* Washington: Georgetown University Press.

Grant, I. (1981) *U202 Inquiry.* Open University UK.

GMP (2002/05) *Race Equality Scheme.* Manchester: Greater Manchester Police Authority.

Grieve, J. (2007) 'Behavioural science and the law: investigation', in D. Carson, B. Milne, F. Pakes, K. Shalev and A. Shawyer (eds) *Applying Psychology to Criminal Justice.* Wiley: Chichester.

Grieve, J. (2008) 'Lawfully audacious: a reflective journey', in C. Harfield, A. MacVean, J. Grieve and D. Phillips (eds) *The Handbook of Intelligent Policing: Consilience, Crime Control and Community Safety.* Oxford: Oxford University Press.

Grieve J. (2009a) 'Developments in UK criminal intelligence', in J. Ratcliffe (ed.) *Strategic Thinking in Criminal Intelligence*, 2nd edn. Cullompton: Willan Publishing.

Grieve, J. (2009b) 'The Stephen Lawrence Inquiry: from intelligence failure to intelligence legacy', in N. Hall, J. Grieve and S. Savage (eds) *Policing and Legacy of Lawrence.* Cullompton: Willan Publishing.

Grieve, J., Crego, J. and Griffiths W. (2007) 'Critical incidents, investigation, management and training', in T. Newburn, T. Williamson and A. Wright (eds) *Handbook of Criminal Investigation.* Cullompton: Willan Publishing.

Hall, N. (2006) *Hate Crime.* Cullompton: Willan Publishing.

Hall, N., Grieve, J. and Savage, S. P. (eds) (2009) *Policing and the Legacy of Lawrence.* Cullompton: Willan Publishing.

Harfield, C. and Harfield, K. (2005) *Covert Investigation.* Oxford: Oxford University Press.

Harfield, C. and Harfield, K. (2008) *Intelligence: Investigation, Community and Partnership.* Oxford. Oxford University Press.

Harfield, C., MacVean A., Grieve, J. and Phillips, D. (eds) (2008) *The Handbook of Intelligent Policing: Consilience, Crime Control, and Community Safety.* Oxford: Oxford University Press.

Juett, L., Smith, R., Grieve, J. (2008) 'Open source intelligence – a case study: GLADA "London – the highs and lows" 2003 and 2007', in C. Harfield, A. MacVean, J. Grieve and D. Phillips (eds) *The Handbook of Intelligent Policing: Consilience, Crime Control, and Community Safety.* Oxford: Oxford University Press.

Laming, Lord (2003) *The Victoria Climbié Inquiry*, Cmnd 5730. London: The Stationery Office.

Lubans, Y. A. and Edgar, J. M. (1979) *Policing by Objectives.* Hartford, CT: Social Development Corporation.

Macpherson, W. (1999) *The Stephen Lawrence Inquiry*, Cm 4262. London: The Stationery Office.

Neyroud, P. and Beckley, A. (eds) (2001) *Policing, Ethics and Human Rights.* Cullompton: Willan Publishing.

Punch, M. (2009) *Police Corruption.* Cullompton: Willan Publishing.

Ratcliffe, J. (ed.) (2004) *Strategic Thinking in Criminal Intelligence.* Cullompton: Willan Publishing.

Ratcliffe, J. (ed.) (2009) *Strategic Thinking in Criminal Intelligence*, 2nd edn. Cullompton: Willan Publishing.

Richards, L., Letchford, L. and Stratton, L. (2008) *Policing Domestic Violence.* Oxford: Blackstone's Practical Policing.

Roberts, T. (2002) *The Human Factor: Maximising the Use of Police Informants.* New Police Bookshop.

Savage, S. (2007) *Police Reform: Forces for Change*. Oxford: Oxford University Press.

Savage, S., Poyser, S. and Grieve, J. (2007) 'Putting wrongs to right: campaigns against miscarriage of justice', *Criminology and Criminal Justice*, 7(1): 83–105.

Scarman, Lord (1981) *Inquiry into the Brixton Disorders*. London: The Stationery Office.

Smith, S. D. (2008) *A Guide to the Holocaust for Police Personnel*. London: The Holocaust Centre with the Community Security Trust.

Stanko, B. (2008) 'Strategic intelligence: methodologies for understanding what police services already "know" to reduce harm', in C. Harfield, A. MacVean, J. Grieve and D. Phillips (eds) *The Handbook of Intelligent Policing: Consilience, Crime Control, and Community Safety*. Oxford: Oxford University Press.

Summers, D. (2009) 'Johnson to censure police over pair's death', *Guardian*, 28 September, p. 15.

Taylor, Lord (1989) *Hillsborough Stadium Disaster*. London: HMSO.

TSO (1999) *The Stephen Lawrence Inquiry Report, Appendices & Daily Transcripts*. London: The Stationery Office.

UK Government (2009) *CONTEST Strategy*. London: The Stationery Office.

Walker, P. (2009) 'Police errors contributed to tormented mother's suicide', *Guardian*, 29 September, pp. 1–3.

Chapter 20

Young offenders and public protection

Kerry Baker

'Millions will scarcely believe such things possible in a rich, educated society by children so young.' (*The Times*, 4 September 2009)

Introduction

At the time of writing, the case of two boys aged ten and eleven convicted of committing serious acts of violence and abuse against two other boys aged nine and eleven, to which the quotation above refers, is attracting considerable press and public interest in the UK. It immediately prompts critical questions relating not only to the children who carried out the abuse but also about the role of communities and professionals in terms of our collective social responsibility towards children and young people.

Such examples of young people committing heinous acts of violence or sexual aggression vividly illustrate the 'paradox of the child-criminal' (McDiarmid 2007: 129). Young people can themselves be vulnerable and in need of protection, yet they also have agency and the ability (to varying degrees, depending on age and maturity) to make choices about their actions. Societal responses to this tension have varied enormously over time and across jurisdictions. There are striking differences within the western world in the way young people who commit very serious offences are treated. On the one hand, legislation in some states in the USA means that children as young as seven could receive a mandatory sentence of life without parole (Deitch *et al.* 2009), while on the other, the welfare-based approach of countries such as Norway means that young people under the age of fifteen would not be prosecuted for any offence, no matter how serious, but would instead be seen as needing help and support (Carmichael 2003).

While there is much to be learned from looking at comparative approaches to serious offending by young people, this chapter will (for reasons of space) focus primarily on developments in England and Wales in relation to children and young people aged ten to seventeen. The literature on public protection in the UK has tended to concentrate on adults (for example, Nash 2006; Kemshall 2008) and although there has been some discussion looking more specifically at young people (Nash 2007; Baker and Sutherland 2009) it is an area that has not perhaps received as much attention as it deserves.

The chapter is divided into four main parts. The first looks at the type and extent of behaviours by young people that might fall under the umbrella of public protection. The discussion then moves on to consider the formal frameworks and structures set up to respond to such behaviour, and then looks at some of the practical issues that arise in the operation and implementation of these procedures. Finally, the chapter concludes by reflecting on the implications of serious offending for our perceptions of 'youth' and by considering some potential lessons for the future development of the apparatus of public protection.

'Risk' and 'dangerous' behaviour by young people

One important debate in the literature on 'risk' has been about the extent to which such concepts are socially constructed (Lupton 1999). Ideas about 'dangerousness' have changed over time with a move from a fear of (primarily property) crimes committed by the 'dangerous classes' to the current preoccupation with sex offenders, particularly paedophiles (Pratt 1997). A similar pattern can be seen in the way that previous social panics in relation to, say, the risks associated with joyriding by young people have been superseded by concerns over the use of weapons. The 'elasticity' of concepts such as risk and dangerousness (Robinson and McNeill 2004) is further illustrated by the way in which additional categories of behaviour such as terrorism and domestic extremism are now being explicitly included in public protection systems (Ministry of Justice 2009), alongside the more typical concerns about sexual and violent offenders. In addition, policy documentation tends to define these concepts in terms of offences committed by adults and does not always acknowledge the nature of adolescent behaviour. For example, there is often little mention of dangerous driving (Ministry of Justice 2009), yet this could be one of the ways in which young people are most likely to cause death or serious injury to others. Thus there are elements of fluidity and uncertainty in terms of what types of behaviour should be assessed and managed as part of the public protection agenda.

Nature and prevalence of serious offending

As there is no single definition of what would count as 'public protection offences' the data and evidence summarised here are something of an approximation and based on the relatively limited data available about the prevalence of serious offending by young people in England and Wales. Data in relation to young people who sexually abuse, for example, indicate a gradual increase over time in the number of sexual offences by young people being dealt with through the criminal justice system, notwithstanding the fact that these kinds of offences are typically under-reported (Grimshaw *et al.* 2008). For 2007–08, there were 2,088 sexual offences committed by young people that resulted in a formal sanction (YJB 2009b). During the same period there were 53,930 offences for violence against the person leading to a disposal, 1,232 for arson and 122 for death or injury by dangerous driving (YJB 2009b). The weakness of these figures, however, is that they include offences of varying degrees of seriousness and it is difficult to ascertain how many would be serious enough to trigger public protection processes. More generally, other data indicate that although there has been a reduction in violent crime overall (HM Government 2008), serious violence has been 'the most resistant to improvement' (Squires *et al.* 2008: 8). The impact of serious violence on young victims needs to be noted with, for example, data indicating that between 2003 and 2007 stab-related hospital admissions for under-sixteens increased by 63 per cent (Home Affairs Committee 2009).

It quickly becomes apparent that 'public protection' is a term that can cover a diverse range of offences and there will be significant heterogeneity in the backgrounds, characteristics and offending patterns of young people convicted of such crimes. Understanding these behaviours requires familiarity with research relating to specific types of offences, and although there is still less evidence than for adults, there is a growing knowledge base in relation to young people who sexually abuse (Grimshaw *et al.* 2008) and young people engaging in violence (Burman *et al.* 2007), for example. While it is not possible to generalise across all these types of offences, it is worth mentioning two common traits of young people's behaviour that help to distinguish it from that of adults. The first is that of impulsivity and recklessness, as illustrated by a recent case of young people setting fire to a tourist's hair on a train (Greenwood 2009). The consequences were potentially very serious, but from the information available it appears to have been an impulsive act rather than a premeditated use of instrumental violence. The second feature to mention is the influence of groups and peers on adolescent behaviour, with this being one of a number of factors identified as contributing to gun and knife crime among young people, for example (Silvestri *et al.* 2009).

Profiles of young people who commit serious offences

Accounts of specific high profile cases of young people who have killed (Morrison 1997; Sereny 1998) have shown a disturbing background of neglect and sometimes abuse. More generally, studies looking at the backgrounds of young people serving long custodial sentences for serious offences show a high incidence of experiences of abuse and loss (Boswell 1996; Falshaw and Browne 1997). Dent and Jowitt highlight the prevalence of 'severe and multiple traumatic events' in the lives of young people convicted of homicide and serious sexual offences' (2003: 87). A study by Bailey of twenty adolescent murderers in the UK found that this particular group 'showed family backgrounds characterised by mental illness and violence within the family' (1996: 36) and mental health problems in young people themselves are often a significant factor (Bailey *et al.* 2007). Clearly, not all cases will fit this pattern but the available evidence does seem to indicate a prevalence of troubled backgrounds and experiences of victimisation among young people convicted of serious offences.

Public protection and youth justice

The increased political focus on public protection has led to a continually expanding set of measures and systems for assessing, managing and monitoring those offenders considered to present a significant risk to others (Kemshall 2008). The aim of this section is to provide an overview of these measures in so far as they apply to young people, beginning with a brief overview of the current youth justice system in England and Wales.

Youth justice

The Crime and Disorder Act 1998 introduced major reforms to the youth justice system in England and Wales. Section 37 of the Act stated that it shall be 'the principal aim of the youth justice system to prevent offending by children and young people', and all those who work within youth justice are required to have regard to that statutory aim. The Act introduced new multi-agency youth offending teams (YOTs), which bring together professionals from a range of disciplines including children's services, the police, probation and health.

The 1998 Act also established the Youth Justice Board (YJB), an executive non-departmental public body with responsibility for promoting good practice, setting minimum national standards, monitoring performance, commissioning research and purchasing places in the secure estate for young people sentenced to custody. In relation to public protection the YJB's monitoring role is seen, for example, in the requirement for YOTs to report on any serious incidents involving young people under their supervision (YJB 2007) and its role in promoting good practice could be illustrated by the publication of an annual summary of lessons learned from these reports (YJB 2009a).

Youth justice powerfully illustrates the care/control dilemma (Muncie 2004) with commentators arguing that developments in recent years, particularly those outlined below in relation to public protection, indicate a more punitive turn (Smith 2007). In contrast, however, the adoption of the Every Child Matters agenda (HM Government 2004) in youth justice could be seen as evidence of a pendulum swing back towards a greater concern with 'needs'. Opinions will differ but the tension between meeting the needs of young people and protecting the public from those who would cause serious harm is one that permeates practice and, hence, this chapter.

The apparatus of public protection

The legislative framework is an obvious starting point and young people have been affected by the recent toughening up of sentencing in relation to violence. Examples would include the increased maximum penalty for knife possession and the creation of new offences such as 'using someone to mind a weapon' which can apply to young people aged sixteen or over (Violent Crime Reduction Act 2006).

Arguably, the more significant trend has been the expansion of long-term custodial sentences. Young people convicted of murder will receive a mandatory life sentence under section 90 of the Powers of Criminal Courts (Sentencing) Act 2000, while section 91 deals with sentencing for a range of other grave crimes. Although originally intended to be used in exceptional cases only, the scope of the section 91 provisions has gradually expanded over time to cover a wider range of offences (NACRO 2007). In addition, the public protection sentences introduced by the Criminal Justice Act 2003 – and subsequently amended by the Criminal Justice and Immigration Act 2008 – also apply. Young people convicted of a 'specified' offence (as defined in the 2003 Act) and assessed by a court as 'dangerous' can receive a sentence of Detention for Public Protection (s226) or an Extended Sentence (s228) if the court considers that no other lawful sentence is adequate to protect the public. These sentences have been controversial, particularly in regard to the indeterminate nature of the section 226 sentence and, for example, the impact this can have on a young person's mental health (Prison Reform Trust 2007).

Young people serving indeterminate sentences (s90 and s226) cannot be released from custody unless the Parole Board deems it to be safe for them to return to the community. Criticism of the unsuitability of an adult-focused approach for young people (Howard League 2007) has recently prompted changes to parole procedures with more young people now offered oral hearings and specific guidance on the process available for children and young people (Parole Board 2008).

With regard to risk management in the community, young people can be subject to multi-agency public protection arrangements (MAPPA). The eligibility criteria for MAPPA and thresholds for MAPPA management levels are the same for adults and young people, as is the requirement for information about MAPPA cases to be recorded on the ViSOR database (Ministry of Justice 2009). Few accurate figures are available on the number of young people subject to MAPPA although it has been estimated that the figure is around 2,000.[1] More reliable data should become available in future now that MAPPA coordinators are required for the first time to provide a breakdown of data by age (Ministry of Justice 2009). The evidence currently available (Kemshall *et al.* 2005; Sutherland and Jones 2008; Baker and Sutherland 2009) indicates some difficulties in YOT/MAPPA collaboration and noticeably variable practice quality. In some areas 'junior MAPPA' have been established to try to make the process work more effectively but there is little robust evidence available to date about how these developments have affected practice.

Young people can be subject to other public protection measures, such as being on the sex offenders register (that is, required to comply with the notification arrangements of part 2 of the Sexual Offences Act 2003).[2] Of the new civil orders introduced since 1997 to assist agencies engaged in public protection work, only sexual offences prevention orders can be applied to young people. Risk of sexual harm orders and violent offender orders cannot currently be imposed on those under eighteen.

Other approaches

In addition to measures aimed at those convicted of offences, there have also been initiatives targeted at young people, families and communities more widely. Raising the legal age for buying a knife from sixteen to eighteen (Violent Crime Reduction Act 2006) is one example of a measure intended to reduce injuries by limiting the availability of weapons. Another example would be the provision of information and guidance for parents about gangs (Home Office 2008). Such approaches could be viewed as part of a public health approach to public protection (Kemshall and Wood 2007) and reflect an acknowledgement that community-based initiatives are required to address the deep-rooted social problems that contribute to youth violence (Payne and Button 2009). These approaches are often used alongside more traditional community justice responses, as seen in the Tackling Knives Action Programme which combined education and prevention measures with enforcement (Ward and Diamond 2009).

Young people: the same and yet different

Given that a degree of 'separateness' from the adult criminal justice system has been an essential attribute of the youth justice system from its inception (Easton and Piper 2005), it is important to consider the extent to which these public protection measures take account of issues such as age, adolescent development and maturity. As noted above, there are some differences in relation to civil measures and the thresholds for sex offender registration requirements. Apart from these, however, key planks of recent public protection policy – MAPPA and the 'dangerousness' sentences – apply to both adults and young people, giving the impression that there is little recognition of any need for differentiation.

A closer look at the implementation of these measures reveals a more complex picture, however. In its guidance on public protection sentences the Sentencing Guidelines Council state that 'the court should be *particularly rigorous* before concluding that a youth is a dangerous offender' (2008: para. 6.5.1). The relevance of adolescent development has been noted by the Court of Appeal, which stated: 'It is still necessary, when sentencing young offenders, to bear in mind that, within a shorter time than adults, they may change and develop. This and their level of maturity may be highly pertinent when assessing what their future conduct may be and whether it may give rise to significant risk of serious harm.'[3] In the same judgment, the Court of Appeal also acknowledged the problems associated with imposing indeterminate sentences on young people: 'In relation to a particularly young offender, an indeterminate sentence may be inappropriate even where a serious offence has been committed and there is a significant risk of serious harm from further offences.' Thus, sentencers' interpretation of legislation appears to take some account of the developmental nature of youth.

Another example can be seen in the recently revised national MAPPA guidance which for the first time includes a section dealing with children and young people. Although the eligibility criteria and thresholds for MAPPA management levels are the same as for adults, the guidance now highlights the fact that young people should be treated differently: 'Children should not be treated by MAPPA as "mini-adults" and should not be managed using the same risk assessment tools or management process' (Ministry of Justice 2009: 140). It is also noted that, as per the Children Act 2004, all agencies involved in MAPPA have a statutory duty to make arrangements for ensuring that 'their functions are discharged having regard to the need to safeguard and promote the welfare of children' (2009: 139). While these are welcome pronouncements, there is still a question about what it means in practice. How will the welfare of young people be promoted within MAPPA? How will we know if the risk management processes are appropriate? The current model means that 'the development of systems and procedures that take account of the particular needs of young people will be heavily reliant on the goodwill of local MAPPA coordinators and chairs. This is likely to lead to pockets of good practice in some areas but not necessarily a widespread improvement' (Baker 2009: 97).

Overall, what we see is a somewhat confused approach to public protection and young people. Why, to take one example, can young people be given a sexual offences prevention order but not a risk of sexual harm order? With no obvious rationale for this difference, one might assume that it is perhaps a failure to properly think through the application of new policies. The current situation appears to be a (typically British?) compromise involving legislation and statutory procedures designed to look tough but where, buried beneath the headlines, are statements and guidelines that acknowledge the need for young people to be treated differently.

On the front-line: public protection in practice

Given the challenging nature of the offences involved, and the mixed messages identified above in relation to how young people are viewed, it is inevitable that practice on the ground will be both complex and variable. This section considers some of the key practice issues that arise for staff working with, and within, public protection procedures.

Risk assessment

Assessment is a key task for, and underpins decisions by, many participants in the public protection process, including YOTs, courts, MAPPA, and Parole Board members. The first challenge in this process is that of *understanding* behaviour. It may, for example, may be difficult to ascertain whether inappropriate sexual behaviour by a young person represents adolescent experimentation or whether it is indicative of more serious problems. Understanding intentions and assessing the extent to which a young person appreciates the consequences of his/her behaviour can be difficult if the offending appears to be primarily impulsive or reckless. A further complexity arises in trying to interpret the significance of a young person's emotional state and level of cognitive ability. Guidance from the Sentencing Guidelines Council states that 'an offender's inadequacy, suggestibility or vulnerability

423

may mitigate his or her culpability. However, such features may also produce or reinforce a conclusion that he or she is a dangerous offender' (2008: para. 6.3.4.1).

The knowledge base is less developed when compared to the literature on adult offenders, which may hinder the process of understanding behaviour. For example, the evidence in relation to 'offence paralleling behaviours' which can inform assessment of behaviour in custody (Jones 2004) has so far focused on adults and it is unclear to what extent it can be applied to young people. There is also a question to be asked about the extent to which practitioners in youth justice are informed about relevant research and evidence where it does exist. Some guidance is available centrally on young people who sexually abuse (Grimshaw et al. 2008) but none of the other YJB-sponsored guidance or training materials cover issues such as violence, dangerous driving or arson in any depth. Lack of knowledge may be a problem for staff involved in MAPPA or parole decision-making where, because the vast majority of cases will be adults, experience of judging young people's behaviour and level of risk is likely to be limited.

Capturing the young person's perspective is important. Research indicates, for example, that some young people perceive significant benefits from joining a gang (Melde et al. 2009), which helps to explain why they might become involved even though it will increase their risk of experiencing violent victimisation. There also needs to be an understanding that young people are not passive in the face of difficult experiences but are themselves often actively engaged in negotiating and navigating complex risks which they may encounter (Sharland 2006; Ralphs et al. 2009).

Second, predicting rare events, such as very serious offences, is known to be difficult with adult offenders (Kemshall 2001) but the problems are exacerbated with young people who typically have a shorter offending history. In such cases there is less information available on which to base judgements about the future. The impact of external and contextual factors on behaviour (Craissati and Sindall 2009) is often particularly important for young people and adds to the difficulty of prediction.

Third, there are questions relating to the use of standardised assessment tools. All YOTs in England and Wales use Asset as the core assessment (YJB 2006) and many also use the AIM2 assessment for young people who sexually abuse although other assessments for this group are also in use (Grimshaw et al. 2008). There is occasional use of the Structured Assessment of Violence Risk in Youth (SAVRY) (Borum et al. 2003) and a number of other assessment schedules are used by mental health professionals or other specialist practitioners working in YOTs and secure settings. With the exception of Asset the use of tools can differ considerably between teams, with some YOTs developing their own in-house assessments (of variable quality) for other specific issues.

Assessments and reports written by youth justice practitioners have been criticised for lacking analysis of information (HMIP 2009), and although there have been improvements, reviews of serious incidents show that there continue to be ongoing concerns in relation to assessment and report-writing practice (YJB 2009a). An analysis of risk of serious harm assessments undertaken by

YOT staff (Baker 2008) revealed some good practice (such as practitioners using information from a wide range of sources) but also weaknesses in relation to a lack of 'whole-case hypotheses' (Sheppard *et al.* 2001) and a tendency to avoid altering the assessment conclusion in the light of new or challenging evidence.

The use of, and significance attached to, standardised tools tends to be less than in adult services. There are perhaps some benefits associated with this, however, in terms of a greater awareness of the continued need for professional judgement in view of the more obvious limitations of the tools (Burman *et al.* 2007). Other positives could include a greater emphasis on contextualisation and individualisation of assessments (Baker 2005) although this is only likely to be apparent in practice if practitioners have adequate training and knowledge.

Interventions

The current provision of services for young people who have committed, or are assessed as being likely to commit, serious offences is a mixed bag. On a positive note, YOT workers typically have smaller caseloads than their counterparts in probation and thus have, potentially at least, more chance of being able to develop the relationships of trust required as a prerequisite for achieving change (Burnett and McNeill 2005). Other aspects are more problematic. Despite increased investment in programmes for young people who sexually abuse, for example, there are still significant gaps in provision (Hackett *et al.* 2003). More widely, there is some evidence of other agencies failing to provide services to YOTs (see, for example, Commission for Healthcare Audit and Inspection 2009). Particular problems can arise in relation to the resettlement of children leaving custody, as illustrated by the case of 'K' in which the parole application of a fourteen-year-old boy was hindered by the reluctance of his local authority to undertake a 'child in need' assessment and to provide appropriate support on his release (Hollingsworth 2007).

It is not possible within the confines of this chapter to look in detail at evidence from evaluations of interventions, so rather than discussing specific programmes it is more useful here to consider two wider issues that will affect the success of interventions. The first of these relates to the focus of interventions in view of the influence of groups and peers as a significant contributory factor to offending by young people. The importance of this is noted by Ho and Gee in their discussion of dangerous driving, who argue: 'At the individual level, intervention strategies are unlikely to succeed if they fail to acknowledge the youthful imperative to increase social status by courting danger to demonstrate courage' (2008: 99). This could surely be applied more widely to other types of reckless or potentially dangerous behaviour by young people and implies that interventions need to give more attention to addressing group dynamics rather than focus solely on individual offenders.

The second key issue is about the extent to which young people are able to participate in the risk management process. 'If an offender understands not just what type and level of risk (or indeed risks) he or she poses, but also how to reduce, monitor and manage that risk and what circumstances are likely to enhance or reduce it, then together we have a better chance of reducing that risk and protecting the public' (Attrill and Liell 2007: 201). This is all very well in principle, but some young people will find this difficult due to limited insight into their own patterns of behaviour. Understanding complex public protection measures – such as MAPPA – could also be a problem and youth justice professionals need to find ways of explaining them to young people if they are to be able to participate in the process meaningfully.

Organisational structures and cultures

Effective assessment and interventions depend not just on individual practitioners but also on team culture, managerial oversight and organisational clarity of purpose (Munro 2008; Carson and Bain 2008). Some of the problems identified from reviews of serious incidents in the community, such as poor enforcement practice, inconsistent management oversight of serious harm cases, inadequate links with MAPPA and problems during transfer of cases between YOTs (HMIP 2005; YJB 2009a), are broader than just individual practice and highlight the significance of organisational factors.

What hold does the culture of public protection have in youth justice? 'It is extremely difficult to say that an organisation has one type of culture or another', Nash argues, but instead it is 'very likely that any organisation will have a number of cultures' (2007: 92). Moreover, the application of 'risk technologies' is often more uneven than anticipated by policy-makers (Kemshall 2003), not least because of the potential for practitioners to subvert an agenda imposed upon them (Barnes and Prior 2009). Overall, the evidence appears to suggest that there has been an increasing acceptance of the risk and public protection agenda within youth justice but it is not necessarily the dominant paradigm and a variety of cultures continue to coexist (Burnett and Appleton 2004; Field 2007). This helps to explain some of the tensions that can arise in multi-agency public protection work where there may be a clash of cultures between YOTs and adult-based services in which the risk paradigm holds more sway (Sutherland 2009).

Young people, serious offending and society

Having looked at the criminal justice measures designed to promote public protection, this section seeks to draw together some key themes to reflect more widely on social perceptions of, and responses to, 'risky' young people.

Perceptions and representations of youth

The chapter began by noting the paradox of the child-criminal and the consequent difficulty of managing the 'tension between vulnerability and agency' (McDiarmid 2007: 160) that is inherent in childhood and adolescence. In policy discourse children can typically be presented as a threat, as victims or as investment for the future (Hendrick 1994) and it would be easy to assume that young people drawn into the public protection process are automatically seen as a threat. The picture is more complex, however. For example, mainstream services such as education might view a young person as being extremely troublesome and impossible to manage but when the same young person comes into contact with systems such as MAPPA, they may be regarded more as a nuisance and not seen as a threat in comparison to adult offenders (Sutherland 2009). In the multi-agency environment of public protection, young people will be perceived in various and sometimes conflicting ways.

The increasing focus on children's rights has sharpened awareness of the vulnerability/agency dilemma. While some would argue that the UK has not gone far enough in implementing the provisions of the United Nations Convention on the Rights of the Child (Children's Rights Alliance for England 2006), there is nevertheless a growing awareness that rights now jostle with justice and welfare for position in the contested terrain of youth justice. One result of this, however, could be that young people are increasingly 'responsibilised' such that 'the extension of the notion of children's rights may have the effect of enlisting children and young people into actively governing their own freedom(s) and hence subjecting them to a much more sophisticated form of adult monitoring and control' (Foley *et al.* 2003: 117). Analysis of these issues in the context of public protection is now beginning to emerge, for example in discussion of the interface between children's rights, the sex offender register (Thomas 2009) and MAPPA (Whitty 2009).

The sharply contrasting reactions across the media to high profile incidents such as the Bulger case (McDiarmid 2007) demonstrate our uncertainty about how to perceive young people who commit very serious offences. This confusion lends support for the claim that the current socially available representations of youth are inadequate and that 'what is required are ways of thinking about the real, lived experiences of children and the complex character of childhood in a changing world' (Prout 2003: 22).

Applying public protection measures to young people

Much of the public protection infrastructure has developed from concerns about, and responses to, adult sex offenders (Kemshall 2008), and young people appear to have been grafted in to this framework in a somewhat awkward way. The use of guidance to draw attention to the importance of young people's specific needs and behaviours within structures that give little formal recognition to these issues is one approach discussed above for dealing with this tension. Another method seems to be to deal with offending and welfare through separate procedures. Young people who sexually abuse can be referred to both MAPPA and the Local Safeguarding Children Board (LSCB), for example. In such cases, MAPPA would be responsible for public protection while the LSCB would have a remit in relation to protecting the young person's own welfare and the task of ensuring that there is no conflict between these processes falls to the YOT (Ministry of Justice 2009). Approaches that recognise that young people have a range of needs and that tackling risk may be a necessary but not sufficient way of reducing reoffending (McNeill 2009) are welcome but the separateness of the processes again highlights the difficulty that the adult-focused public protection system has in balancing the welfare, risks and rights of young people.

The intelligibility of sentences and interventions for young people matters. One of the problems associated with the public protection sentences introduced by the Criminal Justice Act 2003 is their complexity. This was stated in fairly blunt terms by the Court of Appeal who described the measures as 'labyrinthine' and added that 'it does seem to us that there is much to be said for a sentencing system which is intelligible to the general public as well as decipherable, with difficulty, by the judiciary'.[4] If some of the judiciary were struggling to understand these legislative provisions then practitioners in YOTs and the secure estate will also be perplexed, not to mention young people themselves who may find it impossible to work out, and thus work towards, a release date. As noted earlier, there are also challenges for youth justice staff in explaining complex arrangements such as MAPPA to young people. In her discussion of criminal capacity, McDiarmid (2007) argues that court proceedings lack legitimacy if children and young people cannot understand what is going on or participate meaningfully in the process. Such a line of thought must prompt some serious questions about the suitability of applying adult-focused public protection measures to young people.

One final issue to consider is the impact of public protection measures on the prospects for reintegration and reacceptance by society. It would be foolish to suggest that there is no need for some kind of monitoring and supervision that continues after the end of a statutory order, but this should be proportionate and take account of young people's potential to change. Current rules regarding, for example, retaining data on ViSOR until an offender's 100th birthday (Ministry of Justice 2009) send out a message that the slate can never be wiped clean. Under the provisions of the 2003 Sexual Offences Act, individuals subject to notification requirements were placed on the sex offender register for life which again implied that those who had committed sexual offences would be 'labelled for life' (The *Guardian*, 21 April 2010). However, the UK Supreme Court has recently ruled in support of a teenager who argued that this breached his human rights by failing to allow any opportuinity for him to demonstrate a reduced risk of reoffending and hence be removed from the register.[5] In its defence, the Home Office had argued that robust systems are required for monitoring sex offenders but, while this may be a reasonable claim, 'robust' should not mean precluding the possibility of re-assessing cases and young people in particular should surely be given an opportunity to show that they can change. Following the Supreme Court ruling the Government will now need to introduce a review mechanism which should enable this to happen.

Conclusion

Public protection is an emotive subject where complex, and sometimes confused, socially constructed conceptualisations of youth, risk and dangerousness collide. But it is also an area where the age of the young people involved necessarily draws our attention to some important lessons about dealing with risk. Critically, but by no means exhaustively, these include the link between experience of victimisation and serious offending; the significance of families, groups and communities in both contributing to but also preventing serious offending; and the fact that wider needs have to be addressed because focusing on risk may be necessary but not sufficient. These themes are, of course, relevant for working with adult offenders but can all too easily be overlooked in a risk-averse and under-pressure environment where defensive practice may become the norm. In youth justice, the challenge of dealing with the agency/vulnerability tension brings these themes to the fore and makes them much more difficult to ignore.

The current public protection framework in England and Wales reveals a somewhat confusing picture in which young people's specific needs can potentially be addressed through the exercise of professional discretion in the interpretation and implementation of measures that on the surface may only give limited acknowledgement to the differences between adults and young people. Responding appropriately to serious offending by young people matters, not just in terms of preventing immediate serious harm but because without this adult criminal justice services may find themselves having to tackle more deeply entrenched problems at a later date. No system will ever be perfect and it is incumbent on those working with young people – particularly courts, YOTs, Parole Board members and MAPPA – to use their knowledge, practice wisdom and professional skills effectively when dealing with the child-offender paradox in the context of an essentially adult-based approach to public protection.

The commission of very serious offences by children and young people is unsettling, not just because it spotlights our difficulty with formulating coherent perceptions of youth, but also because it challenges our preoccupation with the individual. This challenge applies not only to how we understand offending behaviour and select interventions to address it, but also to our sense of shared community responsibility for young people's development given that youth offending is not just a criminal justice problem but a social issue (Stephen 2009). Policy and debate in England and Wales continue to focus primarily on individualised risk, in contrast to Scandinavian countries, for example, where there appears to be more of 'an acceptance that children are entitled to understanding and respect *as children* rather than as innocent angels or potentially evil beings, and the recognition of collective responsibility for children along with a sense of community' (Carmichael 2003: 128). While no political party here seems likely to propose any fundamental changes to the apparatus of public protection and its application in youth justice, the importance of understanding young people and accepting collective responsibility should surely be seen as reasonable and desirable goals for the rich and educated society that we claim to be.

Selected further reading

Data on the extent of serious violent and sexual offending by young people in England and Wales are available from the Youth Justice Board's *Annual Workload Data* (for example YJB 2009b). Boswell (1996) and Bailey (1996) provide valuable insight into the backgrounds, lives and characteristics of young people who have committed particularly serious offences. For a discussion of key issues in how the criminal justice system should treat children who commit serious crimes (and an interesting overview of how these matters are dealt with in Scotland) see McDiarmid (2007). For an in-depth focus on one example of recent public protection policies in youth justice see Baker and Sutherland (2009). This edited volume considers a range of practical and theoretical issues relating to the inclusion of young people in multi-agency public protection arrangements (MAPPA).

Notes

1 Ministry of Justice, personal communication to the author.
2 For some offences where registration for adults is automatic it only applies to young people if the sentenced received was twelve months custody or more.
3 *R v Lang & Ors* [2005] EWCA Crim 2864.
4 *R v Lang & Ors* [2005] EWCA Crim 2864.
5 [2010] UKSC 17.

References

Attrill, G. and Liell, G. (2007) 'Offenders' views on risk assessment', in N. Padfield (ed.) *Who to Release? Parole, Fairness and Criminal Justice*. Cullompton: Willan Publishing (pp. 191–201).

Bailey, S. (1996) 'Adolescents who murder', *Journal of Adolescence*, 19(1): 19–39.

Bailey, S., Vermeiren, R. and Mitchell, P. (2007) 'Mental health, risk and antisocial behaviour in young offenders', in M. Blyth, E. Solomon, and K. Baker (eds) *Young People and 'Risk'*. Bristol: Policy Press (pp. 53–71).

Baker, K. (2005) 'Assessment in youth justice: professional discretion and the use of Asset', *Youth Justice*, 5(2): 106–22.

Baker, K. (2008) 'Risk, uncertainty and public protection: assessment of young people who offend', *British Journal of Social Work*, 38(8): 1463–80.

Baker, K. (2009) 'MAPPA as "risk in action": discretion and decision-making', in K. Baker and A. Sutherland (eds) *Multi-Agency Public Protection Arrangements and Youth Justice*. Bristol: Policy Press (pp. 93–110).

Baker, K. and Sutherland, A. (eds) (2009) *Multi-Agency Public Protection Arrangements and Youth Justice*. Bristol: Policy Press.

Barnes, M. and Prior, D. (2009) *Subversive Citizens*. Bristol: Policy Press.

Borum, R., Bartel, P. and Forth, A. E. (2003) *Manual for the Structured Assessment for Violence Risk in Youth (SAVRY) Version 1.1*. Tampa: University of South Florida.

Boswell, G. (1996) *Young and Dangerous*. Aldershot: Avebury.

Burman, M., Armstrong, S., Batchelor, S., McNeill, F. and Nicholson, J. (2007) *Research and Practice in Risk Assessment and Risk Management of Children and Young People Engaging in Offending Behaviours*. Paisley: Risk Management Authority.

Burnett R. and Appleton C. (2004) 'Joined-up services to tackle youth crime', *British Journal of Criminology*, 44(1): 34–54.

Burnett, R. and McNeill, F. (2005) 'The place of the officer–offender relationship in assisting offenders to desist from crime', *Probation Journal*, 52(3): 221–42.

Carmichael, K. (2003) *Sin and Forgiveness: New Responses in a Changing World*. Aldershot: Ashgate.

Carson, D. and Bain, A. (2008) *Professional Risk and Working with People*. London: Jessica Kingsley.

Children's Rights Alliance for England (2006) *The State of Children's Rights in England*. London: Children's Rights Alliance for England.

Commission for Healthcare Audit and Inspection and HMI Probation (2009) *Actions Speak Louder*. London: Healthcare Commission.

Craissati, J. and Sindall, O. (2009) 'Serious further offences: an exploration of risk and typologies', *Probation Journal*, 56(1): 9–27.

Deitch, M., Barstow, A., Lukens, L. and Reyna, R. (2009) *From Time Out to Hard Time: Young Children in the Adult Criminal Justice System*. Austin, TX: University of Texas at Austin, LBJ School of Public Affairs.

Dent, R. and Jowitt, S. (2003) 'Homicide and serious sexual offences committed by children and young people: findings from the literature and a serious case review', *Journal of Sexual Aggression*, 9(2): 85–96.

Easton, S. and Piper, C. (2005) *Sentencing and Punishment: The Quest for Justice*. Oxford: Oxford University Press.

Falshaw, L. and Browne, K. (1997) 'Adverse childhood experiences and violent acts of young people in secure accommodation', *Journal of Mental Health*, 6(5): 443–55.

Field, S. (2007) 'Practice cultures and the "new" youth justice in (England and) Wales', *British Journal of Criminology*, 47(2): 311–30.

Foley, P., Parton, N., Roche, J. and Tucker, S. (2003) 'Contradictory and convergent trends in law and policy affecting children in England', in C. Hallett and A. Prout (eds) *Hearing the Voices of Children: Social Policy for a New Century*. London: Routledge (pp. 106–20).

Greenwood, C. (2009) 'Youths set fire to tourist on train', *Independent*, 19 August. Online at: www.independent.co.uk/news/uk/crime/youths-set-fire-to-tourist-on-train-1774306.html (accessed 20 September 2009).

Grimshaw, R., with Malek, M., Oldfield, M. and Smith, R. (2008) *Young People who Sexually Abuse (Source Document)*. London: Youth Justice Board.

Guardian (2010) 'Sex offenders win appeal against indefinite inclusion on register'. Online at: http://www.guardian.co.uk/uk/2010/apr/21/sex-offenders-register-life-appeal (accessed 7 June 2010).

Hackett, S., Masson, H. and Phillips, S. (2003) *Mapping and Exploring Services for Young People who have Sexually Abused Others*. London: Youth Justice Board.

Hendrick, H. (1994) *Child Welfare 1870–1989*. London: Routledge.

HM Government (2004) *Every Child Matters: Change for Children*. London: The Stationery Office.

HM Government (2008) *An Action Plan for Tackling Violence*. London: The Stationery Office.

HM Inspectorate of Probation (2005) *Inquiry into the Supervision of Peter Williams by Nottingham City Youth Offending Team*. London: HMIP.

HM Inspectorate of Probation (2009) *Joint Inspection of Youth Offending Teams: End of Programme Report 2003–2008*. London: HMIP.

Ho, R. and Gee, R.-Y. (2008) 'Young men driving dangerously: development of the motives for dangerous driving scale (MMDS)', *Australian Journal of Psychology*, 60(2): 91–10.

Hollingsworth, K. (2007) 'Protecting the rights of children leaving custody: R (on the application of K) v Parole Board and R (on the application of K) v Manchester City Council', *Journal of Social Welfare and Family Law*, 29(2): 163–75.

Home Affairs Committee (2009) *Knife Crime: Seventh Report of Session 2008–08*. London: The Stationery Office.

Home Office (2008) *Gangs: You and Your Child*. London: Home Office.

Howard League (2007) *Parole 4 Kids: A Review of the Parole Process for Children in England and Wales*. London: Howard League for Penal Reform.

Jones, L. (2004) 'Offence paralleling behaviour (OBP) as a framework for assessment and interventions with offenders', in A. Needs and G. Towl (eds) *Applying Psychology to Forensic Practice*. Oxford: Blackwell (pp. 34–63).

Kemshall, H. (2001) *Risk Assessment and Management of Known Sexual and Violent Offenders: A Review of Current Issues*, Police Research Series 140. London: Home Office.

Kemshall, H. (2003) *Understanding Risk in Criminal Justice*. Maidenhead: Open University Press.

Kemshall, H. (2008) *Understanding the Community Management of High Risk Offenders*. Maidenhead: Open University Press.

Kemshall, H. and Wood, J. (2007) 'Beyond public protection: an examination of community protection and public health approaches to high-risk offenders', *Criminology and Criminal Justice*, 7(3) 203–22.

Kemshall, H., Mackenzie, G., Wood, J., Bailey, R. and Yates, J. (2005) *Strengthening Multi-Agency Public Protection Arrangements*. London: Home Office.

Lupton, D. (1999) *Risk*. London: Routledge.

McDiarmid, C. (2007) *Childhood and Crime*. Dundee: Dundee University Press.

McNeill, F. (2009) 'Young people, serious offending and managing risk: a Scottish perspective', in K. Baker and A. Sutherland (eds) *Multi-Agency Public Protection Arrangements and Youth Justice*. Bristol: Policy Press (pp. 75–92).

Melde, C., Taylor, T. and Esbensen, F.-A. (2009) '"I got your back": an examination of the protective function of gang membership in adolescence', *Criminology*, 47(2): 565–94.

Ministry of Justice (2009) *MAPPA Guidance Version 3.0*. London: Ministry of Justice.

Morrison, B. (1997) *As If*. London: Granta Books.

Muncie, J. (2004) *Youth and Crime*. London: Sage.

Munro, E. (2008) *Effective Child Protection*, 2nd edn. London: Sage.

NACRO (2007) *Youth Crime Briefing: 'Grave Crimes', Mode of Trial and Long Term Detention*. London: NACRO.

Nash, M. (2006) *Public Protection and the Criminal Justice Process*. Oxford: Oxford University Press.

Nash, M. (2007) 'Working with young people in a culture of public protection', in M. Blyth, E. Solomon and K. Baker (eds) *Young People and 'Risk'*. Bristol: Policy Press (pp. 85–95).

Parole Board (2008) *Parole for Children and Young People*. London: Parole Board.

Payne, B. and Button, D. (2009) 'Developing a citywide youth violence prevention plan: Perceptions of various stakeholders', *International Journal of Offender Therapy and Comparative Criminology*, 53(5): 517–34.

Pratt, J. (1997) *Governing the Dangerous*. Sydney: Federation Press.

Prison Reform Trust (2007) *Indefinitely Maybe? How the Indeterminate Sentence for Public Protection is Unjust and Unsustainable*. London: Prison Reform Trust.

Prout, A. (2003) 'Participation, policy and the changing conditions of childhood', in C. Hallett and A. Prout (eds) *Hearing the Voices of Children: Social Policy for a New Century*. London: Routledge (pp. 11–25).

Ralphs, R., Medina, J. and Aldridge, J. (2009) 'Who needs enemies with friends like these? The importance of place for young people living in known gang areas', *Journal of Youth Studies*, 12(5): 483–500.

Robinson, G. and McNeill, F. (2004) 'Purposes matter: the ends of probation' in G. Mair (ed.) *What Matters in Probation Work*. Cullompton: Willan Publishing (pp. 277–304).

Sentencing Guidelines Council (2008) *Dangerous Offenders: Guidance for Sentencers and Practitioners*. London: Sentencing Guidelines Council.

Sereny, G. (1998) *Cries Unheard*. London: Macmillan.

Sharland, E. (2006) 'Young people, risk taking and risk making: some thoughts for social work', *British Journal of Social Work*, 36(2): 247–65.

Sheppard, M., Newstead, S., Di Caccavo, A. and Ryan, K. (2001) 'Comparative hypothesis assessment and quasi triangulation as process knowledge assessment strategies in social work practice', *British Journal of Social Work*, 31(6): 863–85.

Silvestri, A., Oldfield, M., Squires, P. and Grimshaw, R. (2009) *Young People, Knives and Guns: A Comprehensive Review, Analysis and Critique of Gun and Knife Crime Strategies*. London: Centre for Crime and Justice Studies.

Smith, R. (2007) *Youth Justice*, 2nd edn. Cullompton: Willan Publishing.

Squires, P., Silvestri, A., Grimshaw, R. and Solomon, E. (2008) *Street Weapons Commission: Guns, Knives and Street Violence*. London: Centre for Crime and Justice Studies.

Stephen, D. (2009) 'Time to stop twisting the knife: a critical commentary on the rights and wrongs of criminal justice responses to problem youth in the UK', *Journal of Social Welfare and Family Law*, 31(2): 193–2006.

Sutherland, A. (2009) 'Youth Offending Teams and MAPPA', in K. Baker and A. Sutherland (eds) *Multi-Agency Public Protection Arrangements and Youth Justice*. Bristol: Policy Press (pp. 43–58).

Sutherland, A. and Jones, S. (2008) *MAPPA and Youth Justice: An Exploration of Youth Offending Team Engagement with Multi-Agency Public Protection Arrangements*. London: Youth Justice Board.

Thomas, T. (2009) 'Children and young people on the UK sex offender register', *International Journal of Children's Rights*, 17(3): 491–500.

The Times (2009) *Uncommon Evil*. Online at: www.timesonline.co.uk/tol/comment/leading_article/article6820880.ece (accessed 20 September 2009).

Ward, L. and Diamond, A. (2009) *Tackling Knives Action Programme (TKAP) Phase 1: Overview of Key Trends from a Monitoring Programme*, Research Report 18, London: Home Office.

Whitty, N. (2009) 'MAPPA for kids: Discourses of security, risk and children's rights', in K. Baker and A. Sutherland (eds) *Multi-Agency Public Protection Arrangements and Youth Justice*. Bristol: Policy Press (pp. 111–24).

Youth Justice Board (2006) *Asset Guidance*. London: Youth Justice Board.

Youth Justice Board (2007) *Serious Incidents: Guidance on Reporting Procedures*. London: Youth Justice Board.

Youth Justice Board (2009a) *Community Serious Incidents: Annual Report (October 2007–December 2008)*. London: Youth Justice Board.

Youth Justice Board (2009b) *Youth Justice Annual Workload Data 2007/08*. London: Youth Justice Board.

Chapter 21

Public protectionism and 'Sarah's Law': exerting pressure through single issue campaigns

Stephen P. Savage and Sarah Charman

'Over the last eight years I have been asking for victims to have a louder voice, and for government to listen more closely to what they have to say.' (Sara Payne, campaigner, 26 January 2009)

'Victims are the most important part in the criminal justice system. We must always ensure that their voice is heard loud and clear by policy-makers.' (Jack Straw, Justice Secretary, 26 January 2009)

Introduction

'Public protection' discourse acts as one configuration of what we might call 'justice agendas'. Justice agendas take different forms and can be subject to transformation when various sets of conditions, events and scenarios come together to push discourses on justice in particular directions, whether they be 'rights' oriented (where the emphasis may be on strengthening protections for those suspected of crime), or 'victim' oriented (where the emphasis may be on protecting the potential victim, or the 'public', if necessary at the expense of suspects' rights). One such transformation of a justice agenda, very much along the lines of public protection discourse, emerged in Britain in the mid-1990s, following in the wake of the murder by two young boys of James Bulger, a two-year-old abducted in a shopping precinct in the full glare of closed circuit television. This event, which was to (further) fuel public anxieties about crime and, matched with an emergent political climate (Savage 2007: 179–80), helped set in motion a justice agenda oriented around a 'populist punitive' ethos (Bottoms 1995), and was associated with a wide range of 'get tough on crime' measures (Morgan and Newburn 2007: 1030–1). The significance of this particular transformation was evident in subsequent reflections from a key player at the time, the Home Secretary Michael Howard, in which he referred to his role in 'ending the 1960s consensus' on crime. In place of the apparently benign '1960s consensus' which assumed crime to be an illness to be cured, Howard claimed to have offered a blunt alternative: 'My approach was simple: to give the police the powers they needed to catch criminals; to give the courts the powers they needed to convict criminals; and to give our prisons the space to take persistent, serious and dangerous offenders out of circulation altogether' (Howard 2004).

Ironically, this ideological shift came hot on the heels of a very different justice agenda that came close to asserting itself at the beginning of the 1990s. In the wake of high profile miscarriages of justice around the cases of the Guildford Four and the Birmingham Six and the deficiencies of the criminal justice system they exposed (Rozenberg 1994), a rights oriented justice agenda was almost discernible, not least in the decision by the Home Secretary (then Kenneth Baker) to hold a Royal Commission of Inquiry into the criminal justice process, fired at least in part by the miscarriages of justice in question and the evident wrongful convictions they involved. However, even at that point the nascent rights-based justice agenda was compromised, because the Royal Commission's terms of reference were to enshrine 'securing the conviction of those guilty of criminal offences' as a core concern of the Commission's work, a clear marker of a potentially different agenda from that hoped for by more rights oriented commentators (Rozenberg 1994: 321–4). As such, Howard's 'ending of the 1960s consensus' was to emerge on ground already shifting in a public protection direction. This development is cited not just out of historical interest; what Howard claimed to have done constituted a quantum leap in the public protection agenda, taking it significantly further along the path of populist punitivism, the consequences of which are still evident in contemporary law and order policy, as many chapters in this book testify. More significantly for the purposes of this chapter, his 'simple approach' – *more* police powers, *more* sentencing powers, *more* prison places, and so on – also acts as a classic statement on the apparent need for 'rebalancing criminal justice', in zero-sum terms away from the rights of suspects and towards the 'rights of victims'. Commentators on the political discourses associated with the so-called 'war on crime' have drawn attention to the ideological refrain of rebalancing or 'reshaping' justice and crime policy – typically towards a more crime-control orientation (Simon 2007: 96–101). Over the past three decades in Britain one of the recurring themes of political rhetoric associated with 'law and order politics' has been the claim, as reflected in Howard's statement above, of the need for readjusting the balance between suspects' rights and the rights of victims more in favour of the latter. There has been little political space for the notion of readjusting the balance in the opposite direction. This has been the climate within which actors involved in engaging with policy change in the crime field have been operating, including those that are the focus of this chapter: victim-led campaign groups.

A justice agenda based on the rhetoric and actions of rebalancing criminal justice in favour of protecting the public and/or victims presents both opportunities and threats for interest groups involved in crime policy shaping; there will be winners and losers, with some 'voices' being heard over others. In this respect the ethos of public protection and rebalancing criminal justice would seem to create a particular space for those seeking to represent the views, concerns and perceived interests of *victims* of crime. In this type of climate the voices of victims may have two functions. On the one hand victims' voices may find a receptive audience among those in authority and be allowed some form of *influence* over crime policy itself – this is a major concern of this discussion. On the other hand, and as part and parcel of that, victims' voices may be *exploited* by those in authority, used as instruments of political rhetoric within the politics of law and order, along the lines of 'we share your concerns'. In both respects what is in question is the power of victim-led justice campaigns in the crime policy-making process.

This chapter examines the roles that victim-led campaigns can play in fuelling and/or shaping the justice agenda(s) associated with the public protection movement. Within the context of the policy formation process, it attempts to situate victim-based campaigns as sources of influence over crime policy, why and how they engage in the business of policy-shaping. In particular, it reflects on the power and potency of *women-as-victims* within public protection discourse and the apparent 'fit' between female-led campaigns for forms of justice and the ethos of public protection. The discussion will reflect on motivations behind and the tactical impact of victim-led campaigns that are driven by women who have been victimised by crime. In this respect it focuses at length on one, arguably totemic, campaign agenda, which was associated with what became known as 'Sarah's Law'. Although the campaign around Sarah's Law met with significant but only partial success, the fact that it was successful at all reveals much about the articulation of a public protection justice agenda and a 'movement from below' that was led by a woman who was the victim of serious crime committed against a family member. As shall also be seen, that movement took a form very different from beyond the traditional model of pressure group campaigns and was oriented around a media-focused, largely single-issue, campaign.

Sarah's law: swimming with the tide of public protection

The campaign for Sarah's Law was named after Sarah Payne, an eight-year-old girl murdered by a known paedophile in July 2000. The campaign was led by Sara Payne, Sarah's mother, although, as shall be seen later, much of the support for the campaign came *via* a national newspaper. Before moving to the campaign itself, it is useful to reflect briefly on the political environment and the politics of law and order either side of the campaign launch, in order to better situate and make sense of the 'power' of victims' voices as expressed by this particular movement.

Reference has already been made to Michael Howard's claim to have turned the tide of criminal justice away from the '1960s consensus'. Whatever the accuracy of this claim, there is little doubting the significance of the dramatically shifting agenda on crime policy that was taking place in Britain in the early to mid-1990s, captured perhaps above all by Howard's 'Prison Works' speech to the 1993 Conservative Party Conference and its '27 point' strategy for tackling crime (Downes and Morgan 2007: 214–15). At a time when the Conservative government was itself in deep electoral trouble following the financial crisis associated with 'Black Wednesday' and seriously challenged by a resurgent Labour Party (Savage 2007: 179–83), this stance effectively threw a gauntlet down to the Labour Opposition as an assertion that the Conservatives were *the* party of law and order. Not only was Labour prepared to respond, it was to do so by matching Howard 'punch for punch' (Downes and Morgan 2007: 214). With the launch of the slogan 'Tough on crime, tough on the causes of crime', Labour (as 'New Labour') had already signalled its intent to go on the offensive over law and order – a field not traditionally Labour's natural territory. It was above all the tough on crime side of the equation that most clearly set out Labour's stall; through this commitment Labour was in Opposition making its own claim to be *the* party of law and order. The most explicit expressions of the tough on crime agenda could be found in Labour's flirtation with 'zero tolerance policing' (Jones and Newburn 2007) and in the concerted attempt to prioritise problems and solutions associated with low level disorder and minor incivilities, or 'anti-social behaviour' (Downes and Morgan 2007: 214–15). Although such an agenda was in some ways more rhetorical than intentional – zero tolerance policing never was translated into concrete policing policy (Jones and Newburn 2007: 135–6; Savage 2007: 60–1) – Labour had positioned itself in Opposition as a party fully prepared to justify its claim to be 'tough on crime', one oriented to a justice agenda based on the ethos of public protection.

On taking office in 1997 Labour would demonstrate that the 'Tough on crime, tough on the causes of crime' commitment always contained within it a more equivocal approach to crime than the wider rhetoric might indicate. For example, while the Crime and Disorder Act 1998 launched what was to become the first of a series of measures to target anti-social behaviour, it also laid grounds for a more strategic role for crime *prevention* in the Labour government's crime policy, grounds that were more directed at crime causation (Savage and Nash 2001: 112–13). Labour was also to introduce the Human Rights Act 1998 which brought the European Convention on Human Rights formally into UK law, thus enshrining a degree of rights-based justice alongside other more public protection oriented measures (Savage and Nash 2001: 122). Yet it is the latter that most coloured Labour's overall approach to crime policy, typified in legislation such as the Sex Offenders Act 1997, which established the sex offender register, requiring various offenders to notify their whereabouts to the police – particularly relevant to the discussion of 'Sarah's Law' – and the range of initiatives associated with the government's 1997 White Paper on youth crime and youth justice, titled revealingly *No More Excuses* (Home Office 1997). These measures were early forms of what was to become a wide range of measures very much steeped in the public protection ethos. However, it was some years later that Labour's commitment to the public protection agenda was to find its ultimate expression: the launch of the 'rebalancing criminal justice' agenda in 2006.

It was perhaps ironical that the Labour government was to talk about rebalancing criminal justice in its second term of office, having entered office with an agenda already explicitly committed to 'law and order' (Jones and Newburn 2007: 111). It was, however, some measure of the relentlessness of its pursuit of public protection that even after introducing the raft of measures it had previously adopted to take criminal justice in this direction,

Labour still found it necessary to challenge those parts of the justice system that were still seen as inadequately oriented to the public protection ethos. Furthermore, as has been noted earlier, the notion of rebalancing justice has been a recurring theme of the justice agenda attached to public protection. The launch of this particular brand of rebalancing came with the document titled, pointedly, *Rebalancing the Criminal Justice System in Favour of the Law-Abiding Majority: Cutting Crime, Reducing Offending and Protecting the Public* (Home Office 2006). While acknowledging that steps had already been taken to 'rebalance' criminal justice (Home Office 2006: 2) the document went on to map out areas where more could be done, including:

- Putting law-abiding people, communities and victims first.
- 'Gripping' offenders to cut crime, reduce offending and protect the public.
- A simpler and swifter justice system. (Home Office 2006: 4–8)

Central to the strategy was better treatment for victims of crime and a greater 'voice' for victims in the justice process. This was to include adjusting the rules for justice processes to ensure that offenders' rights are not given a 'privileged' status relative to the interests of victims or potential victims, whether this be in relation to dangerous offenders, possible terrorist threat or convictions that are quashed on 'technicalities' (Home Office 2006: 15–16). This was to be all part of a rebalancing act that would ensure, in then Prime Minister Tony Blair's words, 'that in a modern world ... criminal justice organisations live up to their duty of protecting the rights of victims and communities. We must build a criminal justice system which puts protection of the law-abiding majority at its heart' (Home Office 2006: 2). This was as clear a statement as possible of Labour's commitment to listening to 'victims' voices'; it was against this political backcloth and what preceded it earlier in the new century that the campaign for 'Sarah's Law' was fought, a backcloth that provided fertile ground for such a victim-led movement for 'justice'.

Sarah Payne disappeared on 1 July 2000 after playing in fields with her siblings in West Sussex, England; her unclothed body was found on 17 July of that year, following a search that had gripped the attention of the public, not just nationally but internationally. Throughout the period between the disappearance and the body being eventually found, Sarah's mother, Sara Payne, and her husband Mike frequently appeared in the media, making appeals for witnesses and so on, so that by the time the body was found they had both become well known public figures, particularly Sara. The police had strong suspicions before and particularly since the body was found that they were dealing with a predatory child sex offender – and a convicted paedophile, Roy Whiting, was eventually found guilty of the murder. In the days following the discovery of the body Sara began to learn about the extent of convicted paedophiles living at large in the community (Payne 2004: 92) and that, despite the introduction of the sex offender register, many such offenders were not actually registered. She had also begun to find out more about what was known as Megan's Law, introduced across many states in the USA just 89 days after the sexually motivated murder of seven-year-old Megan

Kanka in New Jersey in July 1994, and following a high profile campaign by Megan's parents. Megan had been killed by a convicted paedophile who had been living with two known sex offenders in close proximity to her home. The focus of the eventually successful campaign was to change the law to allow people to be informed of the presence of known sex offenders in their localities. Megan's Law was to vary in form state by state, but in essence it did provide for details of convicted sex offenders, including their address, to be made available to the public through internet or other media postings or through local leafleting (Hinds and Daly 2001).

Soon after Sarah's body was discovered, reporters from the national press began to approach the family with financial offers for an interview with them, one of them being Robert Kellaway of the *News of the World*. Sara Payne, having declined to be interviewed for money, suggested to him that he should look into Megan's Law, telling him, 'If you have any ideas about how we might start something like that in Britain, then get back to me' (Payne 2004: 94). Within 24 hours the *News of the World* editor, Rebekah Wade, who had only been in post for two months at that point (Hinds and Daly 2001: 257), had put a proposal together for a 'For Sarah' campaign, which would have two main goals. On the one hand it would lobby for a 'Sarah's Law', aimed at protecting children, at the heart of which was to establish the right of every parent to know details of child sex offenders living in their locality (Payne 2004: 94). On the other hand was a plan to mount a 'name and shame' programme to identify Britain's worst convicted paedophiles and cite where they lived. Sara Payne was keen for the campaign to proceed 'determined that some good would come out of Sarah's death' (Payne 2004: 85).

The following Sunday the *New of the World* ran the headline 'Named Shamed' alongside a picture of Sarah, and inside published the photographs, names and general location (but not addresses) of 49 male and female convicted sex offenders. Wade ran an editorial headlined, 'Everyone in Britain has a child sex offender living within one mile of their home' (see Hinds and Daly 2001: 257). The paper also stated that it planned to publish information on over 100,000 'proven' sex offenders. The *News of the World* also organised petitions for public support to the campaign, and arranged for badges with Sarah's face on them with the slogan 'For Sarah' to be distributed across the country; the public response was extensive and opinion polls indicated widespread support for 'Sarah's Law' (Payne 2004: 97). However, and much to the dismay of the family (2004: 96–7), there were two downsides to the campaign. First, the broadsheet media and professional bodies associated with offenders, such as the Association of Chief Police Officers (initially at least) and the National Association of Probation Officers, came out against the campaign, largely on the basis of it forcing sex offenders 'underground'. Second, and linked to this, the publicity given to details of sex offenders seemed to be behind a series of vigilante attacks and disorderly protest gatherings, most notably in Paulsgrove, Portsmouth (see Golding, this volume), soon after the naming and shaming exercise. Nevertheless, the *News of the World* campaign continued.

The then Home Secretary, Jack Straw, himself a leading light of New Labour's tough on crime agenda while Shadow Home Secretary in Opposition, was initially opposed to the Sarah's Law campaign, but perhaps under media pressure (and ever alert to populist appeal) was to change tack somewhat and state that it should be 'urgently considered' (Hinds and Daly 2001: 258). It also helped that Sara Payne's campaign strategy shifted somewhat away from the *News of the World* driven 'name and shame' agenda and towards a more measured and tactically astute approach:

> The problem was that the naming and shaming campaign was alienating those we needed on our side the most: the police and probation services, the professionals who dealt with child safety issues on a day-to-day basis. We decided that if the proper authorities would back us and help Sarah's Law, we would drop naming and shaming. (Payne 2004: 98)

Following round table meetings with stakeholder groups, including the Association of Chief Police Officers and the Association of Chief Officers of Probation, a refocused and clearly more measured and balanced set of campaign objectives were agreed (Payne 2004: 100–2), based on:

- Controlled access for parents to information about individuals in their neighbourhood who might pose a threat to their child – but measures for penalties for abuse of that information.

- Empowerment measures for victims of sexual abuse, including restrictions on offenders regarding future contact with victims.

- Better preventative measures such as enhanced vetting procedures for those working with children.

- Amendments to the sex offender register to enhance the registration process and more transparency for victims in the sentencing process.

This package was clearly more palatable not just to stakeholders but also to government – it enabled the more obvious political appeal of being seen as supportive of a victim-led, highly populist campaign to be married to a more balanced set of measures that could win support from stakeholders. Arguably, some of the measures contained in the Criminal Justice and Court Services Act 2000 could be seen to reflect in part the ethos of Sarah's Law, with steps to strengthen the Sex Offenders Act, and the family itself saw this Act as at least a 'great start' (Payne 2004: 104). The Sarah's Law campaign was, however, to continue, including a targeting of the political party annual conferences and other focused campaign tactics (Payne 2004: 105–7). It was, however, to be a long game; it was not until 2007 that a more explicit acceptance by government of the thrust of the Sarah's Law campaign was to be acknowledged.

In June 2007 Home Secretary John Reid somewhat surprisingly announced a package of measures that were branded as 'Sarah's Law proposals' (Mulholland and Tempest 2007). Jack Straw, while clearly warm to the ethos of Sarah's Law, was in favour of leaving control of any disclosure of information on child sex offenders to the police and probation services, as he made clear to the Payne family at the time (Payne 2004: 104). Reid was to distance himself from this more cautious approach by stating: 'Information should and can no longer remain the exclusive preserve of officialdom. We will therefore update the law to give the police and other agencies a duty to consider whether a member of the public needs to know about an offender's history to protect the child' (cited in Mulholland and Tempest 2007). Sara Payne hailed these proposals a 'massive step forward' and Reid was content to see them as very much an incarnation of Sarah's Law: 'What we did want to do was address the campaign that Sara Payne put forward … If someone wants to call that Sarah's Law, then I am delighted for her' (cited in Mulholland and Tempest 2007).

Eventually, this embrace of 'Sarah's Law' was to be expressed in a series of pilot schemes run across police forces in England that involved giving parents, guardians and carers access to information about whether people who have access to their children have committed child sex offences. In January 2010, the Home Secretary Alan Johnson announced that early results from the pilots were 'extremely encouraging' and the government indicated its intention to take steps to roll out the scheme nationally (Johnson 2010). The Conservative Shadow Home Secretary Chris Grayling was quick to announce on the same day that the Conservatives also 'supported Sarah's Law' (Grayling 2010). The *News of the World* immediately claimed some of the credit for the proposal. It ran a headline exclaiming 'Success for Sarah', and added the rider that 'After 10 years we win a huge success to protect our children from paedophiles' (*News of the World* 2010). The combination of a grieving mother and a high profile media campaign seemed to have delivered serious policy change.

There is another dimension to the effectiveness of the Sarah's Law campaign. In January 2009 Sara Payne was appointed as Britain's first Victims' Champion, a new 'independent public voice' for victims of and witnesses to crime. The appointment was heralded by the *News of the World* itself by the headline 'Sara's the Minister for Victims' (Kirby 2009). Jack Straw, now Minister of Justice, was a key player in Sara's appointment. One of the post's responsibilities was a review of provision and services for victims and witnesses, and perhaps significantly the end of term report on the review was entitled *Redefining Justice* (Ministry of Justice 2009), very much a refrain of the rebalancing justice theme outlined earlier. The appointment of Sara Payne as Victims' Champion said much. It signalled the deep significance of Sara Payne as a *person* and as a *role holder* for the effectiveness of the campaign she was fighting. Much of the power of the Sarah's Law campaign related to the power and potency of the image of Sara Payne herself as a grieving mother fighting for a form of justice. Although the campaign was fought (and partly won) in a climate of receptiveness provided by the public protection justice agenda, and that climate has to be part of any assessment of why Sarah's Law was to win support politically, we should not underestimate the significance of the campaign itself, with Sara Payne at the helm as a mother fighting for justice, for its successes.

The Sarah's Law campaign was indeed swimming with the tide of public protection, but it was also drawing from some hugely potent forces of its own in doing so. This includes three related dimensions: first, the powerful *motivational* factors driving mothers' (and more generally female-led) campaigns for justice where loss of a family member is involved, and how coping with loss might relate to victim-led campaigns; second, the changing forms of the 'politics of influence' and the significance of pressure/interest groups to policy-making more widely; and third, the power, potency and effectiveness of female-led protest movements as a whole. It is to these three dimensions that we now turn to make more sense of Sarah's Law as a movement for public protection oriented justice. What follows draws to an extent on a wider study by the authors, of the role of gender in campaigns in justice campaigns concerned with miscarriages of justice (Charman and Savage 2009).

Coping with loss: motivation, meaning and campaigning for justice

There is an extensive literature on the subjects of death, dying, loss and bereavement. Although much of it is practice-based, concerned with counselling and self-help, one field of study, 'thanatology' – the study of the social and psychological effects of death and dying – embraces clinical and social psychological research in the area. This includes processes relating to bereavement, grief, mourning and loss. Such experiences can have a fundamental effect on the individual and their conception of their 'social self'. The question is how those experiences are channelled and translated into actions in the form of campaigns and how gender might play a part in campaigns for forms of 'justice' in the light of the discussion so far over Sarah's Law.

Grieving is a process and not simply an emotion. Bowlby (1980) refers to three 'stages' of grief: yearning (or protest), disorganisation, followed by reorganisation. In terms of the latter there tends to be movement towards the resumption of normality. However, in relation to justice campaigns, 'normality' may not be restored or be possible until certain 'end goals' are achieved – a public inquiry, a change in policy or legislation and so on. Even when such significant goals have been achieved, other goals might take their place; campaigners might not be satisfied with a public inquiry until actions have been taken in response to its findings, for example.

It is at this point that we can reflect on *differential grieving*, the extent to which grieving is experienced differently and reflects itself in different forms depending on who is facing loss – and who is lost. There appear to be various cultural, psychological and even physiological factors that can affect or influence the way people grieve and their ability to cope with a situation of loss. Martin and Doka (2000) refer to the importance of personality, social class and age in their effects on grieving patterns and in its impact on the mourner's choice of coping strategies. Perhaps more obviously, but of great significance in this context, the quality of the *relationship* between the bereaved and the deceased and the *role* the deceased played in the life of the bereaved will also influence the degree of loss or grief felt (Schwab 1996).

A further factor contributing to differential grieving is the *nature* of the loss or death. In this respect there would appear to be three main classes of death: anticipated death, sudden accidental death, and criminal death. While there is no simple relationship between type of death and relative pain of the bereaved, there will clearly be different reactions to the different types of death. Rando (1995: 239) argues that certain factors can complicate or exacerbate the mourning process, three of which are highly significant for our purposes: a sudden and unanticipated death, the loss of a child, and a death that is believed by those bereaved to have been preventable (Rando: 1995: 239). Where one or more of these factors are present, then the pain of loss may be particularly acute and the grieving process more extended. These complicating factors will inevitably play their part in reactions to loss; the case of Sarah Payne figures large in these respects.

Paul Rock (1998) alludes to the notion of compound grief in his study of the collective responses of those whose family members are the victims of homicide. A campaigning organisation set up the UK in 1984 called Parents of Murdered Children (POMC) had originally been part of the much wider group, The Compassionate Friends, which was a support group for all parents who had suffered the loss of a child. POMC had felt the need to organise themselves separately because of the gulf in understanding between those suffering grief through a 'normal' bereavement and those suffering grief through 'complicated' bereavement, associated with the fact that their child had been the victim of murder. While not wishing to mitigate the pain felt by those suffering 'normal' bereavement, what separated the two types of grief was *anger* (Rock 1998). A respondent in Rock's study referred to being driven by 'anger, pure anger' (1998: 219).

A small but potentially highly significant part of the thantological research literature focuses on the question of the relationship between gender and bereavement. This revolves around the themes of the differential intensities of grief, the differential reactions to loss, and the variations in coping strategies between the sexes (Scott Kenney 2002). Research indicates that there are significant differences in the levels of intensity of grief experienced between men and women and in particular between fathers and mothers (Martin and Doka 2000; Schwab 1996; Archer 1999; Fish 1986; Parkes 1996; Gilbert 1997; Bohannon 1990–1). This research indicates that *mothers* feel greater levels of grief intensity than their male partners. Much of the research relies upon the Grief Experience Inventory, a 'measure' of grief that relies upon an inventory of statements to which the respondent must answer 'true' or 'false'. Significant results were obtained from studies using this method. Mothers' scores were typically higher than fathers' scores on a range of issues including feelings of despair, guilt, loss of control, sorrow and fear (Gilbert 1997; Schwab 1996; Bohannon 1990–1). What these studies fail to provide, however, are fully plausible explanations for these differences.

It would seem, therefore, that men and women *tend* to exhibit marked differences in their reactions to the death of a child (Charman and Savage 2009; Scott Kenney 2003; Martin and Doka 2000; Bohannon 1990–1; Gilbert 1997; Stroebe and Stroebe 1991) with one very relevant outcome being a tendency to embark upon an often prolonged and personal investigation into the circumstances relating to the loss (Glick *et al.* 1974, in Archer 1999; Rando 1995; Bright 1996). The coping strategy of some women is commonly felt to be a 'search for meaning'. Women often embark upon a relentless quest to answer what is often unanswerable and to seek some form of explanation for their loss. This 'passion for comprehension' (Rock 1998: 98) and this quest for understanding and meaning can provide an outlet for grief. Active strategies for dealing with death and loss are often encouraged by those involved in the counselling of the bereaved as a method of regaining some control in an often seemingly uncontrollable situation (Martin and Doka 2000). Those who cope better with grief tend to be those whose focus is less inward-looking and less concerned with the open expression of grief and whose strategies are much more 'active' (Scott Kenney 2003). These grievers are often referred to as 'blended' grievers, not conforming to rigid gender stereotypes but flexibly exhibiting elements of both intuition and instrumentalism (Martin and Doka 2000: 51).

The desire to reach some level of comprehension of death or loss appears to be a common reaction to the enormity of sudden, unanticipated or preventable death, particularly involving from our perspective 'criminal death'. The loss will undoubtedly have caused great levels of distress and suffering in what according to Scott Kenney can be a 'debilitating and lifelong experience that strikes at the core of the survivor's being' (2002: 219). The loss can affect the fine balance of family life (Schatz 1986, in Scott Kenney 2002; Thompson and Janigian 1988, in Nadeau 1998) of which the mother is very often the central character. Any addition or subtraction from a family causes disturbance (Nadeau 1998); in the case of loss through homicide Rock refers to this as 'anomie' (1988: 42). The solution appears to lie in *action*. This is captured in Sara Payne's own words:

> One of the only things that distracted me from my misery in those months [after the murder] and gave me something to get up for in the mornings was the thought that we could do something to stop another family suffering as we were. I was determined that Sarah would not die in vain and it was from this desire that the campaign for Sarah's Law began. (Payne 2004: 89)

As already highlighted, the ability to harness some of the energy and anger experienced by the loss of a loved one greatly increases the likelihood of 'coping' with that loss (Scott Kenney 2003). Couple this with an often overwhelming urge to find some explanation or meaning for this loss and the result is a very powerful mix of anger, grief and desire, which can find its voice through campaigning.

Turning loss into action: the changing face of the politics of influence

Campaign groups and pressure groups have a long history and tradition in the UK. At the 1937 Institute of Sociology address, Ernest Baker is quoted as saying that England was a 'paradise of groups' (Wootton 1978) and 25 years later the *Sunday Telegraph* declared that 'the land is alive with pressure groups' (Wootton 1978). If that was the case then, there appear to be significantly more now, although 'paradise' is probably not the term used by all; James Callaghan referred to them as 'a nuisance, if not a menace' (quoted in Wilson

1984: 17). There are clear difficulties with establishing the amount of pressure group activity in existence in this country: groups are not always organised, no accurate mapping exercise has been completed on group participation, and group membership is not always a reliable indicator of support. However, we can state that the number of pressure groups increased significantly over the course of the twentieth century. The Directory of British Associations records 7,755 such organisations, many starting between the 1960s and the 1990s, a growth period. It is estimated that almost a third of adults in the UK are members of at least one group, with 6–8 per cent of adults 'actively' involved (Dalton 2006, in Jordan and Maloney 2007).

Group activity, especially within the political sphere, has historically been examined by recourse to theories of pressure groups. The study of pressure groups attempts to consider what are the internal formations and external activities of bodies that are assembled around organisations, associations and interests. Pressure group scholars do this in an attempt to appreciate the relative power of these bodies and their influence upon politics and policy-making. Over the years political theorists have categorised pressure groups (alternatively known as interest groups or lobby groups) according to their supposed purpose, with splits made between sectional and promotional groups (Potter 1956; Kimber and Richardson 1974), interest and ideas group (Childs 1935; quoted in Wootton 1978), producer and consumer groups (Beer 1965) or sectional and cause groups (Stewart 1958).

The activities of a pressure group can be dependent on many factors: resources, public support, expertise, membership and motives, for example. However, probably the most defining feature, and in some ways constraint, on pressure group activity is the group's acceptance or otherwise by government. Pressure group analysts have distinguished between the status and strategy of pressure groups by reference to pressure group typologies, the most widely used of which is Grant's (1984, 1989) 'insider' and 'outsider' split (originally formulated by Schattschneider 1935, in Maloney et al. 1994).

An insider group has a regular and consultative relationship with government whereas an outsider group does not, based on either failure to obtain insider group status or a decision not to engage with policy-makers. In order to achieve insider status, it is argued that a decision must be taken not only by government but also by the group in question (Grant 1984; Maloney et al. 1994). Grant rests the majority decision with the government, who make the decision based on three factors: whether the pressure group is needed for implementation purposes, whether the pressure group represents many people and whether the pressure group will play by the rules (Grant 1984).

The 'insider/outsider' typology retained its currency for many years. However, there are a number of fundamental problems with its applicability in the current political world, a fact readily accepted by its creator, Wyn Grant (2000). First, it is based on two variables – strategy and status. Maloney, Jordan and McLaughlin (1994) argue that the two factors are too different and are two separate decisions that cannot then be analysed together. The strategy of a group is something that the group itself makes a decision about (Maloney et al. 1994; McKinney and Halpin 2007), albeit within certain constraints such as membership, resources, the political culture and environment (May and Nugent 1982, in Jordan and Richardson 1987; Ball and Millard 1986). Second, with an increasingly professional consultation machinery within government (see the very detailed Code of Practice on Consultation, 2008), gaining insider status in terms of having a voice within the consultation process is virtually guaranteed for any group. There are relatively few groups, therefore, who could be classed as outsiders all of the time (Page 1999). Third, and of relevance within this chapter, is the changing nature of political participation.

The decline in the number of people voting at general elections (from nearly 84 per cent in 1950 to a low of 59.4 per cent in 2001 – see House of Commons Library 2001) and local elections (averaging 35 per cent since 1995 – ODPM 2002) and the decline in political party membership in recent years (3.4 million to 800,000 between 1950 and the mid-1990s – Jordan and Maloney 2007) have prompted claims of political apathy in Britain (Monin 2009; Belgutay 2009). What is confused in this process is the difference between disengagement with party politics and disengagement with politics *per se*. While it is accepted that there has been a decline in involvement with traditional politics, not to mention a sharp decline in the public trust of politicians (13 per cent believing that politicians 'tell the truth' (Ipsos Mori 2009) – unhelpfully aided by the 2009 MPs' expenses scandal – the issue of political apathy is questionable. A rise in group membership and a decline in party membership is a problem for political parties, not a problem for democracy (Wheaton 2007). What we have witnessed in recent years is a new, and very different, engagement with the political process, of which the campaign around Sarah's Law may be one significant example.

The traditional view of a class-based political system, centred on party loyalty, with elite-directed political activity is largely eroding (Jordan and Maloney 2007). In its place is emerging a system that is much more choice based and activist centred, which is challenging the tightly knit policy communities that have held sway within government for so long (Norris 1992; Grant 2005). This has been identified as a move from the politics of production to the politics of consumption (Grant 2005; Wheaton 2007). The focus of the groups involved is less now about fighting inequalities but more about lifestyle choices – from 'emancipatory politics to life politics' (Giddens 1994). These new social movements operate in very different ways from traditional insider groups, which focused upon the close, consultative relationships with ministers and government departments. Instead, we witness groups with fluid membership, often single goals (Sarah's Law?), who adopt the more traditional lobbying tactics of outsider groups. This centres on the mobilisation of public support and a high profile media presence (Toke 1997, in Jordan and Maloney 2007) – such as that examined earlier in terms of the *News of the World* support for Sarah's Law. The politics of protest, while more brash and less deliberative than some might like, appears to have a foothold in modern politics. The Green Paper *Governance of Britain*, published in 2007, makes only one reference to more traditional pressure groups (Grant 2009). In recent years, this new 'politics of protest' has witnessed calls for change at every level, from environmental issues, to security issues to lifestyle issues, and of relevance in this chapter, to public protection issues.

There is concern from some about the shallowness of this form of politics, which consists of loud demands without much understanding of the wider implications of those demands (Grant 2000). Pressure groups, it is felt, should engage more in a political dialogue rather than a stating of preference (Maloney 2009). This is part of the much broader debate around a 'culture of impatience' (Loader 2006). However, there is no doubting the existence of this form of politics and the need to understand their development, their motivations and their operational practices is imperative. Kenney (2003: 202) argues that we must:

> ... expand our scope of inquiry beyond policy professionals, interest groups, and elites. We need to understand the relationship of insiders and outsiders and tell the stories of grass roots activists. We need to explore the discursive aspects of politics and examine how groups frame their policy proposals. And we need to factor in the emotional and symbolic aspects of politics.

With the locus of who to appeal to now moving from civil servants to the public, pressure groups have found different ways to frame their message and get the issues that they are concerned about into the public consciousness. Kingdon (1984), in writing about agenda setting, focused upon the three stages of identification of problems, the policies and then the politics. It is this first issue, of turning an issue into a social problem that needs addressing, that is perhaps the most challenging task for pressure groups (Stolz 2005). While more traditional pressure groups might utilise techniques such as education, dissemination of information, conferences, dialogue with government departments, the politics of protest works in different ways. The framing of the message is of vital importance in this regard. Problems are personalised, complex arguments are simplified, and in the case of public protection, fears are played upon. Groups must target sympathetic audiences with issues that are already of concern to them and promote the dangers of inactivity (DeGregorio 2009). The proximity of the concern is also important in this regard: how will the issue affect me (Jordan and Maloney 2007)? The *News of the World* campaign for Sarah's Law fits very clearly into this framework. Targeting its readers about child safety issues with the image of a murdered girl on its front cover framed the message in such a way to those readers that inactivity was not seen as an option. People are more inclined to act upon a threat rather than upon a collective good (Mitchell 1979, in Jordan and Maloney 2007) so the role of fear and anxiety in this case clearly plays its part. The 'arousing power of fear' (DeGregorio 2009: 481) should not be underestimated. The proximity of the problem was portrayed as potentially very close. As mentioned earlier, a *News of the World* editorial ran a headline about sex offenders living within a mile of everyone in Britain (2000, in Hinds and Daly 2001: 257). One million people subsequently signed the petition. This leads us to another, related issue thrown up by the Sarah's Law campaign: the use of *emotion*, and in particular the emotion associated with grief, loss and above all a mother's loss, as a powerful weapon in justice campaigning.

The 'moral authority of grief': the emotional power of victims' voices

The use of emotion as a technique in campaigning is not new. Animal rights groups, environment groups, pro-life groups, have all used evocative images to convey their message and to win sympathy from the public. Research analysing 421 press releases found that over half used emotion to convey their message (DeGregorio 2009). This is even more astonishing given that the groups that were part of this analysis were campaigning in the field of energy, tax and education. However, emotion is not merely present as a tool of campaigning. It is also there as a driver for campaigning in the first place. With an increasingly punitive justice system and a 'war on crime' political rhetoric, as we have seen earlier, victims of crime and their families have therefore found a rich avenue to exploit in terms of conveying their demands to the public. The image of the victim of crime has been placed centre stage in any debates or policy change about law and order, and indeed the justification for those decisions (Simon 2007). As Garland (2001) says, 'The new political imperative is that victims must be protected; their voices must be heard, their memory honoured, their anger expressed, their fears addressed.'

The 'moral authority of grief' (Kaminer 1995) in campaigning terms is then a powerful tool and one that can take prominence over what can be convincing evidence to the contrary. Victims of crime or their families who are left behind, and particularly mothers, find themselves therefore in a unique position as symbols of those suffering loss when that loss is transferred to forms of protest. Women, of course, have long been connected with protest movements, from the suffragette movement through to more recent campaigns against weapon-related violence and against drugs. A common thread binding the campaigning of women is a focus of protest on 'social transformation' (Rowbotham 1992); in the UK and elsewhere, women seem to tend to campaign about the needs of others, whether about environmental concerns, social conditions or the welfare of children. In the UK, for example, there are many specifically female campaigning organisations that have pressed for change. This list includes Women Against Fundamentalism, Women's Action for Iraq, Women Against Rape, Women Against Violence, Women Against Hunger, and Women Against Pornography. There are also those groups that specifically campaign as *mothers*. These include Mothers Against Murder and Aggression, Mothers Against Guns, Mothers Against Drugs, Mothers Against Violence, and Mothers Against Injustice. It is interesting in this respect that in his study of the organisation SAMM (Support After Murder and Manslaughter), Rock found that its membership was made up of twice as many women as men, with mothers, sisters, daughters and wives making up the bulk of participants (Rock 1998). As well as the processes of coping with loss raised previously, there is a form of *public representation of private grief* at work in this respect, something that tends, as Riches and Dawson (1996: 149) have claimed, to be a female rather than male strategy: 'The public work of expressing the pain of grief appears to be done, on the whole, by women.' Furthermore, it is arguably a highly potent and effective strategy, particularly when attached to imageries of motherhood.

This alludes to another way in which women, particularly mothers, may act as more powerful advocates of their causes precisely *because* of their emotive and expressive role in the campaigning process. Rowbotham (1992) has referred to the representational force associated with imageries of 'mother and child' in the victim role as a form of 'social power'. Using the example of *'Madres'*, Argentinian mothers who publicly protested their emotions in their own campaigns for their 'lost children', she argues that this expresses 'a social power based on the intensity of the personal bond between child and mother' (Rowbotham 1992: 305). While there is an obvious danger here of motherhood being 'sentimentalised' (Kaplan 2001: 41) or even essentialised, the imageries attached to the status of motherhood when faced with adversity involving their children are clearly potent. Indeed, Kaplan goes on to argue that a part of the appeal of motherhood to audiences is that it may be seen as a non-threatening and safe identity to be confronted with. Perhaps, however, it runs more deeply than that. Rowbotham has commented that in many cultures motherhood is 'revered' (Rowbotham 1992: 306), and harm caused to the mother in turn is seen as potentially damaging to the social fabric as a whole.

Into this mixture we can add the intimate and unique 'knowledge' that women, not just as mothers but also as sisters and daughters, can introduce to a campaign, given their own relational and emotive attachment to family members they have lost. The loss of a loved one as a result of a crime has been referred to as a 'debilitating and lifelong experience' that very few people have experience of (Scott Kenney 2002: 219; see also Rock 1998). This places the survivor in a position of possessing 'knowledge' that is not readily accessible to others. This unique knowledge can be used to the campaigner's advantage. Scott Kenney argues that campaigners for justice will often use metaphors that illustrate their loss but that also have important 'micro-political significance' (2002: 232). Through the use of language and certain expressions, campaigners can evoke a level of sympathy that would be hard for others to achieve. Rock (1998) argues that the public perception of the campaigner as a 'victim' is far more likely to be able to be used to the campaigner's advantage. In a similar way, Clark (1987) argues that for sympathy to be freely given, the combination of a sympathetic character and one who is suffering injustice is likely to prove potent. Females, given their greater emotional and affective proximity to family members than males, are typically better placed to evoke such sentiments of sympathy than men.

It should not be felt that the unique position that women find themselves in as campaigners is something that is unknowingly thrust upon them. Women are deliberately using their metaphors of loss more often than men in order to achieve control of their campaign (Scott Kenney 2002). Women are not passive actors within campaigns but may be seen as deliberate, if not strategic, players whose own personal journey through grief is aided through their work. As Rock has argued: 'Intensive campaigning became a vehicle for the validation, objectification, and articulation of deep feelings, a non-verbal medium to express the inexpressible, a demonstration of an understanding that was more experiential than cerebral' (1998: 220).

Female campaigners bring with them not only resilience and determination, they bring *effectiveness*. The privileged position of motherhood in particular manages to overcome any alternative concerns about freedoms and rights (Nelson 1984, in Kenney 2003). We would argue that this process was at work when the Sarah's Law campaign with the justice agenda attached to the public protection movement.

Conclusion

David Garland (2001: 143) has warned of the dangers of passing laws named, officially or unofficially, after victims, on the basis that they threaten to exploit victims and those who campaign on their behalf for political ends. Such measures are, he argues, 'nothing more than retaliatory legislation passed for public display and political advantage'. There is some support for that interpretation in the discussion presented here, although there is also a sense in which it underestimates the role of *agency* played by those, such as Sara Payne, who have campaigned on a victim-based agenda. What we have presented in this chapter is the process of *interaction* between the political climate on the one hand and the campaigning process on the other. In this respect we have attempted to draw out the significance of the Sarah's Law campaign for understanding the changing politics of influence in a climate of public *protectionism*. We have argued that the ethos of public protection helped create an environment within which a campaign such as Sarah's Law would be 'swimming with the tide'; it was to fall on fertile ground as 'victims' voices' were being increasingly heard, or at least portrayed by politicians as being 'listened to'. However, we have also argued that the success of the Sarah's Law campaign should be seen as more than a matter of receptive audiences. That campaign was an independent as well as a dependent variable. The Sarah's Law campaign can be seen as drawing from a number of combined forces: action driven by the energies of coping with loss, particularly the female experience of loss; the changing face of political influence and the rise of single-issue, media-driven interest movements; and the power and potency of justice campaigns that can draw from the imageries and emotions associated with motherhood, loss and the grieving mother. Those forces seemed irresistible.

References

Archer, J. (1999) *The Nature of Grief: The Evolution and Psychology of Reactions to Loss.* London: Routledge.

Ball, A. and Millard, F. (1986) *Pressure Politics in Industrial Societies.* Basingstoke: Macmillan.

Beer, S. (1965) *Modern British Politics.* London: Faber and Faber.

Belgutay, J. (2009) 'Students vote for apathy over politics', *Sunday Times*, 13 December, p. 18.

Bohannon, J. R. (1990–91) 'Grief responses of spouses following the death of a child', *Omega*, 22(2): 109–21.

Bottoms, A. (1995) 'The philosophy and politics of punishment and sentencing', in C. Clarkson and R. Morgan (eds) *The Politics of Sentencing Reform.* Oxford: Clarendon Press.

Bowlby, J. (1980) *Attachment and Loss, Volume 3, Loss: Sadness and Depression*. New York: Basic Books.

Bright, R. (1996) *Grief and Powerlessness: Helping People Regain Control of their Lives*. London: Jessica Kingsley.

Charman, S. and Savage, S. P. (2009) 'Mothers for justice? Gender and campaigns against miscarriages of justice', *British Journal of Criminology*, 49(6): 900–15.

Clark, C. (1987) 'Sympathy biography and sympathy margin', *American Journal of Sociology*, 93(2): 290–321.

DeGregorio, C. (2009) 'Calling out the troops: interest groups, press releases, and policy promotion through speech', *Policy and Politics*, 37(3): 463–84.

Downes, D. and Morgan, R. (2007) 'No turning back: the politics of law and order into the new millennium', in M. Maguire, R. Morgan and R. Reiner (eds) *The Oxford Handbook of Criminology*. Oxford: Oxford University Press.

Fish, W. C. (1986) 'Differences in grief intensity in bereaved parents', in T. Rando (ed.) *Parental Loss of a Child*. Champaign, IL: Research Press.

Garland, D. (2001) *The Culture of Control*. Oxford: Oxford University Press.

Giddens, A. (1994) *Beyond Left and Right: the Future of Radical Politics*. California: Stanford University Press.

Gilbert, K. (1997) 'Couple coping with the death of a child', in C. Figley, B. Bride and N. Mazza (eds) *Death and Trauma: The Traumatology of Grieving*. Washington DC: Taylor and Francis (pp. 101–21).

Grant, W. (1984) 'The role and power of pressure groups', in R. Borthwick and J. Spence (eds) *British Politics in Perspective*. Leicester: Leicester University Press.

Grant, W. (1989) *Pressure Groups, Politics and Democracy in Britain*. London: Philip Allan.

Grant, W. (2000) *Pressure Groups and British Politics*. Basingstoke: Macmillan.

Grant, W. (2005) 'A politics of collective consumption?', *Parliamentary Affairs*, 58(2): 366–79.

Grant, W. (2009) 'Review of G. Jordan and W. Maloney *Democracy and Interest Groups*', *Public Administration*, 87(1): 142–43.

Grayling, C. (2010) '"Sarah's Law" sex offender alert scheme may be expanded', BBC News. Online at: http://news.bbc.co.uk/1/hi/uk/8477310.stm (accessed 24 January 2010).

Hinds, L. and Daly, K. (2001) 'The war on sex offenders: community notification in perspective', *Australian and New Zealand Journal of Criminology*, 34(3): 256–76.

HM Government (2008) *Code of Practice on Consultation*. Online at: www.berr.gov.uk/files/file47158.pdf (accessed 21 January 2010).

Home Office (1997) *No More Excuses: A New Approach to Tackling Youth Crime*. London: Home Office.

Home Office (2006) *Rebalancing the Criminal Justice System in Favour of the Law-Abiding Majority: Cutting Crime, Reducing Offending and Protecting the Public*. London: Home Office.

House of Commons Library (2001) *General Election Results, 7 June 2001, Research Paper 01/54*. Online at: www.parliament.uk/commons/lib/research/rp2001/rp01-054.pdf (accessed 19 January 2010).

Howard, M. (2004) 'Howard on law and order', BBC News. Online at: http://news.bbc.co.uk/1/hi/uk_politics/3551318.stm (accessed 25 January 2010).

Ipsos Mori (2009) *Trust in Professions*. Online at: www.ipsos-mori.com/researchpublications/researcharchive/poll.aspx?oItemId=15&view=wide (accessed 19 January 2010).

Johnson, A. (2010) '"Sarah's Law" sex offender alert scheme may be expanded', BBC News. Online at: http://news.bbc.co.uk/1/hi/uk/8477310.stm (accessed 24 January 2010).

Jones, T. and Newburn, T. (2007) *Policy Transfer and Criminal Justice*. Maidenhead: Open University Press.

Jordan, A. and Richardson, J. (1987) *British Politics and the Policy Process*. Hemel Hempstead: Unwin Hyman.

Jordan, G. and Maloney, W. (2007) *Democracy and Interest Groups: Enhancing Participation?* Basingstoke: Palgrave Macmillan.

Kaminer, W. (1995) *It's All the Rage: Crime and Culture*. New York: Addison Wesley Educational.

Kaplan, T. (2001) 'Uncommon women and the common good: women and environmental protest', in S. Rowbotham and S. Linkogle (eds) *Women Resist Globalization*. London: Zed Books (pp. 28–45).

Kenney, S. (2003) 'Where is gender in agenda setting?', *Women and Politics*, 25(1/2): 179–204.

Kimber, R. and Richardson, J. (1974) (eds) *Pressure Groups in Britain*. Hertfordshire: Dent and Sons.

Kingdon, J. (1984) *Agendas, Alternatives and Public Policies*. New York: Addison Wesley Educational.

Kirby, I. (2009) 'Sara's the minister for victims', *News of the World*. Online at: www.newsoftheworld.co.uk/news/article144268.ece (accessed 25 January 2010).

Loader, I. (2006) 'Fall of the "platonic guardians": liberalism, criminology and political responses to crime in England and Wales', *British Journal of Criminology*, 46(4): 561–86.

Maloney, W. (2009) 'Interest groups and the revitalisation of democracy: Are we expecting too much?', *Representation*, 45(3): 277–87.

Maloney, W., Jordan, G. and McLaughlin, A. (1994) 'Interest groups and public policy: the insider/outsider model revisited', *Journal of Public Policy*, 14(1).

Martin, T. and Doka, K. (2000) *Men Don't Cry ... Women Do: Transcending Gender Stereotypes of Grief*. Philadelphia: Taylor and Francis.

McKinney, B. and Halpin, D. (2007) 'Talking about Australian pressure groups: adding value to the insider/outsider distinction in combating homelessness in Western Australia', *Australian Journal of Public Administration*, 66(3): 342–52.

Ministry of Justice (2009) *Redefining Justice: Addressing the Individual Needs of Victims and Witnesses*. London: Ministry of Justice.

Monin, J. (2009) 'How Britain lost its way', *Guardian*, 27 January, p. 12.

Morgan, R. and Newburn, T. (2007) 'Youth justice' in M. Maguire, R. Morgan and R. Reiner (eds) *The Oxford Handbook of Criminology*. Oxford: Oxford University Press.

Mulholland, H. and Tempest, M. (2007) 'Reid unveils Sarah's Law proposals', *Guardian*, 13 June. Nexis UK database, accessed 25 January 2010.

Nadeau, J. (1998) *Families Making Sense of Death*. Thousand Oaks, CA: Sage.

News of the World (2010) 'Success for Sarah's Law', 24 January. Online at: www.newsoftheworld.co.uk/news/696503/After-10-years-we-win-a-huge-victory-in-fight-to-protect-our-children-from-paedophiles.html (accessed 25 January 2010).

Norris, P. (1992) *Democratic Phoenix: Reinventing Political Activism*. Cambridge: Cambridge University Press.

ODPM (Office of the Deputy Prime Minister) (2002) *Turnout at Local Elections*. Online at: www.dca.gov.uk/elections/elect_odpm_turnout.pdf (accessed 19 January 2010).

Page, C. (1999) 'The insider/outsider distinction: an empirical investigation', *British Journal of Politics and International Relations*, 1(2): 205–14.

Parkes, C. M. (1996) *Bereavement: Studies of Grief in Adult Life*, 3rd edn. London: Routledge.

Payne, S. (2004) *A Mother's Story*. London: Hodder and Stoughton.

Potter, A. (1956) 'British pressure groups', *Parliamentary Affairs*, 9(4), Autumn.

Rando, T. (1995) 'Grief and mourning: accommodating to loss', in H. Wass and R. Neimeyer (eds) *Dying: Facing the Facts*. Washington, DC: Taylor and Francis (pp. 211–41).

Riches, G. and Dawson, P. (1996) 'Communities of feeling: the culture of bereaved parents', *Mortality*, 1(2): 143–61.

Rock, P. (1998) *After Homicide*. Oxford: Clarendon Press.

Rowbotham, S. (1992) *Women in Movement*. London: Routledge.

Rozenberg, J. (1994) *The Search for Justice*. London: Sceptre.

Savage, S. (2007) *Police Reform: Forces for Change*. Oxford: Oxford University Press.

Savage, S. and Nash, M. (2001) 'Law and order under Blair: New Labour or old conservatism', in S. Savage and R. Atkinson (eds) *Public Policy Under Blair*. London: Palgrave.

Schwab, R. (1996) 'Gender differences in parental grief', *Death Studies*, 20: 103–13.

Scott Kenney, J. (2002) 'Metaphors of loss: murder, bereavement, gender and presentation of the "victimized" self', *International Review of Victimology*, 9: 219–51.

Scott Kenney, J. (2003) 'Gender roles and grief cycles: observations on models of grief and coping in homicide cases', *International Review of Victimology*, 10: 19–47.

Simon, J. (2007) *Governing Through Crime*. Oxford: Oxford University Press.

Stewart, J. (1958) *British Pressure Groups*. London: Oxford University Press.

Stolz, B. (2005) 'Educating policymakers and setting the criminal justice policymaking agenda: interest groups and the "Victims of Trafficking and Violence Act of 2000"', *Criminal Justice*, 5(4): 407–30.

Stroebe, M. and Stroebe, W. (1991) 'Does grief work "work"?', *Journal of Consulting and Clinical Psychology*, 59: 479–82.

Wheaton, B. (2007) 'Identity, politics, and the beach: environmental activism in surfers against sewage', *Leisure Studies*, 26(3): 279–302.

Wilson, D. (1984) *Pressure: The A–Z of Campaigning in Britain*. London: Heinemann.

Wootton, G. (1978) *Pressure Politics in Contemporary Britain*. Toronto: Lexington Books.

Index

NAPPO (National Association of
Probation Officers) 439
Nash, M. 13, 426
National Audit Office
The National Probation Service 115
risk prediction 166
National Intelligence Model 404
*National Objectives for Social Work Services
in the Criminal Justice
System* (Scottish Executive)
273–4
National Standards 220–1
The Nature of Prejudice (Allport) 362–4
Nellis, M. 284, 337, 354
net-widening 237–8
Netherlands
Amsterdam 1012 project 267–8
big events 260
community safety 258–63
comprehensive safety policy
258–9
criminal law 259–60
ethnic minorities 263–4, 265, 268
HALT 264
leefbaar 260–1, 267
mentally disordered offenders
265–7, 269
multi-agency working 259
overview 251–2, 257–8, 269–70
political parties 260–1
prostitution 267–8
Rotterdam approach 260–3
veiligheid 257, 260
youth offending 263–5
network society 344–5
New Labour 62, 342–4, 437–8
new penology 381
New Zealand 87–8, 90, 94, 97
Newman, Kenneth 405, 406
News of the World 237, 239–40, 383–4, 439,
441, 447
Neyroud, Peter 195
NOMS (National Offender Management
Service) 116, 118, 152
Norman [2009] 1 Cr App R 13 106–7
Northern Ireland 399, 407–9

Norway 417
notification
see sex offender notification
NSPCC 244

OASys Data Evaluation and Analysis
Team (O-DEAT) 138
OASys (Offender Assessment System)
in action 141–2
aggregate analysis 155
completed assessments 151
core sections 142–6t
counts and categories 142–8
criticisms of 148–51
overview 83, 85–6, 138, 156
policing 410
O'Connor, Denis 402
O'Connor v Donaldson 1975 319
ODEAT (OASys Data Evaluation and
Analysis Team) 149
offence paralleling behaviours 424
offender behaviour 32–4
Offender Management Act 2007 117
Offender's Tag Association 346
OffenderWatch® company 297
OGRS 3 (Offender Group Reconviction
Scale) 142, 191
Ohlin, L. 137
Oliver, Robert 199
O'Malley, P. 40, 42
open prisons 192
Operation Ballast 407
Order of Lifelong Restriction (OLR) 274
Orend, B. 90
Overarching Principles: Seriousness (SGC)
112
overseas offences 123
Owen, C. 52

Padfield, N. 85, 116
Padgett, K. 352
paedophiles 383–4 *see also* Megan's Law;
Sarah's Law
Pakes, F. 251–2
Pam's Law 296
panoptical systems 210–11